The Impressionist Print

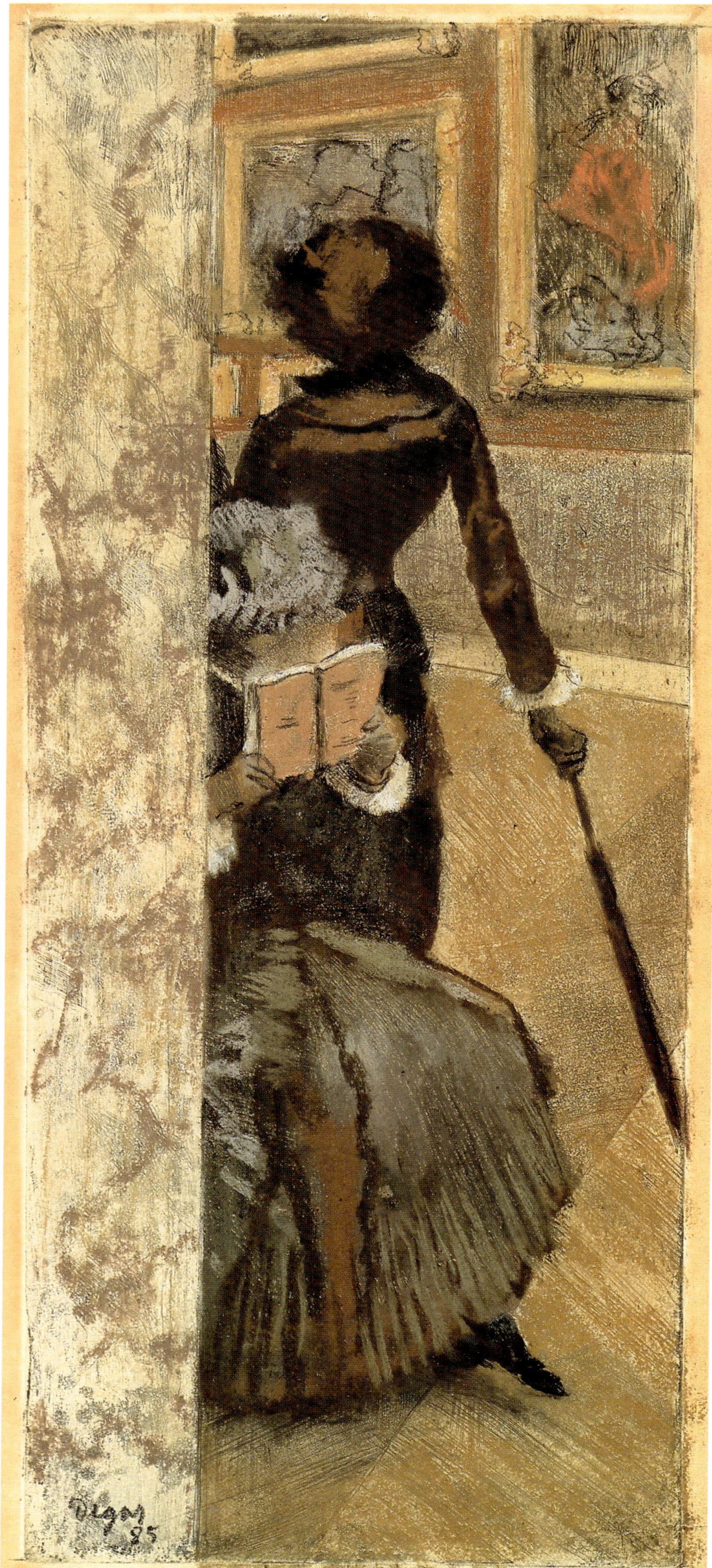

Frontispiece: Edgar Degas, *Mary Cassatt at the Louvre: Paintings*. 1885. Etching, aquatint and drypoint touched up with pastel, 305 x 127 mm. Art Institute, Chicago, bequest of Kate L. Brewster.

The Impressionist Print

Michel Melot

TRANSLATED FROM THE FRENCH BY
CAROLINE BEAMISH

Yale University Press
New Haven and London

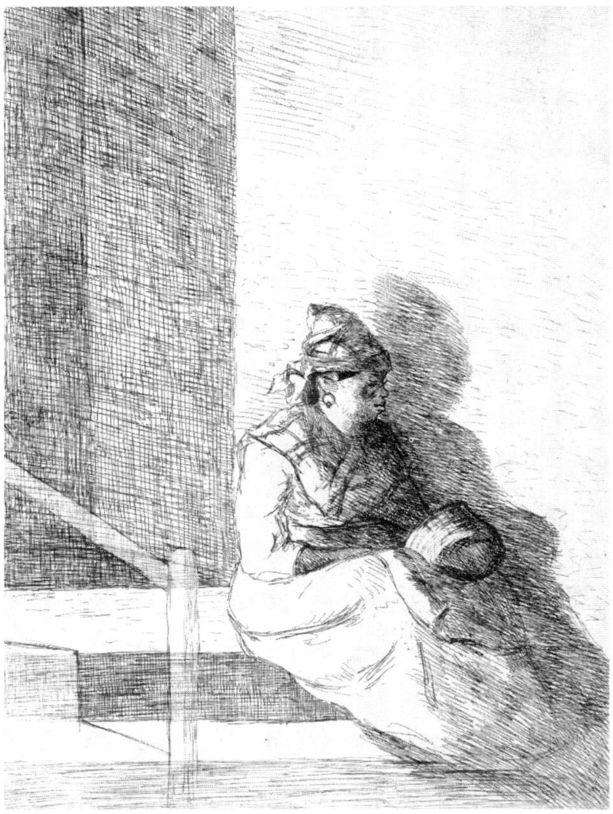

1. Camille Pissarro, *The Negress*. 1867. Drypoint, 307 x 217 mm. Private collection, Paris.

First published as *L'Estampe Impressionniste*,
© by Flammarion, Paris, 1994

Translation © by Yale University 1996

All rights reserved. This book may not be reproduced, in whole or in part, in any form (beyond that copying permitted by Sections 107 and 108 of the U.S. Copyright Law and except by reviewers for the public press), without written permission from the publishers.

Set in Garamond by SX Composing DTP, Rayleigh, Essex
Printed in France

Library of Congress Cataloging-in-Publication Data
Melot, Michel.
[Estampe impressionniste. English]
The impressionist print/Michel Melot; translated from the French by Caroline Beamish.
p. cm.
Includes bibliographical references and index.
ISBN 0-300-06792-5 (cloth)
1. Prints, French. 2. Impressionism (Art)—France. 3. Prints—19th century—France. 4. Art and society—France—History—19th century. I. Title.
NE647.6.14M4413 1996
769.944'09'034—dc20
95-50606
CIP

Figs 309–13 ADAGP, Paris and DACS, London 1996
The publisher would like to thank M. and Mme Prouté for kindly authorising the reproduction of a number of works in their collection.

My work on this book has been facilitated by the many studies that have recently helped to bring completely fresh life to our understanding of the Impressionist print. The book is dedicated to these scholars and friends: to Janine Bailly-Herzberg, to Juliet Wilson-Bareau, to Jean-Paul Bouillon, to Douglas Druick and Peter Zegers, to Alan Fern, to Robert Herbert, to Richard Field, to Jay Fisher, to Antony Griffiths, to Annegret Rittmann, to Barbara Stern Shapiro and to those whom I know only through their writing, in particular Joël Isaacson and Eugenia Parry Janis. To them this book owes anything new that it contains.

Anything that is doubtful in the book is the sole responsibility of the author; in history, as in art, reproduction does not exist.

M.M.

CONTENTS

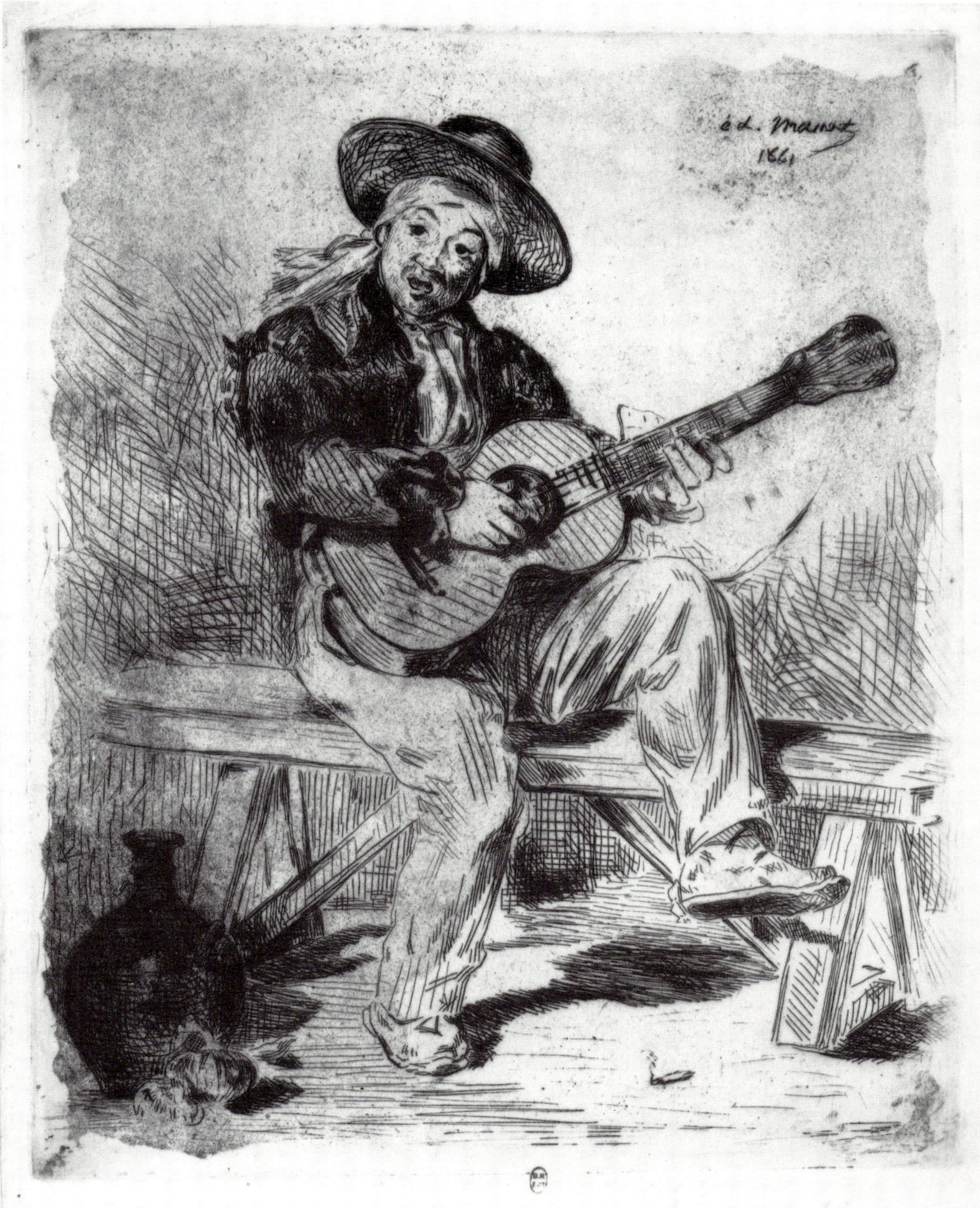

2. Edouard Manet, *The Guitar Player*. 1861. Etching, first state, 298 x 246 mm.
Bibliothèque nationale, Paris.

PART ONE

On the Eve: 1850-70

1. *Introduction*

A print can sometimes tell us more about the history of art than can a painting. The art of printmaking uses techniques that usually involve collaboration, or at least consultation; prints are seldom made in solitude and are therefore more firmly rooted in their period than paintings. Alliances are formed, like those between Bracquemond and Manet, Pissarro and Cézanne, Degas and Mary Cassatt. In addition, the print is designed to reach a large and widespread public, the number of prospective purchasers being anticipated in the size of the edition, with a view to either increasing the size of the audience or to limiting it. This estimate, which is controlled (or at least acknowledged) by the artist, even if he plans to produce only a single proof, obviously has a bearing on his choice of technique, of subject, even of style, and in some ways influences the contents of the work. If the state of the arts reveals the state of society, sometimes in advance, then to the same extent the state of the print reveals the state of the arts.

If one of these engravers, Félix Bracquemond or Edgar Degas, had written his memoirs we should be in possession of a detailed history of Impressionism. We should have had described to us the discussions that led up to the election of a number of engravers to a group that was formed eight times and had to be reconstituted eight times. We should know why the Impressionists were unsuccessful in their attempt to unite in 1874, yet were able to separate successfully in 1886. And we should have an answer to the question raised by their earliest champion, Théodore Duret, in 1878, and reiterated almost at once by Émile Zola in the first articles written in their defence: 'The impressionists were not created by their own hands'.[1]

Who, then, did create the Impressionists? Who played a part in their development? Their critics, certainly, – the rôle of the critics is well-known today;[2] their dealers and their first clients, whose importance has also been investigated.[3] But now that Impressionism has achieved a semi-official position in the artistic canon, the investigation needs to be extended to the less exalted levels of society. The study of engraved prints allows the historian to penetrate a much broader stratum of an as yet unspecified public, whose sense of its own identity was probably enhanced by these prints and who, having grown and prospered, found its lives henceforward mirrored therein. The success subsequently met with by the print, and the fame that Impressionism has achieved today, confirm our perception that a profound change has occurred in our own beliefs, in our perceptions and in our value system, and that the two phenomena were in some way connected.

The new features that constituted Impressionism – the changed relationship with time, objects and techniques, with man and his environment, and with property – which nowadays reinforce our view of the world but which in the nineteenth century took time to gain acceptance, can also be found in the print. They can be found in surface features such as the form and content of a work of art, but also in the inner nature of each work, in the manner in which prints were conceived, produced, viewed and understood; in their subjects, their techniques, their abundance or their scarcity, and in the manner of their circulation -whether very wide or very restricted. Every aspect of a print has significance: the choice of tool is as important as the choice of subject; the method of printing is an important aspect of style, and sometimes the grain of the paper says as much about a print as does the image itself.

A print is much more revealing of the human network involved in its production than is a painting. The mysterious cluster of people requesting to see or possess each print (which they may accept or reject) constitutes a group, but one that forms without its members knowing one another, performs a function without being conscious of performing it and, by exerting imperceptible pressures, creates a ferment in its time. Such nebulous circles have always existed, but the need for them became more obvious and their effectiveness more evident the moment the social classes began to mingle more freely, when the rigid social hierarchy began to crumble and when democracy, fought for tooth and nail, began to be positively encouraged. Art, having belonged to a static élite, gradually became available to anyone wishing to stake a claim. Battles over style, disputes between different schools, with the accompanying development of techniques and also of the art market, became the normal way of life.

No period of history, in France or elsewhere, had known such rapid economic growth; the succession of generations following that of 1830 saw a tremendous acceleration,[4] and social divisions became increasingly fragile, their consolidation adapting well to the appropriation and development of the arts. Artist there had to be, but in the period of upheaval when fortunes were made and lost at such a rate, all different types of people were to be found in the artistic fraternity: breakaway members of the middle classes, déclassé members of the aristocracy, and hard-working artisans seeking to get their feet on the ladder. The backgrounds from which printmakers came were particularly varied and are thus instructive to us today. Bracquemond and Renoir, both from humble backgrounds, were nevertheless diametrically opposed in their ideas and in their method of print-making. The fortunes of Pissarro and Degas, from very different backgrounds, run parallel throughout this volume. Nevertheless, it should not be assumed that social origins have no bearing on the practice of art, itself so completely dominated by individuals. We have to assess the common features of the artists' enthusiasms, inspiration and style by examining their struggle for success and the strategies they adopted to achieve it.

The Impressionists were the offspring of the July Monarchy; the eldest of them, Pissarro and Philippe Burty,[5] the critic and standard-bearer of the painter-printmakers, were born in 1830. Print-making divided them, and the same divisions and dissensions can be observed, curiously enough, accompanying the generations that followed them; secession and ostracism were a constant source of friction in the lives of the Impressionist painters, sometimes poisoning relationships altogether. The greatest print-makers in the group were the oldest: Desboutin, born in 1823, Pissarro in 1830, Bracquemond in 1833, Degas in 1834, Legros in 1837 and Lepic in 1839. In 1874, when the first Impressionist exhibition was held, they were all over thirty-five. The younger Impressionists provided a new generation of painter-printmakers, with Mary Cassatt, born in 1844, Raffaëlli in 1850, and Forain in 1852. Between these two waves there was a dip containing 'pure' Impressionists who only occasionally made prints. In 1874, Sisley and Cézanne were thirty-four, Renoir and Berthe Morisot thirty-two, Caillebotte, born in 1848, died while still young in 1893 and seems inadvertently to have produced only one print, taken from a painting done in 1878.[6] Exactly in the middle of this dividing line comes Claude Monet, thirty-three in 1874 and the Impressionist *par excellence*, who was the only one of them never to have made a single print.

This pyramid of ages did not occur by chance. As Joël Isaacson[7] has pointed out, it conceals (or covers) the fundamental divergences between the two principal sub-groups: the younger group, trained by Monet and Renoir, and the older group, trained by Degas. The fact that it was the admission of a printmaker of the second wave, Raffaëlli, that turned disagreement into dissension and caused the secession is not immaterial. The selection process to which exhibitors were submitted and the problem of aesthetic values were at the heart of these tensions. But behind the question of aesthetics was the question of the use to which a work of art might be put and, as this correspondence with print-making implies, the question of public preference.

The printmakers, who had been trained during a period of economic growth, when images were multiplying, and who had, in addition, been exposed to manufactured art and the expansion of the art market, grew increasingly indignant with members of the group like Claude Monet, for whom the art of painting was sufficient. Monet, though displaying no hostility towards other techniques, appeared unaware of the dilemma faced by the artisan artist, with his original yet reproduced work. Some rethinking took place in about 1870. Colours grew lighter, realism took on a new lease of life, machines – the camera, for example – began to find their niche, and so did printmaking. Manet's spectacular abandonment of printmaking during the Republic is symbolic of the point of no return at which Parisian society had arrived. After this, the Impressionists hurled themselves into what appeared to be a void.

After 1885 printmaking continued to be practised, but in the register of the decorative arts, whose growth had accompanied the acquisition of wealth by a large middle class. The young were growing affluent, and painters who had hitherto shown themselves indifferent to prints and print-making, like Renoir, Sisley, and Morisot, were now required to make their contribution. Between these two periods an aesthetic crisis, the crisis Impressionism went through from 1874 to 1886, became confused with a political crisis, the final irreversible rise to power of the Republicans and, simultaneously, an economic crisis that shook the country to its foundations; the recession jeopardised French economic recovery, threatened the business of Durand-Ruel and brought financial ruin to the younger painters. During this time, any printmakers in the group took up their printmaking again and even tried, unsuccessfully, to launch a review dedicated to the print, *Le Jour et la Nuit*, thus returning printmaking to the bosom of Impressionism.

The fact remains, however, that this period was fundamentally altered by the growing strength of the European economy. Fortunes amassed quietly over the centuries, now began to grow. Between 1850 and 1870 the global wealth of the French people doubled.[8] But being rich no longer had the same significance as before. To add weight to this new significance, all symbolic means were brought into play and representations were reviewed. One of the striking characteristics of these decades was the need for artists. Everyone wanted artists, but not everyone wanted the same artists. Those straining to join the ranks of the bourgeoisie competed with one another, jockeying for position and possession, as if art carried with it an aura that was an indispensable aid to their acceptance. Thanks to the broad section of society that could be reached by the print, we can learn more about its audience than we could from a painting.

2. *The Impetus of Industry*

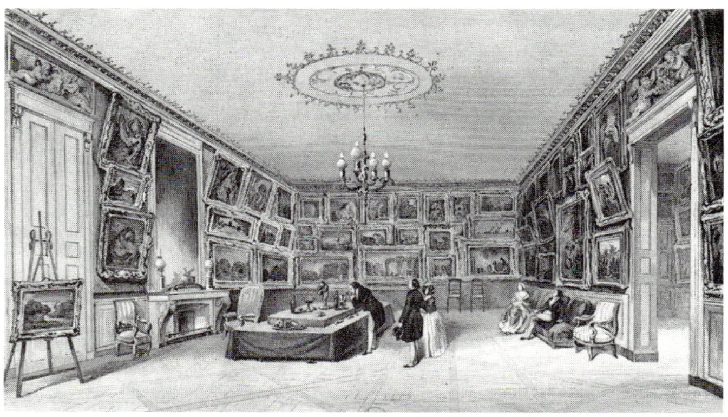

3. Charles-François Daubigny,
The Main Room at the Galerie Durand-Ruel. 1845.
Etching, 128 x 215 mm.
Bibliothèque nationale, Paris.

The oldest of the Impressionist painters belonged to the generation born around 1830. Their youthful experience left them in no doubt about the current success of the arts, and its close connection with the success of industry. They belonged to the generation that used paint in a tube, factory-made glue, paper from a roll, pencils with graphite inside and other early 'ready-made' items; they were also familiar with publicity and photography.[9] They had been brought up with the vigorous, rustic images used in popular illustration, moral and immoral lithography, caricature and the 'picturesque' images in the twopenny magazines. A young painter, Jean-François Millet, arriving in Paris from his native Normandy in January 1837, recalled: 'There was a print seller right there. I looked at his pictures as I ate my last Normandy apple. The lithographs, in the manner of Devéria and Maurin, disgusted me: there were scenes with scantily clad models, women bathing, women at their toilette. They looked to me like the shop signs of fashion shops or perfumeries'.[10]

Lithography was experiencing a boom, offering a fast reproduction service in the alleyways around the Bourse, and filling the shop windows of dealers in the Palais-Royal and the boulevards.[11] Between 1838, the year of the establishment of the printmakers' professional review, *Lithographie*, and 1845, when their professional body was recognised, the number of printer-lithographers in Paris rose from ninety-three to 159.[12] The largest of the printing works, Lemercier, had eighty presses and 159 employees in 1850.[13] While England was sunk in economic crisis, France forged ahead. In 1851, on the occasion of the Great Exhibition of the Works of Industry of all Nations at the Crystal Palace in London, Charles Dupin claimed that France was exporting 40,000 books of lithographs per year, adding that 'gradually the lithograph has purified the taste of the lower orders.'[14] In 1837, Engleman, then Lemercier, perfected the technique of chromolithography. In 1840 a mechanical printing press with automatic inking was invented that could run off 6,000 copies at a time.

The younger artists were brought up to the sound of animated discussions by their elders on the benefits of the democratisation of the arts. This was expansive talk, but had its materialistic side, coming as it did from people earning a regular income, sometimes a considerable one, from illustrated books and reproductions. The young might have heard one of their teachers, Paul Huet, declare: 'the indications are that we should not be addressing ourselves to isolated individuals, but to the sentiments of the populace at large. We have obligations towards them: first and foremost we should enlighten them and earn their approbation . . . I should also like to suggest that our most distinguished artists make copies of works by the great painters . . . . In addition, the techniques for reproducing works of art in quantity are improving by the day, and we should not forget that engraving is one of the ways of popularising art.'[15]

In fact, this kind of discussion divided the art world into two camps. The traditionalist *Journal des artistes* was anxious about the proliferation of illustrations in the press: 'Where will good taste find refuge, if the poor public is swamped to such an extent? . . . And what will become of the exacting art of engraving, so difficult and so worthy of encouragement?'[16] To counter this, the admirers of progress used the assortment of arguments that were to be the mainstay of the doctrine of the realists: 'A picture of a wandering Jew, coloured in red and blue, has far more influence on the morals and manners of the world than any masterpiece tucked away in the study of an avaricious art-lover.'[17] The invention of photography was publicised by Arago in 1839 in similar terms: 'Soon we shall be able to see beautiful prints, previously to be seen only in the drawing rooms of wealthy collectors, adorning the walls of the humble dwellings of artisans and peasants.'[18] This was the atmosphere, enthusiastic but ambivalent, in which the destiny of large numbers (too large, perhaps) was being forged; the inevitable reaction from the next generation was expressed by Théodore de Banville in 1878: 'In the language of the romantics, the true bourgeois worshipped nothing but the hundred-centime piece, had no ideals in life besides the protection of his own interests; in poetry, he liked sentimental ballads and in the visual arts, coloured lithographs.'[19]

The arrival of photography brought the dilemma about prints to a head. For some, photography represented 'the most powerful lever ever put at the disposal of ideas by science; it will allow ideas to become industrialised,' and 'Daguerre [. . .] has become a greater figure, in the eyes of the intellectual, than Michelangelo or Raphael.'[20] For others, photography 'spelled the ruin of art'. In the grand synthesis that he prepared for the Exposition Universelle of 1851, the Comte de Laborde came down firmly on the side of progress. In his opinion, 'painters, assisted by photography which can deliver their creations to all and sundry immediately, will find a highly receptive public even in the most out-of-the-way places.'[21] The Comte's position as a prominent liberal bourgeois of the day illustrates one of the crucial features of the new aesthetic. He wrote: 'With the assistance of art we shall destroy materialism.'[22]

What the print was to painting, scaled-down figures were to sculpture. In 1833 and 1834, Sauvage and Collas patented their first reducing machines, which were used in the great Parisian foundries of Susse and Barbedienne. Critics warmly welcomed this progress in art. The Electrotype process, introduced to France in 1836, was an important step forward for photography (the first photogravures were produced in 1842), and for printmaking (negatives of drawings could be transferred to stone or metal plates), and also for sculpture (Christofle took out a patent on the process of electro'metallic casting in 1840).[23] The market was totally unprepared for the flood of original and reproduction images that ensued. The first art galleries, established under the Restoration, had to adapt themselves to channel the flow. Ingres earned more from the sale of reproductions of his *Odalisque* than he did from the sale of the painting. There were dealers who would buy a painting solely in order to sell reproductions of it, and in 1841 the question of intellectual property was raised in the Chambre des Députés.[24] In 1859, Baudelaire began his great piece on *Le Peintre de la vie moderne* (*The Painter of Modern Life*) with these words: 'There exist in this world, even in the world of artists, people who go to the Louvre . . . and settle down dreamily in front of one of the paintings most widely popularised in print, a Titian or a Raphael; later, they leave, satisfied, often murmuring to themselves: 'I know my museum.'[25]

3. *The Persistence of the Art of Printmaking*

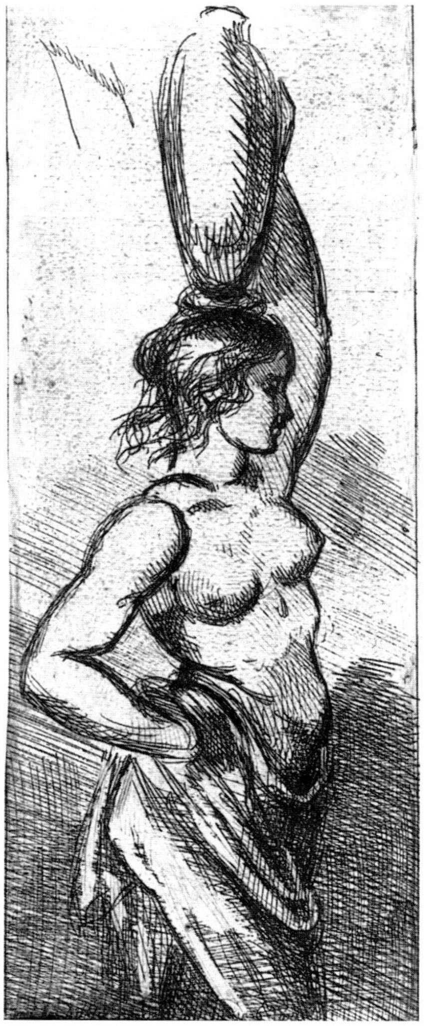

4. Philippe-Auguste Jeanron, *Woman with a Jug*. 1853. Etching, 252 x 100 mm. Bibliothèque nationale, Paris.

The rapid development of the art of reproduction led to the appearance of a new workforce, half artist, half artisan, which excessive confidence and over-investment in the industrialisation of the arts subsequently left at a loose end. The enthusiasm of the 1830s produced a high point in the Romantic illustrated book, and culminated in the invention of photography; this period of enthusiasm was succeeded, however, in the 1840s and 1850s, by a period of nagging doubts about the future, both of art and of the industrial processes that were relied on to propagate it. During this period the bourgeoisie, now greatly increased in numbers and diversity, grew increasingly wealthy and, as they did so, increasingly opposed the democratisation of art; they wanted to appropriate for themselves all the benefits that art offered as a means to legitimising their position and endorsing their individuality.

Artists had continued to make etchings, and indeed the art of etching had known some glorious periods, particularly in Holland in the seventeenth century, when social upheavals comparable to those in nineteenth-century France were taking place. Since the days of the Ancien Régime, before the Revolution, however, the traditional artist's etching had appealed to a very small public. In 1834, Villot was to write in *L'Artiste*: 'How strange are the ways of art lovers . . . They wax tender and lyrical over an etching by whichever old master is in favour at the moment, jump with enthusiasm at the sight of Rembrandt's *Shell* . . . . But these zealous supporters of the etching would smile pityingly at modern attempts at the technique.'[26] The same year, Paul Huet presented a portfolio of six etchings, published by Rittner and Goupil, at the Salon.

At this date a tenuous link still existed with the landscape artists and genre painters of the Ancien Régime, as well as with their admirers. In 1833 Eugène Bléry, who became Meryon's teacher, rediscovered the work of Jean-Jacques de Boissieu in Lyon. Some of the romantics, Decamps and Célestin Nanteuil, and Delacroix himself, had not completely neglected etching. Paul Huet and Charles Jacque had learned to appreciate its charms with the painter Philippe-Auguste Jeanron (Fig. 4). Art historian, director of museums under the Second Republic, reorganiser of the copper plate collection in the Louvre, friend of Daumier as well as of Alfred Sensier, mentor of Jean-François Millet,[27] Jeanron was a member of the circle of lithographers created by publications such as *Le Charivari*, and of illustrators of works like *Les Français peints par eux-mêmes*. Meryon's first patron, Jules Niel, was appointed *sous-préfet* (deputy administrator) in 1830, proof of his support of the new government.[28] The renewal of artists' etchings might be interpreted as the consequence of a revival (by advanced circles after the July Monarchy) of the tradition of the pre-Revolutionary upper middle classes and enlightened aristocrats.

Paul Huet's etchings (Figs 7, 8), some enhanced with coloured wash, were among the works admired by young artists with romantic sympathies. As a painter, Huet preceded the Impressionist movement by a long way and could not therefore be considered part of it. As a printmaker, on the other hand, he bridged the gap, his career dividing neatly into two: before 1838 he was an 'advanced' romantic, and after 1866 showed awareness of pre-Impressionist experiments. In 1828 he breathed a bold resonance[29] into landscape etchings that still clung to the romantic pastoral tradition. In 1866, in the Société des Aquafortistes, he published a plate in the style of the Barbizon school entitled *Near Fontainebleau*, and, in 1868, a second larger folio of etchings. Though still a romantic, he was beginning to develop towards realism and more clearly-defined visual effects. His lightness of touch (*Stand of Willows near Paris*), and his innovative choice of subject (*The Factory*) are sometimes reminiscent of Pissarro.

The large body of work produced by Charles Jacque[30] between 1842 and 1848 also displays an early interest in the techniques favoured by the Impressionists: three monotype proofs of the same print exist, for example, with a first state printed without any embellishment, a second heightened by being worked over with a *roulette* and burnisher, and several intermediary states

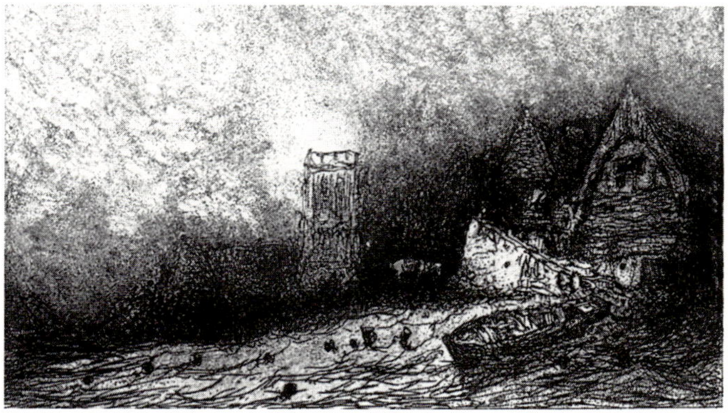

5. Adolphe Hervier,
Etching. 1843.
Etching, 132 x 156 mm.
Bibliothèque nationale, Paris.

6. Théodore Rousseau,
A View in the Berry. 1842 (?).
Etching, 72 x 175 mm.
Bibliothèque nationale, Paris.

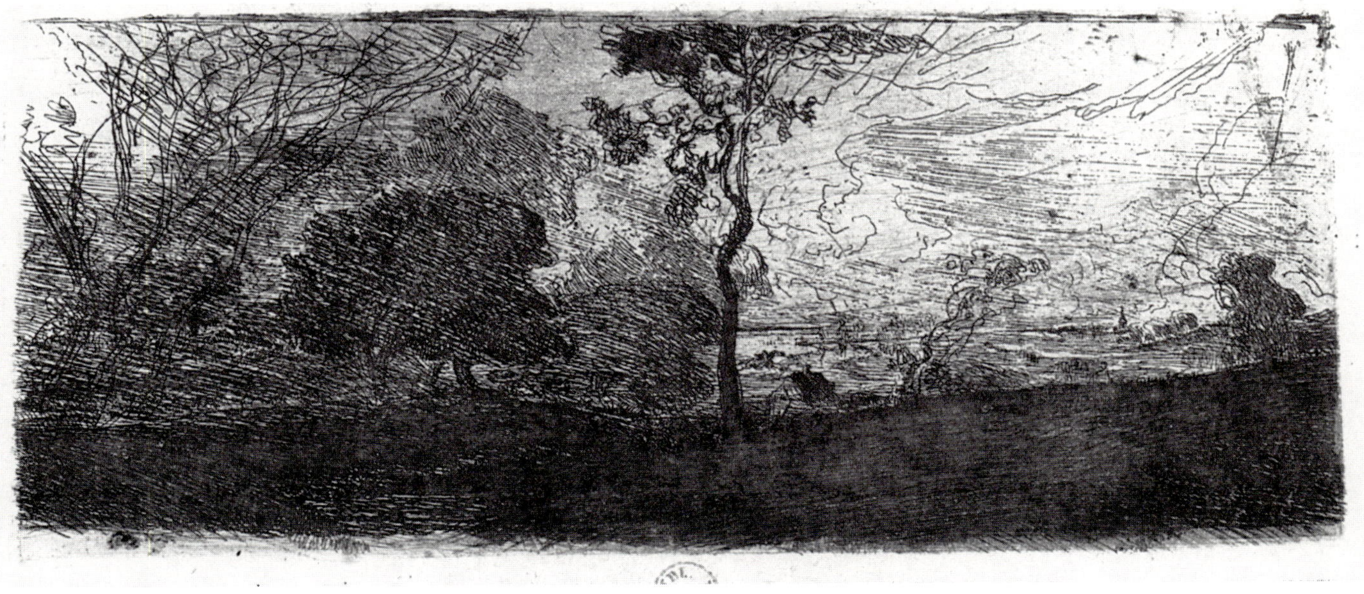

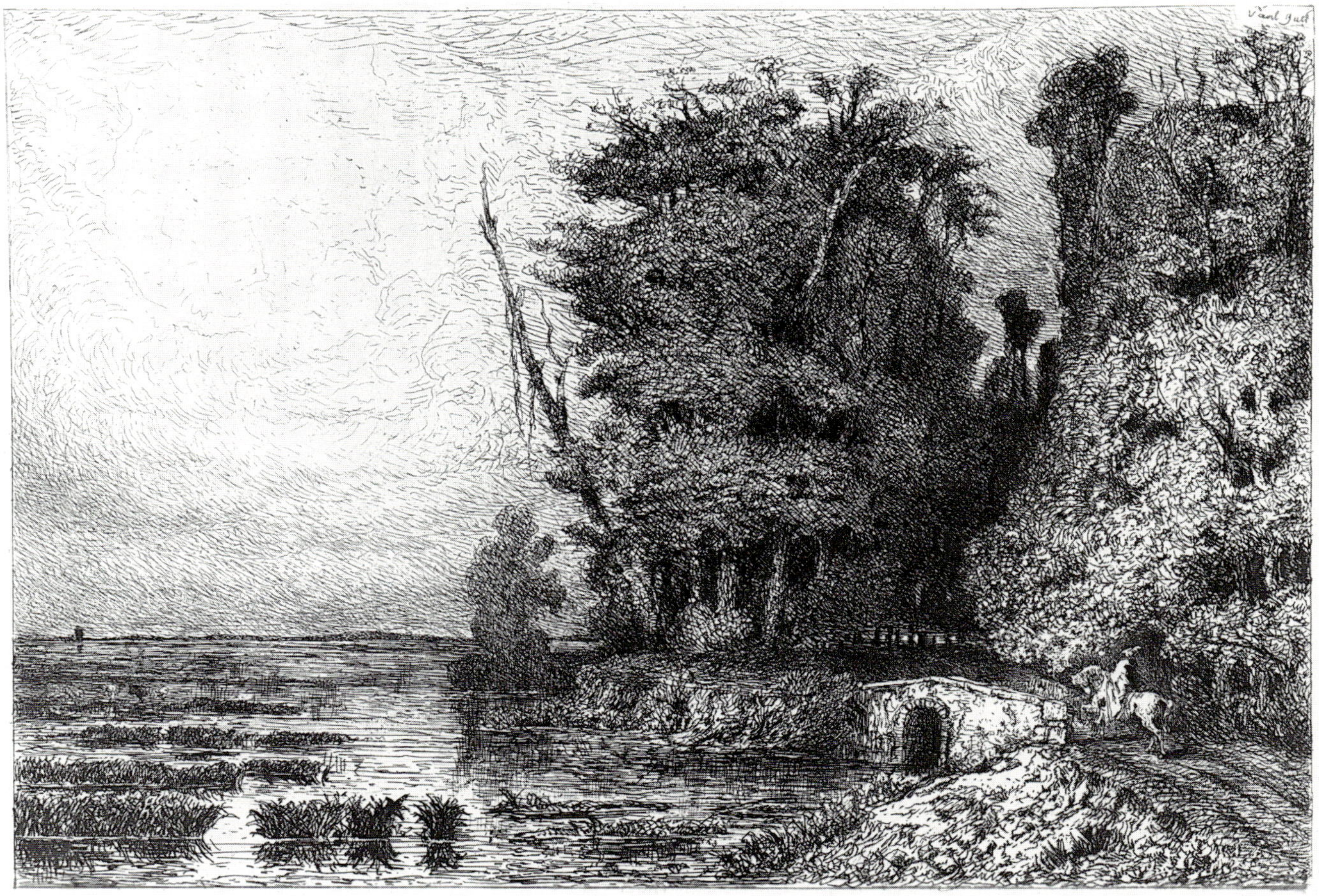

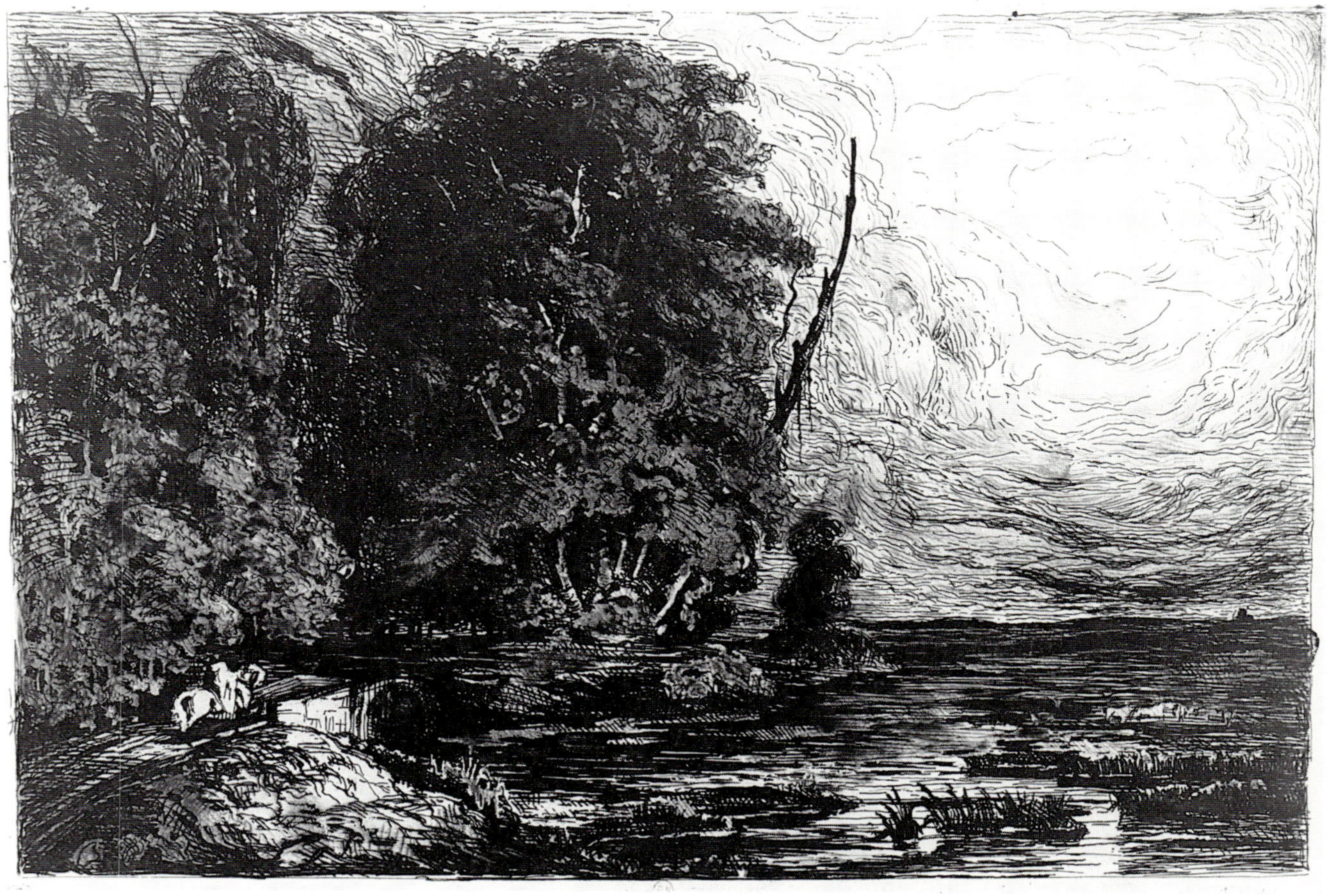

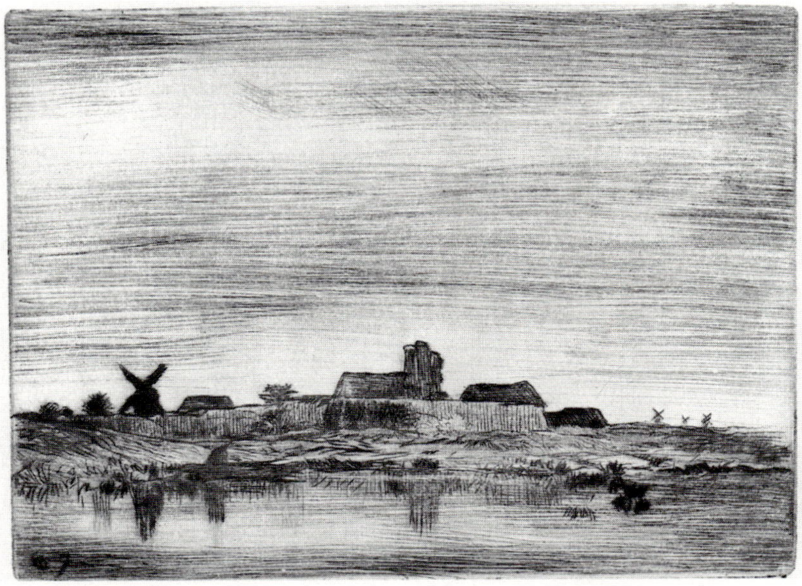

9, 10, 11. Charles Jacque, *Village by the Water*. 1848. Etching, 100 x 133 mm. *Second state*, pale, printed in black and white and printed with inking effect. *Third state*, very heavily inked. Bibliothèque nationale, Paris.

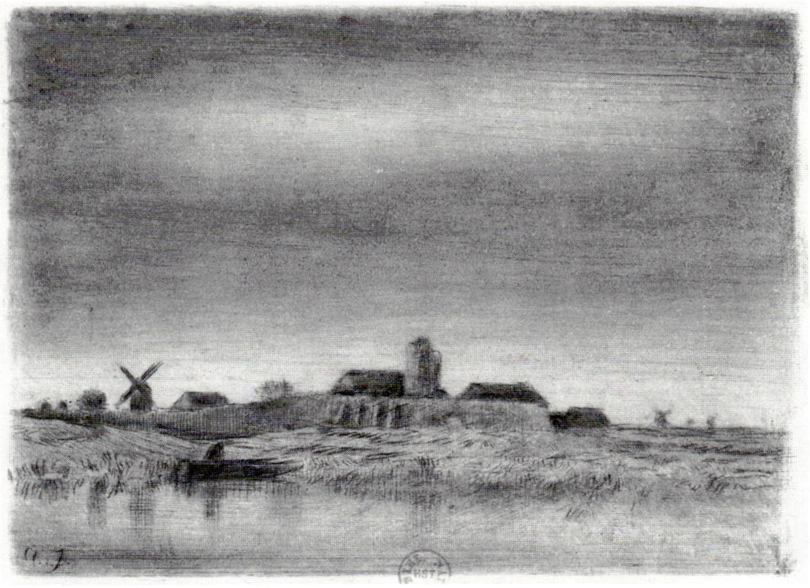

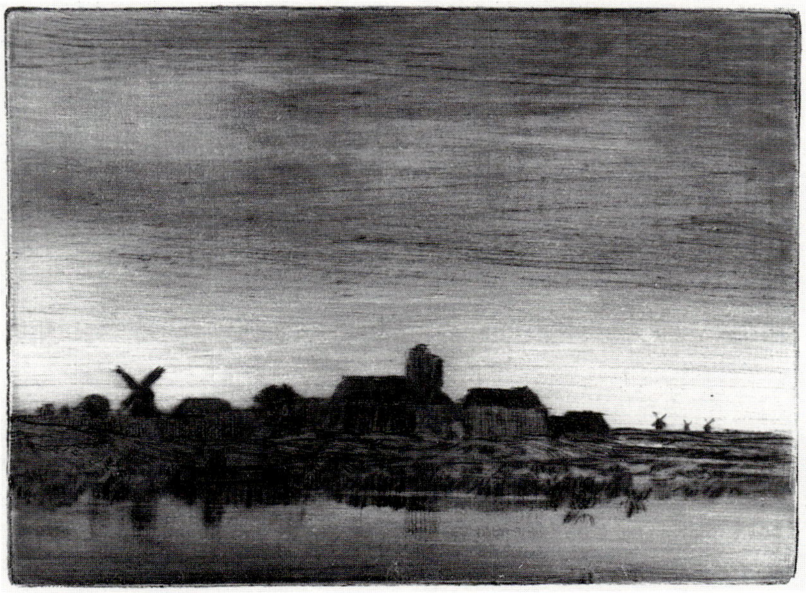

previous page:
7, 8. Paul Huet, *The Horsemen (Evening Storm)*. 1868. Etching and counter-proof printed as a monotype, 173 x 254 mm. Bibliothèque nationale, Paris.

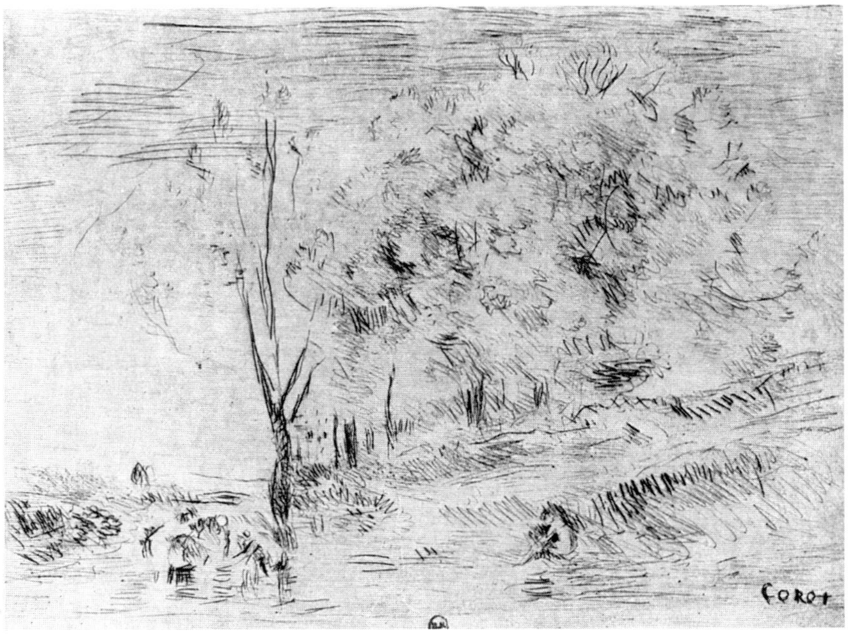

12. Camille Corot, *Bathers*. About 1865(?). Drypoint print of an etching from which the etching ground had been removed, 151 x 196 mm. Bibliothèque nationale, Paris.

printed with various inking effects (Figs 9–11). Charles Jacque, as an artist and as a craftsman, forged a link between the scattered and relatively unsuccessful etchers of the romantic and Barbizon periods and the revival of etching that took root at the end of the 1850s. His prolific output (470 pieces) began to look more experimental in 1843, light being handled with greater freedom using 'manière noire' effects (*Three Mills in Montmartre*, 1846), dry point (*Horse in a Storm*, 1848) and 'clichés-verre'. In fact, his innovations reflect a renewal of interest in techniques that artists, between 1830 and 1850, seemed to have forgotten. This did not prevent Pissarro from disliking quite intensely his facile style and his artificial choice of subjects.

It would be legitimate to assume that it was with Charles Jacque, his neighbour in rue Rochechouart in 1845, that Millet took his first steps in etching. The two left Paris together in June 1849 to set up house in Barbizon. Their earliest, tentative efforts, were completely ignored in the first catalogues. Nothing appeared in the salerooms until Lebrun sold his collection to Keppel in 1886. Lebrun wrote of one of the early drypoint prints, *Sheep grazing*: 'This engraved plate of 1850 is by Millet. . . . Charles Jacque's signature was appended, as a joke rather than an attempt to sell the print, which was executed one evening on the corner of the table in Auguste Delâtre's printing works.'[32] These early attempts are worth mentioning because Millet's prints, six or seven years later, developed in a manner that was of crucial importance to the history of etching.

Adolphe Hervier,[33] a pupil of Isabey (as was Jongkind) and a generally unsuccessful artist, whose work was rejected twenty-three times by the Salon, was inspired by the English romantics (Fig. 5). Viewed with hindsight, his work looks premonitory of things to come: the *Travel Sketches* of 1843 and his album of *Griffonis*, eight prints etched on steel plates, published in 1846, or his *Artistic Lithographs* published by Auguste Bry in about 1850. There were also interesting and very personal interpretations of the romantic etching produced by Harpignie and Célestin Nanteuil. Nanteuil may have been responsible for encouraging Théodore Rousseau (Fig. 6) to produce his first etching, one copy of which is annotated by one of the few collectors of the period, Edmond Hédouin: 'Théodore Rousseau, *Woodland's Edge*, an etching made by him in 1836. First state presented by him to E. Hédouin in 1836. A proof in the same state was retouched by him in black and white pencil and given to Célestin Nanteuil in the same year. I have only ever seen these two proofs and I have reason to believe that the plate was never finished.'[34]

Corot's first etching is characteristic of the 'false starts' at etching made by landscape painters of the so-called 'modern school'. It was executed in two stages, separated by twenty years, according to the story reported by Bracquemond. In 1865 Bracquemond apparently found the designed and prepared (but not etched) plate in a box of nails in Corot's house and offered to etch it and print it for him. The first sketch for this *Memory of Tuscany* was therefore probably executed in about 1845. It is clear, nevertheless, that Corot was uninterested enough in what he had produced to abandon it in its first state.[35] When they did begin printmaking, the Impressionist painters had at their disposal the tools and processes that they had learned from these early, quite paradoxical works (Fig. 12).

4. *A Painter Between Two Worlds: Charles-François Daubigny*

Daubigny's career reached its zenith in 1867, when he was fifty. This was the year when the glory of the French Empire was being trumpeted by the second Exposition Universelle in Paris. Nine paintings by Daubigny were on show in the international art exhibition; he won the gold medal and, later, the Légion d'Honneur. None of the contemporary painters who admired his work had had even a single painting accepted, and the most comfortably off of these, Manet and Courbet, mounted their own exhibition on the fringes of the official one. In July 1865, Daubigny and his dealer (and the publisher of his etchings), Alfred Cadart, dined with Whistler in London. Later, when he returned to Trouville, Daubigny struck up a friendship with Eugène Boudin and a young painter of his acquaintance, Claude Monet, who was later to acknowledge his debt to their brightly coloured, freely painted landscapes. In 1866 Daubigny sat, with Corot, on the jury panel of the recently-enlarged Salon.

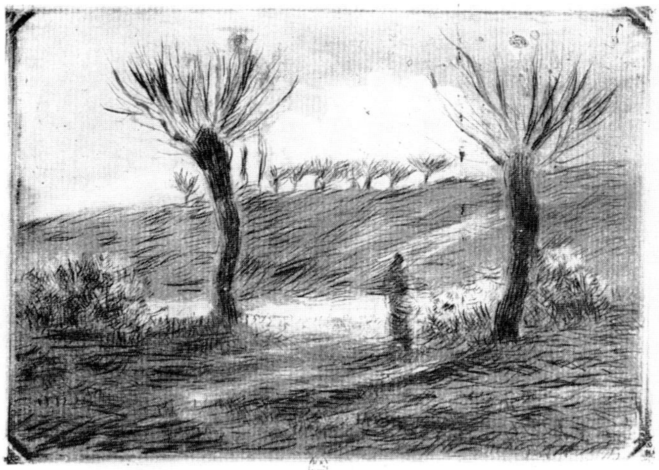

13. Camille Pissarro, *Sunset*. 1879. Drypoint, fourth and final state, 115 x 160 mm. Bibliothèque nationale, Paris.

14. Charles-François Daubigny, *Sunrise*. 1850. Etching, third state, 134 x 233 mm. Bibliothèque nationale, Paris.

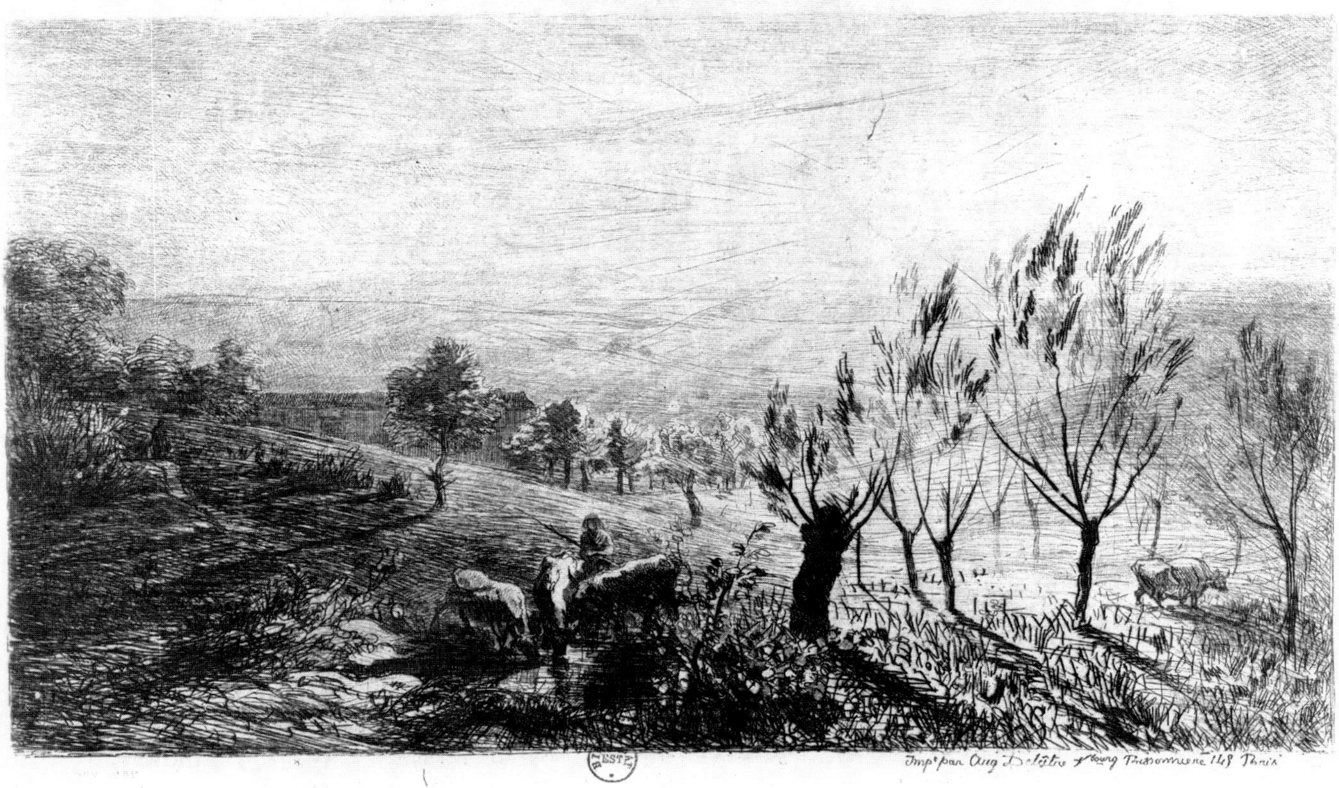

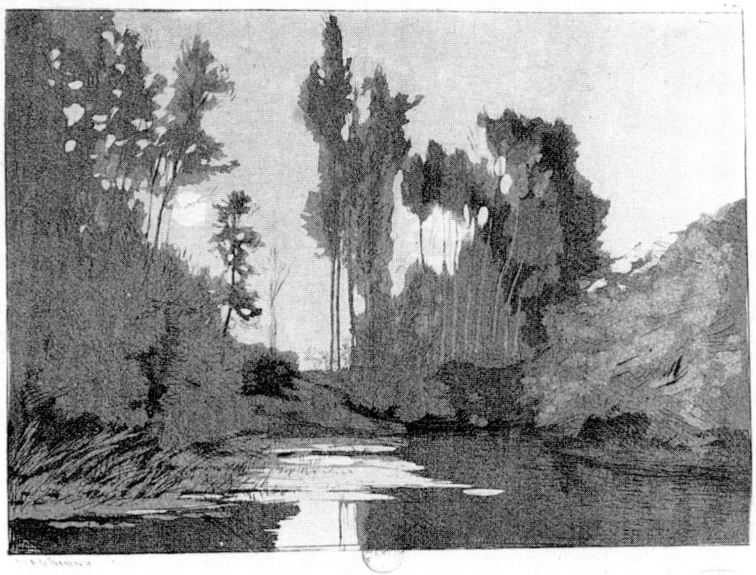

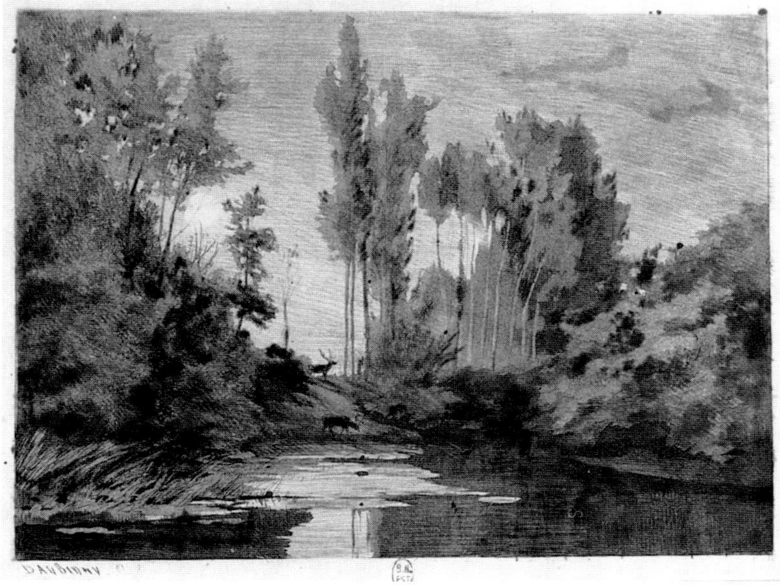

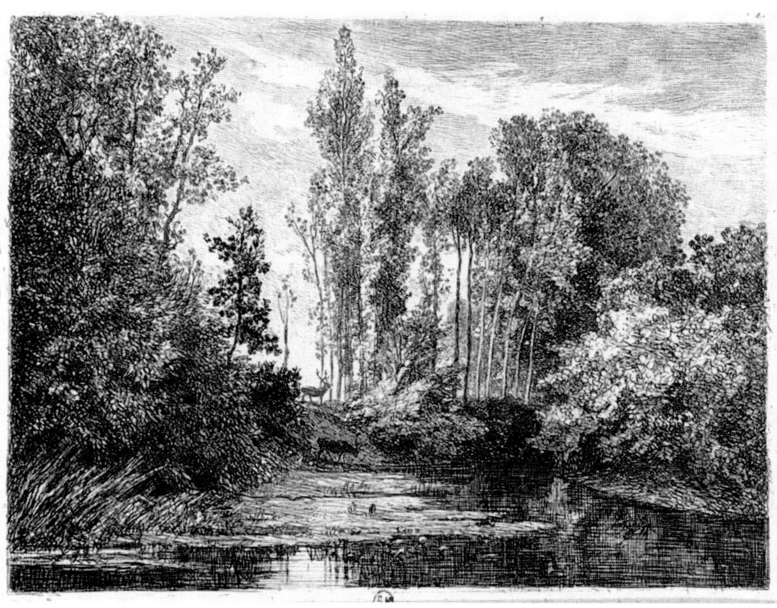

15, 16, 17. Charles-François Daubigny, *Stags at the Water's Edge*. 1848. Etching 'à la cravate' (with fabric), first, second and fifth states, 115 x 154 mm. Bibliothèque nationale, Paris.

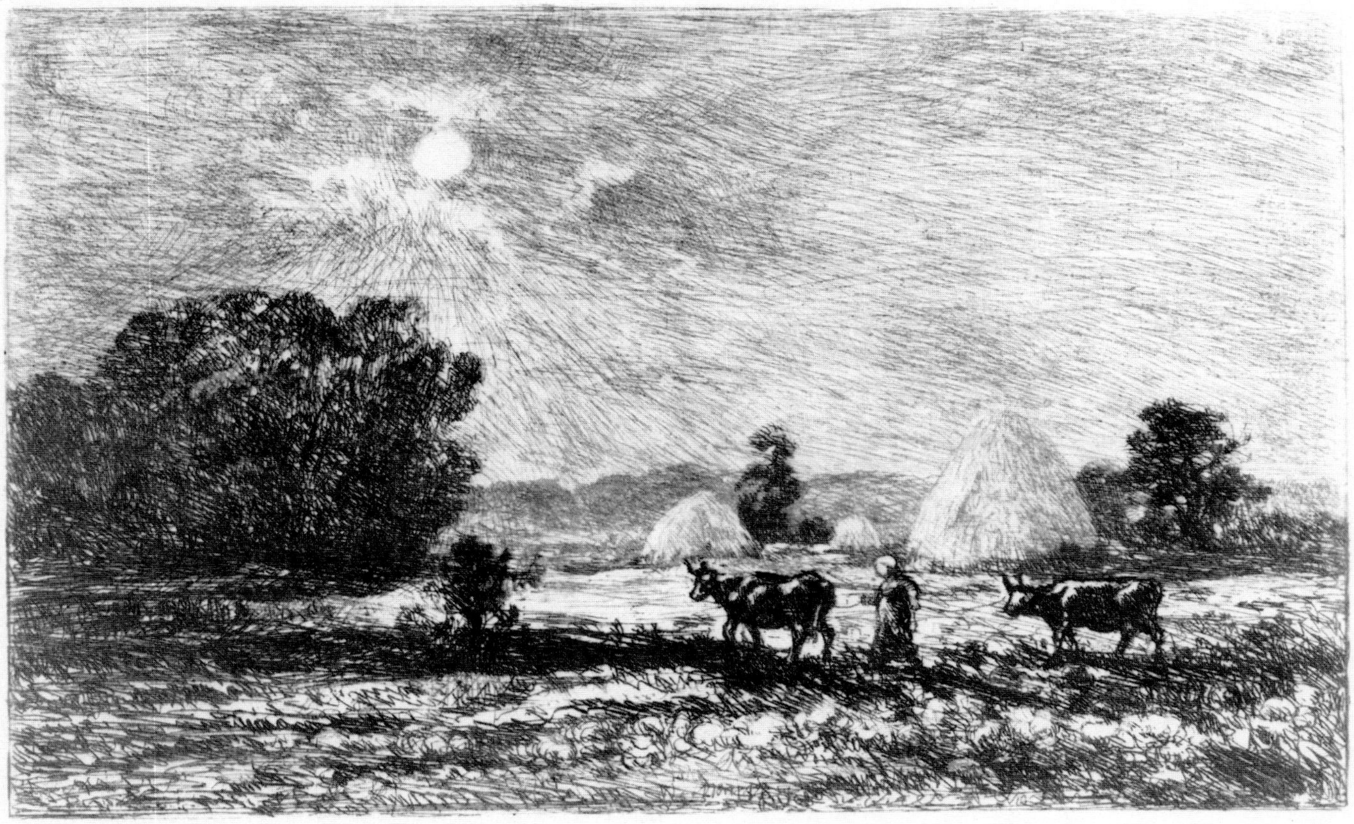

18. Charles-François Daubigny, *moonlight at valmondois*. 1877. etching, 134 x 217 mm. Bibliothèque nationale, Paris.

Cézanne and Renoir, championed by him, were rejected, Pissarro accepted. Daubigny exhibited his paintings of the River Oise, and his etching *The Ford*, just published by Cadart. He also showed some work at the Royal Academy, then went to join Monet at Honfleur. After his success at the Exposition Universelle he was a member of the jury again for the Salon of 1868 and this time was instrumental in securing the admission of Pissarro, Monet, Bazille, Degas, Renoir, Sisley and Morisot,[36] in spite of opposition from members of the Academy and the Minister for the Arts, de Niewerkerke. In his report on the Salon, Castagnary, later a leading supporter of the Impressionists, rejoiced in this 'outburst of freedom.'[37]

In 1866, the year of his success at the Exposition Universelle, Daubigny, to the amazement of his critics, also produced for the popular publisher, Mame, a series of ten wood engravings for a book on gardens. From 1838 to 1847, long before Claude Monet used railways as his chosen subject, Daubigny had begun illustrating guidebooks for tourists in France. These small engraved vignettes won him the esteem of realist critics: 'I know tiny vignettes by him, just a few centimetres square, executed ten or twelve years ago for the railway guides, which display more breadth and skill than many a large, well-known canvas.'[38] Daubigny, who was born between two distinct periods, pursued with equanimity the double career to which these two periods condemned him. In 1838, at the age of twenty, he had set himself up with friends in a kind of commune, all of its members dreaming of fame and fortune: Trimolet made his living with caricatures, Steinheil painted stained glass windows, Geoffroy-Dechaume made designs for goldsmiths. Curmer, the publisher, paid well for book illustrations, which at forty francs apiece represented a source of relative affluence to the community, who shared the task with Meissonier. This income was sufficient for Daubigny to treat himself to a trip to Italy, after which he turned his hand to etching. His reasons have probably been correctly analysed by his first biographer, Henriet, who wrote in 1874: 'It was in about 1839, on his return from Italy, that he first tried using an etching tool, probably because he wanted to record Impressions of his journey. It was not disagreeable to him, anyway, to groom himself for the demands of publishers who, at the time, were beginning to have recourse to etchings on steel as an economical, rapid and durable means of reproduction.'[39]

Thanks to his earnings as an illustrator, Daubigny was able to retreat to Bourg-d'Orsans, in the Alps, to paint a *St Jerome* that achieved a modest success in the Salon of 1840. *L'Artiste*, a contemporary review, ordered an etched reproduction of the painting. Encouraged by this, he exhibited a painting, *View from the Banks of the River Furon* at the Salon of 1841, and a frame containing six etchings. Trimolet did the same. In 1843 the second volume of *Daguerrian excursions* appeared, containing the first two photogravures ever published; as the commentary points out proudly, they were executed 'entirely without human intervention'. The remaining plates were aquatints on steel plates, hand etched from daguerreotypes. Daubigny contributed his *View of Bas-Meudon* (Fig. 22), admired by the commentator for its freshness and straightforwardness, its depiction of air and light, 'the rustling of the trees', and its perfect fidelity to the photographic image.[40]

In 1845, Daubigny executed on a steel plate a view of the luxurious galleries belonging to Durand-Ruel, his dealer (Fig. 3); this was a frontispiece to the catalogue published by Durand-Ruel to introduce his clientèle to 'the most brilliant specimens of the Modern School'. Daubigny, the painter, figured in the catalogue, while Daubigny, the printmaker, was its anonymous illustrator.[41] In 1848, Charles Blanc, the Minister for the Arts in the Republican government, revived the idea of a pictorial museum, first proposed by Paul Huet, and ordered a number of printmakers, including Daubigny, to make reproductions of famous paintings. Under the Second Empire this policy of support to printmakers was continued. For the respectable sum of 4,000 francs, Daubigny made a copy of Ruisdael's *The Bush* in 1853. Bracquemond also benefited from this policy in 1853, receiving an order for a *Décor* by Le Pautre, for 100 francs, then, in 1855, for Holbein's *Portrait of Erasmus* (Fig. 75) 2,000 francs; the latter turned up finally on the wall of the Salon des Refusés in 1863.[42]

The generation of 1840 found itself at the crossroads of pre- and post-industrial civilisation, pursuing a double career that was the daily reality for artists, yet which presented them with a huge dilemma. In 1851, Daubigny successfully published a *Book of Etchings*;[43] this ran into eleven editions, each from a different publisher. The style looks forward to the Impressionist style with its clarity, its rapid simple drawing, and its use of new techniques to convey sensations with spontaneity and truth. Daubigny uses the 'cravat' technique, a method of obtaining a grain by applying a piece of fabric to the etching ground, which gives light variations to the inking (Figs 15–17). The technique, designed to imitate the aquatint, was inherited from etchers of the romantic period like Célestin Nanteuil. By 1874, when his career ended, Daubigny's work was in harmony with the work of the budding Impressionists. His *Rising Moon* and *Villerville, Sunset* won him the Légion d'Honneur. Henriet published a catalogue of his etchings in the *Gazette des Beaux-Arts*. Between 1874 and his death in 1878 he made six more etchings, very close in style to Impressionist etchings. They are small in size and lively; he even uses dry point in his *Apple Trees at Auvers* (1877), so similar to Pissarro's *Landscape at Pontoise, Apple trees* (1873). Similarly, Daubigny's *Sunrise* (1850; Fig. 14) presaged Pissarro's *Sunset* (1879; Fig. 13). Daubigny's last etching, *Moonlight at Valmondois* (Fig. 18), was left unfinished; He intended to burnish it, 'to tone down the sheaves of corn and the clumps of vegetation that edge the horizon'.[44]

5. *Mechanical Reproduction*

Impressionism, the fruit of the Third Republic, began to germinate in the fertile soil of realism during the Second Empire. This was a period of uncertainty and conflict, the fate of the arts in a troubled democracy being as yet unsealed. Realism, as an aesthetic doctrine, exists only in relation to the number of enthusiasts wishing, in the name of the populace at large, to define it as such. Bold statements about the unity of art and industry were soon followed by statements about their separateness: 'The more the theory of social art, the art of ideas, progresses, the more the notion of art for art's sake gains ground', wrote Pierre Georgel.[45] The authoritarian period of the Second Empire perpetuated out-of-date ideologies and brought back censorship, providing no solution to these problems. Courbet's realist manifesto (1855) was followed by the prosecution of Flaubert and Baudelaire for offences against public morals (1856). In 1855, the Exposition Universelle provided a show-case for industrial progress; the eyes of the world were trained on Paris and the French achievement. A young artist arrived from the Dutch East Indies to visit the Exposition Universelle and to see the French art which he so much admired, in particular the paintings of Corot; this was Camille Pissarro, whose family were of Portuguese Jewish origin and whose own nationality was Danish – in effect, he was stateless.

The consummation of the marriage between industrial progress and the fine arts was slow to take place: the process that would permit the printing of photographs to make photographic prints was awaited with impatience. Without this discovery, however, photography remained almost a hobby and engraving an art reprieved only until the sword of Damocles of photogravure fell on its neck. From 1850 onwards the competition between different types of mechanical processes became urgent, even stifling. Nevertheless, in 1851, in order to illustrate printed books with photographs, Blanquart-Évrard, the publisher from Lille, was perfectly willing to print hundreds and hundreds of photographs, drying them in the sun before having them stuck, one by one, by a team of women, on to the pages of each volume.[46] This operation was as costly as printing an edition of an etching and the stability of the images was not guaranteed – the latter problem operating strongly in favour of the continuing success of the 'hand-made' print. In 1842 Fizeau and Charles Nègre had discovered how to

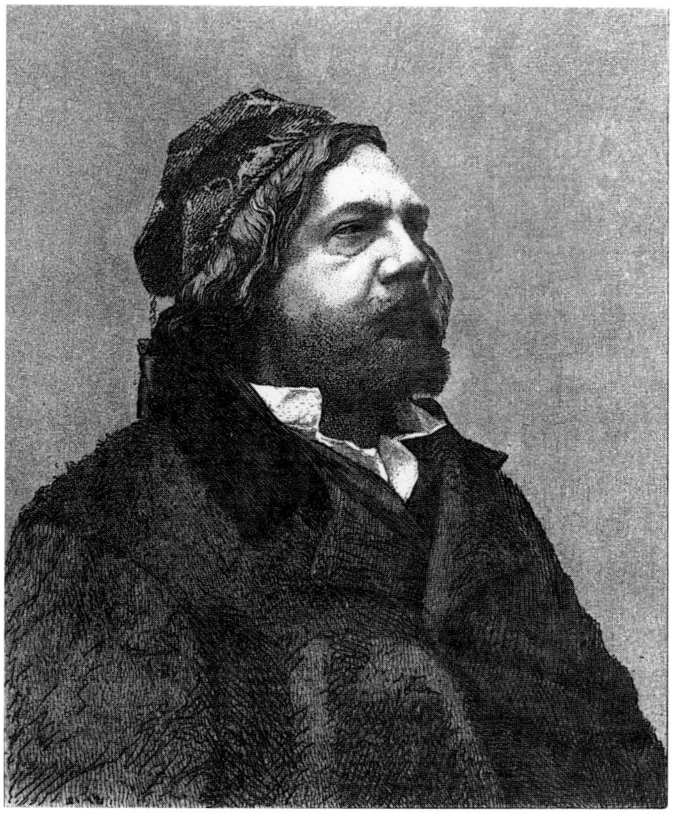

19. Félix Bracquemond,
Portrait of Théophile Gautier, after a photograph by Nadar. 1857.
Etching, 157 x 124 mm.
Bibliothèque nationale, Paris.

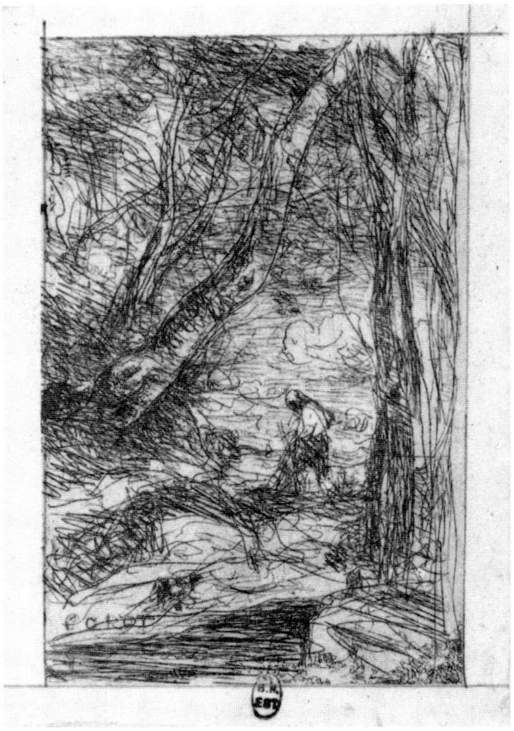

20. Camille Corot,
The Little Woodcutter, after Rembrandt. 1853.
Hand photogravure by Charles Nègre,
from a glass print, 99 x 62 mm.
Bibliothèque nationale, Paris.

engrave and print daguerreotypes, but the process was so complex and costly, and so unreliable, that it was impossible to carry it out on an industrial scale.[47] On the other hand, electrotyping now made possible the reproduction of drawings executed on paper and transferred to stone or metal plates.[48] The Gillot process, referred to irreverently as 'gillotage' by artists, spread to ordinary publishing houses after 1850. Between 1840 and 1860 block printing processes multiplied in the printing works. Each printer had his favourite: Tissier (acid on stone) from 1841, Heims, Coblentz, Comte, Dulos, Didot, Smée, Plon could all by and large meet the demands of the book trade and the illustrated press. The Piaud process gave eternal life to the wood engravings of Gustave Doré. No-one could have guessed that research begun on the screen, a highly complicated, indeed almost inexplicable process, would not reach a successful conclusion until 1885. After 1855 enthusiasm began to wane and research projects to mark time. In 1856 a patron, the duc de Luynes, offered a large sum of money to anyone finding the solution. The final date for the competition was fixed at 1 July 1859, but by then no candidate had come up with an answer. The prize was eventually awarded to Albert Poitevin in 1862 and medals to Charles Nègre and, among others, Lemercier in 1867.[49]

This represented hope to some, a grave threat to others. Artists were divided into two camps, those who were violently opposed to industrialisation and those who accepted and worked with the new processes: from their coupling a new, hybrid style of print was born. One of them, Constant Dutilleux, formed a group of like'minded artists in Arras to pursue the uses of photography in design, and came up with the 'cliché-verre' (Fig. 21): the group consisted of L. Grandguillaume, who taught design at the technical school in Arras, Adalbert Cuvelier, an oil manufacturer and amateur photographer and Charles Desavary, a painter and photographer. All were admirers of Corot, from whom Dutilleux had bought a painting in 1847.[50] Dutilleux obtained drawings on glass from Corot and from them made not only photographs but also photogravures. The glass plate of Rembrandt's *Little Woodcutter* (Fig. 20) reproduced by Corot, of which a proof exists bearing the note 'C. Corot, 1st attempt at glass drawing for photography, May 1853', was sent to Charles Nègre to be transferred to a metal plate and printed like an etching.

Kindly Corot participated willingly in this experiment and his 'engravings' consist of sixty-seven glass plates made between 1855 and 1874 for fourteen copper-plate etchings. Other artists of the 'Modern School' were encouraged to take part: Delacroix, Daubigny, Millet, Théodore Rousseau etc. all had a go at the cliché-verre. Corot alone, however, drew directly on to the glass and also on to the opaque etching paste that was painted over the glass plates, obtaining lighting effects not seen

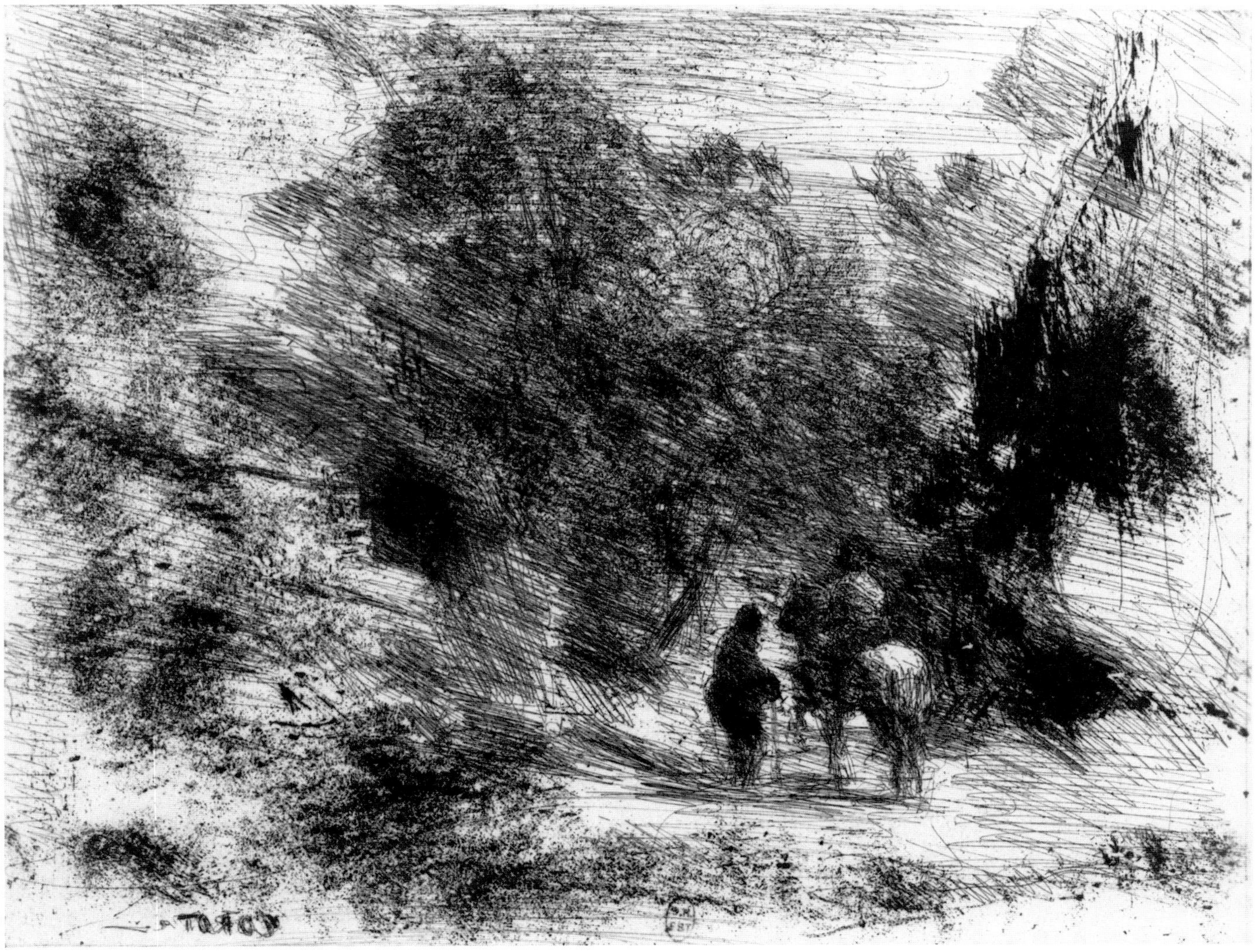

21. Camille Corot,
The Rider in the Forest. 1854.
Glass print, 150 x 186 mm.
Bibliothèque nationale, Paris.

before in print'making; the printing process enhanced the lighting effects by using the glass inverted with the light shining through it. Both in its principles and its results cliché-verre printing was allied to Impressionism. The monotypes subsequently executed by Degas using celluloid plates were not very different. The cliché-verre print, half print, half photograph lingered for years in an artistic limbo, well described by the remark of a collector of prints: 'The presence of photography in this process brings us into the realm of mechanisation, and the finished product is therefore of no interest.'[51]

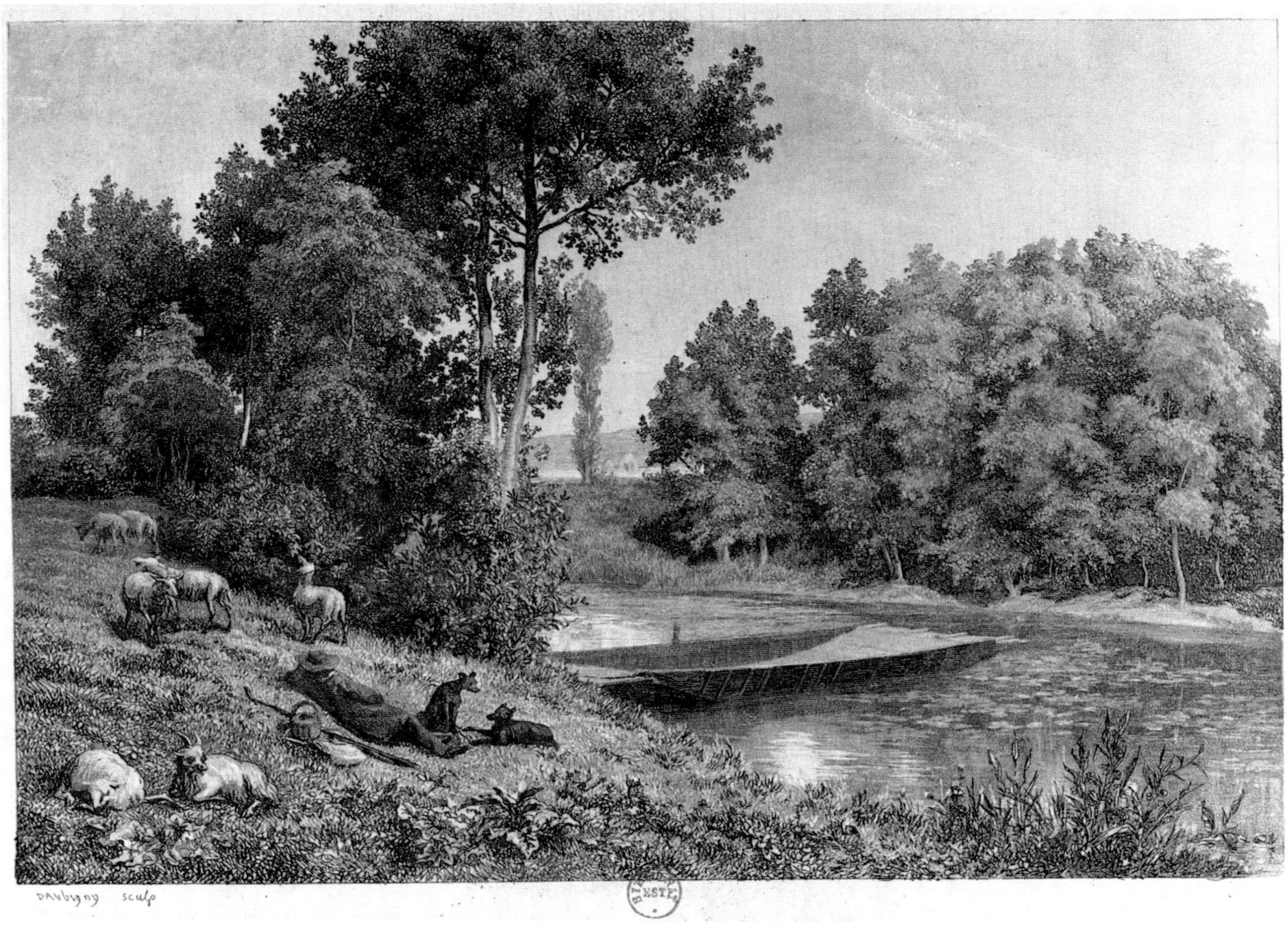

22. Charles-François Daubigny, *View of Bas-Meudon*. 1843.
Aquatint and etching from a daguerreotype, 143 x 203 mm.
First published in *Excursions daguerriennes*, vol. 2, Paris, 1843.
Bibliothèque nationale, Paris.

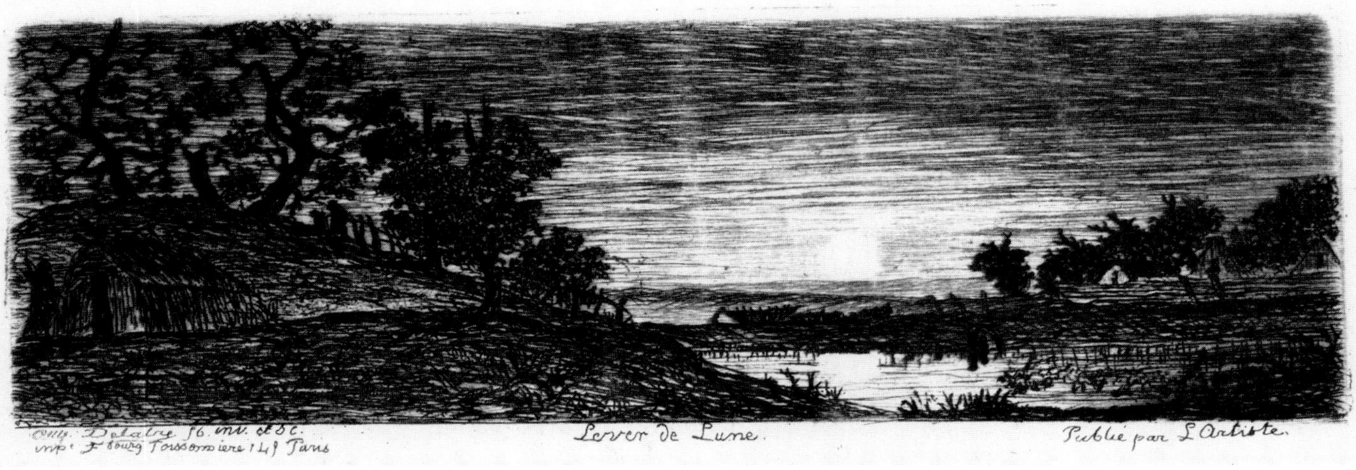

6. *1850–2: Delâtre and Meryon*

While Firmin Gillot was engaged in developing his 'paniconographic' printing process (later a boon to the newspapers but a disaster for illustrators), and Blanquart-Évrard in Lille his 'photographic factory' (thanks to which books could be illustrated with real photographs), a printing shop of a third type had quietly opened its doors at 38 rue Rochechouart in Paris in 1847; it was very near the studio, at 42bis, where Charles Jacque and Millet worked. In 1848 Auguste Delâtre moved the printing shop to the rue Saint-Jacques. He was then twenty-six years old.[52] At twelve he had been an apprentice in the printing works where his father worked but, having been ill-treated by the boss there, had gone from door to door looking for employment. In 1843 he found work with Charles Jacque, whose landscape etchings, made in collaboration with Marvy, had attracted enough buyers for the artist to be able to transfer the handling of the printing to someone else. In 1848, Delâtre was manning the barricades. Charles Jacque gave up print-making at this time, proposing to Delâtre that he take over the press (on credit) and keep Jacque's clientèle. Before becoming the semi-official printer to the Impressionist print-makers, Delâtre did the printing for all the painters of the 'modern' school: Corot, Delacroix, Millet, Daubigny and Charles Meryon, all now starting to take an interest in etching. By taking on this rôle, Delâtre helped lay the foundation stones of their careers.

In 1850, the recent revolution having brought about political and economic changes, the three methods of reproducing images (mechanical reproduction, photography, artists' prints) diverged, each henceforth following its own route. The last-named was by far the most modest in scale – a footpath rather than a major

23. Auguste Delâtre,
The Rising of the Moon. 1856.
Etching. 54 x 152 mm.
Bibliothèque nationale, Paris.

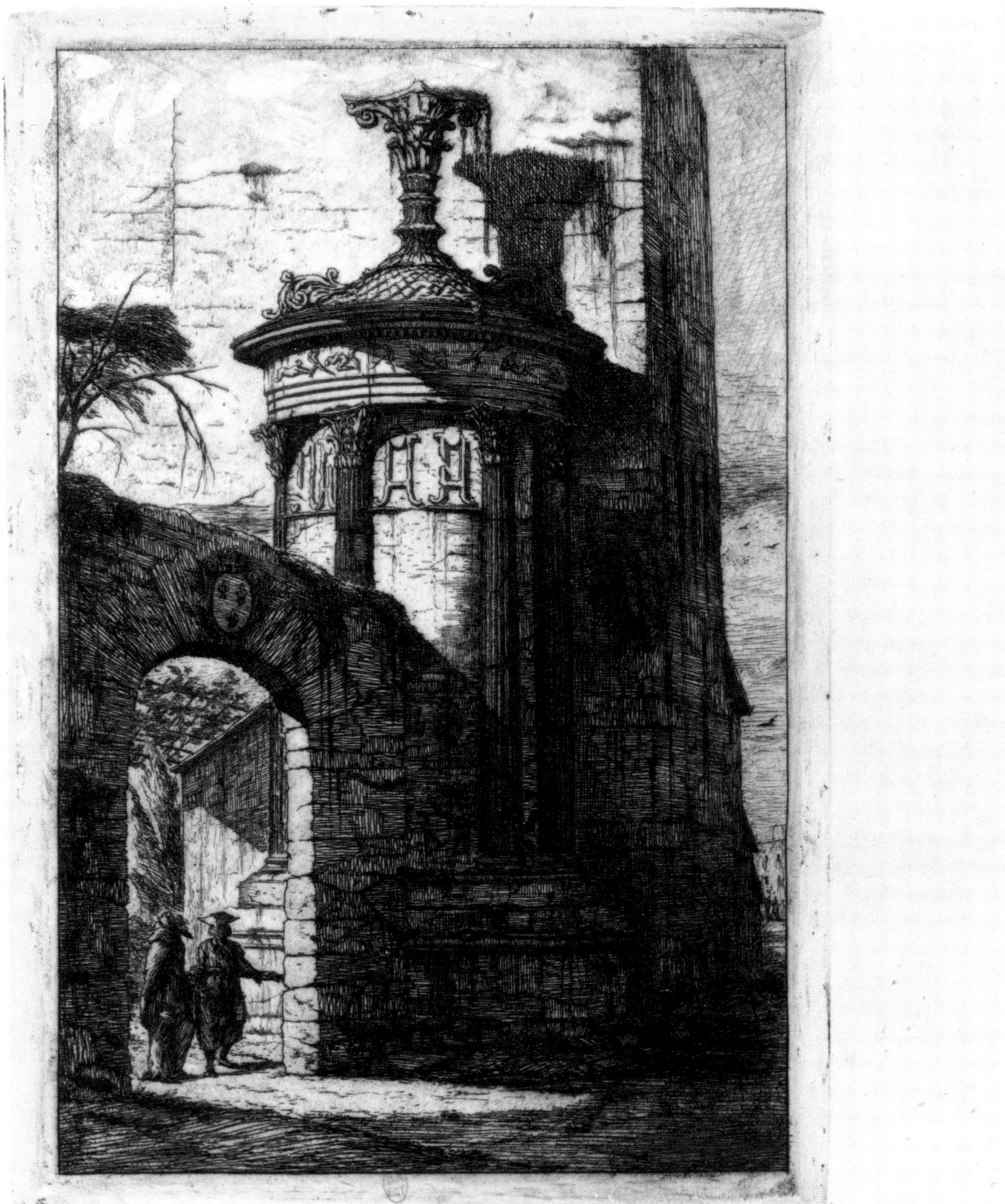
à Monsieur Niel
C. Meryon

route, which, throughout the decade, artisans, critics and artists had to fight hard to keep open. With works like Bracquemond's *Top of a Double Door* (1852), Degas's *Self Portrait* (1856; Fig. 42) and Whistler's *French Set* (1858) the beginnings of the Impressionist print were starting to appear. This period coincided with the first ten years of the Second Empire, the spectacular revival of the French economy and a return to moral and political order.

The minor flurry of excitement now gathering around the print affected the critical fraternity as well. In 1852, Théophile Gautier praised the aquatints of Adolphe Hervier and the post-romantic engravings of fairly peripheral artists like Bresdin and Meryon.[53] He was joined by the Goncourt brothers and then by a young critic whose career was to be closely involved with the engravers of his generation, Philippe Burty. The attention paid to them, however little, served to give hope to those involved in etching, who were the casualties of the conflict between art and industry. Some idea of the fragility of this first sortie is given in a short story published by the Goncourts in *L'Artiste* in 1856 entitled 'The Late M. Thomas' (later changed to 'An Etcher').[54] The character in question is an unsuccessful artist, who, before going mad, confesses: 'I am a printmaker, Sir, a miserable position to be in, as you can see: stains, holes, clothes like tinder on which someone has stuck a match. . . The dealers! Oh, the dealers! I have to beg them to pay me fifteen francs a plate!. . .'. This character was inspired by Meryon, whose prints (Fig. 24) the Goncourts had been examining a few days earlier at the house of Jules Niel: 'They are admirable, amazingly realistic'.[55] Meryon's work does not quite justify the title of Impressionist, but the Goncourts' printmaker voices a thought that inevitably connects him with the Impressionists: 'a glow, as you know, has no outline'.

It was at about this time, after the Exposition Internationale of 1855, that the Goncourts' fictional character, Coriolis, in *Manette Salomon*, one of the numbers of painters produced by the July Monarchy, feeling his career running out of steam, turned instinctively towards print-making: 'He tried to sublimate the agony of those hours in the repetitive labour, the heartbreak, of mechanical art; he was overcome by a violent urge to make an etching.'[56] Meryon's work, in the words of Beraldi, 'is not the free and impulsive work of the painter-etcher; it is a superb example of the engraver's art. Meryon makes original prints and is essentially an engraver: he carves images.'[57]

Meryon's work marked a very important stage in the development of artists' printmaking, which the Impressionists supported. For reasons that it would be fascinating to understand better, Meryon was the first maker of original prints of his day to owe his reputation entirely to printmaking rather than to painting. Such a phenomenon was sufficiently unheard of to have generated a number of hypotheses, our information about

25. Auguste Delâtre,
Night. 1883.
Monotype print of drypoint, 158 x 118 mm.
Bibliothèque nationale, Paris.

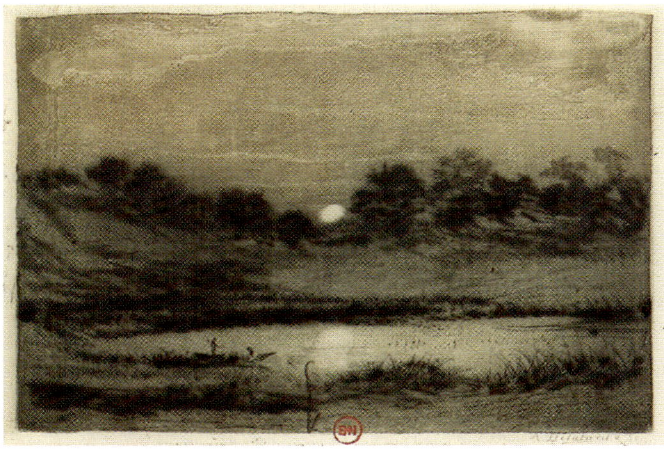

26. Auguste Delâtre,
Landscape. About 1880.
Monotype print of drypoint and roulette etching, 93 x 133 mm.
Bibliothèque nationale, Paris.

previous page:
24. Charles Meryon,
Entrance to the Capuchin Convent in Athens. 1854.
Etching, first state, 178 x 110 mm.
Bibliothèque nationale, Paris.

Meryon's sources being somewhat scanty. The burning question is: how could an artist in 1850 decide to make his career as a printmaker without being a painter, an illustrator or a copyist-engraver? Meryon, like the rest, wanted to be a painter but it has been suggested that, because he was colour-blind, he had to choose black and white; or, alternatively, he was unable to transfer the cartoon he had made for the Salon of 1848 to canvas; or, perhaps, he decided to learn printmaking with the aim of publishing the drawings he had done going round the world as a sailor between 1842 and 1846. The truth is that he was forced to leave the navy on health grounds and became an apprentice-engraver in the studio of Eugène Bléry, who thought highly enough of him to entrust him with the title page of one of his albums. Philippe Burty and Delteil mention his illness and his inability to paint.[58] The success he won with his first series of views of Paris in 1852 is an indication of the new attitude towards original prints on the part of certain collectors. Meryon was admired by various artists, including Bracquemond and Seymour Haden; in Beraldi's words, he was 'unfortunate, but not totally neglected'.

In 1852, in *Le Magasin pittoresque*, Charles Jacque published a series of technical articles in which the subtleties of printmaking as compared to mechanical engraving already seemed to be the object of curiosity, a quaint technique from the past.[59] The rejection of industrialisation and the appearance of a new clientèle looking for modest but authentic works of art stimulated new ideas, at least, even if there was no real market for them.

The rôle played during this period by art periodicals should be emphasised, principally because their readership consisted of the intellectually curious who were in favour of the circulation of art via the print, and who were waiting for reproductive prints to achieve the status of the works that they reproduced. *L'Artiste*, the review that had made romanticism official in 1830, regularly published reproductive prints, but these gradually gave way to original works. A painter like Jules Dupré, for example, presented lithographic versions of his paintings in 1835 and 1836, but then seems to have emancipated himself from reproduction, proposing to the paper in 1836 that they print new lithographs, not directly connected with his paintings.[60]

The earliest prints by etchers involved in the revival of the skill, like Charles Chaplin,[61] were found in *L'Artiste*. Jules Laurens published work in this review in 1858, 1859 and 1860, before becoming an enthusiastic member of the Society of Etchers. In his memoirs, he is at pains to recall how 'even before he launched the journal of the Society of Etchers, acid flowed like water in the studio of the publisher Cadart'.[62] Links were forged by these people with Georgel's 'romanticism of the 1860s' and the beginnings of Impressionism.

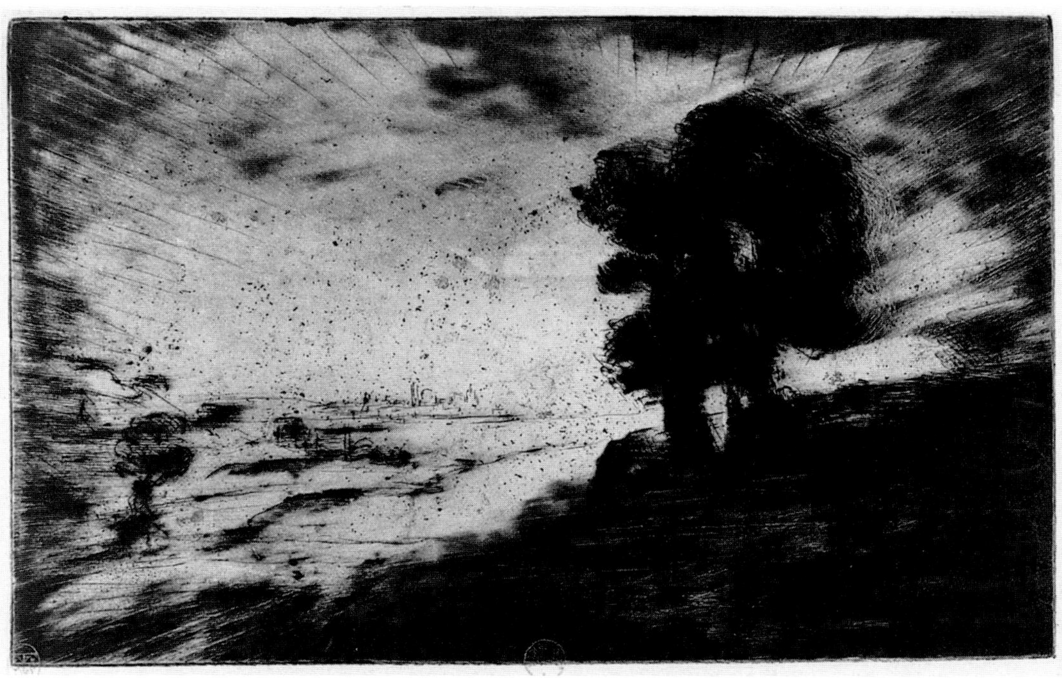

7. *1852–7: Bracquemond, Millet, Legros*

As a young man, Félix Bracquemond was employed as a lithographer and craftsman etcher. In 1842, having lived in hope that a new artistic track was opening up in front of him, he discovered to his disappointment that the art market was a closed shop and that, in order to live by printmaking, it was necessary to accept modern methods of reproduction, in other words to accept industrialised methods.[63] He made an etched plate, *Top of a Double Door* that was unusually daring for its day on four counts: its realism, its clarity, its unprepossessing subject and its large size. All through the 1840s Bracquemond's example gave direction and meaning to other artists' search for new subjects, adapted to contemporary life. Whether it can be judged successful or not, what is striking about his output is the way he doggedly pursued innovation. He experimented constantly in a variety of styles and techniques, moving from sketches copied from Marvy (*Sketch of a Landscape, after Marvy*, 1849; *Old Passageway at Meudon*, 1850) to 'griffonis', hitherto confined to the private sketchbooks of draughtsmen (*Rough Sketch, etched*, about 1855; *The Lake in the Bois de Boulogne*, about 1858), to plates etched with deliberately perfunctory lines (*The Acrobats*, dry point, about 1855–60). In addition to his portraits (*Portrait of Meryon*, 1853), sometimes copied from photographs[65] (*Théophile Gautier after a Photograph by Nadar*, 1857; Fig. 19), he seemed to want to get away from the posed portrait, producing sketches flung awkwardly in the corner of a copper plate (*Sketch of Joseph Guichard*, 1853). Many a bold experiment was born in his studio (Fig. 28), and the Impressionist desire to substitute an individual view of reality for the reality itself can already be sensed, particularly in Bracquemond's astonishing *Sunset* (about 1855?; Fig. 27), executed in a special kind of 'manière noire' probably achieved with glass paper or emery; as Jean-Paul Bouillon remarked, 'the process is its main feature'.[66] He comes close to the kind of style that his Impressionist friends developed later, in, for example, his *Small Boats beside the Seine* (1858), reminiscent of Cézanne's boats at Bercy (1873; Fig. 109); as with Cézanne, 'the preparatory sketches prove that this is drawn from life'.[67]

During this period Bracquemond continued to publish albums, printed by Delâtre.[68] In 1859 Delâtre registered seven of Bracquemond's etchings for copy-

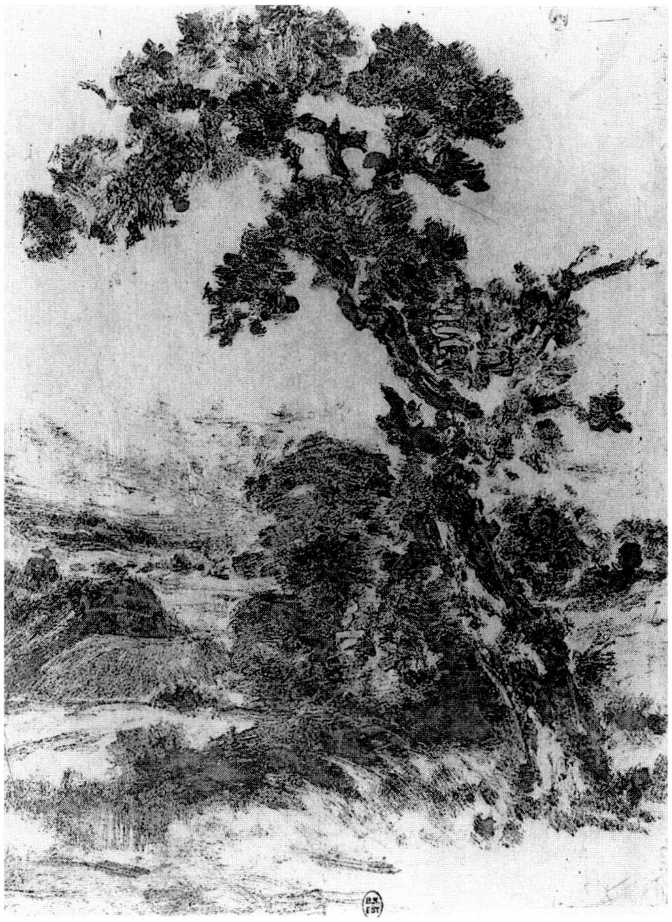

28. Félix Bracquemond, *Experimental Print*. Undated. Sulphur engraving (?), 231 x 216 mm. Bibliothèque nationale, Paris.

previous page:
27. Félix Bracquemond, *Sunset*. About 1855 (?). Mezzotint and drypoint, 135 x 216 mm. Bibliothèque nationale, Paris.

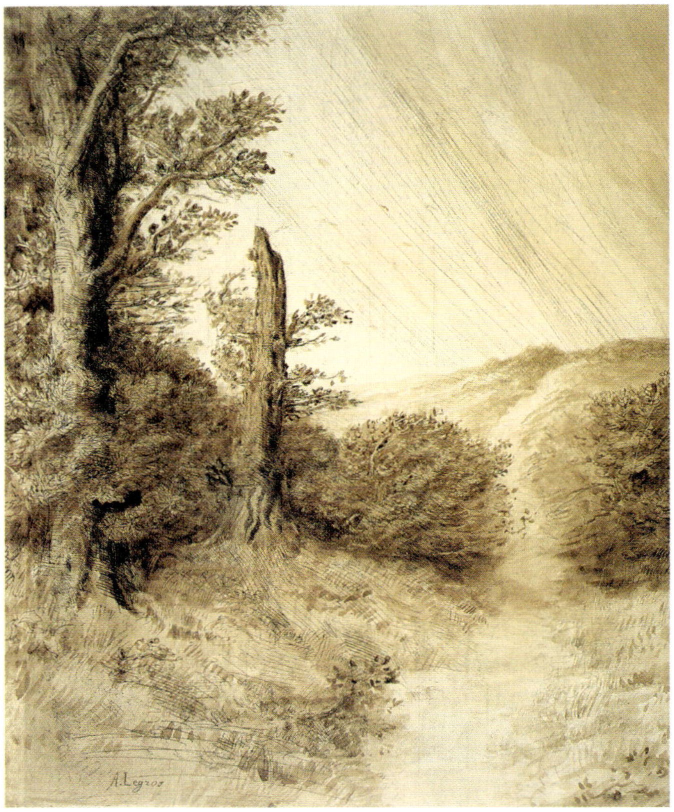

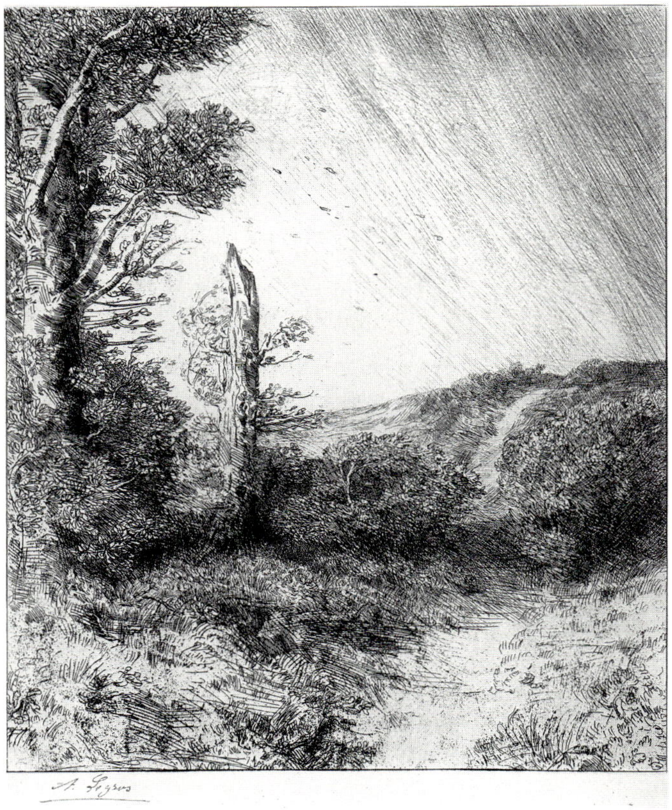

29, 30. Alphonse Legros, *The Gust of Wind*. Undated. Wash on a first state etching, and etching, final state, 613 x 470 mm. British Museum, London.

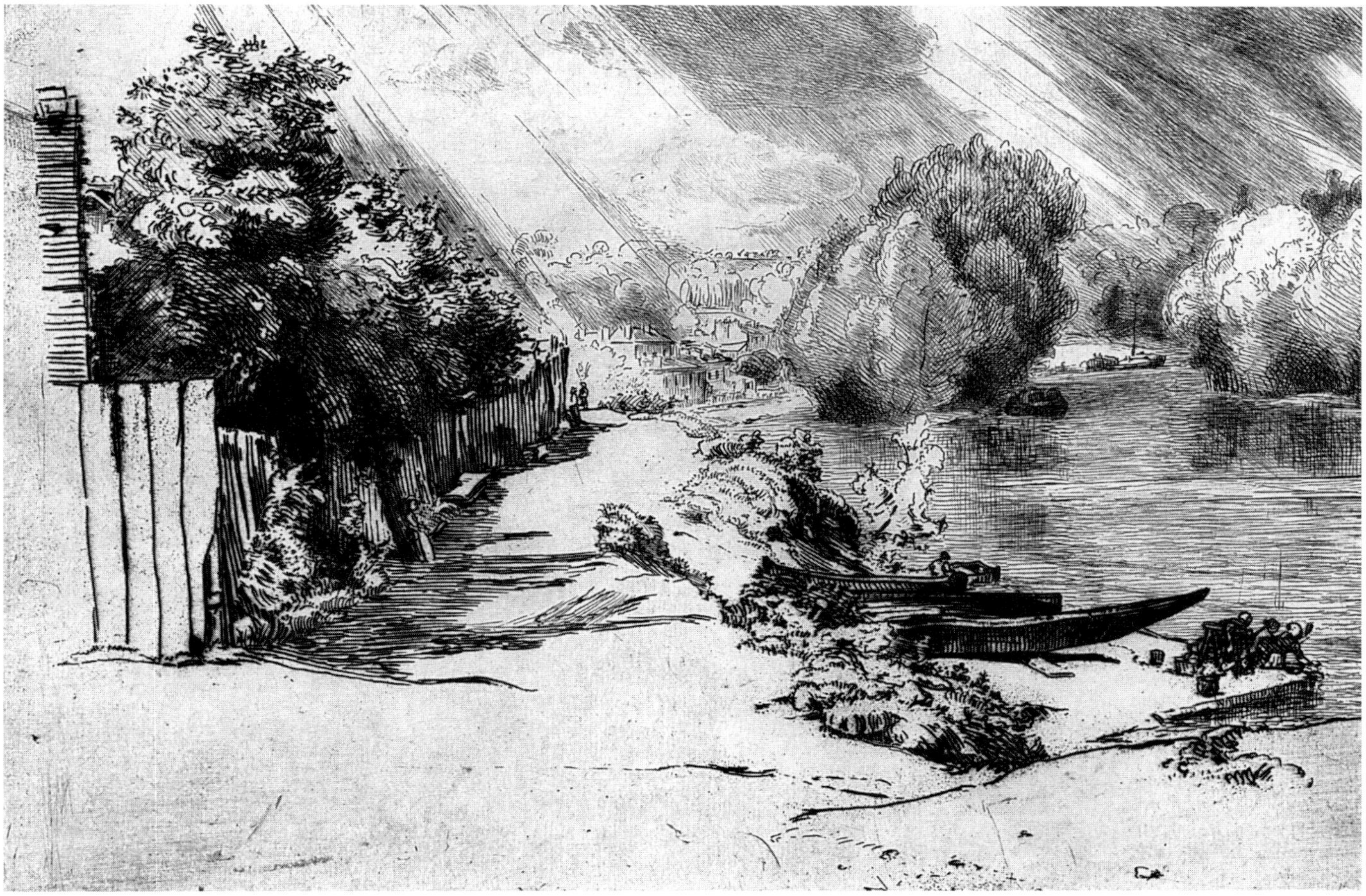

31. Félix Bracquemond, *The Seine at Bas-Meudon*.
1868. Etching, 155 x 227 mm. Bibliothèque nationale, Paris.

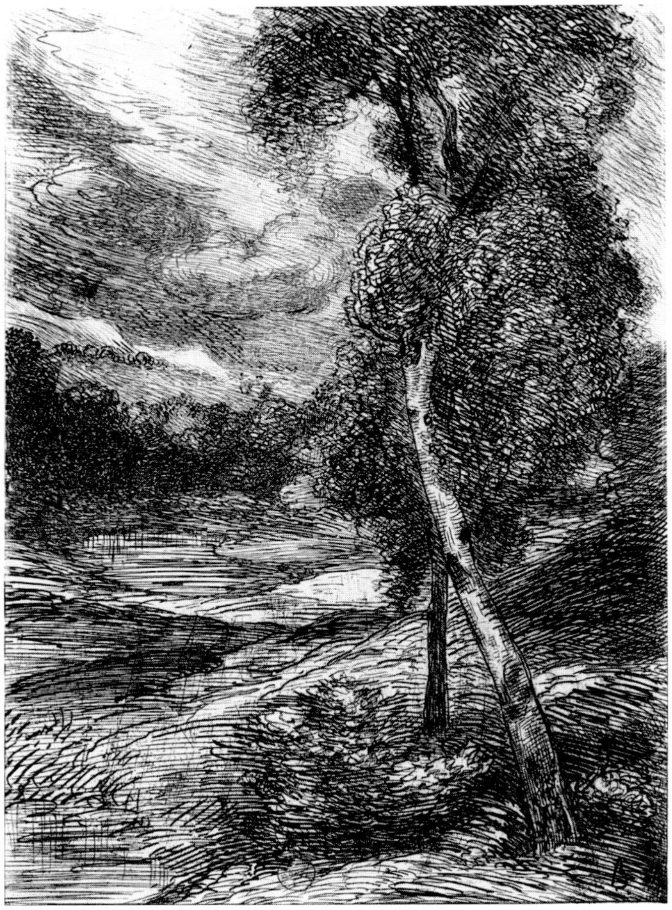

32. Félix Bracquemond, *Landscape with Birch Tree*. About 1863. Pen engraving, 212 x 163 mm. Bibliothèque nationale, Paris.

right, a gesture interpreted by Bouillon as 'a desire to precipitate matters'.[69] The time was ripe, in fact.

A new threshold seemed to have been crossed in the emancipation of the engraving when, in 1856, Bracquemond took the decision to acquire his own printing press. In 1856 this was easier said than done: printing was kept under strict surveillance, and all printers, whether artists or not, were objects of suspicion. On 3 May Bracquemond put in a request for authorisation, giving an original justification for such a request. He wished to print his engravings himself 'because there were no good printers left'.[70] He was authorised to print providing he did not compete with the dealers. This was not his intention, however. By printing his own work, Bracquemond was exploring a new, untapped market: he recognised the decline of craftsmanship, killed by industrialisation, and was hoping to revive it in the name of art. The first result was Bracquemond's withdrawal into his own studio: 'Production oscillates between rare and extremely rare', wrote Jean-Paul Bouillon.[71] Later he was able to shift from rarity based on necessity, to planned rarity: 'I must make this general observation once again: all Bracquemond's first state etchings are very rare and have never been printed commercially', Beraldi is at pains to emphasise.[72] During the second phase the effect of this subterfuge was to attract the kind of client for whom this meagre diet had conferred upon Bracquemond's prints the qualities of uniqueness and authenticity that (under the ambiguous title of originality) define a work of art.

After the experiments carried out in collaboration with Charles Jacque from 1847 to 1850, Millet's career as an etcher made perceptible progress.[73] Five more elaborate plates were begun during the winter of 1855–6 (Fig. 34), inspired by Alfred Sensier who had worked with Jeanron and who saw this as a way of diverting resources to his friend and enhancing his reputation. These plates betray their authorship very clearly, even though some of them, *The Seamstress*, *The Woman churning Butter*, *The Peasant returning from his Midden*, are not copies of any known painting; they remain nevertheless in the tradition of the prints that painters used to circulate in order to make their work known. This explains the etching taken from *The Gleaners*, the original of which was presented in 1857 (Fig. 35).[74] Letters from Sensier to Millet mention this painting and seem to suggest that work on it continued into 1857. In July of that year the etchings were ready, but Sensier makes it clear in a letter of 8 February 1858 that he does not want Delâtre to take the copper plates away; he wants to be present at the printing.[75] He was eager to supervise the quantity as well as the quality; clearly there was pressure to limit editions and this shows that the market for numbered contemporary prints was beginning to build up. In this same letter, Sensier also writes: 'Delâtre is in clover. He is director of the studio printers Gide et Baudry, at a salary of 1800 francs plus four hours a day, and four printing

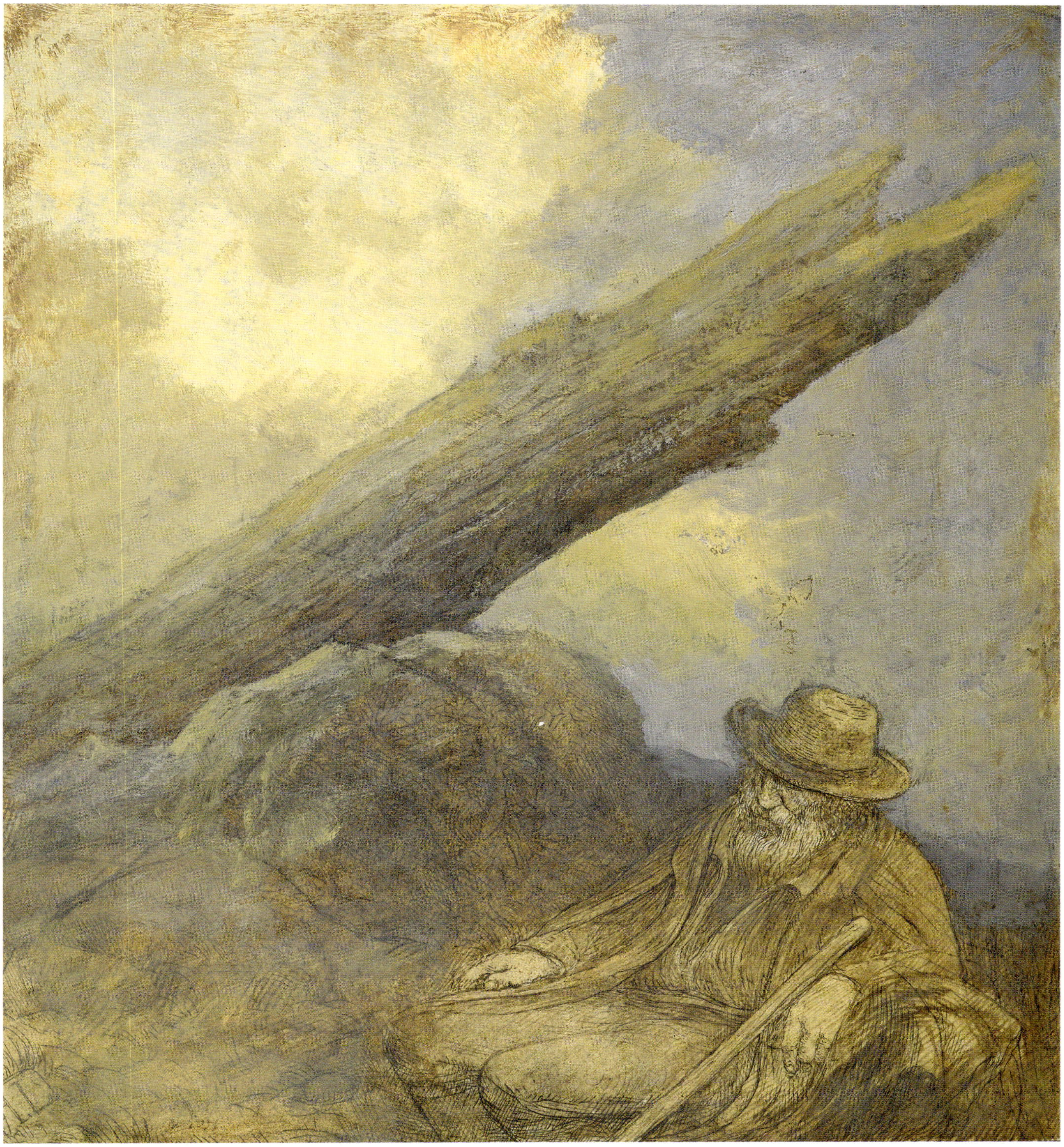

33. Alphonse Legros, *The Shepherd's Repose*. Undated. Etching touched up with oil paint, 338 x 307 mm. Private collection, Paris.

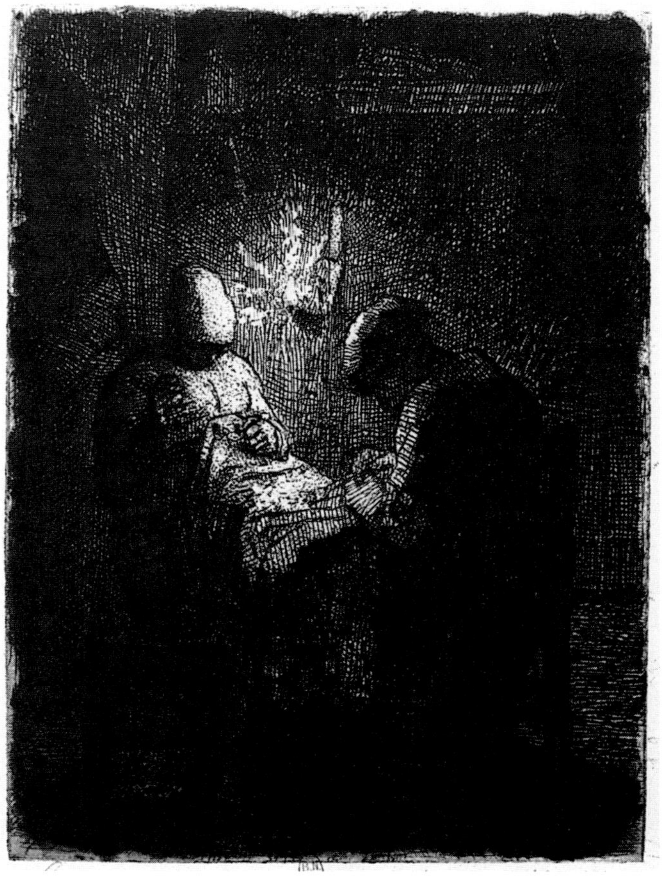

34. Jean-François Millet,
The Vigil. 1855–6.
Etching, 151 x 110 mm.
Bibliothèque nationale, Paris.

presses.' The aesthetic of the 'artist's proof' now drew the buying public. 'Delâtre has printed a collection on old paper which he hopes that you will give him to present to M. About, who is sponsoring his entry into the Chalcographie du Louvre (the copper plate collection)', wrote Sensier. Millet's reply was: 'It would give me a bad conscience to stand in the way of Delâtre's happiness for the sake of a few proofs on old paper. . .' In 1860, the request was confirmed: 'Diaz possesses at least 40 copies of your Diggers and Gleaners, and we should get the other subjects printed too but I definitely blame Delâtre. Meryon, who has a press, offers to print them for you free. He is an honest and serious man to the highest degree and prints very well.'[76]

The Salon of 1857 presented a new champion to the supporters of realism, the painter Alphonse Legros, then aged twenty; he excited the enthusiasm of Champfleury, then Baudelaire, with his religious paintings.[77] He enjoyed the same success in 1859 with an *Angelus* that was bought by Seymour Haden, and in 1861 with his *Ex-voto*. Encouraged by Bracquemond and Burty and by Baudelaire (who, in 1862, praised his 'big, bold prints')[78] and also by the publisher Poulet-Malassis, Legros had begun print-making in 1857, producing the same energy and strength that was to be found in his paintings. Poulet-Malassis commissioned four etchings to illustrate Duranty's realist novel, *Le Malheur d'Henriette Guérard*, published in 1861. From a modest background, like Bracquemond, Legros worked in Dijon, his home town, as a housepainter and hand colourist.

Although, with Bracquemond, Legros became one of the two main engravers to the first group of Impressionist painters, his reputation has suffered because of the style of his etchings: the lines are thicker than the lines normally made by a burin, the subjects more conventional even than those of Manet, with whom he was linked and who on occasion assisted him with his printing. His reputation in France was not helped by his emigration to England in 1863, on Whistler's advice; he pursued a successful career in England as an artist and teacher. Although Legros's drawing has none of the lightness of the Impressionists, his printmaking, influenced by memories of Rembrandt and the art of Spain, followed the same lines as that of his contemporaries: a limited number of editions, but different states sometimes numbering as many as eleven.[79] He used dry point with increasing frequency and relentlessly retouched his printed proofs by hand, with a pen or brush, thus confusing prints with drawings and even oil paintings (Figs. 29, 33). This habit was invariable and began very early: an early print, *The Ambulance*, dating from 1861, shows signs of retouching, as does his *Session with the teacher*, annotated as follows by Poulet-Malassis: 'Proof, retouched with the brush, by Legros for Baudelaire'.[80]

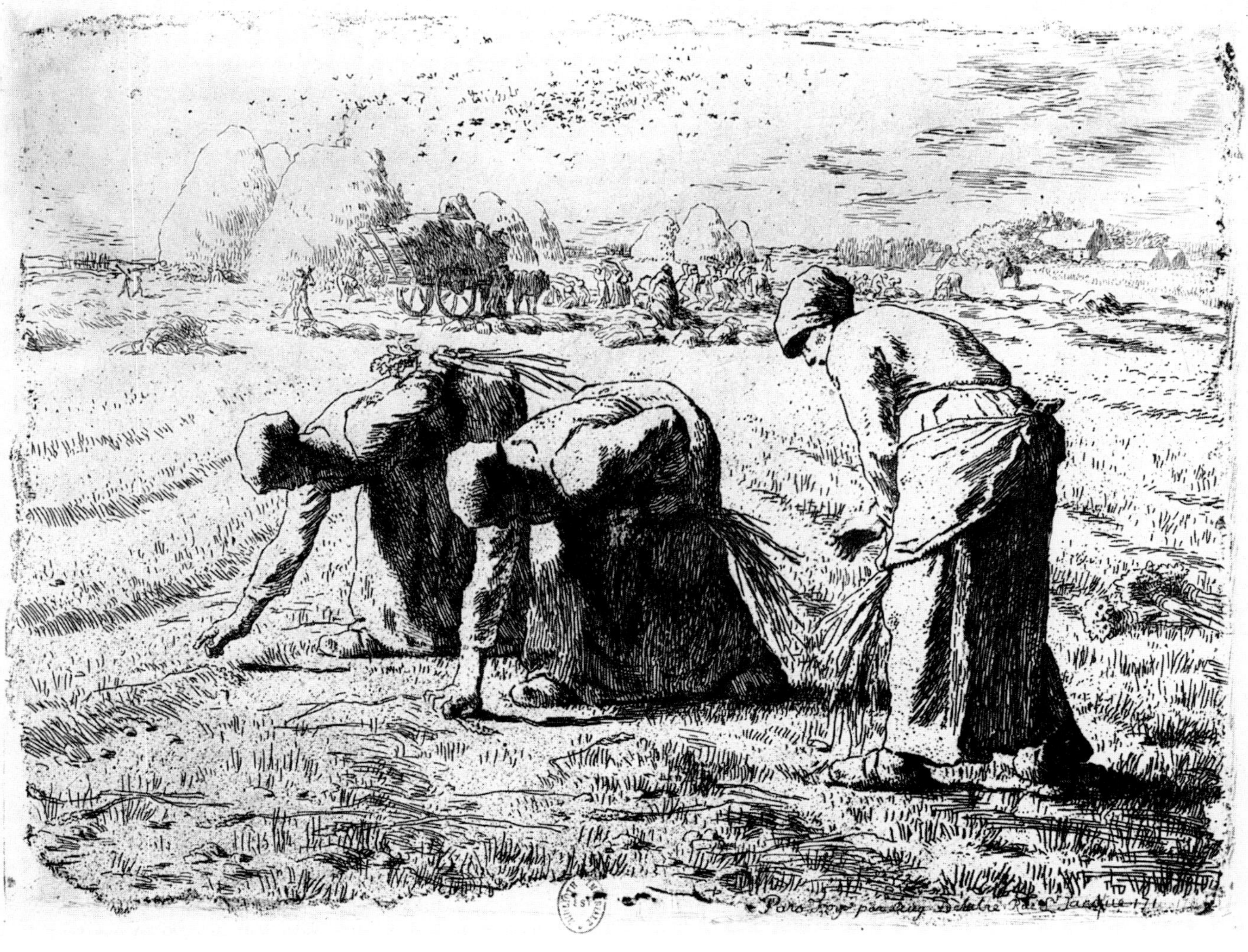

35. Jean-François Millet, *The Gleaners*. About 1857.
Etching, 190 x 252 mm. Bibliothèque nationale, Paris.

8. *Whistler and Seymour Haden*

The Exposition Universelle of 1855 was the first public manifestation of France's new prosperity. The Salon was an integral part of the Exhibition and on that occasion was international. In the section devoted to English engravings, under the name 'Etching Club', could be found 'a frame containing steel and copper plate etchings by various members of the Club'.[81] Engraving in England was reputed to be more highly developed and its outlets better organised than in France. There was also an evident renewal of interest in the art of etching there in about 1850. French artists, in particular romantics like Isabey, had adopted the English print as their model. However, with the recovery of the French economy, a movement in the other direction also established itself. One sign of this reverse movement was the arrival in Paris, in the late summer of 1855, of a twenty-one-year-old American, James McNeill Whistler who, after a brief sojourn at West Point, and a spell learning geographical engraving at the U.S. Coast Geodetic Survey, had decided to become an artist.[82] He frequented the Louvre, and courses run by Lecoq de Boisbaudran and Gleyre, making friends of his own age there, including Degas and Fantin-Latour. Since leaving Washington he had continued to etch family portraits. He carried on with etching in Paris, with Meryon as his mentor; his first Parisian prints bore Meryon's imprint. In 1856 he made a journey to Alsace, where he produced *The Kitchen* (Fig. 36) an etching in which the spirit of Impressionism in its first realist period is clearly perceptible. There is a distant flavour of the school of Rembrandt in the etching too, with its theatrical back lighting, its strong contrasts, obtained by a dense network of carefully shaded lines, and the use of dry point to heighten the tones and add effect. Rembrandt's influence is coupled with the more recent influence of the realist painter Bonvin, who specialised in domestic scenes. Whistler's etched lines are airy and relaxed, the drawing does not enclose the objects; he allows the light to circulate and the white paper to take over at the focal point.

Opinions about Whistler's 'Impressionism' are divided, and *The Kitchen* demonstrates the contradictions into which the artist was to fall. His sincere concern for realism, which led him to make etchings in the open air, is combined with a pronounced taste for spectacular effects, manifested in dry point lines,

36. James McNeill Whistler, *The Kitchen*. About 1838. Etching, third state, 225 x 155 mm. Bibliothèque nationale, Paris.

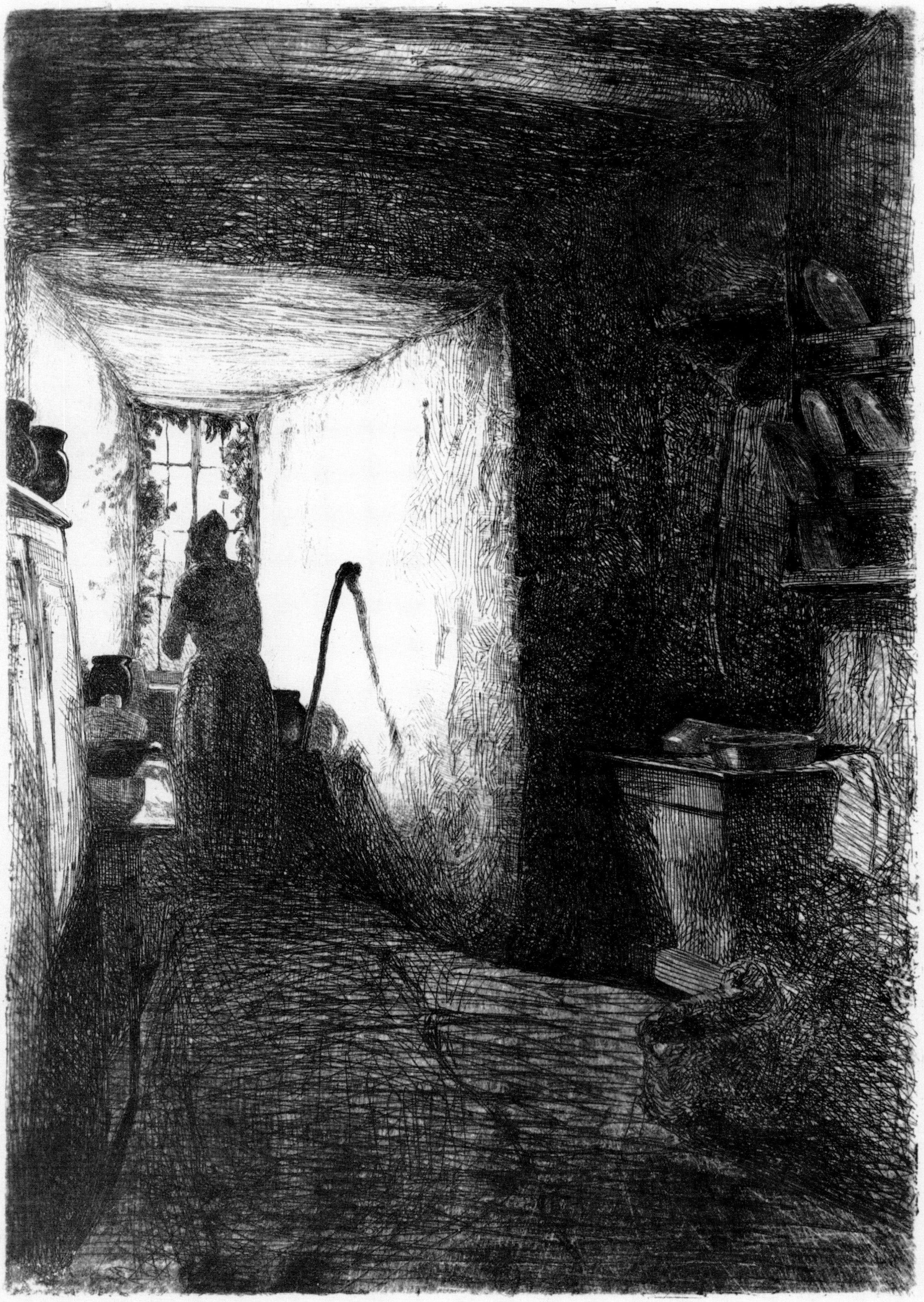

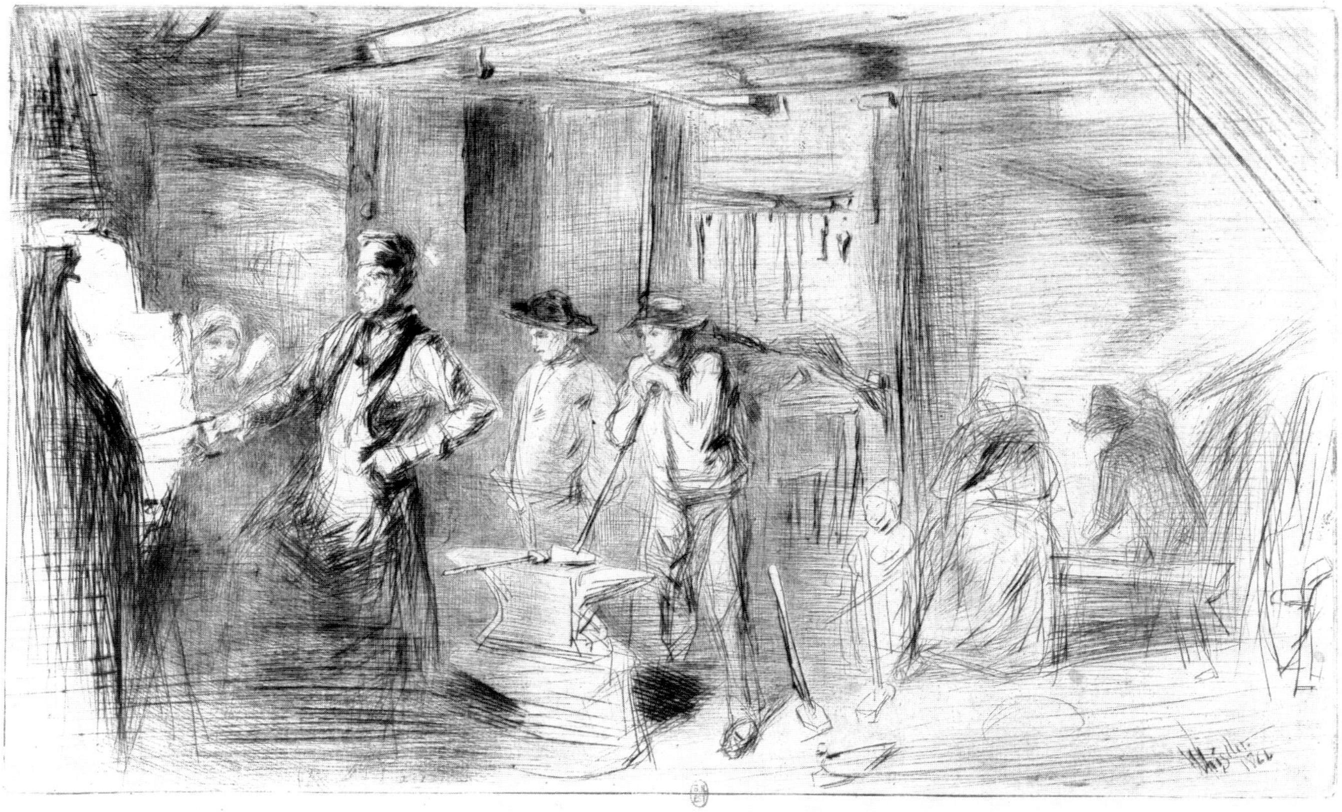

37, 38. James McNeill Whistler,
The Forge. 1861.
Drypoint, two third and fourth states, 193 x 320 mm.
Bibliothèque nationale, Paris.

aquatint and inking over the drawing; because of this taste he was suspected of the kind of romantic leanings that Degas and Pissarro were trying so hard to avoid. *The Kitchen* is the twelfth and last plate of the 'French Set', a series of etchings and dry points that Whistler decided to publish in an album for the relatively high price of fifty francs in 1858; he was probably encouraged in this by his printmaker friends, Bracquemond and Legros, the critic Burty and the printer Delâtre, who printed the edition. In 1859 Whistler submitted two etchings and a painting to the Salon: the etchings were accepted and the painting rejected. Whistler showed it eventually in the studio of François Bonvin.

The 'French Set' was dedicated to Francis Seymour Haden, sixteen years Whistler's senior and a celebrated London surgeon, owner of a collection of etchings by Rembrandt; he was a typical aristocratic, Tory art fancier, exigent and cultivated, for whom nothing was too good. Haden had practised printmaking in the gentlemanly tradition, widespread in French and English society since the eighteenth century. These amateur etchers usually produced family portraits and picturesque landscape views of their travels, and were close relations of the miniaturists and watercolour painters. He had produced six small etchings inspired by the Venetians during a tour of Italy in 1844. In 1846, Seymour Haden married Deborah Whistler, James's sister. Meeting his brother-in-law encouraged him to take up printmaking again and the two worked together

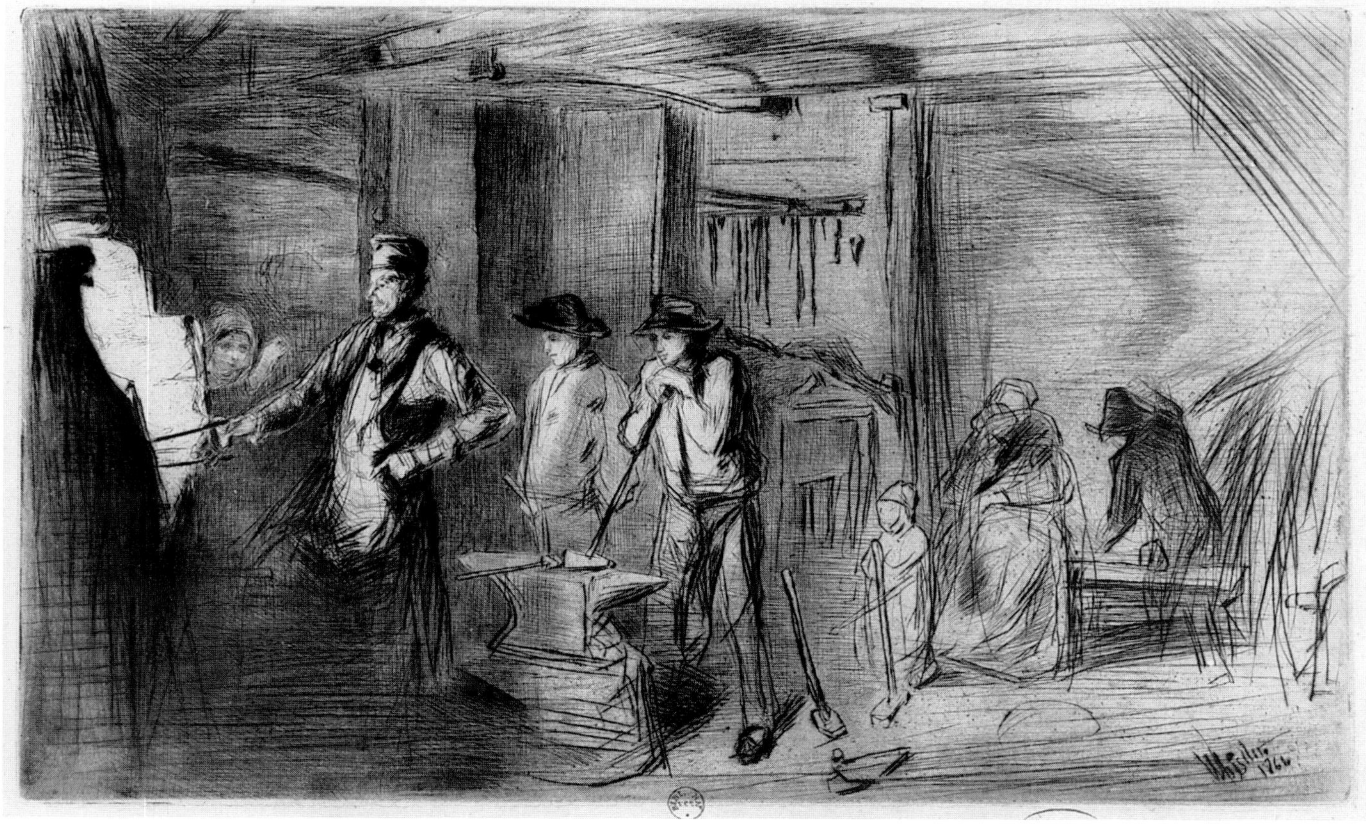

during the Christmas season of 1857; Whistler spent Christmas in the surgeon's comfortable house in Chelsea.[83]

Haden's technique owes a lot to Whistler. He enjoyed working from nature on landscapes that were always 'picturesque' in the conventional manner; he would make alterations, filling them with drypoint additions, romantic light effects and inking. The stylistic devices criticised in Whistler's work by the Impressionists are even more pronounced in Haden's etchings. Haden knew France well, having studied there, and from 1857 to 1859 the two artists travelled continually between London and Paris. Like Whistler, Haden presented an etching, *Thames Fisherman No. 1*, at the Salon in 1859. In the same year Whistler had exhibited two prints at the Royal Academy, although engraved reproductions were not accepted there. Encouraged by this, Haden submitted two etchings to the Royal Academy in 1860; they were accepted and exhibited under the pseudonym of Dean.

As in the case of the French printmakers, it was their innovative techniques rather than their style or subject matter that made these etchings original. Haden's good taste satisfied the demands of the new clientèle, as explained by Philippe Burty. Between them, Burty and Haden worked out most of the theory behind the 'original print'. The flattering techniques of Whistler (Figs 37, 38) and Dean lent themselves to it better perhaps than the more austere offerings of Bracquemond or Legros. A first sketch traced with a point on the copper, like a sketch in a drawing book would then be systematically worked over with dry point and burnisher, re-etched, heightened with aquatint to dramatise the lighting and create atmosphere; areas were deliberately left unfinished for effect, and the weather conditions carefully noted. In 1859, on the same day, Seymour Haden completed two different etchings of the same landscape view: *A Water Meadow* and *On the Test*, the first at midday and the second in the evening (Figs 39, 40). It is evident from the results, and from the various subsequent states made from them, that, like Claude Monet, although he painted the same motif twice, his primary aim was to represent a time of day rather than a landscape. This rather self-conscious aestheticism matched the exigencies of the new collectors, who were ready to accept the etching provided it could be distinguished from a mass-produced product. In 1859, in London, Whistler republished the 'French Set' for the price of two guineas with the support of a patron'publisher, the lawyer Thomas, who summoned Delâtre. But Whistler was growing keener and keener to print his work himself in order to keep an eye on the effects of inking. It is possible that he may have owned a small press in his Paris studio, in rue Campagne-Première. Auguste Delâtre went on working in London in 1863 and 1864, at the request of Seymour Haden. Their passion for printing stimulated competition, and Frederick Goulding set up a rival studio; he became to London what Delâtre was to

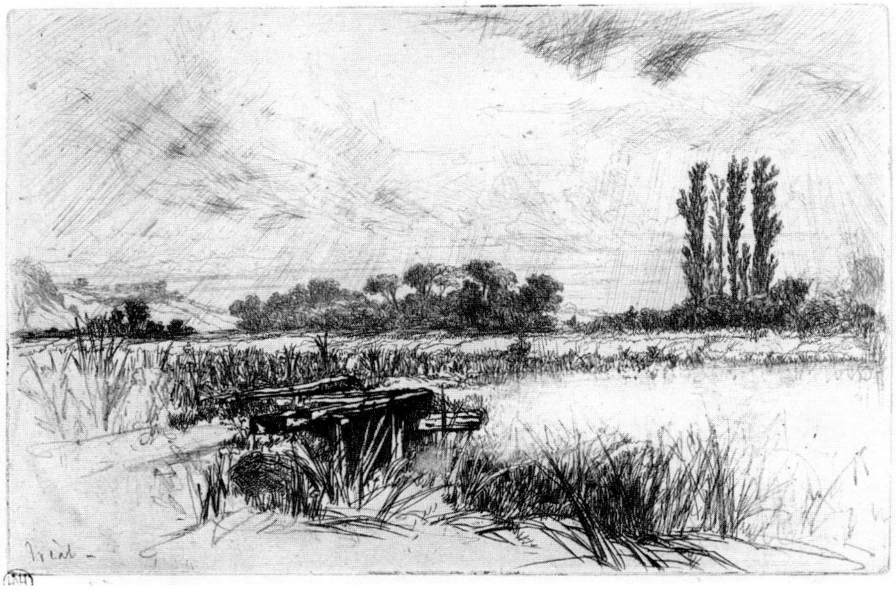

39. Francis Seymour Haden, *A Watermeadow*. 1859. Etching and drypoint, 150 x 213 cm. British Museum, London.

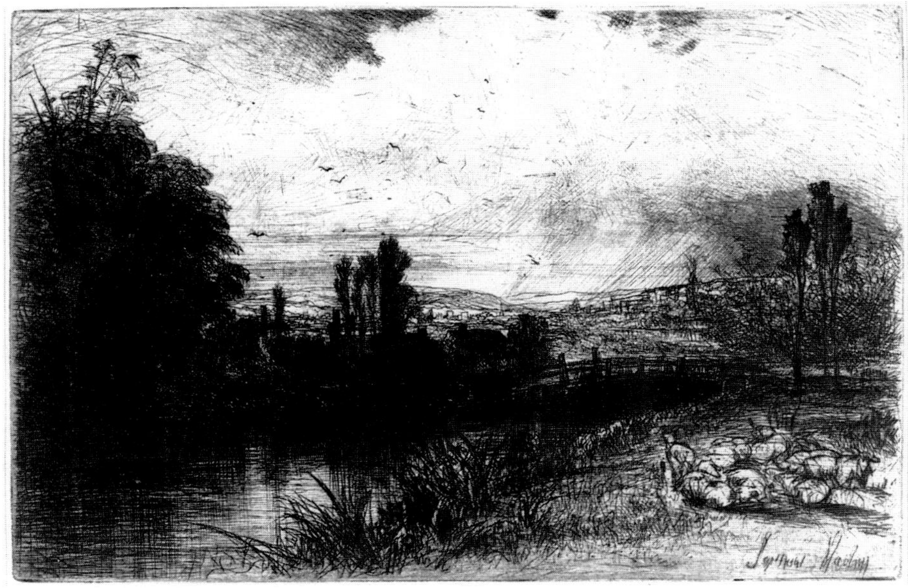

40. Francis Seymour Haden, *On the Test*. 1859. Etching and drypoint, 150 x 213 cm. British Museum, London.

Paris. Philippe Burty, who had already published a catalogue of Seymour Haden's etchings in the Gazette des Beaux-arts in 1864,[84] before Haden had produced very much work, encouraged him to publish his first album in 1865, advertising a limited edition of 250 copies. Later Seymour Haden explained his principles in a personal statement: 'My practice is to keep my plates in my own possession and to print from them only as long as the copper, which is not steel-coated, can go on providing a clear image; then I destroy the plate.'[85] In fact, Haden supervised the printing of his work very closely. In his catalogue of 1880 Drake mentions plates that have been suppressed. It appears that in 1850 Haden, like Meryon, began signing his proofs in manuscript to authenticate them. Like his contemporaries, he wrote handwritten dedications, another way of signing something without actually appending a signature to the work itself.[86] Seymour Haden's letters to Philippe Burty appeared in the *Gazette des Beaux-Arts* in 1864,[87] before the publication of a much longer essay, 'About Etching', published in 1866;[88] with Burty's writings and prefaces to the albums published by the Society of Etchers, this constitutes one of the manifestos of the new ethos surrounding printmaking, an ethos consciously and wholeheartedly embraced by the Impressionist printmakers. It could be said that the historical importance of Seymour Haden was connected more with his actions than with his art – if it were possible to make such a distinction.

9. *Degas's Self Portrait*

He is the son of a banker who wants to become an artist (Fig. 41). He wears the look of a man who is naive yet disenchanted; his gaze uncertain, the set of his mouth proud under his shy moustache. He is wearing an artist's soft trilby, a hat that is neither distinguished nor vulgar, and has his hands in his pockets. He was described, as an older man, by Paul Valéry in these words: 'An unusual character and a great artist, severe and very strongminded with an exceptional intelligence, lively, refined and questioning. Behind the strength of his opinions and the severity of his judgments lurked an intangible self-doubt, a desperate fear of not living up to his own expectations, both painful yet noble sentiments instilled in him by his extraordinary familiarity with the work of the great artists, his desire to possess their secrets, his continual awareness of the contradictory nature of their perfection'.[89]

He studied the classics at the Lycée Louis-le-Grand. He liked literature and art, particularly Ingres, and his family, particularly his mother and his sister. Bound tightly and permanently into the web of family relationships he found it impossible to break away; he was on bad terms with his father and adored his mother, keeping her wedding dress until the day he died. He was never to marry. He could never forget his mother's irritation with his father; his father would take his coat and leave the house.[90] He was never sure how his name should be written, nor what his style should be: De Gas, de Gas or Degas? He thought of himself as an aristocrat, yet was perfectly aware that his grandfather had made a fortune speculating in grain during the Revolution and had then fled to Naples where he founded a bank, later becoming a servant of the Empire. He was brought up among men of progress. He was interested in industry, photography, politics and horses. His brother worked in the bank and used the aristocratic version of the name, with its 'noble particle': de Gas. He chose the other, more plebeian version: Degas.

What pose should he strike with such insecurity lurking in the mirror? He chooses the modern one, the three quarter face. He has learned from Ingres that drawing and position should not be confused. The old fashioned self portraits that abounded in Italy were less concerned with scenery and setting: just a face, a head and shoulders usually. But in the Exposition in 1855 he saw the superb self portrait by Ingres, itself inspired by David's

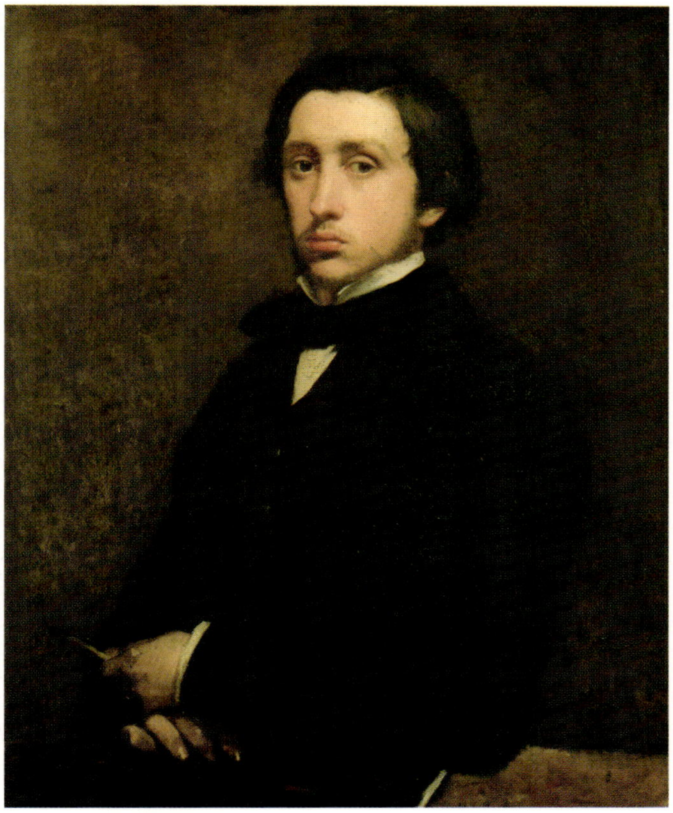

41. Edgar Degas, *Self Portrait*. 1855. Oil on canvas, 81 x 64 cm. Musée d'Orsay, Paris.

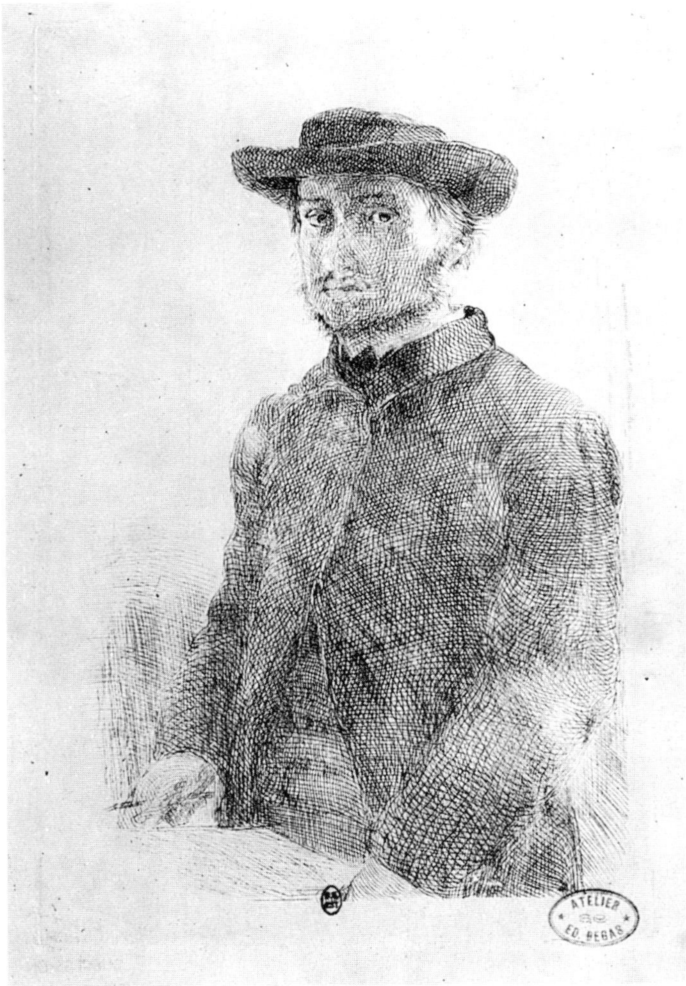

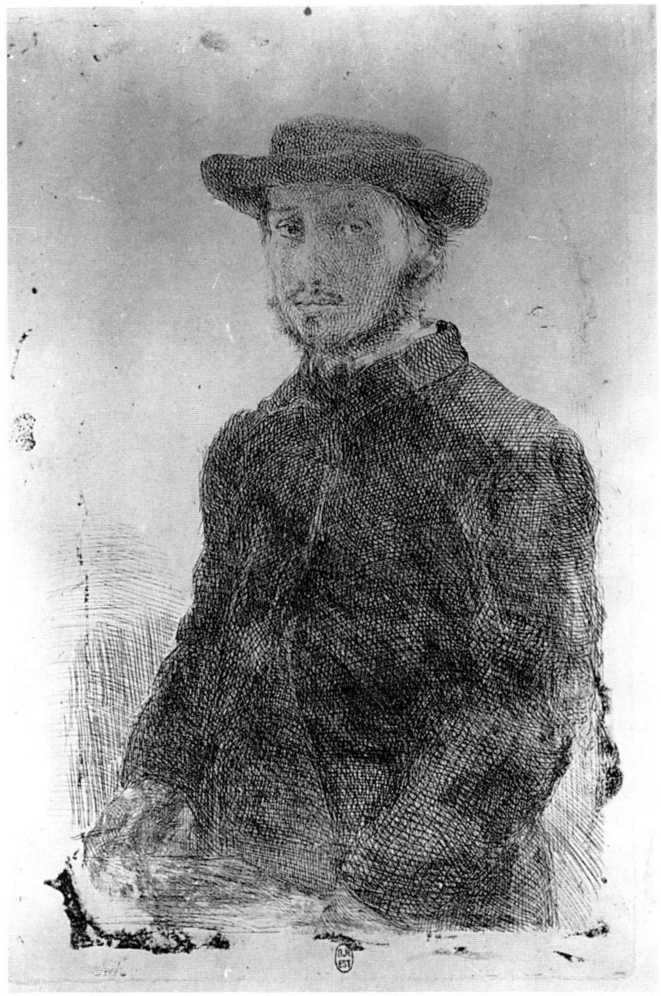

self portrait, a masterpiece of dignity and suppleness. He imitated the pose, but the drawing is different, consisting of a dense web of lightly etched lines illuminated as if from within. He also drew himself with the light behind him as, at a later date, he would take photographs in a mirror, blinding the reflective surface with his floodlight.

The subject of a self portrait is evidently the author and the subject, at one and the same time; an attempt at transfiguration is being made, a bid for a new character from a different family background. In a self portrait the artist is hallucinating, standing well back from his own image and trying to depict himself as if he were dead. Then he offers himself to the spectator to reassemble. The spectator is the object of the exercise: what status does the artist want accorded to him? what kind of view of himself does he want to project? The glimpse caught in a mirror acts as a kind of block. The living image in the reflection cannot abolish the past and memory. Forgotten aristocracy does not become proletarian, a huge fortune is no guarantee of legitimacy. Degas still believes in progress; he loves order and liberty; he also loves Delacroix. He is alone, skilfully posed. The light breaks up his person. The glass that would normally receive such a projected image has just shattered into minute splinters on the varnished copper plate: this is the 'mirror' stage of Impressionism.

At twenty-two, Degas arrived in Italy in order to learn to paint. His father had finally given way: he had ideas about art as well, and his own father lived in Naples. Like everyone else, he went to Rome. Anything and everything could be learnt in Rome, including caricature and etching, the latter a somewhat superficial skill appreciated, collected and sometimes even practised in a mild way by polite society under the Ancien Régime. The romantic painters cultivated etching as well, enjoying the freedom and contrast it offered, and the mixing of genres. Prince Soutzo, an aristocrat and amateur etcher who was a friend of the Degas family, showed him his collection of etchings by Rembrandt, Van Ostade and Claude Lorrain. Degas recorded his 'great conversations' with him in his notebooks.[91] He enjoyed working on some small copper plate engravings with him, gluing the prints made from them in his notebooks. He met an engraver in Rome, Joseph Tourny (Figs. 47, 48), who was finding a commission to reproduce the ceilings of

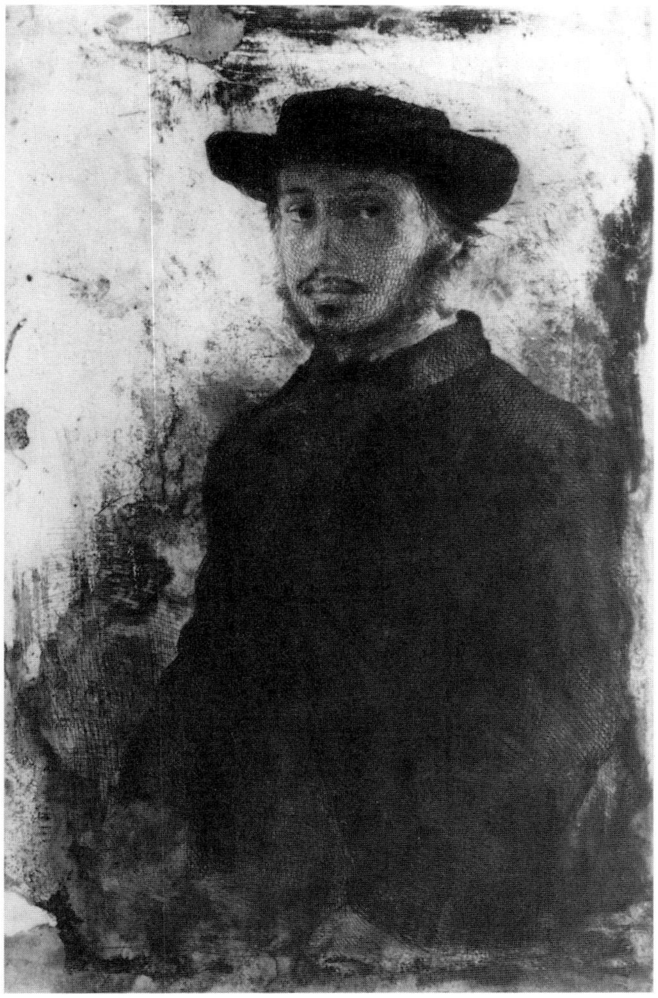

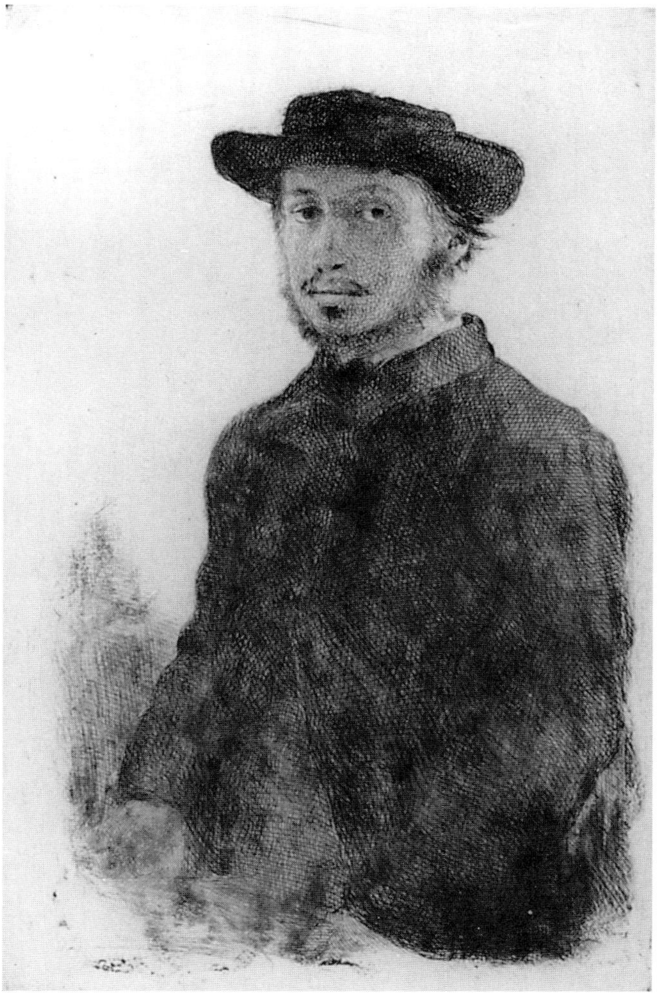

the Vatican very tedious. Tourny was a virtuoso printmaker and exhibited two original etchings, both portraits, at the Salon of 1857.

In his studio, Degas made a scrupulously accurate copy of Rembrandt's etching *Seated Young Man in a Velvet Beret* (Figs 49, 50). He worked hard on the downcast eyes, on the serious mouth and the air of melancholy. With Tourny as model he transposed the scene, replacing the hat with the big beret, but not altering the lighting. He studied the effect of using a brush. Then he tried his Neapolitan grandfather. He was only interested in human subjects (Fig. 46) and their surroundings. He asked Tourny to pose for him again. This was on 8 November 1857 in Rome; he had visited the Corsini Gallery that day and, as Valéry remarked, coveted the skills of the old masters. The greatest etcher of all was Rembrandt, with his extremely free handling of light - light that crosses the etching or withdraws from it completely, sometimes disappearing into the whiteness of the paper, sometimes into the black of the ink. On the first printing he completed in Tourny's studio he was still trying to add value with his brush, around the face, on the clothes and even on the face itself, applying

42–45. Edgar Degas,
Self Portrait. 1857.
Etching, first state, second state,
third state, fifth state, 230 x 144 mm.
Bibliothèque nationale and
Bibliothèque d'Art et d'Archéologie, Paris.

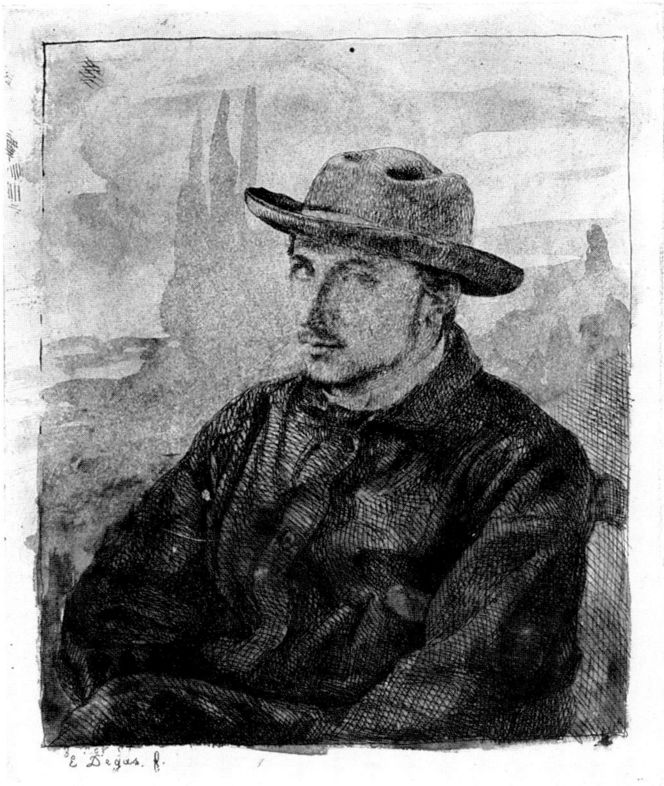

46. Edgar Degas,
Portrait of an Unknown Man. 1857.
Etching, proof retouched with wash,
115 x 92 mm.
Bibliothèque nationale, Paris.

the wash lightly and allowing it to drip down the etched lines to show the path the light should take, through the web of lines made by the etching tool. Rembrandt's etchings issued from a studio that supplied the middle classes of Amsterdam, the first republic in the world since Rome; they give the feeling, particularly in their lighting, of an art that is modern and wealthy, yet at the same time brutal and harsh. Rembrandt is a better reference than solemn, religious Rome. He never went to Rome. That displeased some of his clientèle, but later those who recognised themselves in his independence of style and proud drawing technique were flattered. Rembrandt was surrounded by disciples. He never ceased to look at his own reflection in the mirror, inquiringly and without complacency. Degas looks at his own reflection, alone, in Rome. He would love to see Rembrandt in the glass, right across Italy, across Ingres, and the far side of himself.

So he took a bigger copper plate than the ones he had used before, and threw himself confidently into a self portrait (Figs 42–5). Beyond the looking glass is Rembrandt and also Goya, whom he studied in 1853 in the print room of the Imperial Library; Van Dyck and Velázquez as well. Degas, like everyone else, is in Rome, as Édouard Manet had been the year before, like Gustave Moreau, Chapus and Bonnat, who had come to Rome in the same year to study art history – to try and appropriate it rather than to copy it. He introduces himself through his self portrait. Not in the same way as Bracquemond, who painted himself as an etcher in a picture that seems to have learned nothing since Holbein; not like Whistler, who portrayed himself as a dandy with romantic colour and brushwork effects. He presents himself naturally, like Goya or Rembrandt, not frozen to attention; he allows his own insecurity, his uncertainty about his position, to show that he is an artist.

The first state (Fig. 42) is well positioned and well lit but too pale and timid. It needs more acid. In the second state (Fig. 43) clumsy spills of acid have bitten in to the copper here and there. Will the figure vanish behind this leprous overlay, or disappear, corroded away? Degas repaired and renewed the etching ground. When he dipped the plate into the acid for the third time (Fig. 44) he had no idea what kind of inferno his portrait was plunging in to. He took a risk, but the first state was wasted by this time anyway. The future was uncertain but he had nothing to lose. In the third state the acid bit too aggressively, like a storm that darkened the delicate contrasts of light and shade in brutal fashion. All was not lost, however. Degas enjoyed experimenting with technique, using skill and judgment, making mistakes and rectifying them, reacting to ordeals and challenges. He patiently closed up the wounds on the plate, smoothed its scars with the burnisher and cleared the background again. The portrait re-appeared, looking more dignified and more detached, cleansed of its blemishes (Fig. 45). The head has not been touched.[92]

When he returned to Paris in 1859, Degas may have been surprised to note that, with the assistance of improved prosperity, the French art market was improving in leaps and bounds and that, oddly enough, the etching was coming back into fashion as it had done under the Ancien Régime. In fact this was not of great importance to him, as his ambition had never been directed towards becoming a printmaker. But his experience with etching had taught him something new: that in printmaking, as in painting, there is no such thing as reproduction.

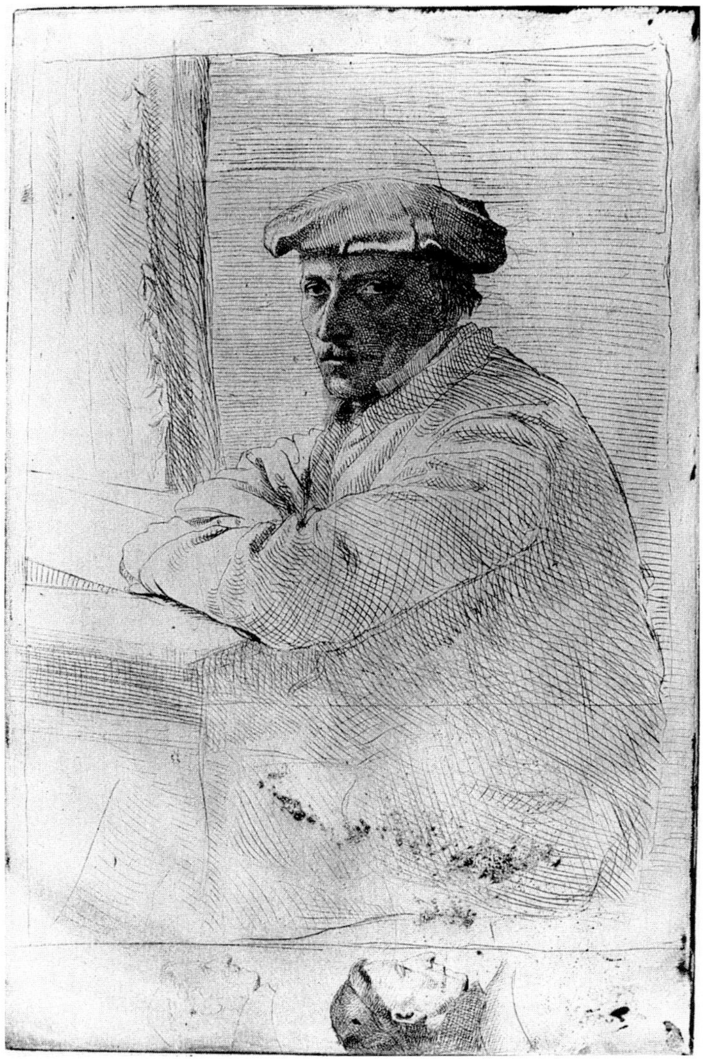

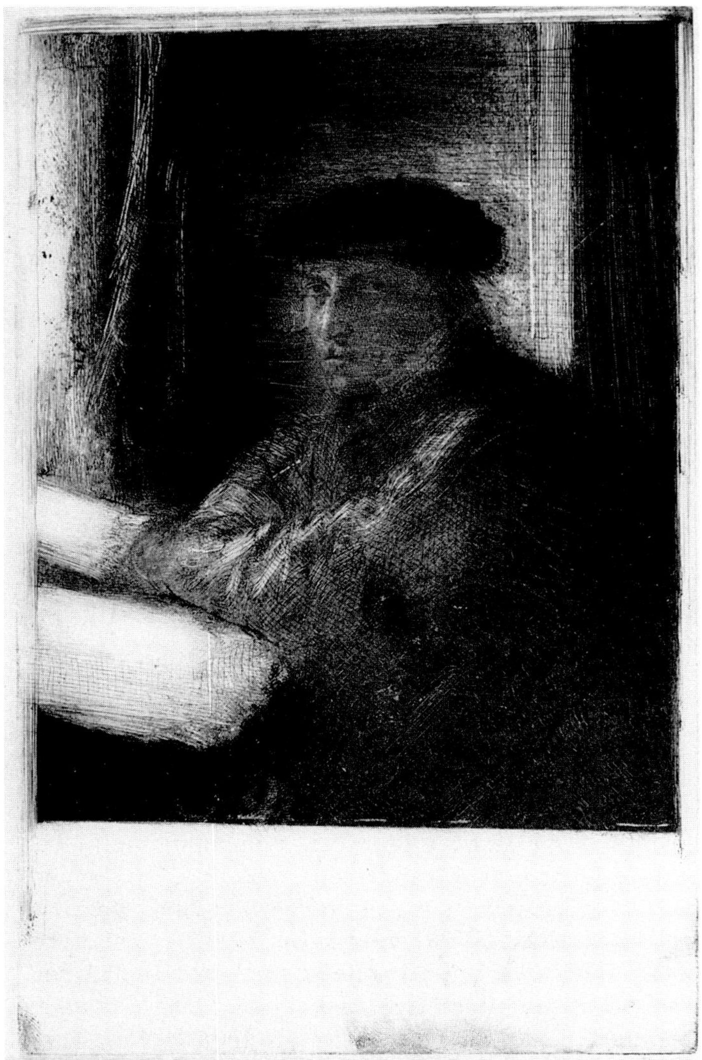

47, 48. Edgar Degas,
Portrait of Joseph Tourny. 1857.
Etching, 228 x 143 mm.
First state, National Gallery of Art,
Washington, Rosenwald Collection;
monotype proof, Metropolitan
Museum of Art, New York, Harris Brisbane Dick Fund.

10. *1859: The New Art Market*

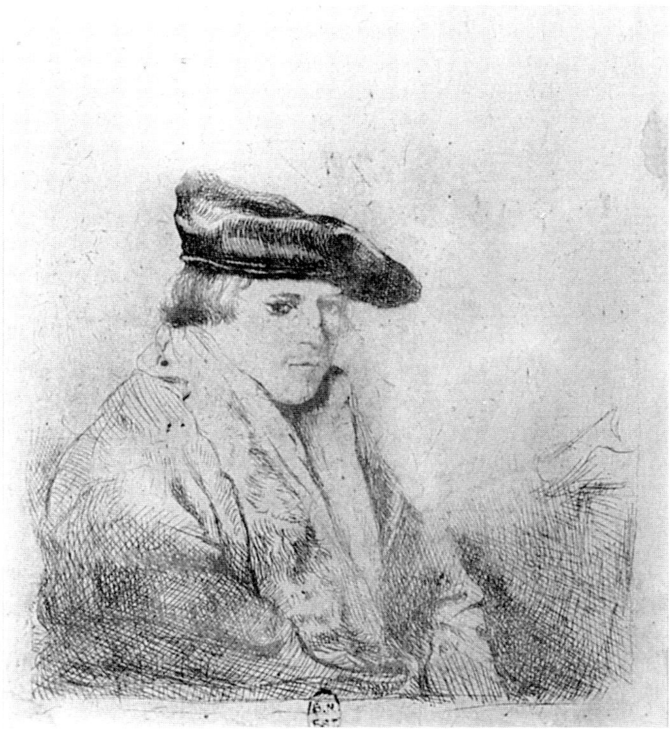

49. Edgar Degas,
Seated Young Man with Velvet Beret,
after Rembrandt. About 1857.
Etching, 105 x 85 mm.
Bibliothèque nationale, Paris.

In his first editorial in the review he launched in 1859, Charles Blanc explained the expansion of the art market in straightforward terms: 'The founding of this review, the *Gazette des Beaux-Arts*, would not have been possible fifteen years ago; it would not have attracted so many as eight hundred subscriptions. Now, if things go as planned, it will easily achieve ten thousand. What has caused this change? What has happened in the world? What has made this huge audience, that has appeared so quickly, so eager to take an interest in artistic matters? It cannot be that our sensory perceptions have quickened unexpectedly, or that our minds have suddenly grown more refined. . . France, however, has recently seen the emergence of instant wealth, as at the time of Law.'[93] Just as it had done at the time of Law, and sometimes on the same terms, the print had arrived to satisfy a clientèle of patrons of the arts who were the product of a greatly enriched middle class. Renewed interest in the eighteenth century, and in books and libraries,[94] and Manet's revival of Watteau's themes (for example) show how even the most advanced of the middle classes under the Empire would hark back to their forefathers, in spite of three revolutions.

At mid-century, tradesmen, government officials and intellectuals wanted access to works of art that would endorse their new social situation, and confer on them the status of owners of *objets d'art*. They helped maintain the progress of the original print by recognising themselves in its shifting identity, and trusting that others would recognise them in it as well. As Philippe Burty observed in 1863, 'the etching bridges the gap between painting and engraving'.[95] The tastes of this new class were generally conservative, and this prevented their admiring craft products. The most daring of them sought realism of the anecdotal kind, that echoed the contents of the newspaper. They continued to appreciate the values of the romantic period, indeed their own virtues were based on them, but this did not automatically signify that they were all repelled by Charles Jacque's pigs or by Bracquemond's chickens. They were admiring of the printmaker's art, but even more so of the technical skill that made constant innovation possible and demonstrated that progress existed in art as well as in more mundane fields; they liked a certain sturdiness of composition and straightforwardness of expression. All wished to draw a firm line between the products of art and the products of industry. They particularly appreciated skilled printing because it helped distinguish an original print from a mass produced item, and gave each print its value.

The new society found its own trademark among the new kinds of *objets d'art*: Zola, writing in 1847, said: 'Art could be said to be fragmented; this great kingdom has broken into a series of small republics . . . Art has become like a great sweet shop, with sweets to suit every taste.'[96] The writer notes the concomitant fashion for small works of art and domestic subjects.[97] In the 'great sweet shop', demand was not met immediately. Under the Second Empire the market was still sluggish; as Jean-Paul Bouillon explains with reference to Bracquemond, artists were forced to fall back on their own resources and to experiment, each trying to find his own way by trial and error.[98] Bracquemond found himself, with potential purchasers of his work, seated 'between plaster casts of antique sculptures and the chicken run.'[99]

Publishers at this time required illustrations for elegantly produced books (in the eighteenth-century tradition), and this gave Bracquemond and his fellow printmakers reason for hope. Poulet-Malassis, Baudelaire's editor, commissioned frontispieces and went to Delâtre for the printing. At the end of 1859 he was planning an illustrated edition of *Les Fleurs du mal*, which had been condemned in the courts two years earlier. Bracquemond provided a portrait of Baudelaire and remained in contact with Poulet-Malassis until the publisher's death; he had played a vital rôle in the encouragement given to etchers and engravers by the illustrated book. He had a drawing by Courbet made into a print by Bracquemond for Champfleury's *L'Œuvre nouvelle* in 1859; the following year he employed Carolus Duran to make prints for his *Rabelais*, and for *Le Salon intime* by Zacharie Astruc; in 1861 he gave Legros the job of illustrating Duranty's realist novel, *Le Malheur d'Henriette Gérard*.

The Salon of 1859 provided Baudelaire with the opportunity to make a wide-ranging 'aesthetic appraisal'.[100] For the first time in a Salon there was a section for photography, which was thus welcomed officially into the world of art. The critic, Louis Figuier, wrote: 'We may have been spared the argument between ancients and moderns in this century, but we have certainly had the argument between engravers and photographers. . . Photography was born twenty years ago, and for twenty years lithographers and engravers have battled against it.'[101] The fight was not over yet, but the outcome was no longer in doubt. In Zola's great sweetshop there would be a counter for photography and another for original prints; industrial products would be kept at arm's length, in the 'expositions universelles'. The coexistence of different techniques, manual and mechanical, is exemplified in 1859 in the first publication by a new dealer, Alfred Cadart, who

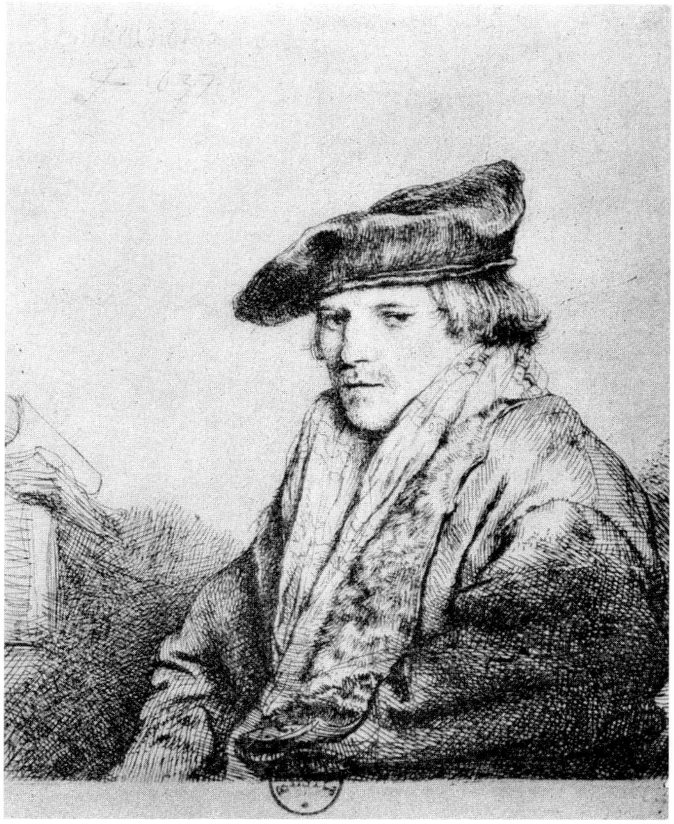

50. Rembrandt,
Seated Young Man with Velvet Beret,
1637.
Etching, second state, 93 x 83 mm.
Bibliothèque nationale, Paris.

reproduced the work of his brother-in-law, the painter Chifflart. Chifflart's album consists of sixteen photographs of paintings, one original lithograph, one original etching and a reproduction.[102] It is a portfolio made to sound out the preferences of the new clientèle and demonstrates clearly the uncertainty into which the arts of so-called 'reproduction' had fallen. Just as indicative of the ambiguities of the period was Chifflart's second publication, a series of original etchings made between 1859-60, commissioned from a craftsman printmaker, Léopold Flameng, and entitled: *Paris qui s'en va, Paris qui vient* (*Paris going and Paris coming*).

The year 1859 also saw the arrival in Paris of a South American millionaire, Arozarena, who in two years established a large-scale speculative business in artists' etchings. By systematically outbidding other buyers in the sale rooms he managed to accumulate 297 prints by Rembrandt, eighty-six by Van Ostade, fifty by Dürer, fifteen by Van Dyck, and almost a complete set of the works of Claude Lorrain, etc. In total, 818 prints which he sold by auction at four sales between 11 March and 28 May 1861,[103] leaving afterwards for Cuba. The catalogue, edited by Clément, Paris's most celebrated dealer in old master prints, carried a preface by Émile Galichon, one of the staff of the *Gazette des Beaux-Arts*. In it he praised the artist's print: 'having become aware of the distance that exists between a print coming from the artist (who puts his heart and soul into it) and one, which may perhaps be more meticulously executed, from one of those 'translators' who do nothing but make cold reproductions of other peoples' masterpieces.'[104] Another dealer, Rochoux, proclaimed his indignation against those people for whom 'a high price replaces sentimental value',[105] and was particularly incensed by the idea that a value could be attached to prints that were not reproductions. 'Today only the great masters are worthy of admiration. Tomorrow it will be the turn of the printmakers', he wrote, with some irony, in a pamphlet published just after Arozarena's sales.[106]

The principal arguments on which the value of original prints was founded were set out in this preface. The first one is an ethical argument: the artist 'puts his heart and soul' into an etching, says Galichon. Burty also declared, in 1863, that 'the original outline must be drawn by the artist, and by 'artist' I always mean someone acting on his own inspiration'.[107] The second argument is technical and makes the distinction between craft and industrial production, linking craft production with objects that are either unique or produced in very small quantities and are therefore liable to become very rare if they are bought and sold. Some of Rembrandt's prints have ragged edges, or different inking or paper – something that differentiates each print from any other, thereby conferring on it the quality of uniqueness. Philippe Burty condensed all his writing about prints into a famous article entitled 'La Belle épreuve';[108] Impressionist engravers showed extreme skill in putting it into practice.

11. *1861: The Society of Etchers*

The gallery run by Auguste Cadart in the rue de Richelieu was a testimony to the vigour and diversity of the contemporary art market: Cadart sold paintings, original and reproduction prints and even photographs. He opened the gallery in 1859, when he was thirty-one years old. He had previously been an employee of the railways, and nothing seemed to predestine him for life as a publisher: 'Fifteen or so years ago I was in the army when my marriage to the sister of M.F. Chifflart made me a publisher',[109] he explained. Encouraged by the success of the salerooms, by Burty's rhetoric and Bracquemond's advice, and by the financial advance of the middle classes, Cadart decided to put his money on original etchings by contemporary artists. Times were still uncertain, however, and when he formed a partnership in 1861 it was with a photographer, Félix Chevalier.

In 1861 Cadart, with Manet, Bracquemond and others, was preparing a periodical that was to consist of albums of original etchings provided by any of the painters who was drawn to printmaking. Their allegiance was obvious. The original etching was thus labelled the contemporary work of art par excellence, the victorious rival of photography. Copies did not fade, and their price, between 1F and 1F50, was no higher than the price of photographic prints. An etching involved no mechanical processes and was therefore able to convey either the artist's 'temperament' (the realist version) or his 'soul' (the romantic version).

Théophile Gautier took it upon himself to sing its praises. His preface to the first issue, in September 1862, is a manifesto in support of etching against photography: 'At this time, when photography is beguiling ordinary folk by the mechanical accuracy of its reproduction, art should be manifesting a tendency towards originality and the picturesque.' The goal, once set, was half way to being attained. Théophile Gautier declared quite simply that 'each etching is an original'.[110] His conclusion could not be more clear: 'The Society of Etchers was founded in order to mount a campaign of resistance against photography, lithography, the aquatint and the engraving whose cross-hatching meets in the centre'. The preface to the second album (1863) was by another Romantic writer, Jules Janin, who drives the point home even farther, extolling the etching over the photograph feature by feature.[111]

It was not so much a question of providing the new bourgeoisie of the Second Empire (then at its height) with art that was financially within its reach (reproductive engravings cost as much as original prints) as of providing a 'work of art' that, in spite of its reasonable price, could assume the same symbolic powers of authenticity and uniqueness as a painting. This product of the modern age was able to qualify its purchasers as true art lovers and to give them the chance to collect; they in turn were able to endorse their social status by becoming the owners of works of art. From 1862 onwards the lower middle classes and ordinary people began to reject industrialised art, and the distinction between objects became as subtle as the distinction between the many categories of owners of art, as defined by what they owned.

Artists taking part in this game were recruited from realist circles and formed themselves into a society – this in itself was unusual but, given the swift evolution of the art market, not exceptional. In the same year, 1862, Bracquemond became a founder member of the new Société Nationale des Beaux Arts, another group founded to fill the gap between the Salon, which was too ancient, and the galleries, which were too new. The Society was one method of indicating the solidarity existing between the publisher and the artists who shared the costs of each edition. The Society of Etchers published 300 etchings in five annual albums, divided into monthly issues appearing from Septmber 1862 to August 1867. The pace of production had been settled at five etchings per month at a cost of 1F50 per print, or fifty francs for a subscription to sixty prints annually. Delâtre was the printer, Bracquemond the organiser and consultant.

The first issue contained works by Bracquemond, Lalanne, Ribot and Manet, a choice that left no room for doubt about the aesthetic orientation of the publication. The idea was not, however, to promote any particular school. The choice of artists was based on their interest in etching and the general effort to publish and circulate artistic prints. In his preface, Théophile Gautier says: 'This society has no other common code but individualism. . . No particular genre predominates, no manner prevails.' As it turned out, the subsequent issues included a range of landscape painters of the 1830 generation: Daubigny, Paul Huet, Corot, Charles Jacque;

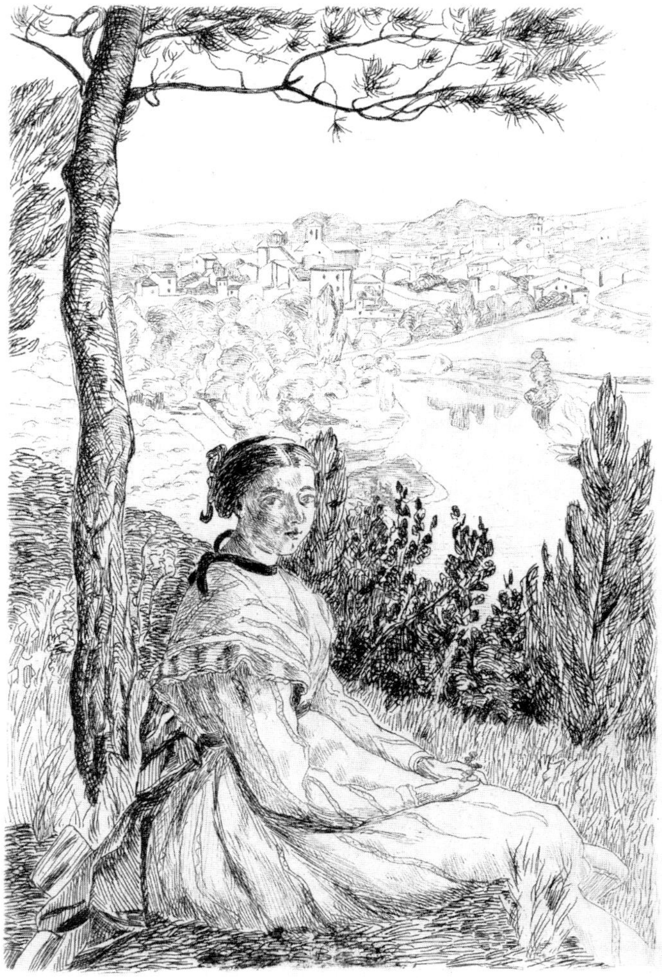

51. Frédéric Bazille,
Seated Young Woman.
Undated. Etching, 235 x 155 mm.
Bibliothèque nationale, Paris.

also, some unknown artists: Appian, Jongkind; established artists: Delacroix, Courbet; young realists: Fantin Latour, Legros and the English etching fanatic, Francis Seymour Haden. In such a compilation the quality of work was bound to strike the critics as uneven. The Society of Etchers was reproached for its eclecticism and non-conformism, the standard criticism levelled against all the Societies that burgeoned within the framework of Impressionism and which were also enjoying the opening up of the art market. Beraldi, the collector, was later to moan: 'Oh, the number of pseudo-Daubignys that have been let loose, who have allowed their etching tools to wander aimlessly, sketching trees in the varnish, or cows and shepherdesses looking as if they had stepped out of a two penny Noah's Ark! Cadart's albums are among these near misses. I am no more in favour than the next person of what Théophile Gautier terms "a meticulous finish, the joy and admiration of the philistine", but in prints as in everything else one must know what to love and what to hate. What we should hate in this case is the rough sketch with a continuous line, in which the plate is barely scratched, but to which the technique gives the status of a system'.[112]

In the name of this cautious aesthetic, Beraldi rejected Corot's 'clichés-verre' as well as Manet's etchings. Conversely, the tolerant attitude we have learnt (from the Impressionists) towards 'sketches' and 'the unfinished' makes us look at the landscapes of certain painters not then redeemed by Impressionism with new eyes. One must not be taken in by the natural-looking light generated by the emotive lines of the etching, bathed in the white of the paper, and label every showily-lit or insufficiently-etched landscape as 'Impressionist'. In the etchings in the collection, however, and particularly in the landscapes, there are often technical skills displayed, and a desire to avoid dramatic effects that foreshadow the spirit of Impressionism. The Barbizon painter Ferdinand Chaigneau's flocks of sheep, etched in dry point, give off light in little gusts, like a breeze.[113] The etchings of Xavier de Dananche, on the other hand, are very dark, demonstrating a strong effort to make shadow look natural.[114] Vollon should be mentioned here, as should Jules Michelin who, in 1863, had a set of sixteen etchings published by Cadart and was influential in guiding Corot, Manet and Pissarro.[115] Courbet's experiment was not followed up, but the etched work of Manet, Fantin-Latour and Legros had its source in the Society of Etchers, and Jongkind's work was almost entirely bound up with the Society. There were absentees too: Degas must certainly have been aware of the enterprise but was probably suspicious of associations of artists and was not a member. Pissarro was in touch with the society and indeed was a member, but published nothing with them, although his first large plate, *At the Water's Edge* (Fig. 52), heavily influenced by Corot, could have been designed expressly for their albums.

Cadart's enterprise was a success. In 1864 the Society of Etchers was prospering. In 1866 Cadart paid a visit to America. Goupil, the most important gallery in Paris, had successfully represented the French School there since 1848. Cadart took some paintings with him: Courbet, Corot, Monet, Jongkind, Boudin, plus some sculpture and his collection of etchings. His stay in Boston and New York was influential in persuading American collectors like George Lucas (who bought seventy-eight bronzes by Baraye from him), and Samuel P. Avery, to spend large amounts of money on contemporary French art. Encouraged by his success, Cadart returned to America eight months later with 800 pieces. Auspices seemed good for his exhibitions in New York, Boston, Philadelphia and Baltimore. Alas, by February nothing had been sold. This was probably because the imperialist policies of Napoleon III in Mexico had stirred up anti-French feeling among American art-lovers. On 9

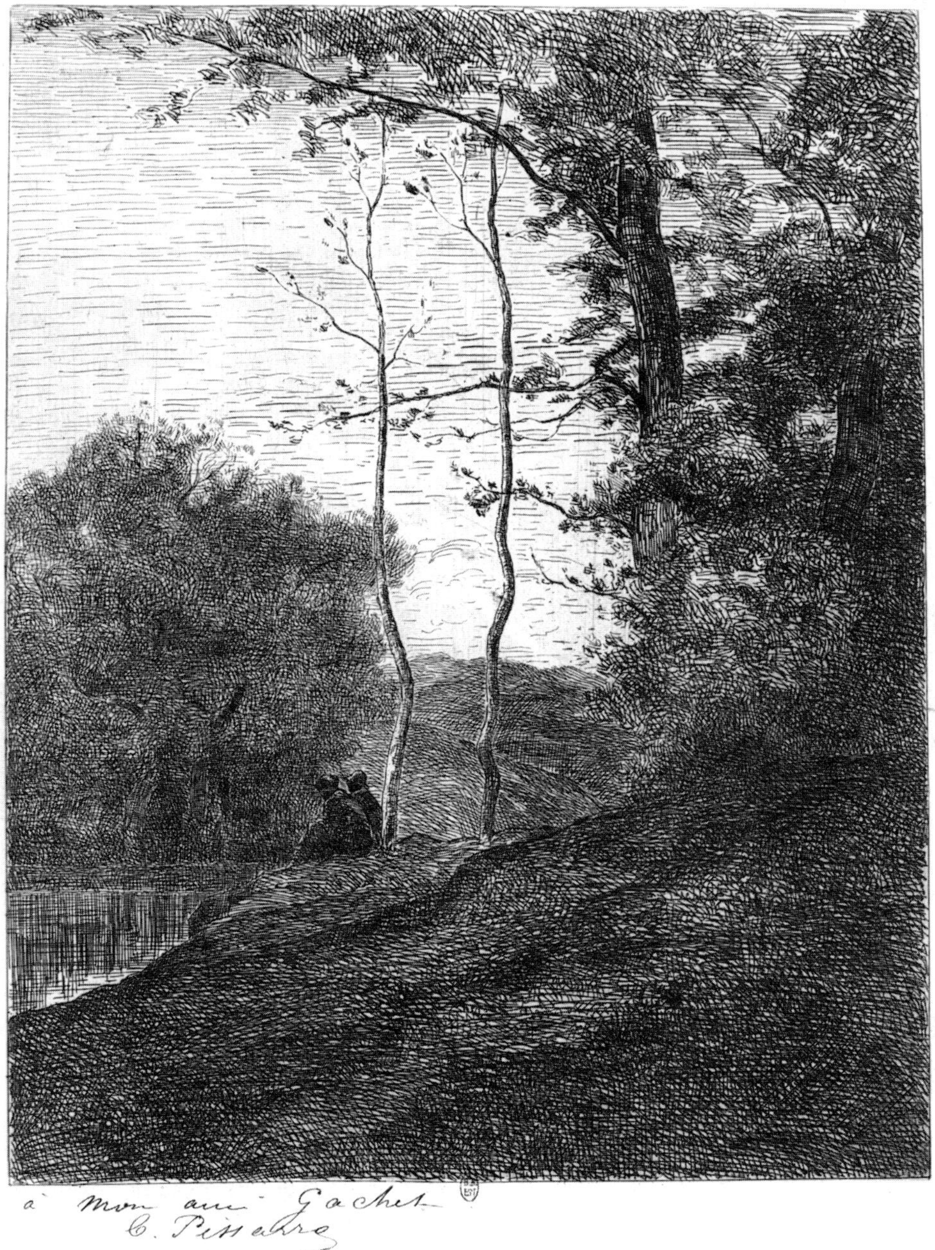

52. Camille Pissarro, *At the Water's Edge*. About 1863. Etching, single state, 283 x 217 mm. Bibliothèque nationale, Paris.

December 1866, the day after the exhibition opened, Cadart complained about political events jeopardising his enterprise.[116] He then organised emergency public sales. He re-boarded the liner with his crates and a loss of 80,000 francs, a disaster for the painters, for the 'French Etching Club', and for their dealer, who was obliged to dissolve the society on 6 September 1867. This did not put an end to Cadart's publishing. In 1868 he started a new set of albums: *L'Eau-forte nouvelle*, for the first of which Bracquemond concocted a grandiloquent title page. It may have been for this new publication that Frédéric Bazille produced his only etching (Fig. 51),[117] taken from a painting shown in the Salon of 1869, shortly before the young painter's death on the battlefield. So much adversity eventually ruined what had been a promising enterprise.

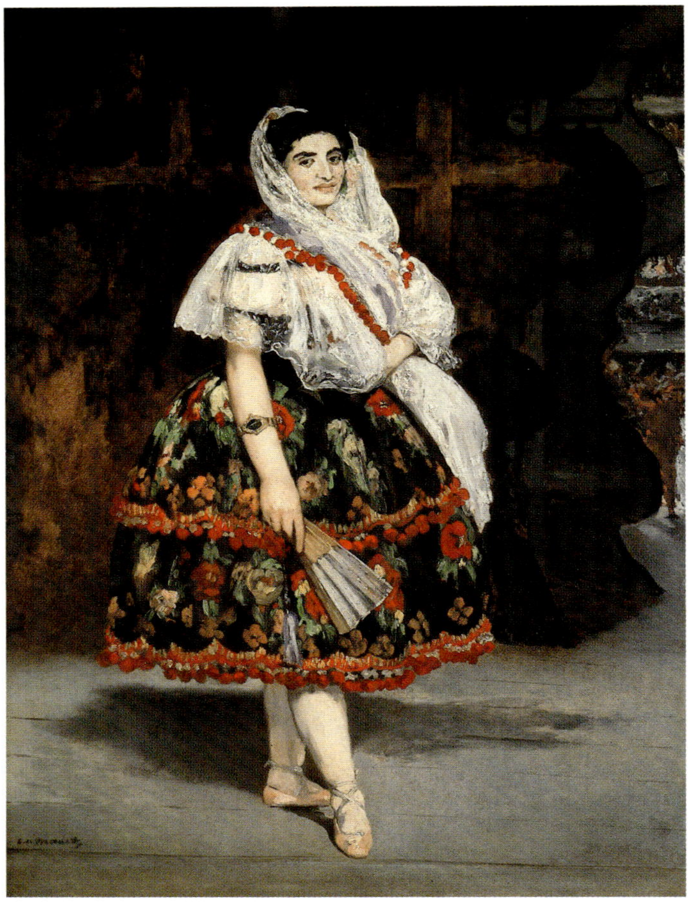

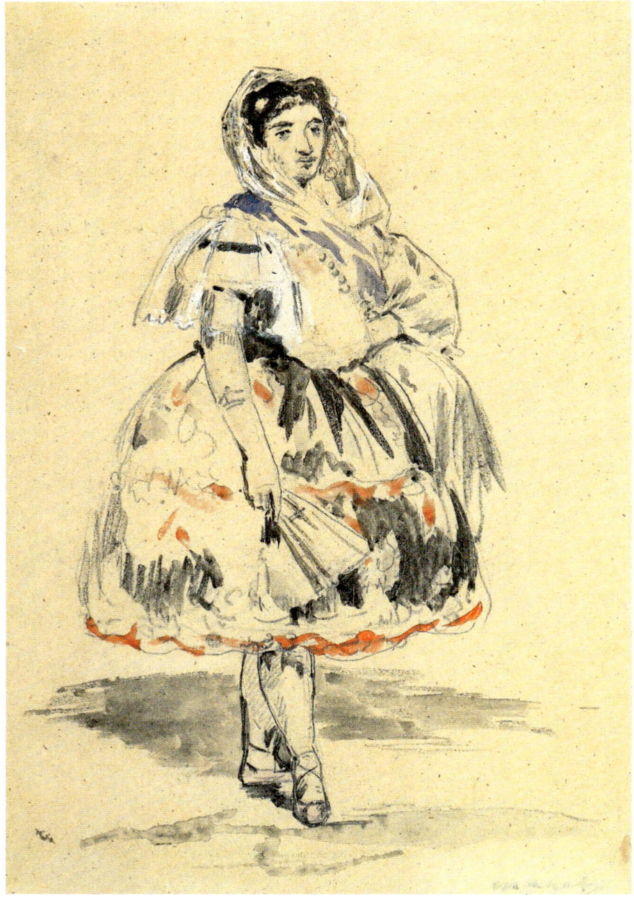

12. *Manet and the Etching*

53. Edouard Manet,
Lola de Valence. 1862.
Oil on canvas, 123 x 92 cm.
Musée d'Orsay, Paris.

54. Edouard Manet,
Lola de Valence. 1862.
Pencil, ink, Indian ink, water colour, gouache, 256 x 173 mm.
Musée du Louvre, Paris, Cabinet des dessins.

55. Edouard Manet,
Lola de Valence. 1863.
Etching and aquatint, sixth state, 235 x 161 mm.
Bibliothèque nationale, Paris.

56. Edouard Manet,
Lola de Valence.
Lithograph, 195 x 185 mm.
Bibliothèque nationale, Paris.

To be modern in 1860 meant to build something new. If Haussmann had wished to be completely modern, he should have conducted an archaeological investigation into the 'vanishing Paris' whose ruins provided inspiration to the etching fraternity. The modernism of Baudelaire is full of nostalgia. To Baudelaire, to be modern meant 'to extract from fashion the poetry contained in its historical aspect, to sift the eternal from the transient'. Manet applied these strictures quite literally. To be modern meant to transform the world, to mix history and the present day, to mix the genres and the classes, to mix places of entertainment and relaxation, the alleyways where people stroll, paintings, prints. . . Any public place was a suitable subject to the modern artist – in fact Manet's etchings fitted the bill exactly – and this why the period needs to be studied in detail, keeping firmly in mind the complicated relationships that formed and dissolved so constantly between

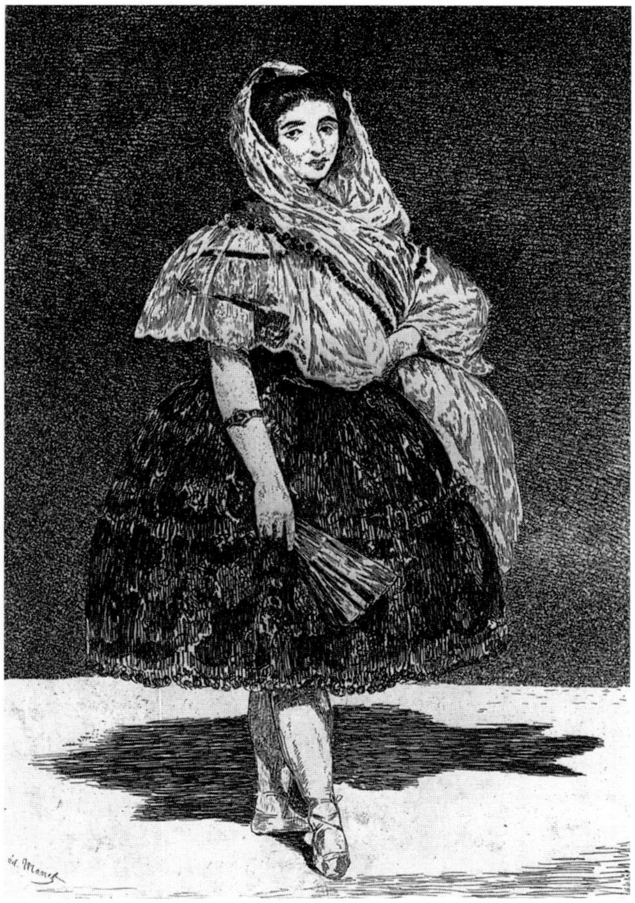

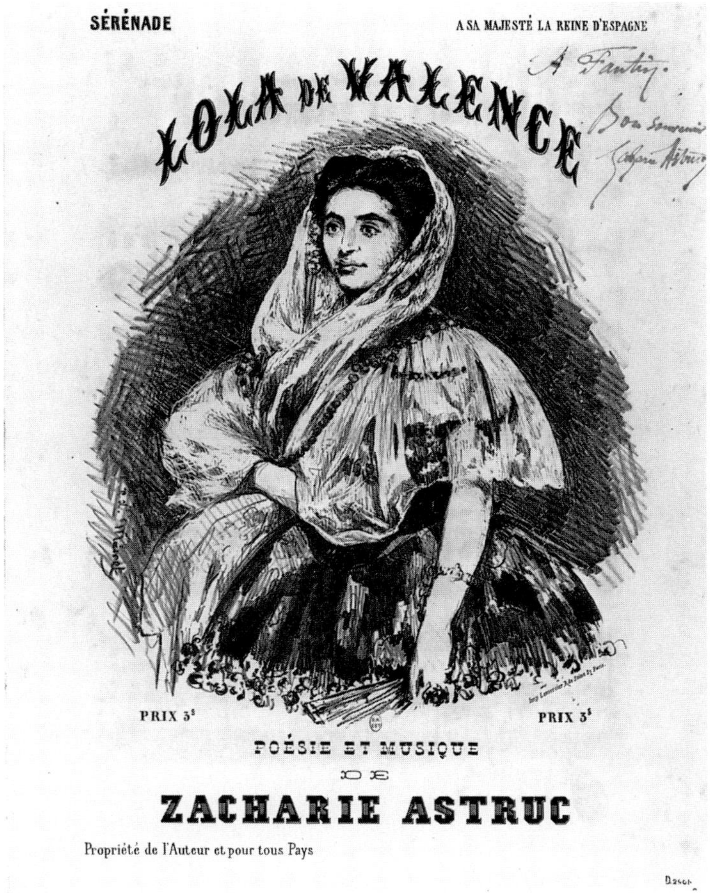

painting, drawing and printmaking. Nor should the occult rôle of photography and the fast-developing rôle of the mechanical reproduction be forgotten.

Manet's earliest etching is a rough reproduction of a fresco by Fra Angelico, taken from a drawing brought back from Italy in 1857. Only a modern artist would have turned a fresco into an etching. A subsequent etching is a scrupulously accurate rendering of a daguerreotype of a portrait of Baudelaire (Figs 57–60).[121] Again, only a modern artist would have given the same respect to a daguerreotype as he did to Fra Angelico. Later Manet took up etching more seriously, producing about forty plates, more than half his total output of prints, between 1860 and 1862, under the aegis of the Society of Etchers. At the publication of the Society's first issue in September 1862, Cadart also published an album of eight etchings by Édouard Manet.

The first large plate to be published, *The Little Horsemen*, is a reproduction of a painting in the Louvre, executed in 1855, after a painting attributed at the time to Velázquez.[122] The painted reproduction of Velázquez is a very free reproduction, not a copy, and it is therefore difficult to decide whether, in his etching, Manet is interpreting Velázquez or copying his own work; is it a reproductive print of his own painting or an original etching? To complicate matters further, there is a hand coloured version of the *Little Horsemen*, and this firmly places the print in the category of drawing and painting. Who are these 'little horsemen' who have dismounted, these little clusters of friends, together yet apart, not a group yet behaving like one? The portraits are almost identifiable and yet curiously anonymous, well placed, well lit and yet located in an indeterminate and unfinished background. The figures are modern, more modern perhaps than the ones visible in the crowd in *Music in the Tuileries*, the great painting of the modern movement on which Manet was already at work; the *Little Horsemen* has often been regarded as a preliminary study for *Music*.

The second etching by Manet to be published by the Société des Aquafortistes was *Lola de Valence* (Fig. 55), another work qualifying as modern because of its Spanish exoticism, its relationship with the theatre where the dancer performed, its reference to Baudelaire (he wrote a quatrain in its praise), and its technique, which was even more 'brutal' than last time. In addition it was accompanied by a lithograph designed for the cover of a popular novel (Fig. 56). The relationship between this etching and the painting is much more complex (Fig. 53): a watercolour served him as a model

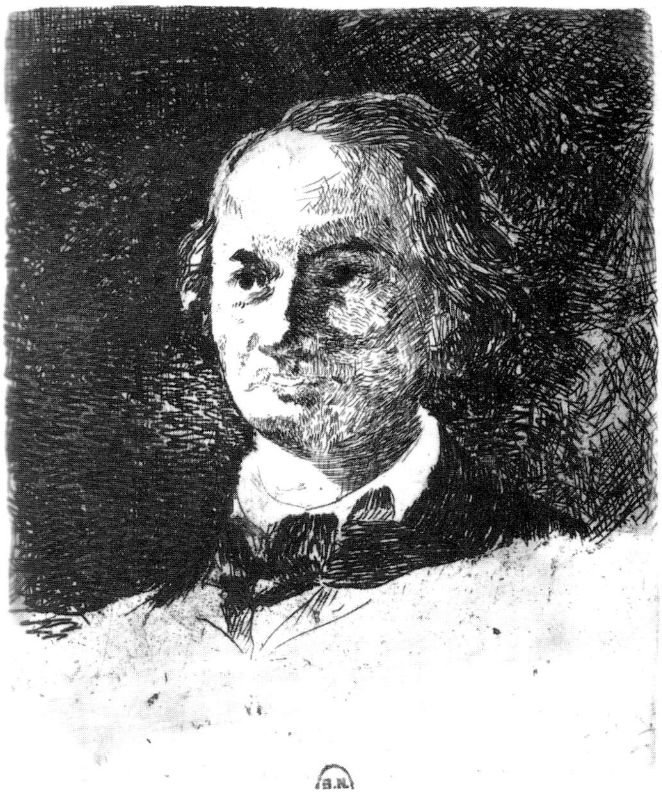

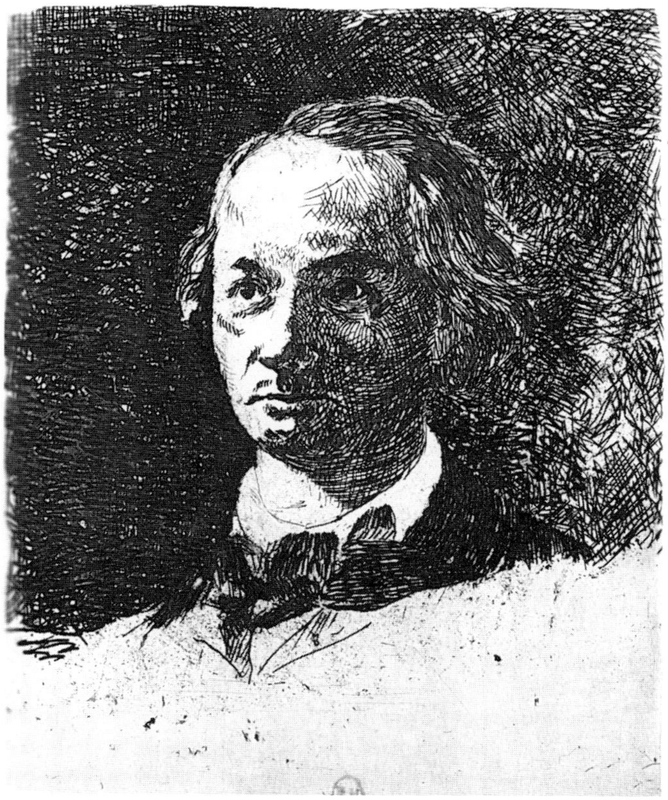

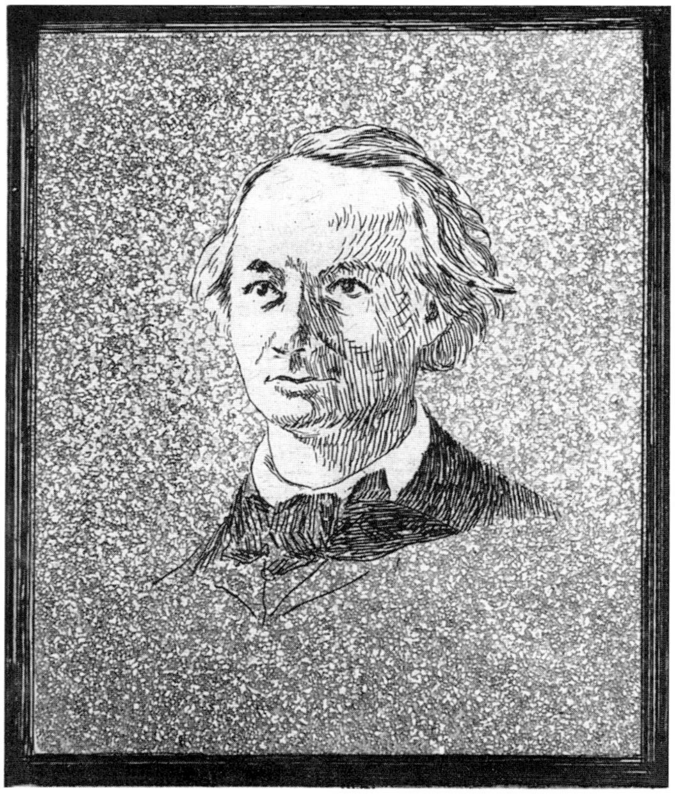

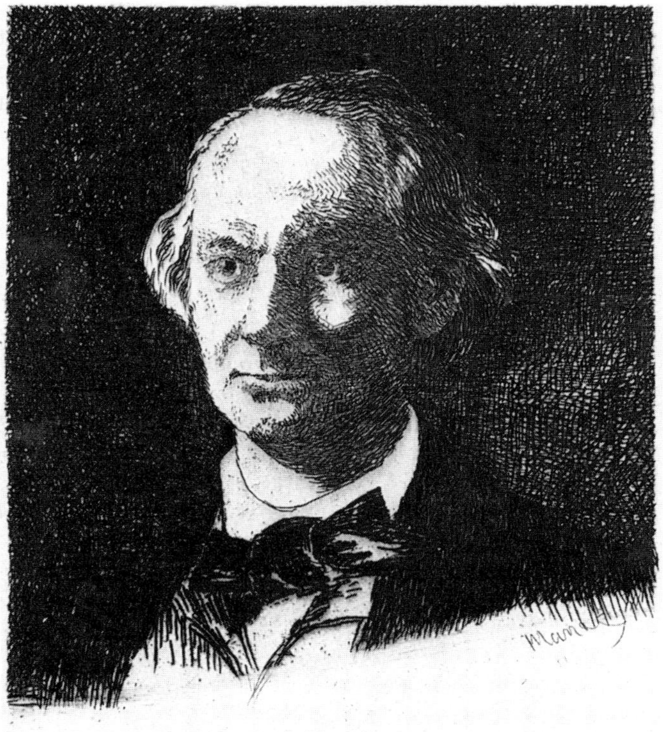
Point et Gravé par Manet 1865

(Fig. 54), and the imprint of the point with which he traced the outline on to the copper plate can still be seen. Manet was to use this technique of copying a picture directly on to a plate more than once, subordinating the watercolour painting to the requirements of the print. To ensure the success of the transfer of the drawing to the print, of the paper on to the copper, Manet used a simple grid, still visible on the sheets of the *Gitanos*, *Philip IV* or the *Candle Seller*. In the way of a busy modern painter, Manet then took to using photographs. Photographic proofs of *L'Espada* or the *Child with a Sword (turned to the left)* prove that he used 'reproductive' photography after the appearance of the album in 1862.[123] Later he regularly had his work photographed, sometimes re-touching the photographs, in the same way that all the photographers of the *quartier* would re-touch or hand-colour their photographs. The *Absinthe Drinker* (Fig. 61), in the album of 1862, is another completely modern work in its reference to the age-old theme of 'beggars', or 'ragged-trousered philosophers', unearthed by Manet, and its realism (which won him critical opprobrium). A watercolour exists that is half way between the painting and the etching. There is no coloured proof in existence but in 1868 Manet returned to the plate and produced a third state (Fig. 62), re-etched and covered with aquatint; this differs entirely from the second published state in that the dark aquatint augments the black of the strokes made by the etching tool. The 'Tiepolo effect' has been replaced by a 'Rembrandt effect'.[124]

By now the etching had won its independence. Manet's mentor was Goya.[125] His earliest prints all stem from the contemporary hispanicism that he shared with a number of realist artists including Legros and the other etcher from the Salon des Refusés, Louis Lombard. Goya's art, looing back at a Spain frozen into the eighteenth century, reflects the position of progressive French artists stifled by the authoritarianism of the Empire, with its censorship. Manet looked upon Goya as a true spiritual father. There were several new editions of his etchings after 1855, including the *Majas* and the *Blind Guitar Player*.[126] Manet's *Guitarrero* dates from the year following the publication of Goya's etching. The critics were less caustic about the *Guitarrero*, accepted by the Salon of 1865; the etching had already been published in the album of 1862. A water colour played the rôle of intermediary in this case as well. The different states of the *Guitarrero* are very different from one another, and the watercolour used for the tracing of the etching looks like a supplementary state. From the sketch to the painting and from the painting to the etching as it was finally published – as a plate in *L'Artiste* in 1867 – the work proceeds through a number of metamorphoses that constitute the modern aspect of Manet's art.

It is interesting to see how Manet coped with the confusion between painting and drawing, the print and

57, 58, 59, 60. Edouard Manet,
Portrait of Baudelaire.
Etching, 98 x 77 mm.
First plate, 1861 or 1865,
first and second states;
second plate, 1869;
third plate, 1869,
fourth and final state.
Bibliothèque nationale, Paris.

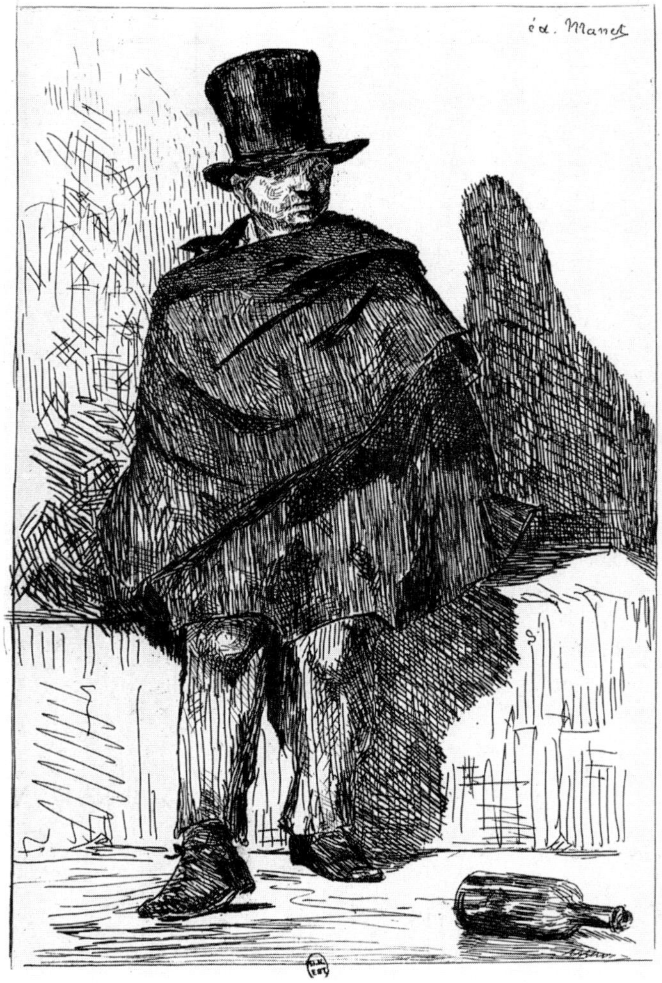

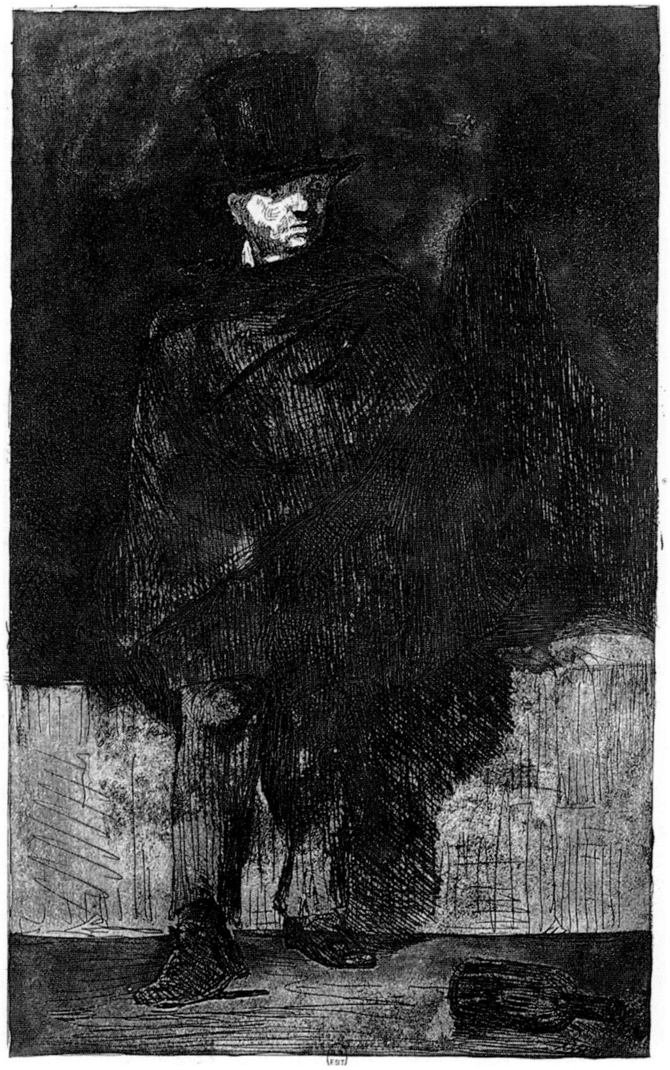

61, 62. Edouard Manet,
The Absinthe Drinker. 1862.
Etching, first and third states,
252 x 152 mm.
Bibliothèque nationale, Paris.

modern methods of reproduction, even if he did not manage to separate the media entirely. Whether it was deliberate or not, the etching emerged with the same status as a painting or drawing, and this meant that the technical side, the application of the aquatint or the acid, could be left to a professional. Bracquemond,[127] Legros and Guérard took it in turns to lend a hand. Alphonse Legros, for instance, was responsible for managing the *Boy with a Sword*, Bracquemond the *Olympia*, the *Dead Bullfighter* (Fig. 64) and many others, including one curious experiment in pen engraving which served to add to the confusion between the techniques of drawing and intaglio techniques. His last plates were etched in the studio of Henri Guérard. This collaboration did not reduce the value of the etching any more than did the use of photography. On the contrary, it served to emphasise the importance of the artist in the genesis of the etching.

Manet's etchings, all of them (except one) produced before 1871, belong to the period when the etching had

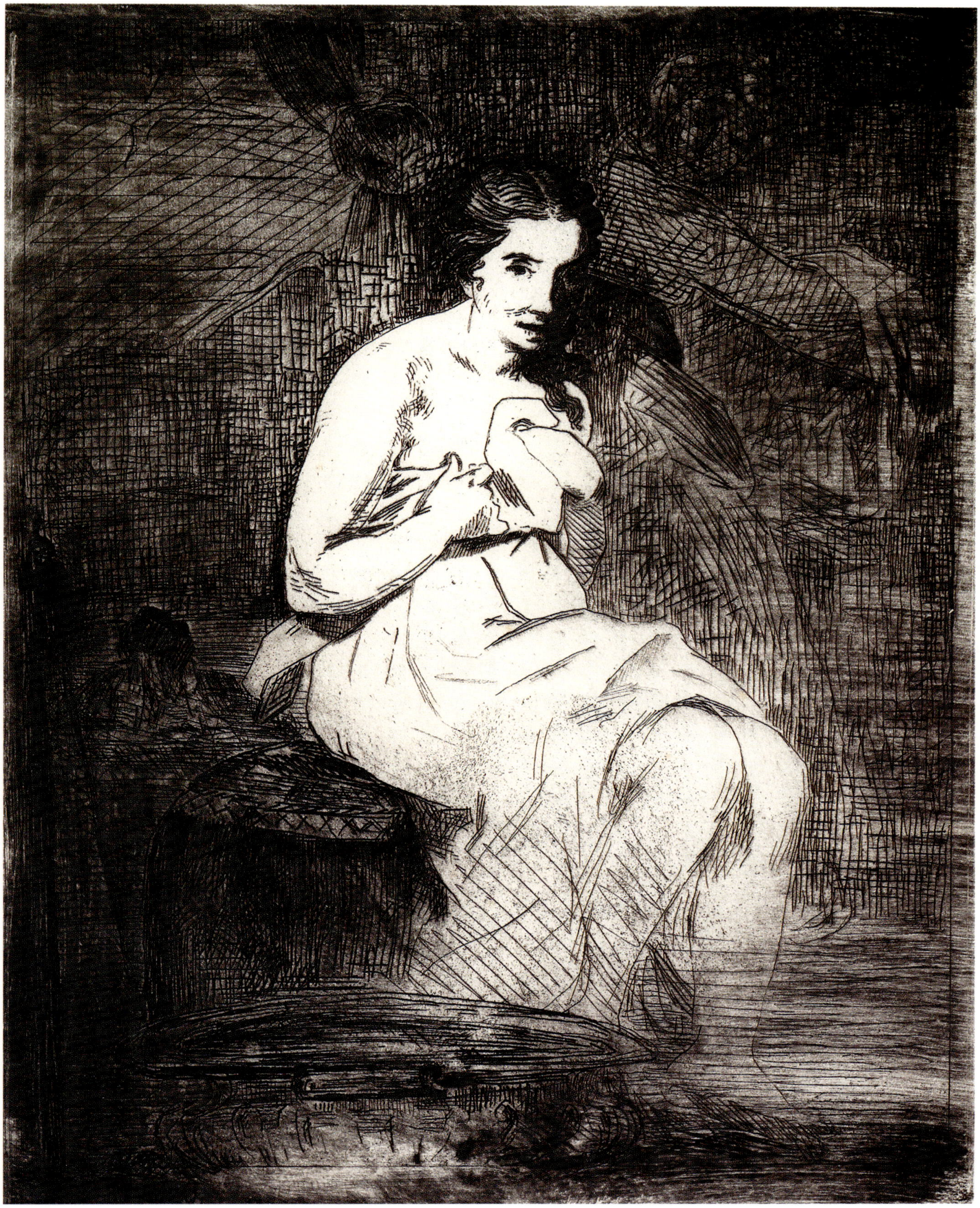

63. Edouard Manet, *The Toilette*. 1862. Etching, first state, second proof, 283 x 224 mm.
Private collection, Paris.

not yet become an independent art form although, thanks to its assimilation with the art of drawing, it was on the way to becoming one. Manet's etchings are almost all connected in some way with his paintings. A few plates, *The Child with a Dog*, *The Candle Seller*, *The Man in the Straw Hat*, *The Queue at the Butcher's Shop* (Fig. 101) and *At the Prado* have no painted version. Unlike the etchings that painters of the previous generation made from their own paintings, Manet's etchings look less and less like a debased version of a painting, a re-play of the painting in a minor key. As Jay Fisher rightly comments, they are equivalents, not substitutes. One proof of this is the position Manet gave to his etchings at his exhibitions. Not only did he present them at the Salon at the same time as his paintings (including the Salon des Refusés in 1863) but he included them in his personal exhibitions as well, at Martinet's gallery in 1862, or in his show in the avenue de l'Alma in 1867.

Besides being linked to painting, etchings were also linked to publishing. Surreptitiously and probably unconsciously, the painter-printmaker was assembling the technical and stylistic wherewithal that would allow him to transform a published work into something individual and unique. Almost all of Manet's etchings were published or were intended for publication. Exceptions were few and far between: the first one, after Fra Angelico, and a few others could count as unfinished exercises in technique. Others were finished but were compromised in one way or another. The revival in aquatint of some of the plates, including the *Absinthe Drinker* in 1868, when no new edition was planned, takes on a particular importance. The attention paid to the different states, as for example with the *Dead Bullfighter* which exists in seven or eight states, testifies to something above and beyond the passion for technique displayed by someone like Bracquemond.

One extraordinary proof of *The Toilette* (Fig. 63), an etching from the first album of 1862, exists in which an overlay of ink bears witness to the artist's search for a monotype effect. In this way the print joins the drawing as an unique work of art, owing nothing either to the printer or to chance.

Unlike Bracquemond and the painter-printmakers of the 1880s, Manet never signed his proofs by hand. Nevertheless his interest in the value set on them by collectors is demonstrated by the way he selected different paper for different clients. To the routine edition by Cadart on Holland paper he added editions on Japan and one edition on China in 1863, the latter printed for his friends. This personalisation and sophistication of the series are also facets of Manet's modernity.

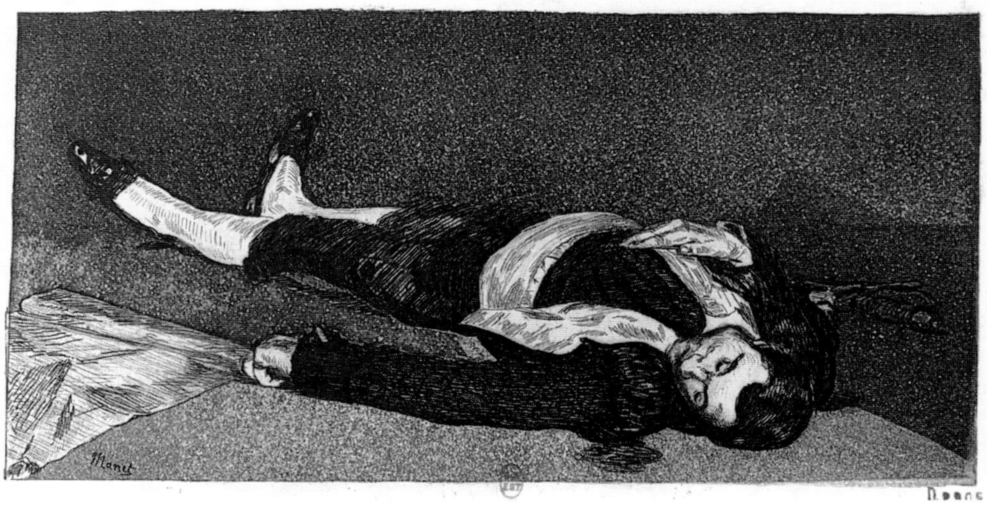

64. Edouard Manet, *The Dead Bullfighter*. 1868. Etching, sixth state, 95 x 193 mm. Bibliothèque nationale, Paris.

13. *1862: The Artist's Lithograph*

The *Gazette des Beaux-Arts* was by now definitely the spearhead of the print trade. Alongside the controversy raging since the Arozarena sales between Émile Galichon and Rochoux, the dealer, Philippe Burty published regular updates on the fortunes of the print. He drew up the first catalogues of etchings, Millet in 1861, Meissonier in 1862 and Meryon in 1863. In March 1861 he wrote a preface to the catalogue of another sale that made a stir, the sale of the Parguez collection of lithographs by Romantic painters.[129] Parguez had been collecting artists' proofs of the lithographs of Delacroix, Géricault, Ingres, Vernet, Bonington and Charlet from the start. It was he who commissioned Delacroix to tackle the Faust legend. The Parguez sale demonstrated to collectors and artists alike that the lithograph was worthy of interest in spite of the disrepute it had been cast into (as a commercial means of reproduction) by industrialised and mass production. This sale and the sale of the collection of Colonel de la Combe which followed in 1863 aroused just as much interest as the Arozarena sale.

In his preface Burty reiterates the arguments he had used to sanction the etching as a creative work of art: 'Lithographs are the most spontaneous expression of the painter's thoughts, and convey these thoughts with the vigour and freshness of an original drawing.' For lithography, however, which was still used for a wide range of reproductive processes, the contention rang slightly less true than it did for etching. Burty nevertheless embarked on it boldly. It was true that these were printed proofs of works by painters who were already well known. Burty wrote: 'The print run is never very considerable. The stones wear out quickly and begin to give a blurred reproduction; they cannot be retouched in the same way as copper plates or wooden blocks and finally their size and weight make it necessary for the publisher to obliterate them after a few years.' Such a statement caused dismay to more than one dealer. Quite a number of collectors and printers felt as infuriated as Rochoux by such extraordinary statements, 'an outrage to the art of printmaking'. Besides, it was known that the new printing presses could produce thousands of copies with the utmost fidelity. This was the weak link in Burty's argument; if he wanted to persuade his clientèle that a lithograph, a humble scrap of paper, could become a rare and precious object, he would have to

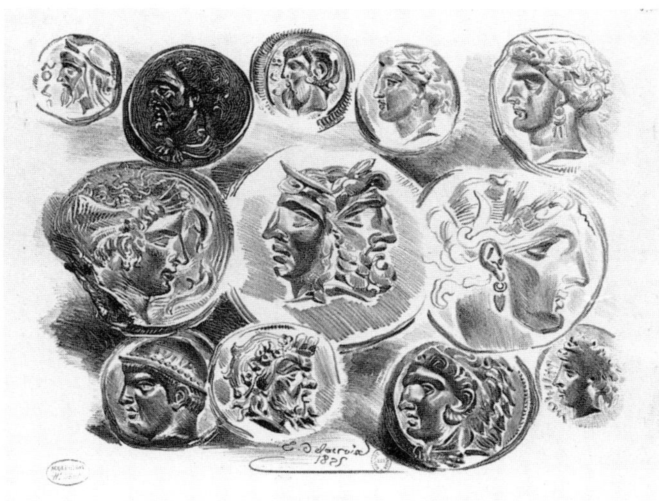

65. Eugène Delacroix,
Sheet Showing Twelve Classical Medals. 1825.
Lithograph, first state, 240 x 305 mm.
Bibliothèque nationale, Paris.

66. Eugène Isabey,
Fishermen's Return. About 1844.
Mezzotint lithograph,
first state, 273 x 412 mm.
Bibliothèque nationale, Paris.

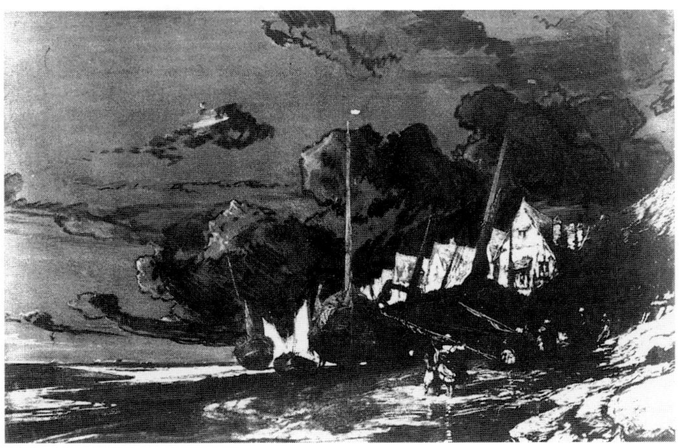

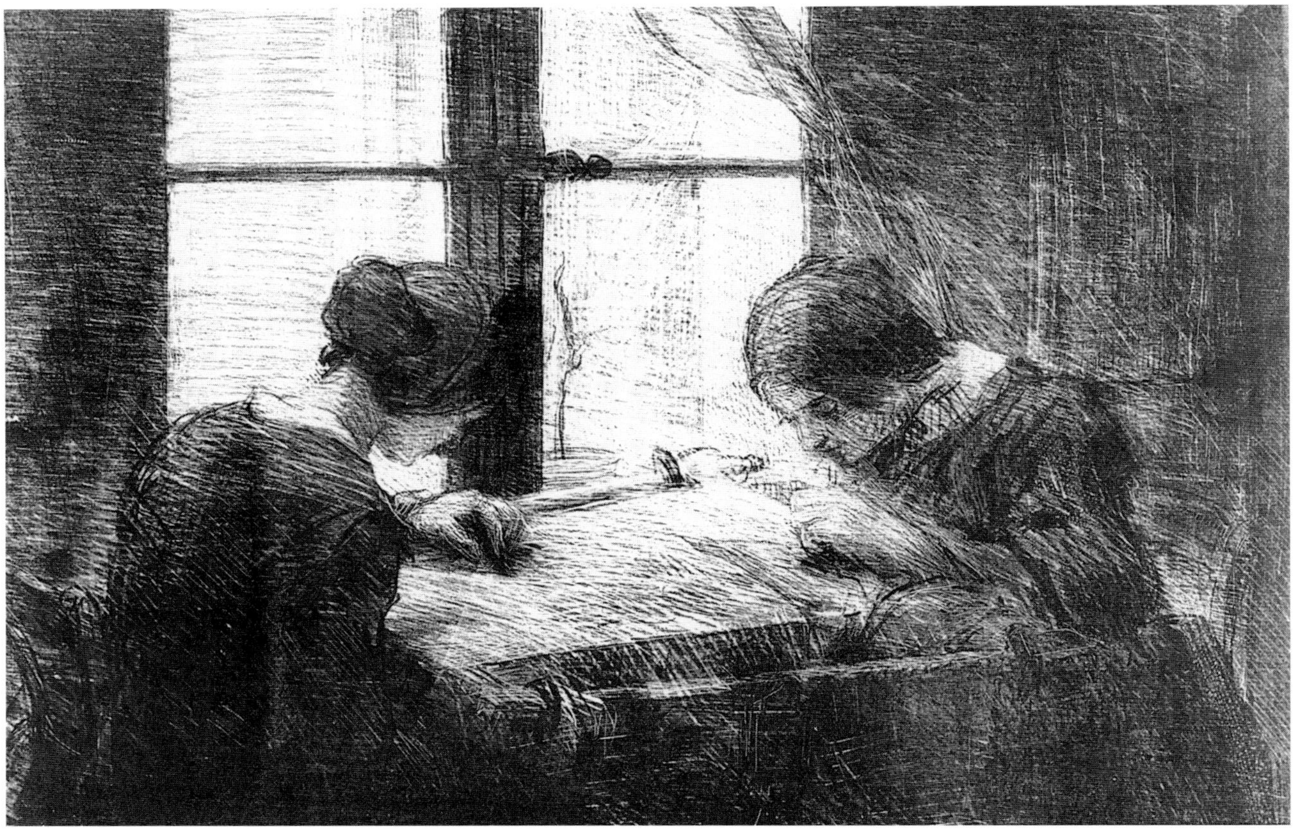

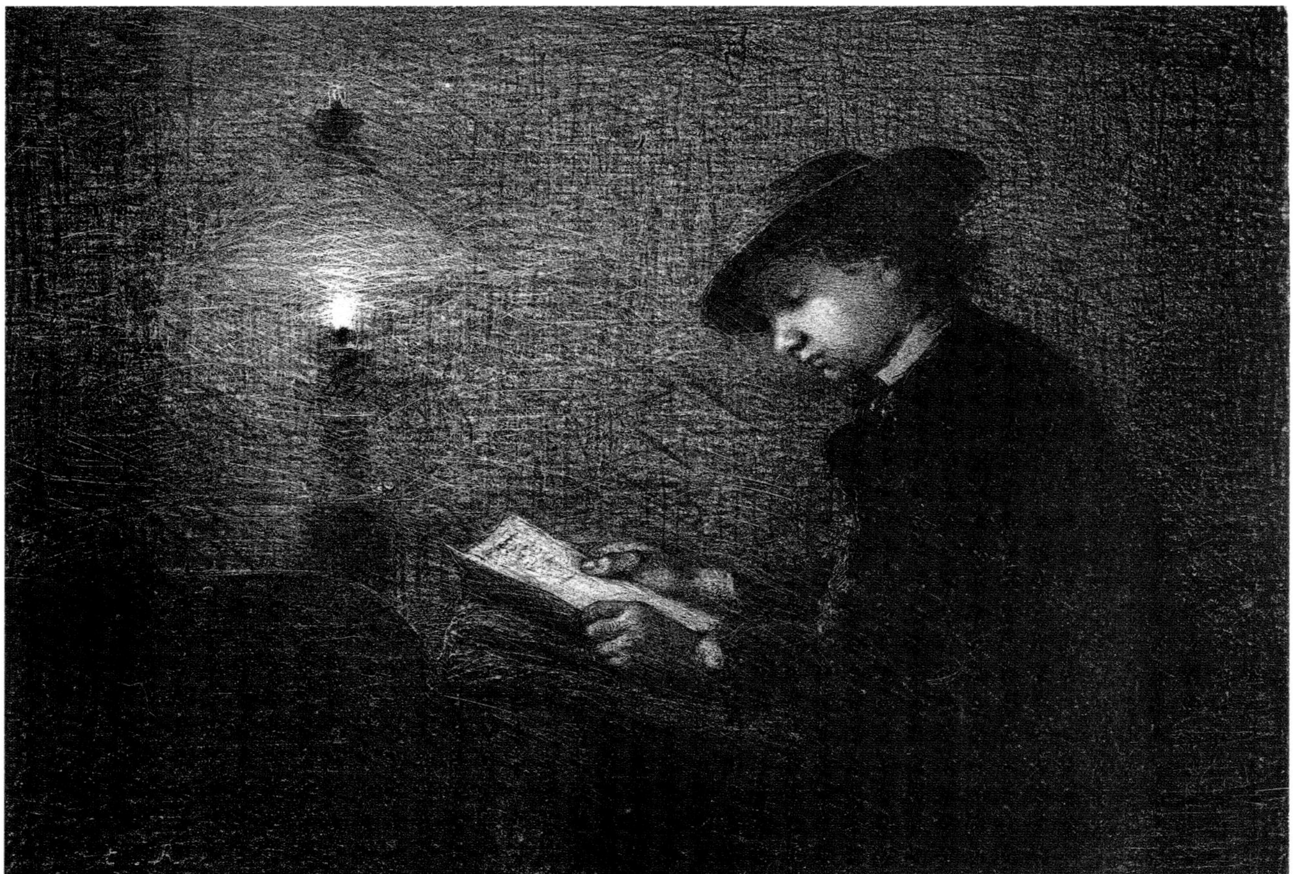

find a better one. A final argument followed this one, which Burty also summed up: 'there is no doubt that in the near future good lithographs will command excessive prices.'

In spite of its exaggerations, this essay was timely. The industrialisation of the lithograph relegated the original craft techniques to the production of backward-looking collectors' items. The future of photo-lithography, invented by Poitevin and Lemercier, rewarded for their invention by the Duc de Luynes in 1862,[130] was no longer in doubt. In addition, the clientèle seemed ready: these consisted of rich or at least comfortably-off collectors (or sometimes quite modest folk) who preferred to buy something suitable to their situation: something less solemn and more personal than a painting and which could be collected in greater quantity. Many collectors still lived under the shadow of the great Romantic painters. Burty was the editor of the *Journal* of Delacroix, the standard bearer and mentor of all modern painters. Most lithographs by Romantic artists had lurked in the corner of the artist's studio, or in a box in the houses of a few collectors; when they came out of exile after 1860 they had gained in stature. Their lessons had been absorbed by Fantin-Latour, in whose collection they figured.

Pissarro, when he sent Delacroix's *Sheet showing Twelve Classical Medals* (Fig. 65) to his son, said 'I am sending you ten lithographic drawings by Daumier and a lithograph of classical medals by Delacroix. These are very rare and I am very attached to them. I often look at them . . . ; as lithographs they have never been surpassed.'[131] The *Classical Medals* lithograph was the only one by Delacroix in Degas's possession. Delacroix had chosen the difficult task of depicting objects in very low relief, and volumes without sharply defined contours, by the use of low-angled lighting. In his *Portrait of Baron Schwitter*, or in some of the diabolical plates he made for *Macbeth*, he made use of the *manière noire* by scratching on the stone.

The lithographs of Richard Parkes Bonington contain the same experiments in the rendering of atmosphere by different treatments of the stone - washing, scumbling, scraping - which were the Impressionsts' first lesson. A scumbled effect is used for mist or fog, and craquelure for old stonework, as Pissarro used it in his views of Old Rouen, half a century after Bonington.[132] Jongkind, who arrived from Holland in 1843, learnt his technique in Isabey's studio. Isabey's lithographs (Fig. 66), with their washed, scumbled and sponged effects, foreshadow the work of Degas and Pissarro. To explain the fleeting reawakening of interest in the artists' lithograph at the beginning of the 1860s the reappearance of Daumier needs to be taken into account; since the *Charivari* had been rendered insipid by censorship, like all the opposition press, he had been almost forgotten. In his new weekly journal *Le Boulevard*, Carjat gave Daumier a full page, in 1862, which the artist used to show the twelve lithographs that are considered his masterpiece. The Impressionists judged that Daumier had managed to translate movement directly on to paper. Pissarro praised Daumier's lithographs: 'The construction is admirable!'[133] Degas possessed almost the whole set in his collection, although actually preferring the work of Gavarni.

The success of the Parguez sale encouraged Cadart to try his luck at publishing lithographs by contemporary artists. In September 1862 he invited five artists from the Society of Etchers to come along, bringing their own lithographic stones. His plan for an *Album lithographique* did not work out, however. Public taste for lithographs stopped short at the Romantic artists, and at artists' proofs that were by definition very rare; Lemercier himself did not follow up the prints made from the stones entrusted by Cadart to Manet, Legros, Bracquemond, Fantin-Latour and Ribot. Trial proofs still exist of them, however. Manet produced *The Balloon* (Fig. 69), Ribot *Reading* (Fig. 68), and Bracquemond some *Horsemen crossing the Forest*. Legros returned to a drawing of 1855, *Quarrymen of Montrouge* to produce his *Plate with Four Landscapes*. Fantin-Latour proved the most diligent, producing four drawings on three stones: *Tannhäuser*, *The Embroidresses* (Fig. 67) and *Love disarmed and the Education of Love*. Burty tried to promote these prints by demonstrating their direct relationship with the romantic lithographs so popular with collectors: 'Generally speaking they are produced with a scraper, the patches of light and the grey being scratched with a penknife, probably on blackened stone.'[134] In spite of all his efforts, it was another ten years or so before the reputation of the lithographic work of well-known Romantic painters could eclipse that of lithographic work devoted entirely to propaganda, journalism and caricature.[135]

67. Henri Fantin-Latour, *The Embroidresses*. 1862.
Lithograph, first plate, 270 x 407 mm. Bibliothèque nationale, Paris.

68. Théodule Ribot, *Reading by Lamplight*. 1862.
Lithograph, 102 x 162 mm. Private collection, Paris.

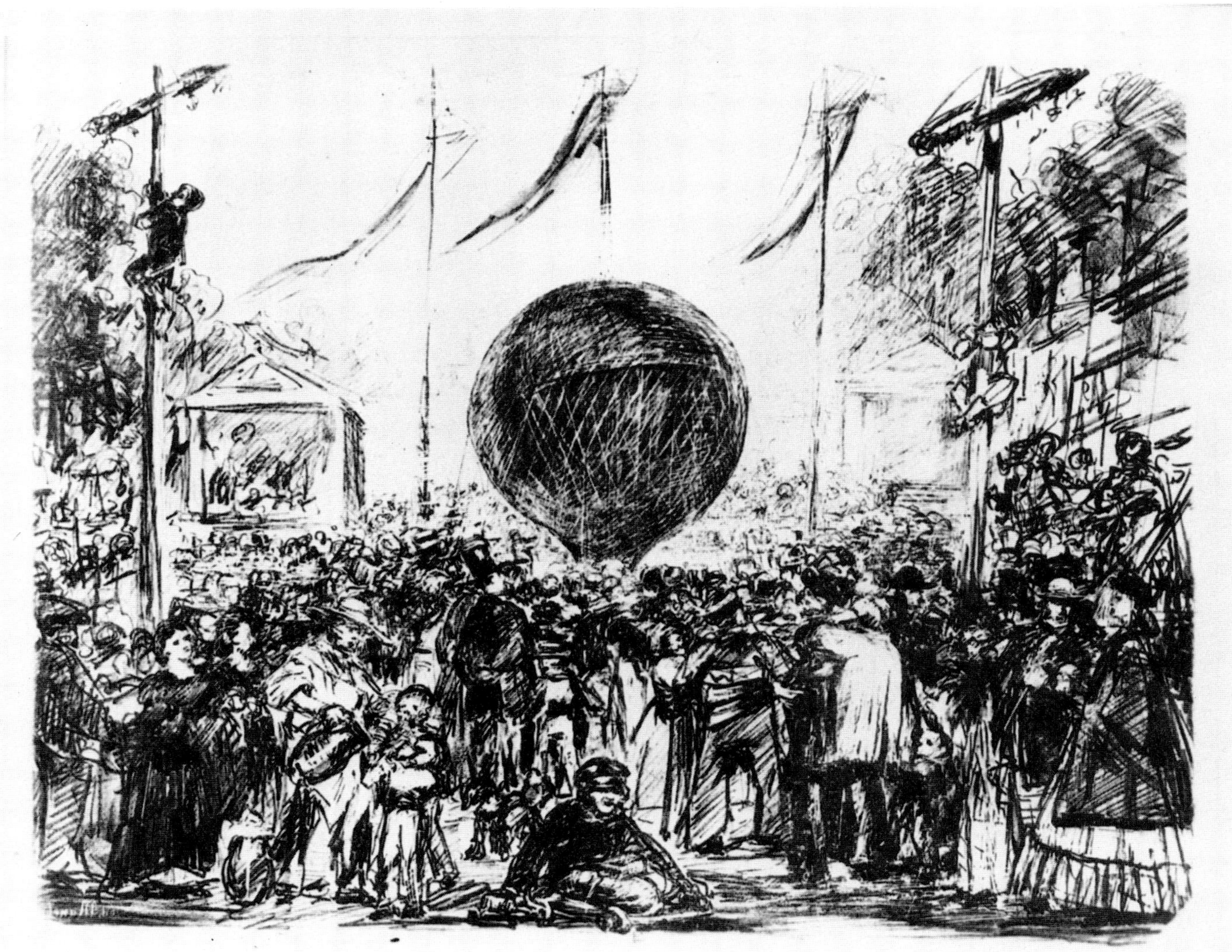

69. Edouard Manet, *The Balloon*. 1862. Lithograph, 403 x 515 mm.
Bibliothèque nationale, Paris.

next page:
71. Edouard Manet,
The Cats' Meeting-Place. 1868.
Lithograph, poster for Champfleury's book,
525 x 415 mm.
Bibliothèque nationale, Paris.

70. Advertisement in
La Chronique illustrée of 25 October 1868,
print after the lithograph by Edouard Manet,
440 x 335 mm.
Bibliothèque nationale, Paris.

14. *Manet the Lithographer*

Lithography crossed the path of the movement towards modernity, but we have seen why it met with such resistance. Édouard Manet saw nothing wrong with publishing a lithographed caricature of Émile Ollivier in the review *Diogène* on 14 April 1860. When Cadart sent him a lithographic stone and requested a 'work of art' he stayed within the register of political satire which was so closely associated with this popular method of reproduction. But he gave it such an allegorical, and at the same time such a realistic twist that historians today are still trying to fathom the significance of *The Balloon* (Fig. 69), the lithograph he sent to Lemercier, the printer.[136] It shows the tremendous throng on the esplanade of Les Invalides on 15 August, when the anniversary of the Emperor Napoleon I's birthday was celebrated. At the vanishing point is a hot air balloon, the star attraction, still on the ground, surrounded by standards, greasy poles and puppet theatres. The crowd scene was close to Manet's heart at this time as an image of modern life – a confused mass – and gave him the opportunity to make a design that was full of movement, and to treat the lithographic stone with unaccustomed vigour. Various categories of spectators can be seen in the foreground grouped around the main character, who is posed in the centre of the lower edge of the page exactly under the balloon, as static as the balloon amidst the jostling crowd – a legless man on a little trolley. The brutal juxtaposition of objects and shapes makes this print a key to the period, and to the Second Empire, and its art history. Lemercier, the printer, refused to print from the block, apparently because he was alarmed by the wild nature of the drawing; he may also have been put off by the subtly subversive allusion made in it to the dictatorship of the Emperor.

Maître Couture is said to have observed to Manet: 'You will never be anything more than the Daumier of your day'; Baudelaire echoed his words: 'You will never be anything more than the first step towards the decline of your art.'[137] Lithography was inextricably linked in people's minds with political imagery and vulgarity. Just as he was hoping to publish his *Album lithographique*, Cadart was also producing the first issues of albums by the Society of Etchers, with a preface by Théophile Gautier in which he inveighed (in the name of art) against the vulgarity of the lithograph. Manet had no problem addressing his work to different levels of soci-

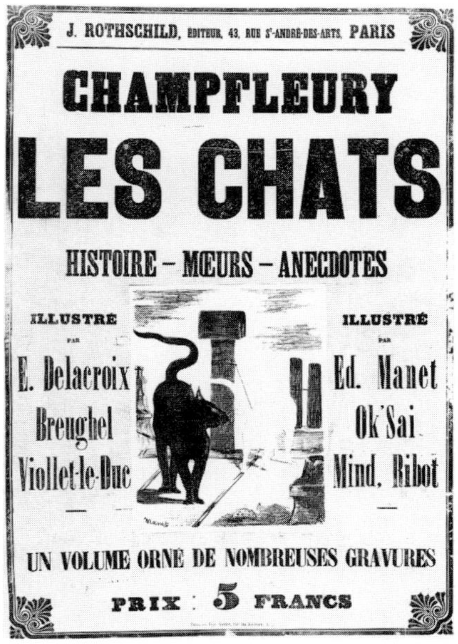

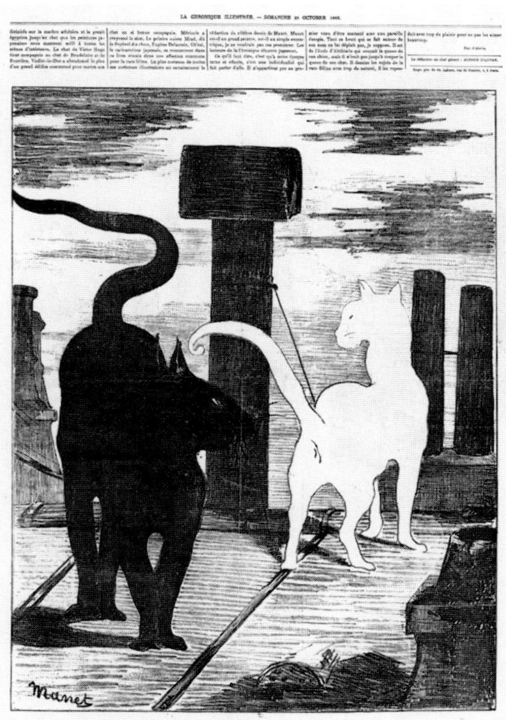

LE RENDEZ-VOUS DES CHATS. — DESSIN ORIGINAL DE MANET.

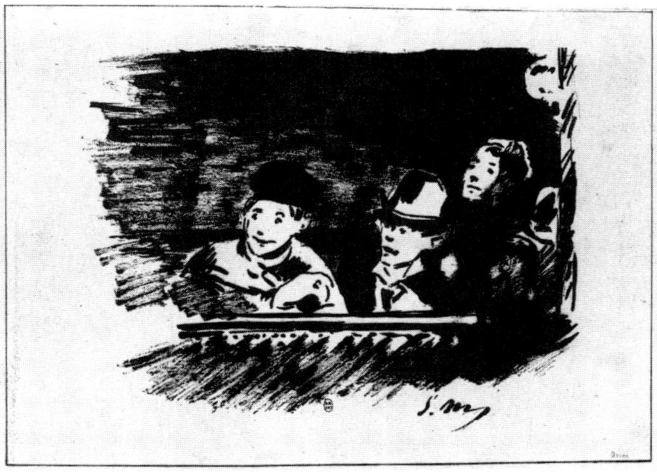

72. Edouard Manet,
In the Gods. 1880.
Autography, 243 x 340 mm.
Bibliothèque nationale, Paris.

ety. After having produced a popular version of a lithograph of *Lola de Valence* (Fig. 56) for the cover of a song, he switched to his *Moorish Complaint* and then produced a poster for a bookshop advertising a book by Champfleury on *Cats* (Figs 70, 71). His other lithographs, like *The Barricade* (1871; Fig. 104), are political. He picked up his lithography crayon once more to castigate *The Execution of Maximilian* (Fig. 103) in a scene taken from Goya. This tragedy, the outcome of French imperialist policy in Mexico, took place on 19 June 1867 at the time when Manet was organising an exhibition of his own work in a building in the avenue d'Alma. Lemercier, the printer, was no more courageous than he had been in 1862. Antony Griffiths has drawn attention to documents revealing that 'when copyright was registered by the printer Lemercier, orders were given not to put this composition on sale, even though it had no title'.[138] On 21 February, Manet protested: 'Monsieur, the Maximilian affair . . . is growing more complicated. Lemercier, the printer, is refusing to return the engraved stone to me and has asked my permission to efface the image. Of course I have refused. . .'. On 28 February Lemercier let Manet know that he could collect the stone from him. The mixing of genres went even further: *The Execution of Maximilian*, or, to be less specific (as the *Chronique des arts et de la curiosité* pointed out maliciously), *A Fusillade in Mexico*, was not just a lithograph. It was an intermediate version, designed as anti-imperialistic propaganda, between a huge topical painting in the tradition of the *Raft of Medusa*, or the *Massacres of Scio* or, especially, *The Second of May* by Goya and other painted versions that were preceded by a sketch. It was not published during Manet's lifetime.

These large plates were drawn on stone, at a period when a process using a stereotype block was beginning to replace traditional lithography in modern studios. Between 1865 and 1868 a publication that used such means of reproduction, *L'Autographe au Salon*, requested sketches from artists which they hoped to pass off as original works. The drawing by Manet that was reproduced in 1865 after *The Man drinking Water* is the only one not to have been printed from a stereotype block made from the artist's drawing but rather, it seems, from a photographic reproduction. Manet nevertheless did not refrain from providing 'autograph' drawings to be reproduced from metal blocks. He did it in 1867 for *L'Art de Paris*, and for a reduced version of his poster for *The Cats*, for the *Chronique Illustrée* (Fig. 70) in 1868 and for the *Revue de la Semaine* in 1877. He even contributed a portrait of Claude Monet and some other drawings to *La Vie Moderne*, in 1880, on the occasion of an exhibition of Monet's paintings in the gallery belonging to the paper.[139] He managed to extract the maximum expression from techniques regarded as 'humble', which dispensed with shading. The sole aim of the deliberate confusion of styles, genres and tech-

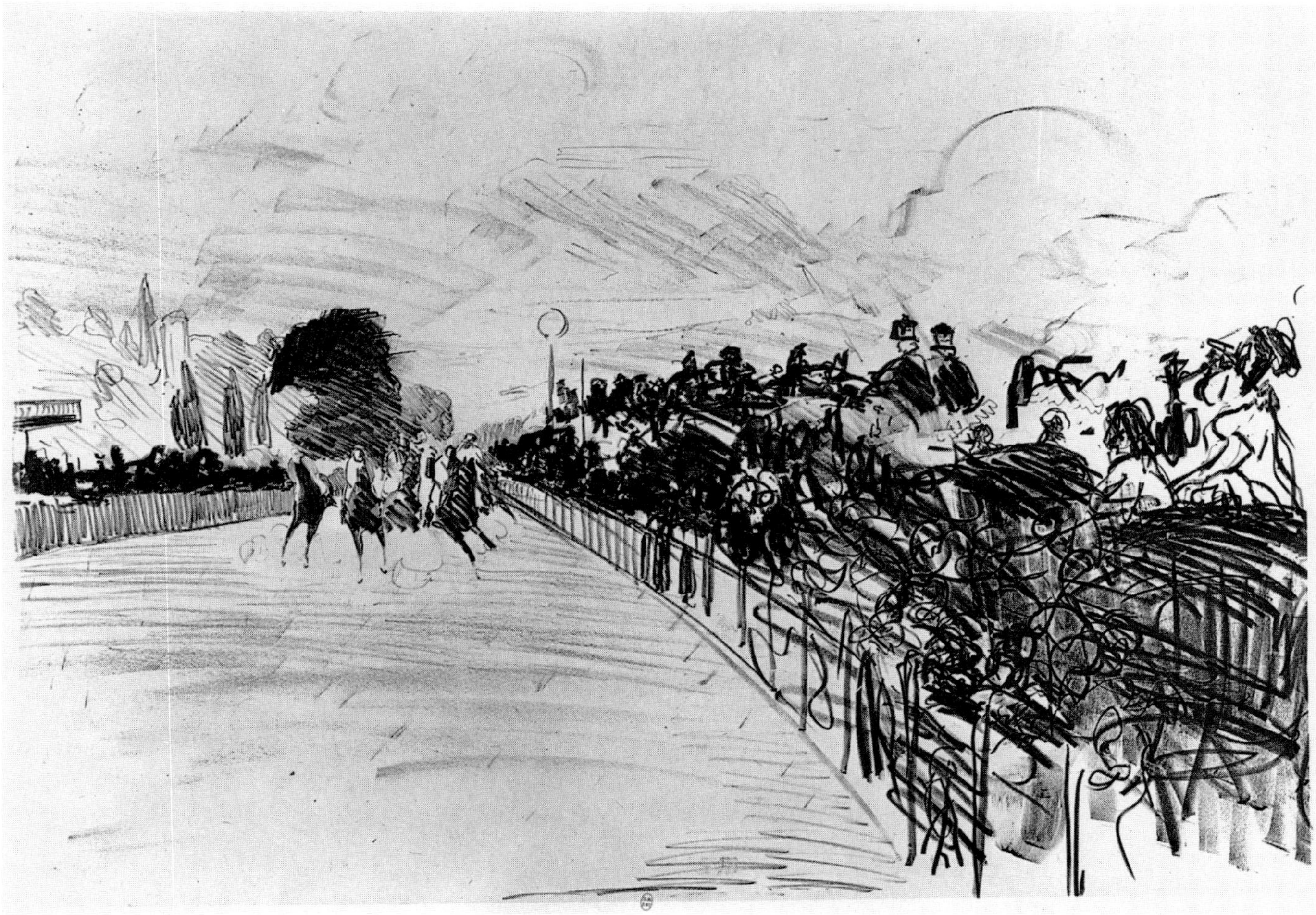

73. Edouard Manet, *At the Races*. 1864–5. Lithograph, 360 x 510 mm.
Bibliothèque nationale, Paris.

niques was to confuse the public, hastening the appearance of a new society.

The story of Manet's last engraving sums up all his previous experience. At the Salon of 1882, the last in which he was to participate (he was by then already paralysed) Manet presented *The Bar at the Folies-Bergère* and a portrait of a woman entitled *Jeanne: Spring*. He made an etching of the latter (Fig. 74) which was not published in his lifetime, appearing in the *Gazette des Beaux-Arts* only in 1902. There is also a watercolour drawing of the same motif, executed on the back of a photograph of the painting which has been printed backwards so that the drawing, traced from the photograph, returns the portrait to face the original direction. The etching is smaller in size than the half watercolour, half photograph and it is difficult to see why the watercolour/photograph should be the model (in the artist's usual fashion); it would have been very easy to print the photograph to the same format as the etching. The conclusion reached by Carl Chiarenza in his detailed analysis[140] is that this photograph was not made for the etching but for reproduction in the *Gazette des Beaux-Arts*, to illustrate the article by Manet's friend Antonin Proust.[141] We have, therefore, an oil-painting, an original etching reproducing the painting (though it was never printed), a 'reproduction' water colour to be used to make a metal block based on a photograph of the canvas. And that is not all. One of the principal supporters of Impressionism, the dealer Ernest Hoschedé, published his *Impressions of my trip to the Salon in 1882*, nothing more than a long paean of praise to Manet, in the form of a small volume with a reproduction of Manet's *Jeanne* on the cover. This reproduction is an incunabulum: it is the first photograph printed in colour, by the process recently invented by Charles Cros.

Manet had had nothing to do with this, but was it not nevertheless his crowning achievement, his most modern work? Manet had handed over his etching to his friend Henri Guérard. Probably in response to the receipt of a trial print of the etching from Guérard, Manet sent a brief note, the end of this tale and of Manet's work as an engraver: 'Thankyou, my dear Guérard. The etching is no longer any business of mine. Give it a good going over with the etching tool and best wishes.'[142] The work in hand was finished and the workshop shut down.

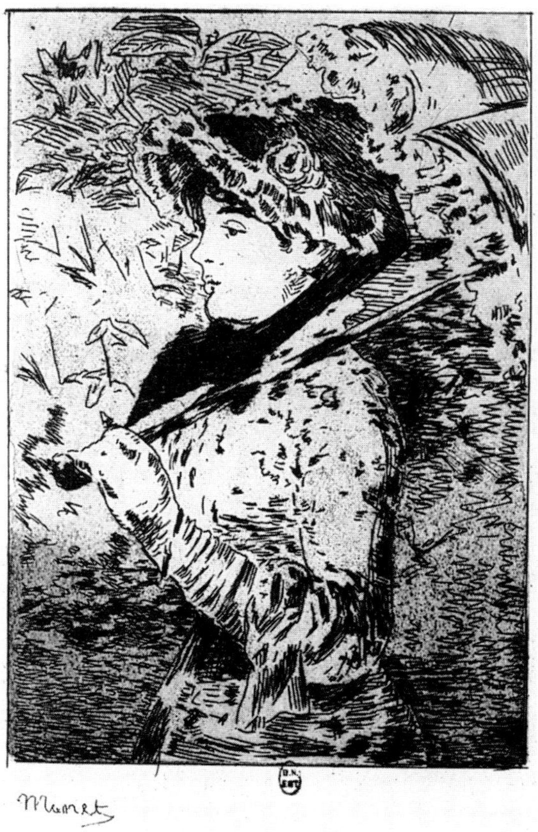

74. Edouard Manet, *Jeanne: Spring*. 1882. Etching, single state, 155 x 105 mm. Bibliothèque nationale, Paris.

15. *The Salon des Refusés*

At the Salon of 1863 Manet entered, for the painting section, *A Young Man dressed as a Majo*, the large *Déjeuner sur l'herbe*, and the *Portrait of Victorine Meurent* and they were all refused. These could all be found, under the titles *The Bath* and *Mlle V. dressed as an Espada*, in the *Catalogue des ouvrages de peinture, sculpture, gravure, lithographie et architecture refusés par le jury de 1863 et exposés par décision de S. M. L'Empereur au Salon Annexe, Palais des Champs-Élysées, le 15 mars 1863,*[143] (*Catalogue of the works of painting, sculpture, engraving, lithography and architecture refused by the jury of 1863 and exhibited by decree of His Majesty the Emperor in the Annexe, Palais des Champs Elysées, 15 March 1863*). In the 'engraving' section could be found *The Little Horsemen* (Figs. 76-9) , *Philip IV* and *Lola de Valence* (Fig. 55). The two government commissions of Félix Bracquemond, the engraved reproductions of Holbein's *Desiderius Erasmus* (Fig. 75) and Rubens's *The Tournament*, both etchings, were turned down. A number of other etchings were turned down as well, including some (*The Borriqueros* and *Spain* by Louis Lombard) that had been published by the Society of Etchers.

The conservatism of the print jury was as intense, that year, as that of the paintings jury: we know that the latter refused more than 4000 paintings, including work by Cals, Chintreuil, Manet, Vollon, Fantin-Latour, Harpignies and Jongkind (who had won a third class medal in 1853), in other words by all the artists considered to be 'modern'. The composition of the jury had not altered. The same four members were appointed to Section IV (printmaking) as had been appointed for previous Salons: a certain Achille Martinet, François Forster, aged seventy-three - one of the pure engravers admired by the dealer Rochoux; he was the author of the portrait (after Winterhalter) that immortalised Queen Victoria;[144] Henriquel-Dupont, aged sixty-six, the undisputed master of the reproductive engraving,[145] and Jacques-Édouard Gatteaux, an engraver of medals.[146] None of these should have been particularly surprised by the 'impulsiveness' of the artist's etching. In fact neither Forster nor Henriquel-Dupont took part in the meetings of the admissions committee. In 1861 the jury rewarded one printmaker who could be described as worthwhile: Édouard Girardet;[147] a disconcerting decision and a diffi-

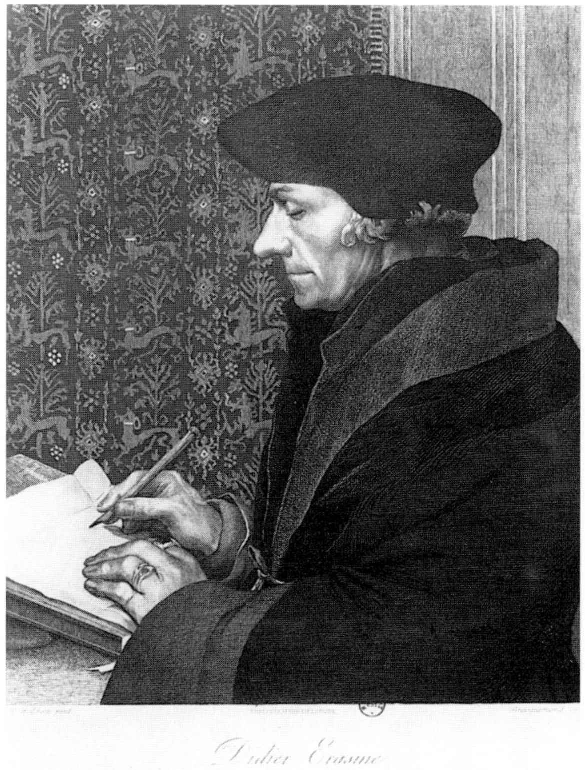

75. Félix Bracquemond,
Desiderius Erasmus, after Holbein. 1863.
Etching, 248 x 197 mm.
Bibliothèque nationale, Paris.

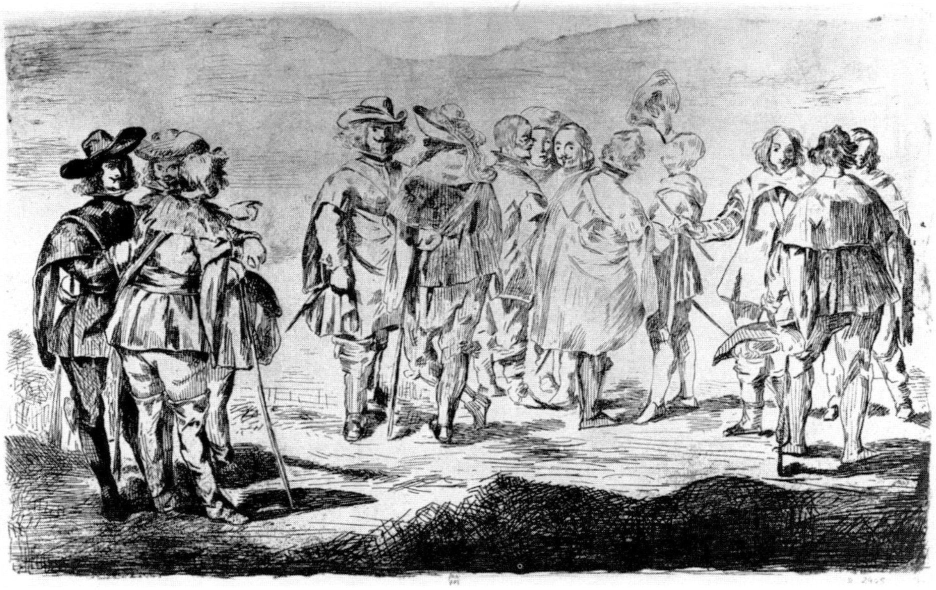

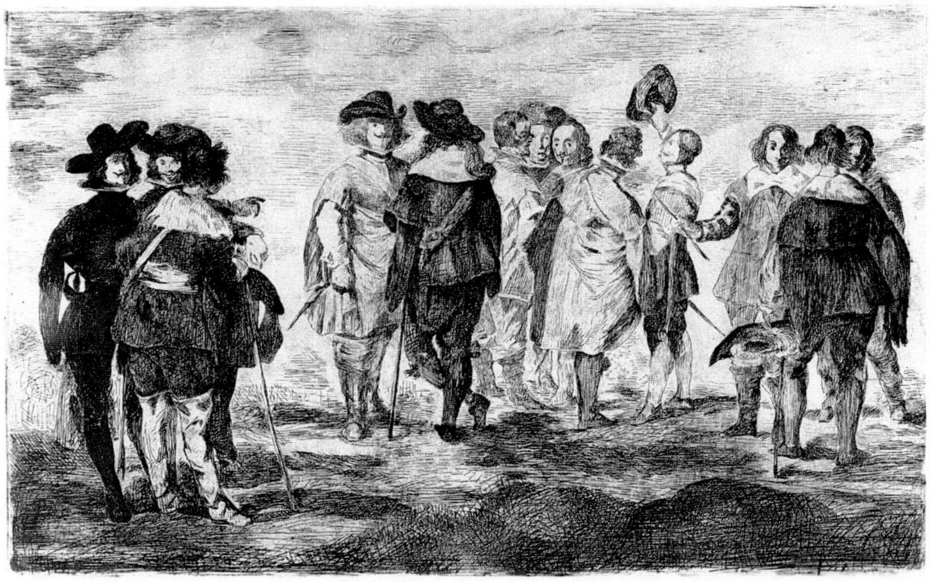

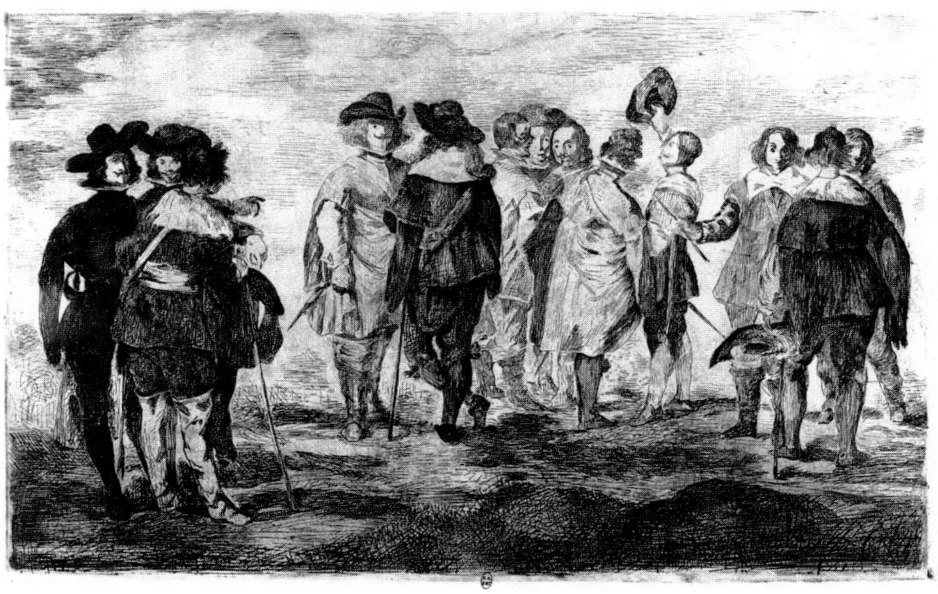

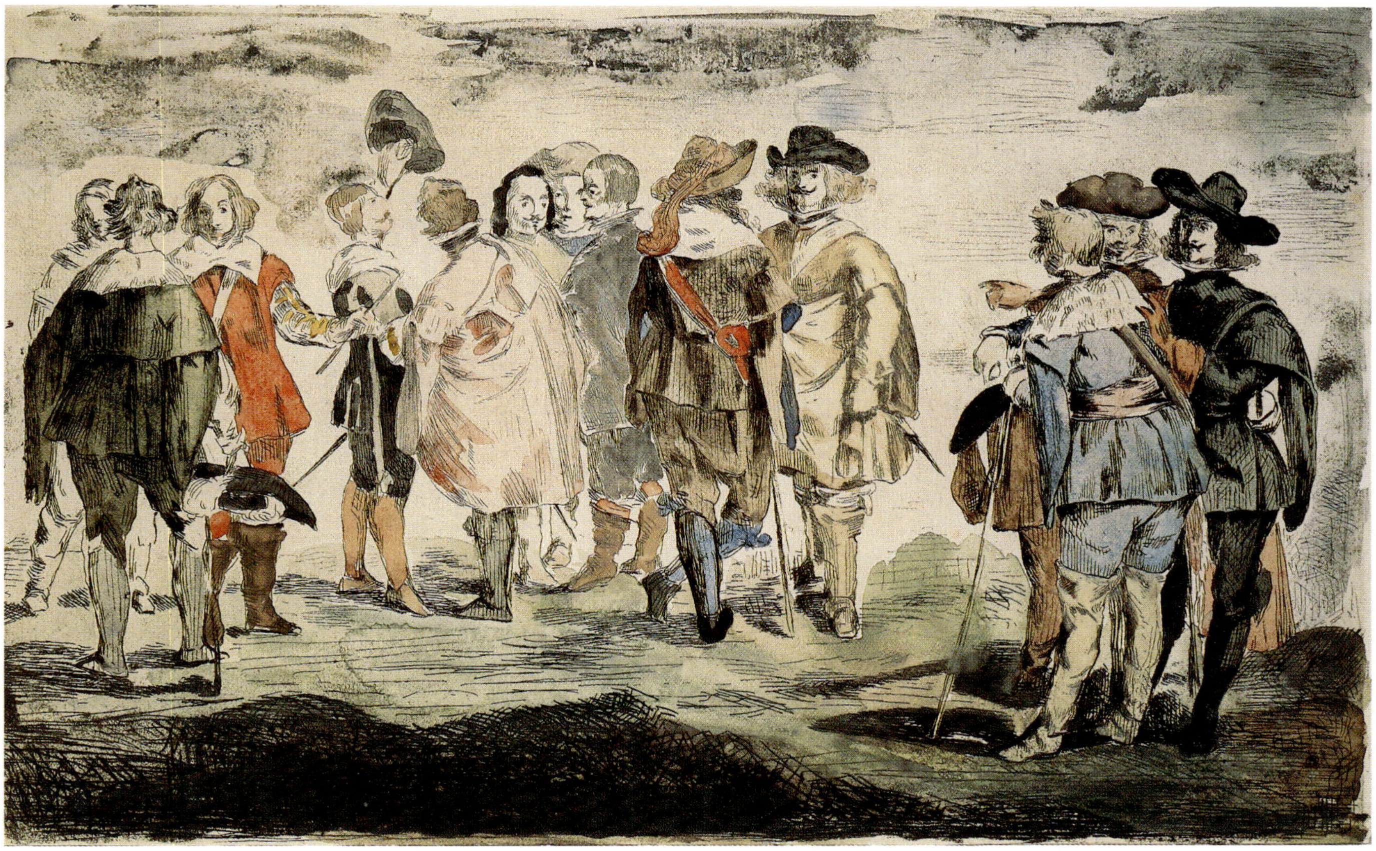

cult one to account for today. Among the 185 prints accepted there were in fact a number of free 'etchings': three by Eugène Bléry and three by Meryon, some by Charles Jacque (who won a third class medal in 1861 and recall of his medal of 1851), some by Charles Chaplin and Xavier de Dananche, by Jules Jacquemart and Maxime Lalanne and other members of the Society of Etchers, Jules Michelin and the realist Ribot. Etchings by Vicomte Lepic and a certain Jules-Alfred de Goncourt, a pupil of Gavarni, appeared in the catalogue of the official Salon of 1863. Finally, the jury had accepted three very sketchy *Views of the Banks of the Thames* by Whistler.

The jury dealing with prints cannot be accused of the unusual severity that may have prevailed in the painting category because of the excessive number of entries, the robust state of the market having caused immoderate expansion. We do not have any idea of how many prints

76, 77, 78, 79. Edouard Manet,
The Little Horsemen. 1861.
Etching, 242 x 375 mm.
First, second and third states.
Bibliothèque nationale, Paris;
first state, proof touched up with watercolour,
Museum of Fine Arts, Boston, Lee M. Friedman Fund.

were submitted, though there were certainly more than for previous Salons. 185 were accepted in 1863, as against 159 in 1857, 146 in 1852, 87 in 1852(?), a growing number in absolute terms but probably not a growing percentage of acceptances. The activities of the Society of Etchers had certainly increased the number of competitors, but the selection shows no bias against their members – rather the opposite. It is easy to imagine that Manet's style might have caused surprise. Bracquemond's *Erasmus* (Fig. 75) on the other hand was not in the least controversial compared with other etchings accepted by the jury, and could be included with work testifying to the persistence of the classical tradition.[148] It has been suggested, without foundation, that the etched reproduction of an old master deserved this fate. A more likely explanation might be that the political allegiance of Manet and Bracquemond influenced the jury's choice at a moment when the Empire, facing mounting opposition, was trying to tighten its hold. The fact that the Emperor, embarrassed by the jury's severity, should have decided to organise the Salon des Refusés does not invalidate the hypothesis that the academicians were overzealous; they were motivated less by political opportunism than by the conviction that art should not be contaminated by politics. The Salon des Refusés opened its doors in the overcharged atmosphere preceding the election of May 1863, when three hundred opposition candidates, mainly republicans, were posing the first threat to the imperial régime.

The consequences of the decisions made by the pseudo-jury were nevertheless not so far-reaching for printmakers as they were for painters, the Salon never having been their only show-case. Prints, being linked to the publishing trade, had their own means of circulation, and were much closer to their public and more varied than painting. The fact that a good printmaker could do without exposure in the Salon demonstrates how printmaking had adapted to vastly increased demand. Although the production of prints of all kinds had exploded recently in unprecedented fashion, their representation in the Salons had dropped consistently, declining from 147 engravings and 120 lithographs in the Salon of 1831, to ninety-five and seventy-seven in the Salon of 1835 and fifty-eight and thirty-seven in 1840. During the preceding decades there was no work exhibited by any 'modern' artist, apart from Tony Johannot and, in 1835, Paul Huet. The walls were covered in engraved reproductions. The great names in printmaking at that time were Mercuri, Henriquel-Dupont, Deroy, Calamatta. The critics had been anxious about it for years, as Laviron's alarm signal in his account of the Salon of 1834 makes plain: 'Engraving has fallen so low that it scarcely shows any sign of life. For the most part our engravers do much less well than the English, and they are particularly strong.'[149] Printmakers usually became known through the reviews. In some ways, however, by creating a demand for illustrations for catalogues and reports, the Salon had helped to set studio printmaking free. Under the Restoration, '*Salons illustrés*' or albums of lithographs and wood engravings began to be circulated. In 1831 Lenormant asked the painters themselves to provide their own reproductions, and this was an important turning point both for the recognition of the print as an original form and for free interpretation in printmaking. In 1834 Alexandre Decamps, brother of the painter, published *Le Musée* with the romantic aim of satisfying public demand for reproductions that were not copies of paintings but were interpretations of the work of different authors, bearing their aura and marked with their signature: *Le Musée, revue du Salon de 1834* contains original etchings by Barye, Paul Huet and Célestin Nanteuil.

Was the interest in printmaking that arose in about 1860 evidence of similar aesthetic commitment? The diversity of the artists requested to take part, both of the old and the modern schools, might make it appear so. But the choice of artists is significant. It is a fact that none of the well-known academic painters of that generation, not Cabanel (born in 1823), nor Baudry (1828), nor Gervex (1852), nor even Gleyre (1808) whose reputation among his students was reasonably liberal, nor Jean-Jacques Henner who almost participated in the Impressionist exhibitions – not one of these produced any original prints. The elderly Dubufe, who was born in 1790,[150] permitted himself a few academic lithographs, like Ingres. Couture (born in 1815) agreed to two etchings for particular purposes, one illustration to Arsène Houssaye's *Revue du Salon de 1844*, and a *Portrait of George Sand* for a book published in 1867.[151] Carolus Duran (born in 1838) had several etchings published by Cadart and illustrated two books for Poulet-Malassis but his *Recollections of a Journey to Venice* published in 1863 was more or less without sequel.[152] Bouguereau (born in 1815) also produced a trial etching, somewhat late in 1880, 'a rough sketch with a point' he wrote, on the proof of *L'Aurore*.[153] Gérôme, after his triumphant appearance in the Salon of 1857, published some etchings in the *Gazette des Beaux-Arts* in 1860 and in 1868, after a number of attempts; when writing the dedication on one of these attempts, *Negress, half-length*, in 1876, he added: 'To Monsieur Mene, unrepeatable garbage, thank God!'.[154] He too thought that 'etching was not his business'. In 1867, Zola wrote: 'Because he works for Goupil, Monsieur Gérôme obviously paints a picture simply in order that that picture be reproduced, photographically and as an engraving; the reproductions can then be sold by the thousand. The subject is all important and the painting of no importance: the reproduction is worth more than the original.'[155]

Courbet's absence from the scene is more surprising. He was nonetheless urged and bullied, assisted by Bracquemond with whom he worked at etching in about 1860. Cadart finally published a single copy of one

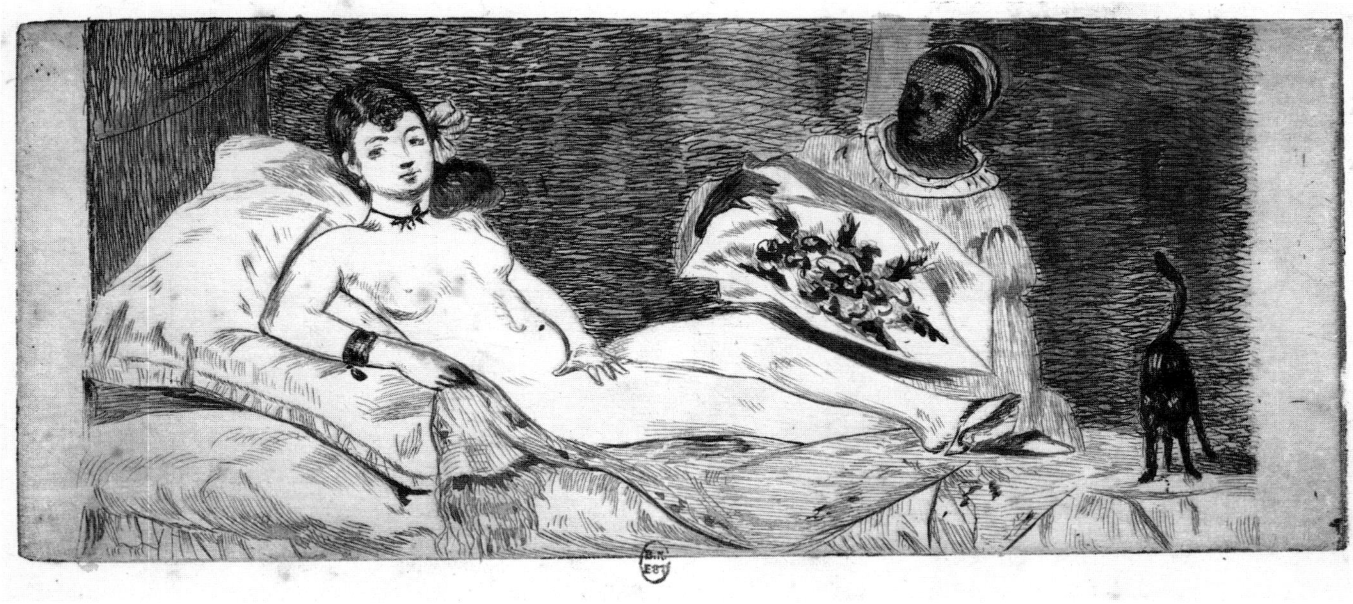

80. Edouard Manet,
Olympia. 1867.
Second plate, proof touched up with wash, gouache and Indian ink, 85 x 172 mm.
Bibliothèque nationale, Paris.

of his plates, *The Village Maidens*, after his painting of 1852, and firmly in the tradition of the engraved version of a painting. He contributed to *L'Autographe au Salon* of 1864 with *The Little Stonebreaker* painted in 1849 and, with Bracquemond's help, produced the title-page for the works of Champfleury, published by Poulet-Malassis in 1859.[156] In spite of his absence it is obvious that the work of the 'moderns', neo-romantics, realists, landscape painters of the Barbizon school, constituted a majority in the development of the original print. Behind the diversity of styles there is a community of feeling amongst the painter-engravers which is not due only to the expanded market offered by etching. The taste for etching was perceived as a bid for modernity, a blow for the opposition and a threat to the academic order of things. Such attributes could not be ignored either by adversaries or partisans. The problems faced by the régime after 1863 made the progress of the 'free' etching as hazardous as it was brilliant.

16. *Jongkind*

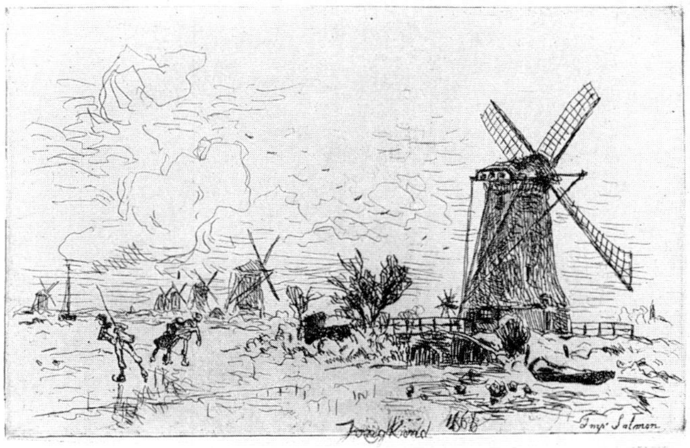

81. Johann-Barthold Jongkind, *Batavia*. 1868. Etching, 123 x 192 mm. Bibliothèque nationale, Paris.

In 1843 Jongkind, the Dutch painter, received a bursary to study in Paris. His career looked promising. He was an accomplished landscape painter and attached himself while in France to Eugène Isabey, with whom he toured the coast of Normandy, then Brittany, in 1851. His efforts were crowned with success: he obtained a medal (third class) in the Salon of 1852 and assumed that his career had taken off. But, unfortunately, the world of art was going through a period of great uncertainty and things were no longer so simple. His subsequent career illustrates the current means of gaining a foothold and the mechanisms being set up to promote particular artists within what has been called the 'critics and dealers' system.[157] The disappointment of realising that recognition at the Salon was no guarantee of good sales discouraged some artists and sent others scurrying back to their studio. In turn, this encouraged the pursuit of 'art for art's sake', raised to the status of a doctrine until new markets were found. Jongkind returned to Rotterdam in 1855 to live with his sister and practise 'art for art's sake'.[158] He continued to send paintings to Paris, to dealers like Père Martin who would accept modern painting. The critics were aware of his move; in *Le Figaro* of 13 September 1857 the critic Jean Rousseau wrote: 'Jongkind treats art as an artist should, and pays no heed to bourgeois proprieties . . . . His careless style of painting is no less pleasing for all that. It is so apt, its nuances so subtle.' The praise encouraged Jongkind's friends to summon him back to Paris to be with them. Like them he submitted work to the Salon des Refusés in 1863; of his painting, *View of the Seine*, the critic Castagnary commented in his review of the Salon for *L'Artiste*: 'His work relies on the Impression it makes.'[159] His friends were the landscape painters of the modern school: Rousseau, Cals, Diaz, Corot, Troyon. In 1862 he met Monet at Honfleur. Many painters were taking up etching, often at the request of members of the Society of Etchers.

Jongkind's output as a printmaker is almost exclusively linked to Cadart's publications; of the twenty prints that he produced, Cadart published seventeen. In 1862 he produced an album of Jongkind's work, advertised with albums by Manet, Legros and Millet on the back of the journal of the Society of Etchers, for twelve francs. On 17 March 1862, Jongkind wrote to Burty to say that 'a folder of six drawings, Views of Holland, has

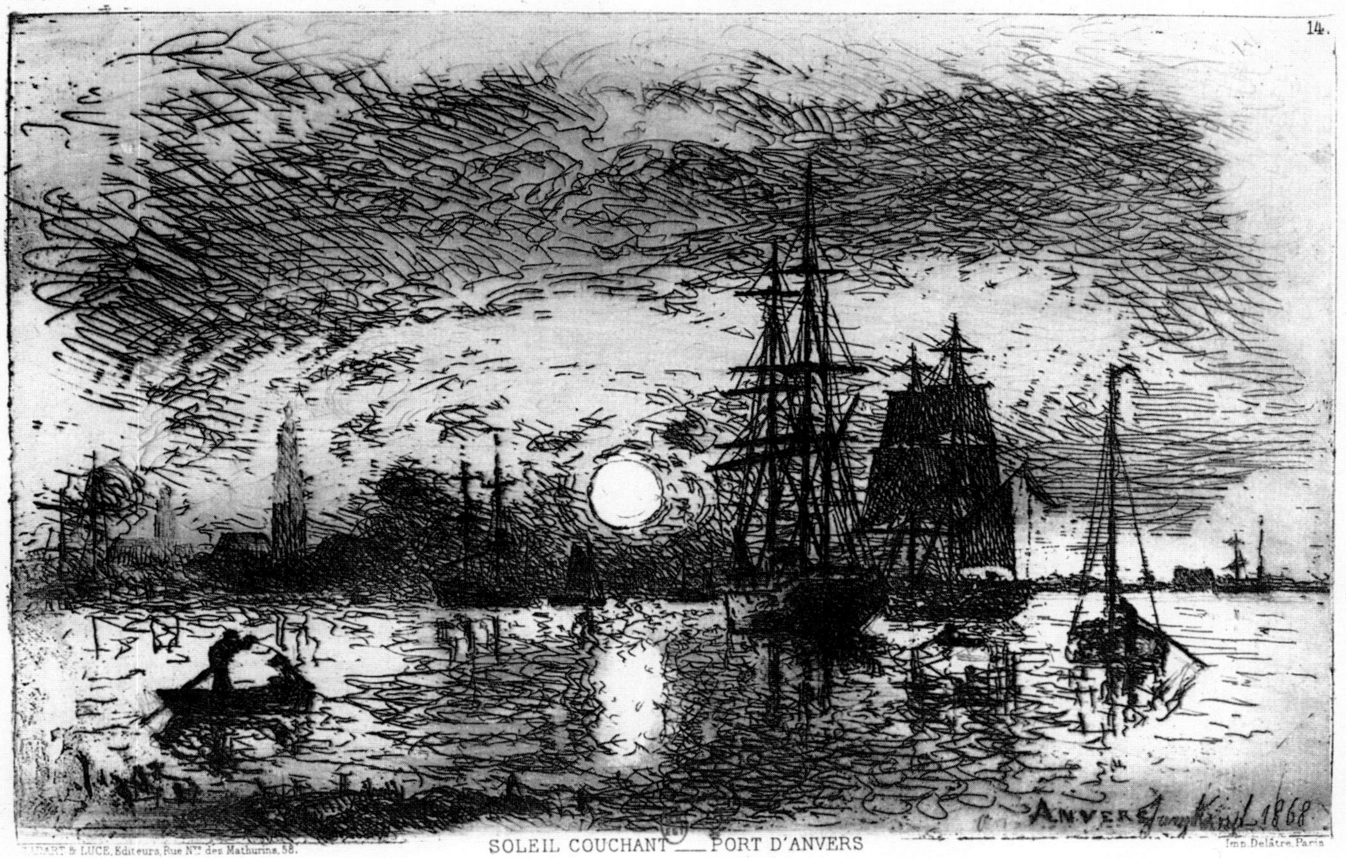

82. Johann-Barthold Jongkind,
Setting Sun, Antwerp Harbour. 1868.
Etching with heavily inked characters, 151 x 233 mm.
Bibliothèque nationale, Paris.

appeared with the caption "etched by Jongkind, 9, rue de Chevreuse and printed by Delâtre, 265 rue Saint-Jacques, price 20F"; these folders can be bought from me or from Delâtre'.[160] This letter is evidence that Jongkind had not quite understood the business of selling: he hopes that the clientèle will come directly to him or to his printer and proposes to sell the album for more than the publisher is asking for it. And he is obviously unclear about the difference (even if he explains it in clumsy French) between 'etching' (which he uses for the engraved title) and 'drawing' (which he uses to designate his etchings).[161] His letter to Burty was intended to provoke an article, and it was successful. The critic devoted a column to him and pursued the confusion between etchings and drawings, but in a deliberate manner this time: 'A few days ago, by chance, M. Jongkind picked up a pointed implement instead of a pencil, a varnished plate instead of a sheet of paper and his etchings have the same qualities as his paintings: skilful use of perspective and a delicate tone broken by some carefully placed patches of black.'[162]

Baudelaire, who was preparing an article on the fashion for etching for *La Revue anecdotique*, also spared some praise for Jongkind, singling out similar attributes for comment: 'curious observations for a painter, sketches which any art-lover accustomed to reading the mind of a painter in his most rapid "scrib-

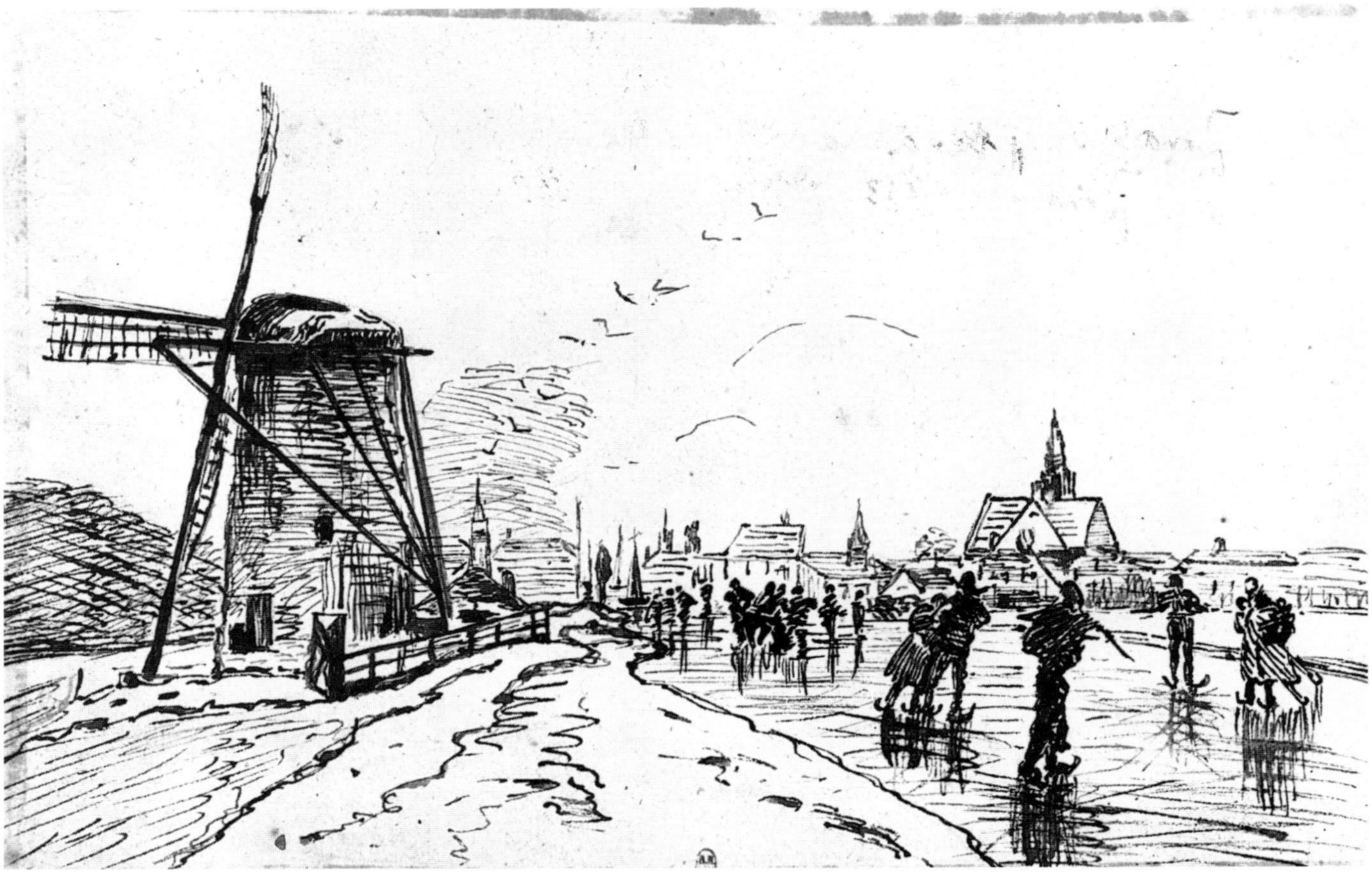

83. Johann-Barthold Jongkind, *View of the Town of Maassluis*. 1862. Preparatory drawing, before inking, 190 x 280 mm. Bibliothèque nationale, Paris.

84. Johann-Barthold Jongkind, *View of the Town of Maassluis*. 1862. Etching, 223 x 312 mm. Bibliothèque nationale, Paris.

bles" will know how to interpret ("scribble", "*gribouillage*", is the term used a little facetiously by the good Diderot to characterise Rembrandt's etchings).'[163] The editor of *La Revue anecdotique* was the publisher Poulet-Malassis, who had revived the use of etchings on the title-page and also, in his most expensive books, as illustrations. Baudelaire introduced him to Jongkind.[164] Poulet-Malassis failed to buy the pendant to the first picture that Jongkind had sold him and did not publish his etchings; business was bad and he went bankrupt in September. Although this outlet had collapsed, Burty remained and Jongkind's etchings continued to be published by Cadart. 'This last year I have done etchings (for the Society) of the entrance to the harbour at Le Havre and they have been published. I am awaiting the proofs and I should be very happy to offer you, and for you to accept, one each of these drawings as an expression of my gratitude.' One advantage of the printing was that it could be offered as a specimen to patrons. Dürer used them in this way, as a kind of sample of his skill, or a visiting card to be presented to important prospective clients. The value of the print could be increased by the dedication, widely used at this period when much was done through intermediaries; the dedication person-

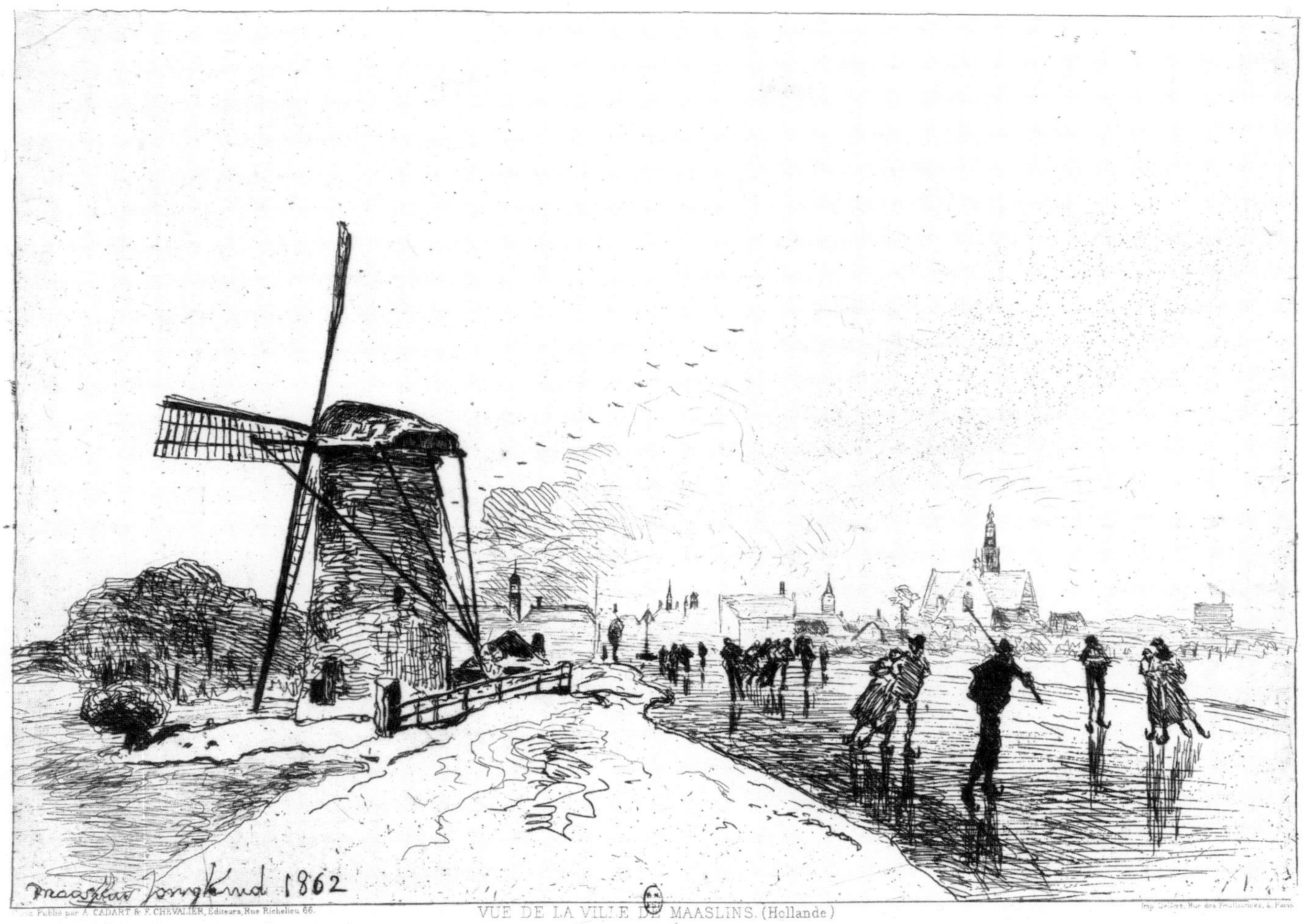

alised the object and foreshadowed the technique of signing each proof by hand, which became more widespread in the years that followed. Burty built up a personal collection of gifts made to him by painters, a habit mocked by the Goncourt brothers, who christened it 'Burtyisme'.[165] Franco-British relations among the Society of Etchers also played their part: in 1864, Hamerton, the English Burty, also published a long article in praise of Jongkind: 'Jongkind does to views and to houses what skilful caricaturists do to men and women – he takes what is necessary to render the expression and omits the rest. Each line is full of character thanks to the artist's unusual ability to select . . . Jongkind is the most skilled of the draughtsmen on copper.'[166]

Cadart continued to sell Jongkind's paintings and to publish his etchings in the publication which took over subscriptions from the Society of Etchers after their collapse, *L'Illustration nouvelle*. Plate number 14 of the first year of *L'Illustration nouvelle*, in 1868, is the most astonishing of Jongkind's prints: *Setting sun, Antwerp Harbour* (Fig. 82) is the etched equivalent of Monet's *Impression, Sunrise* which inspired the name 'Impressionist'. In it the subject is completely immaterial, the atmosphere is what counts. The material objects, boats, quays in the distance, blurred and virtually drowned by the dense network of lines, allow plenty of the white paper to show through. The sea and the sky merge, neither area darker than the other, like two layers of luminous fog; there is no perspective. It could be said that in this plate Impressionist printmaking discovered one of its modes of expression. But it is nevertheless not complete. Although he was a painter and a printmaker, Jongkind had not quite reached the expertise of the painter-printmaker, able to apply the techniques of a painting, a unique work, equally skilfully to a copper plate. He uses neither dry point nor aquatint, he does not develop further states nor seek effects by inking. His etching is technically pure, like an etching by Millet, and owes its movement and light effects solely to the etched line.

Jongkind's etchings were accomplished in parallel (as with the Impressionists) with his drawings and paintings, rather than by a process of osmosis. A number of his preparatory drawings are still in existence. Some of them are exact drawings which reduce the process of etching to the meticulous transposition of the (reversed) preparatory drawing. Sometimes an etching will repeat the motif of a previous painting, in the tradition of the

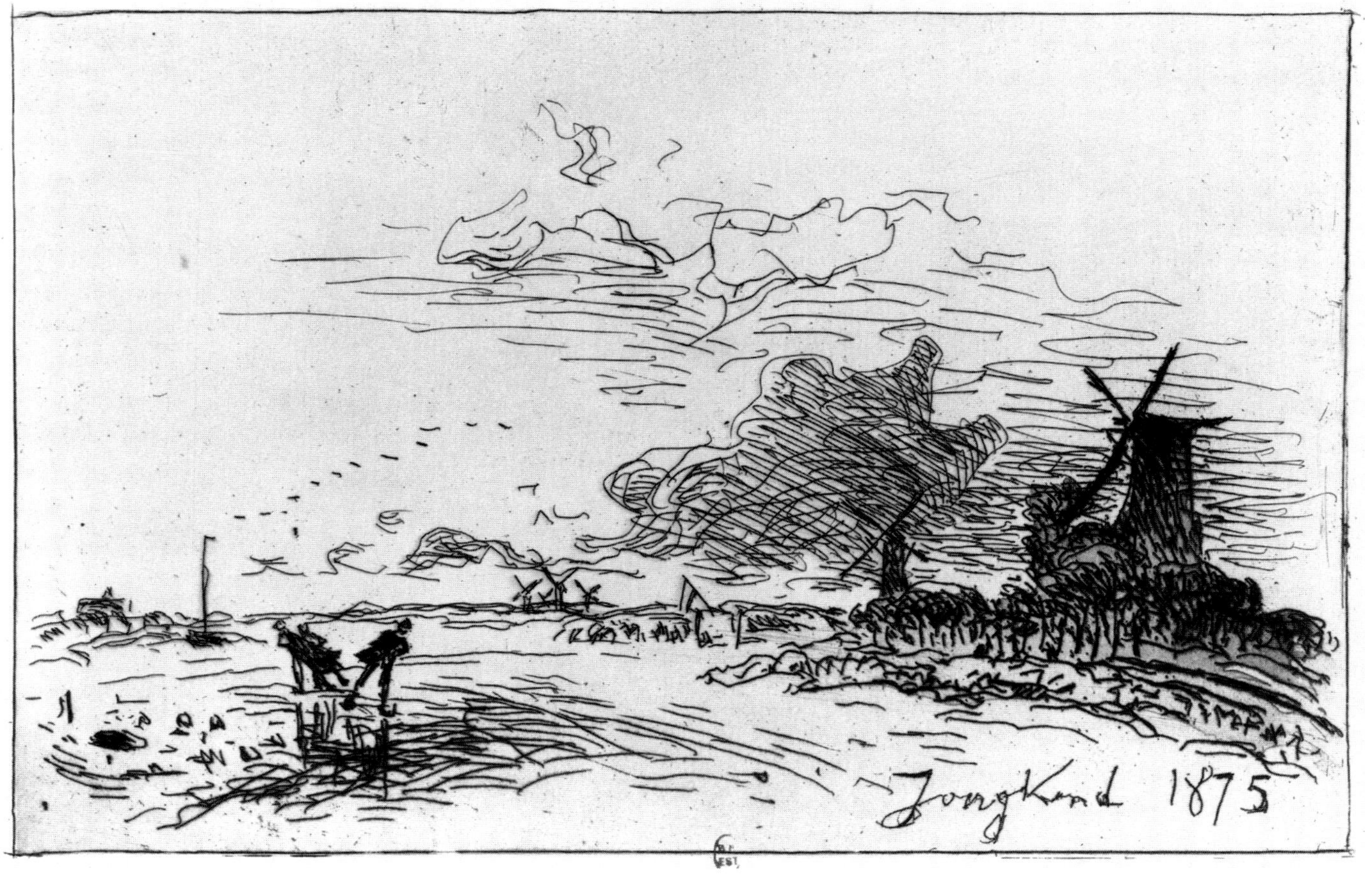

85. Johann-Barthold Jongkind, *Canal near Rotterdam*. 1875. Etching, 1st state 148 x 228 mm. Bibliothèque nationale, Paris.

reproductive print, but sometimes this relationship is reversed: the *View of Maassluis* (Figs 83, 84) follows a painting of 1862, but precedes two others of 1864; the *Entrance to the Harbour at Honfleur*, an etching published in 1863, precedes two paintings of 1864. The etching *Departure from the Harbour at Honfleur*, published in 1864, was used simultaneously in a watercolour and a painting in the same year; and a drawing of the same view, but in a different version, similar to the print, dates from 23 September 1865. Three paintings and a pencil drawing accompany the *View from the Port to the Railway in Honfleur* (1867), and there are many other examples of duplication.

Jongkind's etchings are delicately executed, with a spareness of line that reveals the gleam of the paper; they satisfy the requirements of the publisher as well as the public taste for refinement: 'As for etchings,' he wrote to Burty in 1871, 'I have no more good ones. It is too expensive for me because I have to pay the printer. Otherwise I should have liked to make a series of two portfolios, each containing six pictures of Holland, since I was born in Holland and I have made numerous drawings and picturesque landscape studies.'

Jongkind did not abandon the old tradition of bright, lively landscape etchings (Figs. 81, 85) – in fact he used their expressiveness to the full. He though of etching only in terms of publication. He still had the 'picturesque' in mind. In 1870 he was still signing himself: 'Jongkind, pupil of Isabey'.

17. *Appian and the School of Lyon*

Like the forest of Fontainebleau near Paris, the countryside around Lyon attracted landscape painters. East of Lyon, towards Bresse and the Dauphiné, the villages of Crémieu, Morestel, Artemare and Optevoz had become places where, after 1852, painters from Paris like Corot and Daubigny, and Ravier from Lyon, used to meet. The artists of Lyon had never abandoned the etching, perhaps because the inhabitants of the city were very good customers of the landscape painters, and they may also have tolerated this subsidiary form because it suited their taste as well their purses. The memory of the etcher Jean-Jacques de Boissieu remained very green: he sold his landscape prints all over Europe during the Revolution and, later, during the Empire, at a date when etching had been more or less abandoned in Parisian studios.[167] He still inspired imitators, and it was an artist from Lyon, Baron, who exhibited one of the scarce original landscape etchings to be seen in the

86. Hector Allemand,
The Valley of Optevoz. 1868.
Etching, 183 x 295 mm.
Bibliothèque nationale, Paris.

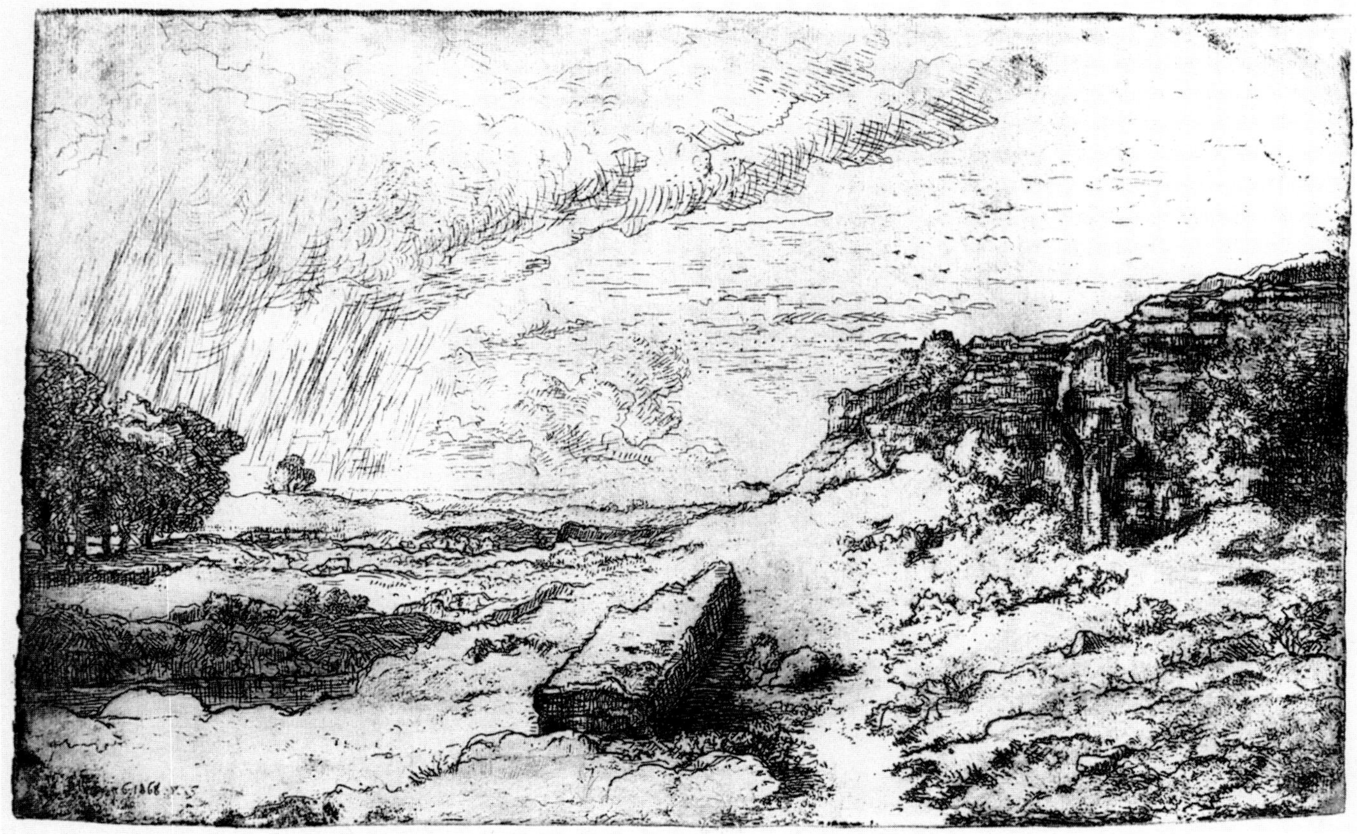

87, 88. Adolphe Appian,
The Etang Neuf near Creys (Isère). 1864.
Proof printed as monotype of first state, and etching, final state, 137 x 266 mm.
Bibliothèque nationale, Paris.

Salon of 1824. Lyon continued to supply etchers, and the link between the eighteenth-century tradition of picturesque landscapes and contemporary landscape painting – Romantic, Realist, then Impressionist – continued unbroken. Louis-Hector Allemand is perhaps the best example of the School; he was born in 1809, a year before the death of De Boissieu, and from 1846 exhibited (in both Lyon and Paris) paintings and etchings whose vigorous line and lively lighting developed the genre in the direction of 'modern' taste (Fig. 86). After his death in 1886 his collection of 10,000 prints, including work by the great Dutch artists, Ruysdael and Rembrandt, and of course De Boissieu as well, was broken up.[168]

The most productive and arguably the most modern of these artists from Lyon was Adolphe Appian, who produced etchings in an unbroken stream from 1853 until his death in 1898. His very first etching, of 1853, is a fairly conventional view of a pond or lake in Bresse or the Dauphiné, bristling with short, straight lines;[169] it already demonstrates his tendency to represent landscape by Impression rather than by description. As with Jongkind, the white of the paper illuminates the centre of the composition and brightens the surroundings. The other etching Appian produced at this period is a study in grey which highlights the contrast between the tradition of bucolic landscape and the new fashion for conveying an atmosphere. Although he did not abandon conventional perspective, his lakesides and hills, woodland and ancient cottages with the odd mill unfurl at their leisure; his work definitely tends to highlight the non-material elements of the landscape. The mountains are rendered by their shadow or by their reflection in water rather than by their rock structure; scrub woodland is represented by its transparence rather than by its opacity; the sky is busier and more charged with movement than the land. An etching can render all these effects. Appian specialised in charcoal drawing and easily translated its contrasting black and white and its porosity into thick printing ink.

Appian was the son of an Italian plasterer (Appiani) who had gone to work in Lyon. Jacques-Barthélemy (who called himself Adolphe) joined the Ecole des Beaux-Arts in Lyon at the age of fifteen. His career seems to have progressed smoothly, perhaps more smoothly than it would have done had he lived in Paris, where he nevertheless went to exhibit his work in 1859. His friendship with Corot and Daubigny lasted throughout his career and he painted with them in the Dauphiné in 1852 and 1853, then joined them at Fontainebleau, working there in 1854 and 1856. The Society of Etchers once again acted as an institutional focus. Appian's work first appeared in their publication Number 4, in May 1863, when he contributed his *Way into the Village of Artemare, Ain*; the title is completed by an interesting addition, the word 'autumn'. The school of Lyon was well represented in Cadart's publications. In 1867 Paul

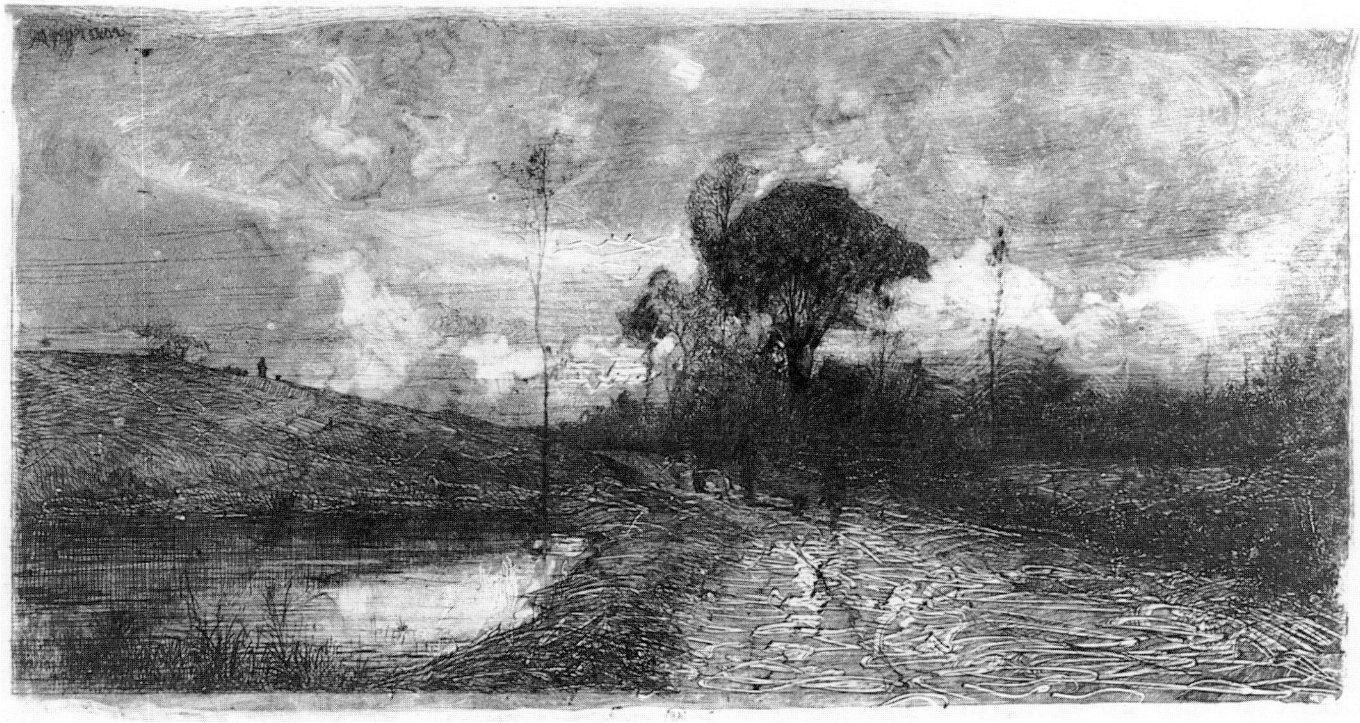

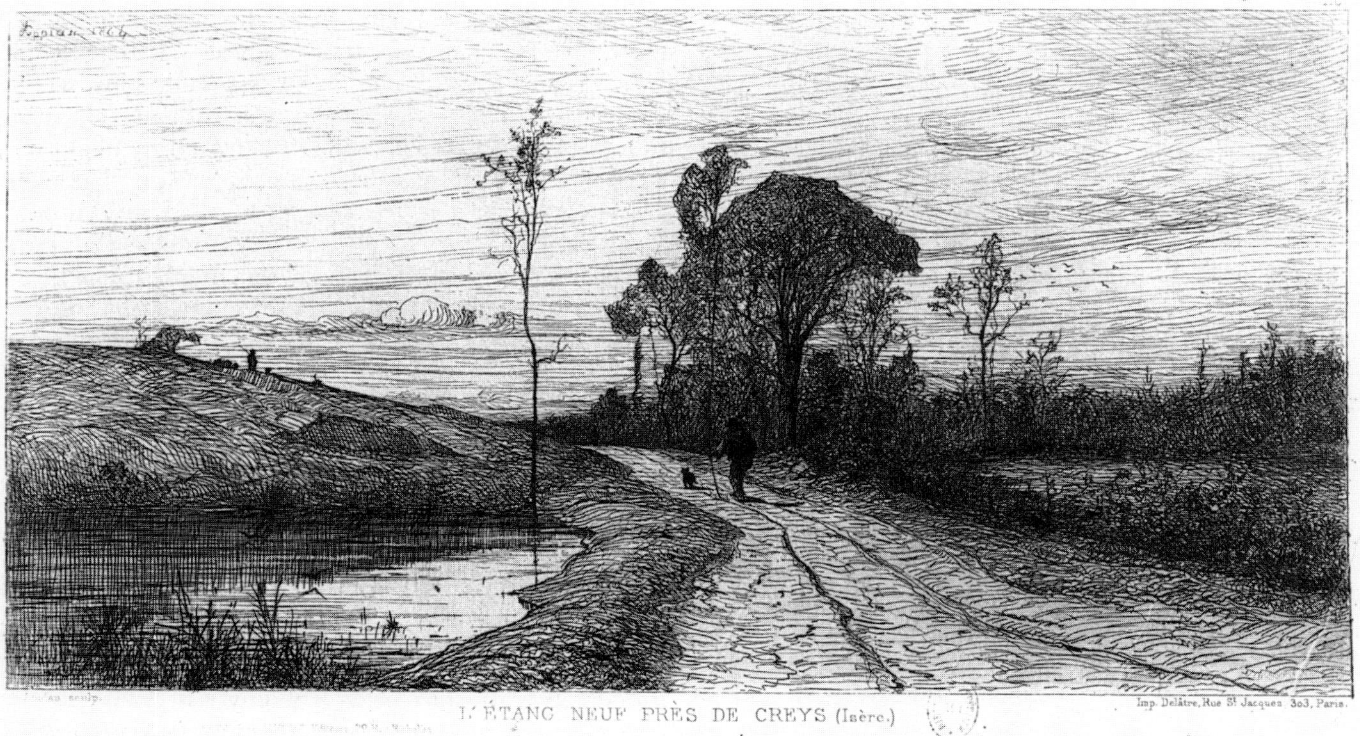
L'ÉTANG NEUF PRÈS DE CREYS (Isère.)
Imp. Delâtre, Rue St. Jacques 303, Paris.

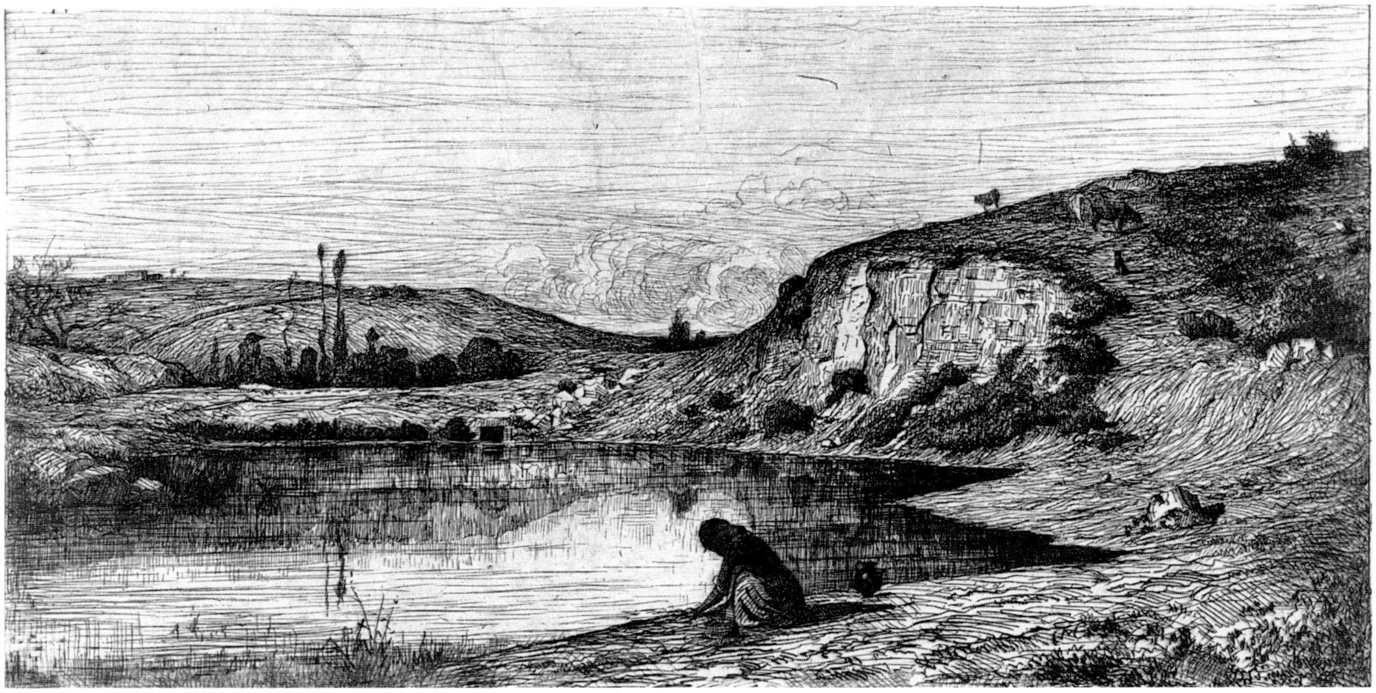

Borel,[170] author of vigorous, almost violent etchings, published a *View of Monaco*, a subject also treated by Appian for Cadart's *L'Eau-forte en 1874*. Also to be found are Soumy and Ponthus-Cinier from Lyon, and above all Vollon who was a leading member of the realist group and introduced Appian into the Society of Etchers.[171] The exhibitions held by the Société des Beaux-Arts de Lyon constituted an alternative Salon; Philippe Burty discovered the etchings of Appian here in 1862.[172] At this date his reputation as a painter and artist in charcoal extended to his etchings and reached Paris, although Appian himself never considered leaving Lyon. Cadart was his dealer, for both paintings and prints, which all sold well; from Cadart's point of view their low price was an added advantage.

Appian's printed work would not find a place in the history of Impressionist art if it did not contain the first example of one of the processes favoured by the Impressionist printmakers: the monotype. The Curtis-Prouté catalogue listed, out of seventy-four etchings, fourteen proofs 'printed after the manner of the monotype'.[173] Among these there are prints in which the ink is so thick that it produces an effect of veiling, or which are so completely covered in ink that the etched line has disappeared. There are also true monotypes – i.e. plates that are not engraved at all but are covered in ink applied with a brush, a rag or a pointed tool and then printed off to give single copies of images with very pronounced night-time or misty effects. The catalogue listed two 'pure' monotypes in an appendix. Twenty-four others appeared in the Gruyer collection and these had the added interest of having for the most part been signed and dated by Appian between 1863 and 1864 (Figs 87, 88). An inscription on one of these states that it is a 'unique example' and produced 'without engraving or etching'. The monotype print of Paul Huet's last etching, *The Cavalier*, cannot date from before 1868,[174] which means that we are dealing with the first known monotypes since Castiglione practised the technique in the seventeenth century. In addition the existence of a 'monotyped' proof of the first state of the etching, *A Rock on the Common at Rix (Ain)* (Figs 89, 90), of which a later state was published by the Society of Etchers in 1866, makes it clear that Appian was using inking effects systematically before that date. This was neither a whim nor an accident: the forty or so monotypes or monotyped prints left by Appian demonstrate a quite deliberate and dogged adherence to the technique, even though the results remained within the family and were not sold. He was certainly responsible for inventing the genre.

If Appian's work is studied closely it becomes evident that between an over-generously inked print ('*saucée*' (gravied), the printers called it), to cover or to add mystery to a view as Whistler used to do, and the idea of printing a plate solely in order to spread a cloud of ink over the paper (achieving thereby a single Impression), there is a very narrow dividing line. To cross this line the notion that a print was created to be published and not simply printed had to be dropped very sharply. The

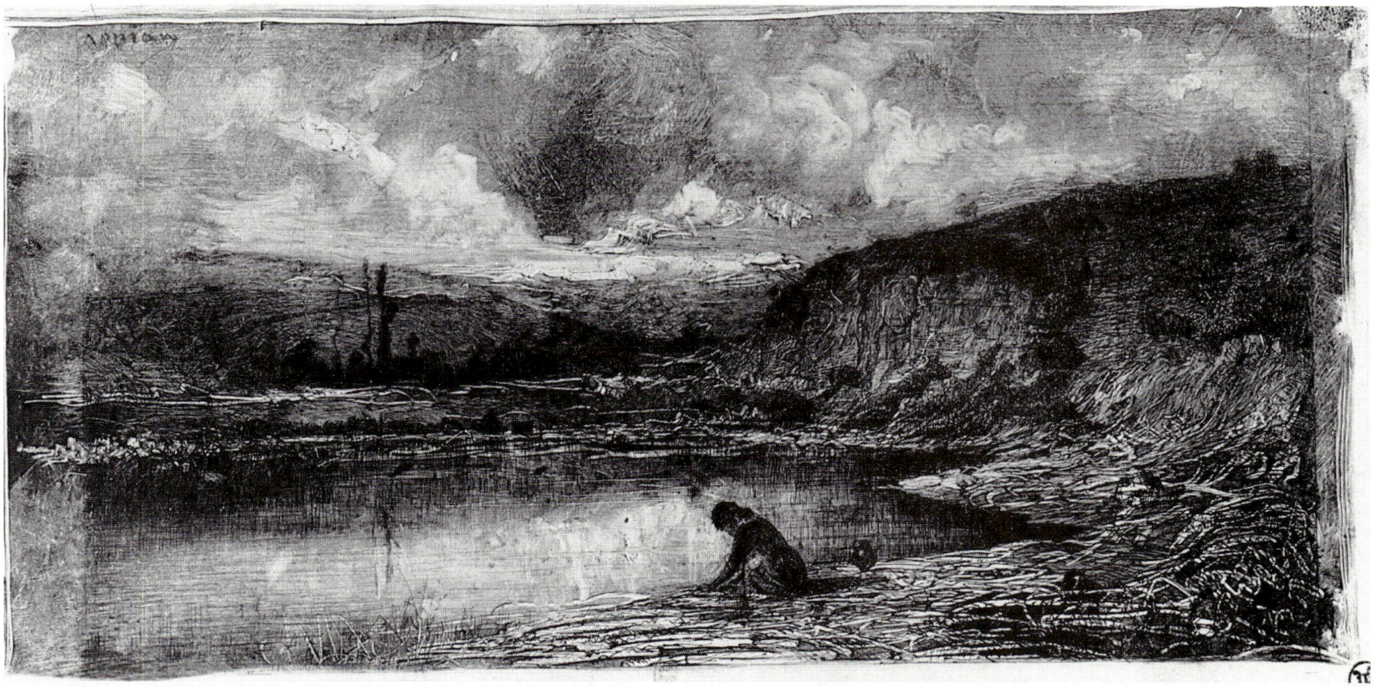

89, 90. Adolphe Appian,
A Rock on the Common at Rix (Ain). 1862.
Etching, first state and monotyped proof, 120 x 255 mm.
Bibliothèque nationale, Paris.

monotype reduces a print to an *Impression* in both senses of the word; the effect obtained is flattering, superficial, incapable of precise detail – it leaves the spectator with an Impression of the scene depicted. The aesthetic desire of the printmaker merges with the public's wish for individualised prints. The 'perversion' of the print by the monotype technique caused it to join the ranks of 'unique works of art', along with the drawing. So where is the advantage of tampering with the plate, or with the printing press, or over-inking, in order to obtain an effect that could, in fact, be obtained in a gouache or a water colour? Monotypes were never produced in great numbers. For the purchaser a drawing would fit the bill just as well. For the artist, however, the approach is quite different: he submits his sketch to a second *Impression*, a mechanical one, which gives it added mystery. Appian saved his monotypes, as Degas generally did, regarding them as experiments or games. It did not matter that they were not circulated; their very existence was enough. The word 'print' carries with it the notion of 'pressure' but not, strictly speaking, of multiplication or even engraving. The monotype brought the print into the domain of unique works of art; thus artists could produce monotypes without feelings of remorse and purchasers could buy them without apprehension.

18. *Constantin Guys*

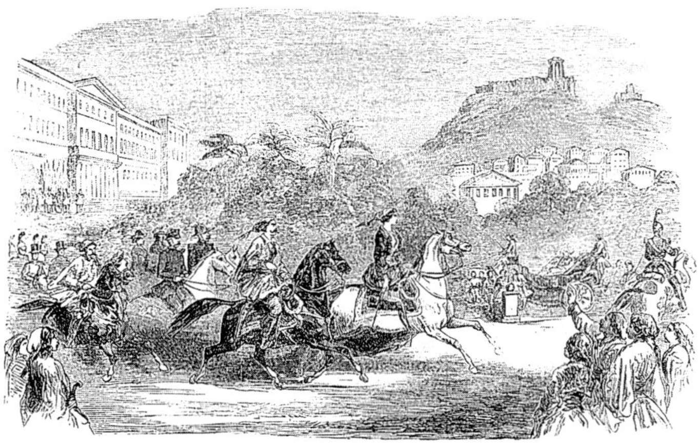

91. Constantin Guys,
Otho, King of Greece, and his Retinue.
Engraving from the *Illustrated London News*,
18 March 1854.

By the end of the Second Empire the printed image had become the business of illustrated magazines. In 1832 the first illustrated daily paper, *Le Charivari*, successfully launched a school of lithographers who were to have a profound effect on the art of their time: Daumier, Gavarni, Grandville, Charlet, Traviès, all praised by Baudelaire.[175] New publications appeared constantly, offering new and sometimes lucrative employment to artists. Paul Delaroche and Horace Vernet collaborated on the *Pictorial Times* (1843–88) and the first number of *L'Illustration* (1843) carried a reproduction of a drawing by Raffet.[176] The first illustrated weekly was the *Illustrated London News* in 1842, which was an immediate success. The formula was repeated the following year by *L'Illustration*, the first illustrated magazine in France. Constantin Guys was living modestly in London at the time, giving drawing lessons. He was employed in 1843 by the *Illustrated London News* and became one of the busiest artists on the paper, to the extent that in 1851, when the director decided to bring out a special French edition of the magazine for the Great Exhibition, Guys was appointed its editor. Censorship cut short the experiment with a French supplement and Guys left London for the Near East to follow the Crimean War.[177]

The profession of press artist was a new one, requiring skills that not all artists possessed. At the newspaper headquarters the work was carefully organised. Readers soon got bored with drawings from stock, and draughtsmen-correspondents had to be sent to cover events on the spot; they never had time to finish a drawing and would send back a rough sketch of their first Impressions of a scene. The reporter would jot down his Impression of an event he thought important or historic, as photographers do now, and send it back to the paper where a second draughtsman would transfer it to a block of wood, correcting it and adding emphasis in a manner appropriate to an engraving. The block would then be cut up and distributed round the workshop where an army of engravers would set to work mechanically on the separate pieces. Then the swiftly engraved pieces would be reassembled and reconstituted before being transformed into a plate or being sent directly to the press. The engravers worked day and night under artificial lights, and were strictly supervised, in order to provide the sixteen pages sent every Saturday to the

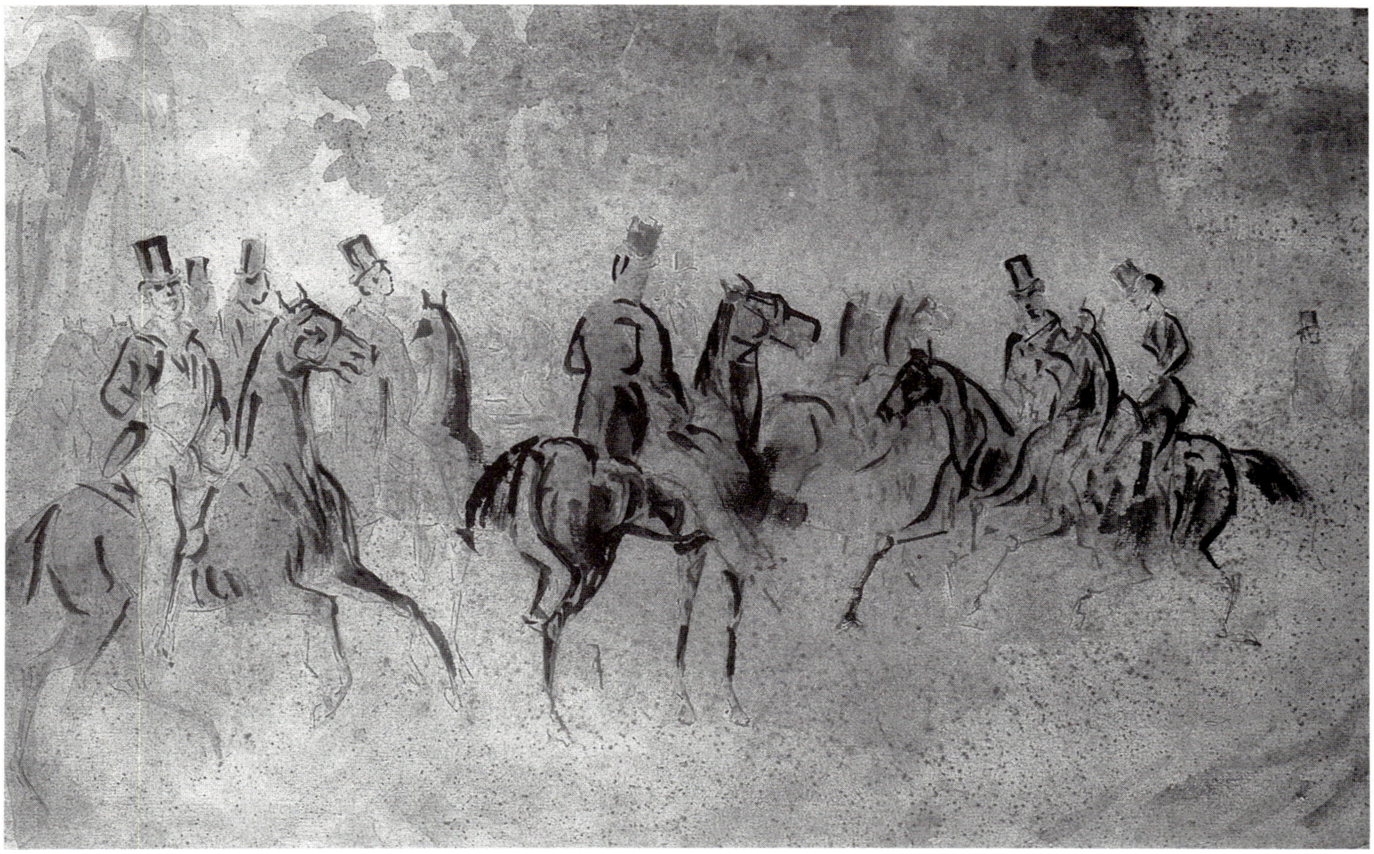

92. Constantin Guys, *Riders*. Undated. Wash and gouache, 240 x 375 mm.
Private collection.

sixty thousand subscribers.

It is impossible to open a magazine of this period without noticing the similarity between the themes chosen by journalists and by the realist painters, although the latter worked in a completely different register. Most of the subjects dealt with by the Impressionists can be found, often in almost identical form, in newspaper illustrations. Manet's studies in particular, abound in examples of such parallels between painters and illustrators. Manet, as we have seen, occupies a very specific position in the evolution of the subject matter of art, which led on occasion to confusion; none of the Impressionist printmakers, even when the situation had become clearer, was spared this occasional collaboration. In a fascinating study,[178] Joel Isaacson has made a preliminary inventory of these iconographic parallels: horse racing, masked balls, cafés, the Moulin de la Galette, boating, the theatre etc. This gives an indication of the community of interest, if not of taste, between subscribers to the magazines and purchasers of contemporary art; it affected the repertoire of paintings more than the repertoire of prints.

The subjects used by printmakers were more likely to include detailed studies of domestic life, family portraits or scenes of intimacy, and this distanced them from journalistic illustration, which shared an interest in public affairs and historical events with painting. A feature of realist painting was the treatment of themes from everyday life as if they were historical or mythological. The divergences are also worthy of note. Because of the autonomy of painting as an art form, the subject of a painting bears a generalised message in contrast to the anecdotal message of a press illustration, even when the subjects are identical. When Daubigny drew a train drawing into a station for a railway guide it was entitled *Pavilly*, the name of the station. When Monet painted the same subject he entitled it *The Train*.[179] This illustrates the different status enjoyed by both pictures, even when there is nothing external to differentiate them.

In fact, the relationship between journalistic illustration and Impressionism is not limited to similarities of iconography, which can be easily explained. The style of the illustrators inspired, opened the way for and endorsed the style of the painters. 'Spontaneity' and 'freshness', immediacy of line and of touch were preoccupations shared by both. Each group reinforced the other in its search for new ways of seeing: high angled views and very low ones, close-ups, panoramic views, sudden centring of an image to suggest the indiscretion, audacity, ubiquity or infallibility of the observer. They shared an obsession with movement; the cinematographic vocabulary used to define their innovatory techniques bears witness to this obsession. Joel Isaacson writes: 'And in so doing, it alienated itself from the very audience it otherwise sought to attract.'[180] The painter, Mason Jackson, who became artistic director of the *Illustrated London News*, explains the position clearly: 'The artist who supplies the sketch has, after long years of practice, acquired a speedy method of working. With a few strokes of his pencil he can give an idea of an event, using a kind of shorthand which is then translated and amplified in the final drawing. . . . All this must be accomplished without traducing the general truth of the representation and while keeping a strict account of the degree of finish, the distribution of light and shade acceptable in an engraving and the rapid Impressions.'[181] The term 'Impression' is used here in the sense of 'printed reproductions' (the plural proves this); its double meaning is emphasised by its use in this context. Constantin Guys was nevertheless at pains to underline the distinction to be made between the skill of the journalist and the talent of the artists; for instance, in a letter to Gavarni in 1847: 'Firstly the newspaper is not just a purely artistic collection of illustrations, it is a serious newspaper, a real one. It reproduces the events of the week. If an item proves to be irrelevant to any particular person or thing it would not be published on grounds of artistic merit alone.'[182]

The character of Constantin Guys illustrates this story of attraction and repulsion between art and modernity; Baudelaire thought he was celebrating the union in a long article he devoted to Guys.[183] Guys returned to Paris in 1848 to cover the Revolution and decided he wanted to stay. No longer young, and constantly short of money he thought of selling the sketches he had produced by the hundred since his youth. Baudelaire wrote that he 'regarded them with the greatest disdain'. Picot sold them in lots in the Passage Vérot-Dodat, one franc for the biggest and fifty centimes for anything smaller. Nadar tells us that the artist 'took pains to conceal himself as others take pains to show themselves'.[184] In fact, he was travelling and was in Paris only briefly between trips. He was in the Crimea at the Battle of Balaklava; at celebrations in honour of the Sultan of Constantinople; in Spain, Italy, Egypt, Bulgaria, Greece. He managed to achieve the status of 'an enigma', and was named by Baudelaire 'the painter of modernity'. He was a strange painter, none the less, rejecting his status as an artist, refusing to sign his watercolours or be named in the articles written about him. 'Such a painter does not exist,' said Baudelaire, who saw it as a sign of dandyism. This mysterious figure was known by everyone in Paris. Nadar was a friend of his, the Goncourts talked about him, Delacroix wanted to buy one of his early drawings, Burty entertained him, Théophile Gautier wrote for him, Champfleury appreciated him. He was neither a painter (he rejected the title of artist) nor an engraver (he sent his watercolour sketches to commercial engravers); it was true, he did not exist, he had 'no place in any art gallery' (Nadar). Manet's admiration for the manner, often so similar to his own, in which he produced quick, rough sketches, described by Nadar as 'sketches that are skilful and childlike at the same time', was no real help. The artist of the modern age was Manet, even though Guys was a forerunner of both Toulouse-Lautrec and Picasso and of the press photographers of today (Figs 91, 92).

For his contemporaries the constraints of drawing for the illustrated press had their consequences: 'unity of Impression', 'obedience to the Impression': the word 'Impression' recurred insistently when Baudelaire wrote about the work of Guys, and really summed up his opinion: 'Interpreting his Impressions with great fidelity, M. Guys emphasises the key features, or the salient points of an object with instinctive energy'.[185] In spite of his success, and his career was, by any standards, a dazzling one, Constantin Guys' old age was long and unhappy. At the age of eighty-three he was surviving modestly on the remains of a pension. An inveterate wanderer, he wanted to go home one evening on his own and to take one last look at the carnival, his 'passion being to mingle with the crowd' (Baudelaire). He was knocked over by a horsedrawn cab. He was taken to a hospice and died there, seven years later, almost forgotten, on 13 March 1892. Later, on 17 April 1895, his friends organised an exhibition of his drawings in the Galerie Georges Petit. He was modern in 1860 when Baudelaire was writing about him; he was too modern for the future, or perhaps the future proved to be less modern than might have been hoped.

19. *The Eleventh Subscriber*

In the 1860s, a group of collectors of etchings focused their enthusiasm on the plates produced by Millet in the winter of 1855–6 with the aim of popularising his paintings. Sensier wrote to Millet on 16 May 1863: 'I've seen some more people; two young enthusiasts. They are asking for your etchings. I've told you already, your name is rising and rising.'[185] The enthusiasts made their requests known and Sensier began building up collections. 'I won't print any more proofs until you have been sent two hundred francs for seven collections' (8 July 1863).[186] At this time Millet was beginning to replace his merry peasants, from the rustic tradition of bucolic painting, with peasants who appeared weighed down by exhaustion and poverty. This adverse social comment[187] won him the mistrust of many and the sympathy of a few. His sympathisers were generally members of the opposition, and were more or less the same people as those who felt that the print should be regarded as a genuine work of art. Millet practised etching in a traditional manner, tracing adaptations of his paintings on to copper plates. Cadart made him offers as well, according to Sensier's letter of 31 July 1862: 'Cadart, the publisher of the Society of Etchers, has been to see me again, and told me that you had authorised him to have a number of your etchings printed by Delâtre, and that he would sell them for you. You talked to me about this a while ago but I do not remember what conclusions you came to. Here are his proposals: 1) to return the plates to Delâtre and request him to make ten copies of each plate; 2) to leave the plates with him for him to sell; 3) he will pay his own expenses, to be deducted from the selling price; 4) the price will be set at thirty francs for the collection, of which thirty-three per cent will be his. If you agree to all this, write to me so that I can get the printing done before I leave for Barbizon which will be before 10 August, I think'. Millet replied to Sensier on the same day: 'This is what you should do with Cadart: if he wants my etchings, he should buy them and make as many copies as he likes. Only I don't know how much to sell them to him for.' Millet was in an awkward position, between a public that was hostile to his paintings and a public traditionally in favour of prints, but whose reaction to scenes of labour, harshly depicted and far removed from the conventional bucolic peasant imagery, could not be anticipated. Between these two camps were a few supporters, not enough for a large edition, but willing to pay a high price for each print. Sensier therefore had the idea of a subscription: he gathered the ten supporters he knew into a 'society', and Millet undertook to etch a large plate for them.

This was the *Departure for Work* (Figs 93, 94), a well-chosen scene, realistic but not aggressively so, begun in November 1863. The fact that this etching, which was more or less made to order, is one of Millet's most luminous, is not irrelevant; it is the etching whose style most closely foreshadows the Impressionist style. The elliptic effect was deliberate, as Millet's letters show: he was concerned to simplify the line, to lighten the bite of the etching tool and not to ink the print too heavily. On 3 November Sensier wrote to him: 'Press on with the etching. I have high hopes for it, very high. I want everyone to want one; I want to exhibit it to demonstrate your mastery of the medium.' On 9 November: 'Tell me when the etching is finished . . . . The Ten are expecting your etching to appear at the end of the month. We'll see about the etching for the Twenty: perhaps it would be a good idea to think about a scene with lots of labourers: The Return of the Last Load of the Harvest, Interior View of the Farm, etc. Whatever you like in this rustic vein.' Finally, on 15 December: 'I will also send to Monsieur Rousseau (the father) the ten first copies of the first state of your etching, so that you can write the following note on each: 1st state. M. Jules Niel, November 1863. J.-F. Millet. The nine others are: Théodore Rousseau, Henri Tardif, Charles Forget, Théodore Sensier, Michel Chassaing, Philippe Burty, Moureau, Charles Tillot and myself. Please include the first names as I have shown them, in pencil, in whatever position you like. . . Do this at home, on your own. The numbers on each proof do not matter because they all date from the same day.'

This letter might be thought of as the foundation stone of the marketing of the modern print, established ten years later by the Impressionists, with handwritten notes testifying to each print's originality, i.e. to its autonomy. That juncture, however, had not yet been reached: Sensier still viewed the print as propaganda for painting and he had every intention of distributing it well beyond the Ten, who had only purchased the right to possess the first edition; moreover, he made suggestions for suitable themes with a subject strangely reminiscent of the most outmoded romantic iconography, the *Arrival of the Harvesters in the Pontine*

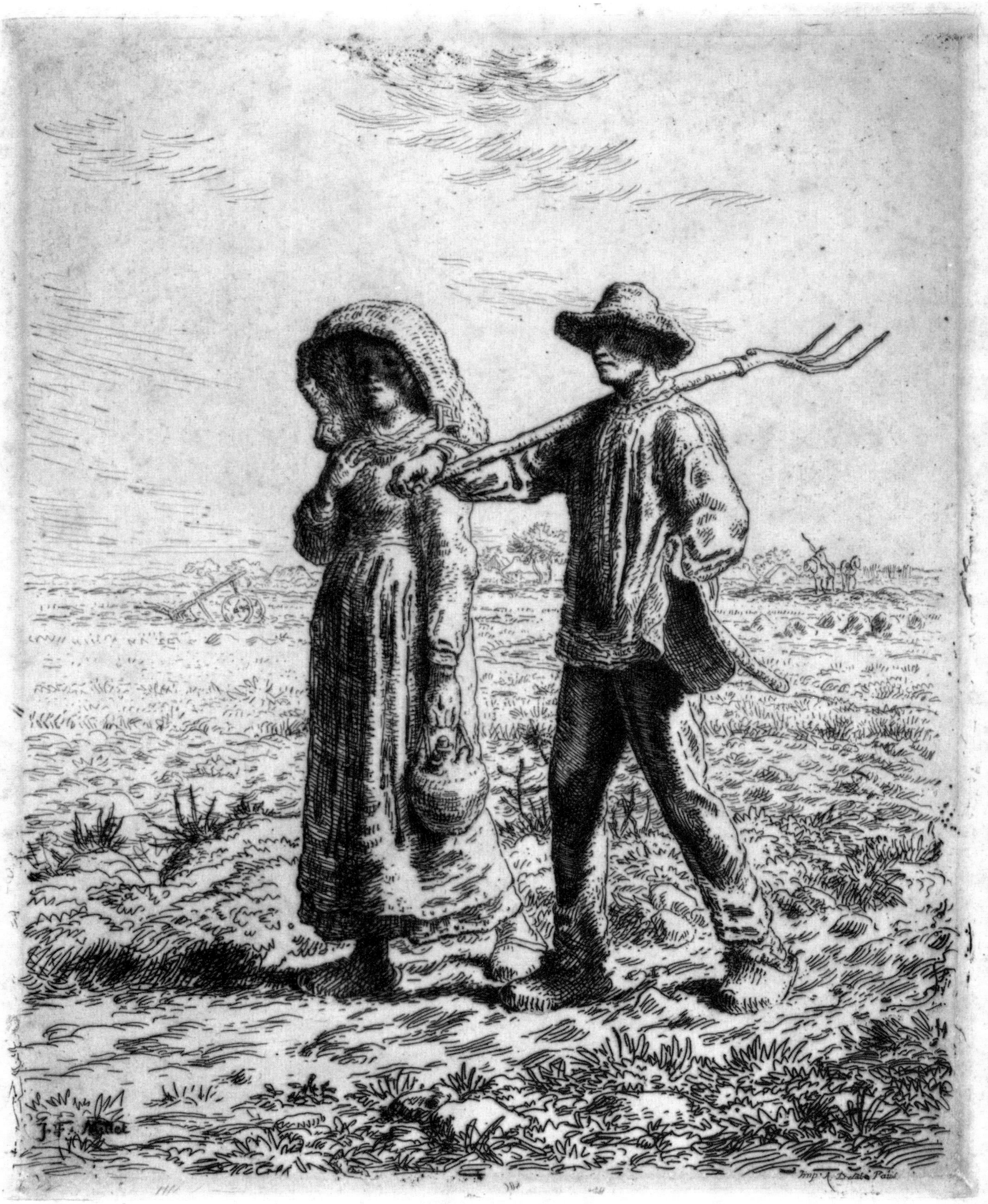

93, 94. Jean-François Millet,
Departure for Work. 1863.
Etching, 310 x 385 mm, second state,
Art Institute, Chicago,
Alice H. Brown Bequest. Fourth state,
Bibliothèque nationale, Paris.

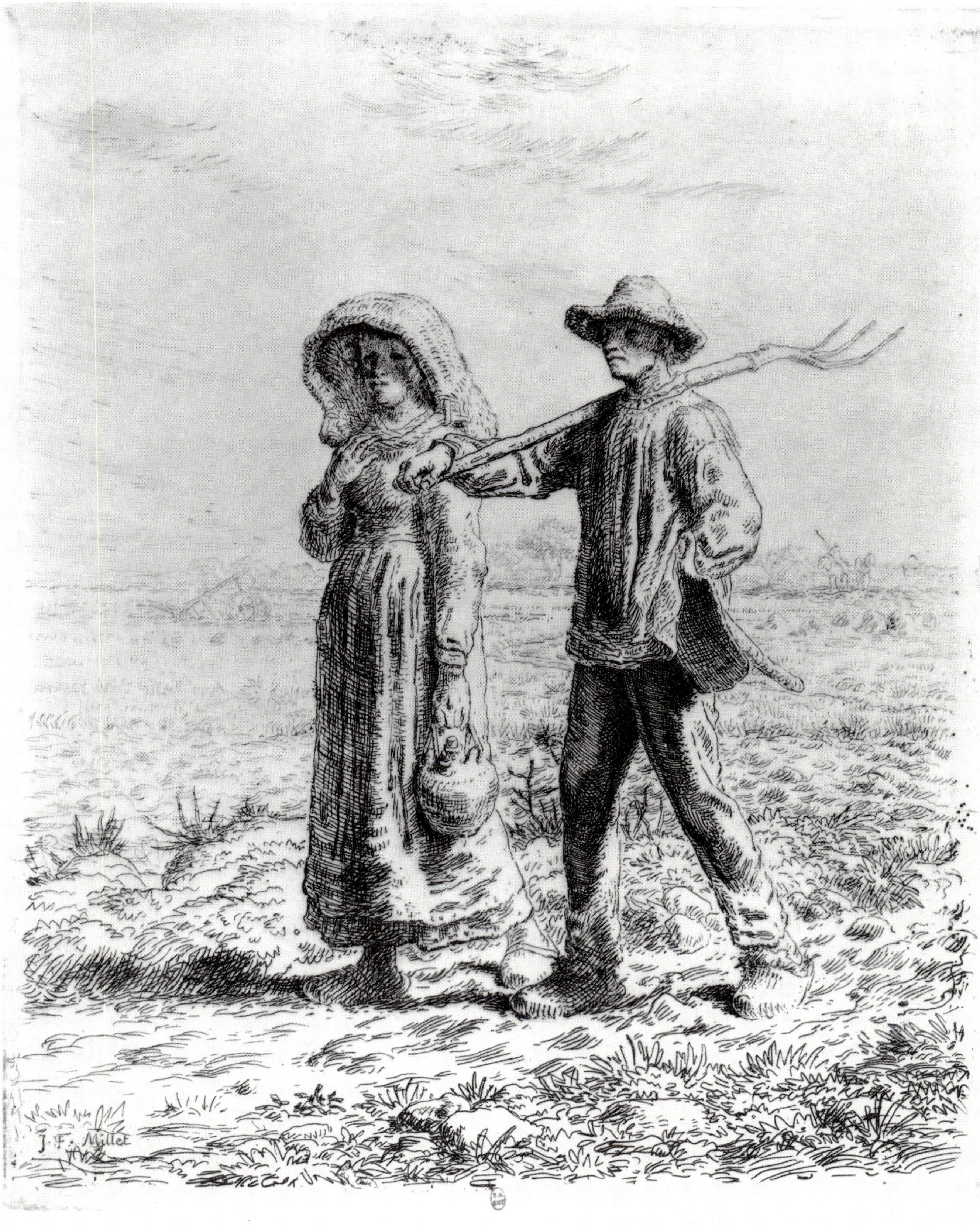
J.F. Millet

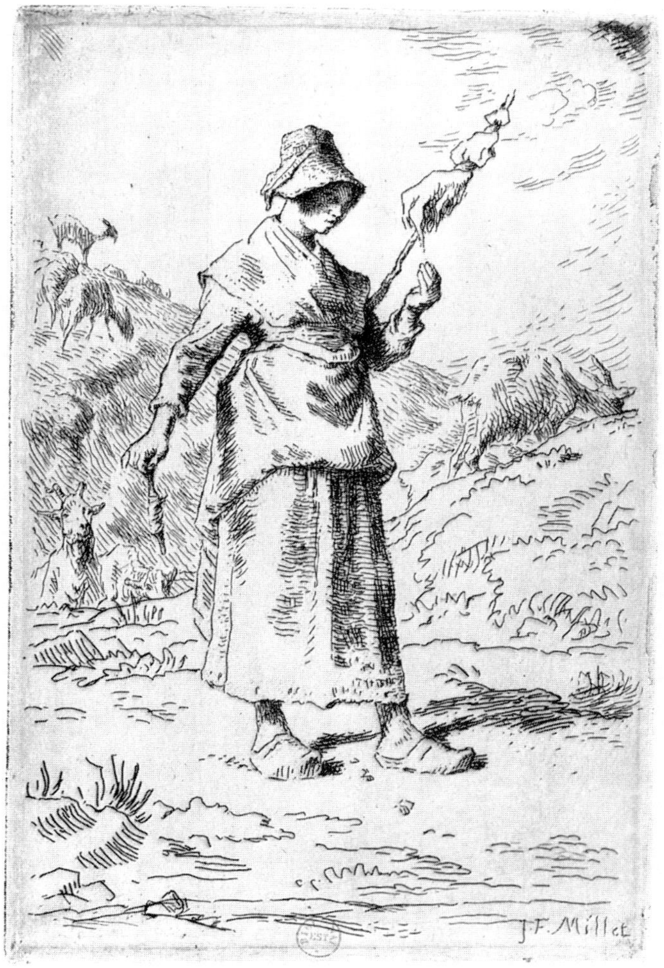

95. Jean-François Millet,
Spinner from the Auvergne. 1869.
Etching, 199 x 129 mm.
Bibliothèque nationale, Paris.

Marshes, which had made the fortune of the painter Léopold Robert at the Salon of 1831, and that of his engraver, Mercuri, as well. The new clientèle wanted much more. Burty had understood this when he insisted that the plate be deleted after ten copies had been printed. Sensier was irritated by his insistence because it completely contradicted his plan, and his concept of the print as well. He replied to Burty: 'I must inform you that nine of the subscribers are of an entirely different opinion: they do not want the plate to be destroyed' (2 December 1863). Faced with such a curious demand, one wonders what Burty needed, or what he was afraid of in refusing possession of a copy of the etching to anyone but the first ten subscribers. Who was this eleventh subscriber, now in competition with the first ten, and whom Burty wanted to exclude?

The idea of limited editions was not new. The artistic review *L'Artiste*, taking advantage of renewed interest in the lithographs of the Romantic masters in the early 1860s, announced that they had bought Isabey's 'drawing on stone', and had printed one hundred copies on large sheets of paper for their subscribers and had then deleted the stone.[188] The limitation of editions first arose in similar conditions, just under a hundred years earlier when the print market, after 1760, enjoyed a similar vogue and was subject to similar excesses. Plates were used until they were almost worn out, prints were made hurriedly and forgeries abounded. In 1751, the engraver Fessard announced an edition of a series of engravings that was to be limited to 760 copies, 260 of which he would sell, the other 500 to be reserved for subscribers. After this the plates would be scratched out in the presence of one of the subscribers. In 1776, infuriated by a forgery of one of their successful prints, *Lunch at Ferney*, the engravers Née and Masquelier decided to sign every one of their proofs by hand.[189] Dealers like Basan organised societies of buyers who took it upon themselves to monitor the exploitation of the copper plates, guarding against forgery and excessive print runs, so that they would retain their value. The Society of Friends of the Arts announced in their brochure of 1790: 'The plates will be broken after 1200 pulls in order that our subscribers should be the sole possessors of the prints, and also in order that, because their number will not increase, they should gain more value.'[190] When David was approached, the Society decided to do a deal with an engraver 'to obtain the agreed number of prints, and the plate will be broken.'[191] How can the difference between a limited edition of 1200 copies and one of ten be explained? The technique of etching had not altered. On the other hand the demands of the clientèle with regard to editions were insatiable, as Burty's demands to Delâtre demonstrate. It was the business of the engravers of the following decade to adapt their practices to these demands; the reason for this remains to be discovered.

The recently-enriched middle classes picked up the art market where the Revolution had put it down, choosing to turn a blind eye to the industrial revolution, the growth of cities and the emergence of new social classes, and to identify with the pre-Revolutionary bourgeoisie, as if it represented some sort of golden age. The revival of a book market in the style of the eighteenth-century prepared the way for the launch of works of contemporary bibliophilism which the mechanisation of publishing and the numerous attempts at creating a luxury, or semi-luxury, industrialised book trade had caused to disappear. As with the print, there was a return to groups of subscribers and a search for ever more refined techniques. It appears that Philippe Burty first produced the idea in the early 1860s. He was combining his efforts with those of Bracquemond who, with the publisher Poulet-Malassis, was trying to include a small number of etchings in printed books. The collapse and exile of Poulet-Malassis inhibited the development of the most ambitious projects, but his place was taken by another publisher, Alphonse Lemerre, whose resources were less limited; Bracquemond fulfilled the same rôle as artistic adviser to Lemerre as he had to Poulet-Malassis. In 1869 Bracquemond was, according to a note from Asselineau to Fantin-Latour, the 'big boss' at Lemerre's publishing house. Conditions were ripe for Bracquemond and Burty to approach their painter-etcher friends for a publication in which etching would play a leading part. Each artist was invited to compose an etching, of a set size, to accompany a poem which would serve to emphasise the etching. Bracquemond himself, Corot, Carolus-Duran, Jongkind, Manet, Millet among others, set to work and Lemerre was able to publish, in 1869, the collection entitled *Sonnets and Etchings*.

The quarrel between Burty and Millet sprang to life again on this occasion. It was agreed to limit the edition to 350 copies on laid paper, plus a few copies on Chinese paper, loose leaf or bound, black or brown, and two or three copies on parchment.[192] First Millet refused to take his inspiration from his allotted poem and used a subject from a painting he had just finished, a *Spinner from the Auvergne* (Fig. 95). Later he tried to prevent the destruction of the plate, required by Burty who was in charge this time, but in vain. On 15 January 1869 he confided to Sensier: 'I gave my consent to the destruction of the plate in spite of my wish to hold on to it. . . Between ourselves, I find this destruction of plates excessively brutal and barbarous. I am not competent enough at business to understand what the outcome is supposed to be, but I do know that even if Rembrandt and Ostade had each made one of these plates they would still be annihilated. That's enough about all that.'

Sonnets and Etchings was published at the very end of the Second Empire and in some ways heralded the Commune and the contradictions of the Republic. It could be assumed that the print had now acquired its status as an autonomous work of art and had achieved total independence from the reproduction. The 'eleventh subscriber', apparently so alarming to Burty, had been excluded. It should not be forgotten also that, twenty years later, Millet's peasants were to become symbols of the Republic, reproduced endlessly in chromolithography, on household china, even on ladies' embroidery. The precautions taken by the Republican Burty, who gave Millet's engravings their artistic legitimacy, protected the new breed of collector from the other kind. Not everyone had forgotten the Revolution.

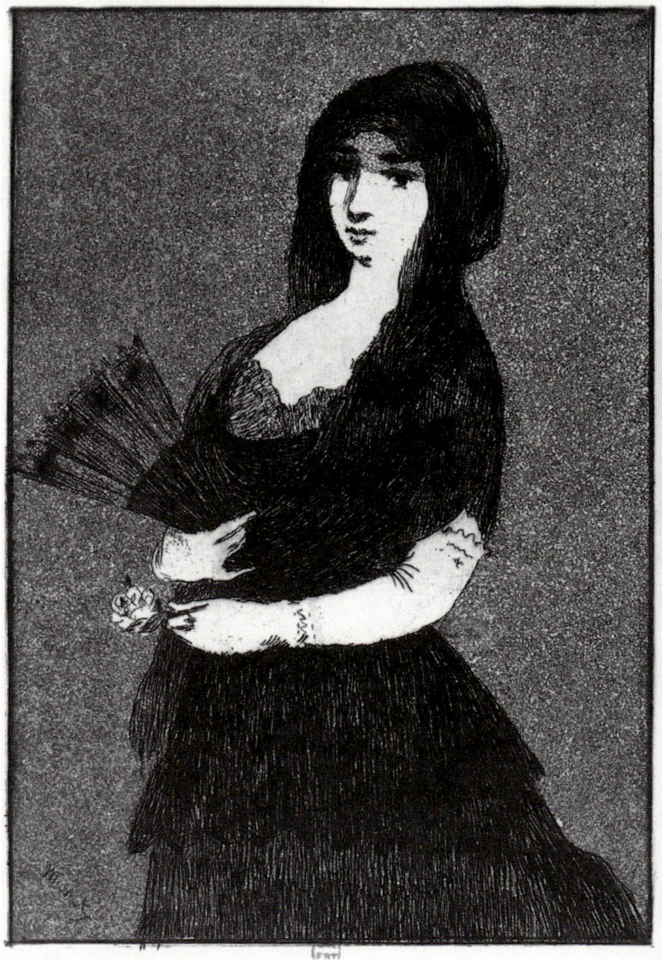

96. Edouard Manet,
Exotic Bloom. 1868.
Etching and aquatint, second and final state,
162 x 104 mm.
Bibliothèque nationale, Paris.

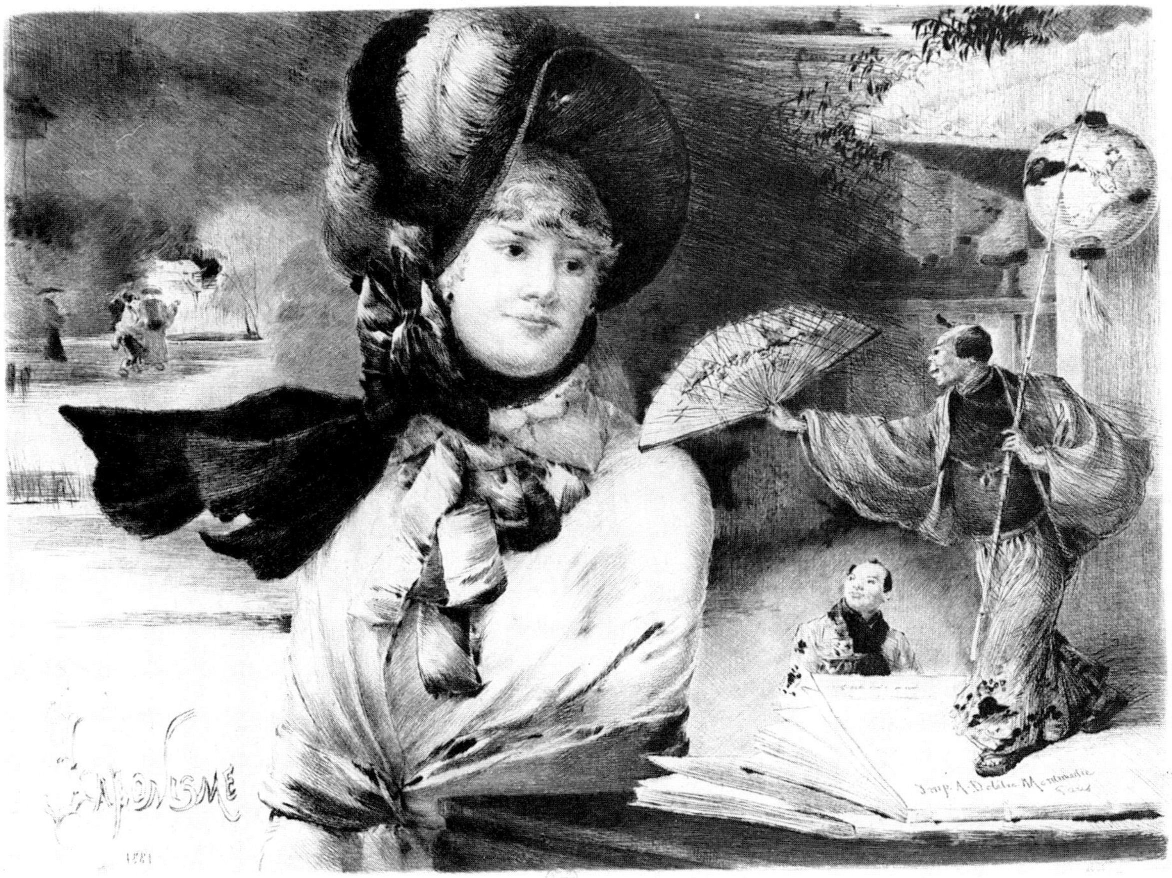

97. Henri Somm, *Japonism*. 1881. Etching, 240 x 318 mm. Bibliothèque nationale, Paris.

20. *The Discovery of Japan*

Baudelaire wrote that 'modernity is all that is temporary, fleeting, contingent; it is that half of art whose other half is eternal and immutable'.[195] An aesthetic existed that answered exactly to this definition, the Japanese aesthetic. Until 1850 Japan had been closed except to a handful of missionaries and explorers. The Second Empire coincided with the opening and rapid development of diplomatic and commercial ties between Japan and the West; in Japan this was a period that saw the decay of the feudal system and a civil war that ended the power of the *shogun*, opening the way to the Meiji period.

Japanese art began to be known to European artists at the end of the 1850s. Its formulae were so attuned to the questions then being asked, so close to the positions from which they were arguing that for many it came as a revelation. From 1860 on, 'modern' artists like Manet, Whistler, Bracquemond, Jacquemart and the critics Burty and Astruc began to collect the exotica that was thrown on to the European market at a negligible price by Japanese decadence; this was sold in the Chinese shops of the rue Vivienne, Bouillette, 'A la Porte chinoise', Decelle, or 'À l'Empire chinois', until, that is, the opening in 1862 of Desoye in the Rue de Rivoli, a shop specialising in Japanese merchandise.[196] Japanese albums had appeared in France even before the establishment of diplomatic relations in 1858 (relations with America opened in 1854); for example, the albums owned by Raoul Duseigneur,[197] the silk merchant from Lyon and father of the etcher Georges Duseigneur. In 1859, Bracquemond used paper imported from Japan (printed by Delâtre); Rembrandt, interested in learning about the East, had already tried the same paper for his etchings. At this time Hokusai's *Mangwa*, a collection of models for artists, was in circulation in artists' studios.[198] In 1861 Jules Jacquemart, an engraver specialising in the decorative arts, and the Goncourt brothers visited the museum in Leiden where they saw the collection of Van Siebold, author of the *Nippon Archiv*, who had returned from Japan in 1830. The presence of Japanese artefacts in the Universal Exhibitions in London in 1862 and Paris in 1867 set an official seal on their entry into the art market.[199] Articles by Ernest Chesneau, Champfleury (*La Mode des japonaiseries*) and Burty (Fig. 98) in 1868 inaugurated a long tradition of writing about *japonisme*.[200] Besides Bracquemond, Manet (Fig. 96) and Whistler, less celebrated artists like Jules Jacquemart, the virtuoso etcher, and Henri Somm (Fig. 97), whose work is occasionally to be found in Impressionist exhibitions, soon took advantage of what the Japanese had to teach. They learned the 'fan' style of layout, which ignores the vanishing point and the laws of perspective; they learned economy of line, varied and more mobile points of view, the taste for ornamentation and the two dimensional. They took from Japanese art only what they wanted to learn, working on areas of which they already had some inkling: the extension of composition all over the page, with the flat surface substituting for the illusion of depth of field; the significant and structural use of the white paper; the arbitrary placing of the edge of the paper, seeming to seize as if by chance upon a slice of life which overflows and escapes from the frame.

The infatuation that followed cannot be accounted for *in vacuo*. '*Japonisme*', the word applied to it by Burty, served as a justificatory, a reference and a model for the new ways of representing reality as well as for the new way of thinking about works of art and the context to which they belonged; Bernard Franck was correct when he wrote that '*japonisme* was primarily an aesthetic matter, but the intimation it brought of a marvellously fresh and renewing universe was certainly not devoid of moral and spiritual aspects'.[201] In popular literature and theatre, allusion to 'Japanese prints' remains, to this day, a reference to the pornographic prints permitted in Japan when Europe was only just beginning to take the

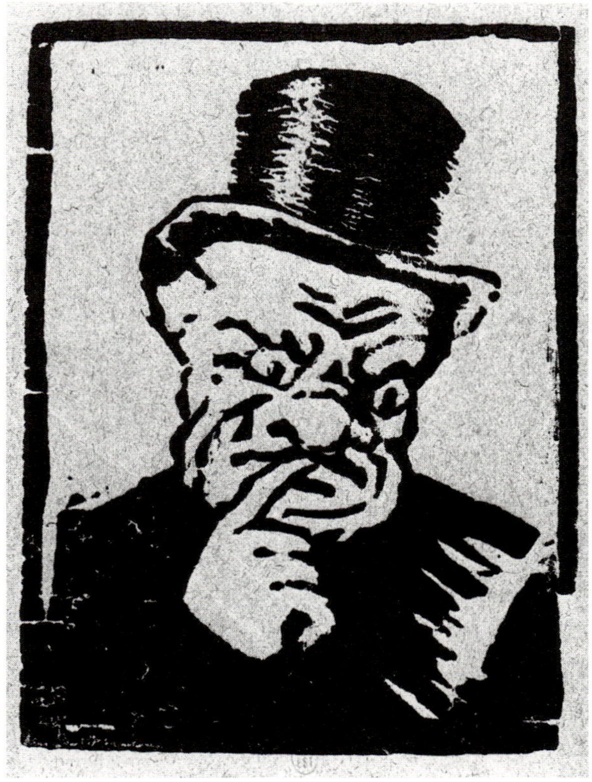

98. Henri Guerard,
Philippe Burty Wearing a Japanese Mask.
Undated. Wood engraving, 80 x 65 mm.
Bibliothèque nationale, Paris.

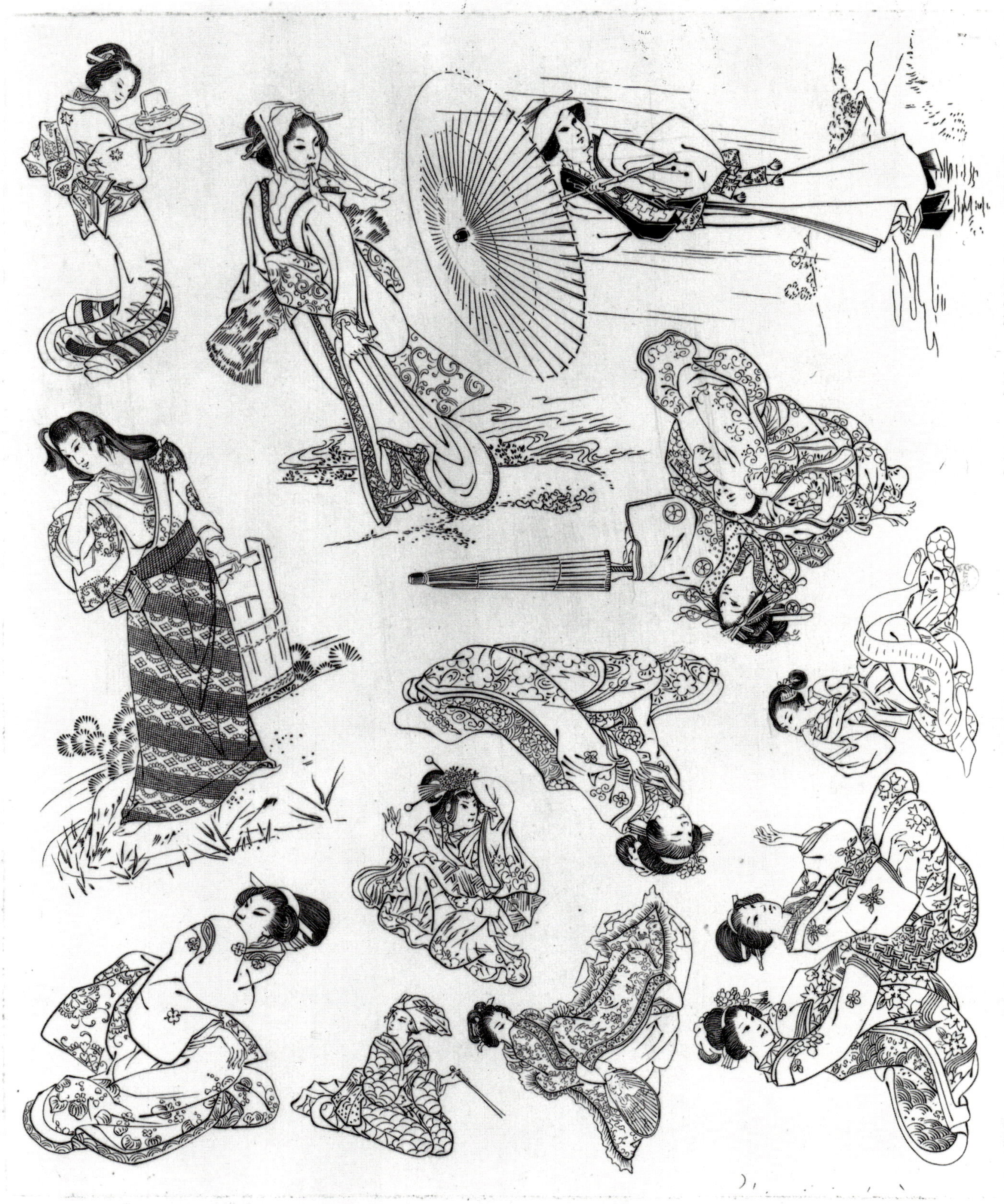

99. Félix Bracquemond, *Thirteen Japanese Graces*. 1866. Etching, 373 x 305 mm.
Bibliothèque nationale, Paris.

odd liberty with religion (without of course renouncing it). The eroticism of the exotic is also linked, in the western imagination, with the return to the consideration of origins as sources of strength and mythical purity: 'Look at the Persians, the Chinese and Japanese. Allow your taste to be formed among men of real strength. Always go straight to the source', Pissarro advised his son Lucien. Provided that the hispanicism that preceded it does not rob it of this claim, Japonisme would appear to be the earliest of the regenerative artistic movements; the 'primitivism' of the 1900s enlarged the field and radicalised the whole approach.[202]

Japonisme was the excuse, therefore, for a new permissiveness, or even a debasement of aesthetic principles at a time when manners of representation inherited from the Renaissance were being shattered by the economic principles of the modern world. Harnessed to *japonisme* in the arts was *japonisme* in philosophy, encouraged by a secular view of the history of religions; this bypassed Christianity and ancient mythology, abused by art for so long, in one leap. 'For the man of science, Japanese civilisation is no less attractive than the civilisation of the Ancient Greeks', declared Michel Revon in his lectures at the Collège de France.[203] It is easy to see why intelligences like that of Bracquemond, formed in the positivist school, should have been sensitive to this view, as were, generally speaking, all the artists aiming to transform the principles of art. It became second nature to use *japonisme* as an example and to hold it up as a model. In fact, as Jean-Paul Bouillon has so clearly demonstrated for Bracquemond, Japanese formulae applied around 1860 simply endorsed the experiments carried out in previous years with the aim of liberating representational art from the straitjacket of Renaissance principles, which were entirely based on the illusions of perspective and volume (Fig. 99).[204]

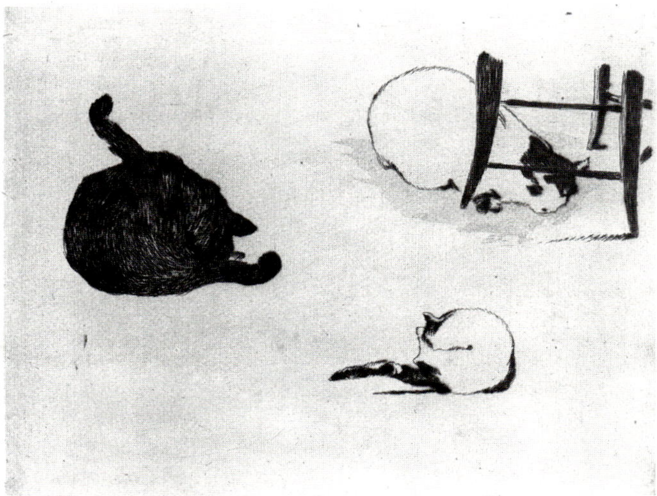

100. Edouard Manet,
The Cats. 1868–9.
Etching, single state, 165 x 210 mm.
Bibliothèque nationale, Paris.

The print was the favoured medium for the meeting of Japanese and Western art. As in the West, the print was born in Japan as the result of a strong surge in the middle classes between the sixteenth and eighteenth centuries; developments in the Orient echoed those in Europe closely, bridging the gap between highbrow and popular art. The low price of prints, and the rustic prints on rough paper that collectors bought to start with, reinforced the Western notion of *Ukiyo-e*, the representation of the 'ephemeral, ever-changing' world, as a form of popular art. Edmond de Goncourt was in no doubt that the art of Utamaro was 'an art born of convention, aimed at the people',[205] although he later regretted that 'industrialised French art, spurred on by Japanese scenes of private life, is killing great art.'[206] The Goncourts' aesthetics have been justly described as symptomatic of the situation of the day, oscillating between opposite poles: popular realism and refinement, decadence and aristocratic symbolism – a duality analogous to the situation pertaining in Japan when

Ukiyo-e was developing.[207] In fact, the Japanese print (like line etching in France) had always been identified with the educated classes, with that bourgeoisie that was descended from the people or was open to the people. As Richard Lane has observed, *Ukiyo-e* 'was in no way a product of the working classes. I suspect that our romantic collectors were to blame for this erroneous definition'.[208] In the eyes of Western intellectuals, the Japanese print combined a number of virtues: it was simultaneously decadent and popular, permissive yet refined. It resolved the contradictions in which innovative artists and left-wing critics were bogged down.

A final asset militated in favour of these new objects: their exoticism guaranteed their scarcity, at least temporarily. At a time when the major problem of the fine art trade was to progress the artists' print from a craft object to the status of an original work of art, and to establish proof of its authenticity, the Japanese print could immediately qualify its owners and its admirers with a measure of 'originality', even if the voyage in 1871 of Duret and Cernuschi, who brought back thousands of albums and statues, might have suggested that originality was not the major preoccupation of Japanese artists.

Japanese iconography is curiously closely related to the themes that Western artists were discovering for themselves in the mid-nineteenth century: landscapes seen through their own weather conditions, courtesans and drinking dens, street scenes and scenes of working-class life, portraits of actors. Nothing that could not appear in the repertoire that Manet (Fig. 100), for example, or Degas, or, later, Toulouse-Lautrec and so many others were laboriously building up. It comes as no surprise, since we know that the success of the print occurred in circumstances similar to those that encouraged the success of the etching in France: to satisfy the requirements of a social class poised somewhere between high and low society. Such a transitory and socially mobile public required a transitory world, all artifice and illusion, filled with distractions and fleeting pleasures. This explains why Bracquemond's ducks and grass bear such a strong resemblance to the ducks and grass of Hokusai, why Tissot's ladies resemble *geishas*. Later the European painters constructed a permanent relationship with the Japanese masters. It is interesting to think that *japonisme* served to mask political opposition to a worn-out Empire in France as well as in Japan, as Jean-Paul Bouillon has demonstrated with regard to the curious Society of Jing-lar, a play on the word *jinglard*, one of the slang words for cheap wine.[209] This society gathered together some militantly left-wing supporters of *japonisme* around Bracquemond and Astruc. The rise of *japonisme* accompanied the rise of the new classes, opposed to the current authoritarian régime; the third Parisian revolution of the century was to spring from their midst.

During the siege of Paris in 1870 Manet picked up his etching tool again, no-one knows why, and etched an image that was not intended for sale, apparently, nor was it linked to any of his other works (this was also unusual for him). The *Queue at the Butcher's Shop* (Fig. 101), a tragic yet light-hearted scene from everyday life, is constructed of allusive figures with unfinished outlines, outlines that disappear into the page, under umbrellas whose ribs mingle with the streaks of rain; it is a composition carried out with a few strokes, in which the white paper plays the leading rôle; depth of field is replaced by an ascending curve and contours by criss-crossed lines. In his correspondence Manet describes having seen this and having made more than one sketch of it. He took the trouble to find a copper plate and to engrave this ephemeral image on to it. *Japonisme* had penetrated the West. Civil War had overtaken France.

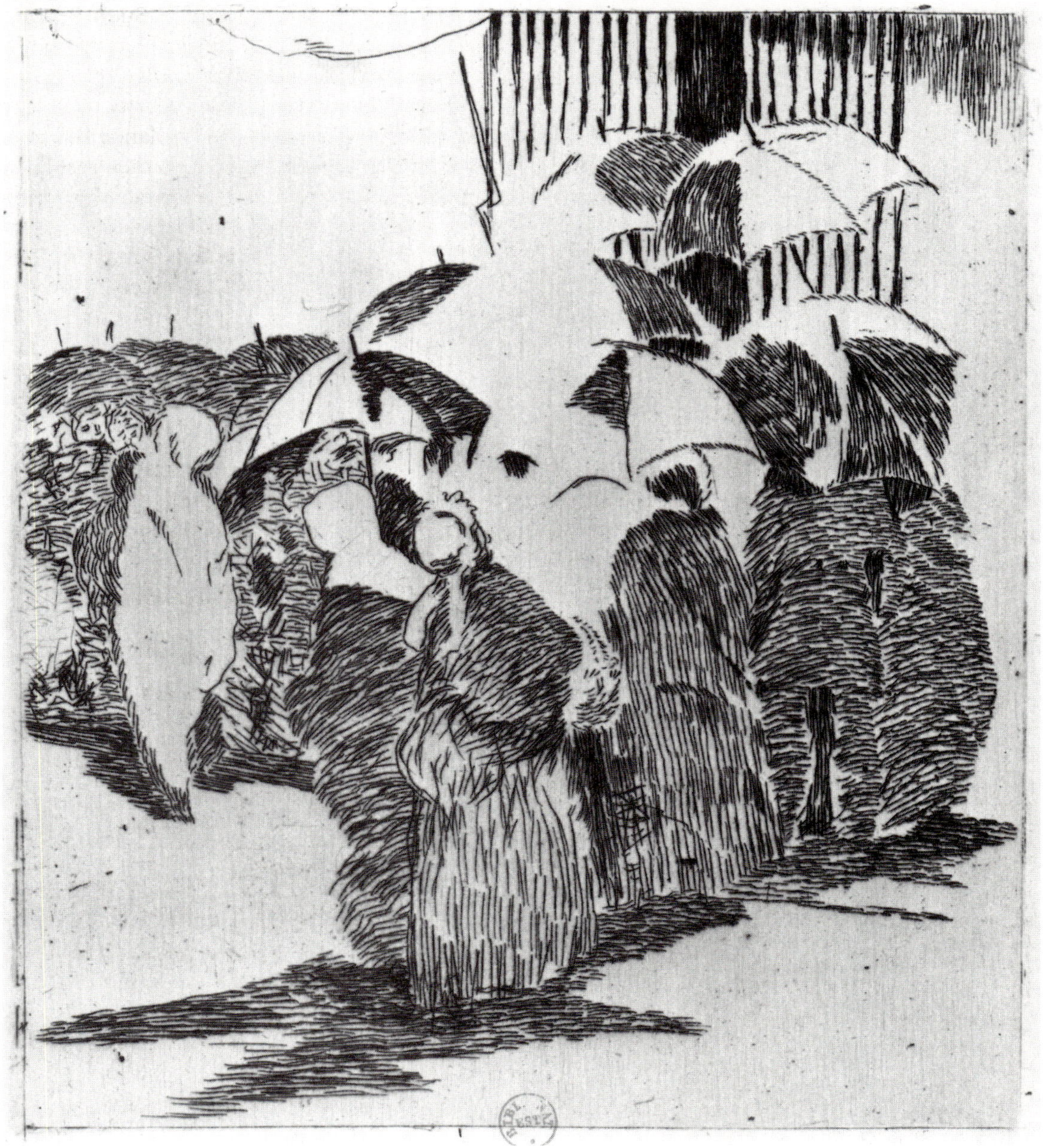

101. Edouard Manet, *Queue at the Butcher's Shop*. 1871. Etching, single state, 168 x 147 mm. Bibliothèque nationale, Paris.

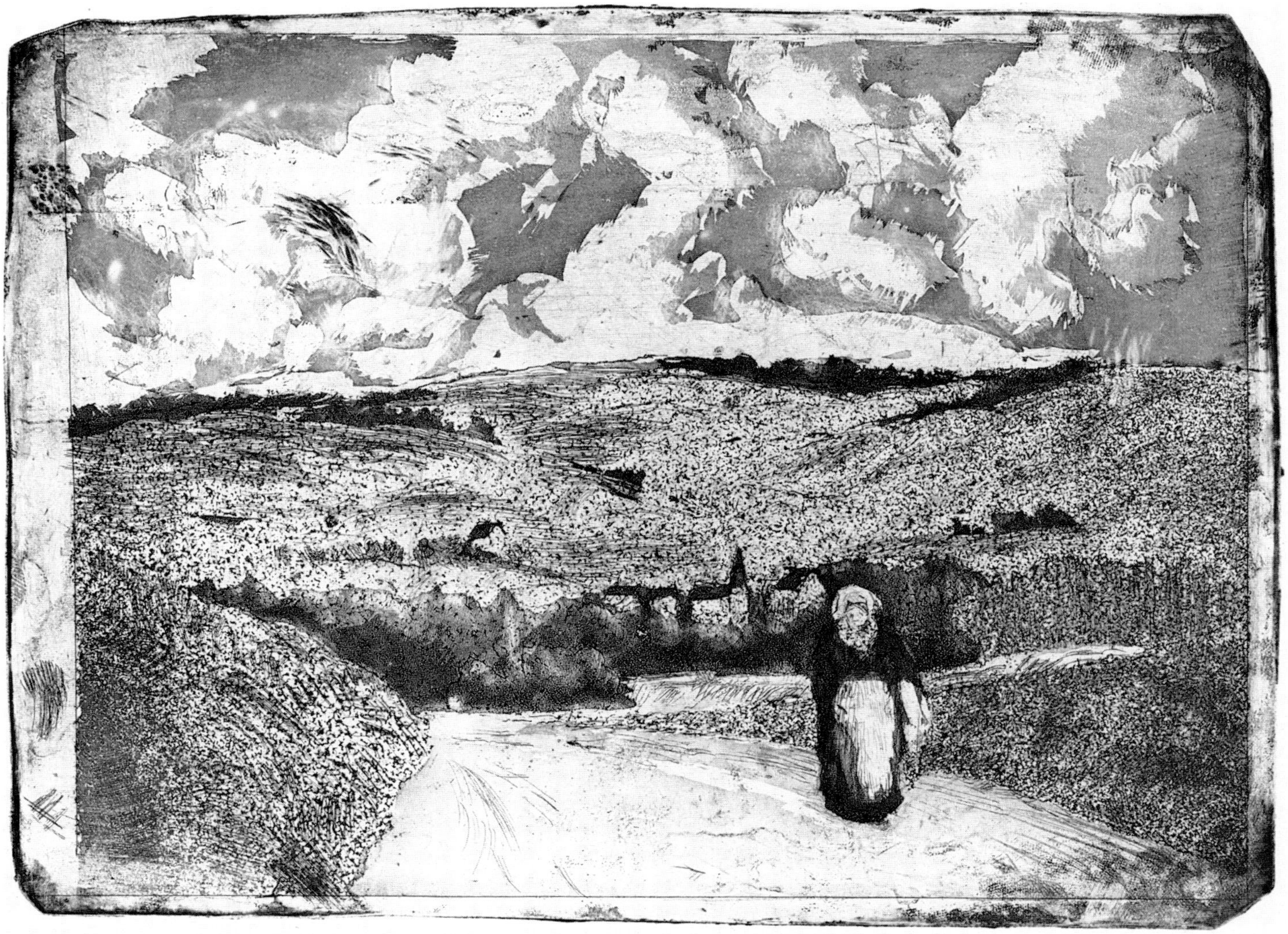

102. Camille Pissarro,
Woman on the Road. 1879.
Etching, fourth state, 158 x 210 mm.
Library of Congress, Washington.

PART TWO

Day and Night: 1870–86

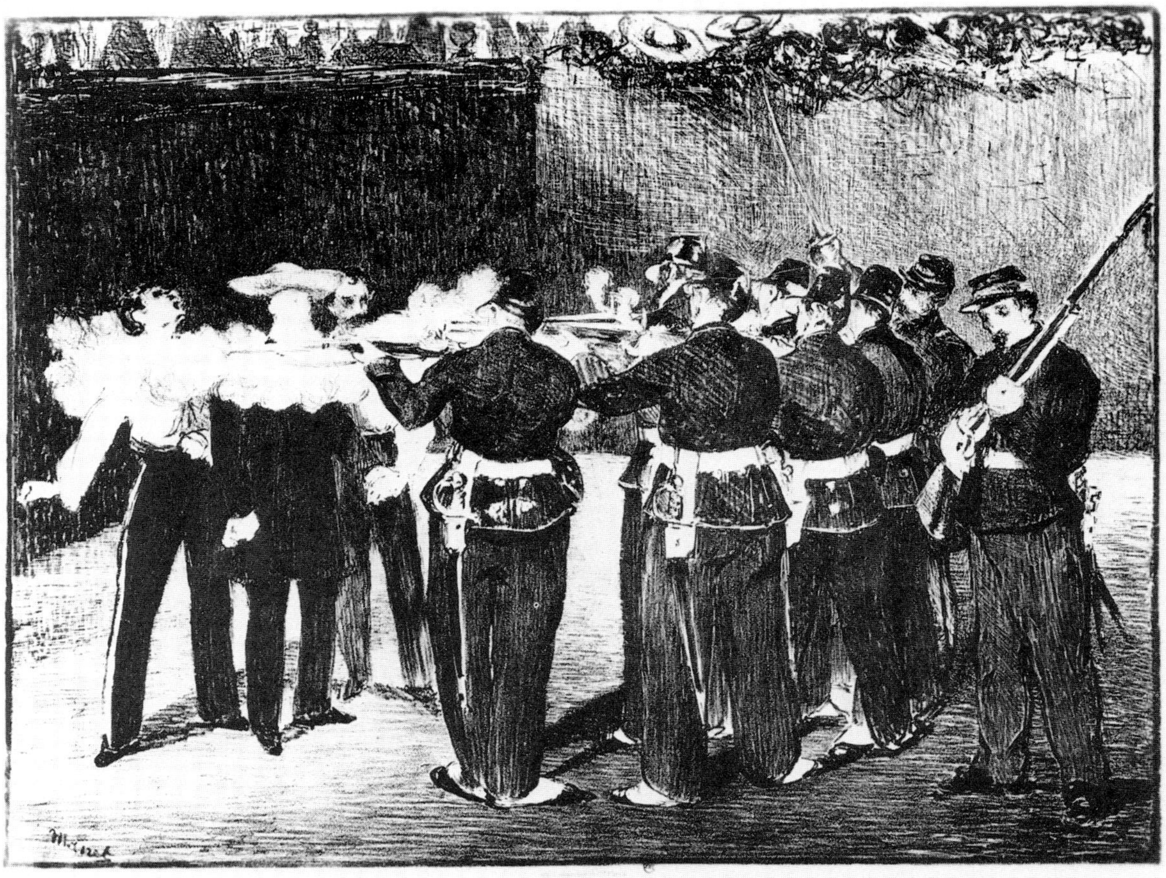

21. *War and Revolution*

103. Edouard Manet, *The Execution of Maximilian*. 1868. Lithograph, 333 x 433 mm. Bibliothèque nationale, Paris.

In the summer of 1870 a fragile republic was established in war-torn France, to be destroyed almost immediately by civil war; the Impressionist painters were approaching their forties, the prime of life, and were looking forward with confidence to the future. The country had been torn apart by rapid growth, and was simultaneously rich and poverty-stricken as a result. In 1867 Edouard Manet, the political dissident, publicly gave vent to his desire to assassinate the government in his painting *The Execution of Maximilian*.[210] He used the same firing squad, borrowed originally from Goya, to denounce government repression of the Commune in his lithograph *The Barricade* (Fig. 104). The oblique corpse of the *Dead Bullfighter* (Fig. 64) became the corpse of a *garde nationale* in another lithograph entitled *Civil War* (Fig. 105). He returned to the medium of lithography for these, the medium of propaganda inherited from the Daumier of the *Rue Transnonnain*; the two lithographs were not published immediately.

While the Second Empire was crumbling in France,

104. Edouard Manet, *The Barricade*. 1871. Lithograph, 465 x 334 mm. Bibliothèque nationale, Paris.

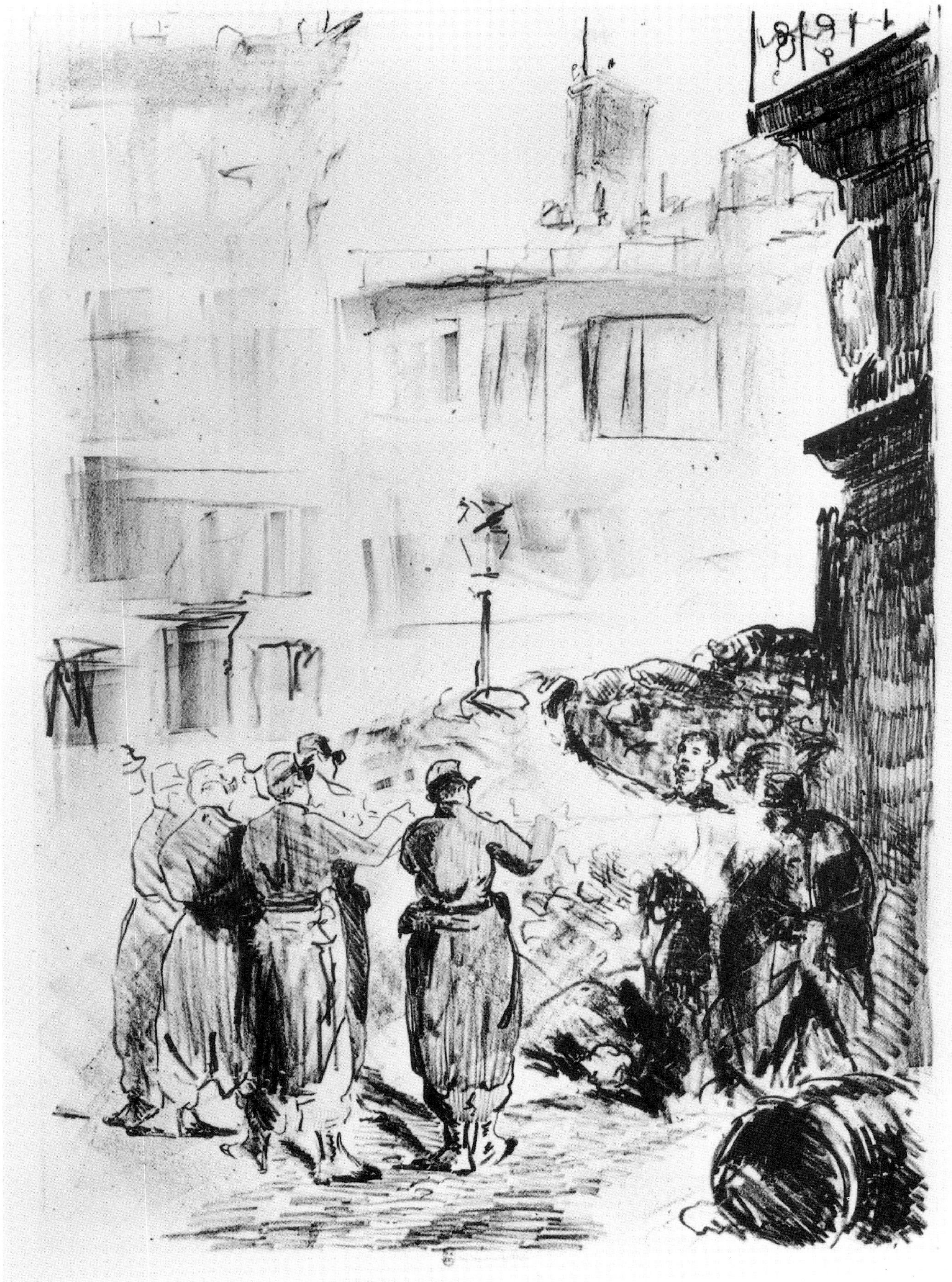

something different was happening in England. Claude Monet and Camille Pissarro left France at the end of 1870, Monet to avoid being called up and Pissarro because his house in Louveciennes had been taken over by the Prussians. Both went to London, Monet because he was in Trouville, in Normandy, at the time and Pissarro because his mother and part of his family were already there. While there, through the intervention of a third émigré, Daubigny, they both met a fourth: this was Charles Durand-Ruel, who was establishing his business in London by holding exhibitions of the work of French painters. Relations between the artists of the two countries were very healthy: Daubigny had been cultivating links with Whistler since 1865. Whistler and Seymour Hadon had formed close ties with Legros and Delâtre, whom they had persuaded to come to London to assist with printmaking. There was already a colony of Parisian artists, including Constantin Guys, living in London. The collector and watercolour painter Edwin Edwards was buying the work of his friend Fantin-Latour, and Legros introduced Durand-Ruel to the Ionides family, who were rich collectors.[211]

Durand-Ruel was getting ready to open a branch in London; in fact it could be claimed that the 'pre-première' Impressionist exhibition took place in London in March 1871, while the Commune was raging in Paris. One of Pissarro's paintings shown there was called *Effect of Snow*. Impressionism was emerging as the gathering of a group of artists around a prosperous and free market, a market now thwarted by the outbreak of war. Prosperity was interrupted, in fact, only on the continent. Durand-Ruel opened his branch in London and, once back in Paris between 1872 and 1873 began regularly buying and selling paintings by the most modern of painters. The story might stop there, with the birth of a style formed in the studios of a society that had become urban and industrial, and which might have developed further in a modern, capitalist republic. The celebrated painting that had given its name to the movement, *Impression, sunrise*, was painted by Claude Monet in 1872.

In 1873, unfortunately, this expansion, sustained for more than ten years and favouring the emergence of a market for art (particularly prints) since 1860, was cut short. Countries that had been thriving were hit by the first great world recession and the subsequent prolonged and progressive depression in trade. The collapse lasted, on and off, for twenty years and had the gravest effect on modern artists because they were dependant on the most recently-acquired wealth and the most modest of fortunes; this was the period when their efforts should by rights have been being rewarded. Just as they were enjoying their first success they experienced the fragility of the new, free art market – or rather, in these sudden adverse circumstances, its hostility.[212] In such an economic climate the artist's print had an important and certainly advantageous role to play; both artists and collectors could fall back on it. Its new artistic status was confirmed and its nature had been altered: in the opinion of many the print was now ripe to be considered as a luxury product.

The Republican victory opened the way to popular art, the applied arts, the popular song and the lithograph. It was a bitter victory, however, and an unstable one, leaving conservatives well provided for and moderates, anxious that their wealth should be, as far as was consistent with democracy, unscathed. In about 1872–5 the well-printed etching, the artist's lithograph and book collecting made their reappearance, but the print's upturn in fortune proved as fragile as the upturn in the fortune of its owners. Cadart's problems, then his death in 1875, before the final collapse of his business on 12 January 1882,[213] made his etchers homeless. The new home provided for them by another publisher, Richard Lesclide, between 1873 and 1876, around another review, *Paris à l'eau-forte*, was a flash in the pan and did not last. In 1875 Durand-Ruel began to feel the effects of the economic depression too and had to close his branch in London; he was dealt a final blow in 1842 by the crash of the Union Générale, a large Catholic bank one of whose directors, Feder, was his most important client,[214] This flurry of bankruptcies affected all artists but was most damaging to those who, like Degas, lived on private means. Degas's father died in 1874, leaving the family bank in desperate financial straits; his two sons were ruined and the artist helped his brother to pay off their debts. This had a detrimental effect on his attitude to life, as well as on his artistic output, particularly on his prints, which were produced henceforth with money in mind.[215] Until now he had turned his back on joint ventures and had never been a member of the Society of Etchers; after the collapse, although he retained his independence of spirit, he became their most active organiser. The dilettante Marcellin Desboutin, who until 1872 led a life of leisure in his house in Tuscany, was then suddenly plunged into poverty in Paris: he is Degas's absinthe drinker, Manet's painter in a garret, the prop and stay of the Café Guerbois, saved only by his talent for printmaking.[216]

The ascending curve that was carrying these artists towards different types of success was momentarily threatened by the war and irretrievably shattered by the recession. The die was cast, however. The values promoted by industry and capitalism were irreversible, as was their symbolic representation, already established through a system specially adapted to the production of *objets d'art*. The visual arts reacted to the situation, and to the change in public taste, more swiftly than music or literature because, supposedly, their existence is intimately connected with the methods of amassing personal wealth: they react to fads and to reversals of fortune, they bear witness to and are symptoms of all life's vicissitudes, and in some mysterious way perhaps may be also part of their cause.

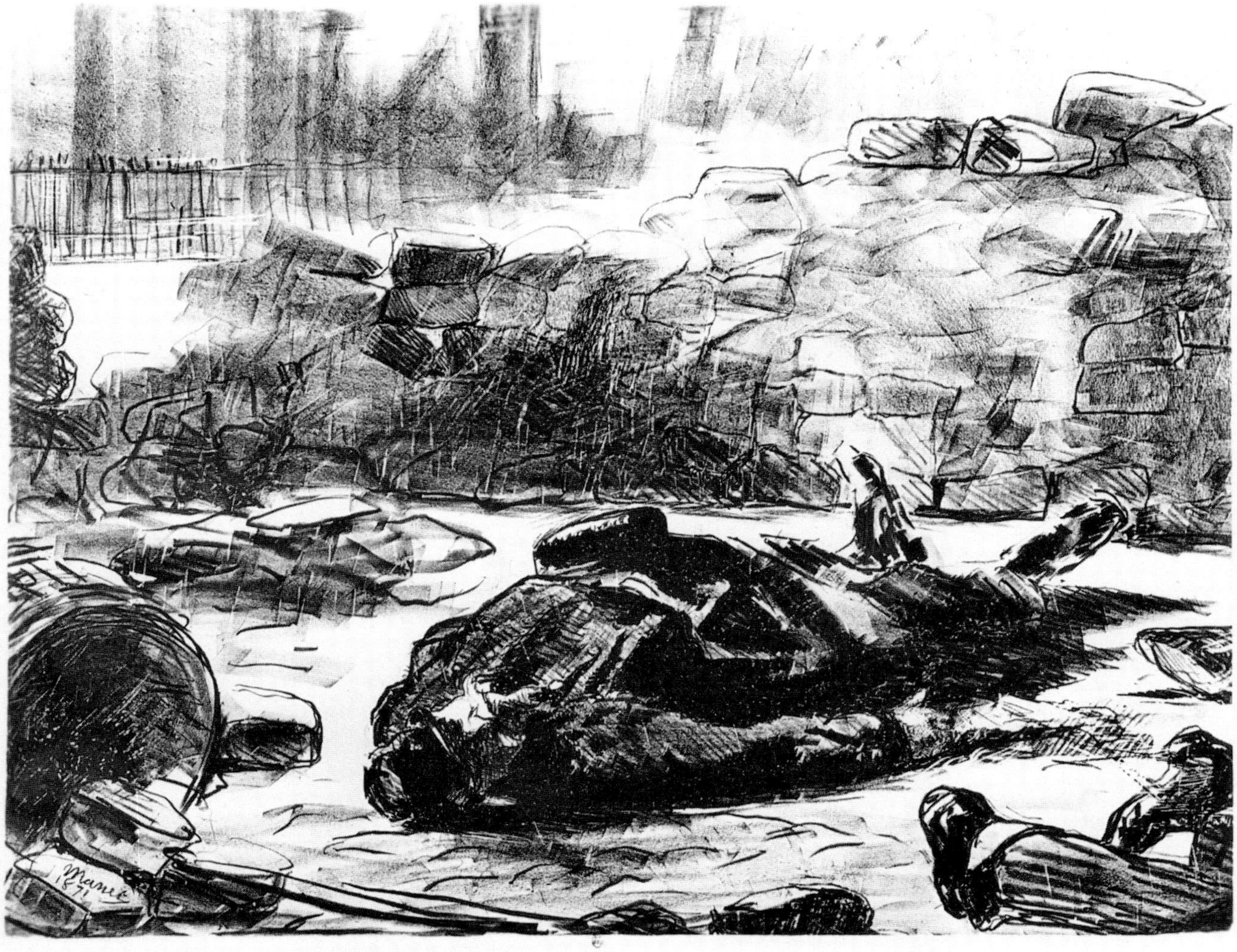

105. Edouard Manet, *Civil War*. 1871. Lithograph, 400 x 520 mm.
Bibliothèque nationale, Paris.

22. *1873: The Auvers Group*

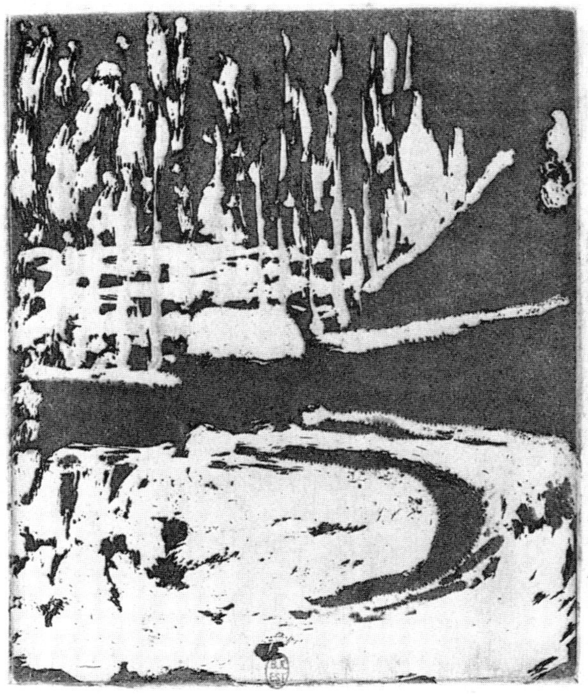

106. Van Ryssel (Dr Paul Gachet), *Garden under Snow*. Undated. Aquatint, first state, 125 x 113 mm. Bibliothèque nationale, Paris.

When Camille Pissarro returned from London in June 1871 and found that his studio in Louveciennes had been ransacked,[217] he moved to Pontoise. In 1872 Doctor Gachet, an amateur artist and etcher, set up his studio in nearby Auvers-sur-Oise. Besides art, Pissarro and Gachet had another common interest: homeopathy. Gachet brought along one of his friends from Paris, Armand Guillaumin, who worked at the Hôtel de Ville and also spent all his free time in artistic pursuits. Camille Pissarro had a young painter from Provence lodging with him, who had come to try his luck in Paris, Paul Cézanne. They would all ramble through the countryside together, stopping to paint from the motif. In the doctor's studio they all tried their hand at etching on copper plates, for the pleasure of the experience.[218] Doctor Gachet lived principally in Paris, where he knew the publisher Richard Lesclide, with whom (and with Félix Régamey, who was interested in Japanese art) he was planning the publication of a review centred around etched illustrations. This was *Paris à l'eau-forte*. The first number appeared on 1 April 1873, subtitled 'Current affairs, the bizarre and the fantastic'. The tone was relaxed and the text of scant importance: 'this magazine is primarily dedicated to etching and wishes to receive no criticism for the modest space allotted to the text, which is there as a foil to the etchings.'[219] A whole edition was devoted to cats. This drew some criticism. The next edition was devoted entirely to the Comédie Française. For seventy-five centimes a week the review, which was printed by Delâtre, provided sixteen pages with eight illustrations which, at the outset, were all by Félix Régamey. Soon other signatures appeared, in the typically Japanese form of anonymous monograms. One of these, a winged creature thought to be a duck, was Doctor Gachet's mark. In August Armand Guillaumin's monogram (a cat) appeared on two vignettes illustrating 'From Paris to Paris by the circular railway'. Gachet introduced Guillaumin to Lesclide. On 6 September 1873, Guillaumin wrote to Gachet: 'M. Richard Lesclide told me that your etchings would appear this month, but I have seen no publicity; have you finished them? If you have, send me a print and in return I will give you those I have done since we met.'[220] Nine or ten small etchings by Guillaumin appeared before the end of the year; they were like small, untidy scribbles, with a tousled mass of lines. Their appearance was far more slapdash than anything 'impulsive' produced by the etchers of the 1860s.

A turning point had been reached: no attempt was made to modify the Impression of abruptness, the note of improvisation, of catching the fleeting moment. The small size of these vignettes, no more than a few square centimetres, intensifies their lightness. The sketches, which a few years earlier would not have fetched anything, were set like precious stones, glued carefully on to Chinese paper in the de luxe edition of the review. Guillaumin's etchings, *Sunken Lane in the Hautes-Bruyères* (Fig. 107) for example,[221] are arresting because they are without any narrative element and make no concession to description or to the picturesque, unlike Régamey's elegant *japonaiseries*, or even Doctor Gachet's slightly similar etchings, illustrating *An Evening with Victor Hugo*. Lesclide knew Hugo and requested (and received) some words of encouragement from him; these were published immediately: '*Paris à l'eau-forte* is an exquisite, admirable publication.'[222] The adjectives were well chosen, refinement being the quality that was sought above all. The editorial proclaimed that 'it seems to us that artists will succeed in producing truly original etchings bearing the stamp of their individuality.'[223] The etchings were also printed separately, on Chinese paper, and subscribers could pay extra for de luxe editions, 'on exotic paper' or on Holland, or order pre'publication proofs glued on to Bristol board; this, according to the publicity, was the 'Connoisseur's edition'. Collections were beginning to be formed (as anticipated) in the way described in an article illustrated by Adeline - i.e. unpredictably, from 'photography at 5 francs to paintings at 20,000.'[224] The way forward for the print was beginning to become clearer.

There is a note of dandyism in prints, like those of Armand Guillaumin, where the leading characteristic is the violence of the artist's line. Oddly enough, the first editorial of the new review makes an allusion to the 'violence' implicit in the title: '*eau-forte* (acid print) is understood in its metaphorical sense.' Metaphor was used to disguise painful memories of recent events. The publisher's plan was to gather together 'some delightful, if slightly precious and self-absorbed characters', and 'to escape from the hurly burly of politics from time to time'.[225] The apparent editorial indifference to politics was deceptive, in fact. In July the magazine spoke highly of Mac-Mahon, 'the glorious victor of Magenta', and featured an etching on page one of 'his calm, serious face'. Do the ten or so etchings made by Guillaumin for *Paris à l'eau-forte*, out of the dozen he made in his lifetime, mark some kind of boundary that could not be crossed? If we remember that neither Cézanne's nor Pissarro's etchings were published in the review, although they were produced at the same time, in the same studio in Auvers-sur-Oise, even on the same day, side by side, and probably in response to the same edi-

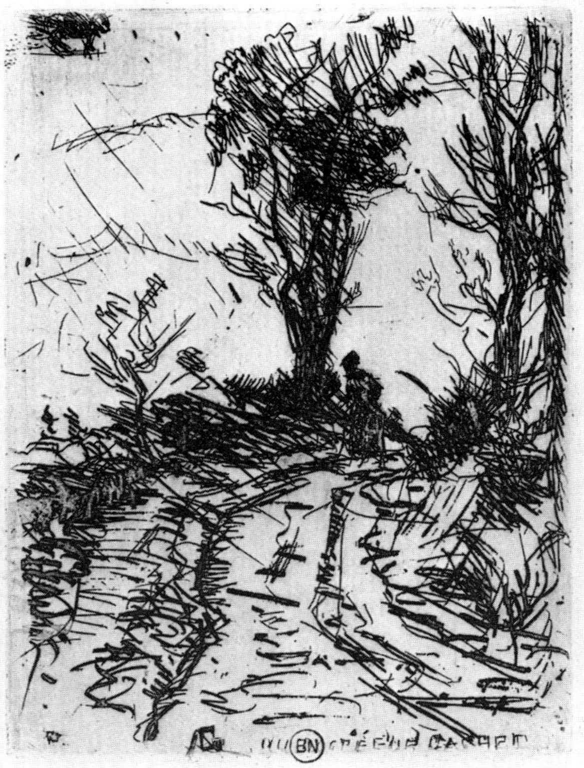

107. Armand Guillaumin,
Sunken Lane in the Hautes-Bruyères, Valley of the Bièvre. 1873.
Etching, 125 x 93 mm.
Bibliothèque nationale, Paris.

108. Van Ryssel (Dr Paul Gachet),
Sunken Lane. Les Hautes-Bruyères, near Arcueil. 1872.
Etching, 115 x 88 mm.
Bibliothèque nationale, Paris.

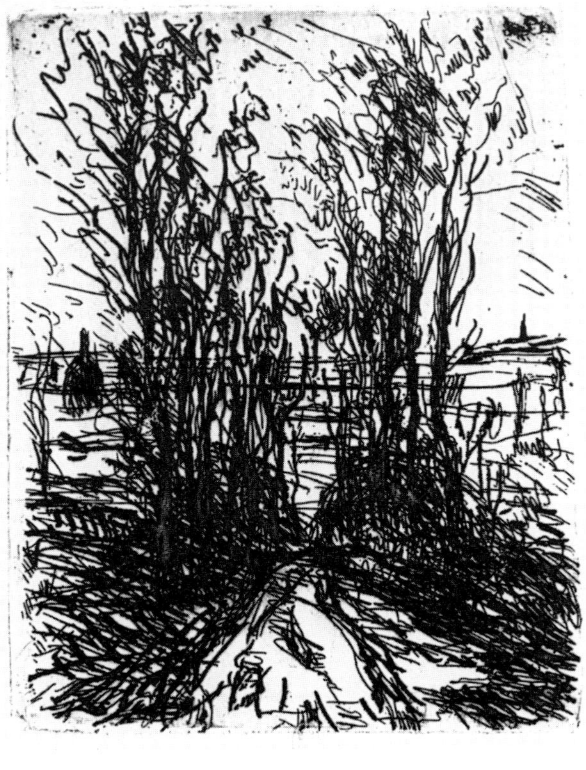

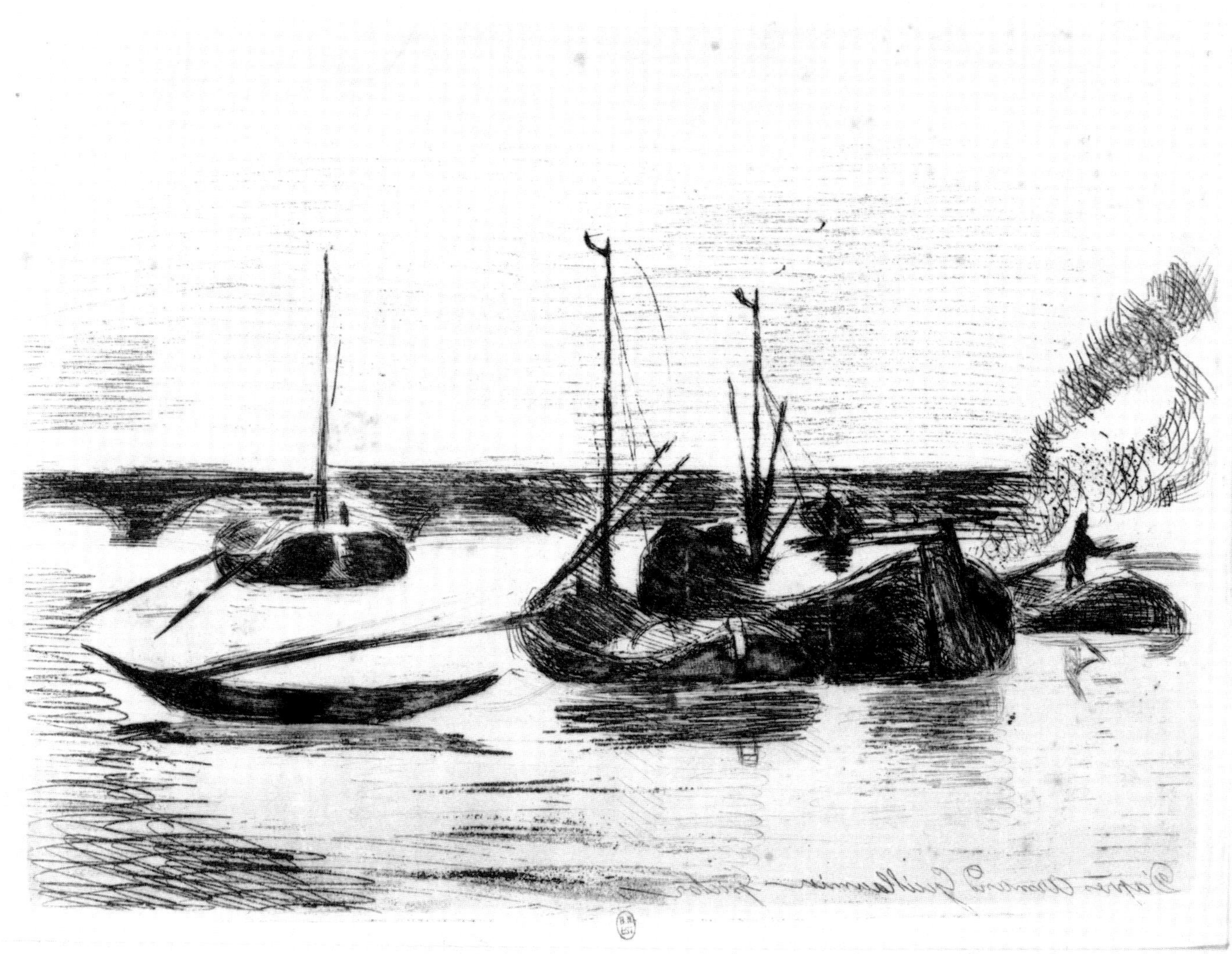

109. Paul Cézanne, *Barges at Bercy*. 1873. Etching, single state, 215 x 265 mm. Bibliothèque nationale, Paris.

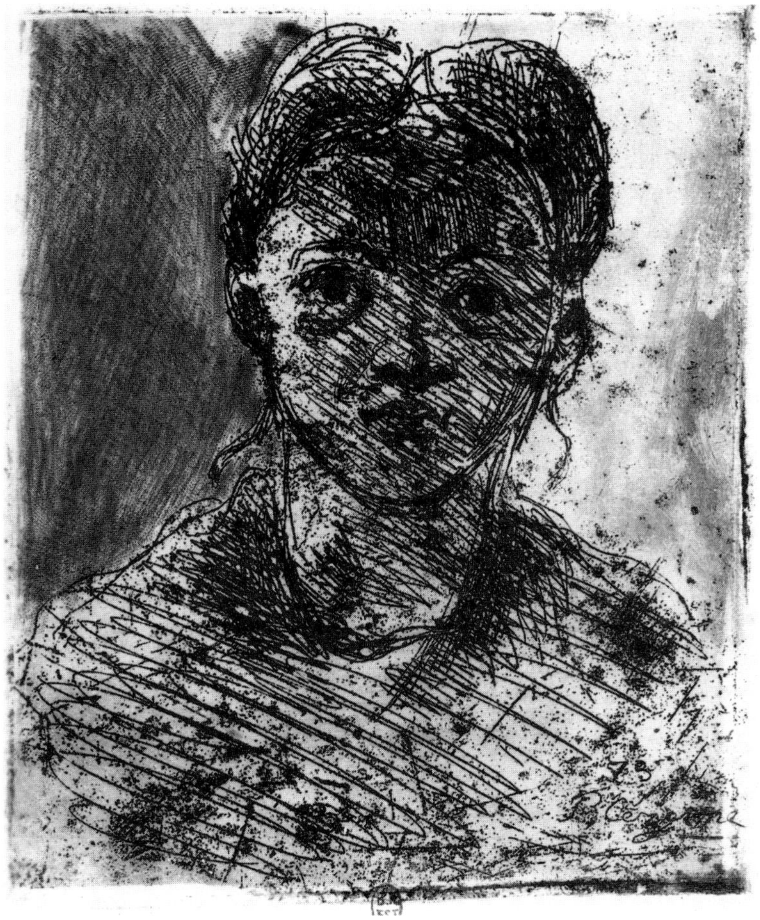

110. Paul Cézanne, *Head of a Young Girl*. 1873. Etching, single state, 129 x 95 mm. Bibliothèque nationale, Paris.

torial demands, then the answer is 'yes'.

Like Guillaumin, Cézanne practised etching only in Auvers, in July 1873, and produced even fewer plates than Guillaumin, a total of five, all exhibiting extraordinary violence.[226] A combination of his unpreparedness for the technique, the mediocre quality of his materials and his temperament resulted in five little plates marking an early but undeniable return to primitivism in printmaking: the plates are hatched and scratched and semi-destroyed rather than engraved. The copper is pitted, it is true, the varnish half torn off, and the paper is not the exquisite exotic paper used by the publisher but the first piece of paper that came to hand in the studio. Gachet printed some of his proofs in red ink. Cézanne shared subjects with his friends, and made sketches with them during their walks: *Landscape at Auvers*, *Garden at Bicêtre* (Gachet had done a *Street in Bicêtre*), *Barges at Bercy* (Fig. 109) (after a painting by Guillaumin), *Guillaumin at the House of the Hanged Man* (at the *'maison du pendu'* in Auvers). The small size of these etchings allows minimal composition and complete absence of depth, yet they are consistent; the subject is condensed into a single area and cut from the block. The tool is handled as if it were a writing instrument. The ill-controlled acid takes the mystery out of the work, and makes these a far cry from any dream landscapes. The most elaborate of Cézanne's etchings is the *Head of a Girl* (Fig. 110), with the shadow in the background worked over with a roulette. Whereas the landscapes are presented without any reworking, this simple, regular face, seen in close up and head on against quite a strong back light with its attendant shadows, has been made more dramatic: the hair is a tangle of lines, there are acid spots everywhere and the eyes are black dots.

Camille Pissarro, as we have seen, was a member of the Society of Etchers and practised etching with them. For some unknown reason (severity on the part of the jury or timidity on the artist's part?) his prints were not published. We can assume, however, from the style and format of his first plate, inspired by Corot in about 1862, and repeated in a second version that proves that

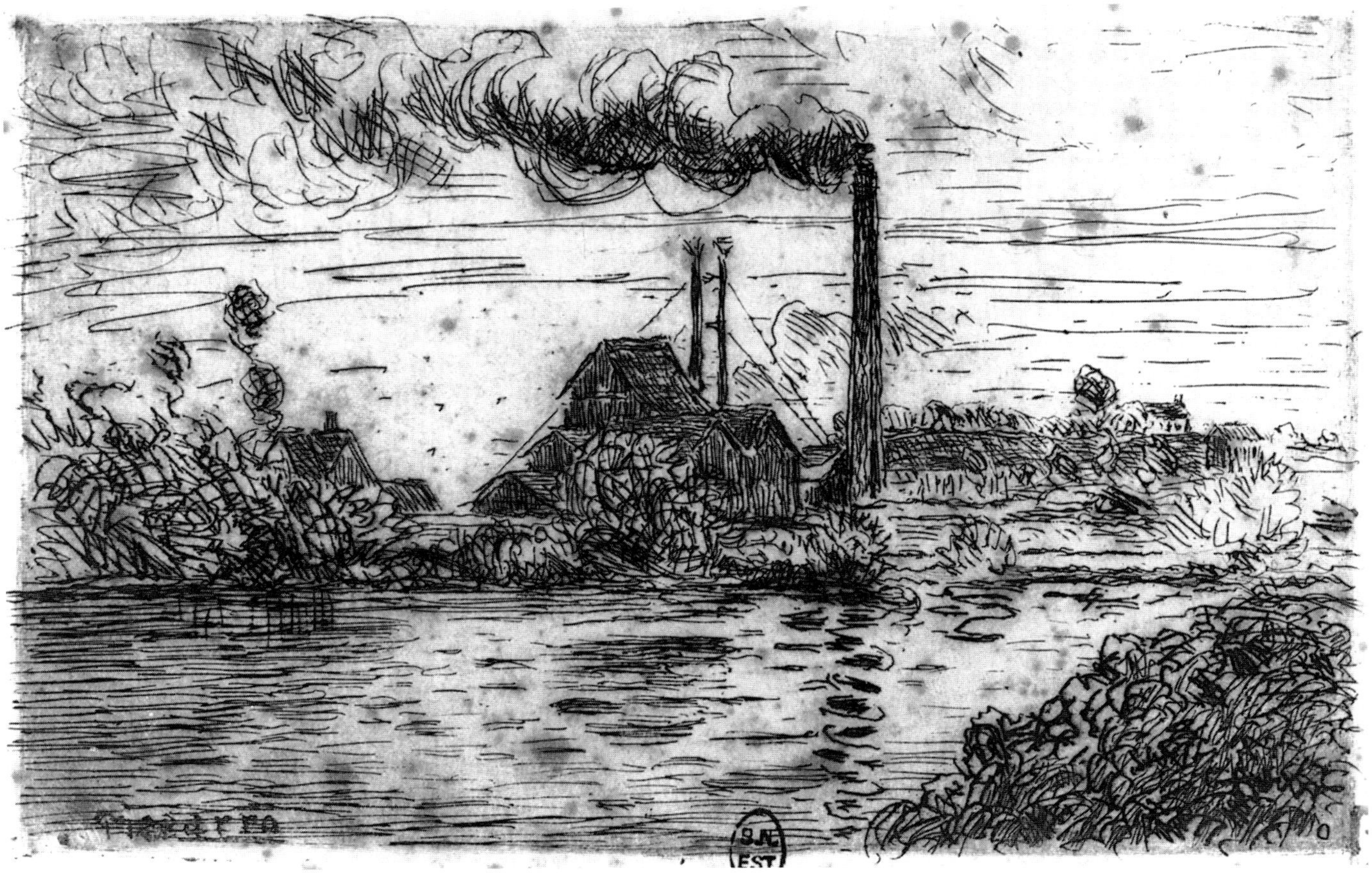

Pissarro was dissatisfied with the first, that the etching was intended for Cadart's publication.[227] The same explanation is valid for the four subsequent large plates, executed between 1863 and 1865 and unpublished. Only one print of the final one, *The Negress*, is known. The style is close to the style used by Cézanne for his head of a girl: bright shadows, busy lines, unfinished composition without depth, a sketch similar also to those of Manet. Neither the six plates of 1862–5 made for the Société des Aquafortistes nor the six subsequent ones made in the studio of Doctor Gachet in the summer of 1873 were published in *Paris à l'eau-forte*. These six small etchings were as ill-served by bad varnish and poor paper as those of Cézanne. To what extent was this due to negligence, to the studied chic of a new style, or to the self-consciousness of artists seeking authenticity? The etchings are spontaneous, using a single application of acid and a single state. Pissarro's work is less abrupt than that of Guillaumin or Cézanne, but like them he seeks an identity through his subjects: an orchard reminiscent of Daubigny (but less romantic), a barge with some sailors (the latter a novelty), a factory with a smoking chimney (Fig. 111). The factory theme had been touched on in the landscapes of Paul Huet and Daubigny but had seldom been used for its own sake; walkers in the countryside (rather than landscapes without figures), and finally a peasant woman feeding her child, after Millet. The eyes of city-dwellers like Pissarro and his friends, unaccustomed to the countryside, were watching the demise of suburban peasant themes, now giving way to towns and urban strollers.[228] These images are different from those of Corot, Huet, Daubigny or even Millet. By now realism was established and did not need flaunting. The humdrum nature of the scenes is conveyed by harsh, exaggerated strokes or, in the case of the interior scene, by a 'sauce' which obscures the room, drowning the two figures in darkness. Guillaumin's offhand style, Cézanne's roughness, Pissarro's sincerity are the new virtues of art. Doctor Gachet's house was certainly one of the seed-beds of Impressionism. Doctor Gachet himself, the architect of this little group, had taken the pseudonym Van Ryssel ('from Lille' in Flemish). His etchings also pioneered new techniques (Figs 106, 108), using thicker ink and

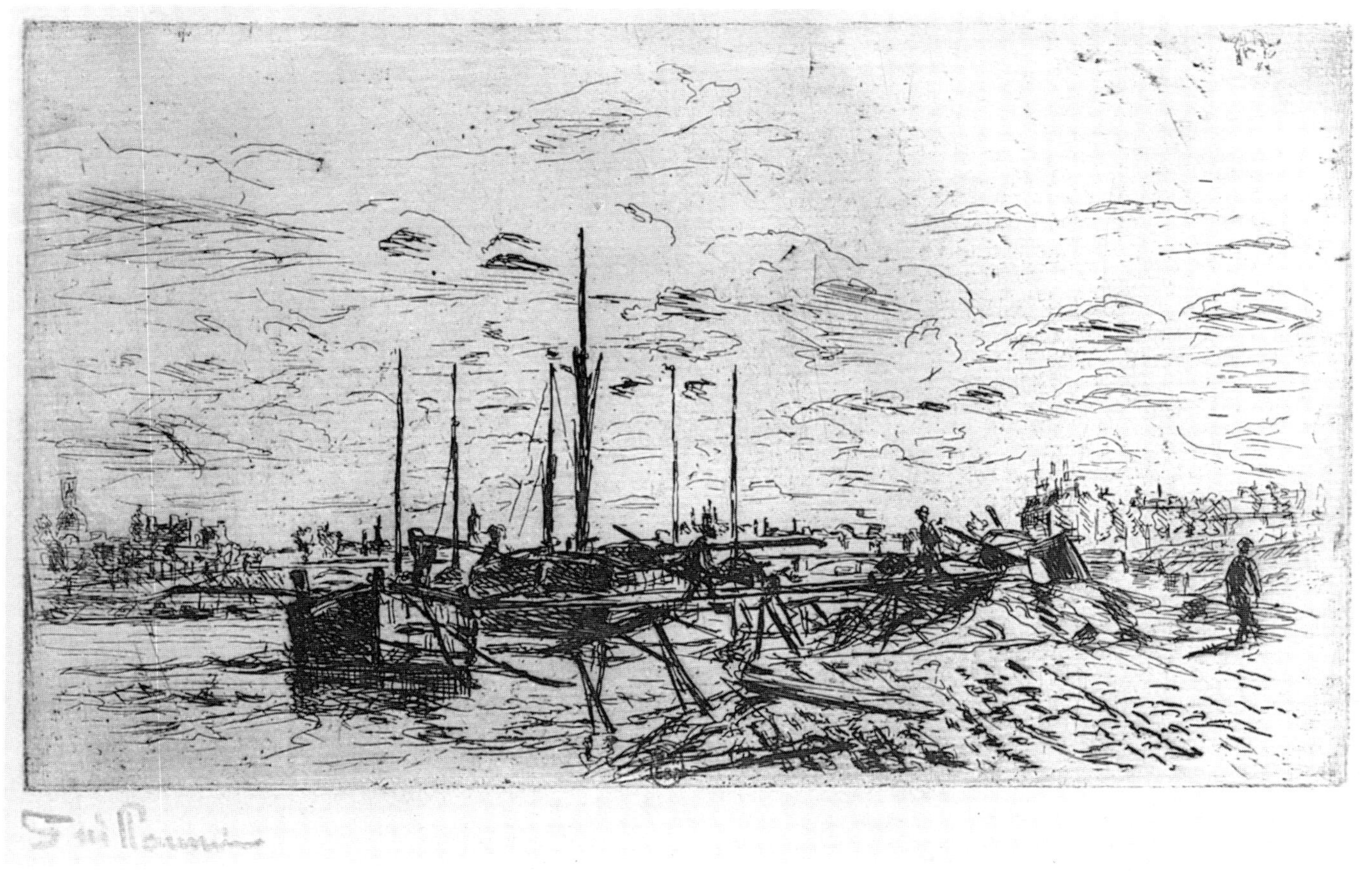

experiments with aquatint; there is one coloured print, *Madame Gachet at the Piano*.[229] He also copied Millet (*The Nurse*, 1874 and *The Woman Spinning*, 1875).

Paris à l'eau-forte was short-lived, ceasing publication in 1876, but the prints came to dominate more and more, because of their size, their variety and the reputation of the printmakers. After Régamey's departure for England the review took on Félicien Rops and André Gill, the mentor of the young Forain who had his first engravings printed there: more importantly, however, they elicited the collaboration of two young artists who were to play a major rôle in the new generation of engravers: Henri Guérard and Félix Buhot. These confirmed the magazine in its vocation as the artistic and experimental field of those 'delightful, slightly precious and self-absorbed characters', just like the public it aimed to attract; the future Impressionists Guillaumin, Pissarro and Cézanne were so near to them at the time, and yet so very far from them.

112. Armand Guillaumin,
Port de Charenton, the 'Deux Lions' Ferry. 1873.
Etching, 82 x 110 mm.
Bibliothèque nationale, Paris.

previous page:
111. Camille Pissarro,
Factory at Pontoise.
Etching, single state, 73 x 115 mm.
Bibliothèque nationale, Paris.

23. *The Return of the Artist's Lithograph*

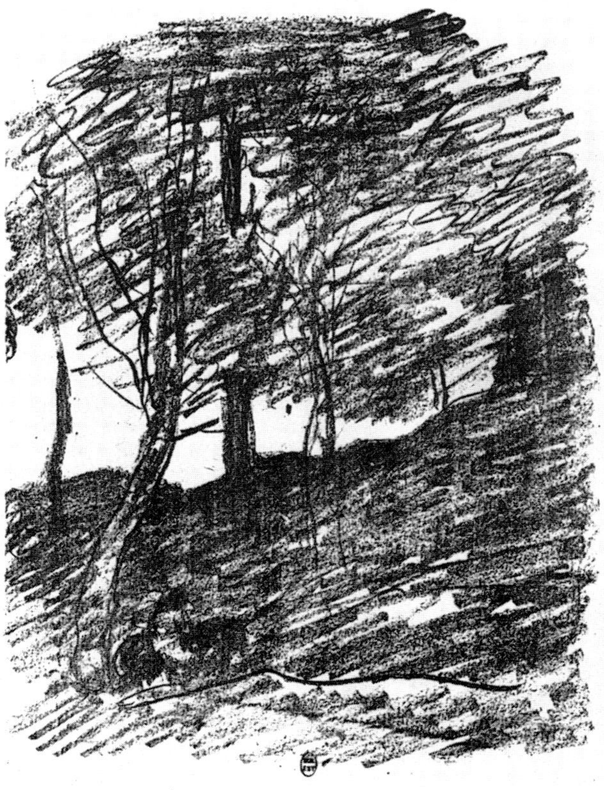

113. Jean-Baptiste Corot, *Woodland*. 1871. Lithograph, 222 x 168 mm. Bibliothèque nationale, Paris.

114. Camille Pissarro, *Portrait of Lucien*. 1874. Lithograph, 203 x 240 mm. Museum of Fine Arts, Boston, Stephen Bullard Memorial Fund.

The 'Fédération des Artistes de Paris', established on 14 April 1871 during the Commune, consisted of an executive committee of thirty-seven members, six of whom were printmakers 'representing the decorative arts, incorrectly termed the industrial arts.'[230] During the turmoil of the Revolution the divorce between art and industry was recognised by the printmakers themselves. Once again now, the history of printmaking moved in two separate directions, one strand joining the slowly developing decorative arts, the other, allying itself tangentially with the archetypal *objet d'art*, the easel painting.

After 1870 it was impossible not to be aware that pictorial reproduction was bound to become industrialised. Photography, the means of mass reproduction at a low price, had yet to be discovered but new inventions were constantly appearing. Poitevin was perfecting his photolithographic processes. The electrotyping of drawings had reached industrial proportions. The Firmin Gillot factory was growing all the time. The small workshop in the rue Chevalier-du-Guet moved twice, first to 23 quai Saint-Michel then to 175 faubourg Saint-Martin. After Firmin's death in 1872 his son Charles continued the business successfully, opening a photogravure studio in 1876.[231] Zinc plates began to replace stone and the use of transfer paper meant that draughtsmen no longer needed to use metal plates; they could also draw subjects as they would finally appear: the transfer of the drawing on to zinc, then from the zinc to the print re'established the drawing in its original direction. Daumier's final lithographs, with their spirited drawing but mediocre printing (*Le Charivari* went over to 'gillotage', or galvanoplasty, in due time) bear witness to these technical developments. Artists were attracted to these modern facilities. Although 'gillotage' meant that nuances were sacrificed and drawings altered, it permitted the growing demand for magazines and albums to be met. The *Autographe au Salon* of 1863–5 was succeeded by *L'Album autographique* of 1867 and later by collections of works of art reproduced by different processes: in 1868, *Le Salon* with artists' drawings, in 1869 *Le Musée universel*, in 1873 *Le Panthéon des illustrations françaises*, in 1874 *L'Album Boetzel*. One of the most remarkable was *L'Art pour tous, encyclopédie de l'art industriel et décoratif*, by Claude Sauvageot, published between 1868 and 1871. The clear objective

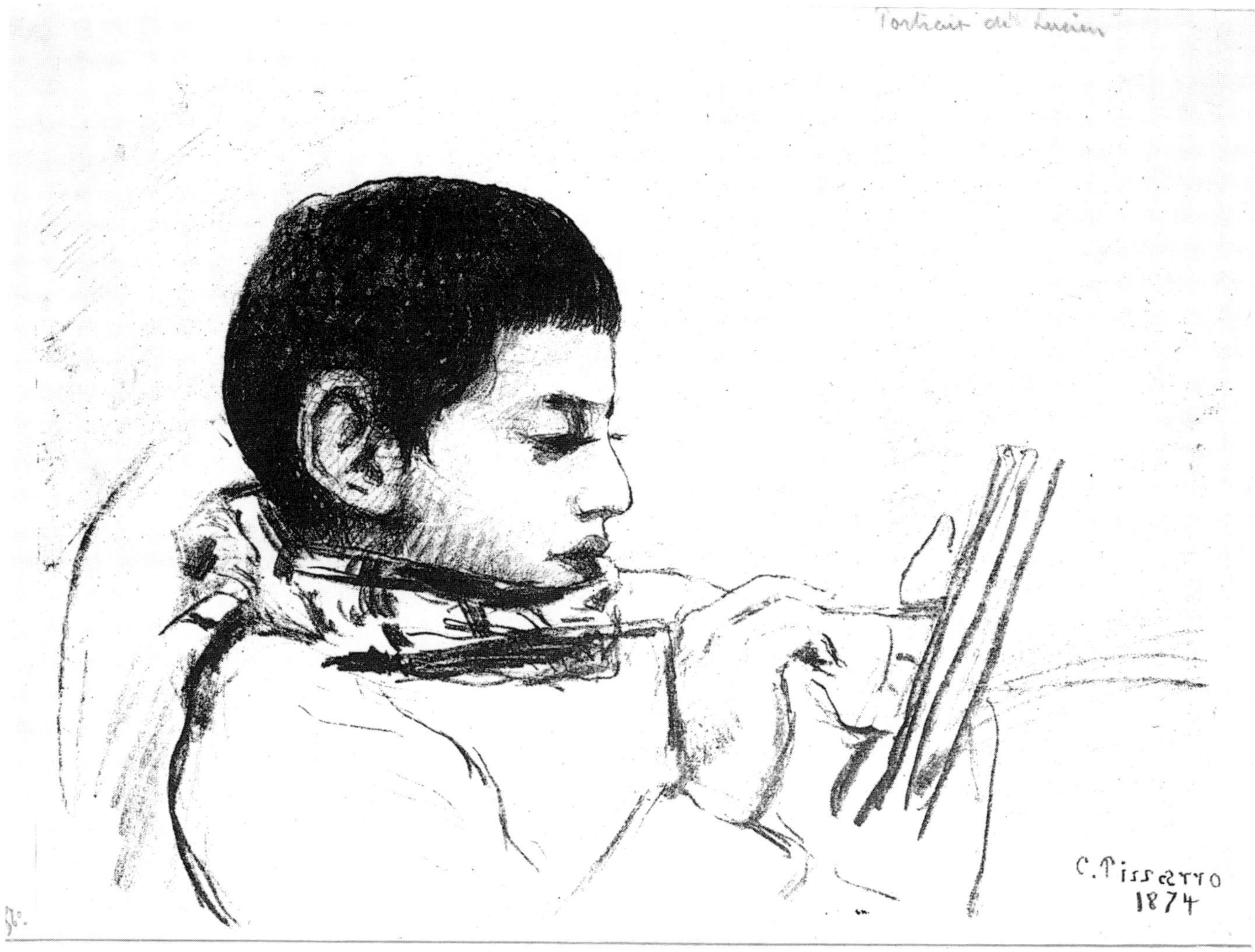

of such publications was to expand the art market, by instilling the appreciation of art into the middle classes. They compensated for the acknowledged inadequacy of the Salons, for which the bell was beginning to toll. The Fédération des artistes de Paris laid the foundations of an independent association. The same spirit prevailed in the Société nationale des artistes français in 1881, in the Société nationale des beaux-arts in 1889, but also in the Société anonyme des peintres, the group formed by the Impressionists, established in 1874.

Corot, like Courbet and Daumier, had supported the Fédération des artistes de Paris. He spent the war in Paris but on 1 April 1871 his friends persuaded him to leave the capital and to join Desavary in Arras, then Robaut in Douai, where he painted the famous *Belfry*. It was in Douai that Robaut, having published a collection of facsimiles of drawings by Delacroix, had the idea of suggesting to Corot that he make lithographs on transfer paper (Fig. 113). Moreau-Nélaton expresses it well: 'the lithographer who was his host put a wax crayon into his hands and he drew charming scenes on autographic paper, which M. Robaut then printed and published.'[232] The cover of the collection bears the title: 'Twelve sketches and original drawings by Corot on autographic paper . . . printed in an edition of fifty copies'. This album, owing so much to circumstances, played a major role in reviving the faith that some artists had placed at an earlier date in the lithograph. As in 1862, the year when Cadart threw himself into the same enterprise, it was somewhat premature, but henceforth the lithograph enjoyed periods of success until the 1890s, when it was condemned finally to death by the preference shown by industry for photogravure; in its turn, however, thirty years after the etching, the lithograph became a desirable and rare collector's item.

Fantin-Latour had been in Cadart's team and was familiar with the lithograph, which suited his generous style of drawing. He owned and admired Corot's collection.[233] He opposed the Empire as solidly as he had opposed the excesses of the Commune; he spent the Siege of Paris studying the old masters and music. Having been requested to paint a picture in memory of Schumann, for the erection of a monument in Bonn, he met with failure and made do with a lithograph, *In*

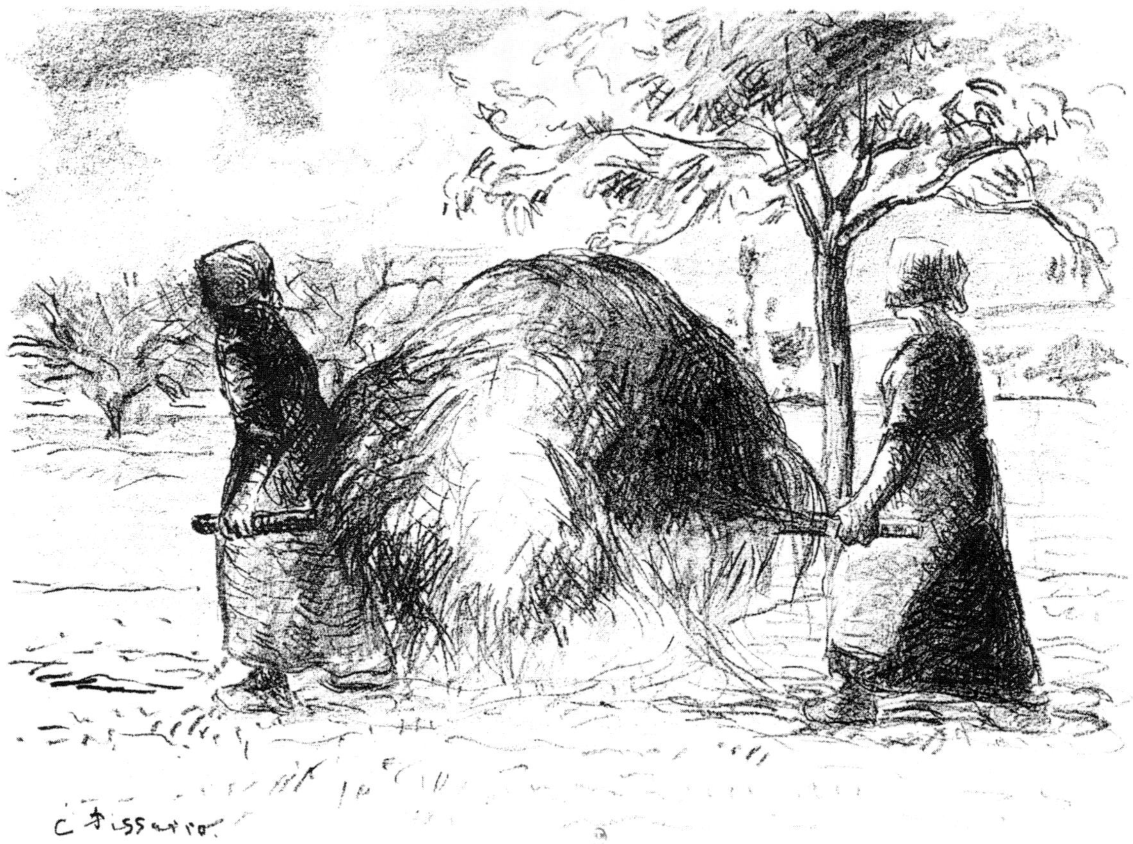

Memory of Robert Schumann, 17, 18, 19 August 1873, then a second one, *The Alpine Fairy*. These commemorative works belong to the tradition of the Romantic lithograph in both style and subject. Fantin-Latour uses Bonington's atmospheric haze, Delacroix's scratched effect and Célestin Nanteuil's contrasts. Nevertheless his work demonstrates a new desire for autonomy. He was an admirer of Whistler and a friend of Manet, and was at the heart of the so-called 'Batignolles School', but was an immediate opponent of the Impressionists. He turned away from Manet, and may have persuaded him not to join the group in 1874; in 1875 he accused him of betraying the realist aesthetic of the 1860s. He regarded Impressionism as a 'caricature' of what the realists had attempted to do, and considered himself 'compromised' by them. In 1875 he tried again with *The Birthday, Homage to Berlioz* (who died in 1869); this produced a painting, a success this time, and another large lithograph.

The realism developed by the Impressionists had nothing in common with Romanticism or Aestheticism; it can be observed in Camille Pissarro's earliest lithographs produced in 1874. During his years in Paris Pissarro lived on an allowance from his mother, but when the family business began to collapse in 1868 he had to take over financial responsibility for himself and his family.[234] In February 1874 he was faced with a difficult monetary situation as well as the tragic illness of his daughter, Jeanne. Pissarro did not know yet that his child was going to die, but his letters to Doctor Gachet are full of foreboding. The doctor's best efforts could not save the child, who died on 6 April. Pissarro and Gachet had worked at etching together in 1873. It is not clear, however, why Pissarro made sketches on transfer paper beside his daughter's bedside and had them printed in Paris by the lithographer Tailliardat. The portrait of Jeanne bears the date 3 February 1874; it was drawn from life. It seems extraordinary that the artist should have chosen for his first attempts at lithography a subject so painfully close to the heart as a portrait of his dying daughter; he also drew his son Lucien (Fig. 114), well wrapped up and also drawing. These family scenes were probably not intended for publication (and this displays quite a different attitude towards art from the traditional attitude of Fantin-Latour) and must have been simply exercises in technique. Confirmation of this hypothesis is provided by the fact that Pissarro used transfer paper at this period, using pen or wax crayon, to make ten other lithographs of rustic scenes, of medium or large, size, which evidently were intended to provide material for an album for publication. The example of Corot must have been influential; Pissarro declared himself a pupil of Corot and his first etchings were inspired by him. Only one, two or a maximum of three copies were printed of his first twelve lithographs, and his hopes that this series would produce some income were deceived. The series forms the third stage (after those of Corot and Fantin-Latour) in the emancipation of the lithograph. The style is unhesitatingly modern: the subjects are deliberately rustic and the style, even in the pen lithographs *The Oise at Pontoise* (Fig. 116) and *House at L'Hermitage*, provocative. The pictures of labourers in the fields, done with a lithographic crayon, including *Haymakers*, *Women carrying Hay* (Fig. 115), go beyond realism in their search for raw sensation and a brightness in which the paper plays an important part. These features make them the first lithographs that can be qualified properly as Impressionist.

It was Whistler who cleared the next hurdle, the fourth. In 1878 he picked up his lithographic crayon again (Fig. 118), having abandoned it since his youthful exercises in 1855 in the United States. We know exactly in what circumstances Whistler took up lithography again – as we did not with Pissarro. His biographer, Pennell, recounts that 'in 1878 he made his first experiments in lithography. His attention had been called to it by Mr Thomas Way, who did more than any other man to revive the art in England . . . . (Way) prepared stones for them, explained processes and would not hear of difficulties . . . Mr Way appealed to Whistler, who tried the stone, grasped its possibilities and was delighted. In his first five lithographs he did things never attempted before and found the medium suited him. During the year he made nine prints on the stone, though his later work was done on lithographic paper. He proposed to publish this first series as *Art Notes*, but there was no demand and the plan fell through. *The Toilette* and the *Broad Bridge* were printed in *Piccadilly* (1878) edited by Mr Watts-Dunton, and they had hardly appeared when the magazine came to an end.;[235]

Whether in the hands of Corot, Fantin-Latour, Pissarro or Whistler, the lithograph continued to be a commercial, publishers' item. The market for lithographs was so patently linked to reproduction that it would have been impossible not to suspect artists practising the technique of being primarily interested in gaining an income from it. Before he emigrated to Canada on 17 June 1873, Rodolphe Bresdin had transferred his eight precious etchings to stone, with the intention of creating a stock of prints to sell off like popular prints.[236] When Odilon

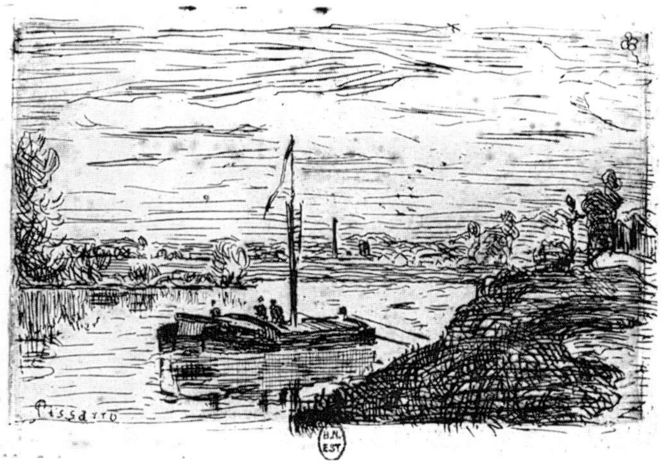

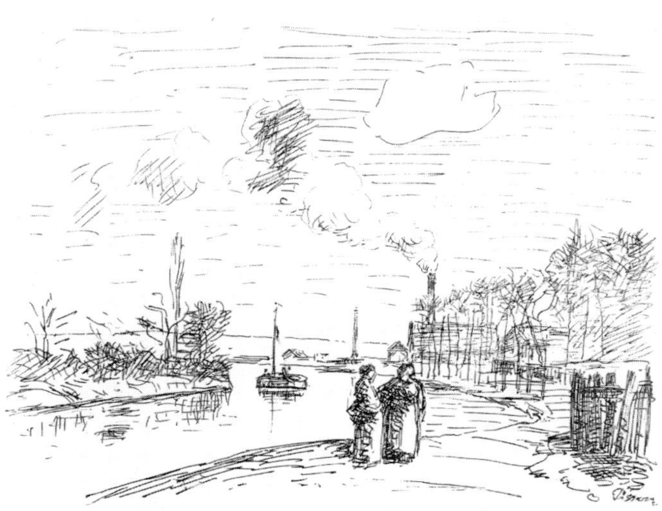

116. Camille Pissarro,
The Oise at Pontoise. 1874.
Etching, single state, 75 x 115 mm.
Bibliothèque Nationale, Paris.

117. Camille Pissarro,
The Oise at Pontoise. 1874.
Lithograph, single state, 218 x 278 mm.
British Museum, London.

Previous page:
115. Camille Pissarro.
Women Carrying Hay on a Stretcher.
About 1874.
Lithograph, single state, 215 x 292 mm.
Bibliothèque nationale, Paris.

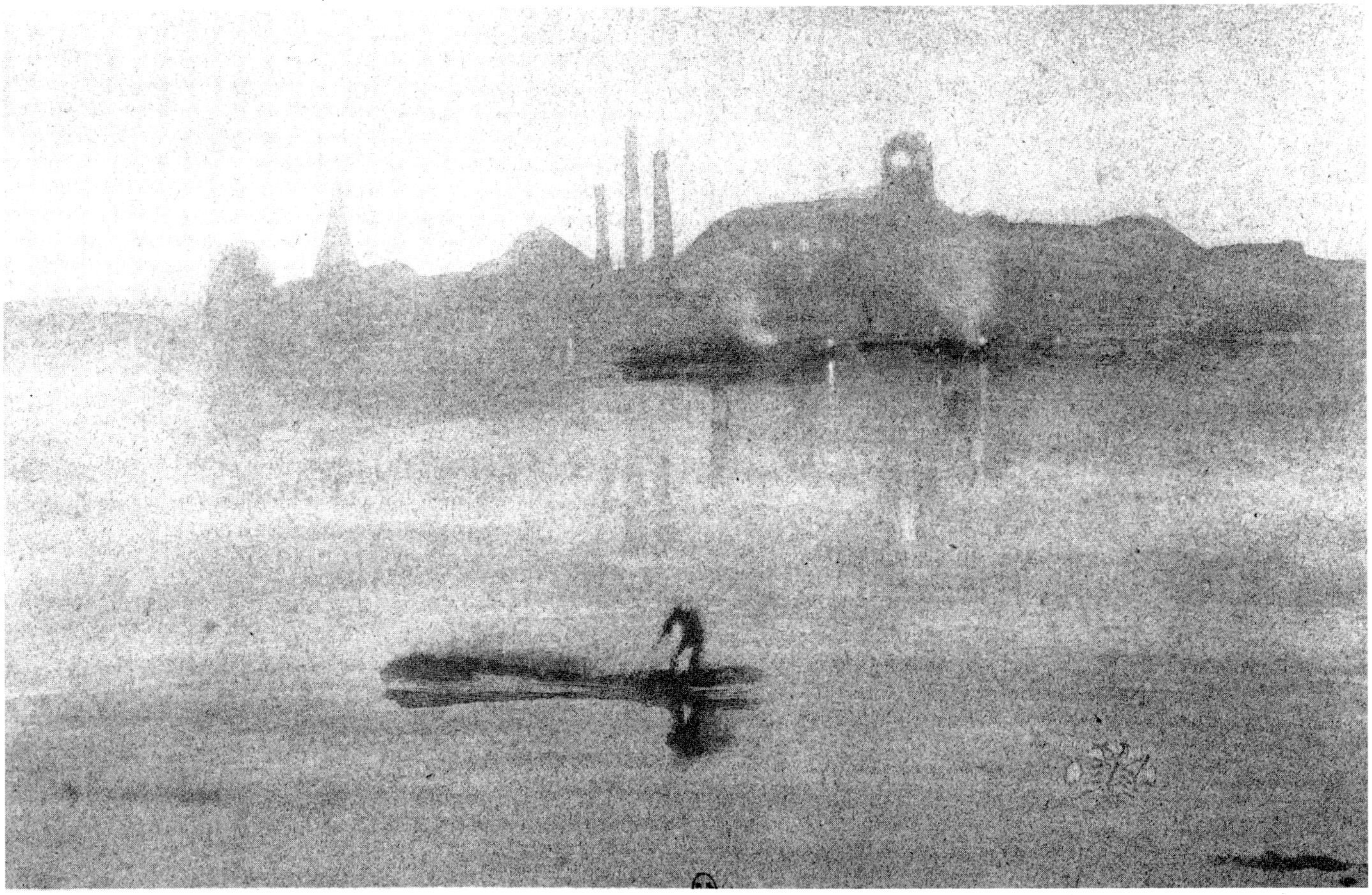

118. James McNeill Whistler, *Nocturne: the River at Battersea*. 1878. Lithograph, first state, 170 x 257 mm. Bibliothèque nationale, Paris.

Redon decided to produce some lithographs in 1879 he too was looking for a means of circulating his drawings as widely as possible. We owe his lithography to the heretical example of his teacher, Bresdin, to whose example should also be added that of Daumier, fervently admired by Pissarro and Degas. After 1870 Daumier's lithographs began to develop towards Impressionism: the drawing became more restless and more inclined to improvisation; light (including larger tracts of blank paper) began to invade the page, the latter development being perhaps imposed by the Gillot process and the printing machinery. If Daumier can be categorised as a forerunner of Impressionism it is more on account of the extreme simplification of his last drawings than of any concern for lighting effects or realism; all the artists of his generation shared these concerns. Daumier was involved in the industrial reproduction of pictures, he was a journalist, and as such was forgotten by the critics and spurned by collectors; it was not until after his death, when the lithograph was accorded the status of a work of art, that he was rediscovered. This reversal of opinion can be seen in the work of Odilon Redon, starting in 1879,[237] the year when the half-blind Daumier died in Valmondois, in the little house given him by Corot, his death going unnoticed by his colleagues.

24. *1874: The First Impressionist Exhibition*

The period of recession that followed the economic expansion of the Second Empire led to a general reorganisation of artists into different groups; the artists had become too numerous and too diverse for the Salon to represent them all in any significant way, and the welcome they were beginning to receive from the first private galleries, fragile even before the recession, was now no longer available. Printmaking faced the same double handicap. The Salon had never been the mainstay of their market, but now that competition from mechanical methods of reproduction was slowly killing the engraved reproduction, honoured for years in the Salon and the academies, the artist's print was meeting the same difficulties with publishers as other works of art were meeting with their dealers. It is no surprise, therefore, to find printmakers, with Bracquemond in the lead, the most abundantly represented group in the first exhibition mounted by the 'Société anonyme coopérative des artistes peintres, sculpteurs, graveurs, etc.' at 35 boulevard des Capucines, in premises rented by Nadar, from 15 April to 15 May 1874.

A nostalgic vision, to a great extent the fabrication of an over-indulgent history of art, has transformed the Impressionist exhibitions into a sort of golden legend of modern art. Recent historiography (post-1974, or thereabouts)[239] has trimmed down these excesses which, to quote Nathalie Heinich 'were based more on celebration than on information'. Their effect was 'to desert the history of art in order to vindicate a style',[240] in the words of Jean-Paul Bouillon, who rightly considers the first exhibition by the group to have been, in many respects, a 'non-event'. It might have sunk without trace if a minority of artists in the group had not doggedly persevered with their so-called 'Impressionist' style, a style whose roots, in fact, had struck well before and extended well beyond the ephemeral event historically viewed as its début.

The treasurer of the Société anonyme coopérative, the sculptor Auguste Ottin, in whose house the headquarters of the society was located, was already running a movement entitled the 'Intransigeants du Pinceau' in Montmartre; his son Léon, the only person to have exhibited a lithograph in 1874, had taken part in the Commune. It was certainly not style (theirs was very traditional) that brought these artists into contact with

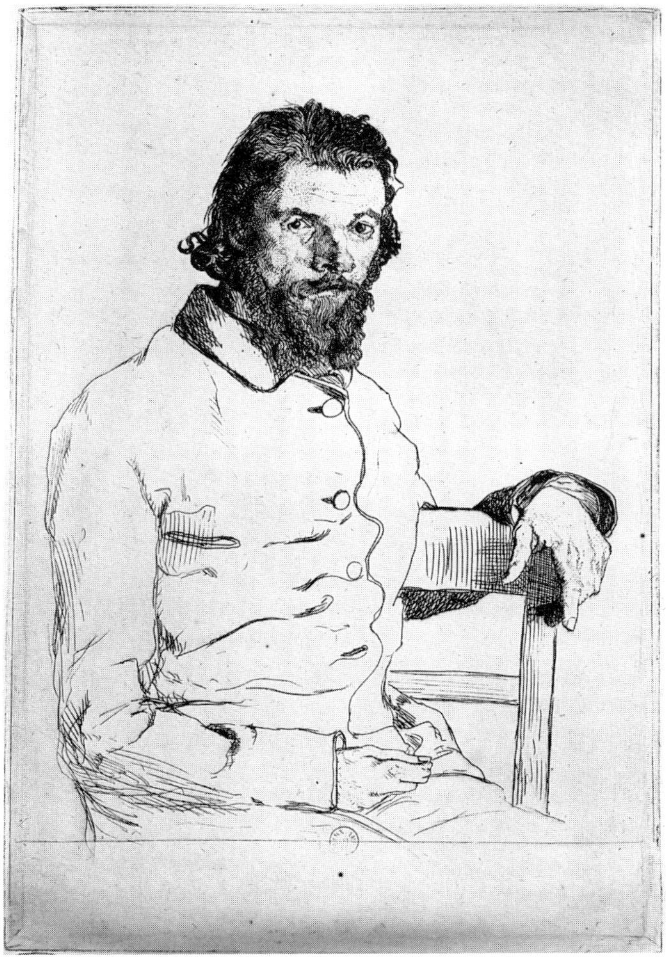

119. Félix Bracquemond, *Portrait of Meryon*. 1853. Etching, 230 x 154 mm. Bibliothèque nationale, Paris.

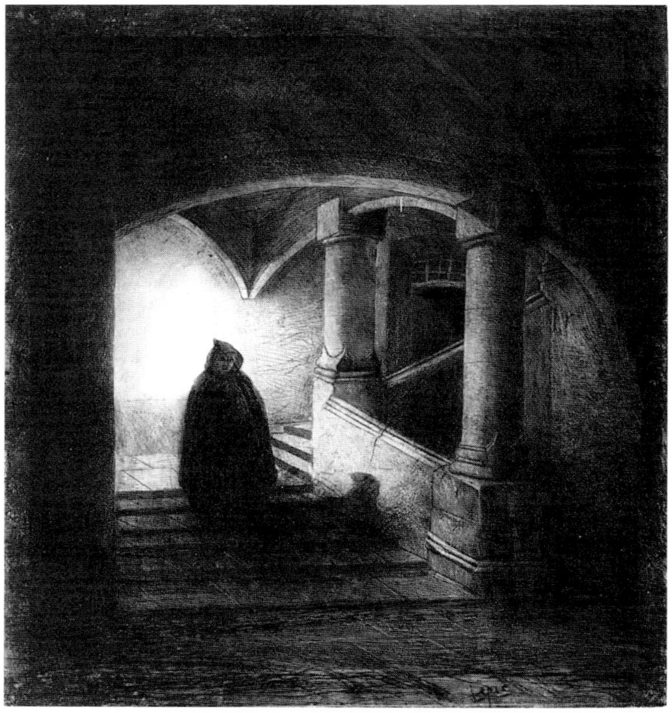

120. Viscount Lepic,
Staircase in the Château d'Aix-en-Savoie. 1863.
Etching, 460 x 385 mm.
Bibliothèque nationale, Paris.

the 'Argenteuil Group', the future Impressionists, known at the time as the Révoltés.[241] The absence of any overriding doctrine, strongly insisted upon by Degas at their first, highly eclectic, exhibition led to a situation of gathering conflict until, in the 1880s, it brought about the decline of the group, which the condition of the market had by now made redundant in any case.

The whole gamut of styles was not represented at the exhibition in the boulevard des Capucines; reaction to academicism was something of a common denominator, but it was not over-emphasised. Marginal organisations attract marginal people, and the Impressionist exhibitions were a focus for opposition activities, sharing the disputed territory already fought over by the etching fraternity. Successful opposition was, however, broadly accepted by this time, even looked forward to by a large number of intellectuals and eagerly anticipated by a class of new collectors who welcomed the new forms of art; their only problem for the next ten years or so was to be insolvency.

It is not possible to make a systematic contrast between the academic Salon and an avant-garde group. With regard to modernism, the print section of the official Salon of 1874 had nothing to be ashamed of. Félix Bracquemond would have fitted in well. Included were a number of 'free' etchers, forerunners of Impressionism: Adolphe Appian, who continued to support the Salon for years, Xavier de Dananche, Maxime Lalanne, Edwin Edwards and a young artist, Henri Guérard, introduced as a pupil of Berthon but who was to become a faithful follower of Manet and the valued assistant of his declining years.

To this new, more accurate analysis of Impressionism should be added a few comments concerning printmaking in particular. Printmakers, like sculptors, were expressly mentioned in the title of the 'Société anonyme coopérative des artistes peintres, sculpteurs, graveurs, etc., and in this 'etc.' lies an important indicator of the more open attitude to the plastic arts; we know what use the future was to make of this 'etc.'. It is striking to notice in the catalogue the large number of works on paper – drawings, pastels, watercolours in addition to the prints. Zola's image of the 'sweetshop', used to characterise the diversity of styles required to satisfy the needs of the purchasers of modern art of the day, is embodied here. Paintings constituted only half the works on show. Techniques were not divided according to hierarchy, as they were in the Salon. The blending of styles and techniques redeemed the print and this redemption was later sanctified by the Société des peintres-graveurs (the Society of painter/printmakers).

A second observation concerns the support that the system of print dealers could offer to the developing free market for painting. Unlike paintings, prints had for years benefited from a comprehensive network of commercial distributors. It seems extraordinary that, in order to cope with the first expansion of the art market in the

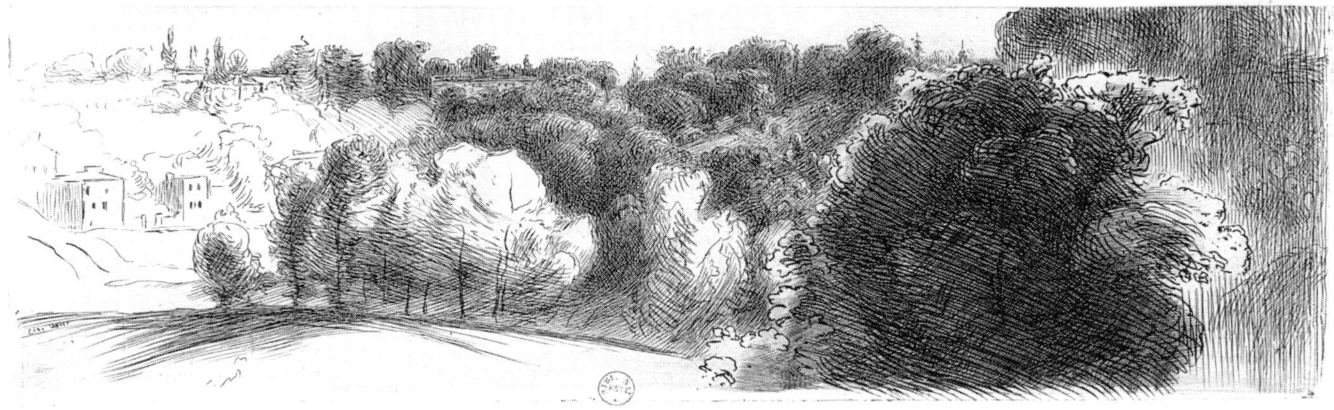

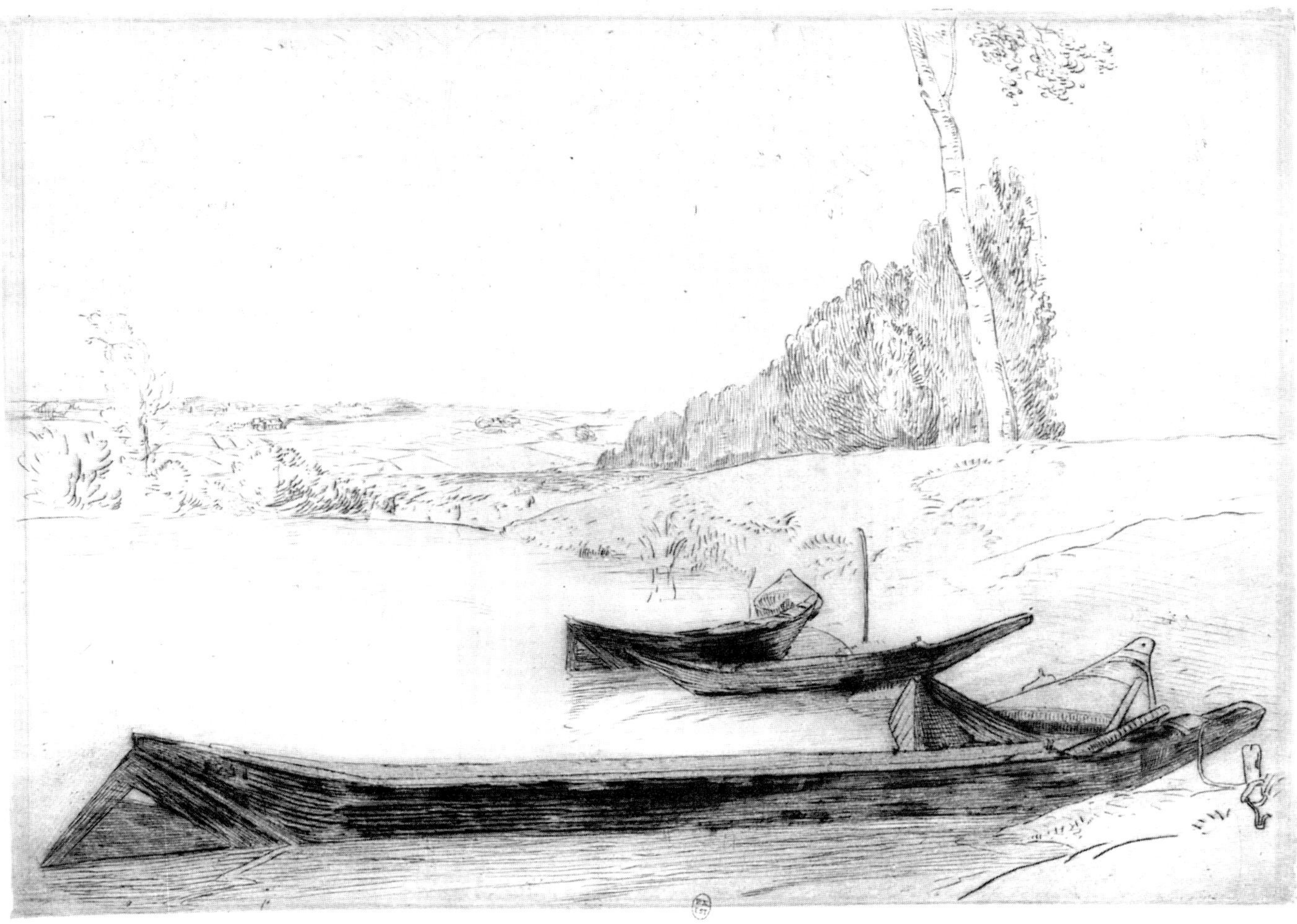

121. Félix Bracquemond,
Uphill Road in Bellevue. 1873.
Etching, 99 x 316 mm.
Bibliothèque nationale, Paris.

122. Félix Bracquemond,
Punts by the Seine. About 1858 (?).
Etching, 250, 250 x 349 mm.
Bibliothèque nationale, Paris.

early 1860s, the groups of 'free' artists linked to galleries (one to Martinet, the other to Cadart) used the shop window of two publishers and print dealers, thereby aiming at the same clientèle. This new combination, a group of artists and a dealer, was inspired by the well-established combination of two existing structures: the societies of print collectors, financed by private subscriptions since the eighteenth century, and certain dealers like Basan. Such a system was well-suited to the print: the process of reproduction and publishing assumes quite a far-flung clientèle. In the mid-nineteenth century painting was confronted by the need for such a system for the first time. The method of having groups of artists linked to particular dealers did not last, and neither did the artists' cooperatives proposed by Pissarro and based on the bakers' cooperative in Pontoise. In fact, as soon as there was a market, dealers began to appear.

Only four of the thirty artists who exhibited in the boulevard des Capucines presented any prints, and three of these four presented very few: a lithograph of a sheepfold by Léon-Auguste Ottin, three etchings by Vicomte Lepic (Fig. 120) and two by Stanislas-Henri Rouart, who had brought ten or so prints, the sum total of his known printed work, back from a trip to Venice.[242] The ever-present Bracquemond was there, of course, with five large frames of etchings, each containing several prints, a total of thirty-two in all chosen to represent all the registers of the medium. The collection of portraits (Fig. 119) alone constituted a salute to contemporary printmaking, comparable to the mixed portraits painted by Fantin-Latour for his friends. Bracquemond's spiritual leaders were on show: Auguste Comte, the philosopher of progress, his patrons Meyer, Heim, Hoschedé and Edwin Edwards, the illustrator Charles Keene, the engravers Legros and Meryon and the critics Théophile Gautier and Baudelaire. The second frame contained etched reproductions of paintings, paying tribute to the original artists with their free style: Manet, Rubens, Ingres, Leys, de Balleroy and above all Turner's astonishing steam engine (Fig. 123). The boldness of the painting *Rain, Steam and Speed, the Great Western Railway*, which had been the toast of the Royal Academy in 1844, became part of the aesthetic of the Impressionists. Bracquemond's interpretation of the picture, what is more, was presented in an unfinished version as if to provoke the spectator even further. The third frame presented the genre that had recently won praise in both etching and modern painting: landscape (Figs 121–2), and Bracquemond's use of drypoint, mentioned in the catalogue, foreshadowed the Impressionist handling of the same theme. The fourth frame contained examples of illustration, with the title page of *Les Fleurs du Mal* and a scene from *Capitaine Fracasse*. Finally, the last frame held the famous portrait of Erasmus (Fig. 75), after Holbein, refused by the Salon in 1863, with a variant crucial to the understanding of contemporary printmaking: two different states of the same print were presented side by side, fulfilling the dealer Rochoux's prophecy. Rouchoux was indignant at the thought that reproductive engravers would shortly be contesting their artistic prowess with that of painters, or might be taking their place, or, perish the thought, even becoming 'authors'. Bracquemond's participation in this exhibition was more than just a presence: it was a manifesto, a retrospective and a programme for the future.

It would be a mistake to regard the print as being represented in the first Impressionist exhibition solely by the works on show there. Many of the painters taking part were also printmakers: Cézanne showed *The House of the Hanged Man*, a *Landscape at Auvers* and *A Modern Olympia*, a sketch belonging to Doctor Gachet; Guillaumin showed a painting that also belonged to Doctor Gachet; and in particular De Nittis, Degas and Pissarro, although they had only recently started out as printmakers. Among those not represented, some printmakers would certainly have found a place: first Desboutin, who showed his drypoints in the second exhibition in 1876, with thirteen works, six of which were drypoint *Portraits and Studies*; Alphonse Legros only joined the group for the second exhibition, with two lithographs and a massive display of twenty-five etchings and drypoints of which, following Bracquemond's example, two only were presented in their first state alone ('Death, first state before the drypoint', states the catalogue).

Other members of the group had had experience in print making or were aware of its potential. Some of these had emerged from the armies of artisans employed by the printing workshops on which the industrial production of images had conferred such prosperity. Adolphe Cals began his career as an apprentice to the engravers Ancelin, Ponce and Bosc.[243] Jean-Baptiste Léopold Levert, a friend of Rouart and Degas and a regular exhibitor with them, took part in the first, second and third exhibitions and the fifth, in 1880; as well as paintings he showed a frame of etchings in the fifth. Others had been made aware of the print by lithographs published in *L'Artiste*: Ludovic Piette published a lithograph, *The Phantoms*, in 1859 and Louis Debras *In the Appennines* in 1861. Finally Jean-Baptiste Millet presented some wood engravings from compositions by his brother Jean-François in the second exhibition in 1876. These occupy a position of particular importance as the incunabula of the artists' woodcut, which did not become really successful until the last decade of the century. Gustave Colin, who took part in the first Impressionist exhibition, was a painter from Arras, a pupil of Dutilleux, who had been showing *Scenes from Spain* in the Salon since 1867; he was also the part author (with friends from Arras) of glass prints influenced by Corot.

It should be pointed out that only half of the thirty participants in the exhibition have been mentioned here. The other half paid no heed to printmaking. This lack of

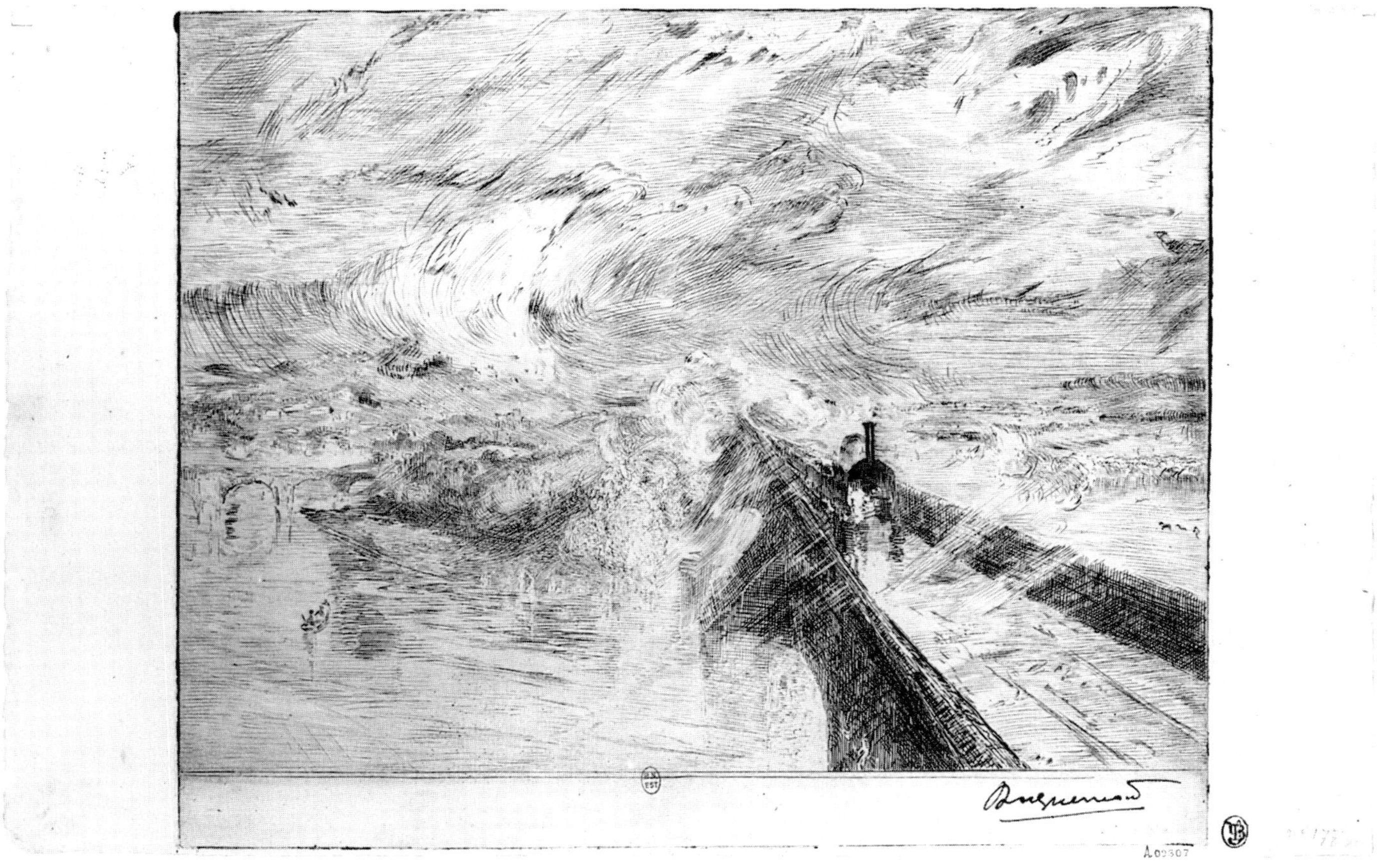

interest diminished with the years and the presence of important engravers such as Forain or Raffaëlli was later to cause problems.

123. Félix Bracquemond, *Locomotive, after Turner*. 1873. Etching, first state, 202 x 263 mm. Bibliothèque nationale, Paris.

25. *Henri Guérard*

The notion of the 'painter-printmaker' came into being in the 1870s and continued to develop throughout the 1880s. What was a 'painter-printmaker'? Initially it meant a painter capable of turning his hand to printmaking; by the end of the century, however, it had come to mean an artist printmaker who could turn his hand to painting. Henri Guérard's work illustrates this transition. He made his first appearance at the Salon in 1870, when he was twenty-four years old, with a painting entitled *The Well*; ten or twenty years earlier he would have made a career as a landscape painter.[244] Like many others, he had tried engraving. As Beraldi puts it, circumstances led him to 'scrape a few plates' from about 1867 onwards.[245] Thereafter he joined the profession incorrectly termed 'artisan-artist', of which Bracquemond is perhaps the best example; he wanted an alternative to painting and chose the field of the printed illustration, producing reproductive prints as well as his own work. This conjunction lent an artistic aura to the craft of printingmaking, and a technical foundation (because of the number of different processes involved) to painting.

Prints took over from painting at different levels. The reproductive engraving lost its importance, as mechanical reproduction and photography took over; it did not disappear completely, however, remaining an academic criterion of technical skill and legitimacy. The original print, meanwhile, gained in importance. Between these two poles the printing trade was sustained by two sectors that were increasing in importance: book publishing, and the production of prints in connection with the burgeoning field of 'decorative arts'. The print was by now an essential element of the publishing business, even if its assimilation was sometimes sacrificed to the nobler art of painting. The major rôle played by publishers in the revival of interest in the etching and in the art trade has been discussed already: Poulet-Malassis was the first of these, followed by Lemerre at the end of the Second Empire, then by Lesclide in the 1870s. *Paris à l'eau-forte*, as has been shown, recruited painters with a knowledge of printmaking; Lesclide has described his encounter with Guérard: '. . .Thereupon Guérard showed me his press and a series of etchings the plates of which unfortunately have been destroyed and he has only kept two or three copies.'[246] The publisher's interest was aroused by work that was already on its way

124. Henri Guerard,
Mill at Montmartre. 1870.
Etching and monotype, 215 x 137 mm.
Bibliothèque nationale, Paris.

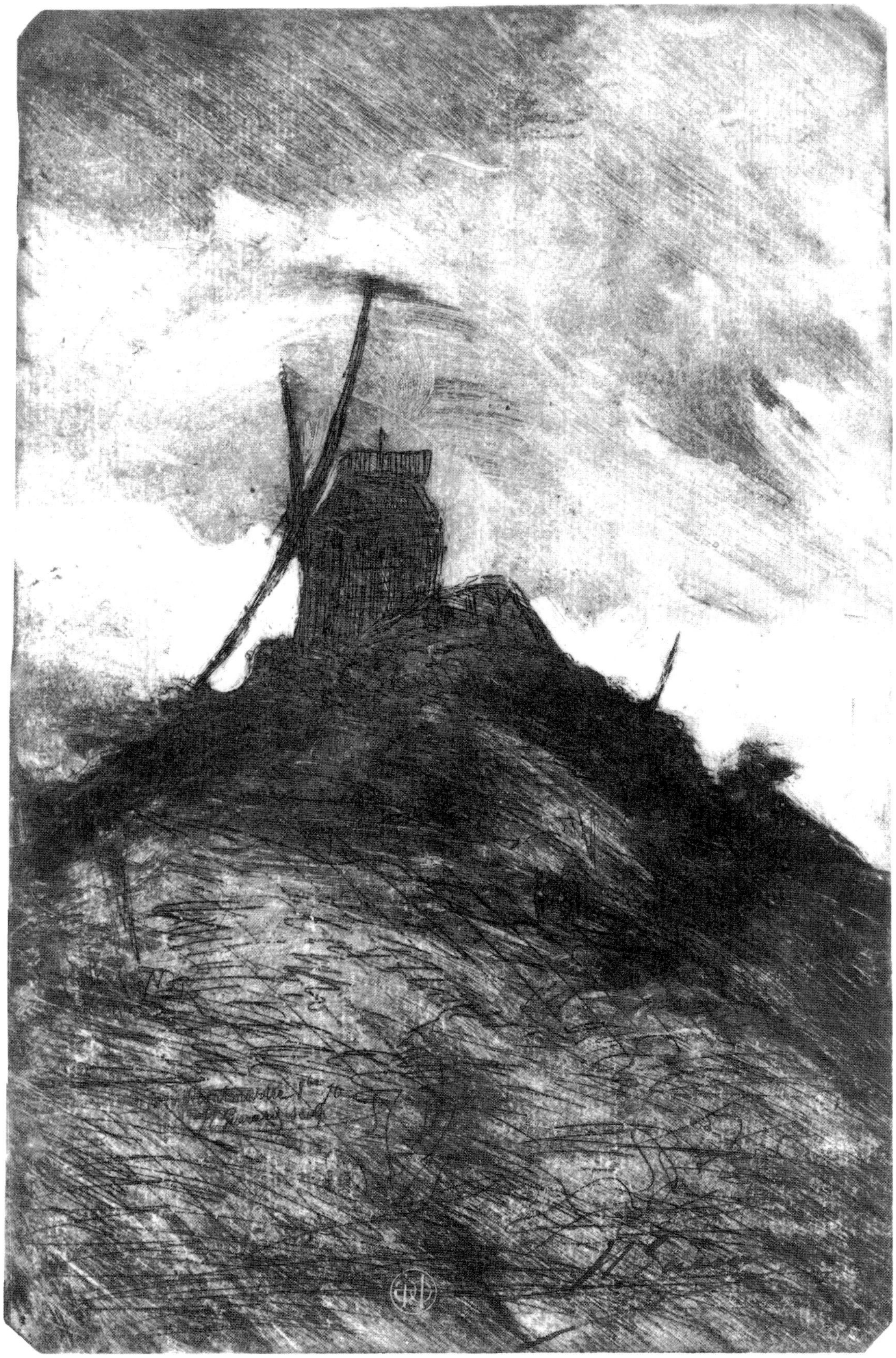

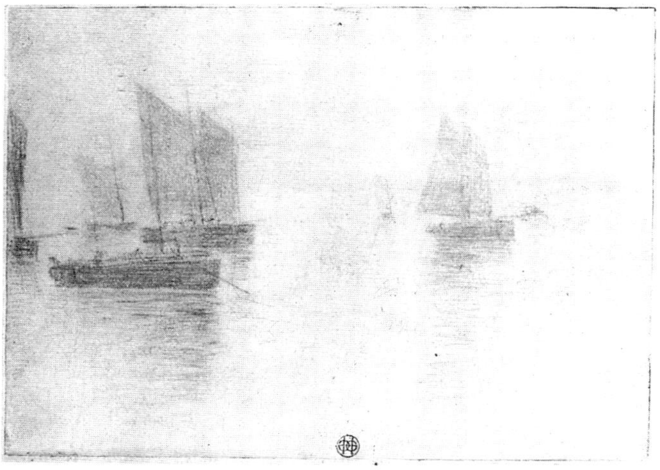

125. Henri Guerard,
Return from the Fishing Grounds, Honfleur. Before 1888.
Etching and wash on green paper, first state, 150 x 205 mm.
Bibliothèque nationale, Paris.

126, 127. Henri Guerard,
Return from the Fishing Grounds, Honfleur. Before 1881.
Etching, state before aquatint and
third state with aquatint, 98 x 130 mm.
Bibliothèque nationale, Paris.

to being rare. *Paris à l'eau-forte* served as a launching pad or as a shop window for the original print. Guérard's output included 106 book illustrations, 101 reproductions or 'interpretations' and 498 original works, the majority of which were never published and remained in his studio for years after his death.

Art reviews had become the official channels of communication between artists, publishers and the public, and by focusing on the print they made an important contribution to the expansion of the decorative arts. Henri Guérard was chosen by Louis Gonse, the editor of the *Gazette des Beaux-Arts*, to illustrate a large book on *Japanese Art* for him. The *Gazette* had taken over from *L'Artiste*, which had been brought low by lithography and by reproductions so badly printed that they no longer met the standards set by the readership. Jules Jaquemart, 'one of the most astonishing printmakers of his day' (Beraldi),[247] had been the star printmaker of the *Gazette*, with his exquisitely faithful rendering of jewellery, furniture, jade, porcelain, weapons etc. culminating in his album of sixty plates, made for the Louvre in 1864, illustrating the *Gems and Jewels of the Crown*. His 400 printed works include forty original etchings. After Jacquemart's death in 1880 Henri Guérard took his place at the *Gazette*. Beraldi admonished Jacquemart in unambiguous terms: 'Please, no contributions with vague titles and subjects; no sketches, outlines, Impressions from nature, scribbles, experiments with different processes etc. . . the plague of collections of prints.'[248] He speaks of Guérard in quite a different tone: 'When he is working for a publisher he pursues a high degree of finish and since the demise of Jacquemart he has taken on the reproduction of works of art. When he is working for himself Guérard is a modernist, an Impressionist, a follower of Manet, a landscapist, seascapist, *japoniste*, fantasist, an alchemist, and an experimentalist. . . like many painters who take up printmaking he is enthralled by the different processes and 'progressive equipment.'[249]

'Progressive equipment' was certainly in fashion, having been developed over a period by Bracquemond. Following his example, Guérard diversified and loosened his technique. In his private work he constantly experimented, for better or worse, torturing his plates in order to get as much out of them as possible: mezzotints obtained using unconventional tools (*The Mill, Montmartre*; Fig. 124), plates worked over with a roulette (*Return from the Fishing Grounds, Honfleur*; Figs 125–7), scratched with glass paper or emery (*Leaving the Port, Le Havre*), or washed directly with acid (*Lines of Boats*). There are a number of monotypes (*Interior in the Auvergne*) and finally, after 1880, experiments with colour etching, some of them very successful (*In the Cornfield*).[250] His seascapes are the most interesting examples of this technique.[251] Guérard employed all kinds of methods to convey an Impression of mist, troubled skies, reflections and fleeting effects.

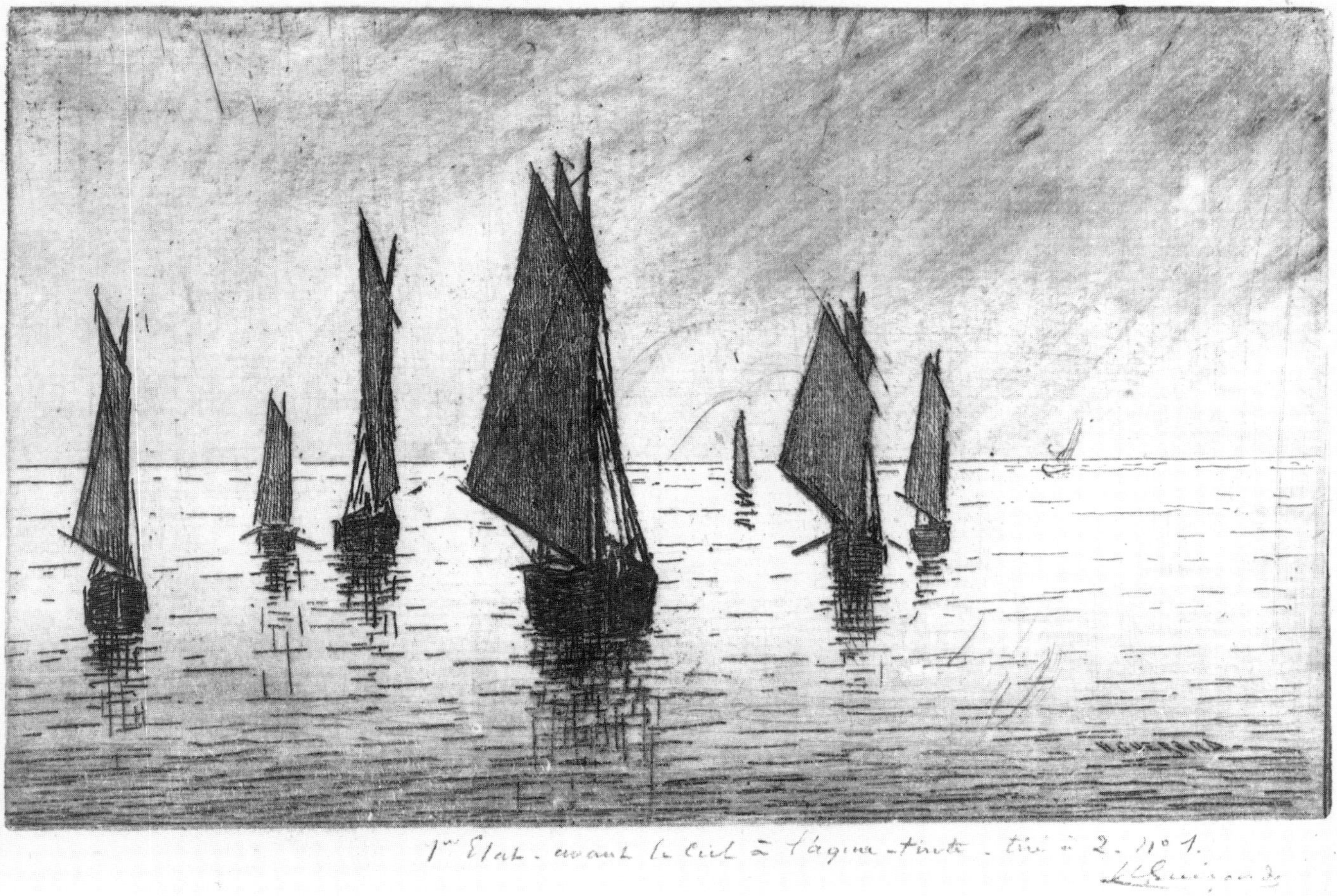
H GUERARD
1er Etat - avant le ciel à l'aqua-tinte - tiré à 2. No 1.
H Guérard

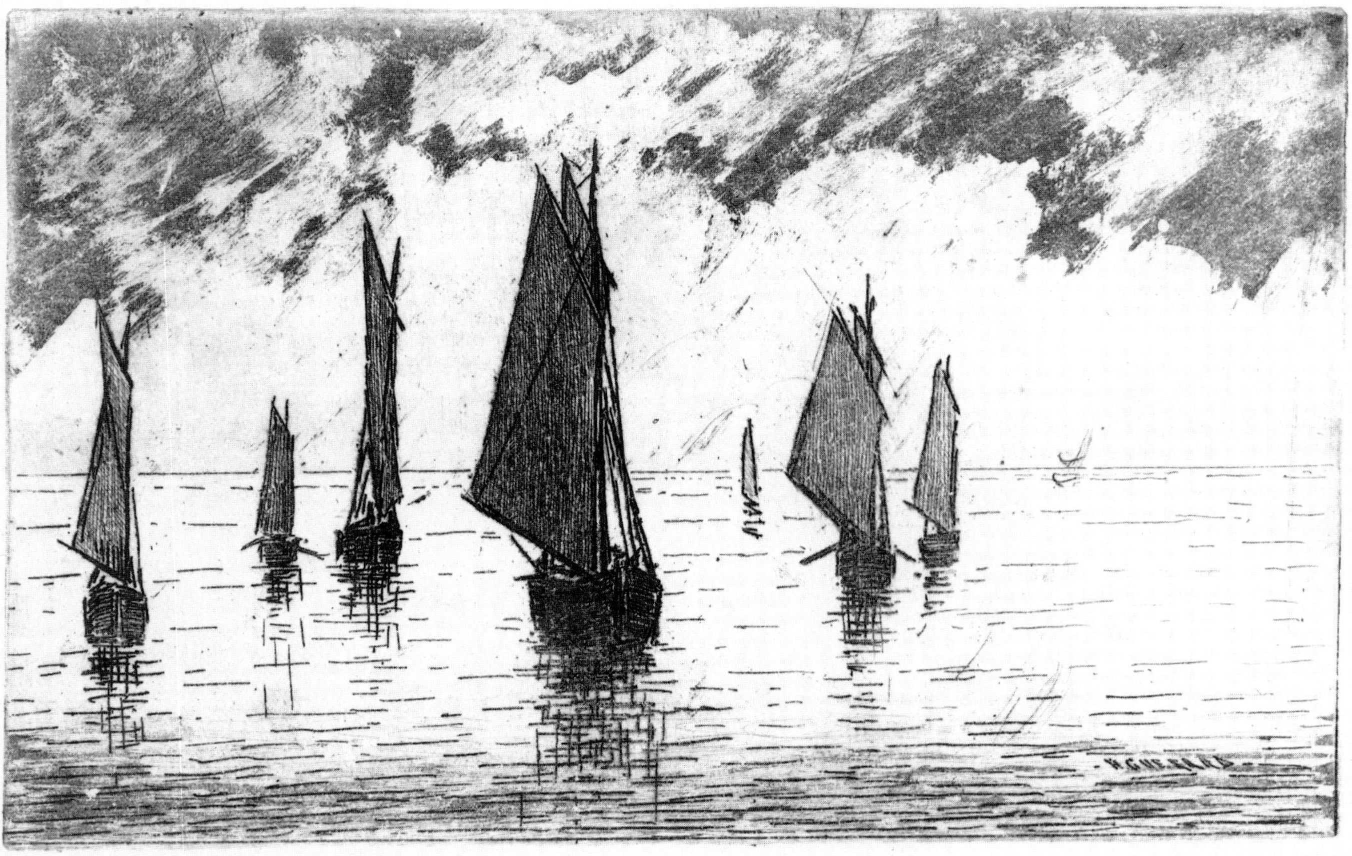
H GUERARD

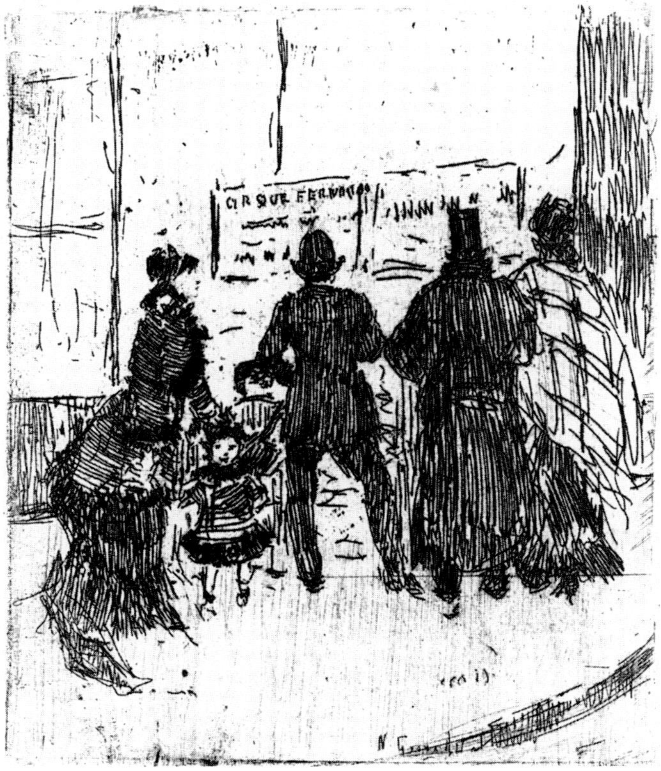

128. Norbert Goeneutte, *Crowd Reading a Poster*. 1875.
Etching for *Paris à l'eau-forte*. 130 x 118 mm.
Bibliothèque nationale, Paris.

Félix Fénéon made express reference to the originality of his series of boats when they were exhibited at the Bernheim Gallery in 1887: 'His seascape paintings of Dieppe and Honfleur and his views of Montmartre are opaque sketches, but the delicacy, transparency and colour so lacking in Monsieur H. Guérard's oil paintings can be found in his prints. The etching, the aquatint and the drypoint, used separately or together, all obey his every whim. They give him mist, snow, rain and sunsets and an indistinct parade of small crafts, engines and passers-by, illuminated by lamps and streetlights.'[252]

Guérard stands at the crossroads of two professions. On one hand he is 'attempting, like the Impressionists, to capture the fleeting, the transient: *Woman Running Along a Boulevard* is an essay in transience; the contours and the details are blurred, the forms undefined . . . In many of his pieces Guérard chooses a subject for its surroundings and atmosphere rather than for the subject itself: this is certainly an Impressionist preoccupation. The processes he uses (monotype, different inking effects) to convey movement and instability are all processes that were familiar to the Impressionists.'[253] On the other hand 'he possesses neither charm nor elegance. . . his strokes are violent and his blacks often opaque.'[254] In all probability he inherited his method (as did Bracquemond) from the requirements of publishers and the reproduction trade; large editions needed deep lines, something for which Manet, and Cadart's publications in general, were also censured. Guérard was unable to overcome this technical defect, and remained on the fringes of Impressionism.

In 1875 *Paris à l'eau-forte* gave a chance to one of Guérard's friends, Norbert Goeneutte who was eight years his junior (Fig. 128). Their early careers were similar: Goeneutte[255] began with an etched portrait of Guérard (*Conversation with Guérard*) and published a small *View of the Boulevard de Clichy* in *Paris à l'eau-forte*. Then, in 1876, Cadart published his *Boulevard de Clichy in the Rain*, entered for the Salon in 1878.[256] Goeneutte, like Guérard, never participated in the exhibitions put on by the Impressionist group. He died young, at forty, in Auvers-sur-Oise in 1894, leaving his work as a printmaker unfinished. Like Guérard he represents the second generation of painter-printmakers who did just as much printmaking as painting.

26. *Lepic and the Mobile Etching*

Viscount Louis-Napoléon Lepic was the second printmaker included in the first Impressionist exhibition, after Bracquemond. He had been encouraged by Degas, a friend with whom he shared a number of attributes including social origins: Lepic's grandfather was created a baron by the Emperor in 1809, but like Degas he was an unconventional aristocrat; like Degas also he had a great fondness for Dutch painting. Degas's admiration for Lepic is confirmed by the way he portrays him in his paintings.[258] Vicomte Lepic has been forgotten as a painter and would also have been forgotten as a printmaker had he not published in 1876 a curious album of prints whose title, *L'eau-forte mobile (The Mobile Etching)*, is more significant than its contents.[259] The portraits of dogs he exhibited in 1874 certainly had nothing to attract the other painters of the group: the seeds of the quarrel that was to break out between the group ten years later had already been sown by Degas, accused by Caillebotte in 1881: 'he maintains that we should all support each other and be able to count on one another (by God!) and then who does he bring along? Lepic, Legros, Maureau. (But he did not castigate Lepic, who has no talent, for his defection, he just forgave him. He obviously would never have forgiven Sisley, Monet and Renoir, who do have talent). In 1878 [he] brought us Zandomeneghi, Bracquemond and Mme Bracquemond; in 1879, Raffaëlli. . ., I'll say no more. What a phalanx of fighters for realism!!!'[260] Lepic showed his work again with the Impressionists in 1876 (the second exhibition), then moved away in order to give more time to sailing, his great hobby.

The Mobile Etching, published by Cadart, begins with a statement by Lepic on *How I became an etcher*. He describes how he was launched by Cadart and by Jadin, the printmaker, in the early 1860s: 'from then I was struck by what was wrong with printmaking . . .: – on one hand it was growing duller and duller as the finish grew more meticulous; on the other . . . it ignored Rembrandt and the powerful effects he achieved by refusing to use printing ink – the only way of achieving such effects'. Fifteen years after making these observations Lepic carried out his plan: 'I organised tools of my own, used neat acid, slammed on varnish, sand, clay – anything to achieve the right black.' The idea underlying the project gradually becomes clear and reflects, in fact, a preoccupation that was quite common: 'I shall make prints like a painter, not like a printmaker.' Lepic sometimes etched no lines at all on his plates but simply painted them with printing ink. 'The artist who uses acid must use his etching tool or his wad of cloth the way a painter or draughtsman uses his brush or pencil.' The important stage in printmaking was by this time the Impression rather than the preparation of the plate. The artist should make the Impression himself, obviously, as it was the culmination of his work: 'The painter emerges from his print, when it is printed. . . only he can bring it to life. . . otherwise etching becomes a trade like any other, that anyone can pursue; it is not difficult to copy a photograph, for example, and to obtain quite an acceptable etching.' The postscript drives the point home further: 'What is the ultimate secret of the etchings that I produce? It is the way I use the ink and the rag; with these two pieces of equipment anything can be wrung from a plate. . . This process has been in existence since the days of the Old Masters and I have revived it. My different versions are filed alphabetically at Cadart's publishing house and can be inspected by anybody. A landscape of the banks of the Escaut has been transformed in eighty-five different ways.' He concluded his introduction without false modesty: 'I proclaim myself the inventor and promulgator of a completely new genre.' In *The Banks of the Escaut*,[261] or *Lake Nemi* (Fig. 129), probably executed in 1870, the print is reduced to a basic smooth plate whose inking is varied by the artist on each proof. The ink can produce a sunrise, moonlight, a storm or rain (Fig. 130). 'By printing my plate of the *Banks of the Escaut* myself, I have made a dream come true. I have obtained a range of very different effects which it would have been impossible to obtain if assistants had printed the etching rather than the artists himself.' These words could have come from the pen of Bracquemond, Degas or Pissarro. The difference is the last three achieved more and talked less; Lepic did not in fact invent anything at all. We have already discussed Appian's interest in monotypes as early as 1863, and in referring to Rembrandt's technique of obtaining picturesque effects by inking Lepic was reiterating something that had become a commonplace among artist-printmakers.

Degas was the keenest proponent of this genre and showed 'drawings done with heavy ink, and printed' at the third Impressionist exhibition in 1877. Other artists

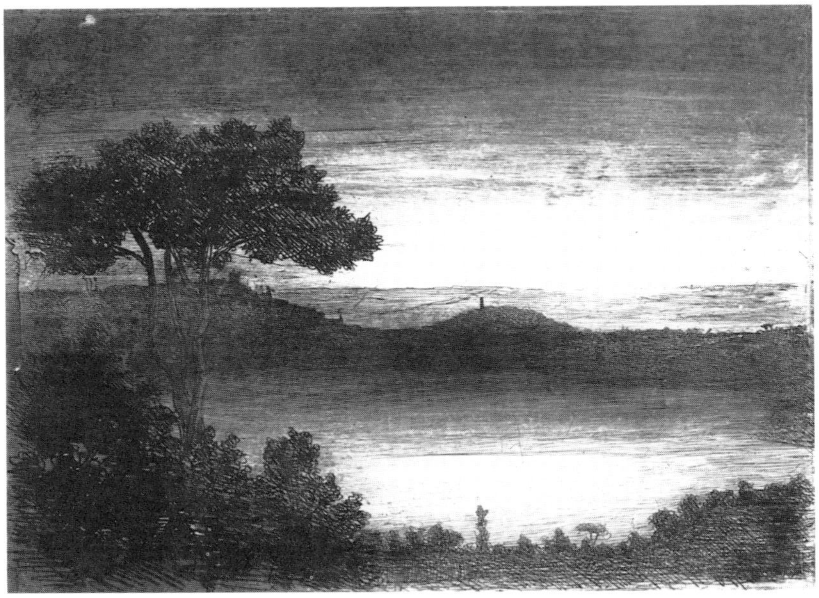

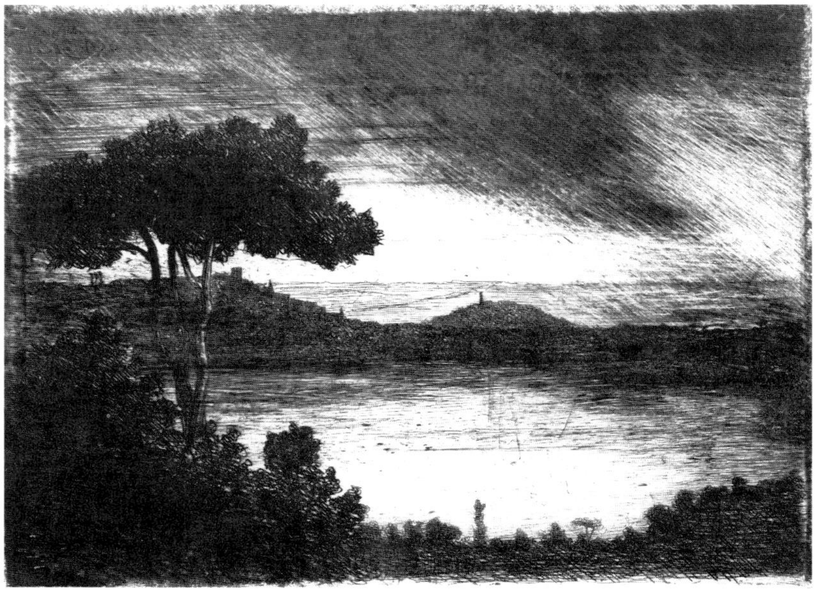

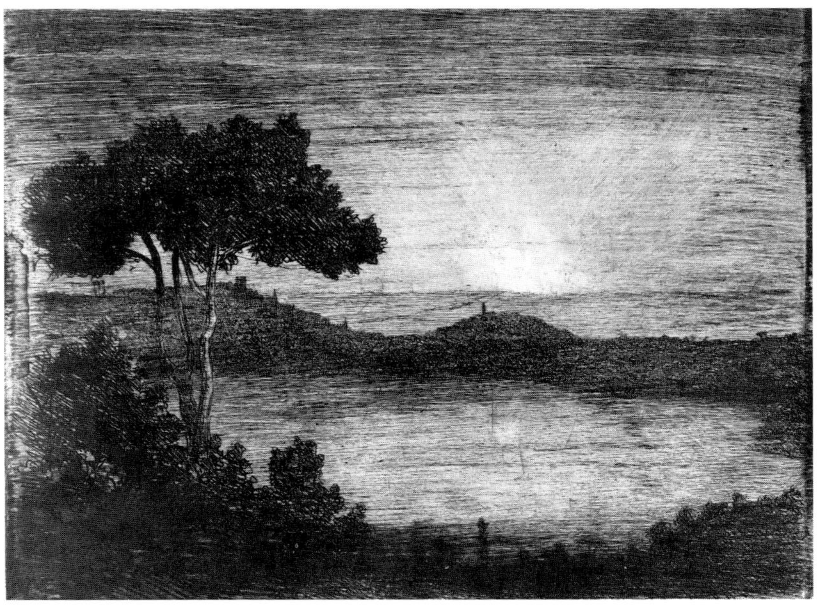

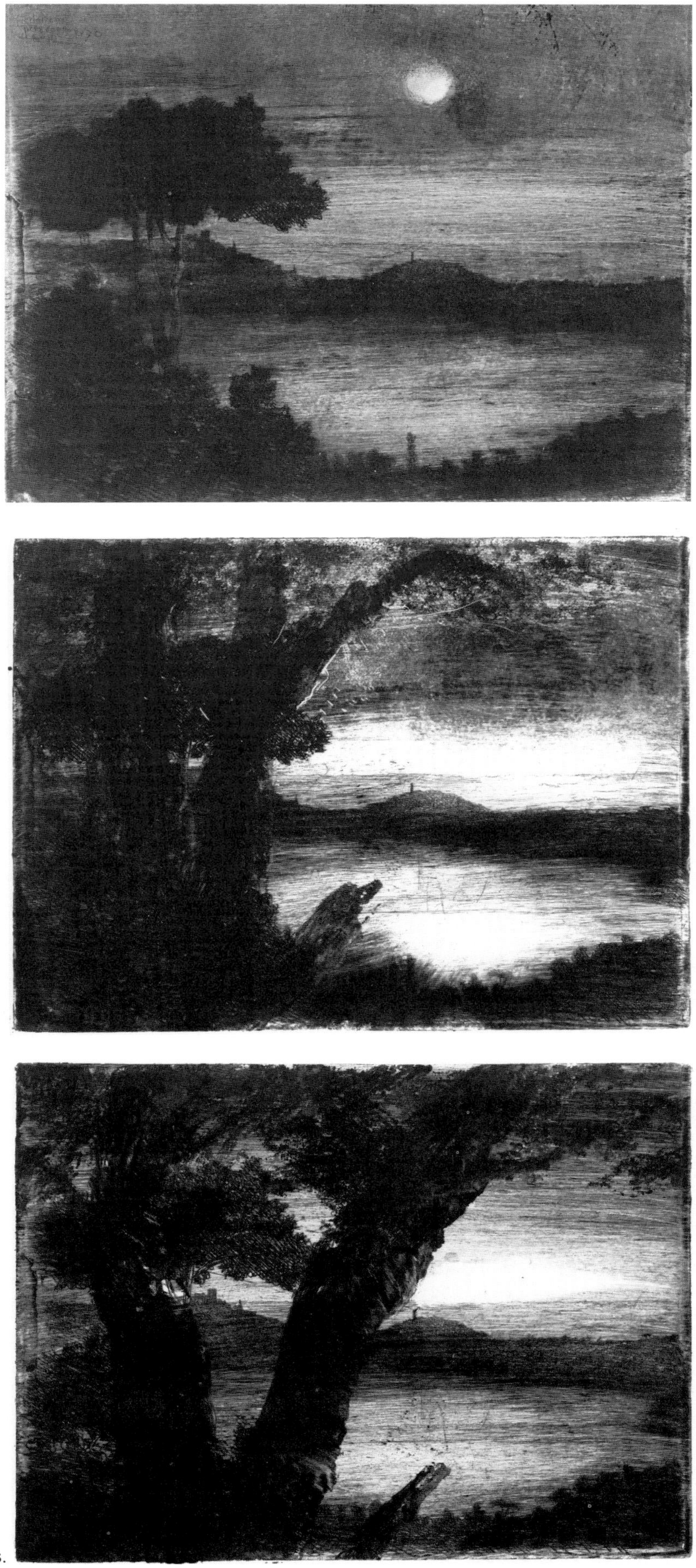

129. Viscount Lepic, *Lake Nemi*. 1870 (?). Etching, six different versions from the same plate, 240 x 315 mm. Bibliothèque nationale, Paris.

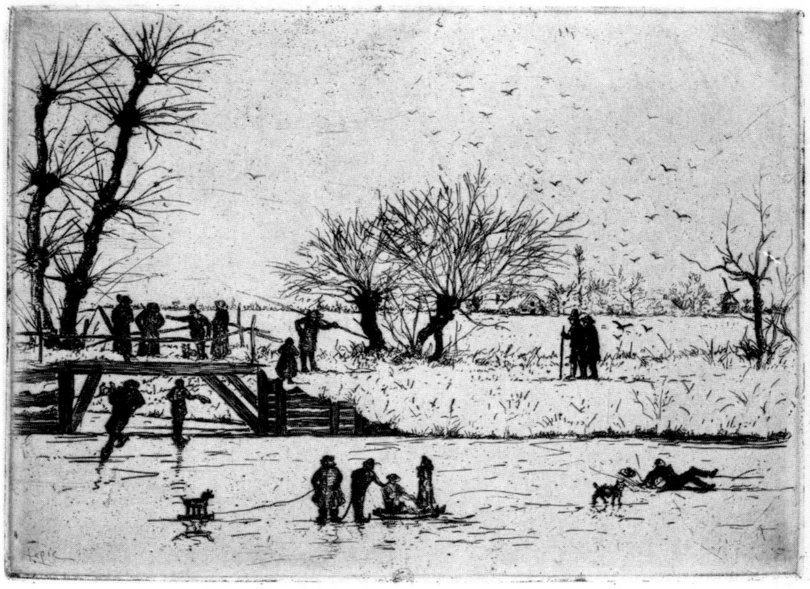

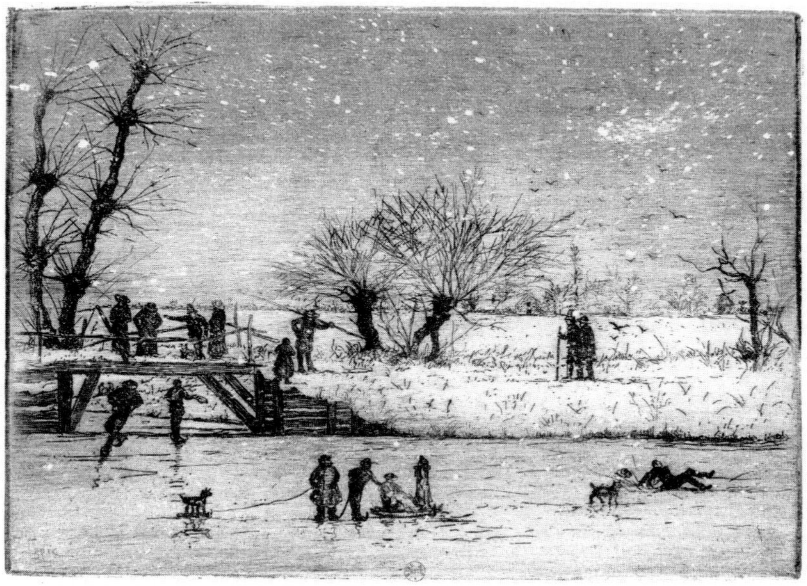

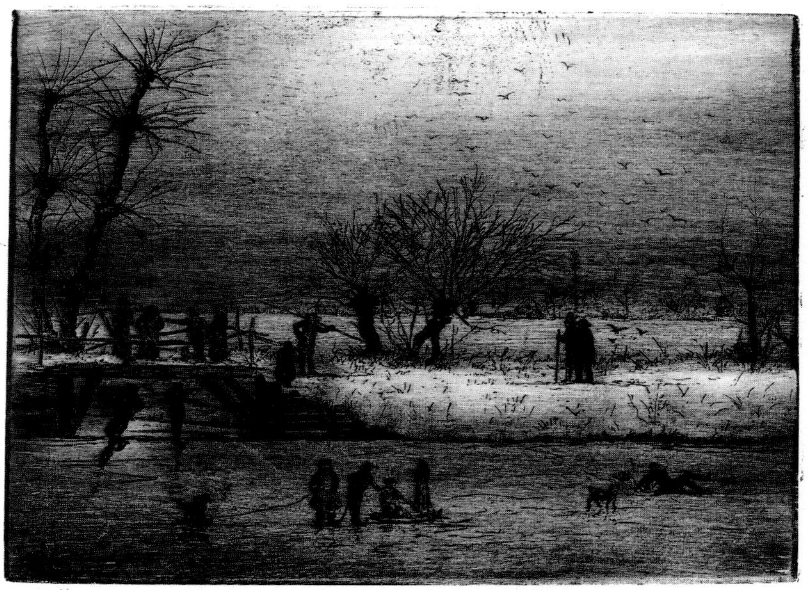

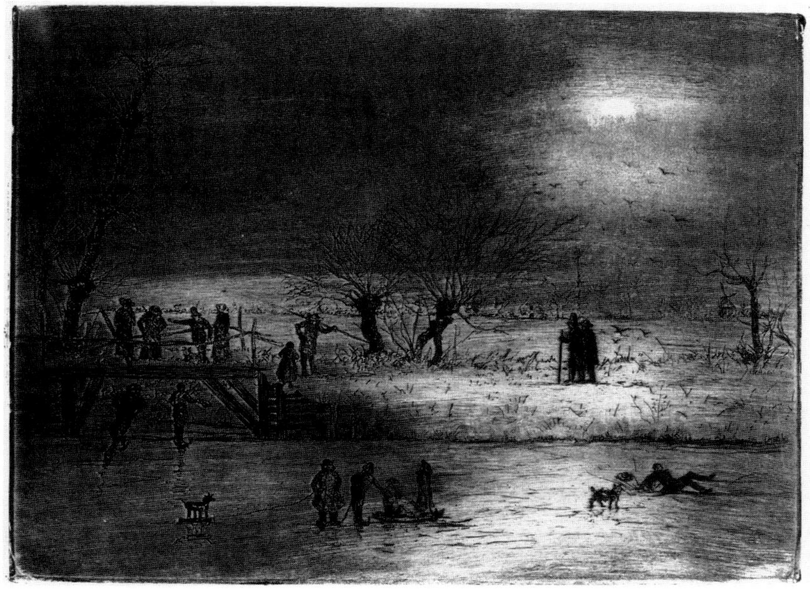

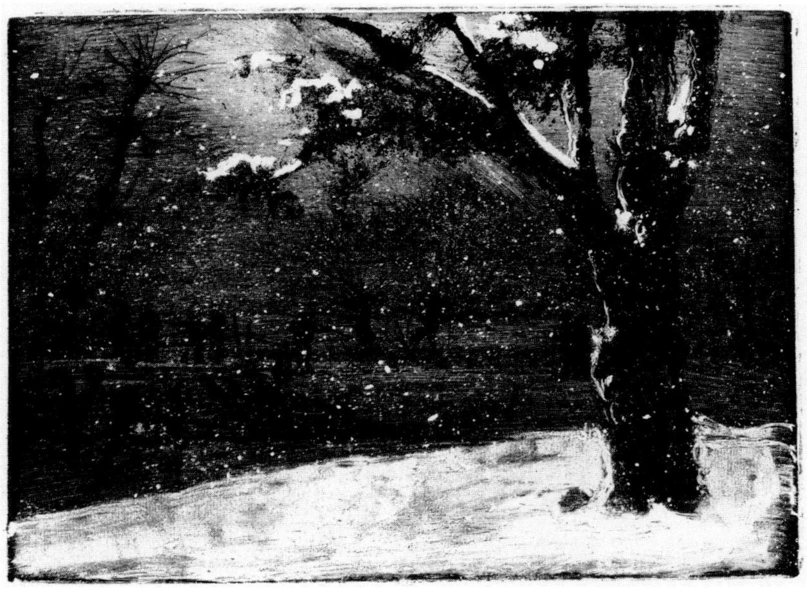

130. Viscount Lepic,
Winter in Holland. Undated.
Mobile etching, 5 printings,
240 x 325 mm.
Bibliothèque nationale, Paris.

went in for it too at this time: among the output of Doctor Gachet – Van Ryssel – there are two monotypes dating from the same period which appear to have been achieved by tortuous means, perhaps with an aquatint as a background; there are other prints in which ink plays an important rôle.[262] The team at *Paris à l'eau-forte* were already interested in this process. Richard Lesclide described how he came upon the painter Henri Guérard busy 'covering a plate with a layer of printing ink. The plate had no signs of any drawing on it. . . . Guérard explained that he was trying a new kind of printmaking with muslin. When he decided that the plate was evenly covered in black ink he took various oily and dirty rags, some rolled into a wad, and some folded into a cone. These he moved about on the copper. After half an hour or so the plate began to shine in places. Patches of light appeared, and gradations of darkness; some heavy columns could be picked out, supporting the arches of a large crypt . . . When at last the artist thought his work complete he lifted the plate, wiped it with infinite care and placed it in the press covered with a sheet of paper three hundred years old. The proof emerged triumphant from its felt overcoat'.[263]

Among the prints left by Auguste Delâtre, the printer, there were some monotypes and he recalls in his memoirs: 'From the same copper plate, [the printer] could make 20, 30 or 40 different versions. On a simple black etching the printer could, for instance, change daylight into moonlight. . . It is he who must repaint the picture for each proof . . . Ideally the artist should print his own work, but as that is not possible. . . there is only one answer – the printer-artist.'[264] For some of his clients Delâtre was bit too much of an artist, 'saucing' their work and distorting it with cheap effects. Millet complained to Sensier about this in the summer of 1853. He accused Delâtre 'of making proofs with too much ink on them, rather than crisp, clear prints.'[265] There was a fashion for softening the line by buffing the ink along the etched lines with a soft cloth when it was being wiped just before being printed. This offended Millet's traditionalist view of the print.

Hamerton devoted a chapter of his treatise *Etching and Etchers* to what he termed 'artistic printing' or 'artificial printing', which he contrasted with 'natural printing'.[266] He returned to the subject when his albums from the *Portfolio* were published. Hamerton mentioned Delâtre's 'interpretative printing', accusing him of adding too much to the proofs. He admired Delâtre more than Ruskin, who thought him untrustworthy. James Tissot also mentions that the printer claimed to have discovered this secret method 'in his study of Rembrandt',[267] and Seymour Haden presented him with Burty's book on Rembrandt (1864), with these words: 'To Delâtre. If he had been alive at the time of Rembrandt the artist would certainly have employed him to print his etchings.'

Whistler, whose habit it was to make semi-monotypes of his prints, protested, according to Pennell 'against the professional printer, his pot of treacle and his couches of ink. But no great artist ever carried the printing of etchings so far or made such use of printer's ink as he did in these plates. Without the wash of ink, they would be ghosts, and he was justified in printing as he wanted to get what he wished. And he used ink in all sorts of ways on the same plate, he tried endless experiments with ever'varying results, even to cover up the weak lines of an indifferent design, as in *Nocturne-Palaces* (Fig. 209), prized highly by collectors, but one of his poorest Venice plates.' To such an extent, concludes Pennell, that for an etching like *The Traghetto*, of which a hundred proofs were made, 'the first proof is different from the last and no two are alike'.

27. *Desboutin and De Nittis*

The fate of Marcellin Desboutin is typical of that of a number of artists in the 1870s.[269] From a life of luxury on his private income he was reduced to penury within a short space of time. From a life of entertaining in his villa in Tuscany, L'Ombrellino, he moved to the smoky corners of the Café Guerbois; from aristocracy – he styled himself the Duc des Boutins de Rochefort – he descended to bohemia; from being a dilettante – he was both painter and playwright – to being an absinthe drinker. Manet and Degas have each left a portrait of him in this guise. Desboutin was a thoroughgoing man of the theatre;[270] when he returned to Paris in 1869 (the Comédie Française was to stage his play *Maurice of Saxony* in June 1870) he found himself in a state of financial ruin in a country in turmoil. It was at that point that he recalled the fact that he was also a printmaker. He had made copies of Rembrandt's work in Amsterdam in the 1850s. With Degas he had done some prints in Florence in 1856 and his prints had been exhibited at the Salon in 1866. Like Degas and other aristocrats with modernist leanings he was passionately interested in heliogravure and photography. Printmaking was now his safety net, fragile enough as it turned out, but he had no choice. Desboutin was a portraitist and won a medal with one of his portraits in the Salon of 1879. The characters portrayed by Desboutin represent the actors on the contemporary the modern art scene: Manet, Renoir, Berthe Morisot (Figs 132–3), Duranty, Zola, Goncourt, collectors like Hoschedé, and the printer Leroy using Cadart's hand press (Fig. 131). Actors and models follow in a celebratory stream, their numbers limited only by the limited number of copies that could be provided by copper plates scratched with the dry point.

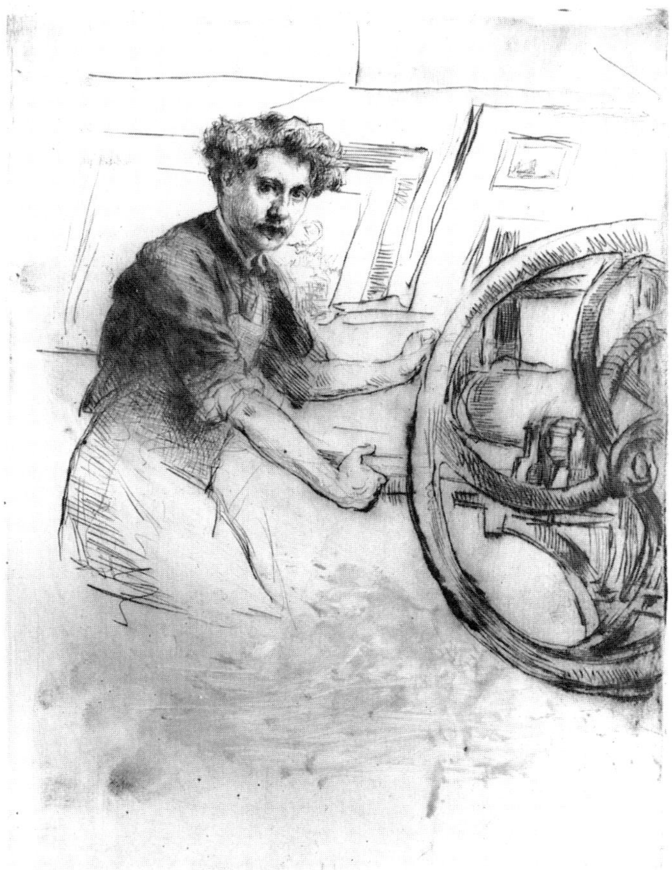

131. Marcellin Desboutin, *Leroy, the Printer*. 1875. Drypoint, 295 x 209 mm. Bibliothèque nationale, Paris.

Desboutin's use of drypoint is lively, warm and velvety with plenty of contrast. He marks the copper plate in a most informal and unaffected manner; ink collects around the mouths and in mens' beards. It is more spontaneous than etching, the latter an indirect process in which the bite of the acid has to be carefully controlled. Drypoint is a direct challenge because it is almost impossible to retouch it once it is done. It can be learned by studying Rembrandt's highlights, although he did not use the dry point on its own. As a process, it proved seductive to the painter-printmakers who exploited its ability to flatter and its sensuality: Tissot with his scenes from bourgeois life and, at the end of the century, Helleu

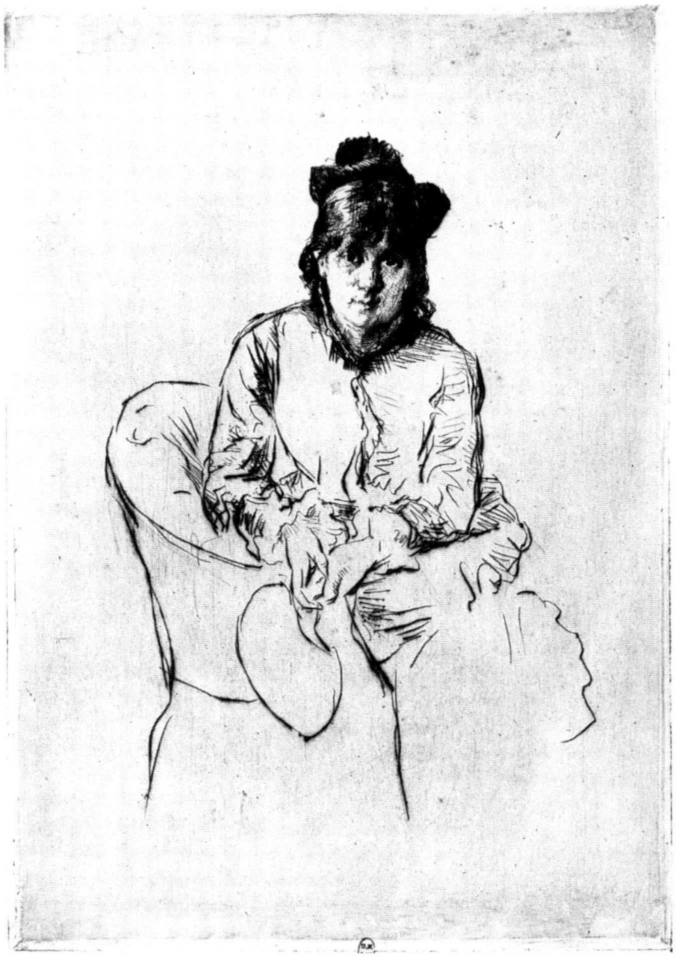

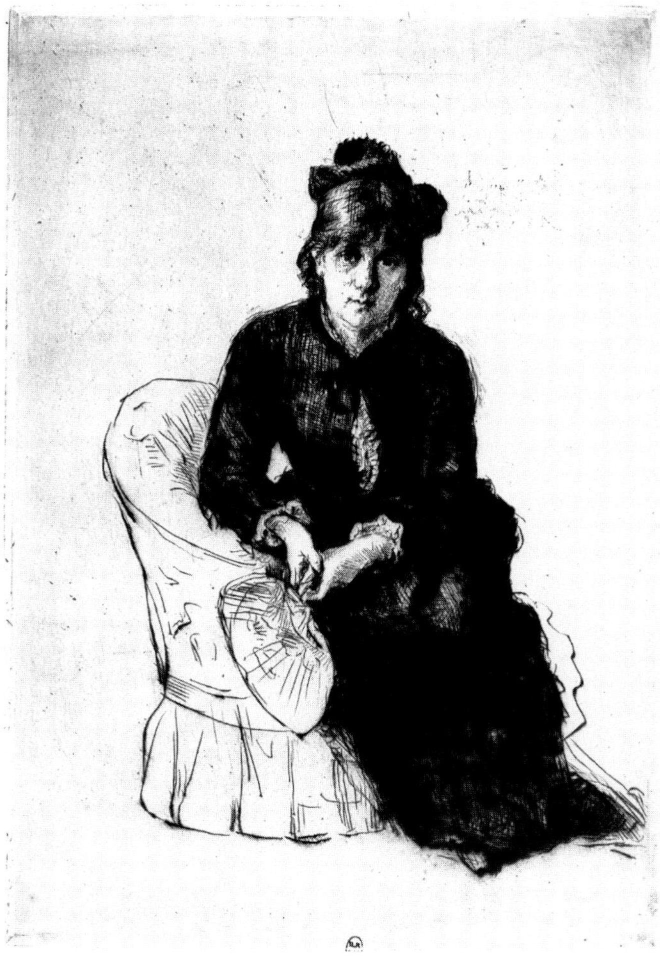

132, 133. Marcellin Desboutin, *Portrait of Berthe Morisot*. About 1876. Etching, first and second states, 260 x 175 mm. Bibliothèque nationale, Paris.

134. Marcellin Desboutin, *The Man with a Pipe*. 1879. Drypoint, 450 x 375 mm. Bibliothèque nationale, Paris.

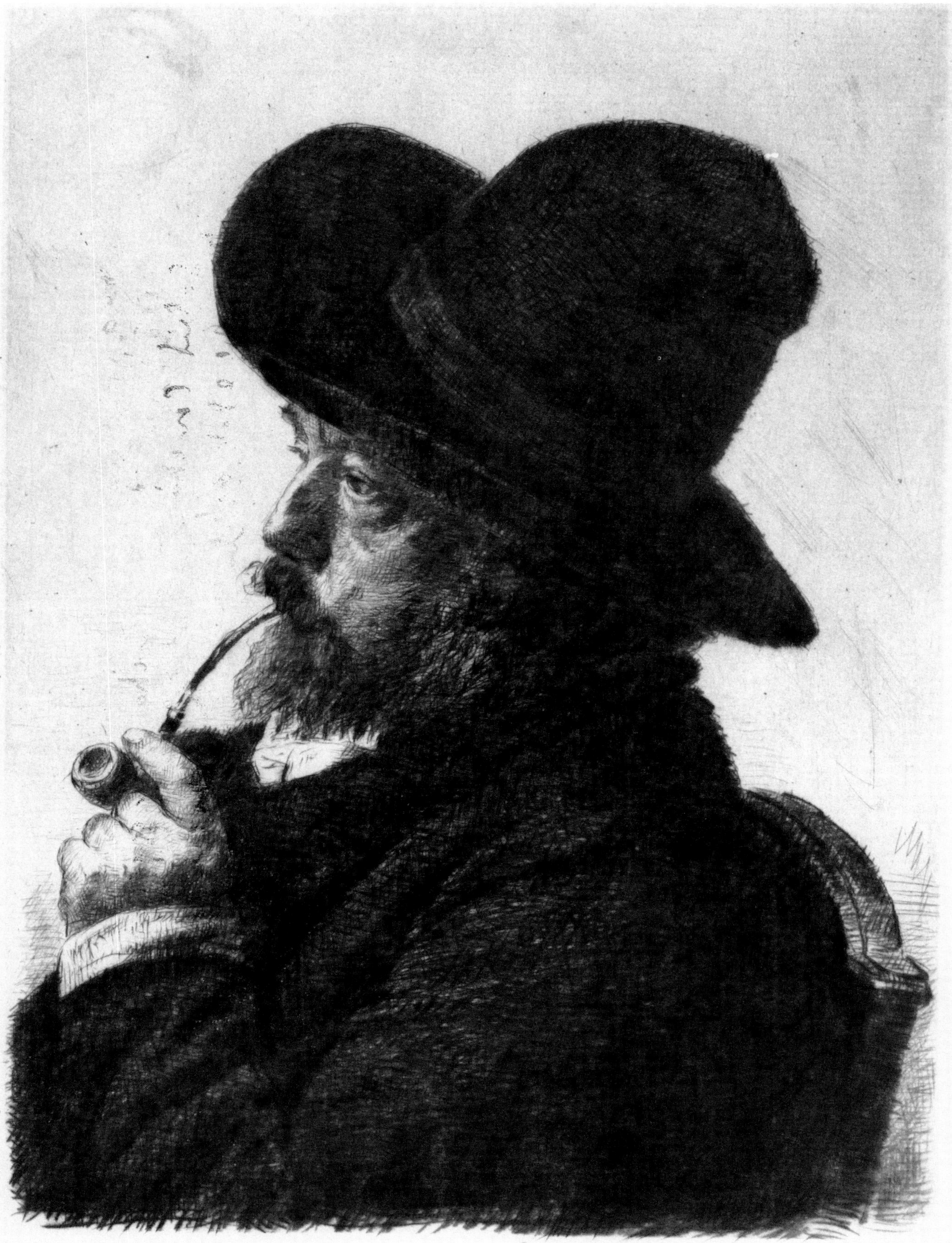

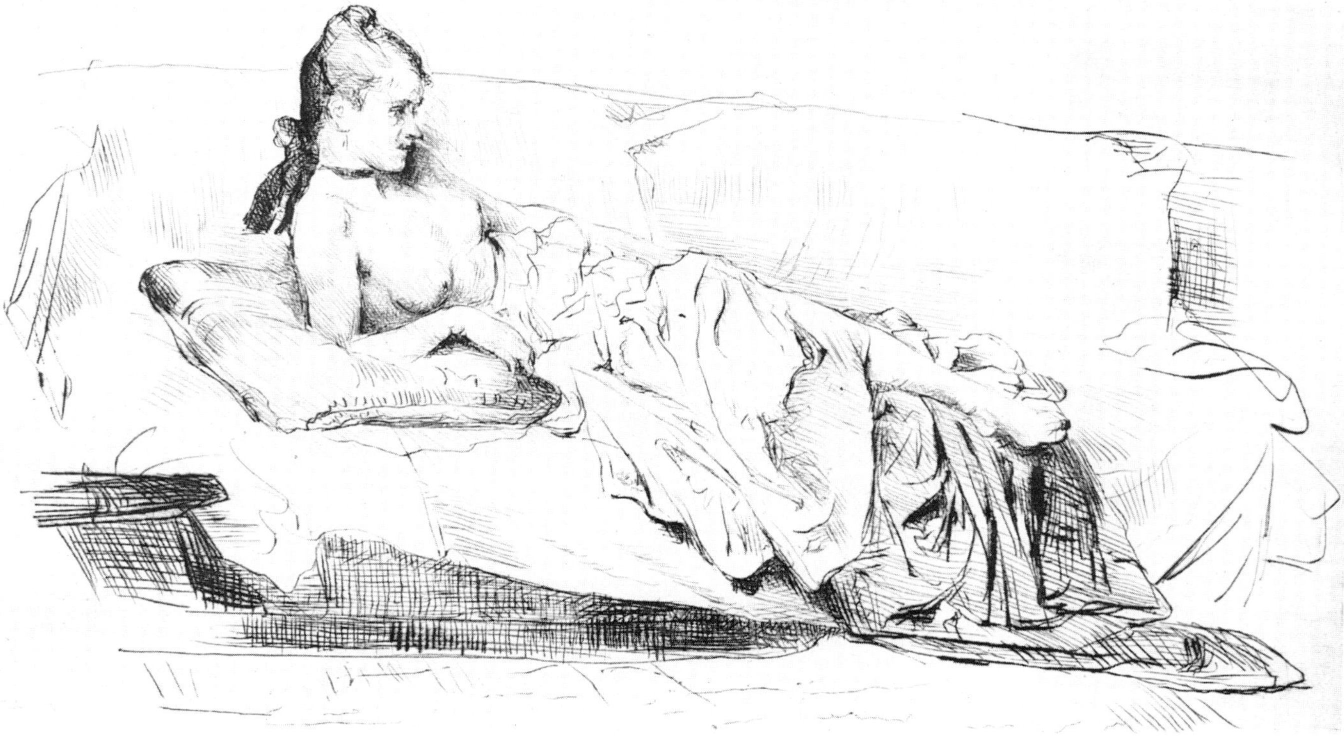

135. Giuseppe De Nittis or Marcellin Desboutin, *Woman Lying Down*. 1874. Drypoint, 160 x 275 mm. Bibliothèque nationale, Paris.

with his languorous ladies. When drypoints are printed, a velvety black emerges from the deeply scored lines and a light grey from the shallow ones. Under Desboutin's direction the dry point produced portraits of a new type of person, a person who, like the etching, is presented as frank, free and politically committed: the modern intellectual. Only the face is shown in any detail (Fig. 134). No effort is spared to define the model's expression and his feelings. The rest is dashed off casually against a completely empty background; the intellectual can stand for himself and needs no décor. He has no attributes – he is not writing or posing, yet his face brightens the page more vividly than in Nadar's portraits. At this period photographs were inevitably posed, photographers were eager to produce official portraits: photographs were less modern than their printed counterparts with their simplicity and informality. The absence of a studio and equipment makes for an intimate atmosphere. A drypoint is produced quickly and printed at once. Photography on the other hand could not dispense with the paraphernalia and pomp that the print no longer needed. Photography ceased to be a rival to printmaking, each technique having staked out its territory. Like Degas, Desboutin was passionately interested in photography, and even more interested in photogravure. When large editions were required he did not reject the contribution that mechanical processes could offer. He also worked with heliographic plates, retouching them by hand and with drypoint; he took them seriously enough to sign them and write a dedication.[271] His engraved portrait of Villiers de l'Isle-Adam is a photogravure of one of his drawings.[272] His portrait of Puvis de Chavannes has an even more complicated history: his original drawing in black pencil heightened with red was transformed into an etching and a heliograph, was reworked in drypoint and published in *La Plume* and in *L'Artiste*.[273] Thanks to his small printing business Desboutin was able to survive, meagrely at first and then more comfortably. An art that gratified its models so greatly could not remain unknown. In 1889, an *annus mirabilis* for painter-printmakers, Desboutin had an exhibition of etchings at Durand-Ruel.

De Nittis was involved in portraiture and domestic scenes. On 3 January 1872 Goupil, the dealers, bought his entire production with exclusive reproduction rights. De Nittis did not exhibit prints at the first Impressionist exhibition, in which his painting was included. He became interested in printmaking thanks

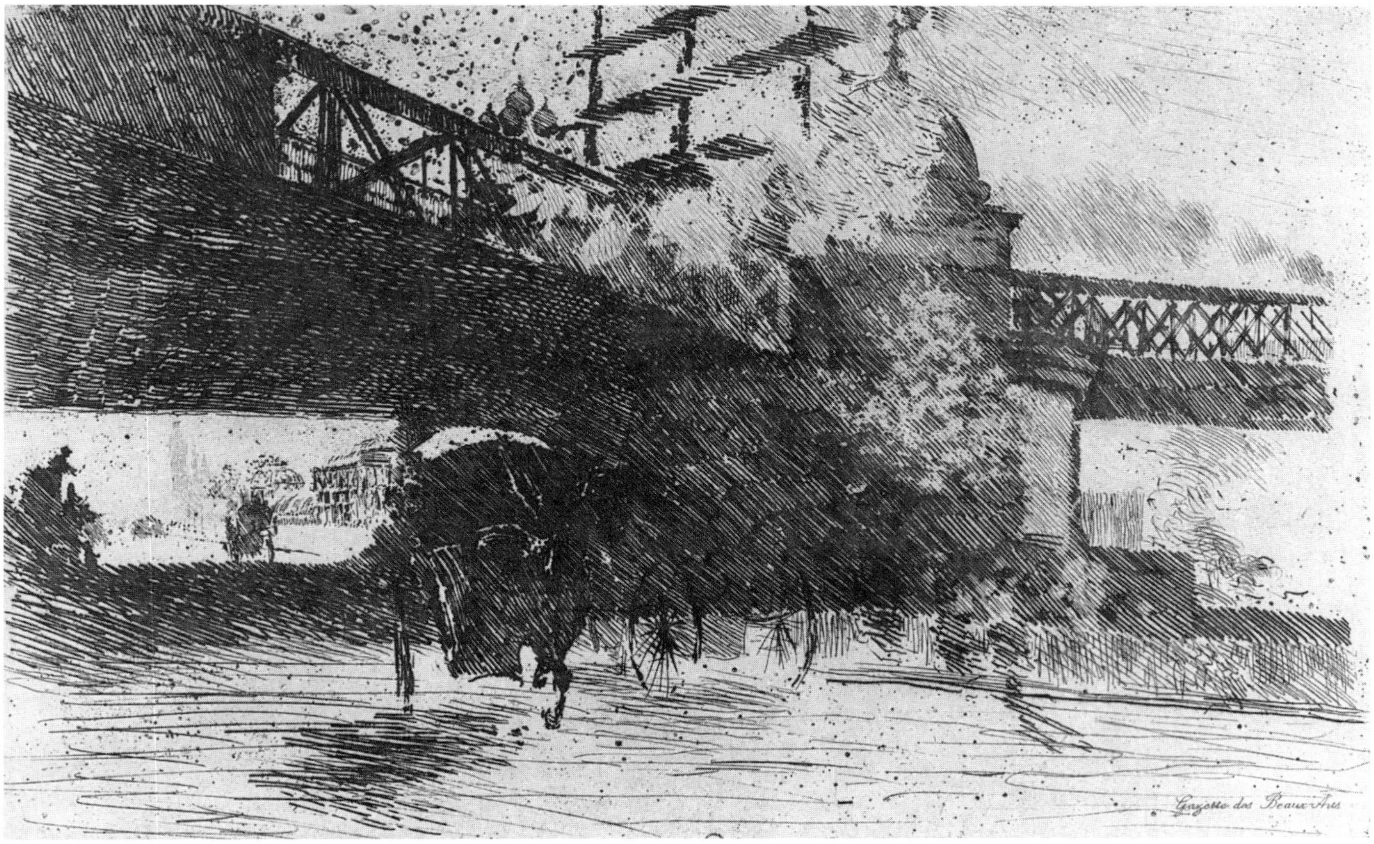

136. Giuseppe De Nittis, *Cab under a Bridge (View of London)*. Undated. Etching, 140 x 220 mm. Bibliothèque nationale, Paris.

to the influence of Desboutin. On 13 April 1875 Desboutin thanked his friend De Nittis for having attempted to launch his prints in London: 'When you next come home, my dear De Nittis, let us give ourselves the pleasure of returning to our sessions with Cadart.'[274] On 18 March he complains about his gloomy life: 'Our friend Degas is my only consolation. Since you left, the semblance of a summer that we have had has permitted me to return to my drypoints, which was interrupted by last winter's illness. I have done a portrait of the Duchess Colonna.' After the second Impressionist exhibition, Desboutin wrote to De Nittis (20 April 1876): 'Our exhibition by a group of artists . . . produced a nice little dividend so that, when all expenses were paid, each of us had his outlay repaid with a little bit on top. The press were very well-disposed towards me this time and this publicity did my humble name more good than ten years of exhibiting in the doorframes of the corridors of the Salon'.[275] He wrote again, on 17 July: 'Durand-Ruel held a black-and-white exhibition here in imitation of the one held in London. As you can imagine, I showed my whole collection of drypoints.'[276] Desboutin, De Nittis and probably occasionally Degas worked at etching together in Cadart's *atelier*, trying out new techniques and effects. De Nittis's output was modest: twelve plates, half of which were of fashionable women, one of them signed on the plate *1873*. Some have been confused with Desboutin's prints. Burty attributed to Desboutin the *Woman lying down* (Fig. 135), a drypoint of 1874 attributed by Degas to De Nittis. Each of them owned a proof of the print. They may have collaborated on the two portraits of Degas, one proof of which, catalogued with the works of De Nittis in the Bibliothèque Nationale, bears the legend: 'the painter de Gas, 20 February 1875, by Desboutin.'[277] De Nittis published a *View of London* (Fig. 136) in the *Gazette des Beaux-Arts* and did not object to the publication of some reproductions of his drawings by photomechanical methods. Degas involved his two colleagues in the Impressionist adventure. On 5 April 1874, De Nittis informed one of his Italian friends that Degas had suggested he join a society devoted to 'realist opposition'.[278] The success of these artists was short-lived, Degas being the only member of the Impressionist group to appreciate their very classical draughtsmanship and their worldly subjects. In 1889 Hoschedé wrote admiringly of Desboutin's prints,[279] but by 1880 Desboutin had moved closer to Italy and was living in Nice, supporting himself by producing society portraits copied from photographs.

28. *Félix Buhot and the 'Fine Print'*

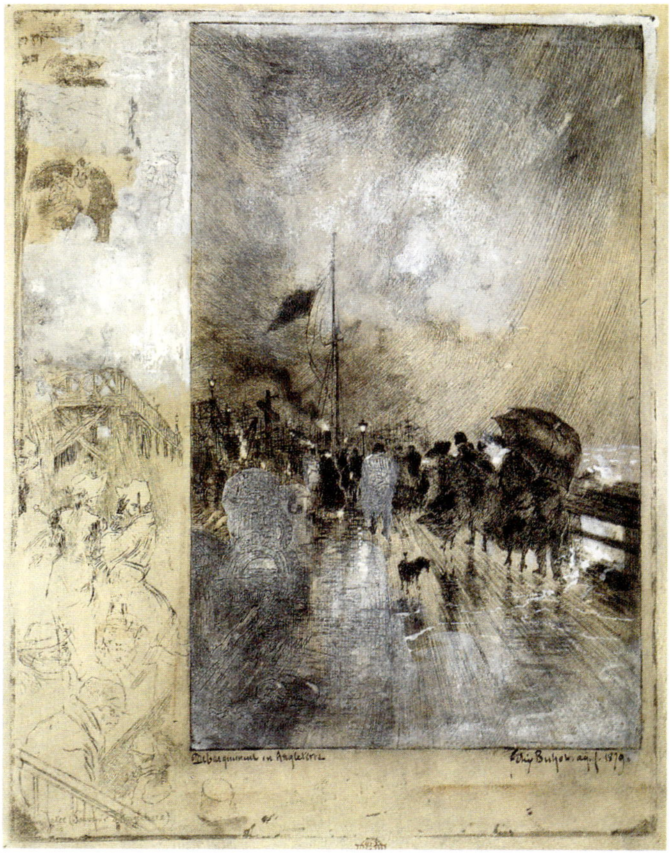

137. Félix Buhot,
A Jetty (Landing in England). 1879.
Etching and gouache, 316 x 238 mm.
Private collection, Paris.

As a result of its being regarded as art in its own right, the print acquired an attribute that was not natural to it: each proof now had to be distinct from the other proofs in a series. Philippe Burty devoted all his critical skills to this distinction, attempting to convince collectors of its importance in his articles in the *Gazette des Beaux-Arts*, his prefaces to sales catalogues and to Cadart's albums. In the mid-1870s the artists' etching was supported by different bodies: the Salon still had a marginal rôle to play, and the rôle of the reviews was expanding. The *Gazette des Beaux-Arts* offered the most active support, with the review founded by Louis Gonse, *L'Art*,[280] which also published original works; the publishers of illustrated books, principally Lesclide and Lemerre, continued to pursue their costly undertakings with some difficulty; finally, the publishing house founded by Cadart survived the death of its founder in 1875. To replace the albums published by the *Société des aquafortistes*, Cadart had launched *L'Illustration Nouvelle* in 1868, and published four, equally eclectic etchings per month. In 1872 he produced an anthology of one hundred plates: *Ten Years of Etching*, with no introductory text. Then in 1874 *The Etching in 1874* appeared, bringing together about thirty etchers, and initiating the Series *The Etching in* . . . . It was in albums like these that the doctrine of the etching as an independent work of art, to be classed with painting on one hand and with the decorative arts on the other, was promulgated, most stridently by Philippe Burty in three manifestos: *The Contemporary Etching in France* (1874), *The Fine Print* (1875) and *What is Printmaking?* (1878).

The attributes of the *belle épreuve*, or fine print, go well beyond the contents of the work as created by the artist: they include the size and shape of the support, the inking, the choice of paper, the printing and even the number of copies produced. The 'artist's proof' is the first proof, when the copper plate is brand new, the ink fresh, on antique paper with broad margins. Burty extols the printing press and its strength, and the temperature of the stove on which the ink is softened. On the choice of paper he expatiates inexhaustibly: 'Charles Meryon preferred greenish paper, and this added to the strangeness of his images; Charles Daubigny would tear out the end papers of fine books printed in Holland in the eighteenth century; François Millet liked strong Italian paper

138. Félix Buhot,
The National Day (30 June) on Boulevard Clichy. 1878.
Etching and aquatint, 315 x 238 mm.
Bibliothèque nationale, Paris.

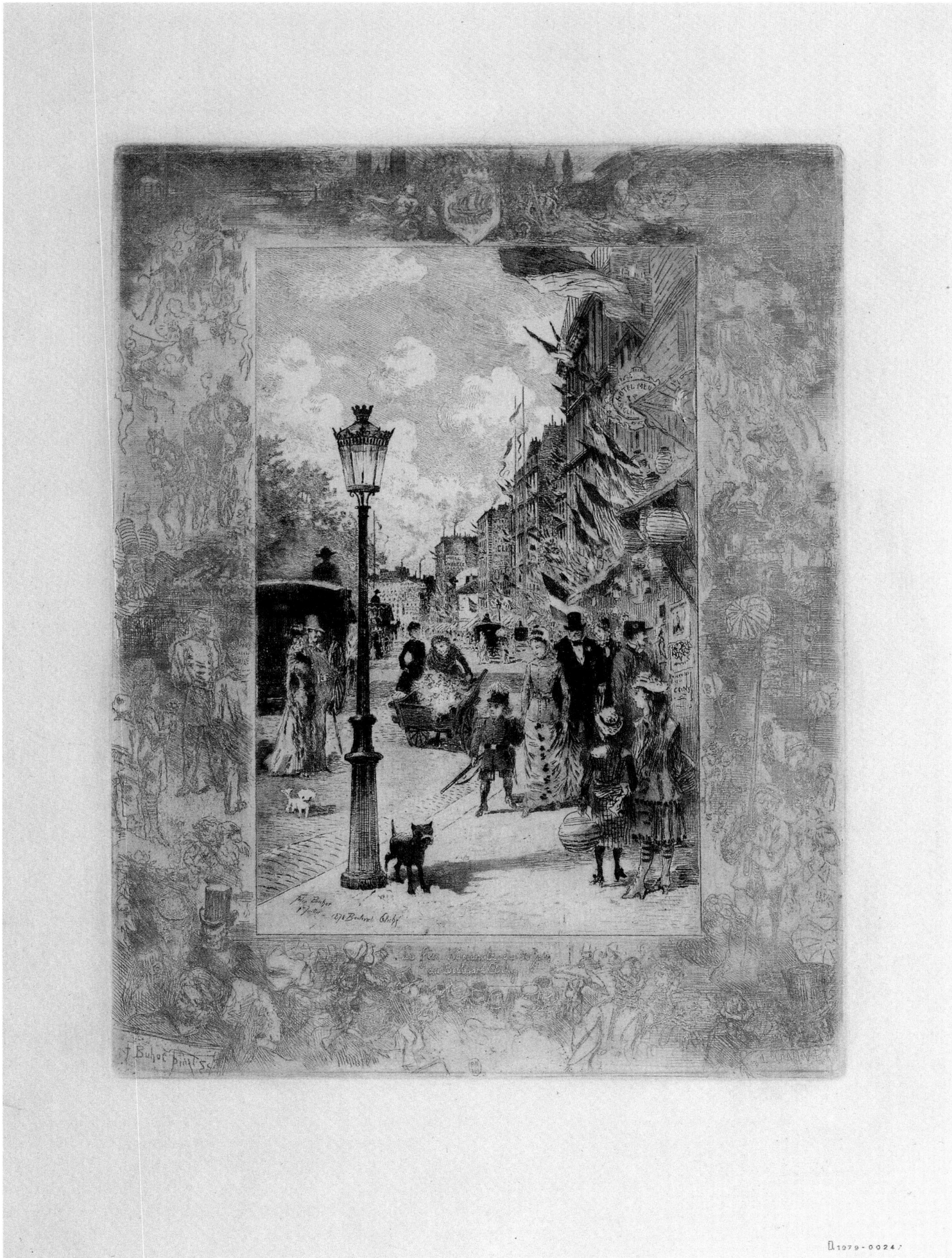

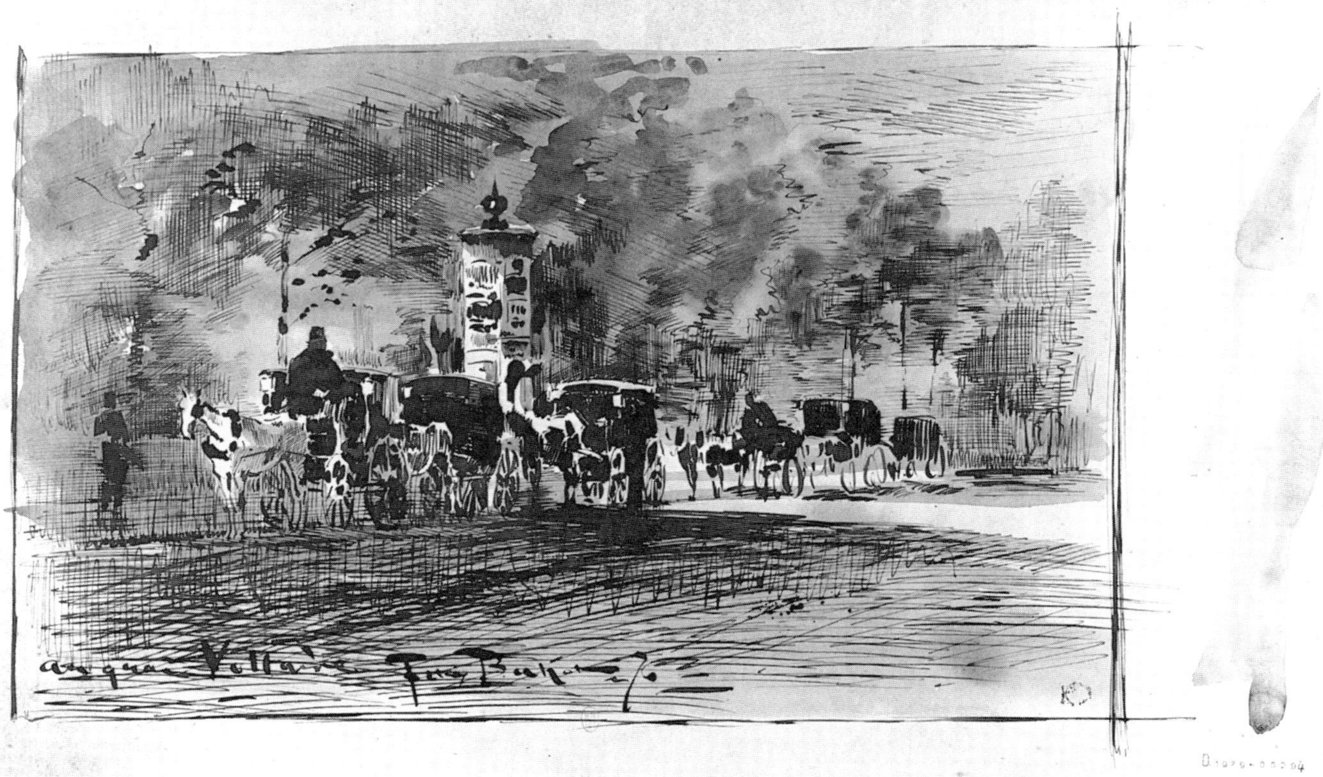

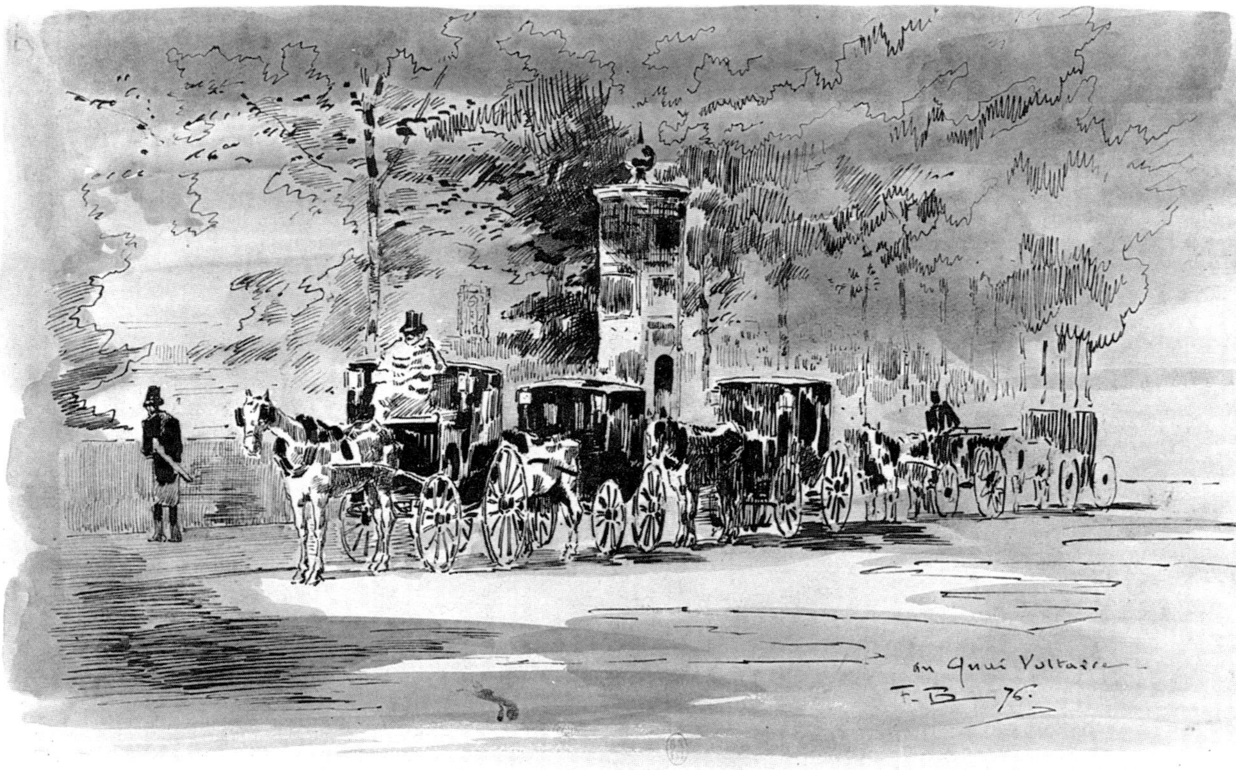

139, 140. Félix Buhot, *Quai Voltaire*. 1876. Ink and wash, 162 x 255 mm. ink & wash 145 x 245 Bibliothèque nationale, Paris.

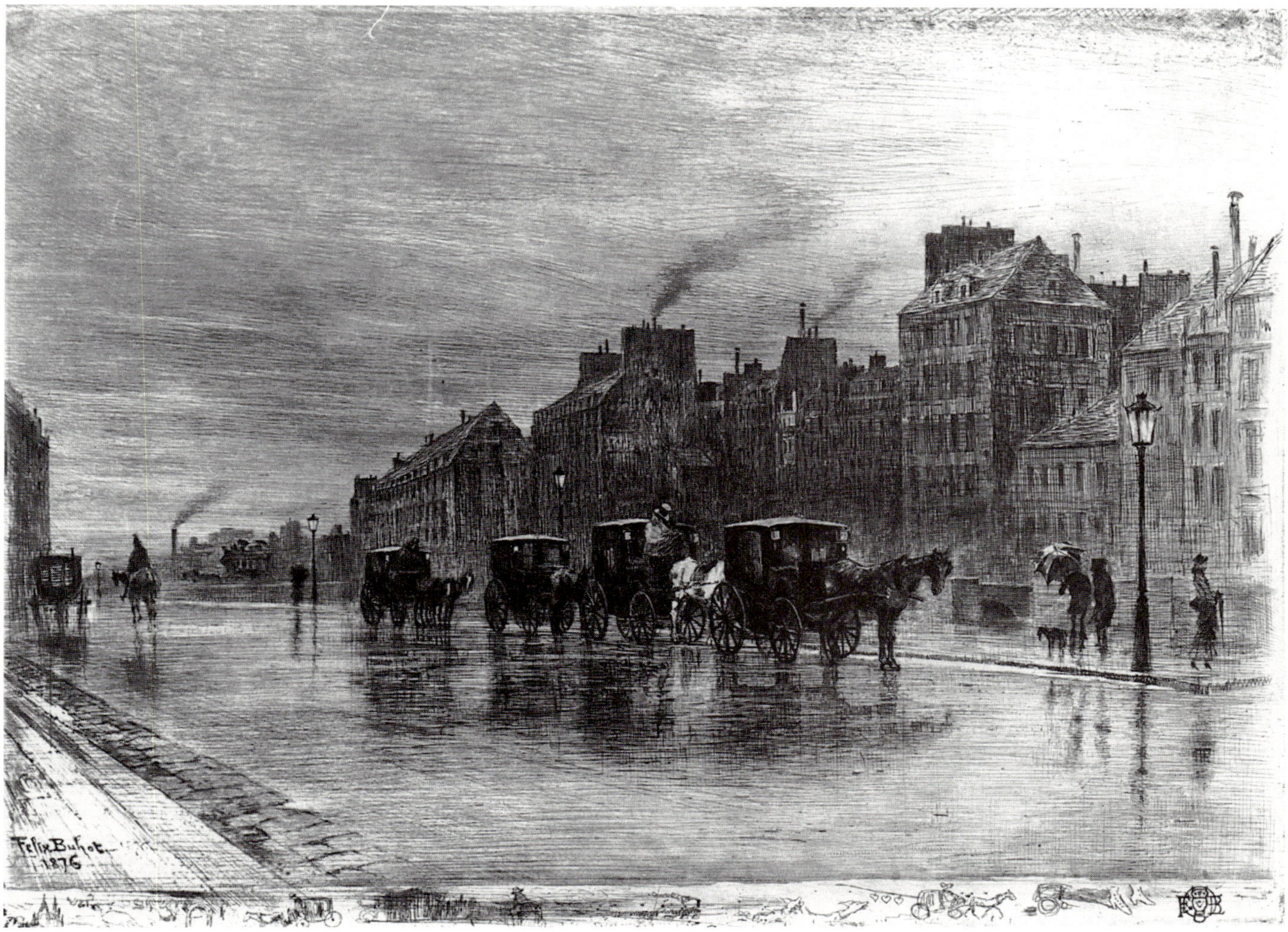

141. Félix Buhot,
Winter's Morning on the Quai de l'Hôtel-Dieu. 1876.
Etching, 240 x 320 mm.
Bibliothèque nationale, Paris.

with a coarse grain. Exquisite prints by Jules Jaquemart can be found printed on parchment. Sir Francis Seymour Haden, passionately seeking his ideal of gallantry, worked his way through the whole spectrum of rare papers. The different states of Bracquemond's *Erasmus* are on Jansenist paper typical of seventeenth century France. Such pieces, on unique papers, are reserved for the enjoyment of the dilettante.'[281]

Burty first met Félix Buhot in 1874, when the young painter from Valognes was earning a living by painting fans and crockery. Buhot had ambitions as a writer and his first submission to Lesclide at *Paris à l'eau-forte* was an article. Lesclide published the text and gave the print-maker employment on his magazine, to which Buhot soon became a leading contributor. Neither the article, entitled *The Calf's Head*, nor the etchings, mainly depicting donkeys, were likely to preserve their author's name for posterity. That same year, however, he published an etched reproduction of a *Bronze Japanese Horseman* in *L'Artiste*, showed work in Durand-Ruel's 'black and white' exhibition and also in the Salon, and also contributed to *L'Illustration Nouvelle*. Buhot had set out on his career as a virtuoso etcher, and dazzled his public with what one critic termed his 'conjuring tricks'.[282]

Buhot's plates in *Paris à l'eau-forte* were followed by larger plates in *L'Illustration Nouvelle*, and here he used all the techniques at his disposal to make each print into a precious object. First he would prepare each composition carefully with a number of small preliminary sketches – in water colour or colour wash, pencil or pastel; the etching had to rival or surpass these. Buhot was never recognised as a painter and, like Meryon, he represented that new breed of artist who owed his celebrity to printmaking alone. Unlike Bracquemond he did not begin his career in the printmaking workshops. His subjects are similar to those of the realist painters of his generation, Guérard or Goeleutte; he depicted street scenes with an emphasis on climatic conditions (Figs 139, 140), as in *The Return of the Artists on a Gusty Day*, or *Place Bréda under Snow*. The most prominent feature of his most famous etching, *Winter's Morning on the Quai de l'Hôtel Dieu* (Fig. 141), is the reflection of the horse-drawn cabs on the rain-soaked pavement. When he chose a subject in the delicate Japanese style he used every known technique. He learned from the eighty-year-old printmaker Frédéric Martens to make two-tone aquatints, and had no reservations about preparing two plates, to be superimposed on one another at the printing stage. He invented what he called the 'symphonic margin', a collection of secondary themes, sometimes etched on a separate plate and used to frame the main picture (Fig. 138). This frame he would prepare carefully with sketches and appliquéd patches that would show the different depths of bite. Then he would choose his tools to give his etchings 'a variety of textures which frequently bore no relation to the objects they represented'. Finally he would choose paper, antique for preference – he made an inventory of about eight hundred different types – even though his work was mechanically printed. He described to Keppel, the American collector, his 'search for textured paper for the reproduction of prints by heliogravure or *gillotage*'.[283] According to Burty's account he would always be present when his plates were printed, and if any proof emerged from beneath the press that failed to convey the gentleness or the vitality, the brightness or the subtlety that he had indicated to the printer, he would destroy it unhesitatingly.[284] The height of refinement was reached when the proof was printed on paper lightly steeped in turpentine, with margins hand gilded, as if all Buhot's production was aimed at Des Esseintes, the hero of *A Rebours* (1884) and the prototype of the decadent aesthete preparing the way for the society of the future.

Buhot's opposition to Impressionism should not mask the features he shared with the Impressionists: the taste for preparatory sketches (Fig. 139), using complicated techniques to capture a fleeting moment (Fig. 137); and above all, the idea of a print as a finished work of art to which the qualities particular to printing and reproduction give a kind of added value. On the other hand the resemblance of his style to that of certain Impressionists should not conceal what distinguishes his work from theirs: his literary preoccupations bring his work closer to the world of illustration than to the spontaneous, non-verbal representation of sensation. He shrouds his scenes in meteorological disturbances, but never abandons the continuity and homogeneity of his subjects, which are always legible and coherent (they can be read like a story) within their artificial frames. He admires Whistler for the unity and harmony of his work, and compares 'dismal' 'Pissarism' with vibrant, glowing' 'Whistlerism'; he defended his 'right to be a storyteller, which apparently the vibrists, decadents, Pissarrists and piss artists are not'.[285]

Unlike the Impressionist painters the young artists who were trying to find a foothold in the growing market for decorative art fostered by the new Republican bourgeoisie and encouraged by Burty never abandoned the Salon and exhibited there quite regularly, sometimes with reproductive engravings and sometimes with original prints. When Bracquemond, who worked at Sèvres and then for Haviland, gave up the Salon after having shown his *Views of Bas-Meudon* in 1870 and his illustrations to Rabelais in 1872, Guérot made his entry in 1874, Buhot in 1875 with reproductions of Japanese art, and Desboutin also in 1875, with portraits of Cadart, Burty, Goncourt and Berthe Morisot. Lepic was accepted by the Salon in 1876 with his *Landscapes on the Banks of the Escaut* and two paintings. The prints of Desboutin, Guérard and Buhot were regularly exhibited at subsequent Salons, as were the illustrations of Paul Renouard and, from 1879, Fantin-Latour's lithographs. There was a perceptible rise in the number of prints in the Salon of 1873 (8.7% of the catalogue entries), but this decreased continuously until 1880 (4.8%). In 1881, however, the increase began again, reaching 8.3% in 1882. Two currents caused these fluctuations, one was the weakness of the market which was favourable to small decorative works, the second the reclassification of the print in relation to other works of art on the market, at the beginning of the economic recovery.

29. *Modern Book-Collecting*

Print collectors were often bibliophiles before becoming interested in the visual arts. Under the Second Empire, the print turned into a branch of the publishing trade. The crucial rôle played by Poulet-Malassis, Baudelaire's publisher and friend, and Bracquemond in the revival of the etching has already been discussed. After his bankruptcy in 1862, Poulet-Malassis continued his activities in exile in Belgium where he encountered Baudelaire and Hugo.[286] Illustrations played only an accompanist's rôle in his books, however. At the close of the Second Empire Lemerre, the publisher of the Parnassian poets, took up where Poulet-Malassis had left off. In *Sonnets and Etchings* the print played more of a duet with literature, but Burty's interests were predominantly visual and the written word was not quite ready to perform on equal terms with the print. The two arts, poetry and printmaking, faced each other on opposite pages in a classic layout. Mallarmé, invited to join in at one stage, was not one of the poets who eventually appeared in the anthology. Manet, well-read and an intellectual, did not perhaps consider it his cup of tea. *Sonnets and Etchings* seems to have been a success,[287] at least its publisher claimed that the first printing was sold out in a week. The great name in illustration at the time was Gustave Doré, an exact contemporary of the Impressionists who, in 1869, had published in quick succession the *Fables* of La Fontaine, Perrault's *Contes*, and Dante's *Inferno* and *Paradiso*; he was celebrated enough to warrant an invitation from the Empress to the opening of the Suez Canal.[288]

After the war the taste for books illustrated in the old fashioned manner persisted. Bracquemond chose to exhibit his illustrations to Rabelais in the Salon of 1872, before opting out for the next ten years. Literature, in particular poetry, was at a high creative pitch, and this was surely an opportune moment for modern writers and printmakers to join forces. Manet frequented the salon of Nina de Villard, the poet, to whom Charles Cros had introduced him, and there were a number of poets to be found there at the time: Villiers de l'Isle-Adam, Mallarmé, Anatole France. Manet's portrait of Nina de Villard lying on her sofa dates from the period when he was working with Charles Cros, who published the first issue of *La Revue du monde nouveau* on 15 February 1874. Mallarmé published his prose poem *La*

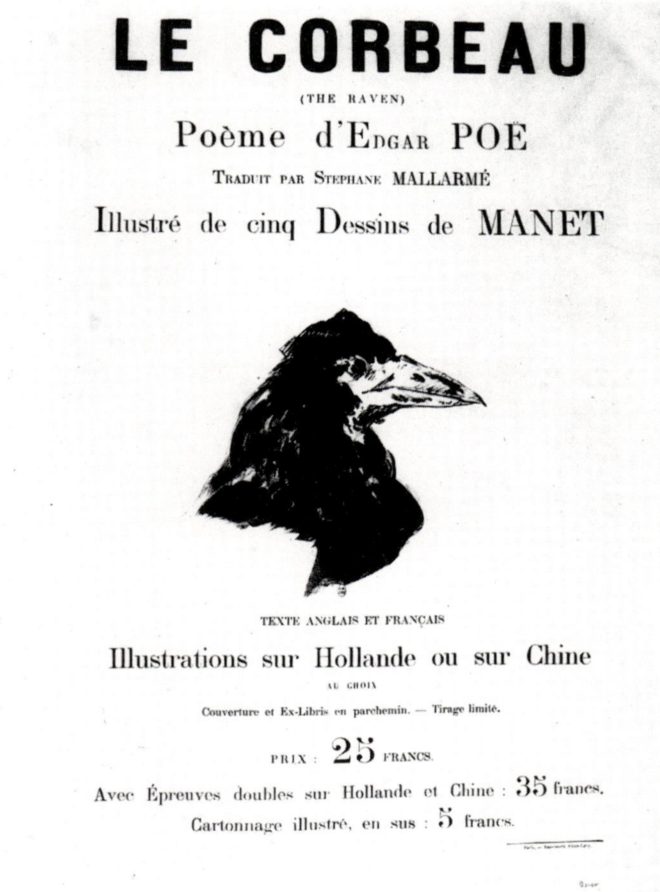

142. Edouard Manet,
The Raven, poster for the 1875
edition of the poem by Edgar Allan Poe.
Typography and lithography, 500 x 360 mm.
Bibliothèque nationale, Paris.

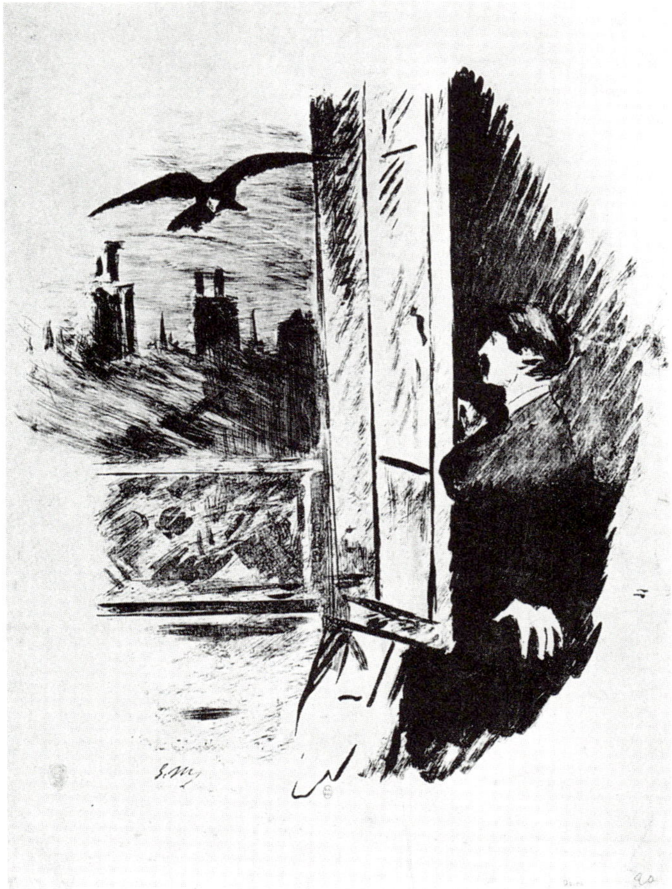

143, 144. Edouard Manet, *The Raven. 'At the Window'*. 1875. Autography, first state and variant, 400 x 300 mm. Bibliothèque nationale, Paris.

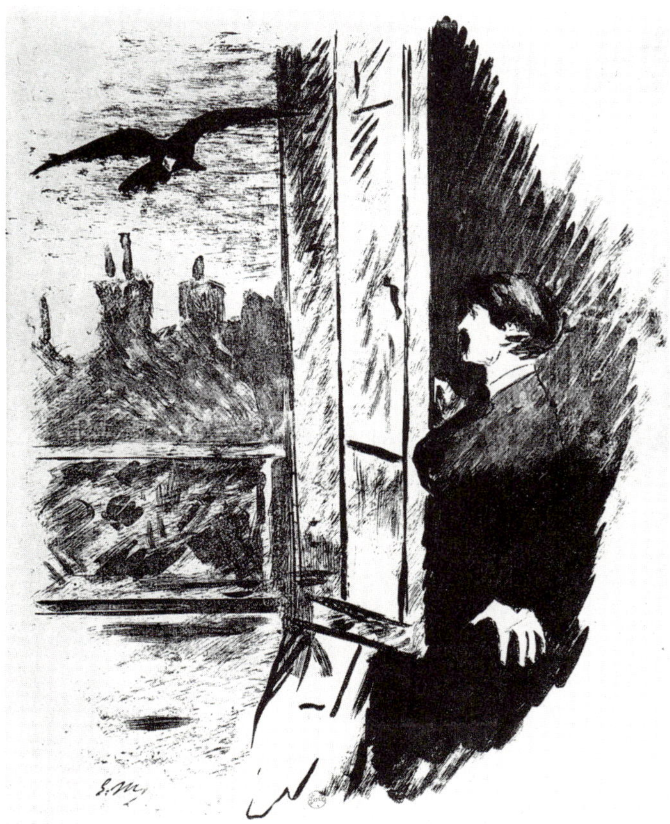

Pénultième in the review, and Manet a wood engraving by Prunaire of a drawing representing a version of his portrait of Nina de Villard, known now as *Le Parisienne*. Cros and Manet were planning to collaborate on a book of etchings illustrating the poem *Le Fleuve* (*The River*; Fig. 145). Charles Cros naturally turned to Lesclide,[289] who agreed to publish the book; an edition of one hundred copies appeared in December 1874 and was sold in the Librairie de l'eau-forte.

For the first time a modern poet and a painter were working as a team. The dialogue between the text and the illustrations is unequal, nonetheless. Manet's etchings consist of eight modestly-sized vignettes and, although the layout offers them ample exposure, they have the same proportions and perform the same function as etchings of the school of Lesclide. Nevertheless the idea of close collaboration between painter and poet has materialised. It was not strictly speaking a new idea: in 1867 Zola had involved Manet in a similar project which he tried to sell to the publisher Lacroix: 'This will be no ordinary book. The artist and I think of it as a work of art, and for you it will be a financial success. My draughtsman is M. Edouard Manet, a highly talented young painter, whose reputation will I'm sure have reached your ears. His critics have tried to depict him as an eccentric and have taken pleasure in deriding his work, just as the early work of Decamps and Delacroix was derided. Tomorrow, I am personally quite certain, M. Edouard Manet will be recognised as a master. I pleaded his cause most fervently in *L'Evénement*, now defunct, and out of gratitude and friendship he has asked to be allowed to provide drawings for my *Contes à Ninon*'.[290] Behind this editorial 'coup' that Zola was proposing to his publisher, there lurked the idea of a collaborative work linking a well-known writer and a well-known painter, a formula that gradually gained widespread popularity.

The culmination came with the collaboration of Mallarmé and Manet over Mallarmé's translation of Edgar Allen Poe's *The Raven*, already well-known in France through Baudelaire's translation. The choice of the American poem, romantic and yet thought'provoking, was not a straightforward one. Mallarmé's translation met with a variety of responses, and was refused by the publisher Lemerre, who later spoke of 'this superb volume which, I now see, would not be easy to sell'.[291] Having looked around for a publisher, Mallarmé returned to Charles Lesclide. *The Raven* (Fig. 142), bringing together the names of Poe, Mallarmé, Manet and Lesclide, is the first book in which the illustrations have the same status as the text. The format demonstrates this at once: Manet's illustrations, in their separate folio, are genuine prints, worthy of being framed (Figs 143–4). The choice of paper was aimed at satisfying the requirements of print collectors. The double handwritten signature of both Manet and Mallarmé on each copy marks the entry of such books

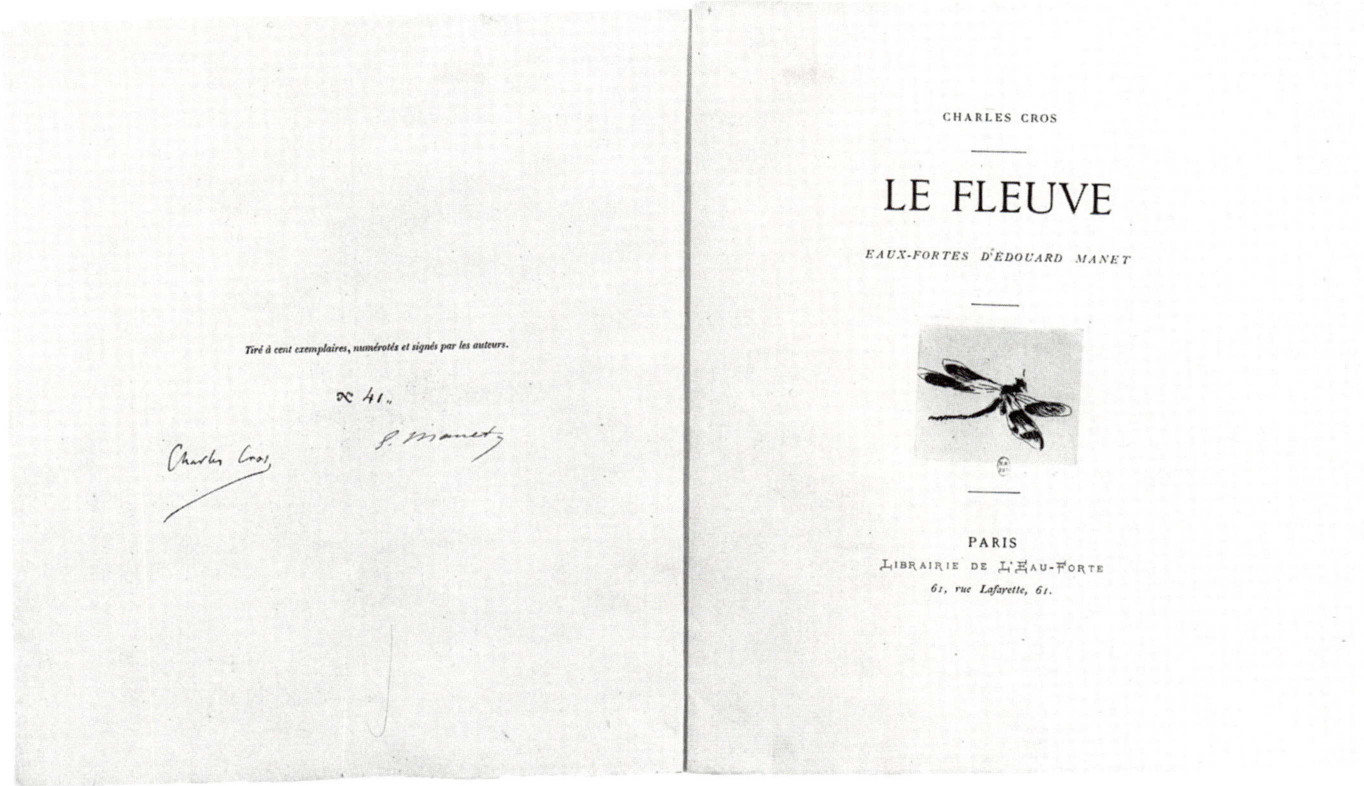

Tiré à cent exemplaires, numérotés et signés par les auteurs.

N° 41.

Charles Cros

E. Manet

CHARLES CROS

LE FLEUVE

EAUX-FORTES D'EDOUARD MANET

PARIS

LIBRAIRIE DE L'EAU-FORTE

61, rue Lafayette, 61.

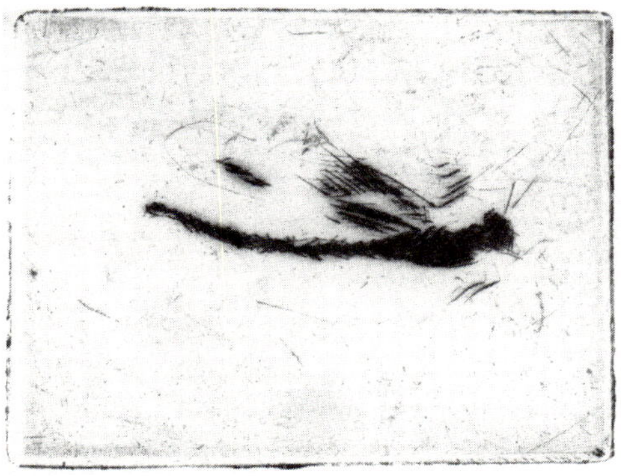

145. Edouard Manet,
illustrations to *Le Fleuve* by Charles Cros. 1874.
Etchings. *Dragon Fly*, 40 x 60 mm;
The Mountain (first project), 78 x 95 mm;
Bibliothèque nationale, Paris.

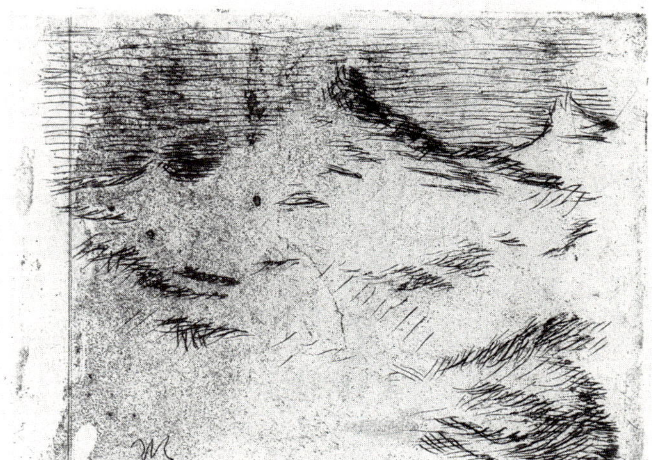

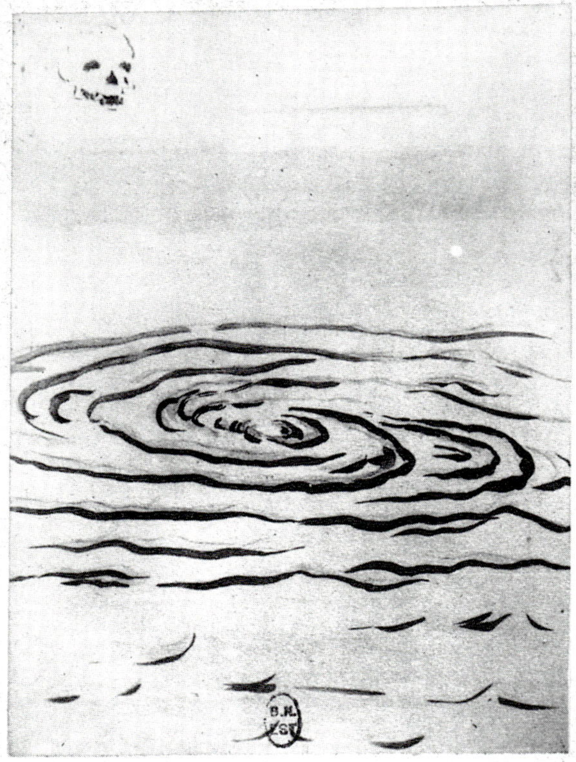

146. Edouard Manet,
illustration to *The City in the Sea*,
poem by Edgar Allan Poe. 1881.
473 x 303 mm.
From *Les Poèmes d'Edgar Poe traduits par S. Mallarmé*,
Paris, Vanier, 1889, p.101.

147. Edouard Manet,
illustration to *L'Après-midi d'un faune*
by Stephen Mallarmé, *Nymphs*. 1876.
Woodcut, 500 x 100 mm.
Bibliothèque nationale, Paris.

into the realm of graphic art; they are no longer simply printed books.[292] Formal innovations like these are matched by a profound alteration to the spirit in which the text is illustrated. Independently of Mallarmé's interpretation, Manet has treated the subject with striking liberty, to the extent that Poe's poem could be subject to two different interpretations, according to whether it is read through Mallarmé's translation or through Manet's illustrations. Ségolène Le Men has commented that 'Manet's graphic transformation cannot be reduced to the same drama of poetic sterility that Mallarmé expresses here and pursues later in *Igitur* . . . . Manet's illustration of *The Raven* proves, in the last analysis, to be a poem in pictures on the theme of the portrait and its metamorphoses, and on the self-portrait.'[293] The starkness and drama of Manet's version is in some ways more original and stronger than Mallarmé's own version. *The Raven* was published in May 1875 and belongs (from the point of view of technique) to the movement instigated by contemporary painters for the revival of the lithograph. Manet chose transfer paper for the reproduction of his drawings, as explained by Moreau-Nélaton, whose information comes from contemporary witnesses: 'with a brush soaked in autographic ink, then transferred to stone'.[294] Unlike the *Sonnets and Etchings*, a more traditional combination published at a more favourable moment, *The Raven* was not a success. Out of a planned edition of 240 copies only 150 were printed and, several years later, Lesclide still had some in stock. In spite of this failure Manet and Mallarmé pursued their collaboration. They planned another work based on Poe, this time on their translation of *The City in the Sea*, to which three drawings by Manet can be attached (Fig. 146); these are even more provocatively wild than his drawings for *The Raven*.[295] Finally in April 1876 the publisher Derenne published an expensive album of Mallarmé's *L'Après-midi d'un faune*, with wood engravings after designs by Manet (Fig. 147).[296]

The illustrations to *The River* came as a revelation to Félix Buhot, Lesclide's favourite artist, and endorsed his idea of what modern illustration should be: 'The sketches scattered by a painter through a text, when the text is purely poetic, should be transpositions, not compositions. The drawings serve as an accompaniment to the main theme. . . Perhaps the artist is seeking to elucidate or to complete the poet's thought; perhaps he is limiting himself to the awakening, by different means, of analogous emotions, in order to produce a harmonious accompaniment.'[297] In this frame of mind he set out to illustrate *The Bewitched*, by his compatriot Barbey d'Aurevilly, with dramatic etchings, to be published in 1877; and he applied the same principles to all his work as a post-Romantic etcher-illustrator (Fig. 148). Odilon Redon drew extreme conclusions from Manet's example, particularly from *The Raven*, cultivating the despised technique of transfer paper and composing lithographs that show no respect for or sensitivity

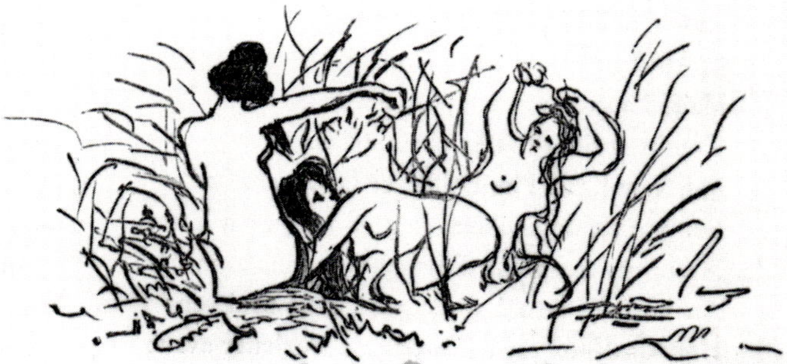

LE FAVNE

Ces nymphes, je les veux perpétuer.

Si clair,

Leur incarnat léger, qu'il voltige dans l'air
Assoupi de sommeils touffus.

Aimai-je un rêve ?

Mon doute, amas de nuit ancienne, s'achève
En maint rameau subtil, qui, demeuré les vrais
Bois mêmes, prouve, hélas ! que bien seul je m'offrais
Pour triomphe la faute idéale de roses —

Réfléchissons...

ou si les femmes dont tu gloses

B.N. EST

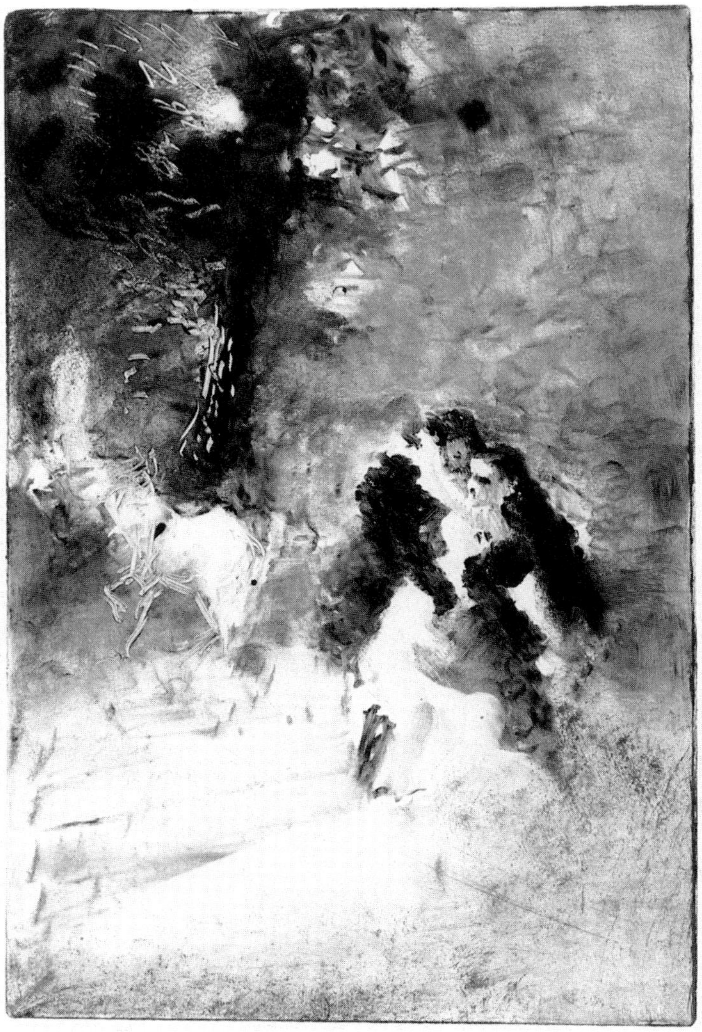

148. Félix Buhot,
illustration to *Une vieille maîtresse* by Barbey d'Aurevilly, *'Ryno and Vellini'*. Undated.
Monotype, 240 x 160 mm.
Bibliothèque nationale, Paris.

towards the author; as illustrator he allowed himself complete freedom to do exactly as he wished. His first series of lithographs, *In Dreams*, appeared in 1879, only four years after *The Raven*; his second, in 1882, was entitled *To Edgar Poe*. His three versions of *The Temptation of St Anthony* (1888, 1889 and 1896), inspired by Flaubert's text, mark the emancipation of the print from the world of publishing and its entry into the realm of *objets d'art*, dragging in its wake the illustration of literary texts as well. Gustave Doré died on 23 January 1883. His last work, published posthumously, consisted of twenty-three plates illustrating the eighteen verses of Edgar Poe's *Raven*. His illustrations are as monumental and elaborate as Manet's are minimal, as extroverted as Manet's are introverted, as explicit as Manet's are allusive, as theatrical as Manet's are undemonstrative. Manet died on 30 April of the same year.

30. *Degas and his Group*

For as long as it has existed, the print has always been a means for artists to circulate their work, even if only in a limited number of copies, apart from a short period in the seventeenth century (around 1625–50), when a growth in urban culture brought with it a surge in the number of rich bourgeois and impecunious collectors, at a period that was not unlike the Second Empire. Never had such care been taken that one print should differ from another as in France after 1870, nor had the taste for variants been so intense that each proof from a single plate was made into something individual and exceptional. Never before had artists responded to such expectations by deliberately creating plates that would not stand up to a second printing. Never before had such a doctrine influenced practices so comprehensively as it did among the group of artists who, on the occasion of the Impressionist exhibitions, congregated around its leading convert, Edgar Degas. As far as Degas himself was concerned, hardly any of his engravings were ever published; this was not for want of a publisher, but because they were not intended for publication. The artist went further than this, out of nostalgia for his life as a gentleman of leisure, perhaps, or because he had some inkling of the use to which works of art might be put in the future, when he pushed arrogance to its limits, asking: 'Is a painting intended to be seen? . . . one works for two or three friends. . . painting is an aspect of private life.'[299] What must he have thought of the print, the focus for such concentrated egoism?

When Edgar Degas lost his private income and fell into debt, he tried to sell what he termed his '*articles*': pastels, fans and, why not, those unusual products of modern technology, the 'rare reproduction' or monotype. According to Henri Loyrette, a quarter of his output dates from this period, between 1873 and 1881.[300] The winter of 1875, between the two first Impressionist exhibitions, found Degas with his engraver friends Marcellin Desboutin, De Nittis and Alphonse Hirsch – the latter an artist but mainly a hanger-on – in Cadart's print workshop. Material evidence of these sessions has survived: the perplexed-looking portrait of Degas by Desboutin (Fig. 150) and De Nittis, and portraits of Hirsch by De Nittis and Degas (Figs 152–2), also in drypoint. This cross referencing of models is more like an exercise in technique than

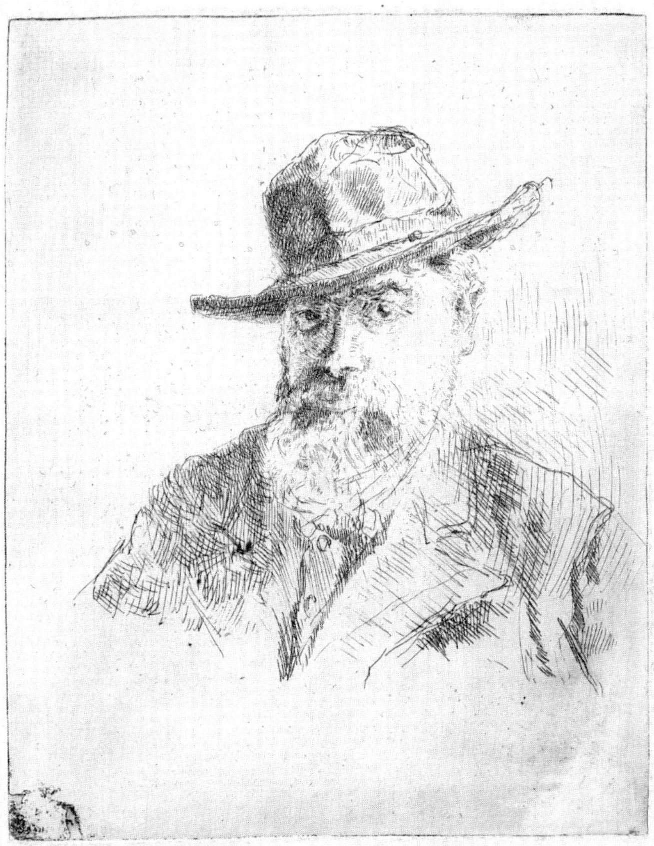

149. Henri Rouart,
Self Portrait. About 1875–80.
Drypoint, 162 x 122 mm.
Jean-Dominique Rey collection, Paris.

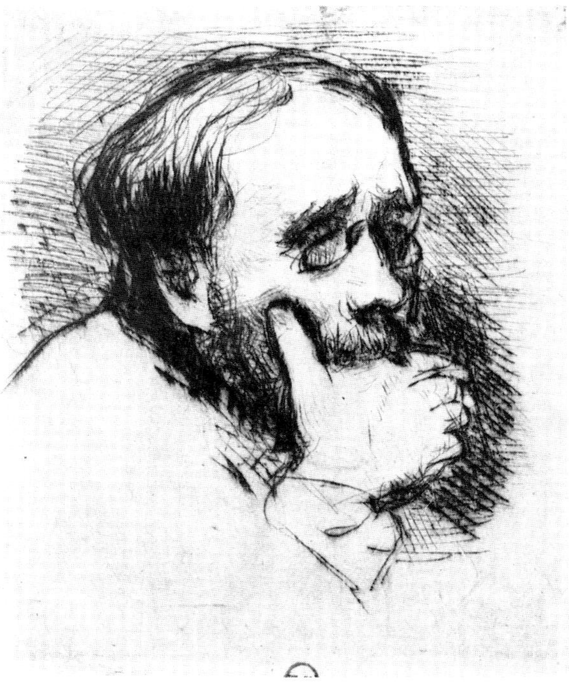

150. Marcellin Desboutin, *Portrait of Degas*. 1875. Drypoint, 90 x 74 mm. Bibliothèque nationale, Paris.

151. Giuseppe De Nittis, *Portrait of Alphonse Hirsch*. 1875. Drypoint, 85 x 70 mm. Bibliothèque nationale, Paris.

152. Edgar Degas, *Portrait of Alphonse Hirsch*, 1875. Aquatint and drypoint, second state, 112 x 60 mm. Bibliothèque nationale, Paris.

sustained work, in an atmosphere that was as friendly as it was professional. This was the year when Degas was given some instruction by his friend Lepic, and together they made their first monotypes. These experiments by Degas and his friends were certainly partly inspired by Duranty's manifesto, *La Nouvelle Peinture* (*The New Painting*) (1876), in which he devotes a passage to what might be called 'the new printmaking': 'Acknowledge the fact that in nearly all respects everything in this movement is new and would like to be free: printmaking too is raddled with processes. One artist will pick up the dry point and use it like a pencil, attacking the plate directly and drawing the etching at a single sitting; another will add unexpected emphasis to an etching by using a graver; a third will vary each print with acid, adding brightness or mystery, sometimes literally painting it with a skilful addition of ink as it is being printed.'[301] The first lines of this allude undoubtedly to Desboutin's drypoints, the second to the experiments made by Lepic and Degas after 1875, and it is Degas who is Duranty's model of the ideal printmaker.

Pissarro was one of those disappointed by the dissolution of the first Impressionist group the day after the first exhibition closed. He had gathered a group of friends around him at Pontoise. To his friends from Auvers, Cézanne and Guillaumin, had been added Edouard Béliard, a participant in the two first Impressionist exhibitions, and Alfred Meyer, with whom Pissarro founded a new cooperative, 'L'Union', along democratic lines.[302] Under the same pressure to earn his living as Degas, but with the additional responsibilty of a family to feed, Pissarro was also interested in '*articles*'. He took up engraving again. In June 1878 he had made enough progress to exhibit the third state of *Woman emptying a Wheelbarrow* at the Dudley Gallery in London, where 'black and white' exhibitions were a regular feature.[303]

Degas was fascinated by the processes of printmaking and eagerly helped himself to some old metal plates found among the refuse of a photogravure workshop. It was then too that he became interested in the 'galvanic pencil', sparks from whose metal point pierced the metal conductor.[304] His notebooks bear witness to these experiments.[305] Desboutin, amazed by the energy Degas (Figs 153–4) expended on investigation into such unorthodox techniques, wrote to his friend De Nittis on 17 July 1876: 'Degas was the only one I saw on a daily basis, and he's no longer a friend, a man, an artist! He's a zinc or copper plate, blackened by printer's ink; man and plate are laminated together by the press, into whose gearing he has disappeared completely. That man's crazes are something quite phenomenal! He's in the metallurgical phase, having his drawings reproduced with an ink roller and is dashing all over Paris in this heat! Hunting for an industrial enterprise to correspond to his obsession! It's an epic in itself! His talk is all of metallurgists, plumbers, lithographers, planers, niliographers! etc. You'll get it when you return. I'm waiting for you to take over from me! Thanks be to God.'[306] As if his conversation were not enough to daze his friends, his letters chased Pissarro to Pontoise and Bracquemond to Sèvres, with requests for information on the mysteries of soft-ground etching or aquatint, the only way of reproducing coloured etchings, whether by hand or by machine.

Bracquemond had found his niche in the Haviland porcelain factory. His experience in craft techniques taught him to explore new market opportunities and the decorative art industry as a whole. He saw the demand for coloured printmaking coming and, first to the post as usual, proceeded to make some experiments. He began by redeveloping the old manual techniques of the eighteenth century whereby different plates bore different colours and were printed by being superimposed one on another. Bracquemond himself took up printmaking again. Having abandoned the Impressionists for their second and third exhibitions he was ready, for the fourth, to submit his experiments with colour etching and three other black and white prints, landscapes, which of all his multifaceted work come the closest to the subject matter and nimble style of the Impressionists. In general, however, his drawing retained its stiffness, making little concession to fleeting sensations, and it was for this reason that he remained on the fringes of Impressionism as it was then perceived. He lost none of his skill, prescribing numerous virtuoso pieces. Only one other printmaker exhibited with Bracquemond in the fourth exhibition in 1879: this was Henri Somm, whose real name was François-Clément Sommier, an illustrator and friend of Buhot. Somm's output, however, was limited in relation to the Impressionist group to the submission of two drypoint 'calendars for 1878 and 1879'; his work displayed little more than a timely Japonism.[307]

Degas found imitators in literary circles and in the cafés where artists congregated. His strong personality made its mark on younger artists looking for a mentor. Jean-Louis Forain, eighteen years his junior, haunted the bohemian world of Verlaine and Rimbaud; rejected by his family, he dropped out of the Ecole des Beaux-Arts and eventually found a home with André Gill, the caricaturist, to whom the post of art editor of *Paris à l'eau-forte* had been offered several years previously. Forain learned etching and newspaper illustration, two acquisitions that could lead to a career, if not a very secure one. He was fascinated by Degas and his cynical view of the world, choosing the same subjects as him, including scenes of low life that appealed to a vast public. Degas involved him in the fourth Impressionist exhibition, to the dismay of some of the other participants.[308] He also recruited a less contentious figure, the rich young American Mary Cassatt, ten years his junior, who had been travelling in Europe for several years. She had made the acquaintance of Joseph Tourny, the print-

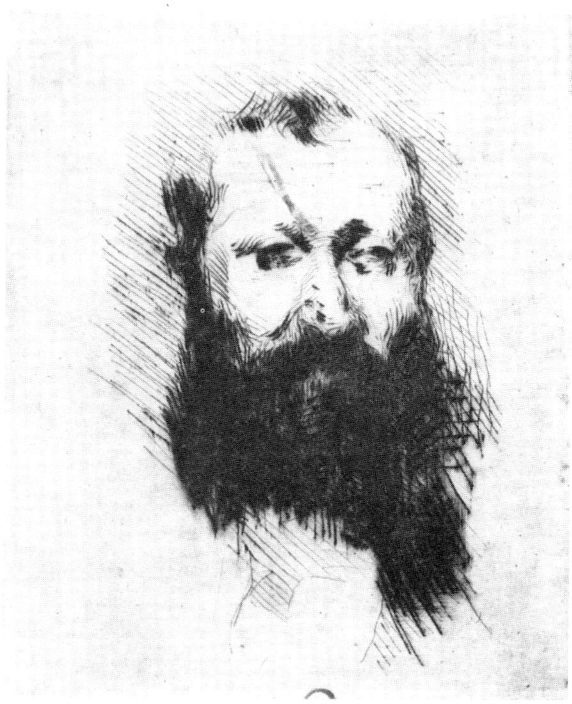

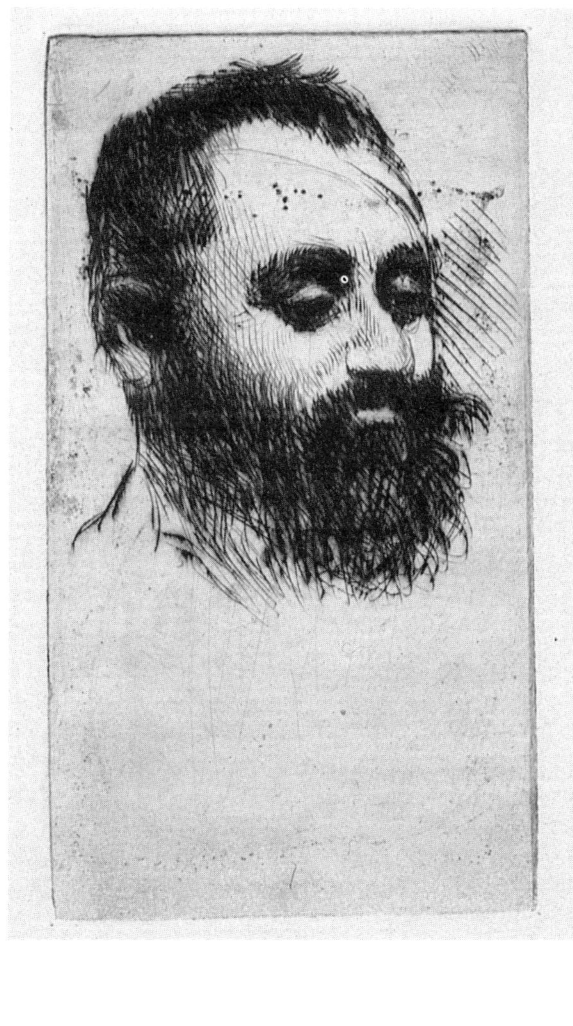

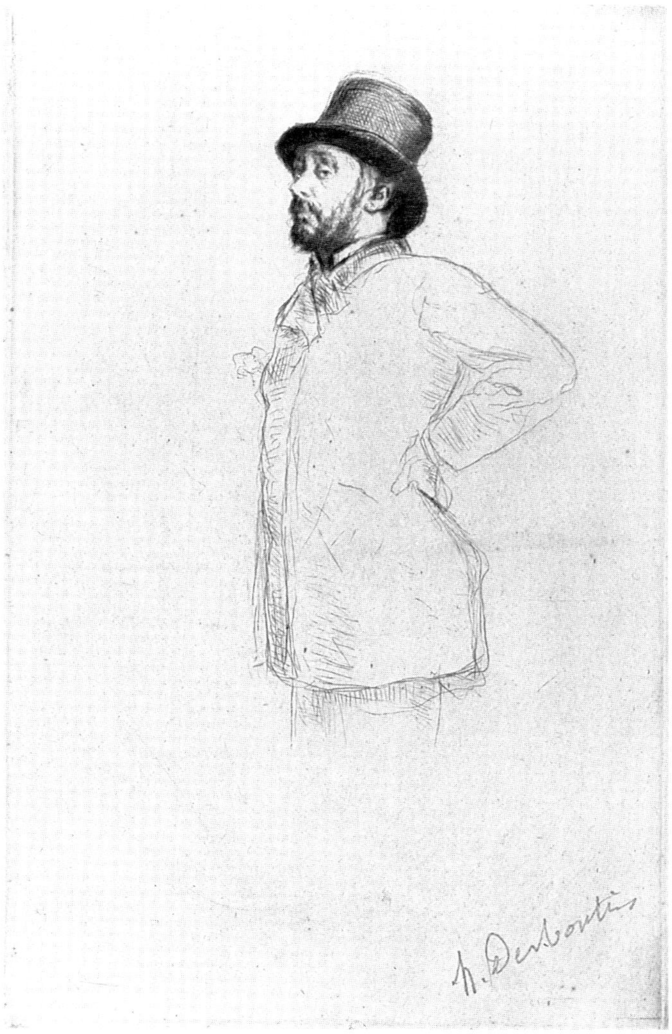

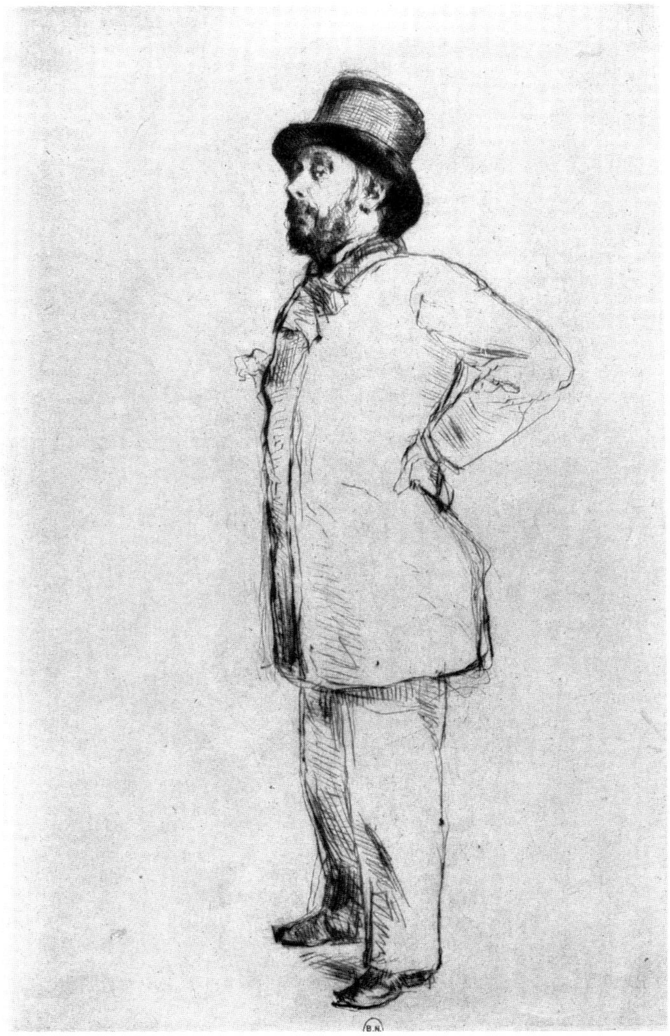

153, 154. Marcellin Desboutin, *Portrait of Degas*. 1876. Drypoint, first and second states, 225 x 144 mm. Bibliothèque nationale, Paris.

maker, in Antwerp in 1873 and he must have spoken to her about Degas. She moved permanently to Paris in 1874, the year of the first Impressionist exhibition, and Degas invited her to participate in the second. She felt ill-prepared and, like Forain, only consented to appear in the fourth; like Degas, she was fascinated by the alchemy of printmaking.

In 1879 everything was in place for what Joël Isaacson has termed 'the Impressionist crisis'. The techniques were ripe, the actors in place. Degas directed the drama. Creativity had become overheated by the dawn of a new age, and matters were made worse by the political situation: the long drawn-out birth of a republic that never quite emerged aroused hope, pain and conflict. The atmosphere at the end of the decade was heavy; the economy was in the doldrums and with it the fragile art market, as revealed by the meagre submissions to the Salon, itself flagging, by the reduced Impressionist exhibitions and other tentative examples of individual enterprise. Several great figureheads of modern art died almost simultaneously: Millet and Corot in the same year, 1875; Diaz in 1876; Courbet in 1877; fifteen hundred admirers followed Daubigny's funeral cortège in 1878, and the republicans showed their continuing displeasure in 1879 by setting up a civil burial for Daumier at which they waved banners bearing his work. All these gave a sombreness to the period; it would be hard to decide if it were the sombreness that precedes dawn or dusk.

31. *Le Jour et la Nuit*

Magazines were in vogue. Most of them were ephemeral and at least some of them still-born. The return to freedom of the press had generated hundreds of new titles.[309] Every movement had to found one of their own, the Impressionists establishing theirs under the editorship of Georges Rivière in April 1877; it too was short-lived. A technical problem, the quality of the reproductions, was the main difficulty facing these magazines. They either had to depend on expensive handprinting, as did *Paris à l'eau-forte*, or on very indifferent electrotyping. Each editor claimed to have found a solution: original etchings and vignettes for Lesclide, or an ordinary printing plus a de luxe edition as with the first illustrated catalogue to the Salon of 1879.[310] Louis Gonse founded *L'Art* in 1875 and *Les Beaux-Arts illustrés* in 1876.[311] Hoschedé founded *L'Art de la mode in 1880.*[312] Emile Bergerat, a friend of Bracquemond and son-in-law of Théophile Gautier, was editor of *La Vie moderne*, launched in April 1879 by the publisher Charpentier; it tried to pitch its appeal somewhere between the mediocre and the elegant publication. Bergerat prided himself on obtaining plates of the very best quality, and promised a journal that would be 'admirably printed on expensive paper, convenient in format, easy to bind and combining the specialist appeal of an art review with the more general appeal of a current affairs magazine.'[313] Bergerat adds: 'It is incomprehensible to me that at a period like our own we are still trying to establish the distinction between art as such and industrial art.'

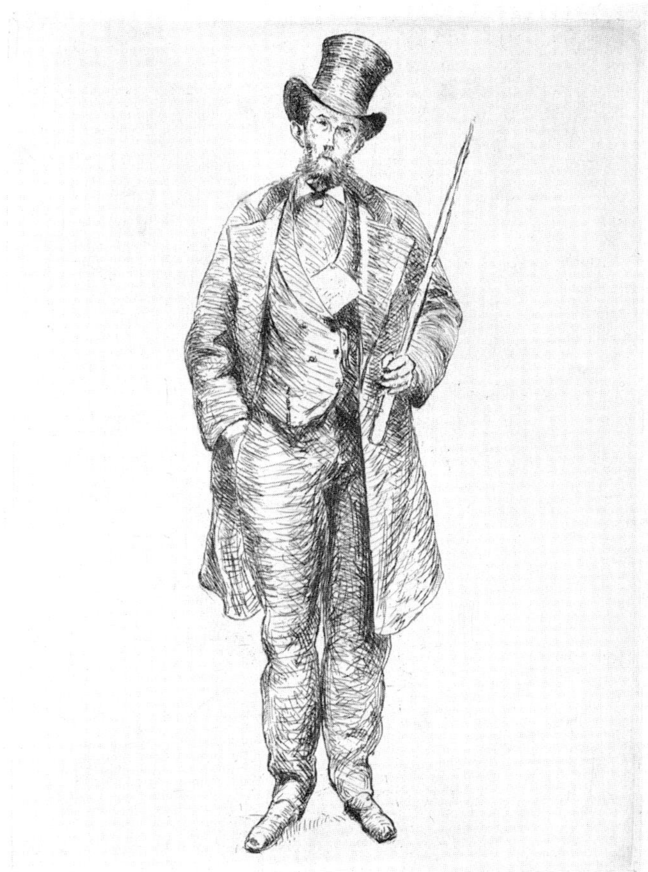

155. Gustave Caillebotte, *Portrait of Paul Hugot*. 1878. Etching, 276 x 198 mm. Private collection, Paris.

Desire for their own magazine also affected those Impressionists sharing Degas's taste for prints and printmaking. They were exploring the money-making potential of 'articles' related to the decorative arts, and it was in this context that they felt that an illustrated review should be attempted; the modest success of their most recent exhibition encouraged them further. *La Vie moderne* boasted the signatures of Théodore de Banville and Alphonse Daudet and, as illustrators, Georges Jeanniot and De Nittis, both friends of Degas. Whether he is to be believed or not, his friend Ludovic Halévy noted in his diary on 16 May, a month after *La Vie moderne* was launched, that Degas's reaction was swift: 'Visit to Degas. Meet him with the independent Miss Cassatt, one of the exhibitors from the rue de la Paix. They are in a state of high excitement. They each

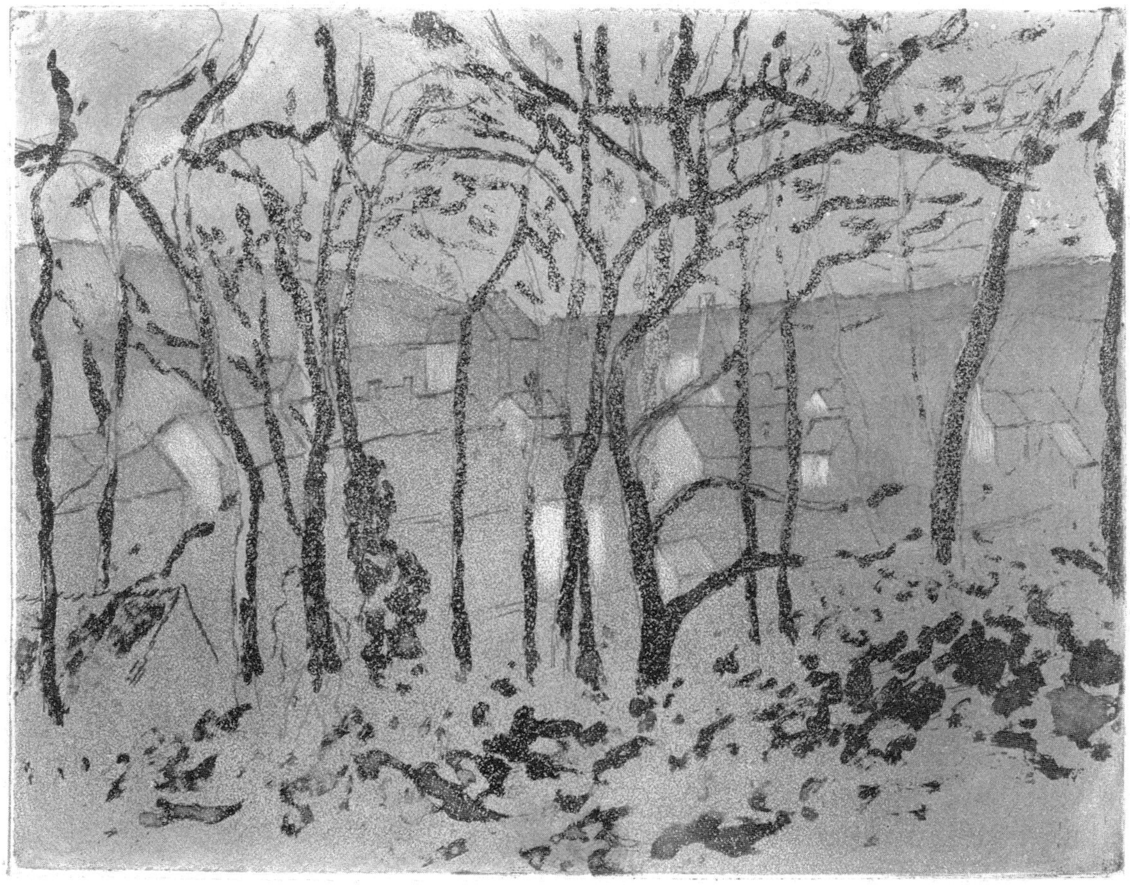

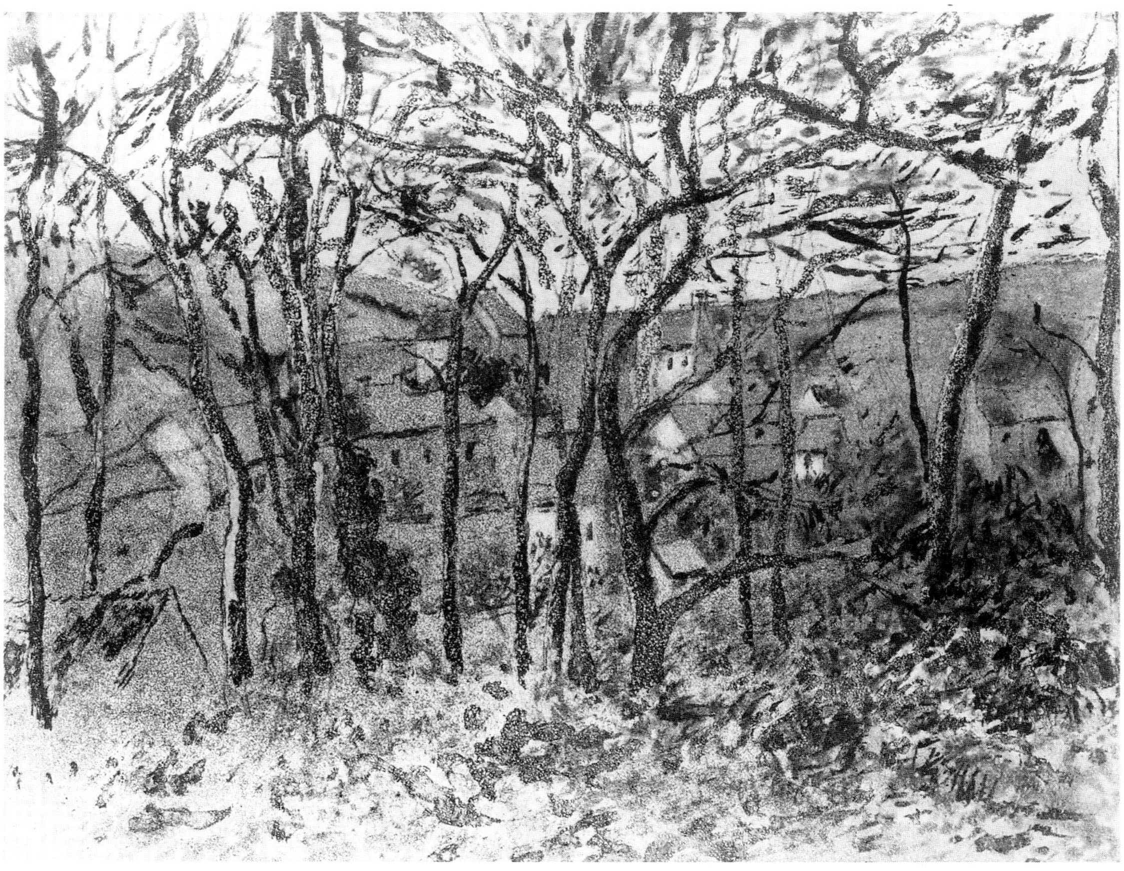

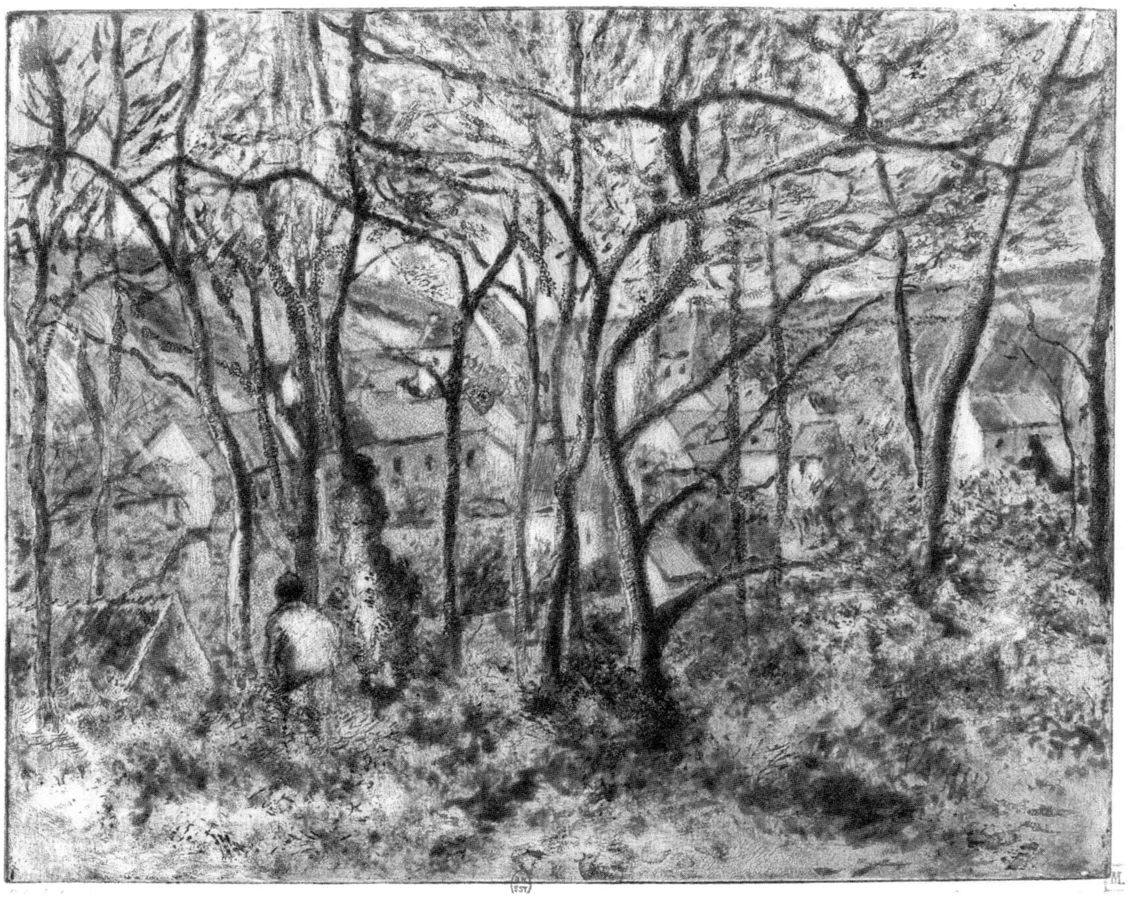

156, 157, 158. Camille Pissarro,
Wooded Undergrowth at L'Hermitage. 1879.
Etching, aquatint and drypoint, 218 x 268 mm. First state, Museum of Fine Arts, Boston, Lee M. Friedman Fund; second state, Library of Congress, Washington; fifth state, Bibliothèque nationale, Paris.

received 440 francs from their exhibition and are thinking of starting a review. I ask if I can contribute.'[314]

A few scraps of correspondence between Degas and Bracquemond, an anonymous article in Le Gaulois and the proof of a cover design by Bracquemond are the few remaining vestiges of an unsuccessful enterprise. But although *Le Jour et la Nuit* did not live to see the light of day, its importance was nonetheless crucial. Even though the crisis was at its most acute, and sales almost non-existent, the Impressionist print can be discussed with more supporting evidence than before; it had reached a point of no return. Artists were making a last effort to have their prints published, but continued to favour techniques that discouraged any kind of reproduction. *Le Jour et la Nuit* could not survive such a contradiction.

The first references to the magazine occur in Degas's correspondence in May 1879, and were followed by an announcement in *Le Gaulois* on 24 January 1880: 'The new school is missing one important thing, namely a journal',[315] and the catalogue to the fourth Impressionist exhibition (1 April 1880), in which Pissarro's prints (Figs 156–8) are described as 'Four states of a landscape, to be published in the first issue of the review *Le Jour et la Nuit*'. The title itself carries echoes of the Symbolists. It

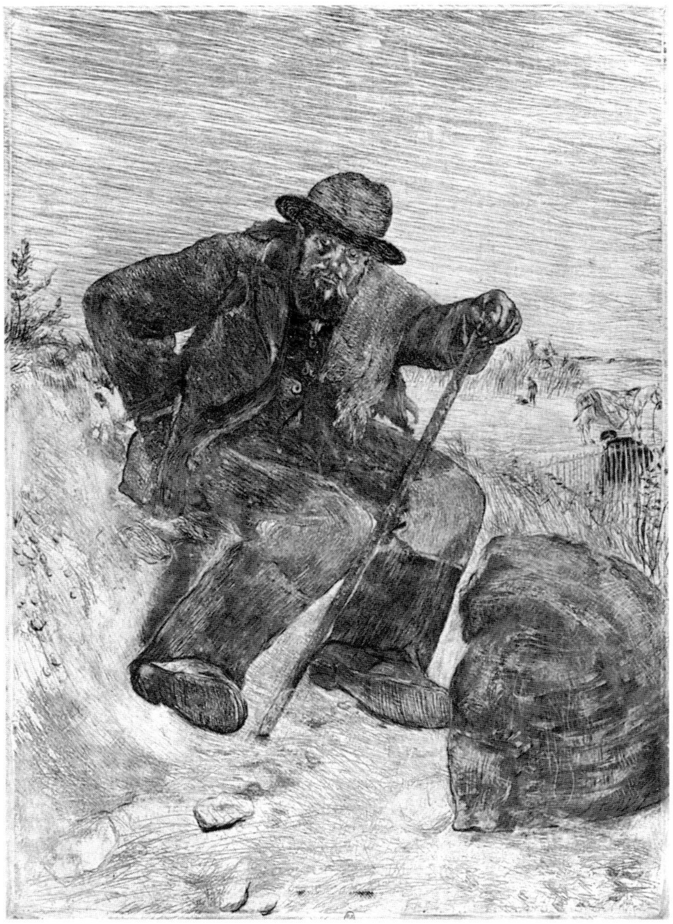

159. Jean-François Raffaëlli, *Old Rag-and-Bone Man*. 1879. Drypoint, second state, 340 x 239 mm. Bibliothèque nationale, Paris.

is not known whose idea it was, but we do now know that Bracquemond, who was still working as a porcelain designer, sketched out a cover design in a style foreshadowing the Modern Style.[316] Bracquemond acted as the artistic director of the review.[317] Degas seems to have been the driving force behind the enterprise, spurring on the artists and visiting Salmon, the printer. The choice of Salmon is instructive: he was less of an 'artist' than Delâtre and was quite heavily involved in mass reproduction. The capital required to set up the review came from two friends, Caillebotte and Ernest May, the banker, both willing to invest in this risky project. From the start, the review was not really a review, and the projected frequency of its appearances was uncertain. In 1903 Degas reprimanded Bracquemond: 'You have forgotten the monthly review that we once hoped to start'.[318] The cover designed by Bracquemond states clearly 'Review to appear "from time to time",' and *Le Gaulois* announced that 'to start with, Le Jour et la Nuit will not appear at regular intervals.' Nor was the format yet decided: J.-P. Bouillon wrote about Bracquemond's design for the cover that 'the measurements of the sheet of paper . . . should apparently not be taken as a reliable indication of the size of the prints that may be going to be included in the first issue.' There was more than one review at the time that in fact consisted of an album of prints, if *Le Gaulois* is to be believed: '*Le Jour et la Nuit* will have no text; it will consist of a cover containing a number of drawings with a short note about the artist.' Ludovic Halévy would have no opportunity to contribute.

The artists advertised were the artists whom Degas had recruited for the Impressionist exhibition: Cassatt, Raffaëlli, Forain, Rouart, plus Caillebotte, their sponsor, Bracquemond and Pissarro. Oddly enough, Desboutin's name was not on the list. The venture was a cooperative one, like the Society of Etchers and also like the first Impressionist exhibition: 'These artists are the proprietors as well as the editors of their paper . . .. Profits or losses will be shared by all those collaborating in the publication.' The techniques to be employed were not laid down either: 'Each artist will be free to employ the method of reproduction that suits him best: etching, drypoint, aquatint etc. . ., even lithography'[319] (the 'even' here conveys a certain condescension, and gives clearly to understand that no-one would stoop to *gillotage* or photogravure). So much uncertainty gave the project little chance of success. The old formula of the album of prints (adhered to for so long by Bracquemond) had to confront the modern formula of the art review; the result was a hybrid, neither old enough nor young enough and thus symptomatic of this crucial phase in the history of Impressionism.

The final handicap threatening the first appearance of the 'journal' was the personality of the man in charge, Degas, who suffered from chronic anxiety and restlessness, according to portraits of him left by his friends; he

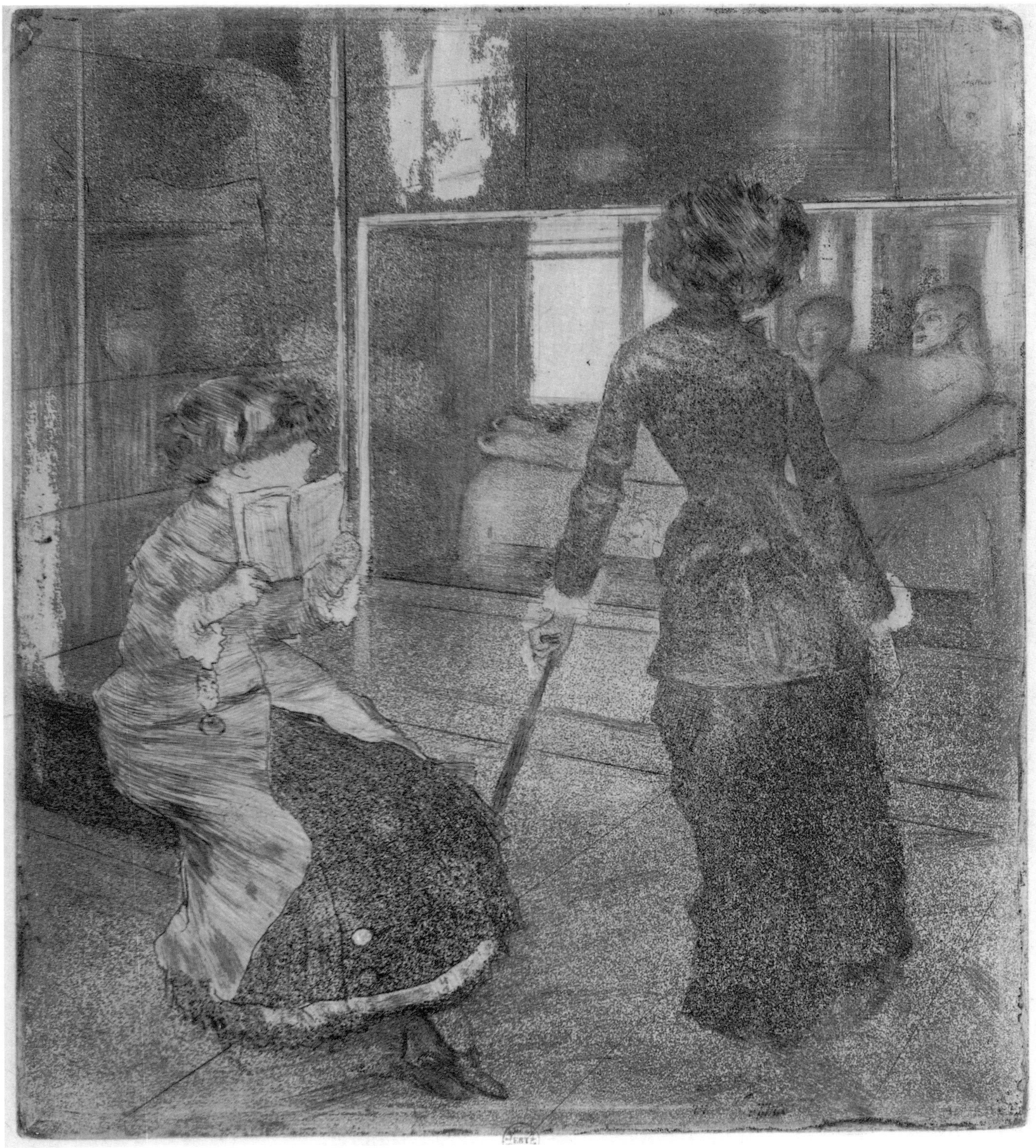

160. Edgar Degas, *Mary Cassatt at the Louvre: the Gallery of Antiquities*. 1879. Etching and aquatint, 270 x 237 mm. Bibliothèque nationale, Paris.

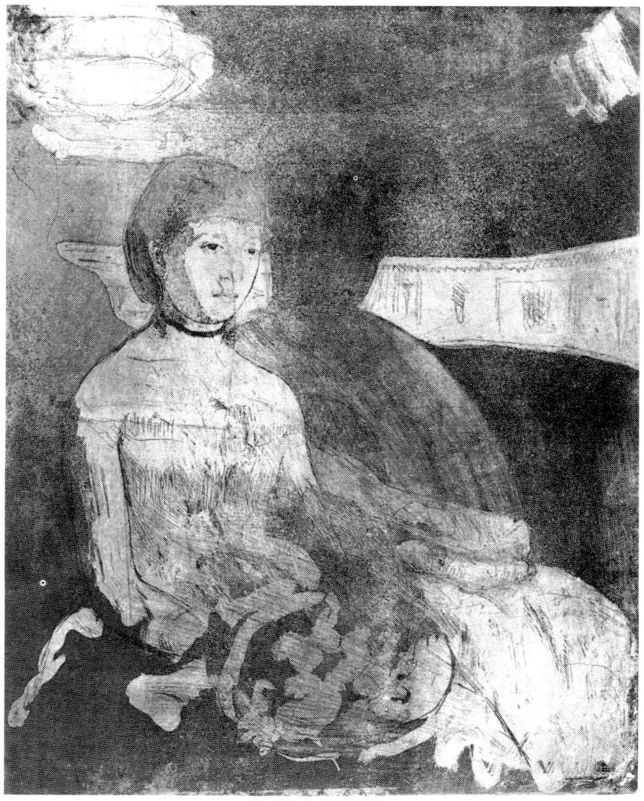

161. Mary Cassatt, *At the Theatre: Mirror Image*. 1879. Etching, aquatint and drypoint, 276 x 217 mm. Bibliothèque nationale, Paris.

was utterly unsuited to business. Mary Cassatt's mother blamed Degas for the failure of the magazine, and it is tempting to believe her: Degas, 'as usual, when the time came . . . was not ready so that Le Jour et la Nuit . . . which might have been a tremendous success, has not yet appeared . . . Degas is never ready for anything – and this time he has caused them to miss a golden opportunity.'[320] In one of his letters, Degas laments Bracquemond's absence and reproaches him with it. In fact it is easy to imagine that if Bracquemond had been involved things would have turned out differently. 'Things are moving, even without you. You should be guiding and teaching us instead of letting us veer from one side to the other.'[321] 'We must talk about the magazine. We did a few trials with Pissarro and have a print by him as a result. Mary Cassatt is hard at it at the moment. With my living to earn it is impossible for me to devote my time to it entirely. Let us arrange to spend a whole day together, either here or at your house. – Is there a printing press at your house?'[322] 'Salmon is getting cross and wants all the plates by Tuesday. A word to the wise is enough. I'm working on my plate, stripped for action. Could you bring your plate over on Tuesday morning or take it directly to Salmon, ready for printing? It is a pity you cannot be there at five because the whole group will be there.'[323] Finally, Degas wrote to Pissarro: 'Mademoiselle Cassatt has made some enchanting prints. Try and come back soon. I have started to publicise the paper in various quarters. We shall cover our expenses with pre-publication sales, or so quite a few print collectors have told me.'[324]

The plates were prepared but it is not known whether they ever arrived at Salmon's workshop. Pissarro's submission had been exhibited in April and can be identified with certainty as *Wooded Undergrowth at L'Hermitage* (Figs 156–8). The proof of Raffaëlli's *Old Rag-and-Bone Man* (Fig. 159), sent with other engravings at the request of the American collector Samuel Avery in 1887, bears the following written note: 'This plate was to appear in the first number of a monthly collection of etchings and drypoints that the 'Impressionist' group had planned to publish in 1880. The collection was to be called "Le Jour et la Nuit". This collection never materialised.' If this document is to be taken literally, it confirms that the publication would have included etchings and drypoints only, and would not have included reproductions produced by electrotype or by any other method; it also implies that the publication was to appear monthly, as Degas reminded Bracquemond in 1903, in spite of the fact the Bracquemond's cover advertised it as appearing 'from time to time'; finally, it suggests that the group around Degas, if not Degas himself, was identified by Raffaëlli with the Impressionists from whom he seems eager to disassociate himself. Raffaëlli's memories could on the other hand be discounted because the note was written seven years after the events and may simply represent his own perception of the unfinished business.[325]

It is generally thought that Degas prepared *Mary Cassatt at the Louvre: the Gallery of Antiquities* (Fig.

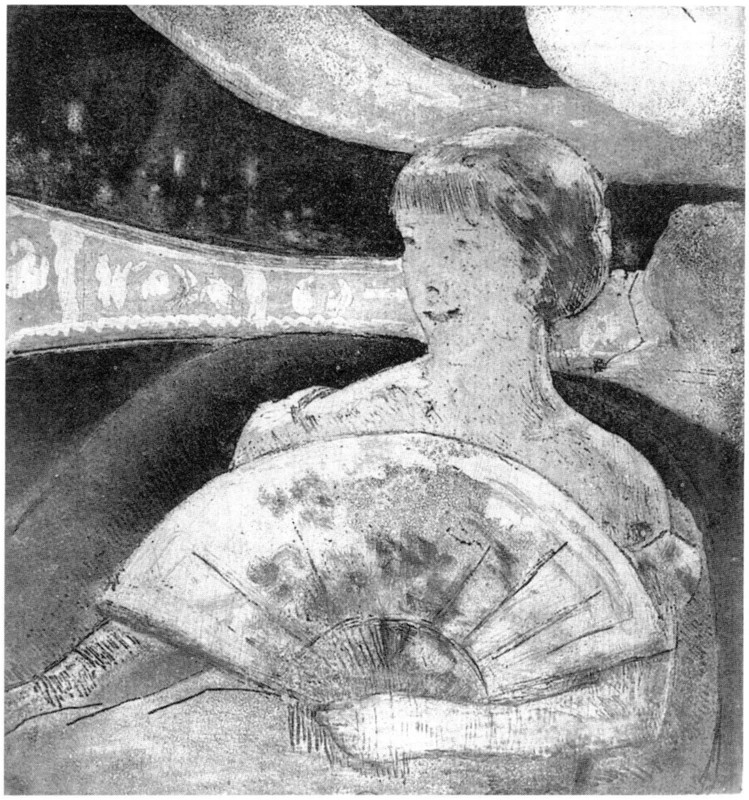

162. Mary Cassatt, *Woman with a Fan (In the Opera Box)*. 1879. Etching, softground etching and aquatint, third plate, 205 x 184 mm. Bibliothèque nationale, Paris.

160), and Mary Cassatt *Woman with a Fan (In the Opera Box)* (Fig. 162). What Bracquemond produced is not known. The format of these prints is relatively consistent.[326] The basic essentials of this abortive project are there: four or five plates in a new style, *Wooded Undergrowth at L'Hermitage* (Fig. 158) and *Woman emptying a Wheelbarrow* (Figs 169–72), or the style developed by Degas after his portrait of Alphonse Hirsch for his more ambitious plates: *At the Ambassadors* (Figs 178–9) or *Mary Cassatt at the Louvre* (Fig. 161); or Mary Cassatt's style in her first large plates: *Woman with a Fan* (Fig. 162) or *The Visit*. The stylistic similarities between these plates are quite obvious, and consist mainly of a heavy use of aquatint, and the direct treatment of simple subjects, framed as if by a telephoto lens. If his correspondence is to be believed, Degas was the instigator of this reliance on aquatint, but his own experience was deeply influenced by Bracquemond, whose support he sought so insistently. These technical analogies do not tell the whole story: through the artist's still shaky mastery of the grain on each ill-smoothed plate a consistent language began to emerge, consisting of unexpected patches of light, subjects illuminated from behind, and scraps of composition laid out in an off-beat manner, drawn directly on to the plate.

These similarities may have been due in part to Degas's powerful, slightly tyrannical personality, which is identifiable in his letters and visible in the work of the friends whom he tried to turn into disciples. At a deeper level, however, the kinship could be attributed to circumstances favouring intensified experimentation by the Impressionist printmakers. It was too late to go backwards.[327] They were unable to unlearn the techniques of the printed black and white printmaking they had practised in their youth, but had not yet managed to reconcile this with the decorative styles into which the print was beginning to be absorbed. Because of this impasse, unpublished proofs would in a few years time be taken almost unquestioningly into museums of art, as original works in the truest sense of the word, whether their authors liked it or not. The crisis in art had reached its climax, aggravating all the other contradictions. Pissarro had had enough of waiting for clients and critics. In 1878, he confided to Murer: 'How am I to get through it? Not a sale in sight, art is bathed in silence. . . It's no good counting on our exhibition, it's going to be a fiasco; at Durand-Ruel, where there is a gathering of masterpieces by our most illustrious painters – not a soul, total indifference. People have had enough of this portentous painting, so demanding that it begs for attention and contemplation – it's all too serious. Progress should help us to see and feel effortlessly, and to have fun. Anyway, who needs art, can it be eaten? No? Well then!'[328]

32. *Pissarro and Degas: Industrial Progress*

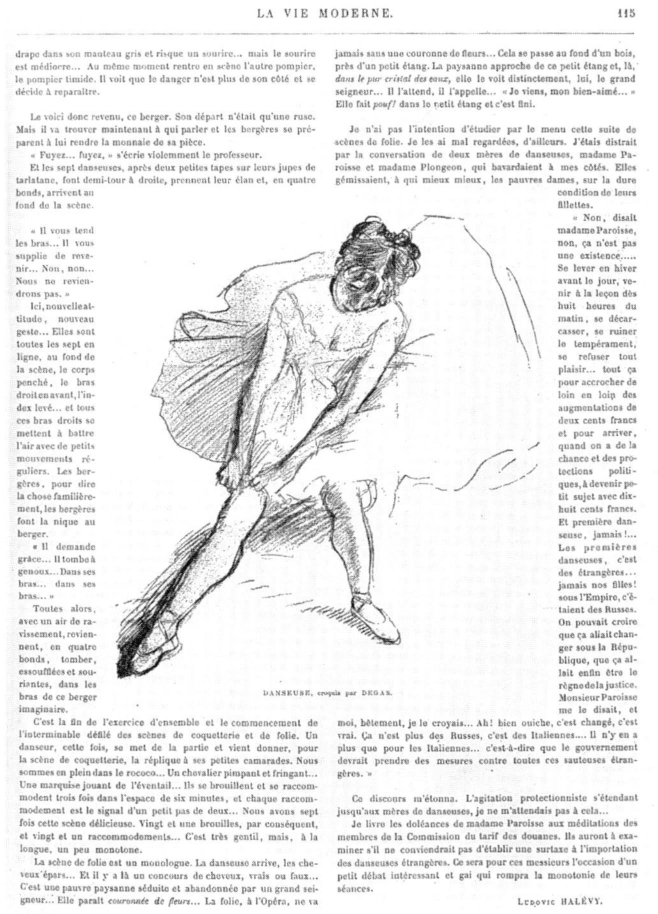

LA VIE MODERNE. 115

drape dans son manteau gris et risque un sourire... mais le sourire est médiocre... Au même moment rentre en scène l'autre pompier, le pompier timide. Il voit que le danger n'est plus de son côté et se décide à reparaître.

Le voici donc revenu, ce berger. Son départ n'était qu'une ruse. Mais il va trouver maintenant à qui parler et les bergères se préparent à lui rendre la monnaie de sa pièce.

« Fuyez... fuyez, » s'écrie violemment le professeur.

Et les sept danseuses, après deux petites tapes sur leurs jupes de tarlatane, font demi-tour à droite, prennent leur élan et, en quatre bonds, arrivent au fond de la scène.

« Il vous tend les bras... Il vous supplie de revenir... Non, non... Nous ne reviendrons pas. »

Ici, nouvelle attitude, nouveau geste... Elles sont toutes les sept en ligne, au fond de la scène, le corps penché, le bras droit en avant, l'index levé... et tous ces bras droits se mettent à battre l'air avec de petits mouvements réguliers. Les bergères, pour dire la chose familièrement, les bergères font la nique au berger.

« Il demande grâce... Il tombe à genoux... Dans ses bras... dans ses bras... »

Toutes alors, avec un air de ravissement, reviennent, en quatre bonds, tomber, essoufflées et souriantes, dans les bras de ce berger imaginaire.

C'est la fin de l'exercice d'ensemble et le commencement de l'interminable défilé des scènes de coquetterie et de folie. Un danseur, cette fois, se met de la partie et vient donner, pour la scène de coquetterie, la réplique à ses petites camarades. Nous sommes en plein dans le rococo... Un chevalier pimpant et fringant... Une marquise jouant de l'éventail... Ils se brouillent et se raccommodent trois fois dans l'espace de six minutes, et chaque raccommodement est le signal d'un petit pas de deux... Nous avons sept fois cette scène délicieuse. Vingt et une brouilles, par conséquent, et vingt et un raccommodements... C'est très gentil, mais, à la longue, un peu monotone.

La scène de folie est un monologue. La danseuse arrive, les cheveux épars... Et il y a là un concours de cheveux, vrais ou faux... C'est une pauvre paysanne séduite et abandonnée par un grand seigneur... Elle paraît *couronnée de fleurs*... La folie, à l'Opéra, ne va jamais sans une couronne de fleurs... Cela se passe au fond d'un bois, près d'un petit étang. La paysanne approche de ce petit étang et, là, *dans le pur cristal des eaux*, elle le voit distinctement, lui, le grand seigneur... Il l'attend, il l'appelle... « Je viens, mon bien-aimé... » Elle fait *pouf!* dans le petit étang et c'est fini.

Je n'ai pas l'intention d'étudier par le menu cette suite de scènes de folie. Je les ai mal regardées, d'ailleurs. J'étais distrait par la conversation de deux mères de danseuses, madame Paroisse et madame Plongeon, qui bavardaient à mes côtés. Elles gémissaient, à qui mieux mieux, les pauvres dames, sur la dure condition de leurs fillettes.

« Non, disait madame Paroisse, non, ça n'est pas une existence..... Se lever en hiver avant le jour, venir à la leçon dès huit heures du matin, se décarcasser, se ruiner le tempérament, se refuser tout plaisir... tout ça pour accrocher de loin en loin des augmentations de deux cents francs et pour arriver, quand on a de la chance et des protections politiques, à devenir petit sujet avec dix-huit cents francs. Et première danseuse, jamais!... Les premières danseuses, c'est des étrangères... jamais nos filles! sous l'Empire, c'étaient des Russes. On pouvait croire que ça allait changer sous la République, que ça allait enfin être le règne de la justice. Monsieur Paroisse me le disait, et moi, bêtement, je le croyais... Ah! bien ouiche, c'est changé, c'est vrai. Ça n'est plus des Russes, c'est des Italiennes.... Il n'y en a plus que pour les Italiennes... c'est-à-dire que le gouvernement devrait prendre des mesures contre toutes ces sauteuses étrangères. »

Ce discours m'étonna. L'agitation protectionniste s'étendant jusqu'aux mères de danseuses, je ne m'attendais pas à cela...

Je livre les doléances de madame Paroisse aux méditations des membres de la Commission du tarif des douanes. Ils auront à examiner s'il ne conviendrait pas d'établir une surtaxe à l'importation des danseuses étrangères. Ce sera pour ces messieurs l'occasion d'un petit débat intéressant et gai qui rompra la monotonie de leurs séances.

LUDOVIC HALÉVY.

DANSEUSE, croquis par DEGAS.

163. Edgar Degas,
Dancer,
published in *La Vie moderne*, no. 5, 8 May 1879, p. 71.
Bibliothèque nationale, Paris.

As a magazine, *Le Jour et la Nuit* promised to be a strange curiosity, and it is not surprising that it never appeared; with its fifty copies, would it ever have survived? To give it greater credibility Druick and Zegers have suggested that a bigger, mechanically printed edition was planned.[329] The first fifty copies would just have been an introduction. Their hypothesis is based on a number of arguments. Although Degas mentions only one printing,[330] and the advertisement in *Le Gaulois* makes no mention of the number of copies but states that 'to start with' the publication will not appear at regular intervals, he must surely have had plans for a longer run and a project more elaborate than just the publication of an album of prints.

The central argument in support of this thesis is based on the great enthusiasm felt by Degas for the process of photogravure. As the letter from Desboutin to De Nittis reveals, this passion was at its height just when *Le Jour et la Nuit* was first conceived. On 13 May 1879, three days before he told Halévy of his project, Degas wrote to Bracquemond: 'This morning I went with Prunaire, the wood engraver, whom I'm sure you know, to see a certain Geoffroy, a celebrated phototype printer in Rue Campagne-Première. He's a strange man, an inventor with bad eyesight. We must quickly take advantage of being ahead of schedule. Boldly forward into the world.'[331] It is obvious that Degas and Bracquemond, who had already transferred one of his etchings, *The Chemin des Coutures, Sèvres* (Fig. 167), on to zinc to be reproduced by 'gillotage' by the printing firm of Yves and Barret, had something in mind.[332] A second argument supports the first one: it seems extraordinary that Degas should have chosen monotype for his illustrations to Ludovic Halévy's short stories (the same Halévy who was to have written for *Le Jour et la Nuit*). In order to transform monotype prints into illustrations the pictures had to undergo either a chemical or a photographic process. Like Manet, Degas had no objection to his drawings being mechanically reproduced. Following Renoir (Fig. 164), who was responsible for the cover of the second issue,[333] Degas (Fig. 163) and Cassatt agreed that *La Vie moderne* could reproduce their drawings using reproductive plates.[334] The hypothesis cannot be ruled out, therefore, that Degas and Bracquemond may have been hatching a plan to bring out a publication with reproductions from drawings specially executed for the purpose, as was happening more and more frequently since Alexandre Decamps launched his publication *Le Musée* in 1834. Although there is no good reason to confuse this more general preoccupation with the project for *Le Jour et la Nuit*, Druick and Zegers have good grounds for pointing out that 'Moreover, far from seeking to distinguish the "original print" from the industrially "printed image", Degas sought to explore simultaneously the resources of traditional and new printing media so as to wed art and industry.'[335] They remind us that the Impressionists, of whatever tendency, were much in demand by their promoters: Degas had permitted a greyish reproduction of one of his drawings, *Dancer at the Barre*, for a full page illustration in the second issue of *L'Impressioniste* (14 April 1877), the journal launched by Rivière to help support them. Drawings adapted from paintings, as were used in the publications reporting on the Salons, by Renoir (*The Swing*; Fig. 165) and Caillebotte (*The Pont de l'Europe*) are used to illustrate the third issue, and by Sisley (*Pit Sawyers*) the fourth and last issue, dated 28 April. Théodore Duret used a 'gillotage' print by Renoir for his pamphlet on *Les Peintres impressionistes* in May 1878, and Duranty, working on the *Beaux-Arts illustrés*, obtained drawings for reproduction by Degas, Cassatt, Forain and even Pissarro: the *Portrait of Cézanne*, an uncoloured etching done as a line drawing. Degas doggedly contrived to complicate procedures to such an extent that his projects seldom reached publication and when they did it was only the smallest ones: a vignette in the catalogue of the Salon of the 'Amis des Arts' in Pau, run by his friend Paul Lafond, in the company of Desboutin, Charles Jacques and Goeneutte.[336]

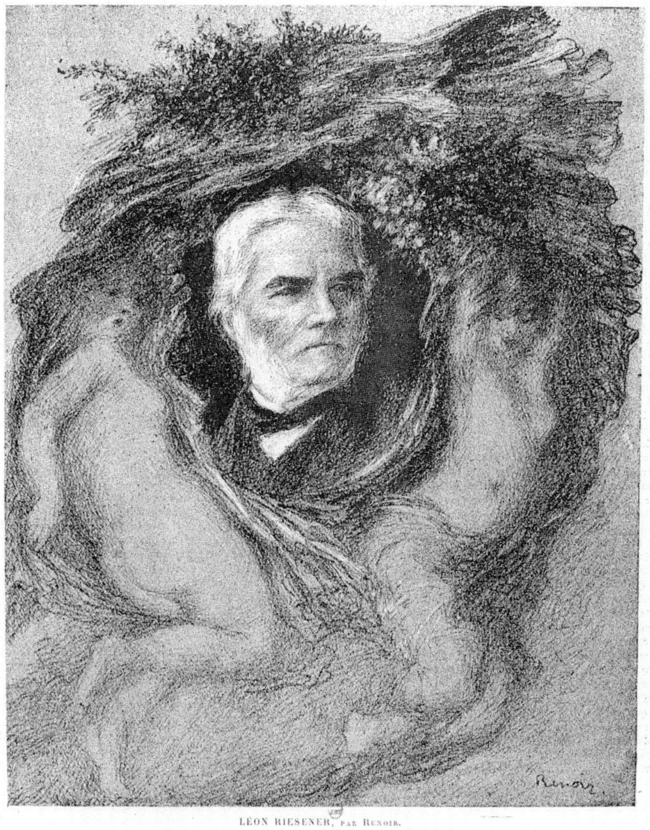

164. Pierre-Auguste Renoir,
Portrait of Léon Riesener,
published in *La Vie moderne*, no. 2, 17 April 1879.
Bibliothèque nationale, Paris.

Unfortunately this final attempt at a marriage between art and industry bore many of the features of a divorce, and produced pieces that bore little resemblance to one another. The work produced by Pissarro for *Le Jour et la Nuit*, exhibited in the fifth Impressionist exhibition, and the monotypes exhibited by Degas in the third have the status of independent works of art rather than matrices for whole series. Degas seems to have been more interested in bringing industry into art than in bringing art to industry.[337] The sincerity of Degas's passionate search for a meeting-ground with industrial reproduction has never been in doubt. Nor is there any doubt that by discouraging it so consistently, and by demanding to control a process whose main aim was to bypass art, he unintentionally caused the inevitable rupture.

In the opinion of Degas the adjective 'original', when applied to a print, has exactly the same strong meaning as when applied to drawings or paintings: these are unique creations. For example, when he wanted to obtain evenly-printed skies using aquatint, he despaired of achieving uniformity and came to the conclusion that: 'If I only wanted to make original prints, art works, it might be simple enough',[338] which must surely mean 'if I only wanted to produce unique prints, each one differ-

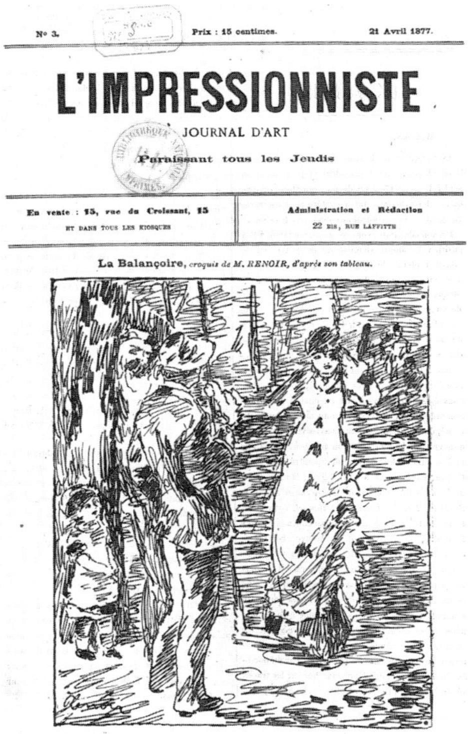

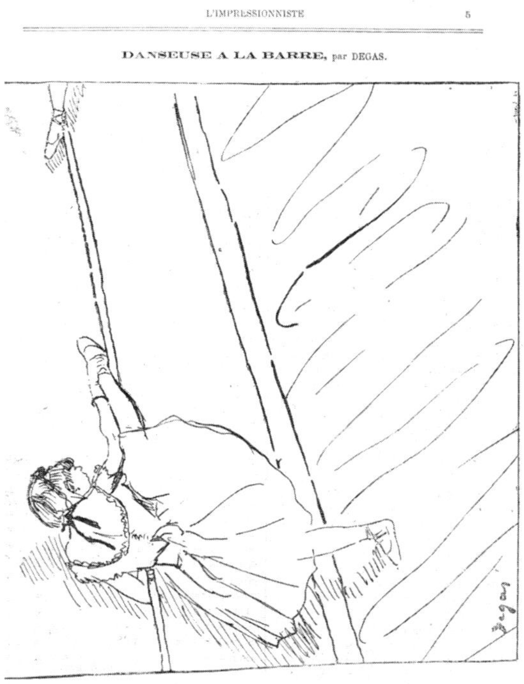

165. Pierre-Auguste Renoir,
The Swing, published on the cover of *L'Impressionniste*, no. 3, 21 April 1877.
Bibliothèque nationale, Paris.

166. Edgar Degas,
Dancer at the Barre, published in *L'Impressionniste*, no. 2, 14 April 1877, p.5.
Bibliothèque nationale, Paris.

ent from the others'. Later, on the subject of proofs of colour etchings, he wrote to Pissarro: 'There is material there for making some original and interesting prints'; it certainly sounds as if he is referring to single prints, each print coloured by stencil, because he proposes 'cutting out designs traced by you on to very light copper. You could then put these templates on to linear prints – etchings or soft-grounds – and print on the revealed areas using a stamp of made porous wood dipped in watercolour'.[339] The close link between the original work and the reproduction, on which the art of printmaking is based, is stretched to breaking point: the original print becomes a unique work of art, a monotype or a 'special edition', and, like a drawing, awaits the invention of a miraculous new reproductive process.

Unlike Degas, Pissarro was openly hostile to reproductions. His attitude was just as complex as that of Degas and his output, in spite of their differences, not dissimilar. He did not reject outright all possibility of low-priced reproductions, but he eschewed any technical solutions that might misrepresent his handiwork, thereby prohibiting the reproduction of any of his work. He admired some of the newspaper draughtsmen, in particular Daumier: 'I often look at them. As a lithographer he has no rival.'[340] He condemned the processes, however: 'At last I have the Figaro engravings that are printed in London. They didn't need to go so far to get them done so badly, it's horrible, horrible!!!'.[341] The artists were not to blame: 'Nevertheless considering those who earn a living by it, it must be acceptable: it can be done, and the Daumiers, Gavarnis, the Henri Monniers, the Keenes all do it well.'[342] 'This is not to say that the process, in the hands of someone like Degas or Keene, is inevitably bad, although the mechanical process is, by its very nature, anti-artistic.'[343] Unlike Degas, he refused to publish in *La Vie moderne*: 'Renoir's brother is the editor of La Vie moderne. His brother does illustrations for the magazine. It's not brilliant. I know from someone that they were counting on me, but I turned them down because of my great dislike of *gillotage*. From the financial point of view it's not worth it; in fact I believe they only reward their illustrators with the publicity!!! I suppose I could have a shot at it.'[344] If Degas, with his enthusiasm, or Bracquemond, with his example, made any attempt to influence Pissarro, it was to no effect. Pissarro's stance was even more intransigent than that of Degas. It must be said that *La Vie moderne*, which promoted itself as a serious journal, upholding family values, trying to dispel the Zola of *L'Assommoir*[345] and ending with a financial section, represented the conservative tastes of the new Republican bourgeoisie; Degas could tolerate these, but Pissarro held them in the greatest contempt.

We shall perhaps never be quite clear what the expectations of Bracquemond and Degas really were when they were planning *Le Jour et la Nuit*, nor what mysterious printing process (certainly not 'gillotage')

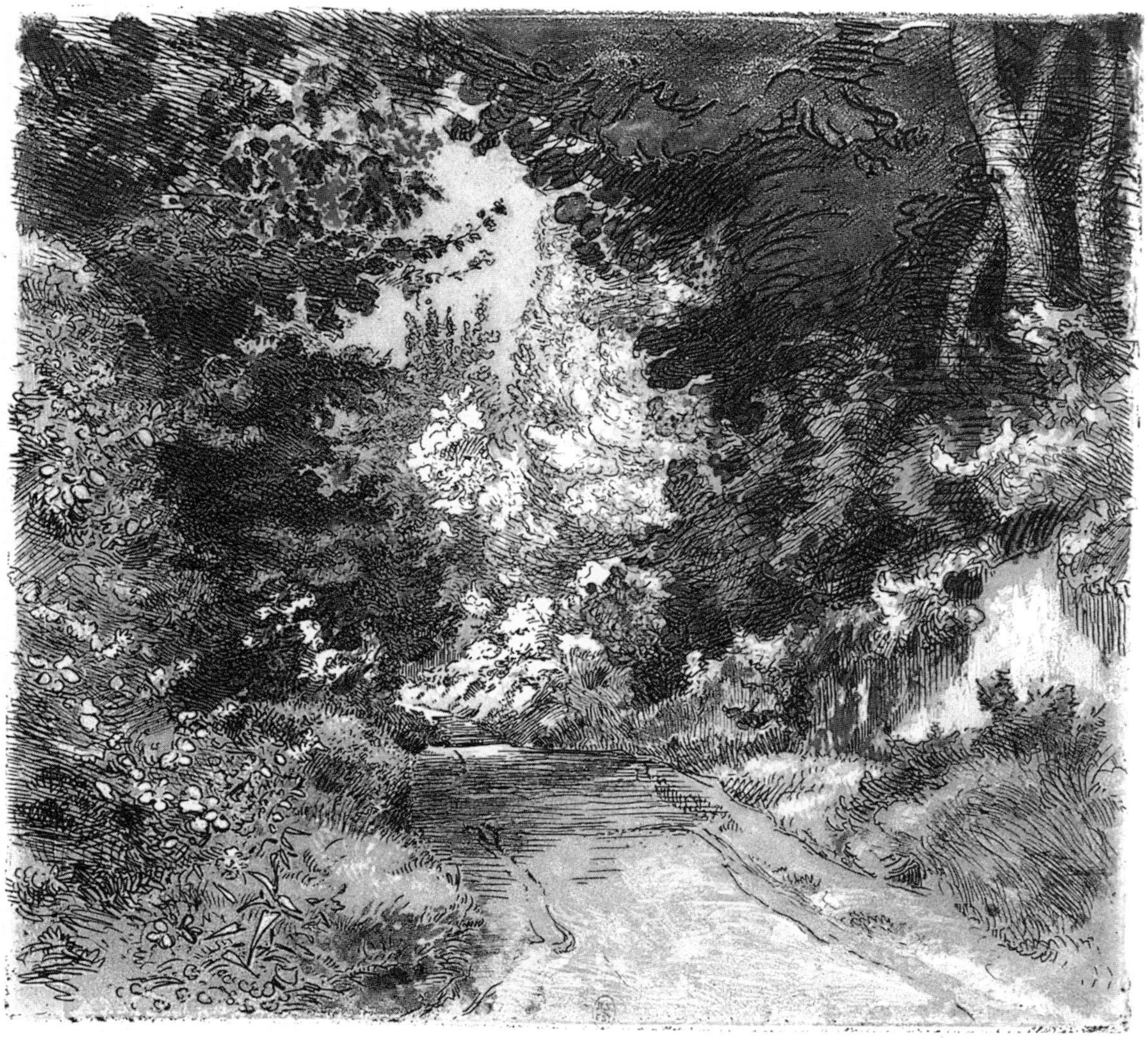

167. Félix Bracquemond, *The Chemin des Coutures, Sèvres*. 1871. Etching, 215 x 230 mm. Bibliothèque nationale, Paris.

they hoped to employ. The surviving documents indicate that they were anxious about the reproduction of their prints, which were increasingly unsuited to mechanical reproduction as they stood, by modern processes. They were plagued by a kind of social conscience, and perhaps by financial misgivings; they looked back nostalgically to the days when Daubigny could carry on his double career without pangs of guilt.

All the evidence indicates that publishing even a small number of copies of *Le Jour et la Nuit* was a dream, at its worst a utopian one. What remains of the project is a collection of prints of such complexity as to defy printing, of such delicacy that even if they had been wiped by hand and hand printed on Salmon's printing press good reproduction could only have been achieved with great difficulty. These prints make no concessions to publishing; they are in the same aesthetic category as pastels and wash drawings, rather than the laborious etchings of the past. These prints are so rare that only a few museums nowadays can afford to wrest the last few copies on the market from the handful of collectors who still have them in their possession. The failure of *Le Jour et la Nuit* signalled the death of a dream in which art, faithfully served by industry, would survive reproduction without being definitively altered.

Neither the steps taken by Degas nor Pissarro's fine words could prevent the involvement of their art in a process of refinement that rendered reproduction virtually impossible: the consequence was the scaling down of editions and the differentiation of proofs. The *objet d'art* was inevitably defined by its differences from a mass produced object. Its quality was incompatible with quantity: only the scarcity of an object could confer the stigma of quality on its owner, only the differences between prints could endorse the differences between collectors. The new bourgeoisie invented this function for art, found its world reflected in it and sought in it minute distinctions and particular delights.

33. *The confection of rarity*

The techniques most favoured by Impressionist printmakers were those least favourable to reproduction: drypoint, aquatint and, to a lesser extent, soft-ground etching. Copper-plate engraving was unknown to them and the use of a pointed tool on etching ground of incidental importance. Etched lines were used for emphasis only. Drypoint does not make too heavy a line, can be used unobtrusively and, because it just scratches the surface, neither interrupts nor constricts the subject. If a little more pressure is exerted its jagged point will soften the sharpness of the line when the line is inked. If it is wielded lightly the grey that appears at the extremities becomes imperceptible. Soft-ground etching was also the subject of research by the Impressionists; its slightly blurred lines were well-suited to the depiction of the immaterial. In 1879 Pissarro tried it in *The Cabbage Patch*, but with little success. Degas encouraged him. He tried again on another zinc plate, but the unpredictability of the process irritated the printmaker. Degas explained to Pissarro how to perfect the technique by covering the plate with resin 'diluted with alcohol, as the photographers do when they pour collodion on to their glass plates' in order to obtain a more regular background, or, for even subtler effects, to press the paper covering the soft ground 'with a stump or a finger, or in any other way' to achieve the delicate 'darkish background tone' that so enchanted Degas.[346]

The series of prints made during the preparation of *Le Jour et la Nuit* is based on the aquatint process, varied *ad infinitum* by all available means to create a luminosity that gleams through the whole composition. Degas, Pissarro and Mary Cassatt served their apprenticeship under Bracquemond. In his *Self Portrait* and his *Portrait of Alphonse Hirsch* (Fig. 152), Degas was already using aquatint as his support. In *Mary Cassatt at the Louvre: Gallery of Antiquities* (Fig. 160) the whole plate has been submitted to the aquatint process. The technique involved agitating the grains so that the whole area was dotted; drypoint was then used to add highlights (the umbrella and the hat). Degas taught Pissarro his new technique: 'Here are the proofs: the blackish, or rather greyish tinge comes from the zinc plate, which has a greasiness about it that helps it to retain the printing ink; the plate is not flat enough . . . . You must practise placing the grains so that, for instance, you get a uniformly grey sky that is even and fine-textured. This is very diffi-

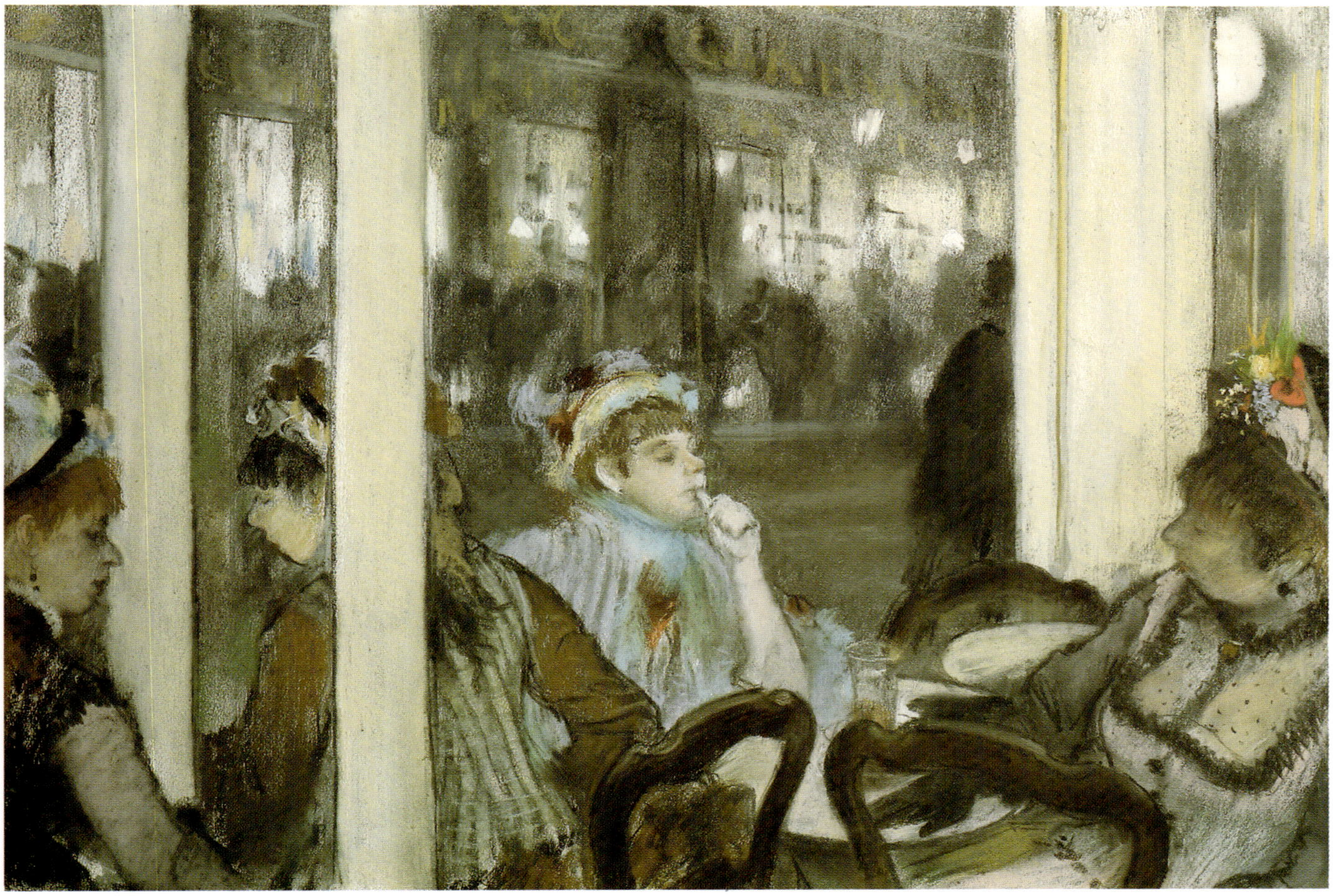

cult, if Maître Bracquemond is to be believed'.[347] Pissarro benefited from these instructions: his *Landscape seen through Undergrowth at L'Hermitage* is built entirely on a jigsaw of aquatint, and Mary Cassatt showed even greater skill. Degas became expert at it quite soon: the vitality of *Dancers on Stage* and *Actresses in the Dressing Room* (Fig. 191) resides in the skilful organisation of the grain of the aquatint. Such variety in the grain and such finely etched lines demanded very careful and sensitive inking that could not possibly have been left to Delâtre nor to any of the professional printers at the print works. These requirements made the production of repeat copies almost impossible. Any means of making the texture more delicate, or of producing subtler greys or more transparent blacks, was permitted. Pissarro practised what he termed his *manière grise*, scratching the plate with glass paper or brushing it with a metallic brush. The effects thus obtained can compare with painted or drawn effects, but an even wider variety of techniques was required. In 1875 Bracquemond did

168. Edgar Degas,
Women on the Terrace of a Café, Evening. 1877.
Pastel on monotype, 410 x 600 mm.
Musée d'Orsay, Paris.

next pages:
169, 170, 171, 172. Camille Pissarro,
Woman emptying a Wheelbarrow. 1880.
Etching, aquatint and drypoint, 319 x 235 mm,
first state, Kunsthalle, Bremen; second state, Museum of Fine Arts, Boston, Lee M. Friedman Fund; sixth state, Library of Congress, Washington; eleventh state, Bibliothèque nationale, Paris.

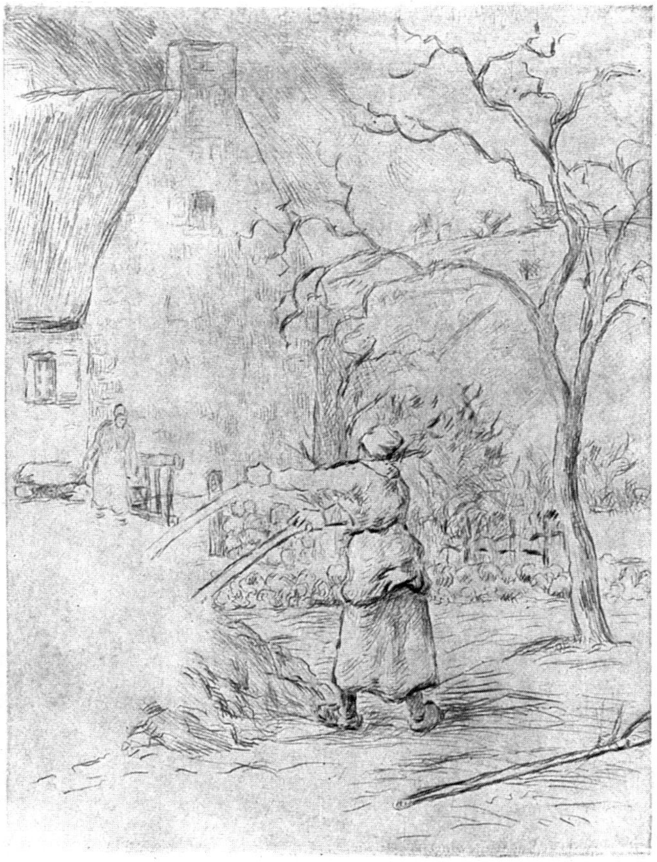

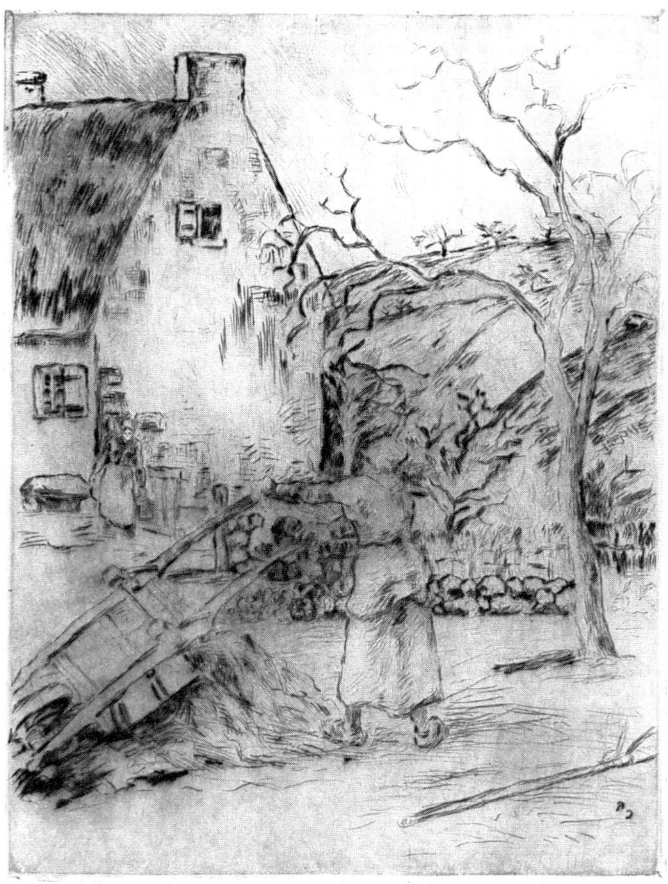

some 'experiments with processes', painting the plate with an acid wash to bite it away.[348] Degas resorted to unconventional methods as well: one day he found a piece of the carbon used in the first electric lamps and scratched the copper with that; the clear, slightly furry line thus produced, softer than a drypoint line, seemed to satisfy him.[349]

The inevitable outcome of courting such problems during the preparation of the plates was that printing them became very difficult and the proofs scarce and valuable. Pissarro wrote to Lucien in 1891: 'You know that these prints are rare, I have only got eight proofs and even those are not very good, the plate is a difficult one to pull.'[350] Later: 'There are only three proofs of this type, the steeling has made the background less responsive.' And again: 'The Woman with the Wheelbarrow is scarce, remember there are only two copies and only one of them is good, the one I'm sending you, it's in my "manière grise".'[351] Pissarro's proofs were sometimes 'printed by Degas', as evidenced by the manuscript note written by Pissarro on some of them, and also by the fact that the plates made at this time were found by him in Degas's studio in 1891: 'I've found my lost plates: the Old Cottage, Père Melon – there was a whole stack of them in Degas's studio, he found them when he was tidying up and has put them at my disposal. I don't know how many there are.'[352] Pissarro was excited by the discovery of his old plates in 1891, a period when the clientèle for contemporary and rare prints was growing. Re-printing might have been a possibility, but according to Pissarro the plates were too delicate to survive steel facing and the prints would never achieve the quality of 'fine prints'. The conditions of poverty and improvisation in which the plates had originally been executed exacerbated their fragility. The zinc which, as Degas had already warned Pissarro, could not have its veil of ink wiped off with the palm of the printer's hand, gives a different interpretation to each proof. Each print has its own personality and its own variety of minute differences, appreciated by collectors but only if printed during the artist's lifetime or by his direct heirs. The orthodoxy of printmaking, according to which an engraver worth his salt had to produce a plate capable of giving a consistent print for the whole length of a projected edition, had been forgotten. The new practice permitted differences in even very short runs, and each state in its turn was divided into trial proofs, artist's proofs and proofs of that particular state, each making its own particular contribution to the series. The proofs of Pissarro's *Haystacks* (Figs 198–200) sparkle collectively, each facet emitting its inimitable glow.

Because each proof was treated as an original work of art the barriers between printmaking and drawing began to disappear (Figs 168, 173). Degas chose to ignore conventions as far as technique was concerned and liked re-using his work, making a lithograph from a monotype (*Mlle Bécat at the Ambassadeurs*; Figs 178–9), then colouring one of the proofs with pastel. He took a photograph of a pastel and copied it on transfer paper (*The Song of the Dog*) to obtain a lithograph which he inked like a monotype.[353] His *Getting out of the Bath* (Figs 194–7) exists as a print on metal done with the 'electric pencil', a monotype in black and white and two monotypes coloured in pastel.[354] In 1879 Degas began mixing pastel into his paintings.[355] Work exists in which pastel, gouache, oil paint, ink and pencil are combined. In 1890, the period when he was producing coloured monotypes, he tried printing from pastels. Pissarro tried the same technique: one of the five surviving proofs of his drypoint etching of 1883, *Woman emptying a Wheelbarrow* (Figs 169–72) is entirely covered in pastel and gouache.[356] A small painting by Pissarro on a zinc plate[357] exists in reverse on paper, showing incontrovertibly that oil paintings were sometimes printed like monotypes. The monotypes were reworked with a brush evidently, because paint did not have the same adhesive quality as printer's ink.

The ultimate method of distinguishing between proofs was to sign them by hand and number them. The origins of this practice have already been discussed, and Degas and Pissarro simply regularised the system. When Pissarro received his first order for prints from the American collector Avery he set about numbering and dating them, adding notes and an autograph signature as Raffaëlli had done for Avery in 1887. Pissarro and Degas put Burty's rhetoric into action in order to limit editions artificially. Now that the plates no longer bore an engraved signature they had come to terms with the requirements of the new breed of collectors, both artistically and psychologically. Their efforts were rewarded in the years immediately following the crisis. In 1888 Pissarro wrote to his son: 'Watch out that he only prints one proof from each, as well as he can, and pays attention to the sky in the "Small Port at Rouen" which I have reworked. The sky must stay white, luminous, just as Jacque, the son, printed it for me, this is imperative. I do not want to wear these plates out with too much printing, I shall have them faced in steel';[358] in 1889, while working on Avery's order, he writes: 'I have not yet got my proofs. I'm having trouble getting good ones; it's a long, long process. . . .'[359] 'As for "The Old Cottage", as you know only six prints have been made. The steel-faced prints are often beautiful, but less rare. I think you are going to have a lot of trouble persuading people that I am not a printmaker and that these are just printed Impressions.'[360] At last the artists' patience matched the demands of their new public.

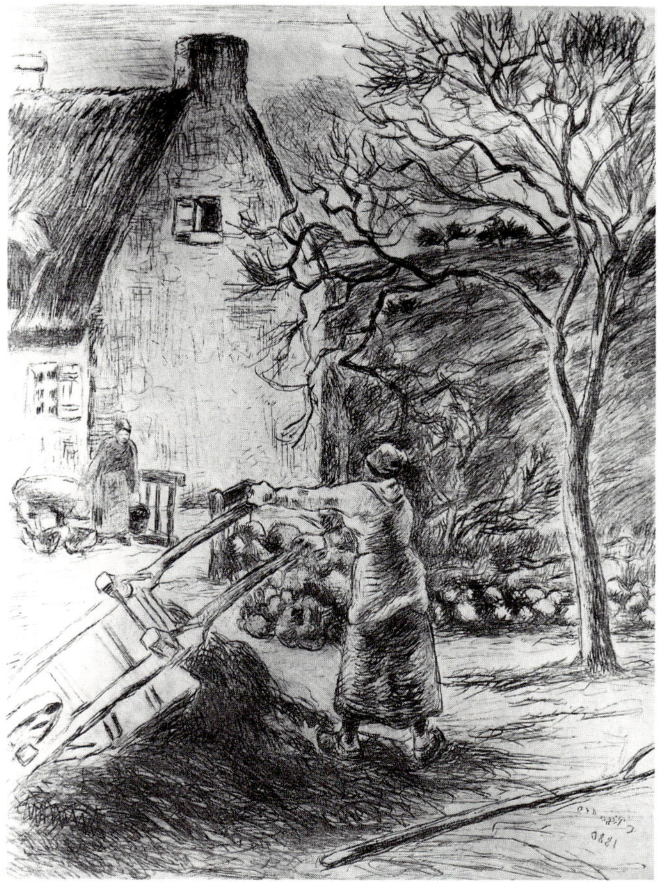

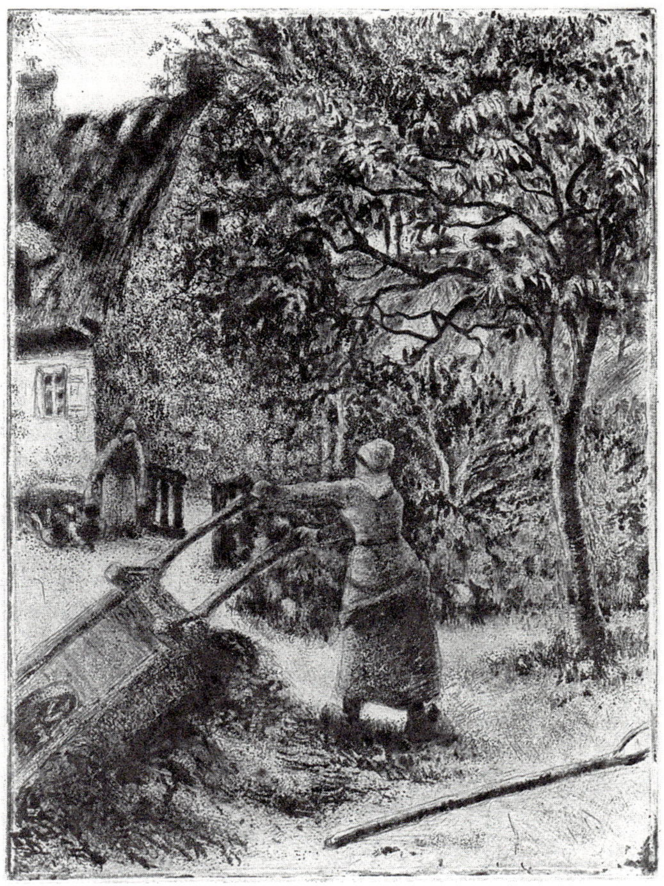

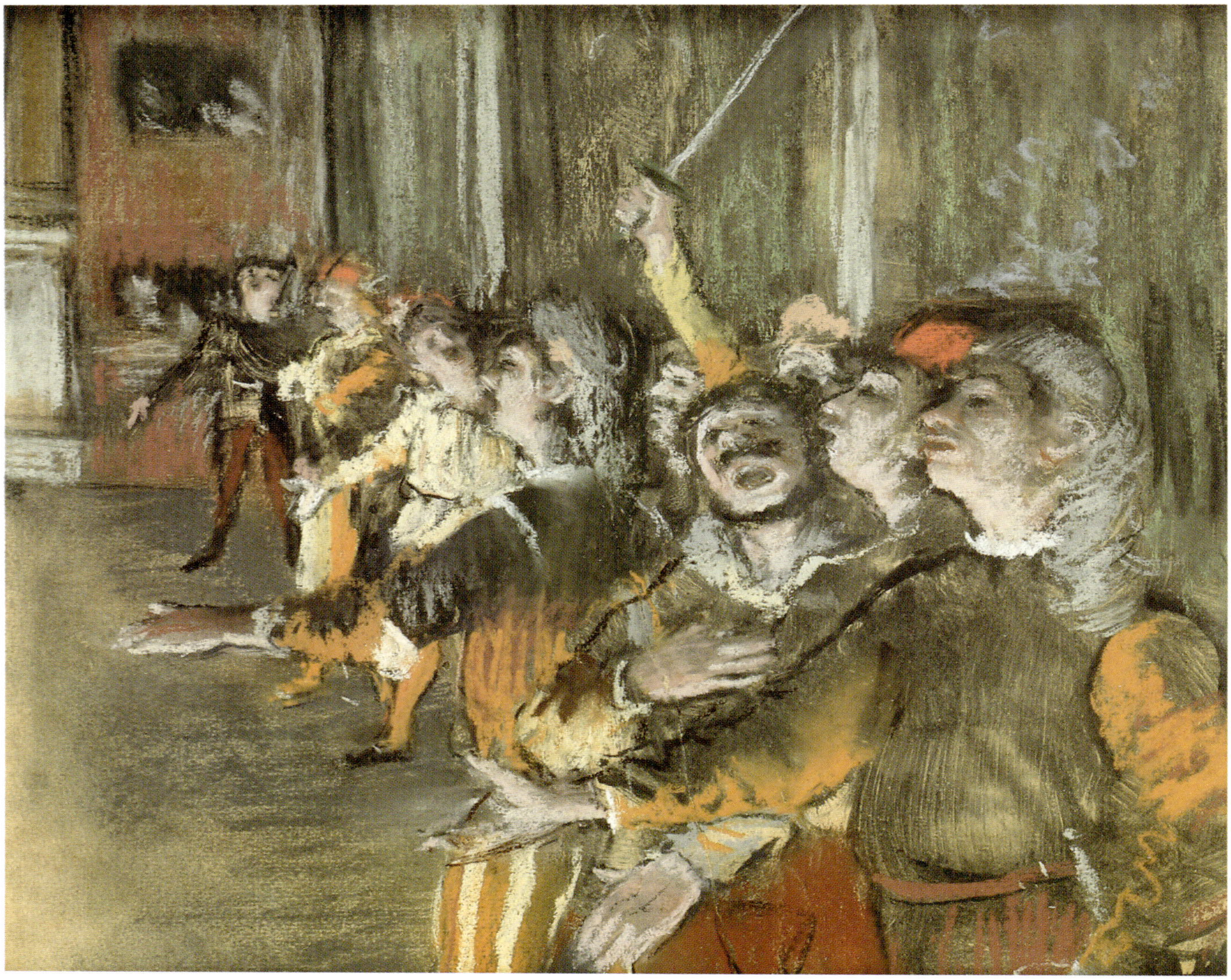

173. Edgar Degas, *The Extras*. 1876–7. Pastel on monotype, 270 x 310 mm.
Musée d'Orsay, Paris.

34. *The Value of the Times*

Pissarro's aquatint of *Evening with Haystacks* (Figs 198–200) is transformed from one proof to the next by the use of different coloured inking. With an edition of fifteen by Salmon, then another posthumous edition of fifty, the print is a rare one. Lucien Pissarro possessed a copy in Veronese green, another of his sons, Ludovic-Rodo, a red-brown one. The Bibliothèque Nationale has proof number 8 with a handwritten comment: 'impr. chez Degas, brun Van Dyck'; the National Gallery of Ottawa has number 2 with 'epr. d'artiste, imp. par Degas' written on it. In each example the aquatint image, coloured all over, forms dark shadows against the light of the setting sun. If all the proofs of *Evening with Haystacks* were lined up the effect would be similar to the effect sought by Claude Monet in his contrasting views of the façade of Rouen Cathedral (1892–3). Pissarro's etched stacks have their counterpart in Monet's painted ones (1890), the difference being that the lighting effects in the prints are consistent. The Goncourt brothers wrote an imagined account of this system: 'If I was a painter I would have a hundred proofs printed on art paper and I should amuse myself painting them in watercolours with all the tints that appear in the misty vapour from the Seine, all the magical colours of autumn, or winter with its plaster grey and rusted stone horizons.'[361]

The ability of an image to be reproduced, even if only once, does not negate the principle of each transfer print having its own significance. One of the main themes of Impressionism was the gap between reality and the perception of reality. The word 'Impression' aspires to embody this projection of reality on to the retina of the spectator, as the etched plate will later be projected on to the paper. Impressionism captures that moment when consciousness wavers between a fixed, rigid world imposed upon man, and a world which man allows himself to manipulate and reconstruct. At this period subjective (and fleeting) consciousness began to be seen as the only scientific form of consciousness; this had been expounded in 1860 by Emile Littré, the most accessible of the positivist philosophers. The fresh eye of the painter, responding to immediate stimuli, forestalls psychological analysis, and aims to precede language, or even to disregard it. The motif and its representation are no longer interchangeable: there is a time lapse between them, the subject has seized the moment and will reproduce it for eternity. The contradiction between subjectivity and realism has been resolved. As Richard Shiff has pointed out, truth has two sides: truth to nature and truth to oneself.[362] Impressionist prints, stable enough on the plate but varying with each printing, demonstrate this ambiguity. As history will show, it is an ambiguity that allows plenty of leeway. The printing press and the transferred image, inescapable even for a monotype print, amplify the Impressionists' Impressions as an echo chamber amplifies sound. Engraving became the art of variation at this time. In 1891 Pissarro wrote to Lucien: 'As for the collectors, I'll tell you what they really admire – Charles Jacque, Buhot, Bracquemond, or Legros when he's in his Rembrandt mood, and the same goes for Seymour Haden. But not printmaking dealing with sensations. And that's what I'm trying to do with my feelings.'[363]

The technique of printmaking, concerned as it is with the representation of movement, has another advantage. A print is produced through a succession of 'states', and it is possible to halt the representation at a certain stage, commit this stage to memory by printing a copy, then to continue work on the same support, print again, do some more work on it and so on, for as long as is required: twenty 'states' of *Mary Cassatt at the Louvre: Paintings* (Figs 201–6) by Degas are known, eleven of *Woman emptying a Wheelbarrow* (Figs 169–72). It is not unusual for a print of this period to exist in ten or more states. Like Bracquemond at the first Impressionist exhibition and Legros at the second, Pissarro exhibited prints in different 'states' at the fifth: 'Martinmas Fair, 3 states; the Old Cottage, 3 states.' The first state sometimes consisted of a shapeless mass of aquatint with the vaguest of outlines just visible: *Effect of Rain* (Fig. 174) in its first state is a haze of aquatint; *Ile Lacroix* in its first version just a block of shadow (Fig. 185). *Woodland Landscape* has only three different aquatint textures and no lines; from this uniform background each of the six subsequent states produces shafts of light, as if a morning mist were dispersing before our eyes. When prints of this period by Degas exist in only one or two states the suspicion must be that he abandoned them. *On the Stage* has four: it was produced in 1877 for the booklet to the Salon de la Société des Amis des Arts de Pau, run by his friend Paul Lafond. *Dancers in the Wings* has nine and here the fragmentation of the subject is at its most

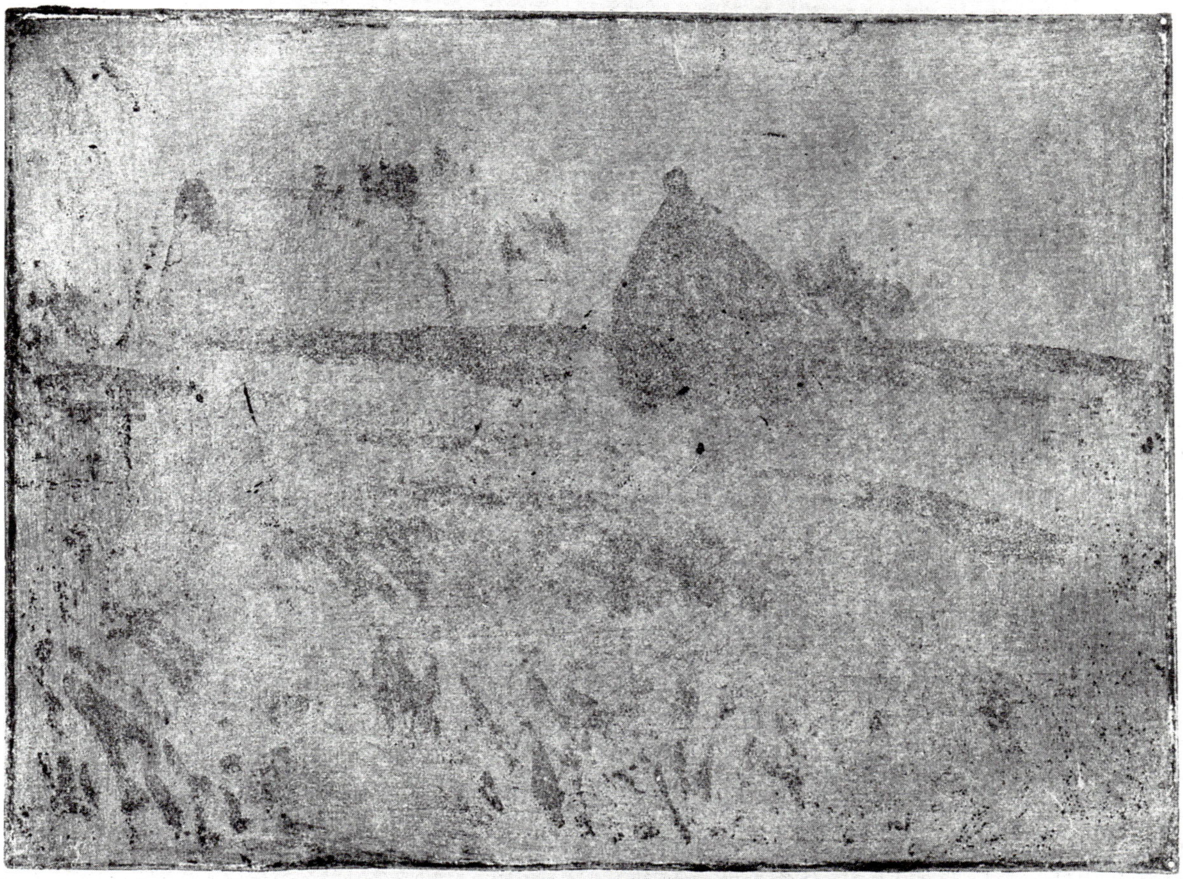

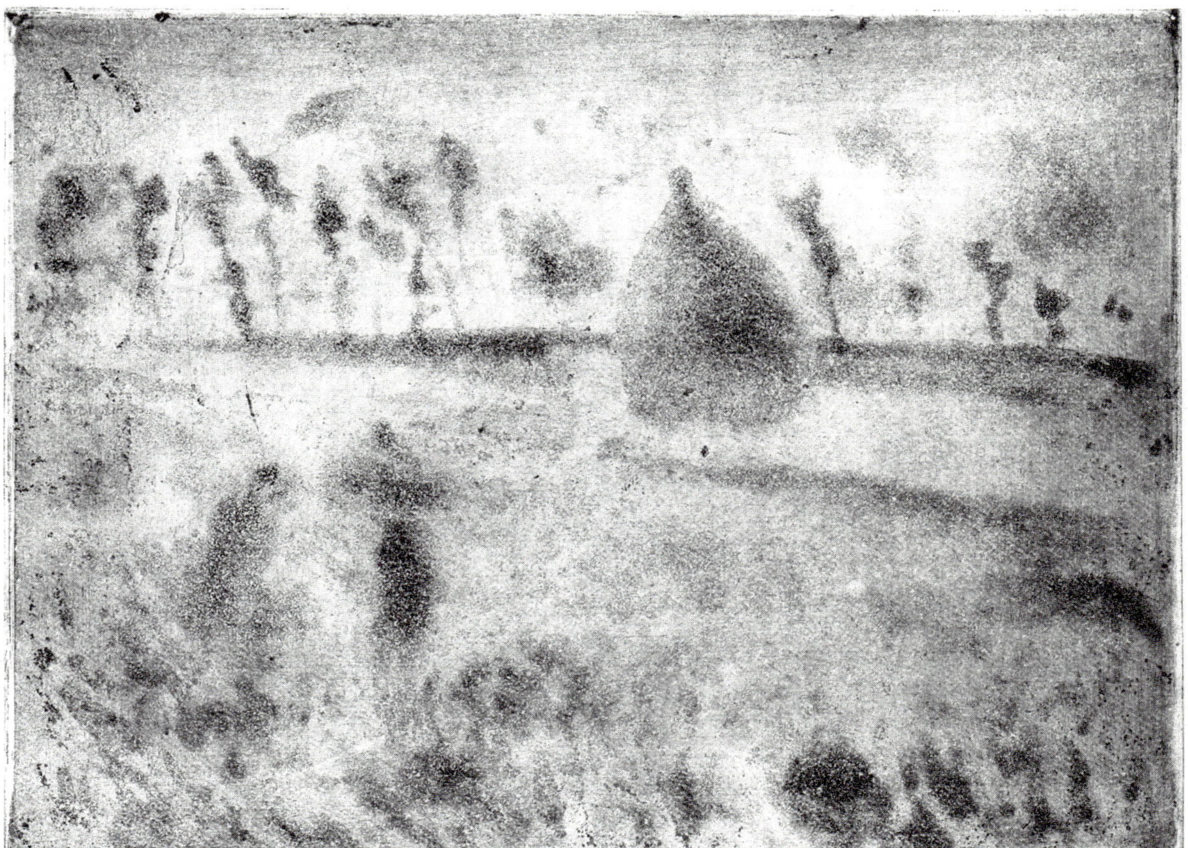

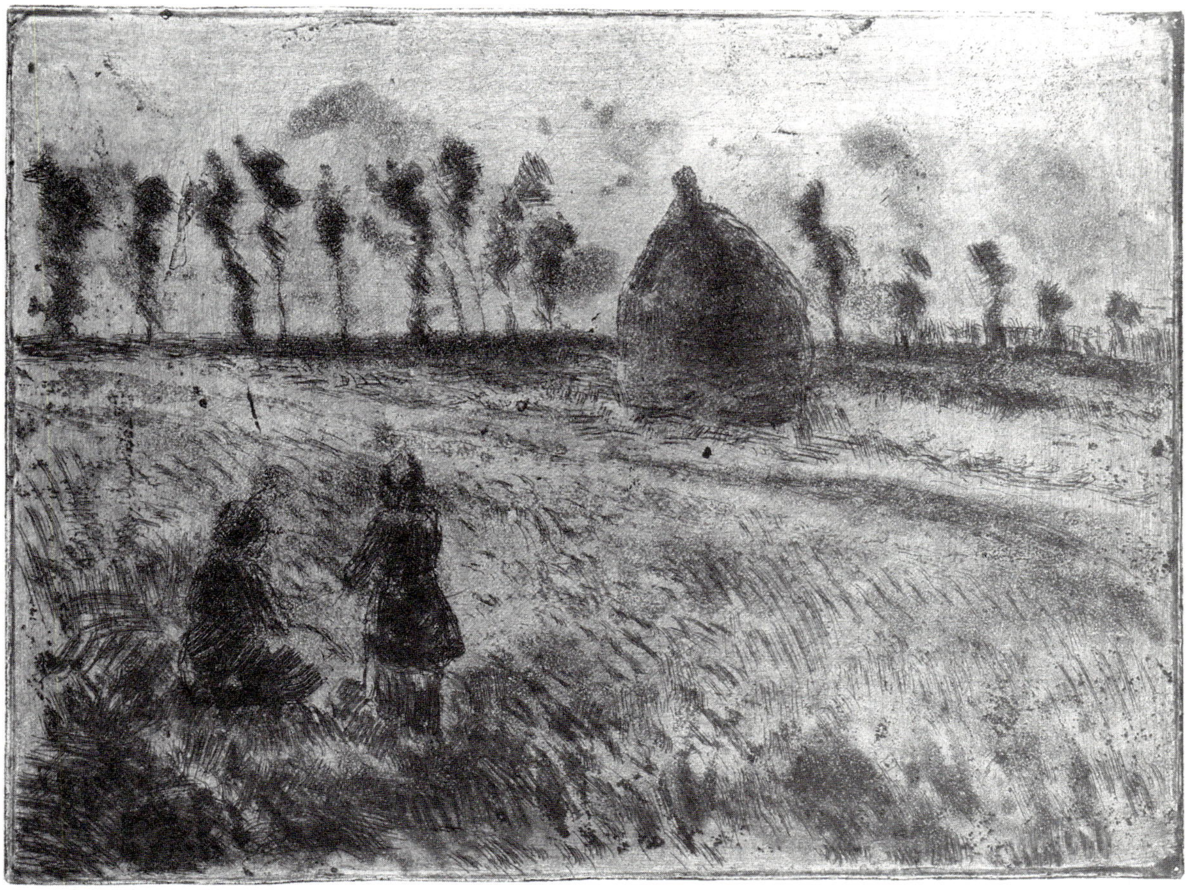

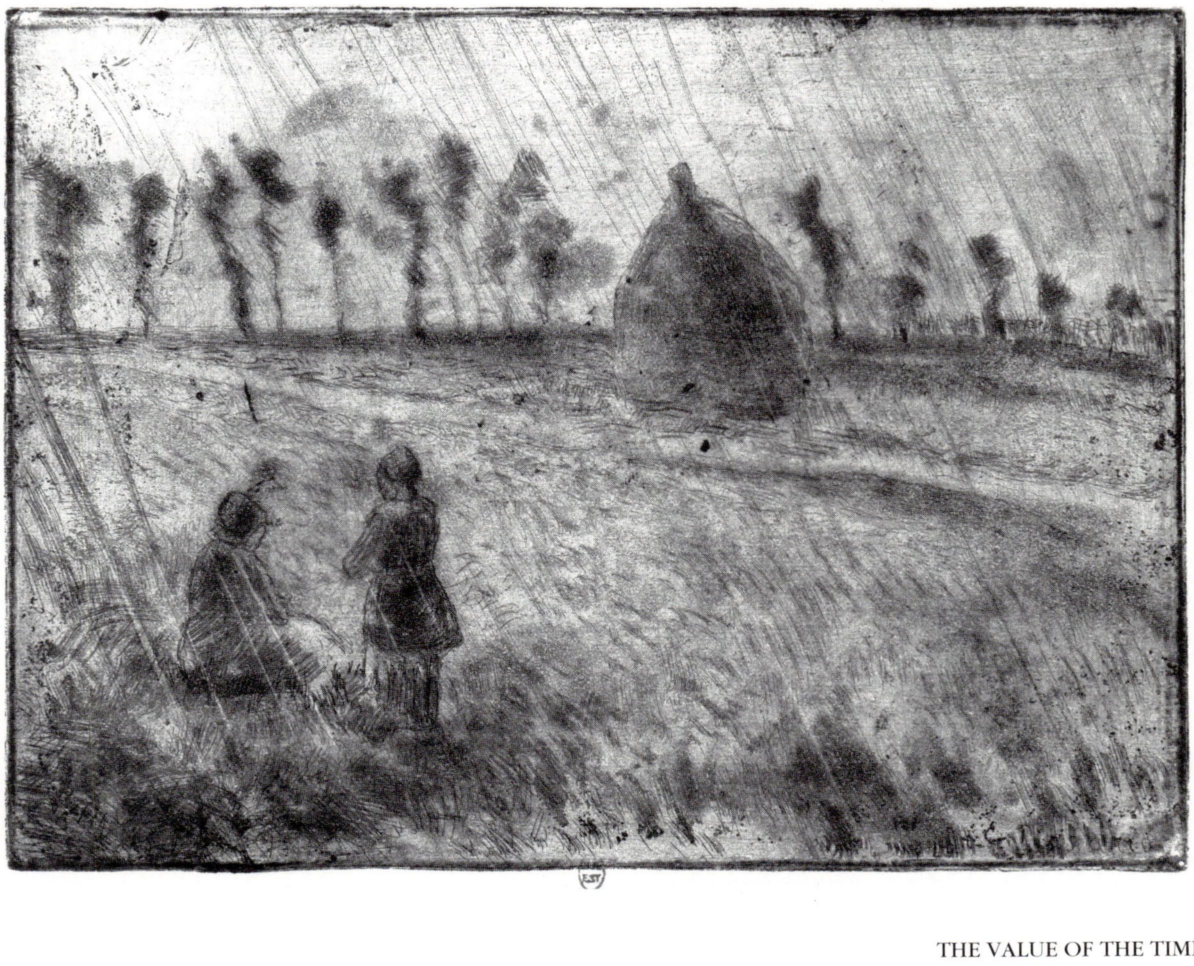

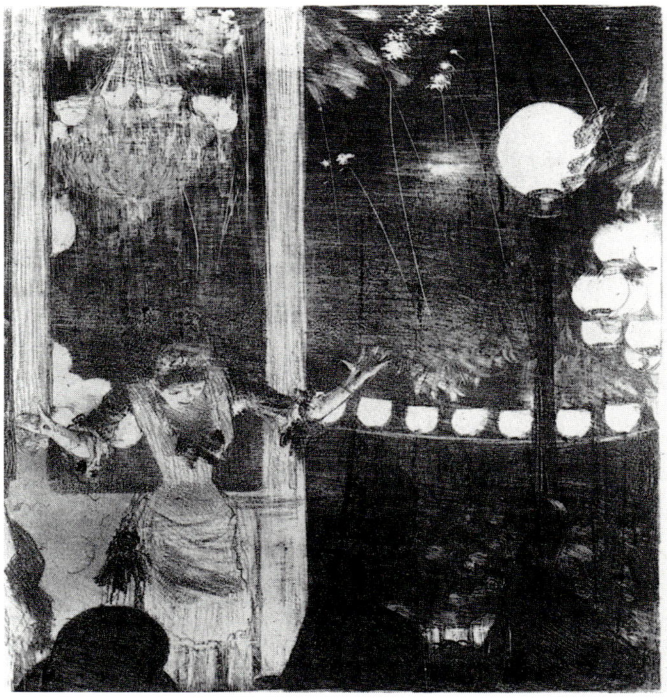

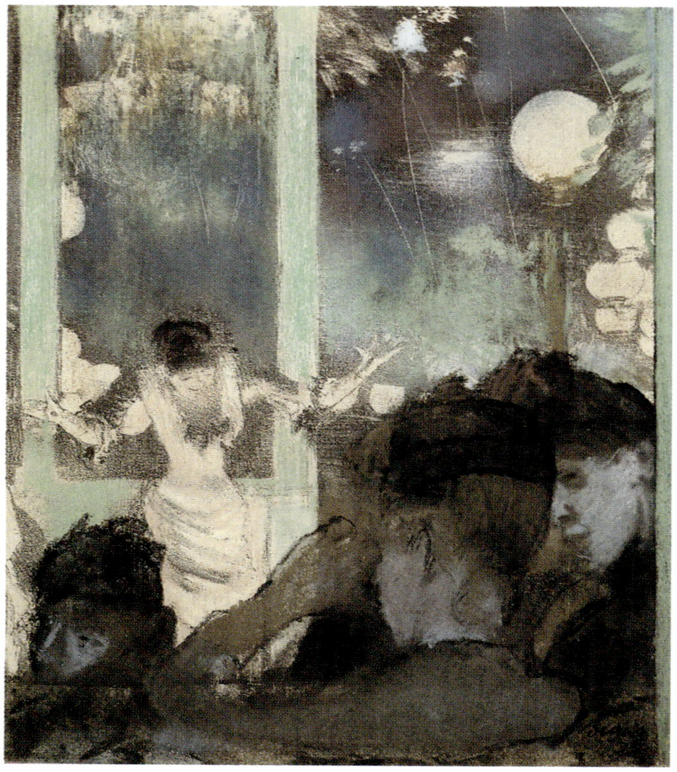

174. Edgar Degas,
Mlle Bécat at the Ambassadors. 1877–8.
Lithograph, 230 x 200 mm.
Bibliothèque nationale, Paris. Proof touched up with pastel, 1885. Collection of Mr and Mrs Eugene V. Thaw, New York.

Previous pages:
174, 175, 176, 177. Camille Pissarro,
Effect of Rain. 1878–9. Aquatint and soft-ground etching, 162 x 213 mm, first state, Kunsthalle, Bremen; second state, Yale University Art Gallery, New Haven, E. V. Meeks and S. Carlton Clark Funds; third state, Städelschen Kunstinstituts, Frankfort; sixth state, Bibliothèque nationale, Paris.

acute: the print is entirely composed of a mosaic of aquatints, with the odd glimpse of a figure drowning in aquatint. *Mary Cassatt at the Louvre: the Gallery of Antiquities* has six states; *Actresses in their Dressing Rooms* five (Fig. 191), *Women Ironing* four, and so on. The states can differ quite considerably. The first three states of Pissarro's *Martinmas Fair* shows the fairground empty. In the fourth numerous figures have appeared. In *Effect of Rain* (Figs 174–7) the first states are hazy; only in the sixth is the rain falling. Conversely the first states of *Woman Emptying a Wheelbarrow* (Figs 169–72) are drypoint sketches, but from the eighth onwards these are virtually obliterated by patches of aquatint and it is not until the tenth or eleventh that the balance is redressed. For the Impressionists the state had ceased to be a rough copy, the preparatory stage through which the definitive representation is gradually achieved. The definitive state is simply the state at which a piece of work is abandoned; it is an accumulation of the previous stages in the same way that a poem by Mallarmé is an accumulation of the layers of meaning contained within it. The dissolution of the accepted meaning of a work of art is manifested in this great output of states, existing independently of the finished work – as there is no 'true' version of a poem by Mallarmé. Reality is fragmented into a series of relative views, none of them perfect.

The Impressionists selected subjects that gave scope for the representation of the immaterial. The Impressionist style is partly the product of their concentration on weather conditions. Pissarro, like Monet and Sisley, was particularly interested in climatic effects: *Effect of Rain* or *Evening with Haystacks*. The scratches of the metal brush on the plate represent streaks of rain, the aquatint is the mist into which the figures disappear. Romantic weather is alternately dramatic and nostalgic, whereas for the realists it is a meteorological statement. Weather, for the Impressionists, equals emotional well-being and has an almost ethical quality. For Degas the weather is embodied in the gestures of his characters as well as in the changeable structure of his images (in the Japanese manner); his play with light emphasises the randomness of the composition. In *Actresses in their Dressing Rooms* (Fig. 191) the figures appear at the edge, seen from behind, cut in half, in motion, disappearing off the edge of the picture, while the middle of the print defies description: it consists of a succession of reflected surfaces, like half-open mirrors, cut by huge shadows. The representation of weather conditions in art accompanied the growth of interest in the idea of relativity, which began to permeate contemporary science between 1890 and 1900, before it was formulated into a theory.[364] The notion of a world preconceived for the eye of the painter had lost its credibility. Permanence and the existence of reality independent of its interpretation (the fundamental principles of classical art) had exploded into successive (or simultaneous) fragments of

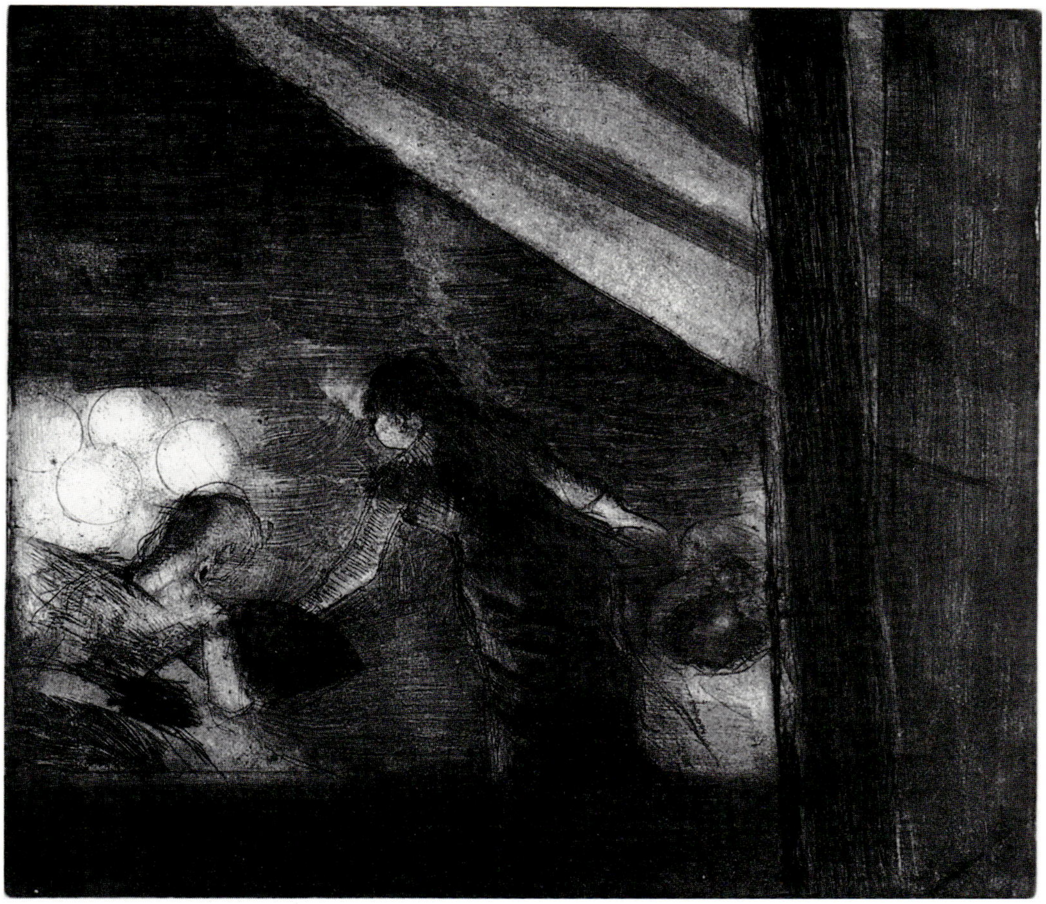

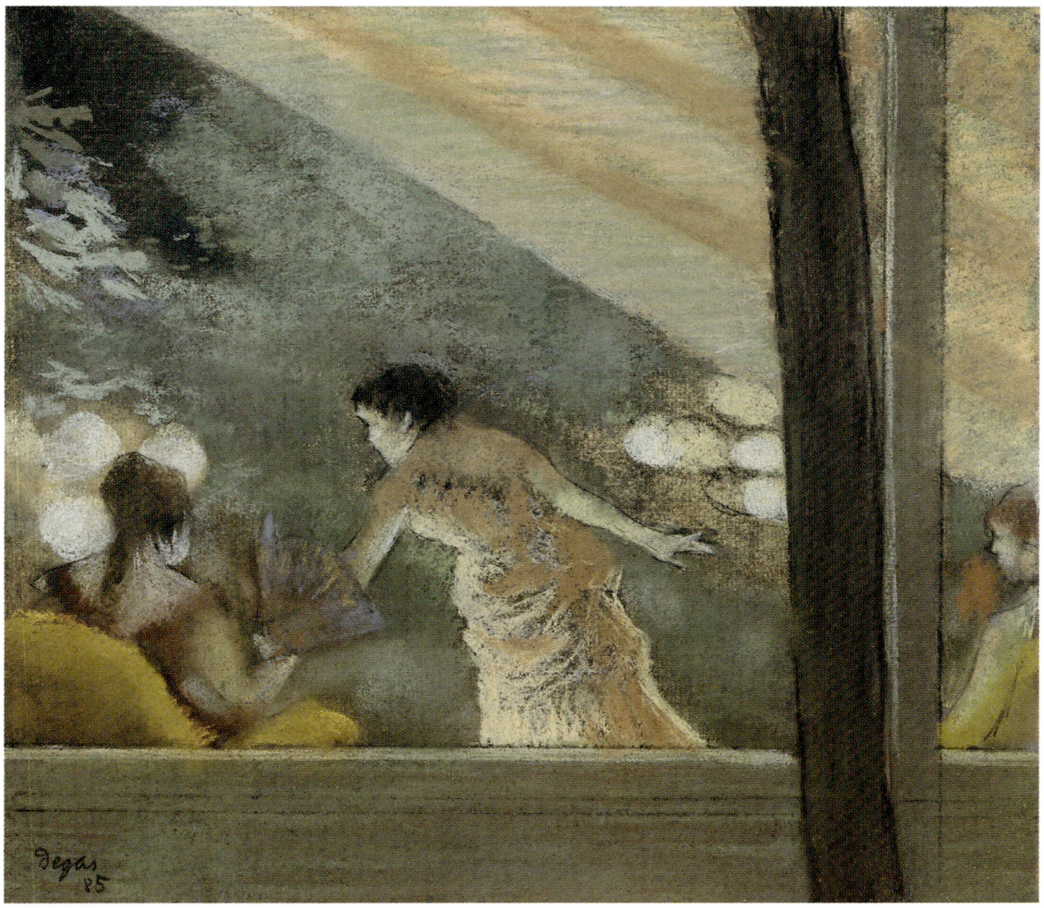
Degas
85

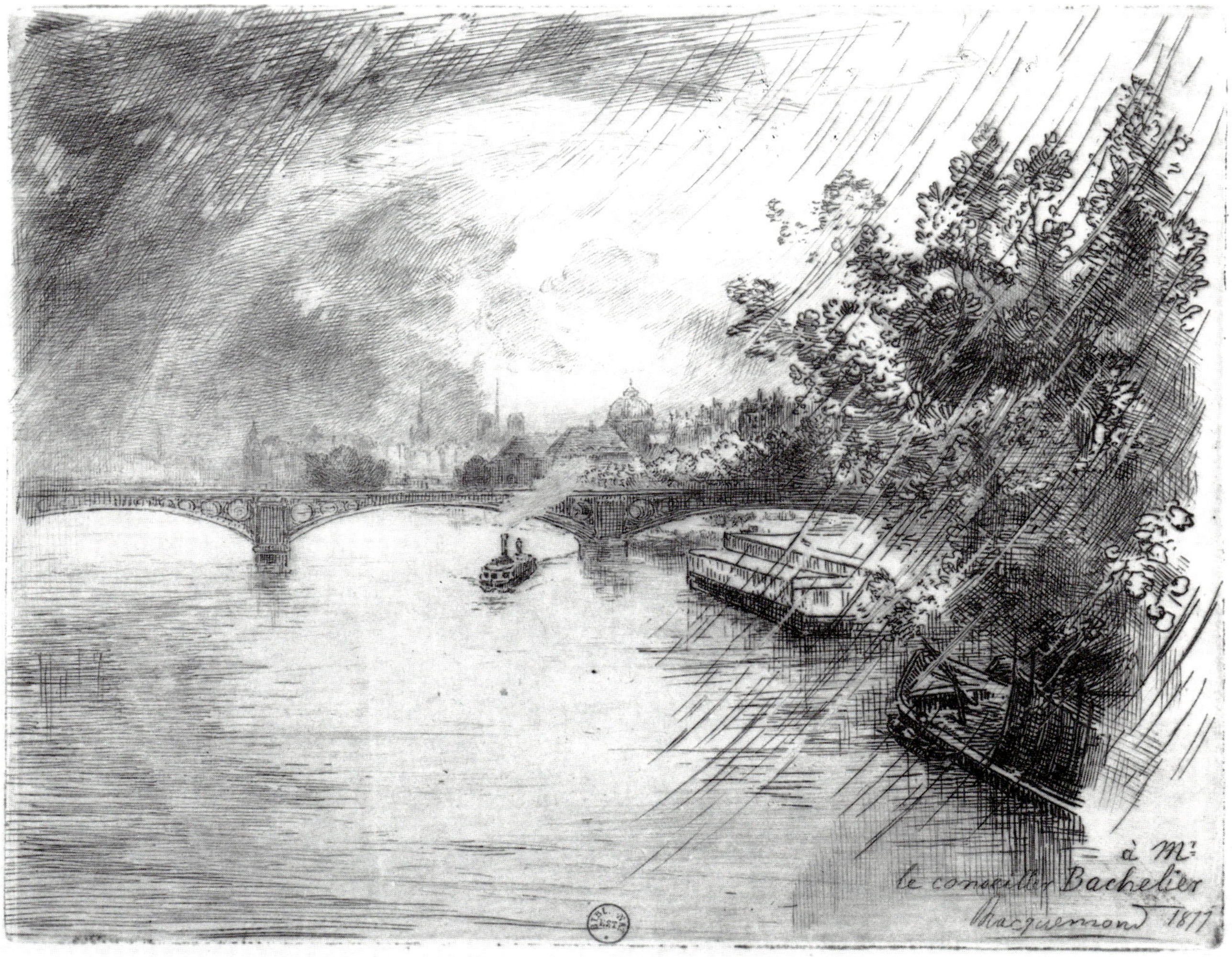

182. Félix Bracquemond,
View of the Pont des Saints-Pères. 1877.
Etching, 200 x 250 mm.
Bibliothèque nationale, Paris.

reality, all of equal value. It had to be recognised that the world was not finished, and that its history, without beginning or end, was the history of its evolution. After the publication of *The Origin of Species* in 1859 evolutionary ideas, in which Degas had already shown an interest,[365] gave birth to numerous scientific versions of the genealogy of the living world. Mathematicians were beginning to introduce time into their calculations, and Bergsonian philosophy was directed at the analysis of this new concept of time. It was a creative concept: from it followed the refutation of determinism and its corollary, the invention of personal liberty.

Previous page:
180, 181. Edgar Degas,
At the Café des Ambassadeurs. About 1877. Etching, aquatint and drypoint, 265 x 295 mm.
Bibliothèque nationale. Proof touched up with pastel, 1885.
Musée d'Orsay, Paris.

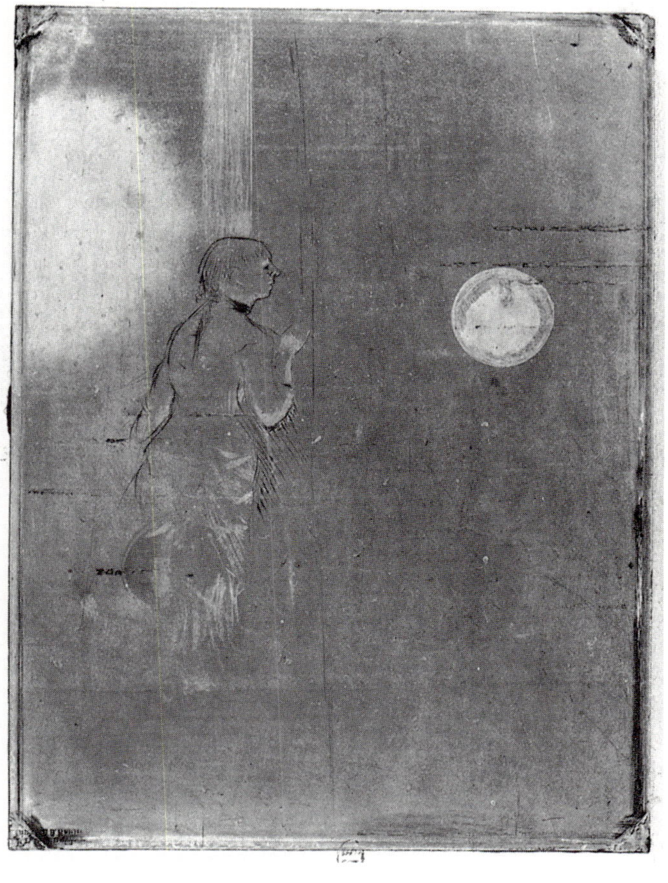

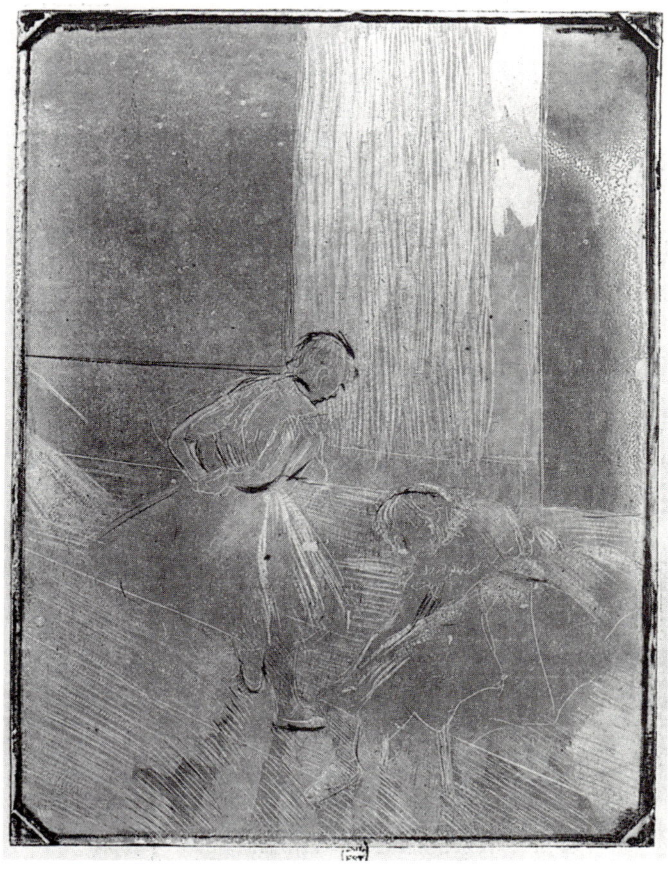

35. *The Obliteration of the Object*

The main theme of the work of the Impressionists was not movement, a favourite theme for many years, but the transience of movement, its passing and the traces left behind by it: the modification or permanent enhancement of the world. Pissarro's climatic disturbances and Degas's gestures possess an inherent value that exists separately from the thematic support offered by the compositions. From now on, movement represented the reality of the object rather than an attribute added to an already existing object. The object appears at the same moment as the movement, disappearing when it disappears. Not only was it now out of the question to represent objects or figures motionless (as the Academy taught), it was no longer even simply a matter of setting them in motion as the Romantic painters had done: motion was not perceived by the Impressionists as an external attribute that would come and disturb the subject for a brief spell. Movement obliterates the model, the passage of time carries the movement forward with it. The ideal of the Impressionist, as we have seen, would be to rework his drawing

182. Edgar Degas,
Behind the Iron Curtain. About 1877.
Drypoint and aquatint, single state, 159 x 118 mm.
Bibliothèque nationale, Paris.

183. Edgar Degas,
Two Dancers. About 1877.
Drypoint and aquatint, 159 x 118 mm.
Bibliothèque nationale, Paris.

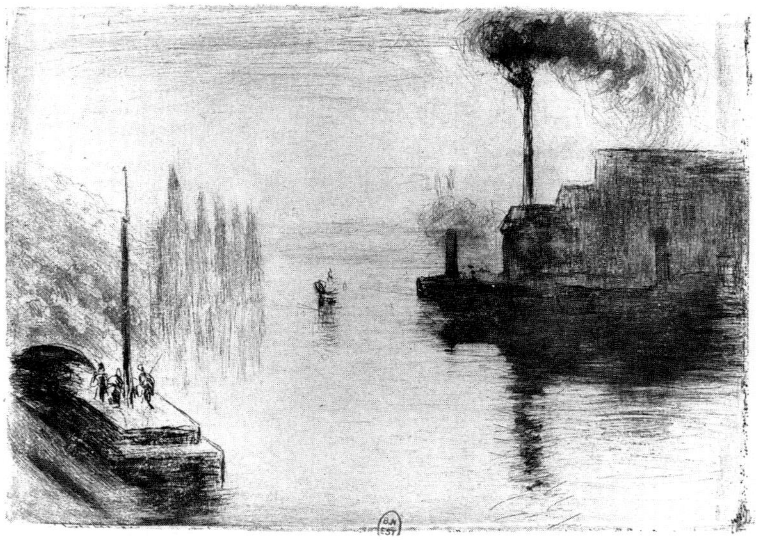

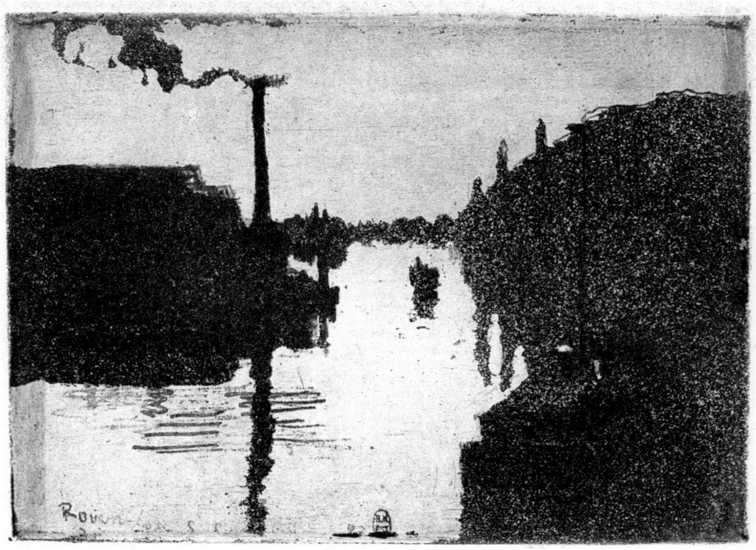

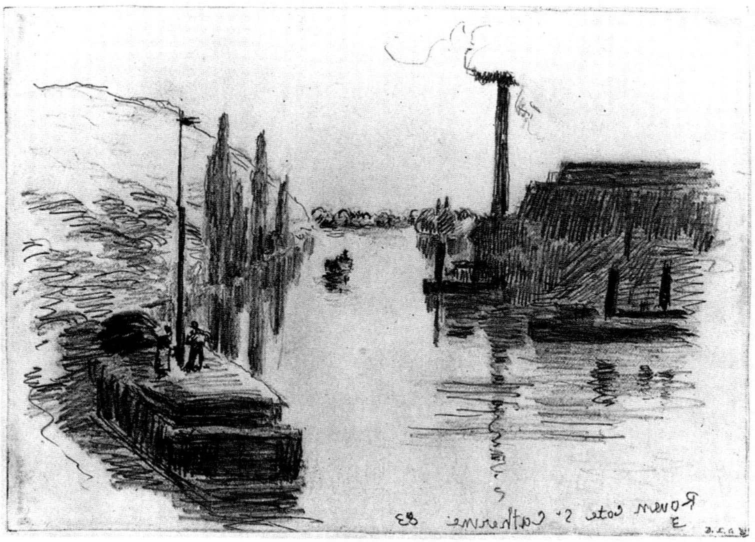

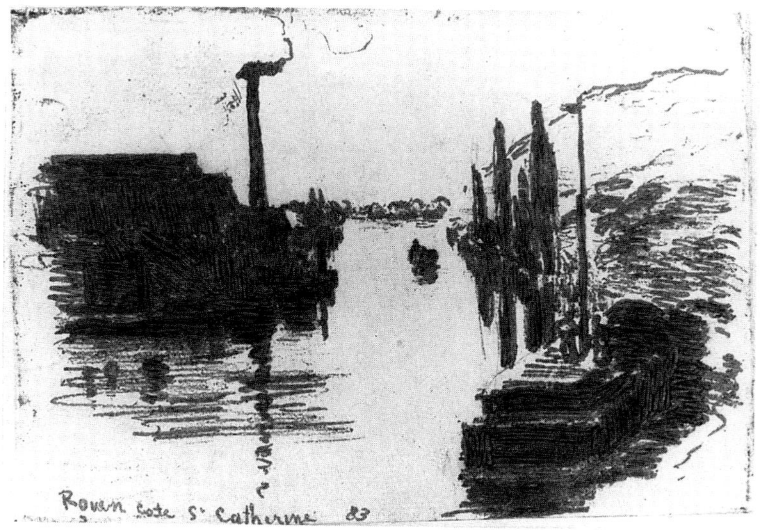

184, 185. Camille Pissarro, *Ile Lacroix*. 1887. Aquatint, first and second plates, 115 x 158 mm. Bibliothèque nationale, Paris.

186, 187. Camille Pissarro, *Côte Sainte-Catherine, Rouen*. 1883. Drawn on soft etching ground (recto) and transferred to soft etching ground (verso), 149 x 181 mm. Ashmolean Museum, Oxford.

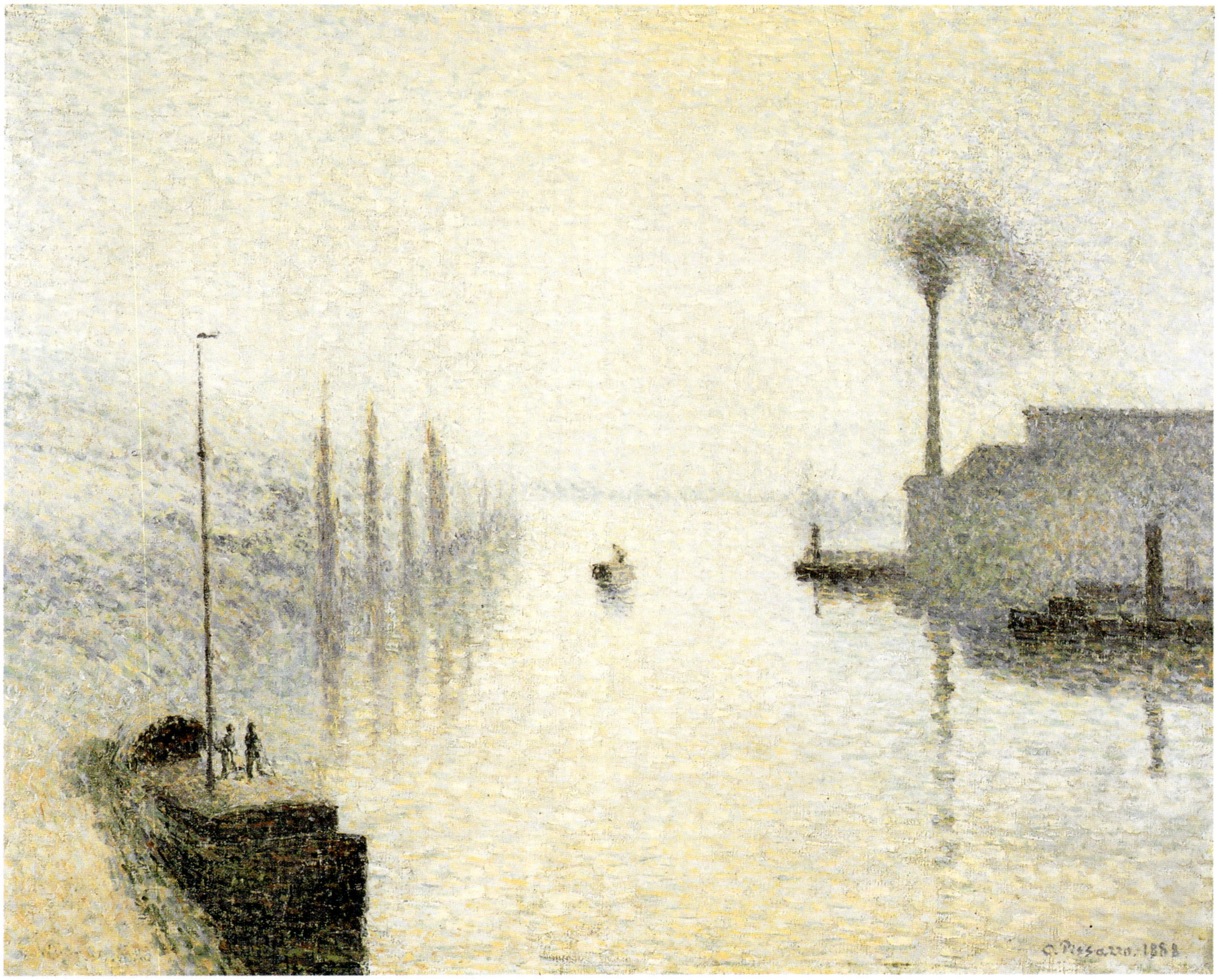

188. Camille Pissarro, *Ile Lacroix, Rouen, fog*. 1888. Oil on canvas, 44 x 55 cm. Philadelphia Museum of Art, John G. Johnson Collection.

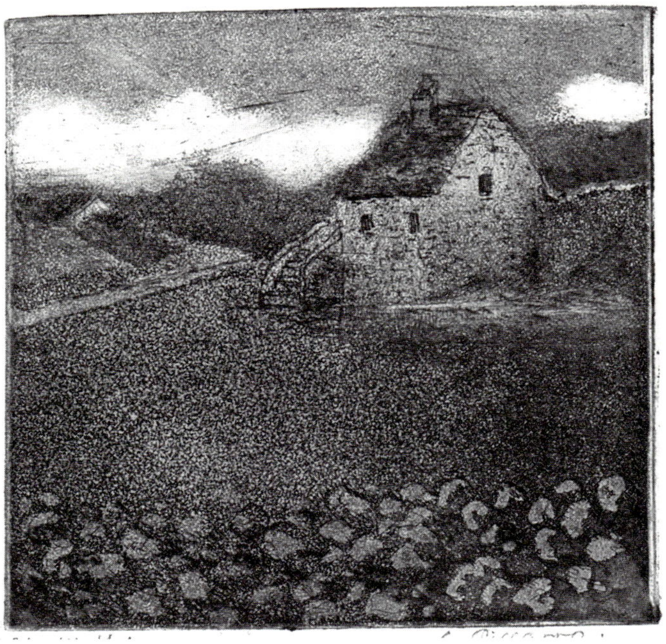

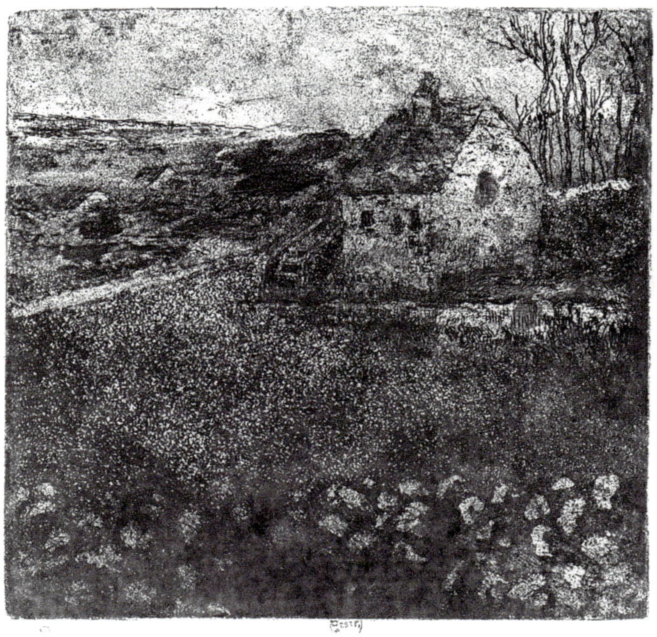

189, 190. Camille Pissarro,
The Old Cottage. 1879.
Aquatint, etching and drypoint, 167 x 170 mm.
Fourth state, Museum of Fine Arts, Ellen Frances Mason Fund; seventh state, Bibliothèque nationale, Paris.

second by second; engraving, paradoxically, could assist in this process thanks to its successive 'states' and the various methods of transfer that could be employed. Colour and light, often considered as the twin touchstones of Impressionism, were in fact only the outward manifestations of these perceptions.

Like movement, colour is not an attribute applied externally to a model; this is the classical Aristotelian view of a world filled with objects that can be repainted. Colour co-exists with and in the model and is responsible for the model's existence. It is not an accessory added in the studio once the outline has been established. Colour is consubstantial with the objects perceived, as the psychologists were quick to recognise, although after the painters. Pissarro represents the blue of the shadows and the blue of the haystacks in the same flow of aquatint. With aquatint, expanses of colour can be varied with different intensities of light, which need not relate specifically to the objects depicted; the objects appear to emerge from darkness or from fog, without regard for distance, order or density. The spectator has to make a mental adjustment to interpret these tactile values. When etched lines play a structural rôle, as in *Women Ironing* by Degas, or Pissarro's *Woman emptying a Wheelbarrow* (Fig. 169), they direct the movement of the subject but do not contain it. Pissarro remembered the drawing lessons learnt from Delacroix. He admired the somewhat austere lithographs in Degas's collection, the *Antique Medals* (Fig. 65) and the *Portrait of Baron Schwiter*.[366] The techniques of etching and inking allow forms to dissolve: trees are indicated by their shady side, their lighted side disappearing. The ground is no weightier than the sky. When the sun sets, the mist has the same specific gravity as the ground. In *Evening with Haystacks* (Figs 198–200) the trees are etched with the same density of resin as the clouds.

Whereas in their paintings colour complicated the fragmented view of their subjects, in their engravings the chief preoccupation of Degas, Pissarro and Cassatt seems to have been an attempt to bring together the divergent elements of their subjects. In *Dancers in the Wings* (Figs 182, 183), as in *Wooded Undergrowth at L'Hermitage* (Fig. 156) or *On the Balcony* (Fig. 193), the foreshortening brings all the elements, the figures and the background forward to the same plane. The overriding interest in the rendering of a visual sensation does away with perspective and the spectator has to replace it mentally: our experience with the displacement and apprehension of objects gives us our ability to perceive distance. Figures undergo the same disembodiment as objects. They blend with the objects, losing the privileged status of elements detached or emphasised by their position or their contours. In the first states of Pissarro's *The Cottage* the subject is just a block, and earth and sky run together (Fig. 189). In the first state of *Ile Lacroix* smoke from a factory chimney and its reflec-

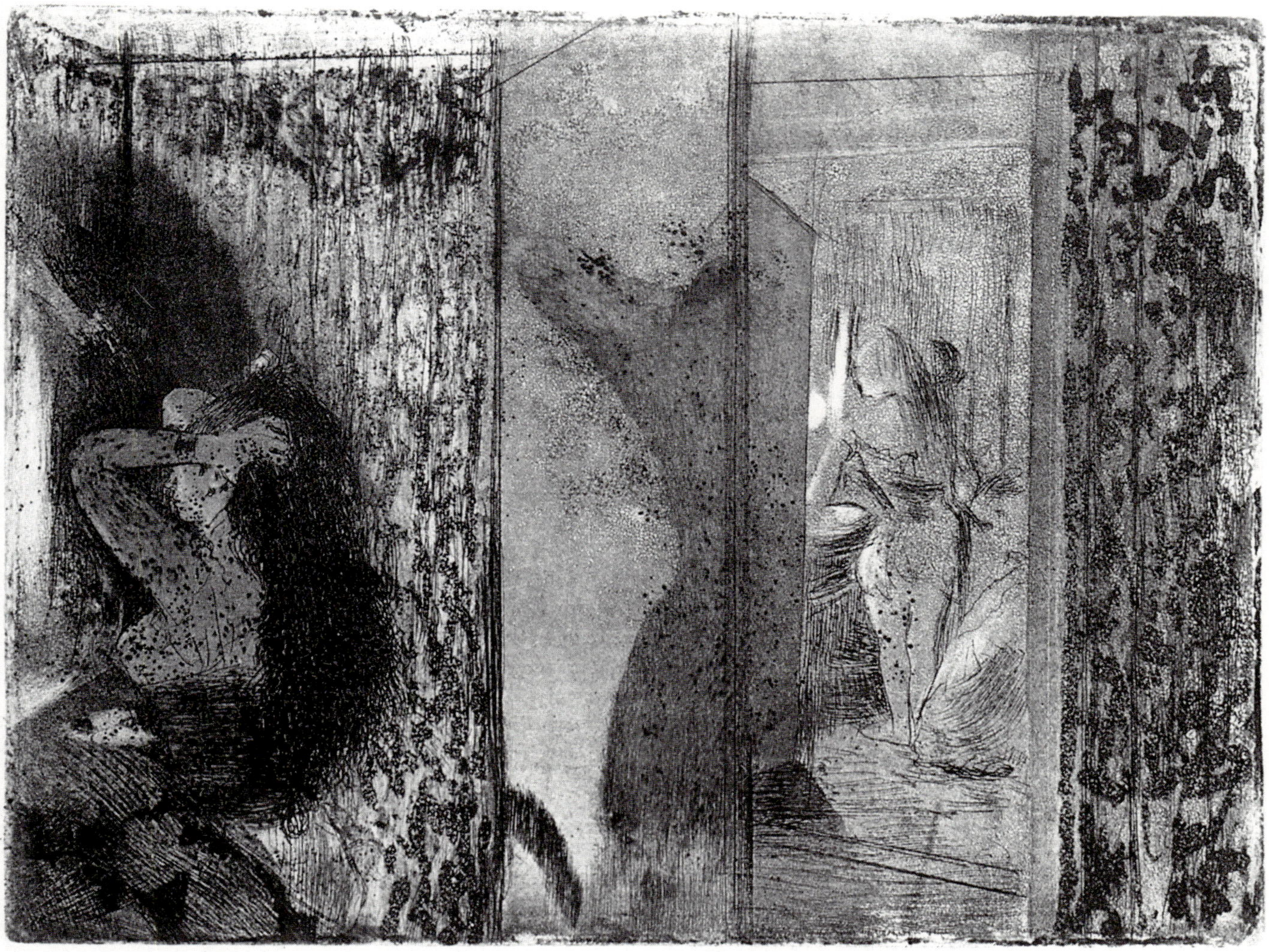

191. Edgar Degas,
Actresses in their Dressing Rooms. About 1880.
Etching and aquatint, second state 160 x 212 mm.
Bibliothèque d'Art et d'Archéologie, Paris.

tion in the water form a solid, very indistinct block (Fig. 184). The embellishments, added with drypoint or glass paper, serve to compound the confusion, denying any individual existence to objects that we identify individually in the normal course of events (Fig. 185). Lucien Pissarro wrote to his father: 'The difficult thing is . . . to know how the drawing relates to the subject . . .' or: 'You have discovered a way of using the metal that is very closely connected to the subject.'[367] Paradoxically the solidity of the metal plates proved far more effective than anything else for the working away at those ethereal effects that inking and printing would transfer to the sheet of paper.

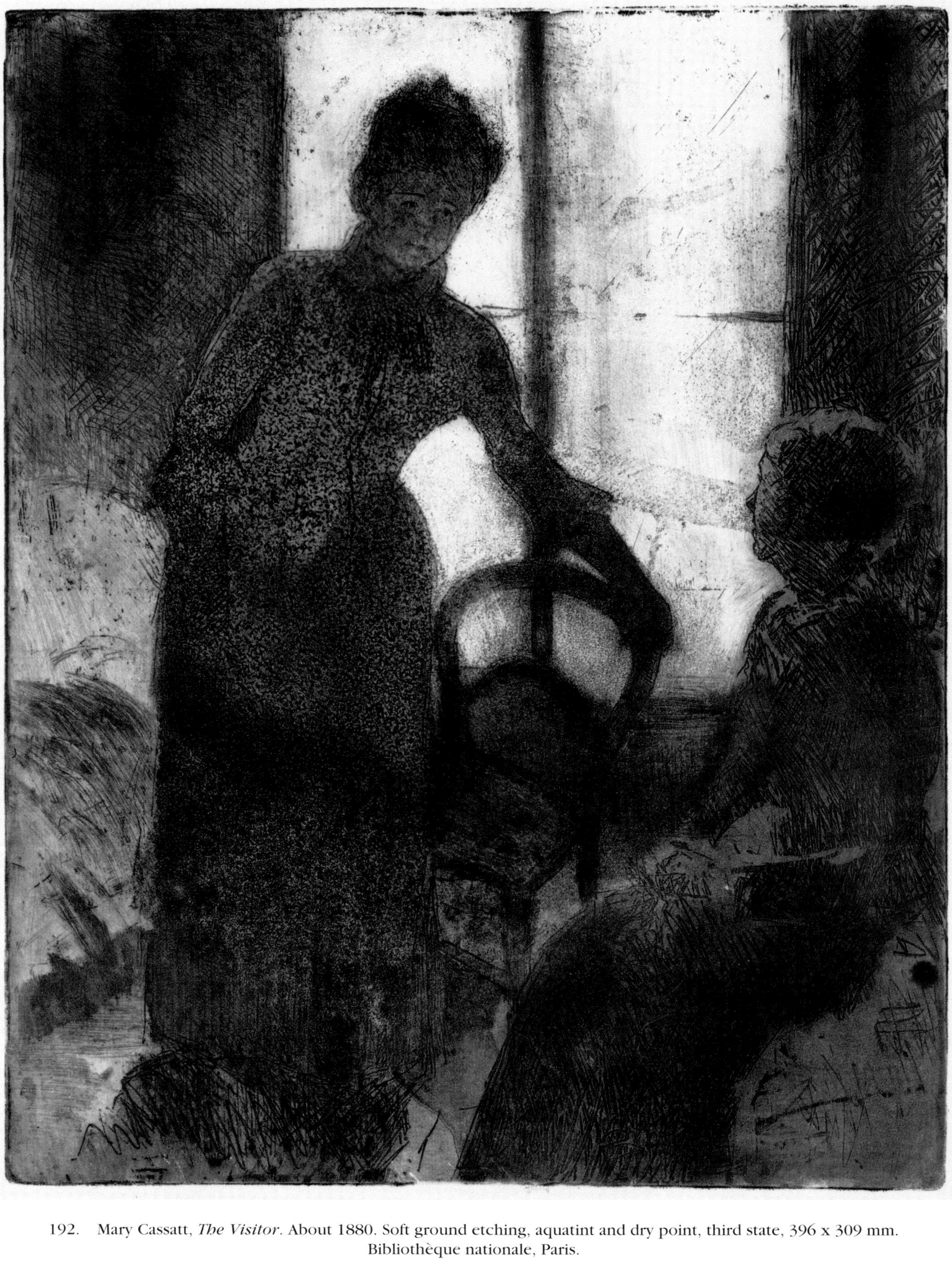

192. Mary Cassatt, *The Visitor*. About 1880. Soft ground etching, aquatint and dry point, third state, 396 x 309 mm. Bibliothèque nationale, Paris.

36. *Scenes from Private Life*

The print might be termed a domestic work of art. With the decorative arts it shares the business of modifying great art, in circumstances that are less solemn than is usual with great art. It helps art to infiltrate normal life and to enter the ordinary household. The Goncourt brothers, and other collectors, have frequently described the solitary pleasures of the print collector. Reproductions are hung on the wall, whereas artists' prints are kept in a portfolio and looked at only by their owner or a few of his friends. They encourage conversation. They are discreet, knowing when to hide and when to reappear. They are particularly suited to scenes from daily life or private life. In her complicated etchings Mary Cassatt depicted the kind of interiors that were later to be the stock-in-trade of Bonnard, Vuillard and Vallotton: a woman sits knitting in front of a bookcase, the bright light from the aquatint throwing the rest into semi-darkness. In others, women sip tea, read under a light or stare dreamily into the fire.[368] These are 'comfortable' prints. *The Visitor* is a curious piece: a woman arrives but is not going to stay (Fig. 192). She is holding the chair on which you have invited her to sit, bending slightly to hold the back of the blackened chair that emerges momentarily from the penumbra. The visitor is looking at you, speaking to you with her back to the light; the silhouette of her dark dress with its thick aquatint grain stands out against the speckled light filtering through the voile curtains, between the vertical line of two drawn curtains. You reply to her with your head turned towards the light, in half-profile, your face almost lost in a blur of ink covered in scratched lines. It is a very skilful image, its complexity combining with the very ordinary nature of the subject in a way calculated to appeal to intellectuals with their fresh way of looking at things. Mary Cassatt discovered the etchings of Degas in 1879[369] and took up the technique more energetically than he did, using the different methods to achieve increasing delicacy and simplicity in aquatints that are weightless and drypoints printed off like working drawings. Her pictures of mothers with children have the lightness of a caress.

Degas grew bored more quickly. After two or three years spent wrestling with the demands of printmaking, his restless temperament made him let go. He took the same pleasure in creating simple images as did Mary Cassatt. *Mary Cassatt at the Louvre* (Figs 201–6), seen

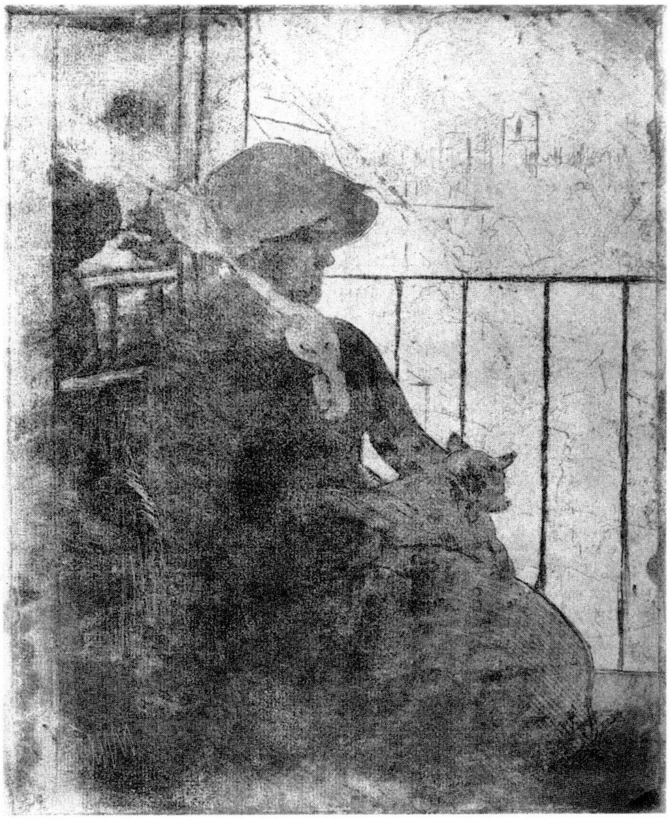

193. Mary Cassatt,
On the Balcony. About 1889.
Soft ground etching and aquatint,
second state, 276 x 216 mm.
Cincinnati Art Museum.

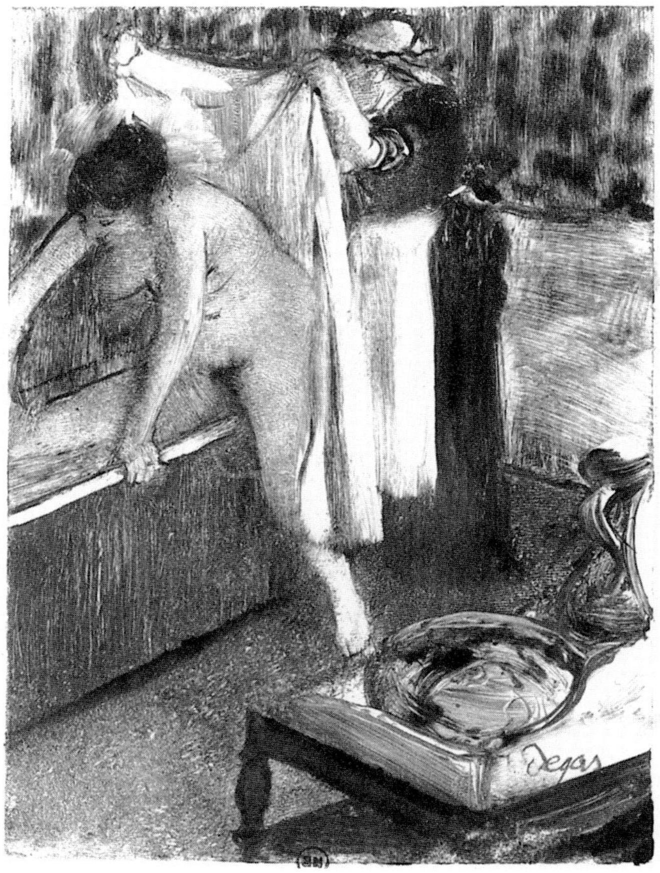

194. Edgar Degas,
Getting out of the Bath. 1877.
Monotype, 157 x 188 mm.
Bibliothèque nationale, Paris.

from behind and cut in half by an opaque panel, is dressed in black like some elegant stranger. She conveys the mysterious quality of a woman glimpsed briefly. Etchings treat figures with a cruelty that cannot have been wholly displeasing to Degas: the smoothness of oil paint is replaced by the bite of the acid. His compositions are cut up even more brutally (if possible) than his paintings, and his figures are systematically dismembered. While he was preparing *Le Jour et la Nuit* he noted: 'For the journal, cut pieces off the dancer, do the arms or the legs, the backside, the shoes, the hairdresser's hands, the finished hair-do, bare feet dancing etc. Do all kinds of everyday items, still bearing the imprint of the man or the woman, corsets just removed, for example, still holding the shape of the body etc. etc.'[370]

Degas shared Mary Cassatt's taste for portraying friends and relations, and they are the subject of a number of his earliest paintings. He liked psychological settings. These are a dramatist's paintings, in which each face is weighed down by experience, in which the silence of the figures bears heavily on their shapes and, in some cases, their posture. The discomfort of dancers at their practice is etched into the metal plate, sometimes so vehemently that the plate is ruined before being completed: faces are permanently scarred by the etching tool, gestures sketched in recklessly and irrevocably. Many of Degas's plates bear witness to this aesthetic aggressiveness: the *Two Dancers* (Fig. 183) are victims of the burnisher, the dancers in *On the Stage* are pursued over three different plates, in aquatint then in soft ground etching. His *Getting out of the Bath* (Figs 248–52), done with the 'crayon électrique', was worked over in an almost obsessional way on several plates. In his boxes fifteen states and forty-three proofs were found.[371] Like Mary Cassatt he loved the theatre (Figs 182, 183); he loved the intimacy of the ground-floor boxes and the orchestra pit (Fig. 213). He inherited this iconography from the Second Empire, with its passionate love of public places where the social classes, thrown together by urbanisation, could make each others' acquaintance, eye each other up and down critically, brush against one another suspiciously and, occasionally, mingle. This iconography was at its most popular among the realists, but was on the wane by the time Degas and Mary Cassatt took it up. Realism had rendered the subjects of great art hackneyed, too hackneyed even for the most ambitious easel paintings. The etched print allowed the taste for more intimate subjects to be pursued further, and allowed the exploration of areas where realist art had feared to tread. Evidence of this was to be found in Bracquemond's earliest prints. The print bears the same relationship to painting as the short story bears to the novel. The print ventures into subjects that are rich in insignificance.

It is interesting to measure the ground that has been covered between Pissarro's peasant pictures and those

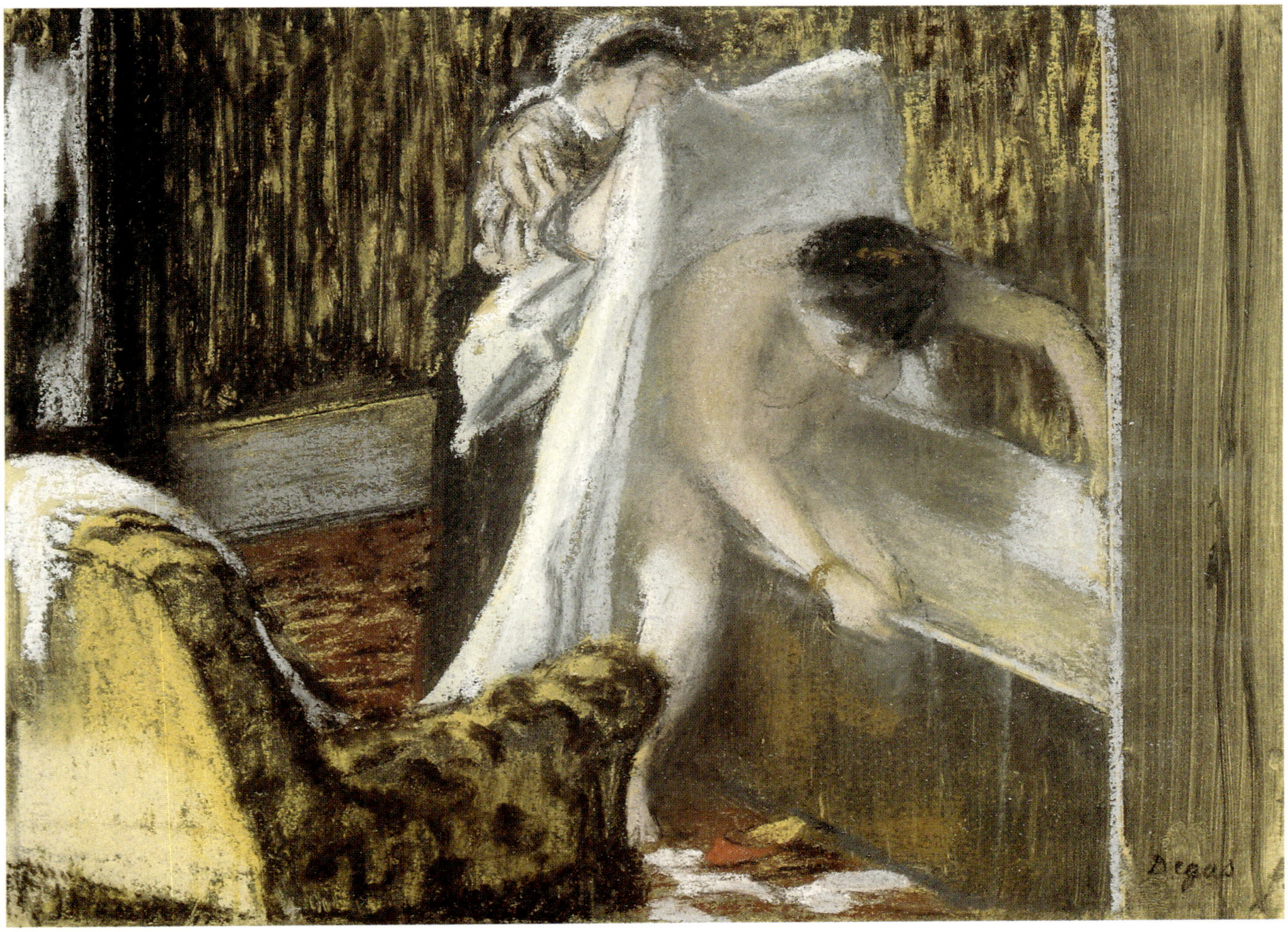

195. Edgar Degas,
Woman Getting out of the Bath.
1876–7.
Pastel on monotype, 160 x 215 mm.
Musée d'Orsay, Paris.

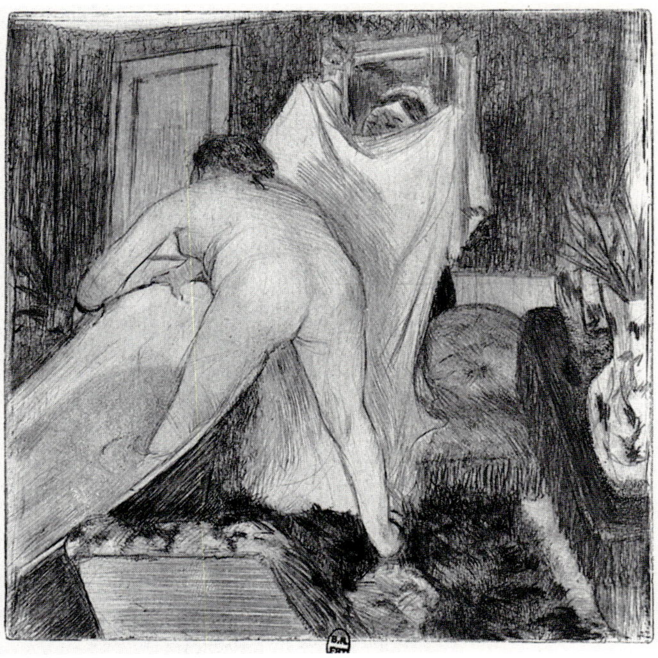

196. Edgar Degas,
Getting out of the Bath. 1880–2.
Etching, drypoint and aquatint, fifth state, 127 x 127 mm.
Bibliothèque nationale, Paris.

of Millet, or the distance separating him from Lhermitte. The figures peopling his landscapes are not destroyed, though they are sometimes cut by the frame, as in *The Chestnut Seller* (Fig. 210). They are sometimes seen from behind (*In the Fields at Ennery*, *Wooded Undergrowth at L'Hermitage*; Figs 156–8), or in the distance (*The Haystacks* Figs 198–200, *Woman on the Road*); they disappear into the fog (*Effect of Rain*; Figs 174–7), or sit by the roadside (*Père Melon*). Only the women are seen working, accomplishing their domestic tasks: *Woman emptying a Wheelbarrow* (Figs 169–72), *The Gruel*, *Woman Churning Milk*, *Woman Carrying Buckets*. For the men, labour is replaced by the road as a theme, and comes close to the theme of tramps, travellers, the homeless and others living on the fringes of society, treated later by Pissarro in an explicitly anarchist context in *The Vagrants*. These are peasants trying to escape from their condition, and they are thus different from Millet's peasants with whom they have traditionally been compared.[372] While the humdrum has replaced the grandiloquent and the picturesque, disillusion has replaced enthusiasm. The glorification of labour (*Leaving for Work*), regarded as threatening halfway through the Second Empire, switched from a threat to a promise and Millet's work, taken up in a big way by the Americans, provided Republican imagery for the whole of the 1880s. Pissarro was using the same themes at this period: *The Gruel*, *Woman Churning Milk*, *Woman Carrying Buckets*, *The Sower*, and was certainly influenced by Millet's imagery. His work, however, was free of romanticism, illustrated by a comparison of his *Haymakers* with Lhermitte's *Haymakers resting* (1886). If Millet's *Gruel* is compared with Pissarro's *Woman Feeding a Child*, besides the fact that his title dispenses Pissarro from any allegorical undercurrent, it is noticeable that the mother depicted by Millet at this simple task has a dignified carriage and generous movements and bears a certain likeness to the tutelary figure of the French Republic, as portrayed in official art. Pissarro's peasant women have nothing of the *alma mater* about them, nor indeed does Mary Cassatt's society lady who, in a drypoint, discreetly suckles her child (1899).[373] Lhermitte's tender, bucolic *Young Mother Harvesting* (1903) is the reverse.[374]

Respect for sensations in all their immediacy, at the heart of the Impressionist doctrine, could be interpreted as a withdrawal into introversion and an intensification of personal experience. Intuition henceforth was jockeying for position with learning. The wings in the theatre received more attention than the stage. Dancers do not dance but are seen putting on their ballet shoes; the square in *Martinmas Fair* (Figs 211, 212) is deserted and *The Visitor* (Fig. 192) is on the point of sitting down. The Impressionist perspective gains in clarity what it loses in breadth, like an image seen through a microscope. In this respect, printmaking is a fertile field for experimentation, like a specimen between two pieces of glass. The result is not necessarily intended for public exhibition, nor even for publication. Nevertheless, unlike a drawing, the result will be printed and may eventually be reproduced. The print has become an art laboratory in which the values of the new society can be 'put to the proof'.

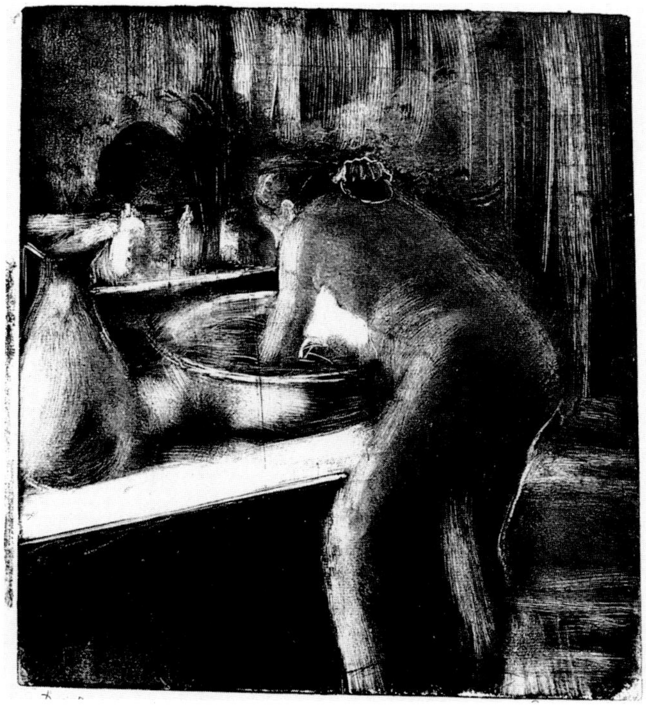

197. Edgar Degas, *Her Toilette*. 1885. Monotype, first proof, 313 x 278 mm. Bibliothèque d'Art et d'Archéologie, Paris.

37. *1881: Revival*

The fifth Impressionist exhibition, held in 1880 on the corner of rue des Pyramides and rue Saint-Honoré, contained a larger number of prints than any of the other exhibitions, the result of hard work done during the winter of 1879–80. The still unpublished etchings prepared for *Le Jour et la Nuit* were exhibited, indicating that the publication was designed as a complement to the exhibition of work by the 'independents', i.e. by the group led by Degas. Degas himself showed a series of 'experiments and plates in different states' – this probably referred to the states of *Mary Cassatt at the Louvre* (Figs 201–6). Mary Cassatt also showed etchings in different states: *Woman reading* and *Woman at the Theatre* in their first and last states. Bracquemond exhibited some 'etchings for the decoration of pottery and porcelain', which implies that his contribution to the review, apart from the preparatory sketch for the cover, had not yet been completed. Thanks to pressure brought to bear on the other members by Degas, Jean-François Raffaëlli appeared with the group for the first time, exhibiting a frame of etchings and drypoints, four etchings illustrating Huysman's *Croquis naturalistes* and the 'successive states' of his *Old Rag-and-Bone Man* (Fig. 159), a plate intended for *Le Jour et la Nuit*. His brother, Jean-Marius, presented six etchings and there was also a 'frame of etchings' by Jean-Baptiste Léopold Levert, a friend of Degas who had exhibited with him in the first exhibition in 1874 and again in the second and third. The most abundantly represented artist was Pissarro, with five frames of prints, each containing a complete set of states of his Pontoise landscapes; the four states of his *Wooded Undergrowth at L'Hermitage* (Figs 156–8) were specifically described in the catalogue as 'part of the first issue of the publication *Le Jour et la Nuit*', proof that at this date the publication had not yet been abandoned.

It was Jean-François Raffaëlli who brought the scandal to a head. His name became the focus of the controversy (already raging in the group) between the so-called 'pure' Impressionists (including Caillebotte, Monet and Renoir) and Degas and his recruits, who followed a more traditional aesthetic.[375] Degas had sponsored the participation of De Nittis (considered to be a society artist) in the first exhibition, and was keen to encourage painters with academic leanings like Tissot, Lhermitte and Henner.[376] Realism seemed a fairly broad criterion, and it was a style that was already well-established. The case of Raffaëlli was bound to cause a storm. Raffaëlli was a young actor turned painter who had retained his sense of theatre. His work was classical in execution, produced in a style that looked back to the genre painting of the age of Louis-Philippe; to accompany it he spun a pretentious yarn claiming to have founded a new school based on the representation of types from all walks of life, the school of the 'beau caractériste'. The *Old Rag-and-Bone Man* was the embodiment of the new school. His doctrine rejected the distinction between 'realism' and 'beauty', the ill-defined notion of 'beauty' now making an unexpected reappearance. His version of realism, in this case, was to choose proletarian characters, dressed in rags. 'Beauty' consisted of portraying them in an idealised manner, worthy of the illustrated albums of the Romantic period. This strange mixture was typical of the 1880s. The Republicans were securely in power and, in a kind of aesthetic of guilt, were exploring and idealising the picturesque aspects of poverty and low-life. Huysmans, an admirer of Raffaëlli's work since the Salon of 1879,[377] was one of the proponents of this attractive but perverse attitude; his was the new face of dandyism under the Third Republic.

Caillebotte and Gauguin contrasted Raffaëlli and Forain, the 'illustrators' championed by Degas, with 'pure Impressionists' for whom realism meant simply working from the motif, and beauty the idea of painting professionally for the sake of art, without any social undertones. Realism and beauty were expressed in a preference for landscape and simple, single figures, far removed from Raffaëlli's 'beau caractériste'. What is of interest in this interchange between the two factions is that the practice of printmaking was almost exclusively confined to the group centred around Degas. Printmaking had its origins in a belief in the social function of a work of art, and this belief justified the passage of the print through the printing press, but, on the other hand, the aesthetics of printmaking had always been opposed to the picturesque and the anecdotal. For the older members of the group – Degas, Pissarro and Bracquemond – such a view was well entrenched, and part of their efforts were devoted to rescuing the print from the picturesque, from illustration and from anecdote in order to assimilate it with the autonomous work of art – with paintings. Raffaëlli accomplished his return to imagery

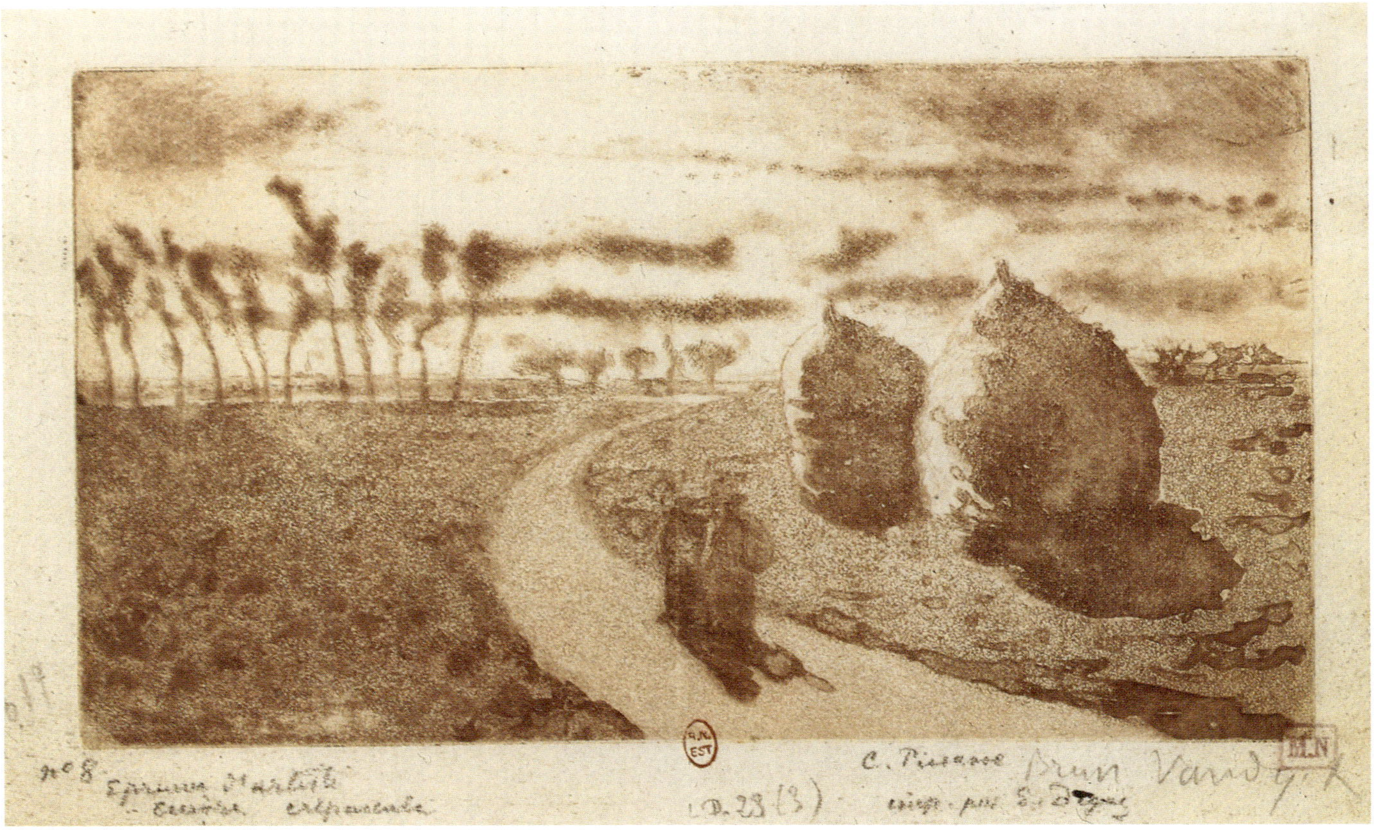

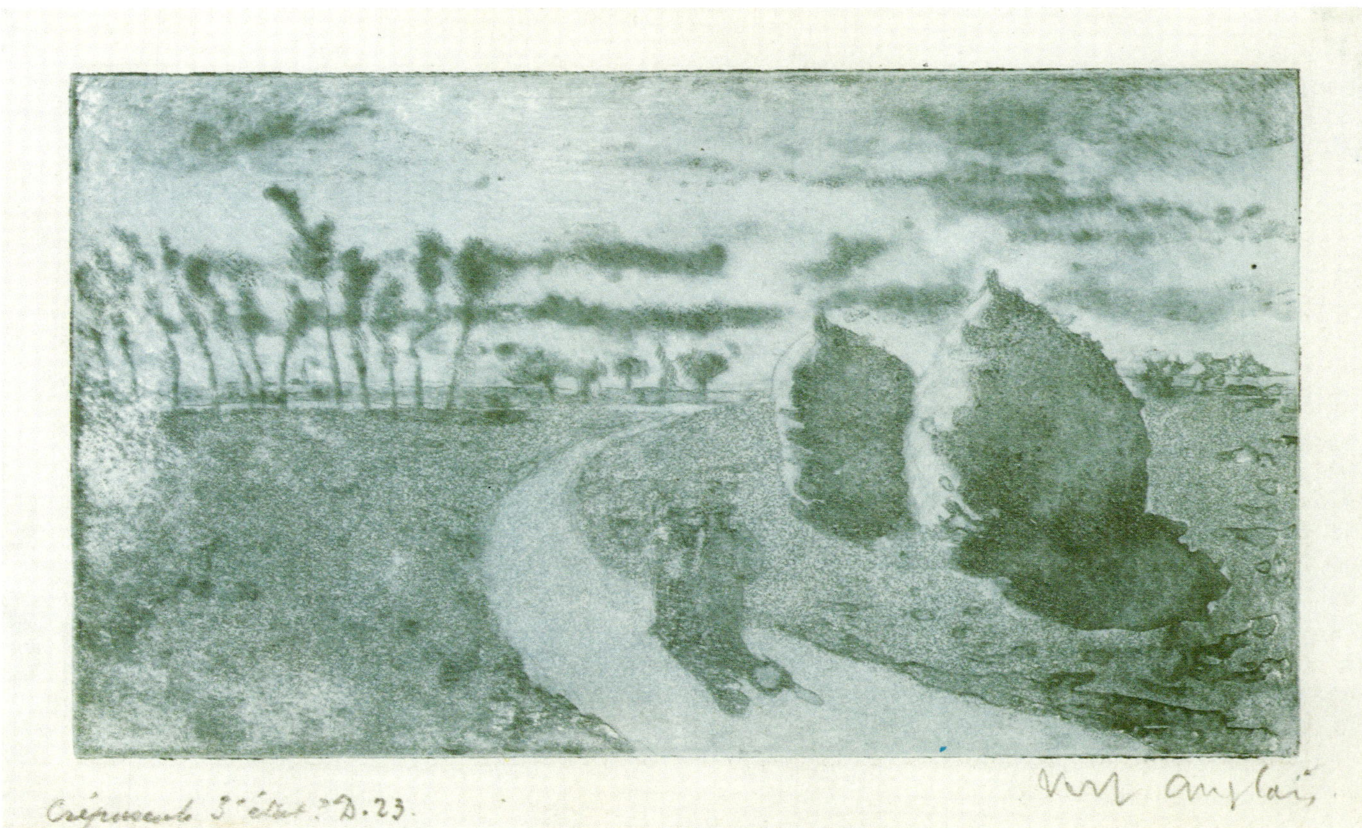

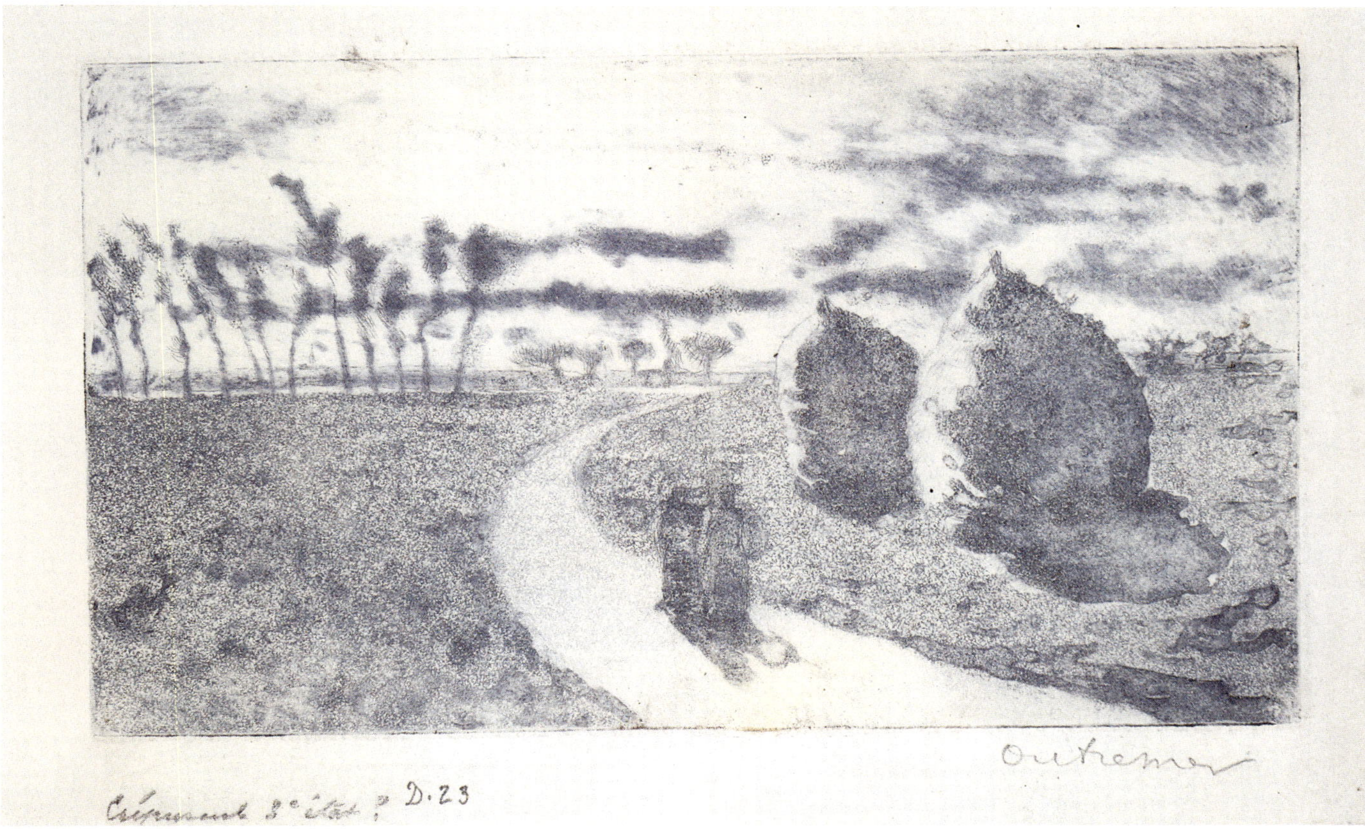

198, 199, 200. Camille Pissarro,
Evening with Haystacks. 1879.
Aquatint and drypoint, 105 x 177 mm. Brown print, Bibliothèque nationale, Paris; green print, National Gallery of Canada, Ottawa; blue print, Ashmolean Museum, Oxford.

from the positions occupied by his elders in the field, but he seemed to distort their kind of imagery, producing something popular and mannered, turning their elegance into vulgarity. These contrasts concerned two distinct groups: the first group comprised the old 'painter-printmakers', Degas, Pissarro and Bracquemond on one hand and the younger printmakers on the other, recruited after 1880 and including Raffaëlli and Forain who were born into an era when the taste for prints had often degenerated into snobbery. In addition to these two sub-groups, linked by their printmaking although a generation apart in age, there was a second group consisting of Caillebotte, Monet and Renoir in whose repertory the print played no part.

It was just at this time (bearing in mind the slant given by Degas) that the critics began to look more favourably on Impressionism. The old-guard softened their attitude

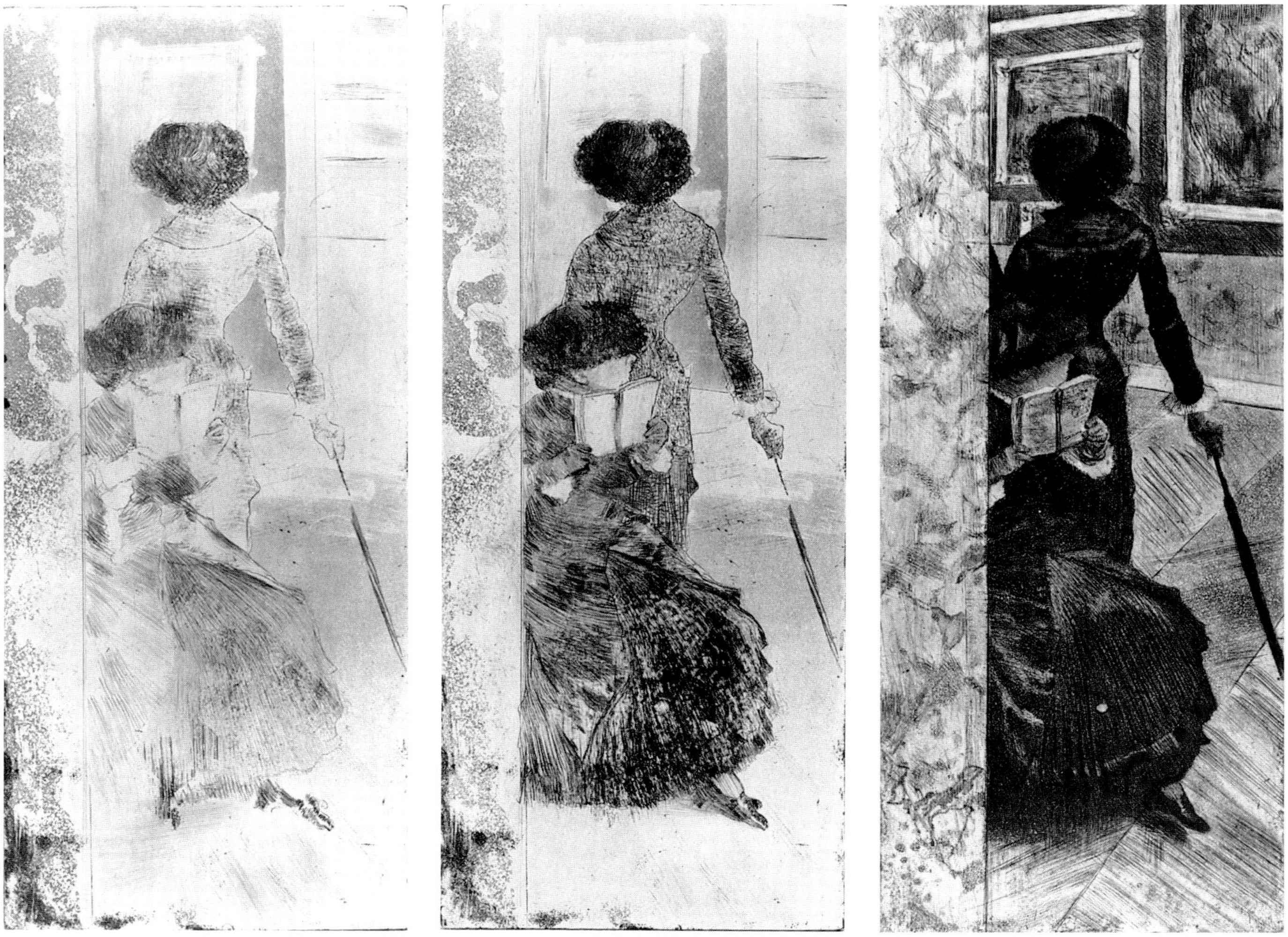

and the younger generation began to appreciate the decorative effects of Impressionist art, the work of Degas and Mary Cassatt in particular, and even more the depiction of contemporary manners provided by Raffaëlli and Forain. Huysmans's *Croquis* exactly translate their favourite themes into literature: the Folies-Bergère for Forain and the sub-working classes for Raffaëlli. When Huysmans saw the etchings exhibited by Pissarro in 1880 he mainly remembered the frames:[378] 'I will omit the engravings of M. Pissarro, with their purple frames and yellow paper – that particular yellow paper on which drypoints and etchings are printed', and devoted his attention to Paul Renouard's *Dancers*. The political situation was settling down, the Republic now permanently installed since hope of a Restoration had been abandoned; the Republicans had won a majority in the 'conservative' Senate. A party was forming around the Republican right wing. Although the economic situation had not fully recovered, France was no longer experiencing the violent recession of the 1870s. The Freycinet Plan, launched in 1878, began to bear fruit in the 1880s. In the same year Durand-Ruel managed to obtain credit from the powerful Banque de l'Union Générale, founded in 1878 by a group of Catholics to compete with the Jewish and Protestant banks that were monopolising the new capital.[379] He began purchasing again, and the Impressionists felt the effects. The revival was short-lived, however. The political struggle intensified under Gambetta between November 1881 and January 1882, the economic crisis was given new impetus and on 19 January came the collapse of the Union Générale and the arrest of one of its directors, Feder, one of Durand-Ruel's best customers. The collapse bankrupted a large number of small Catholic investors; they had rallied to the cause like crusaders and their sorry tale is recounted in Zola's *L'Argent*.

The achievement of the Impressionist printmakers at this time was meagre. Degas, the most determined in his overtures to industry, had published nothing. He had spoiled twenty plates and those remaining that were publishable could be counted on the fingers of one hand. This may explain why he abandoned printmaking for ten years; as Desboutin pointed out, he was subject to 'crazes'. Bracquemond, on the other hand, was a pro-

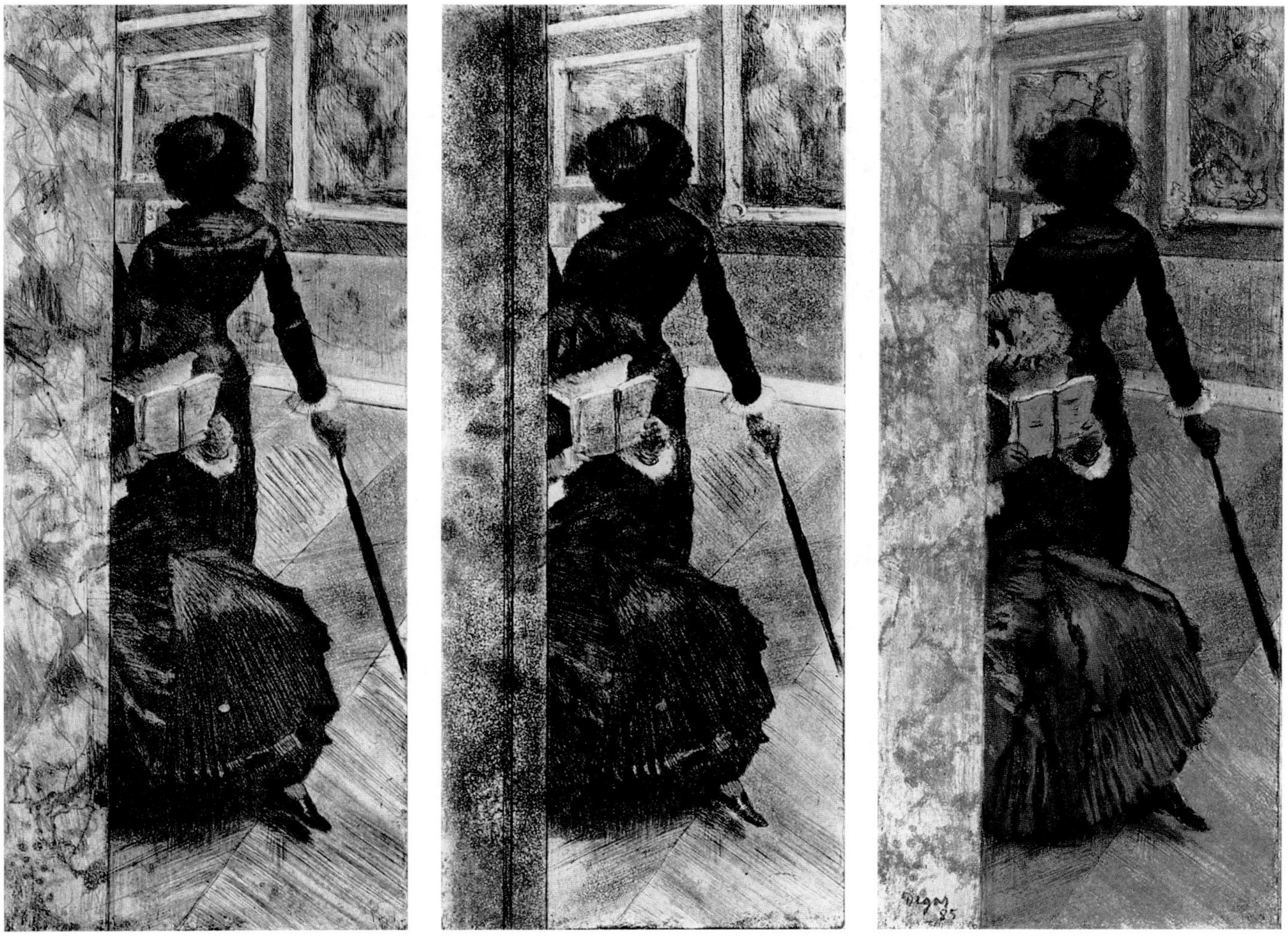

fessional and did not give up printmaking after 1882; Jean-Paul Bouillon states however that 'in this third period his work was of a different nature; large plates, elaborately and skilfully etched, were created in response to official commissions, or commissions from dealers or patrons, and supplanted the improvisations and 'caprices' he had previously produced'.[380]

The sixth Impressionist exhibition, in 1881, without Monet, Sisley or Renoir, contained no prints. The experiment was over. Hopes were pinned on the sale of paintings, after Renoir's success. Degas had imposed his rules. The following year, when Durand-Ruel was in trouble, the opposing faction, the 'pure' Impressionists, Monet and Renoir, returned, splitting the group asunder. Degas and his friends, including Mary Cassatt, withdrew. There were no prints in the exhibition, which was entirely Impressionist: Caillebotte, Gauguin, Guillaumin, Monet, Morisot, Pissarro, Renoir, Sisley and Vignon. Was Zola right in his opinion that, after 1880, the group seemed to have had its day? Burty worded it more strongly still in 1879: 'today the experiment is concluded and we can judge it more harshly'.[381] It is true

201–6. Edgar Degas,
Mary Cassatt at the Louvre: Paintings. 1879.
Etching, aquatint and drypoint, 301 x 125 mm. First state, second state, ten states, Bibliothèque nationale, Paris; thirteenth state, Art Institute, Chicago, gift of Walter S. Brewster; twentieth state, Bibliothèque d'Art et d'Archéologie, Paris; proof touched up with pastel (1885), Art Institute, Chicago, bequest of Kate L. Brewster.

that the need for cooperation and a 'parallel economy' was less pronounced and this caused vacillation and some defections. But, conversely, the crisis closed the ranks, and it could be maintained that Impressionism really started at that time, in 1880. Whatever the truth of the matter, the Impressionists became disunited and disaffected as soon as the goal was in sight. Cézanne returned to Aix, Sisley moved to Saint-Mammès, Monet moved a bit further from Paris, from Vétheil to Giverny, Pissarro buried himself in the country, leaving Pontoise for Osny and taking Gauguin with him; Gauguin had started playing the stock market at just the wrong moment. For the next three years there was no exhibition.

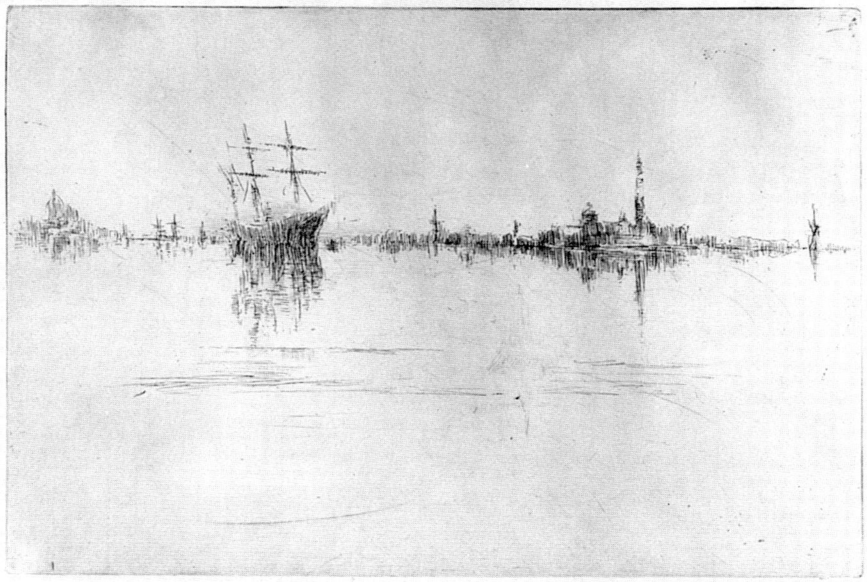

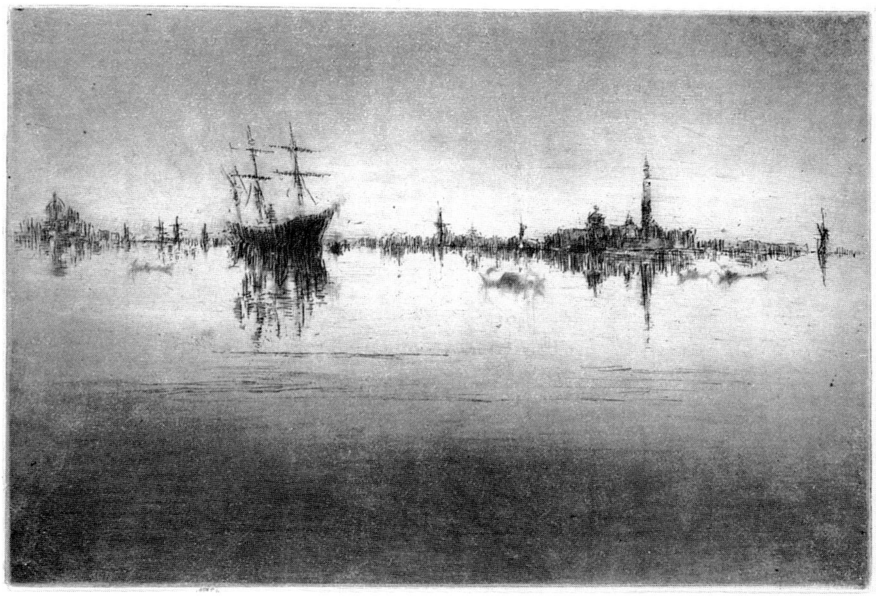

207, 208. James McNeill Whistler, *Nocturne*. 1879–80. Drypoint, 200 x 295 mm.
First state, artist's proof, Hunterian Art Gallery, University of Glasgow, bequest of Birnie Philip;
fourth state, National Gallery of Art, Washington, gift of Mrs J. Watson Webb.

38. *Whistler's Venetian Suite*

According to Mary Cassatt, Degas invited Whistler to join the Impressionist group,[382] but Whistler did not reply to his letter. Degas had hit on someone even more stubbornly independent than himself. After his stay in France, Whistler distanced himself from the group of realists with whom he served his apprenticeship: Fantin-Latour, Bonvin, Legros, Courbet, and was now a member of the group of English aesthetes centred around Rossetti. This development illustrates the impermanence of the dividing line between the idealism of the young intellectuals of the 1880s and the realism of the previous generation; the latter had grown so sophisticated that with the slightest encouragement it toppled over into aestheticism. Huysmans and Edmond de Goncourt provide literary examples of this trend. In 1867 Whistler broke off relations very publicly with Seymour Haden, Courbet and Fantin-Latour. He had not touched etching since 1863. However, encouraged by sales to his patron, Alexander Ionides (also a supporter of Legros) and Frederick R. Leyland, he took up his etching tool again and in May 1871 published *The Thames Set*, 'a series of sixteen etchings on the Thames and other subjects', then, in 1873, produced eighteen etched portraits of the Leyland family. He quarrelled with Leyland in 1877 and in the same year crossed swords with John Ruskin, who accused him of being a charlatan. When financial ruin threatened he took up printmaking again in a style that was becoming more and more allusive; the white of the paper and the lightest of etched marks replaced firm lines and volume. In 1879 he went bankrupt, and sold all his possessions. It was then that the Fine Arts Society, a group of collectors, stepped in: they sent him to Venice, all expenses paid, with an order for a series of prints in the 'vedutista' tradition, still very much alive in England.[383]

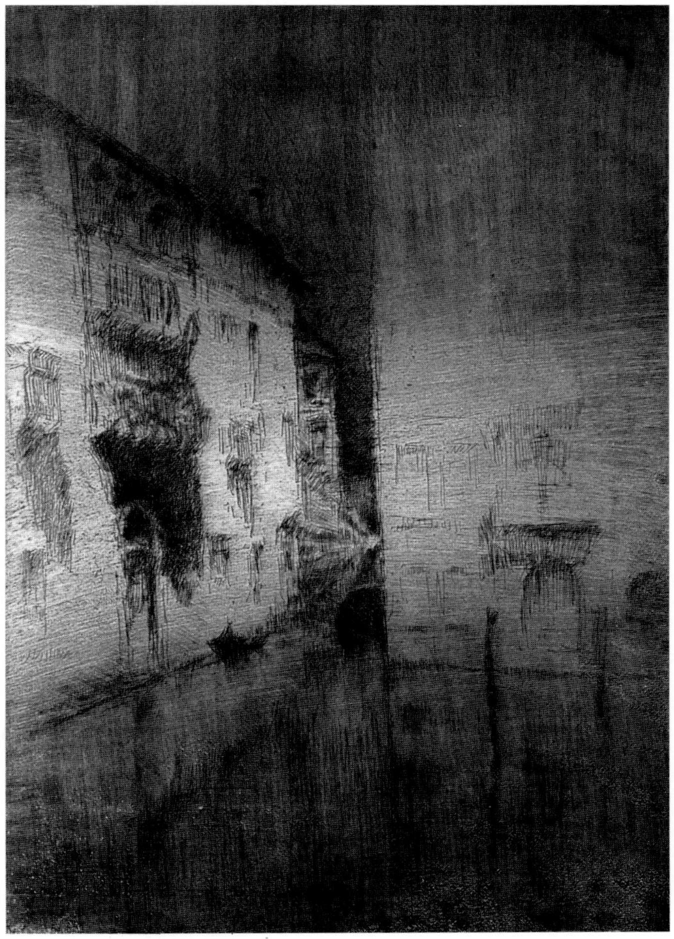

209. James McNeill Whistler, *Nocturne-Palaces*. 1880. Etching and ink, 295 x 200 mm. Bibliothèque nationale, Paris.

Whistler left on 9 September 1879 and, according to his contract, should have returned before 20 December with a series of twelve plates from which an edition of one hundred copies was planned. He came back to London a year late, at the end of November 1880, to the fury of the directors of the Fine Art Society. Once settled in London again he insisted on printing the twelve copper plates himself (Figs 207–9). The lightness of the etched line – referred to by Whistler as its 'delicacy' – meant that the quality of the printed proofs depended on the inking, which Whistler supervised himself. It became clear that the editorial ambitions of the Fine Art Society and the new aesthetic of the original print were incompatible, and the end result was a paradox: 1200 proofs, nearly all of them different, not delivered to the commissioning body until 1901. The artist observed that the beauty of a single proof was sufficient for his reputation; the production of a series from one proof would be madness.[384] As far as possible, Whistler printed on eighteenth century paper, and, in pursuit of refinement, kept the copper plate warm enough during the printing process to impart a silky finish to the paper.[385] Then he trimmed the pages almost to the edge of the image, as was the fashion with old prints, leaving only a tiny margin on which he would print his emblem, a butterfly. His tactics were designed to infuriate existing collectors and to attract a completely new public. In 1880 he refused to join the new Society of Painters-Etchers, founded by Seymour Haden as a counterblast to the Royal Academy, because he was not made president. His outbursts made him more and more popular with the younger generation and, following the publication of a second series of twenty-six Venetian plates, thirty copies of each, he enjoyed growing success with his English publisher, Dowdeswell, and with the American dealer Edward G. Kennedy. In France in 1888 Mallarmé translated his collection of lectures, *Ten o'Clock*, Duret wrote a whole book about him[386] and Durand-Ruel held an exhibition of his work. In 1889 his drypoints and etchings were exhibited in the English pavilion of the Exposition Universelle, but the prize for printmaking was awarded to Seymour Haden. Whistler caught up in 1892 and, thanks to the good offices of Mallarmé, received the Légion d'Honneur and a retrospective exhibition at the Goupil Gallery in London. His travels in the Loire Valley, from which he returned with a series of prints of Renaissance buildings, and his prolonged stays in Paris between 1891 and 1896, during which he produced numerous etchings and lithographs of Paris, made Whistler a figure in French artistic circles. Arguments about him were as acrimonious in Paris as they were in London.

Whistler had gone too far and much too fast into aestheticism to be a member of any Impressionist group, but the Impressionists were impressed by his *savoir-faire.* There were undeniable links: Whistler always referred to his 'Impressionist period', particularly with reference to his Venetian suites. Whistler had adopted Pissarro's technique of presenting his prints in white frames on coloured walls – mauve for Pissarro at the fifth Impressionist exhibition in 1880, yellow for Whistler at the second exhibition of his Venetian pictures (thirty-one were exhibited) at the Fine Arts Society in February 1883. Pissarro made the following comments on Whistler as an artist to his son Lucien, who had seen the exhibition: 'I do regret not seeing Whistler's exhibition, as much for the fine drypoints as for the presentation which, with Whistler, plays a very important part; he puts a bit too much puffism into it if you ask me. Apart from that, I think that white and yellow must be a delightful combination; we were the first people in fact to try out these colour effects: my gallery was lilac with canary yellow borders, without any butterflies. . . . Whistler works mainly in drypoint, sometimes it is ordinary etching, but the fluidity that you remarked on, the smoothness and haziness that you liked so much is a kind of shading done by the printer, who is Whistler himself; no professional printer could take his place, it is very skilled work and complements the work done with the etched line. What the rest of us were trying to do was to achieve the same softness before the printing took place. I've seen two prints shown in Paris, a couple of years ago. They were finely drawn, a bit thin and spindly; I would have had to see a whole collection to judge them properly. There must certainly be some outstanding ones in the exhibition.'[387] A few lines after this eulogy, Pissarro alerted his son to the seductive power of aestheticism, to which the new generation was responding so enthusiastically: 'Aestheticism is a kind of Romanticism compounded with low cunning. . .'.

39. *The Role of the Rebels*

After the failure of *Le Jour et la Nuit* Pissarro, unlike Degas, continued to make etchings; in fact, his printmaking career had only just begun. At the end of 1880, Théodore Duret looked round London for outlets (no longer to be found in Paris) for the work of his friends, and suggested holding an exhibition of etchings there. On 23 December Pissarro replied: 'On the subject of etchings, I have had neither the time nor the means to continue with my efforts, it would have needed two or three years of hard work. We stopped very suddenly! The need to sell my work has obliged me to paint water colours, etching has been forgotten for the time being.'[388] Then, on 4 January 1881, he wrote to his niece Esther, in London: 'I saw M. Duret who is passing through. I have more or less decided to send a collection of etchings to Deschamps, a dealer in London, quite soon; he will exhibit them, if the prints do not alarm the English public too much.'[389]

On 14 January 1881 Duret informed Pissarro that 'a society of painter-etchers is being formed in London . . . Legros, Seymour Haden, Herkomer and Tissot are its leading members. They are holding a big exhibition in April. I've seen Legros and he promised to sponsor your etchings and defend them if necessary. Be sure to send a selection of the prints we did together at your house. We should like to have something by Degas for the exhibition. I said that you were the only person close enough to him to wring something out of him. While we are waiting, could you possibly include in the package of your etchings the two or three rare Degas prints in your possession? I'll be very discreet with them and, if you so require, I'll only show them to private individuals.'[390] Duret received the following reply, dated 17 January 1881: 'On mature reflection, I have decided not to send any etchings or watercolours to London: as for the exhibition you mentioned, it is obviously a good idea to form a group of painter-etchers, but it would not be of particular help to us; or at any rate it would be a waste of time to exhibit work as imperfect as mine there. Nor have I any confidence in the academicians who will form the jury; and besides, we would rather stay in Paris and take part in things here when the time comes. Thank you for taking this trouble on our behalf, if we were on our own it would be a total flop. I've talked to Degas about it and he is absolutely against it. As you know, the English have never seen any of our work! In 70 Monet and I sent work

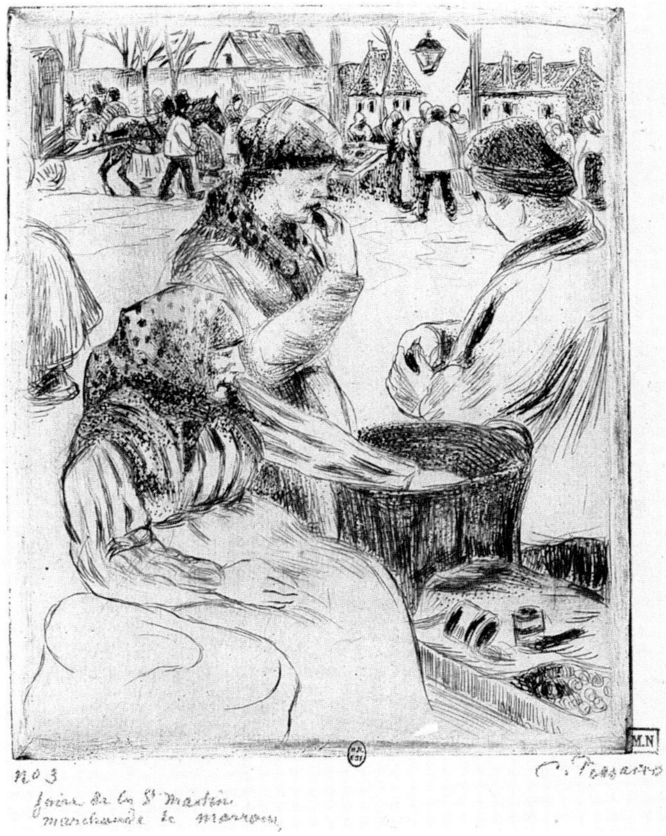

210. Camille Pissarro,
The Chestnut Seller, 1878.
Drypoint, second and final state, 210 x 170 mm.
Bibliothèque nationale, Paris.

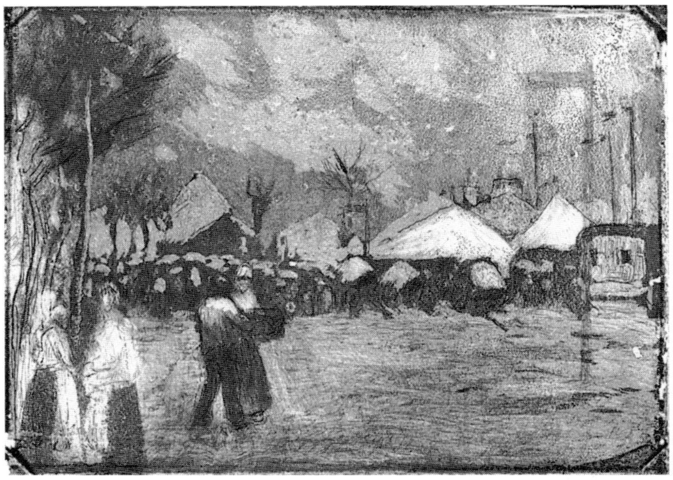

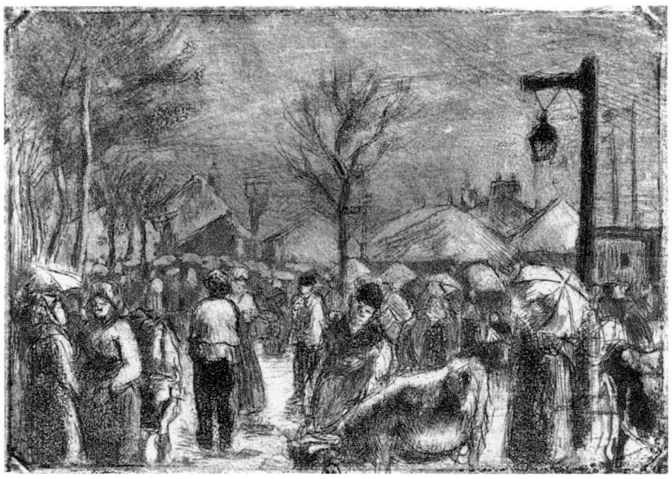

211, 212. Camille Pissarro.
The Martinmas Fair at Pontoise. 1879.
Etching, third and fourth states, 119 x 160 mm.
Bibliothèque nationale, Paris.

213. Edgar Degas,
On the Stage. 1877.
Etching, third plate, fourth state, 123 x 160 mm.
Bibliothèque nationale, Paris.

to the Academy exhibition and the whole lot was rejected; mine was the painting that now belongs to Tissot – it would be even worse with etchings, anyway I'm not keen. I hate officialdom, even English officialdom! Please thank Legros for his offer of sponsorship, it was very kind of him to take on such a compromising responsibility.'[391]

As this letter demonstrates, Pissarro was still working closely with Degas. His attitude was no more accommodating when he turned down a one-man exhibition at Durand-Ruel in 1883,[392] or rejected advances from the Exposition Universelle of 1889, or from Octave Maus for the Salon des XX in Brussels. The intransigence of artists like Degas and Pissarro was an important factor in the establishment of the new criteria that would guarantee the value of work that was not yet widely appreciated. Although they were unaware of it, their shared dislike of officialdom had this effect, whatever their differences and the reasons for their resistance. Pissarro was the son of traders in the West Indies and his family were scattered all over the world, in Portugal, Bordeaux, St Thomas, London, Paris; Degas was the son of a minor banker, half of whose family had emigrated to Naples and the other half to New Orleans. Both came from privileged backgrounds but then were witness to the break-up of their families. Both were temperamentally anxious, felt themselves to be artists and were in a state of rebellion. One, the stateless Jew, was an idealist who was to swell the ranks of the small army of anarchist intellectuals in the final years of the century. The other, the nationalist, was a cynic who, at the same period, was part of the anti-Dreyfus brigade. They remained good friends, bound together by their rebellion against the authorities -embodied in the art world by juries and medals, which both artists doggedly rejected. Without knowing it, they were fighting for the same cause: to make a name for themselves while continuing to have faith in progress. To be 'scientific' Impressionists (in Pissarro's words) but to leave industry to other people. It is the questions raised by their work that make it so rich and engaging, and they are questions whose answers we are still seeking today.

Théodore Duret did not give up his plan for an exhibition in London. On 29 March 1883 Pissarro wrote to his son Lucien, who had been in London since February: '. . . I'm so happy about the good Impression you have made on Duret. We talked a lot about etchings and it has been decided in principle to do something in England; as I said to Duret, the main thing is to produce something that will interest the English buyer. I have been through the work that I have ready: apart from a couple of pieces, there is not really enough to take on such a project. I should like to start work and as soon as I have the money for some copper plates I shall start a series of drypoint etchings on subjects from nature. There are various corners of Pontoise and Osny to be done.'[393] Pissarro did in fact start work. In 1883 he completed

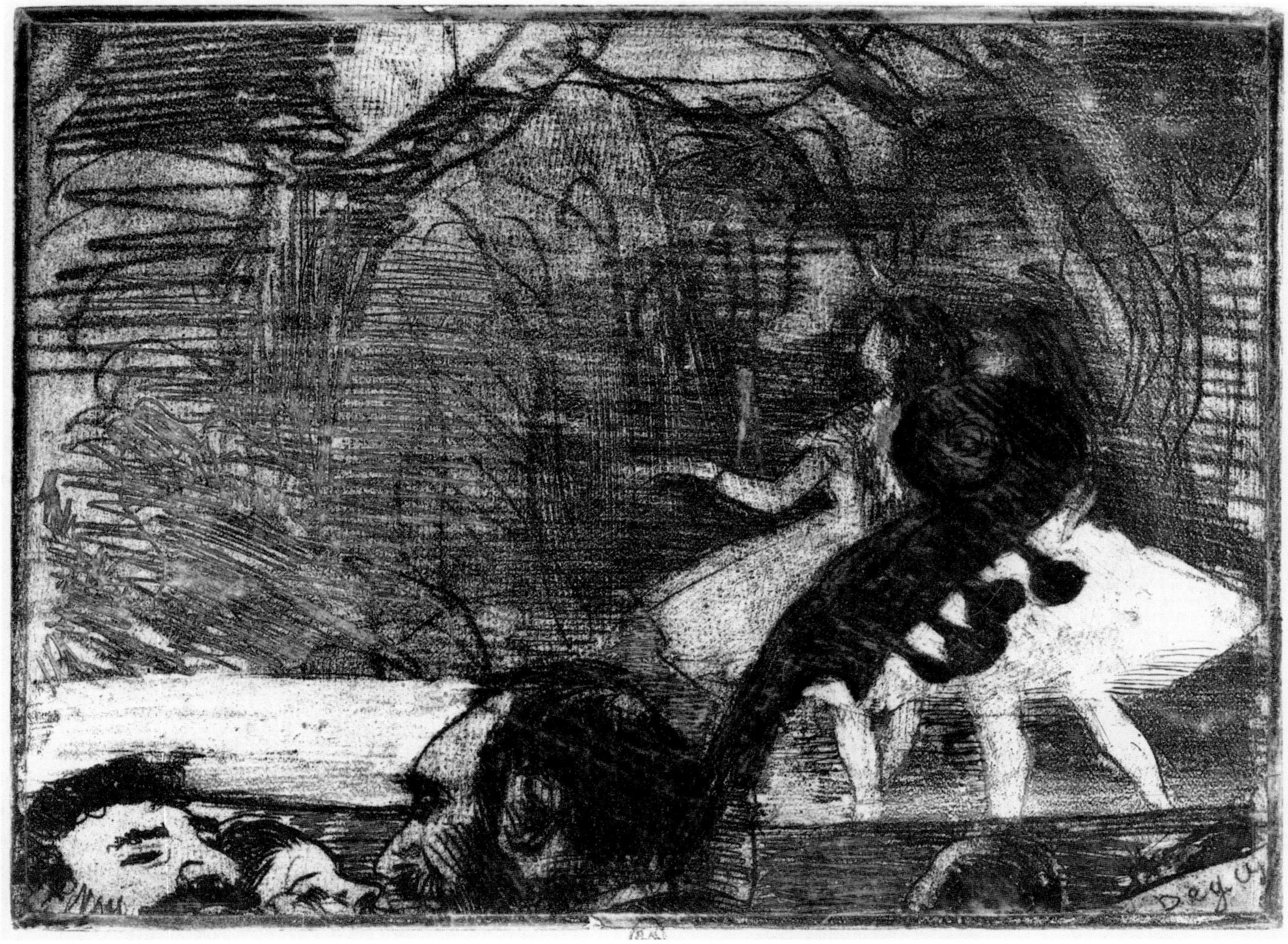

about fifteen views of Pontoise and Osny. In October he went to work in Rouen, staying with his friend Eugène Murer, the restaurant owner, and here he completed another twenty or so plates.[394] The year 1883 therefore accounts for quite a large proportion of his printmaking, and he reprinted and reworked his plates for a long time afterwards. The exhibition in London was never to take place.

The career of the hard-working Bracquemond was quite different. The former apprentice merrily pushed his own social advancement: third class medal at the Salon in 1866, second in 1868, first in 1872. In 1882 the left-wing government rewarded the old republicans, Bracquemond and Manet, who had been 'refused' in 1863, with the Légion d'Honneur. Bracquemond received the Médaille d'Honneur in the Salon of 1884, won a rosette in 1889 and the top prize for engraving in 1900. In 1885, Beraldo wrote glowingly: 'His prints are now collectors' items; the proofs from plates executed by him at present are immediately seized by collectors, who, having been alerted a little too late, will pay any price to get hold of the 'states' of his first etchings.'[395] The *Inventaire du fonds français* (the inventory of the French collection) of the Bibliothèque Nationale ends with this encomium: 'At the end of the last century, no name was more respected than his by those who took pride in their ability to appreciate contemporary French printmaking.'

Two stumbling blocks threatened the rebels: failure and success. Failure encouraged their rebelliousness, success destroyed it. After 1880, success was more threatening to Pissarro and Degas than failure. Both artists kept an eye open for trouble, and took evasive action when it appeared.[396] In a period of breakdown the rebel has a rôle, shouldering responsibilty for the breakdown and then, when others have taken advantage of the situation, continuing to bear the brunt. They form what in military terms is called a 'vanguard' – their death may be necessary but it is only recognised as the supreme sacrifice retrospectively, when victory is won.

40. *1886: the Last Impressionist Exhibition*

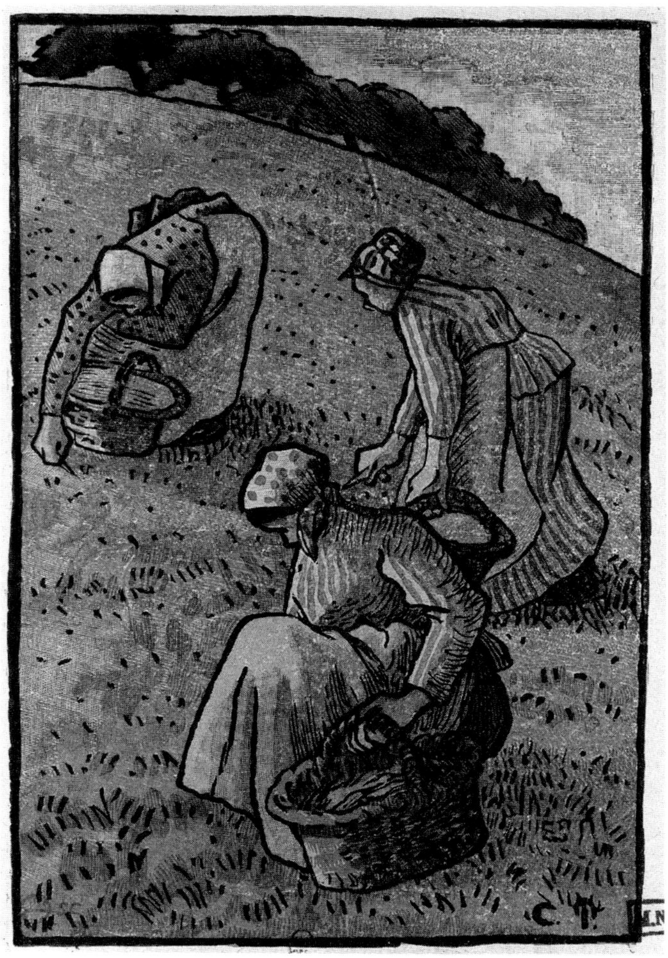

214. Camille Pissarro,
Women Gathering Grass. 1895.
Engraved on wood by Lucien Pissarro, first state, 180 x 120 mm.
Bibliothèque nationale, Paris.

215. Camille Pissarro,
Women Gathering Grass. 1895.
Preparatory drawing for wood engraving.
Ashmolean Museum, Oxford.

The last artist to show prints in the Impressionist exhibitions was not Camille Pissarro but his son Lucien. The father transferred all his thwarted ambitions and frustrated hopes to his son, guiding him firmly towards the illustration of newspapers and children's books, as he guided his second son Georges towards the decorative arts. Lucien began his career as an illustrator in 1885: 'Fifty drawings are planned to start with, etched on zinc then transferred to stone and coloured with lithographic pencils. Although the booklet, devised and drawn entirely by Lucien, was shown by Camille to all his friends, it found no publisher. It was exhibited at the eighth and last Impressionist exhibition; that was his claim to fame.'[397] The period was an auspicious one for illustrators because magazines were multiplying and diversifying in the favourable political and economic climate. Lucien soon did find publishers: Rodolphe Salis at *Le Chat noir* and R.G. Dumas at *La Revue illustrée*. Pissarro *père* showered his son with advice, taking him to visit the wood engraver Auguste Lepère.[398] Lucien has left an account of the meeting: 'I decided at that time to do all the work of engraving myself. With that in mind my father took me to see his friend Lepère who, with his usual generosity, gave me some advice about tools and how to use them. I started work at once and my first experiments were with plates drawn for me by my father.'[399]

The wood engravings exhibited by Lucien at the last Impressionist exhibition are all on themes from his father's repertory: *Head of a Peasant*, *Rabbit*, *Woman in the Grass*, *Woman Reading*, *Pastry Cook*, *Woman selling Chestnuts*, *Peasant Weeding*, *Mending Clothes*, *Parish Priest out Walking*. Some months later (12 January 1887) the discrepancy between the populist spirit of these works and the realism his father had tried to champion became more pronounced. When, for instance, Lucien produced an illustration entitled *The Symbolist*, Camille grew worried: 'By the way, do you think your drawing of the Symbolist is at all topical? New Year's Day is topical, paying the rent, moving house, snow, winter, carnival puppets, war etc.'[400] In April 1886 Gustave Kahn launched the Symbolist journal, *La Vogue*, which ceased publication in December of the same year. On 10 December Camille wrote to his son: 'Apparently Kahn is toying with the idea of transforming the publication. He has suggested that the scientific

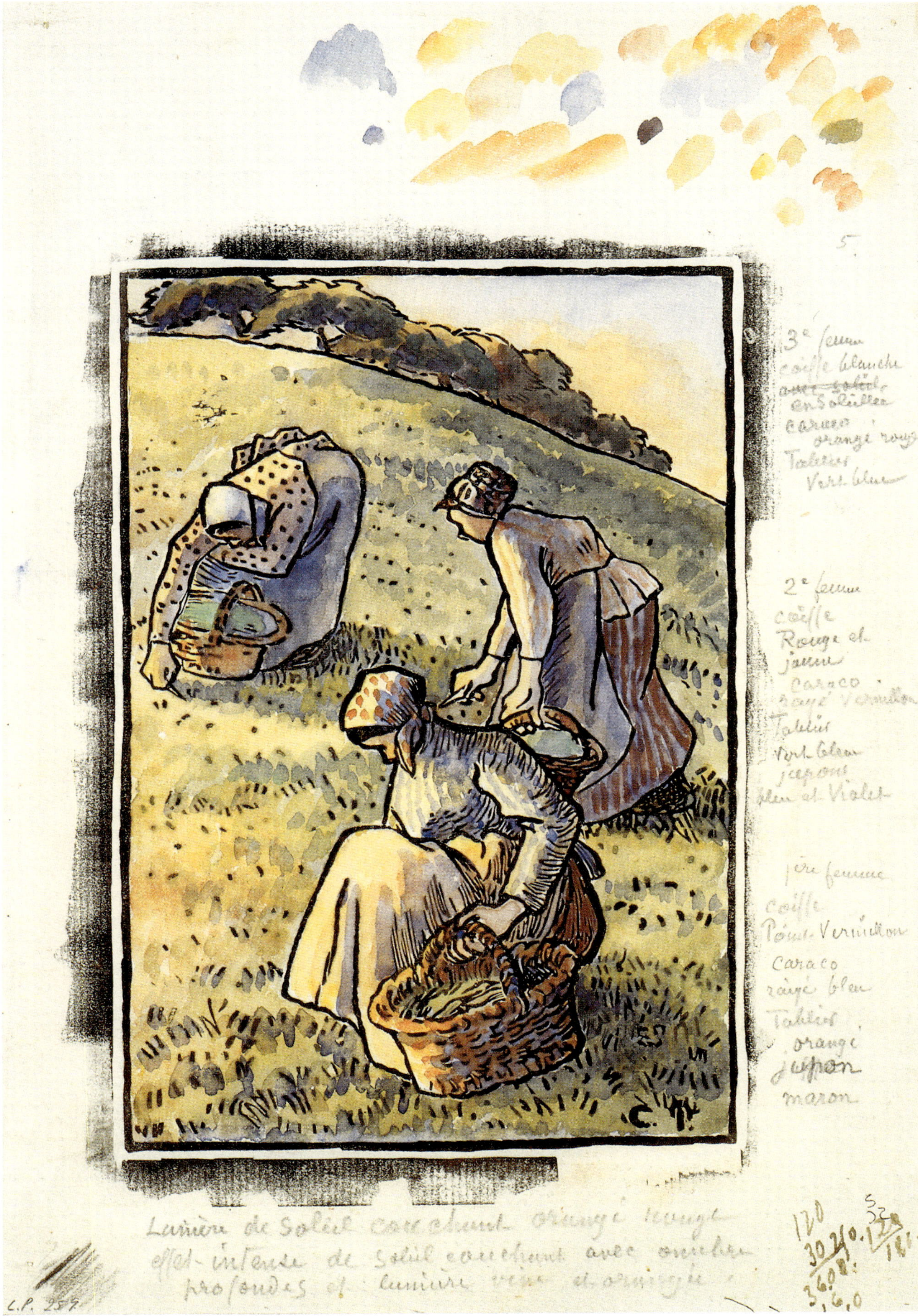
3e femme
coiffe blanche
ensoleillée
caraco
orange rouge
Tablier
Vert bleu
2e femme
coiffe
Rouge et
jaune
Caraco
rayé Vermillon
Tablier
Vert bleu
jupons
bleu et Violet
1ère femme
coiffe
Pois Vermillon
Caraco
rayé bleu
Tablier
orange
jupon
maron
C.P.
Lumière de soleil couchant orangé rouge
effet intense de soleil couchant avec ombres
profondes et lumière vive et orangée
L.P. 257

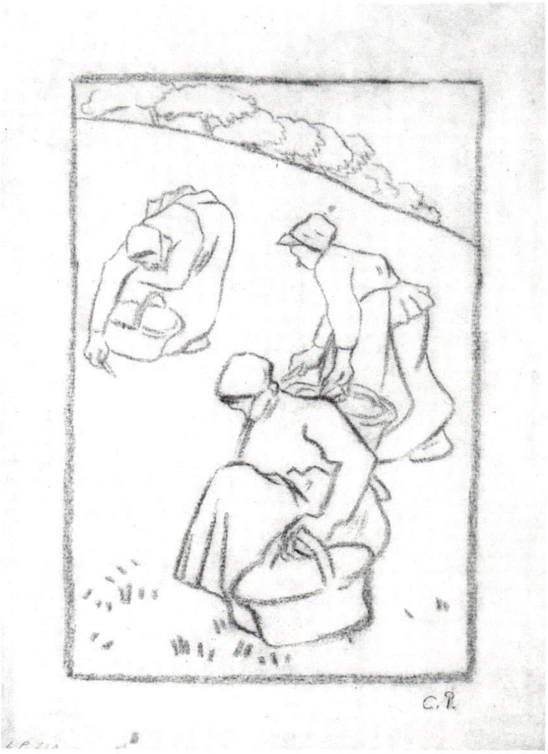

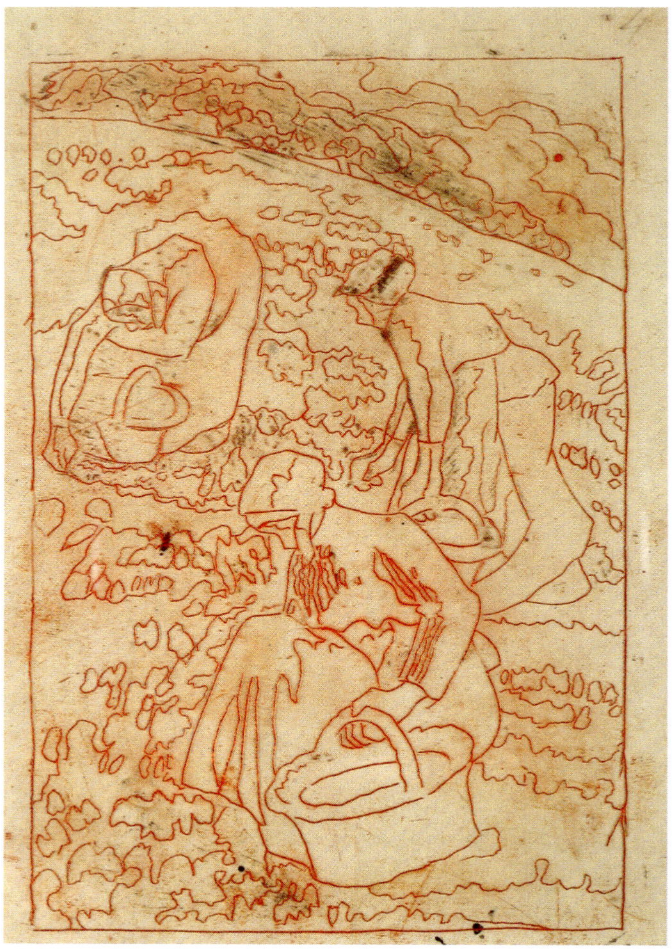

216, 217. Camille Pissarro,
Women Gathering Grass. 1895.
Drawing on celluloid and drawing in Conté crayon, 171 x 114 mm. Ashmolean Museum, Oxford.

Impressionists should do the illustrations. There's only one 'but', which is that for a time he would not be able to pay . . . Nevertheless I think it would be a good show-case for you: *La Vogue* would have a new format and greatly improved paper and printing.'[401]

Raffaëlli rushed to fill this gap in the market, providing the papers with illustrations without concerning himself about methods of reproduction: he contributed to *Le Figaro-Salon*, *Le Monde illustré*, *Les Beaux-Arts illustrés*, *La Vie moderne*, *Le Courrier français* and *Paris illustré*.[402] In a lecture to the Salon des XX in Brussels in 1885, Raffaëlli reinvented the comic strip, making a strong case for 'picture books' at 3F50: 'What is needed now is, in a word, *drawn* not *written* journals, which would be looked at rather than read.'[403] This idea was definitely in the air and, with *Le Chat Noir*, was beginning to be realised. It was the choice of readership that had sown discord amonge the Impressionists, largely thanks to Raffaëlli's anecdotal style, about which Caillebotte and his friends had serious reservations. The print could aim either at wide circulation, or exclusivity, and collectors had not yet come down firmly on one side or the other. Shortly after this, in 1888, Raffaëlli produced ten etchings, each in three states, to illustrate an edition of *Germinie Lacerteux* which Paul Gallimard, the bibliophile, was having published for his personal pleasure (or almost) in three copies. The Goncourts could not get over it: 'That Gallimard is a real revolutionary; he's going to spend 3000 francs, after the example of a farmer general, on producing a de luxe edition of a modern book – and a book of the calibre of *Germinie Lacerteux* -for his sole enjoyment.' On 1 August 1886, *Paris illustré* published twenty-three coloured drawings by Raffaëlli using *gillotage*; Beraldi described them as being 'particularly sought after by bibliophiles.'[404]

In 1889 Raffaëlli published a collection of 179 drawings, reproduced in heliogravure, entitled *Types de Paris*. *Gillotage* and heliogravure were no longer at the bottom of the hierarchy of processes in the reproduction of pictures. The print trade now afforded them a place, half way between original prints, whose virtues were well-known to collectors, and industrialised processes of reproduction. Events that were to have a crucial effect on the printing of images were now taking place. At the burial of Victor Hugo (and on other occasions) the newspapers had made use of photographic negatives directly printed by industrial printing presses, thanks to metal screens which reduced different shades into minuscule black dots. The principle of the screen, although offering little satisfaction from the point of view of accuracy, offered a permanent solution to the problem of the mass production of photographic images.[405]

The establishment of such a large number of art and story magazines was linked to the fragile fortunes of a bourgeoisie that was increasingly split between progressives and conservatives; the effects of this split on the art market began to be perceptible after 1882. The gallery belonging to Georges Petit, the rival of Durand-Ruel, in the rue de Sèze, was amazingly luxurious. It attracted Renoir and Monet. In 1882, De Nittis established the Expositions Internationales there, assembling all that was most respectable in contemporary art while a group of young tearaways founded the Société des Artistes Indépendents; in the same year the Groupe des XX in Brussels was set up under the directorship of Octave Maus. Degas turned his back on public recognition: he refused the one-man show offered him by Durand-Ruel (also offered to Renoir, Monet and Pissarro) in 1883. Pissarro, himself also a confirmed rebel, was reluctant to profit from present circumstances. He did not take up Durand-Ruel's suggestion[406] that he make etched reproductions of his own paintings to illustrate the catalogue of exhibitions sent by the gallery to the United States, a sign, after 1886, of increasing prosperity. Pissarro was still hoping to organise an exhibition of the work of his old friends from Impressionist days, and to include the work of the young Independents introduced by his son Lucien: Seurat, Signac, Dubois-Pillet, Cross, Angrand and Schuffenecker. Degas joined the cause, but without enthusiasm. Eugène Manet staged a fit of anger and the 'pure' Impressionists declined the invitation. The break was finalised.

After the fall of the unpopular Jules Ferry, on 30 March 1885, France was divided into supporters of the left and right who had been radicalised by the failure of the moderate Republic. The anarchist and nationalist factions were favoured respectively by Pissarro and Degas, although without interruption to their friendship. Both found the compromises entered into by the Republican government unacceptable, and particularly their colonial policy. The enrichment of a small percentage of Republicans had not succeeded in halting the economic crisis, which lasted until 1887 and became the focus for working-class discontent. Like a number of other intellectuals, Camille Pissarro, already a keen reader of Proudhon, transferred his allegiance from socialism to anarchy after reading *Les Paroles d'un révolté* published by Prince Pierre Kropotkin in October 1885.[407]

The eighth and final exhibition by the Impressionist group, impressively staged, bore the neutral title of 'Exhibition of Painting', without Monet, Sisley or Renoir but with Degas, Berthe Morisot, Gauguin and Pissarro's new friends: Odilon Redon, Schuffenecker, Seurat and Signac. The group centred on Degas also included Mary Cassatt, Forain, Marie Bracquemond, Rouart, Tillot, Vignon and Zandomeneghi. Only the two Pissarros, Camille and Lucien, showed prints in the exhibition. In the fourth room, not far from them, hung the lithographs of Odilon Redon: *Temptation*, *Beatrice* and *Salomé*.[408] In the same room as Lucien Pissarro's wood engravings, which were typical of the new decorative language, Camille, his father, showed his output of 1883, the drypoints done in the countryside at Osny and Rouen (Figs 186–7), often in several different states; there were thirteen proofs in all, in five frames. In June 1886 Pissarro wrote: 'The exhibition is going very slowly, with negligible admissions. In December he concluded that 'The Impressionists have had it!'[409] Indeed, the Impressionists belonged to the previous generation.

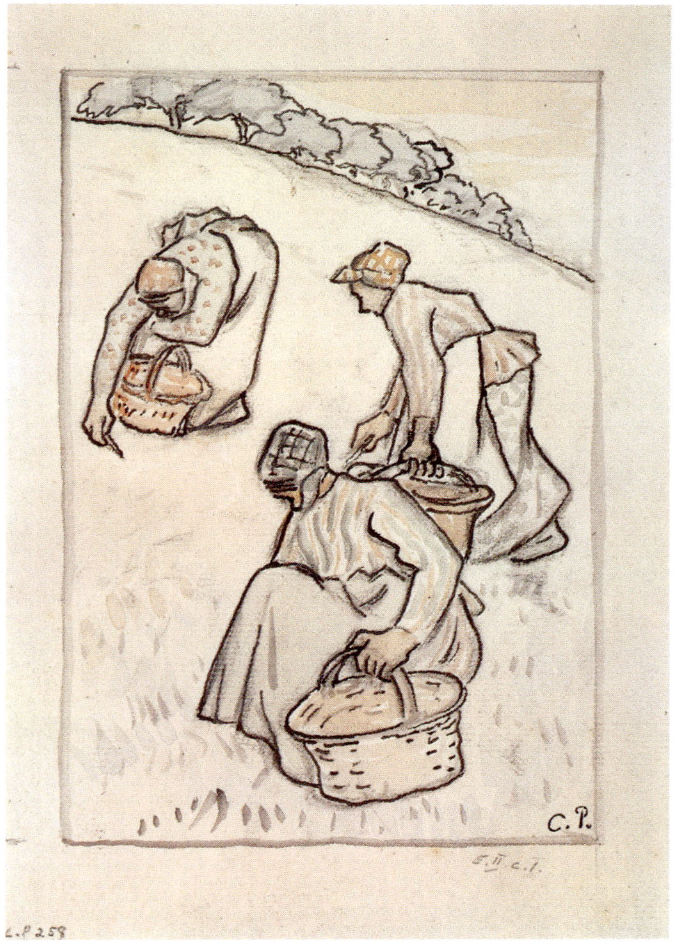

218. Camille Pissarro,
Women Gathering Grass. 1895.
Study, 171 x 114.
Ashmolean Museum, Oxford.

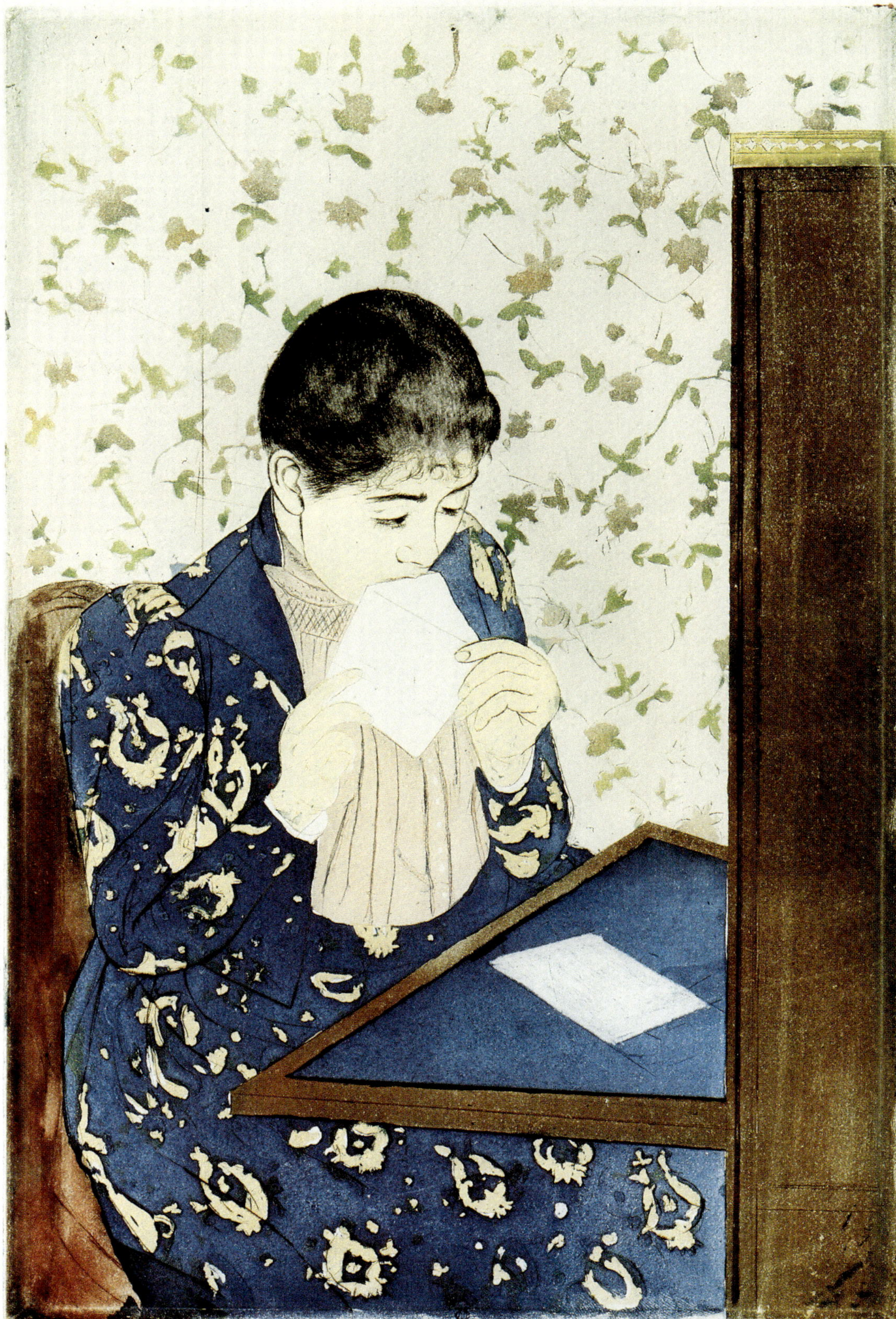

PART THREE

The Next Day *1870-90*

219. Mary Cassatt,
The Letter. 189-1.
Drypoint and aquatint, 346 x 228 mm.
Bibliothèque nationale, Paris.

41. *After Impressionism*

With the appearance of the first photograph ever to be published in a newspaper in 1886, the year of the eighth and last Impressionist exhibition, the image found its industry and the print found conditions favourable to its emancipation (or autonomy) in the art world. The uses to which reproductions might be put were now quite clearly defined and the public seemed satisfied. Durand-Ruel, who had previously only been interested in prints as illustrations to his catalogues, began at last to pay attention to other kinds of print; whereas in 1885 he had asked Pissarro if he would make etchings of his own paintings for an American catalogue[410] (Pissarro refused), in 1889 he commissioned a collection of original prints from him. Pissarro wrote 'I have chosen the artist's proofs and other rare ones, which explains the slightly higher prices of some of the pieces.'[411] Once the print had been accorded the status it deserved, even the most inexpensive methods of reproduction (like the lithograph) acquired a position of dignity in the new hierarchy. William Thornley, the lithographer, asked if he could reproduce Degas's drawings as lithographs, and Degas accepted. The result was a most elegant album published by Goupil, Manzi and Joyant, of which Pissarro wrote: 'I've seen some reproductions of drawings by Degas at the publishers, they are marvellous!'[412] The arguments of the 1890s now shifted to lithography, which offered unlimited print runs and mass reproduction: to what extent should a lithograph qualify as a work of art?

The economic crisis, although not completely over, had settled down. The early effects of colonisation and American expansion were beginning to be felt, particularly in the art market. The first profitable deals were done with the United States just when Durand-Ruel was beginning to make his name there at last. Pissarro's correspondence goes into precise detail on this matter: 'I received a visit from Portier, come to inform me that the etchings I had given him in payment for the hundred francs I owed him had been bought as part of a museum of engravings being set up in New York,'[413] Evidently, therefore, on 26 April 1888 Pissarro knew of the first sale of his prints to the American Samuel Avery, who for years had been in regular contact with Courtier, the broker, and who had already built up a large collection of contemporary French prints.[414] Pissarro claimed never to have sold an etching in his life before and had a problem establishing the right price. He suggested 10 francs for each proof, in a limited edition. He printed a large selection of prints for Avery, each carefully signed and numbered and with hand-written notes; they can still be seen in the New York Public Library. The following year, in 1889, it was the dealer Frederick Keppel, champion of Millet and the French School and a friend of Avery who, on a visit to Paris, became interested in Pissarro's prints; two prints in his new style, *The Goosegirl* and the small *Market* were published in *La Revue independante*. In July of the same year the French collector, Beraldi, who was making an inventory of the work of contemporary French printmakers,[415] asked Pissarro for a complete list of his etchings:[416] sales and cataloguing went hand-in-hand. This gave the artist the opportunity to organise his prints and to number the different states as a collector of original prints might do, regarding each proof as a new work. On 31 July Pissarro sent his catalogue to another American friend of Samuel Avery, Theodore Childs.[417] Childs was the agent for several American dealers and collectors in Paris and the middleman for George Lucas, whose collection can be seen in Baltimore.[418] Pissarro did a deal first with Keppel, for eleven prints, then with Kennedy, and was able to write in 1891: 'Three American dealers now have my work, the three most important, Avery, Keppel and Kennedy'.[419] French dealers were not buying at all.

In retrospect, the final Impressionist exhibition in 1886 seems to have represented the work done by Pissarro and Degas between 1880 and 1883 in quite a coherent fashion. Their careers had apparently come to a standstill before the prevailing favourable conditions set them in motion again. At this period both artists underwent a pronounced change of style, abandoning themselves to decoration and colour (previously rarely seen in prints); even the picturesque began to make an appearance, notably in Pissarro's views of Rouen, along with new themes that were farther and farther removed from realism: different landscapes and an abundance of female nudes in the work of Degas and Pissarro as well as Renoir. The victorious Republic was beginning to build up its own mythology of flags and ceremonial, and its pantheon of dead heroes: Daumier, who died in 1879, and Manet, who died in 1883, were part of it, with Victor Hugo, who died in 1885. Burty and Bracquemond were regarded as official artists to the Republic. Beraldi's monumental work on the nineteenth-century printmakers gives a blow-by-blow account of their differences and their arguments, their triumphs and failures.

Bracquemond worked closely with Beraldi on this project, drawing up a catalogue of his own work for the second volume; he is the artist who bridged the gap between the traditional craft of printmaking and the spirit of the new age. After a last series of birds (*Seagulls*, *Teal*, *Swallows*, *Ducks* etc) and two misty views (*Morning Mist* and *Storm Clouds*) in 1882, after 1884 Bracquemond devoted his attention entirely to book illustration; the national edition of the collected works of Victor Hugo, for example (1885–8), or the Fables of La Fontaine (1887). He returned to individual prints in the 1890s, becoming involved in the activities of the new societies of etchers and being swept up into the fashion for albums. In 1885 he published a manual for the rising generation of artists.[420] His last prints, *The House in the Woods* and *The Question Mark*, date from 1909 and demonstrate no perceptible development in respect of his earlier manner. The 'rebels', on the other hand, fortunately rejected such early canonisation and as a result their success brought them a second wind in the 1890s.

A new avant-garde had grown up by now, reflecting the economic, social and political diversity of the country. To them Pissarro and Degas, approaching their sixties, were patriarchal figures. The banner born by the new critics, Octave Mirbeau and Félix Fénéon, was Impressionism. Fénéon's analysis of an exhibition of prints by Pissarro at *La Revue indépendante* in 1888 is a choice piece which demonstrates how clearly and confidently his art was now understood: 'M. Camille Pissarro prefers zinc plates to copper, because zinc does not have the dull uniformity of copper. The zinc produces a kind of sanded effect and even though only a very small number of good prints can be had from each plate, they are at least richer and smoother than the other kind. The different effects can easily be distinguished if, for example, *Rue de l'épicerie (Rouen)*, on copper, is compared with *Rue Malpalue (Rouen)*, on zinc. M. Pissarro's technique is complex and has a number of idiosyncratic features: at the outset he does not cover his plate with the usual hard etching ground in a ball but uses the soft ground that etchers usually only use to cover completed parts of their plates when retouching. Having outlined his drawing in the soft ground, he abandons his etching tool and continues to mark the metal with glass paper pads (*L'Ile Lacroix*) or, less frequently, with a very aggressive wire brush (the edges of the meadow in *Landscape in the Rain*). Having begun the plate as an etching, he then textures parts of it with resin powder to obtain areas in his 'manière noire' (his *Cows*); or he will use rosin or resin dissolved in ether or alcohol to obtain areas in aquatint. His *Landscape with Church at Osny* is an example of an aquatint finished with drypoint. *The Stone Bridge (Rouen)* was begun as a soft ground etching and finished with emery paper. *Landscape in the Rain* is in mezzotint and aquatint. The dots all over the *Landscape at Pontoise* (there are Japanese prints spotted in the same manner) are applied with an etching needle.'[421]

At the age of twenty-three, Jules Laforgue, secretary to the collector Charles Ephrussi, wrote the first scientific analysis of Impressionism as a phenomenon. He began writing in February 1883 but his text was not published during his lifetime. He attacks the Impressionists' drawing, their perspective and the lighting of their studios – 'the eye should perceive no more than a vibration' – comparing them unfavourably with the tactile values on which classical art was based. He dwells on the 'shifting quality of the landscape and the mobility of the painter's Impressions', compares painting with music and gives the painter a quarter of an hour to produce his painting. In conclusion he demands the abolition of juries, the closure of art schools and the Institute. He claims that 'artists live in anarchy'.[422] The liberty he sought was the liberty of a free market in which the quality of the 'artist' and the 'work of art' should be clearly defined.

42. 1889: The Society of Painter-Printmakers

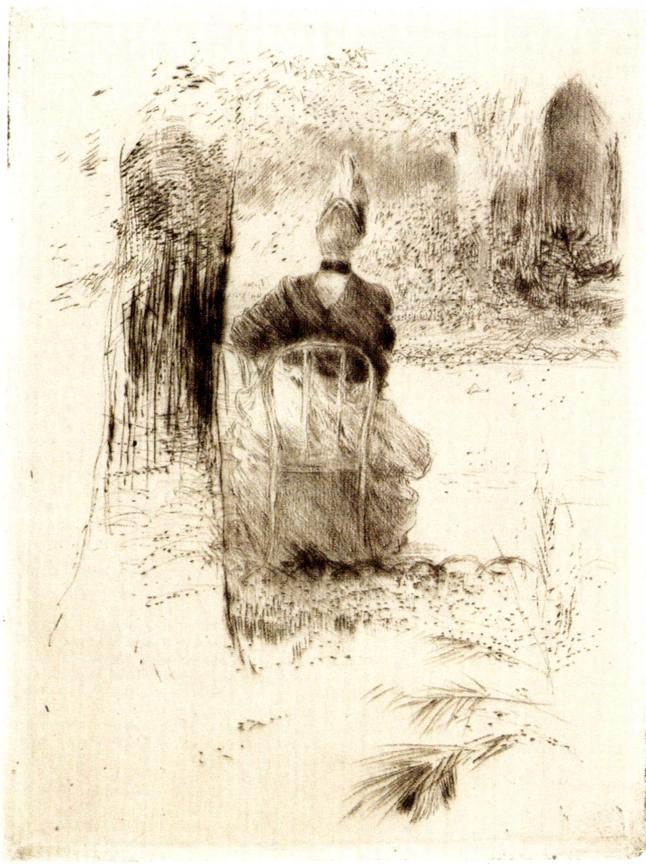

220. Henri Somm,
Woman Seated in a Square, seen from behind. Undated.
Drypoint, 215 x 140 mm.
Private collection, Paris.

The establishment of the Society of Painter-Printmakers during the winter of 1888–9 signalled the triumph of the 'original' print. The statutes of the Society were drawn up by a small group led by Bracquemond and Guérard, who became respectively president and vice-president. The emphasis was on the profession of printmaking and its emancipation, and the two generations engaged in printmaking were to be brought together in one society. The plan was to hang paintings, drawings, pastels and watercolours and prints together in a mixed show, as had happened at the first Impressionist exhibition fifteen years earlier, but this time in inverse proportion. The participants were all printmakers or lithographers, but each brought a painting or drawing along with his or her prints. Mary Cassatt showed a pastel with her aquatints; Tissot showed a watercolour and Pissarro a painting with his etchings; Redon showed paintings, drawings and lithographs. Bracquemond alone showed only etchings and Degas only lithographs. The strategy was obvious: by exhibiting prints with original works the originality of the print was validated and mass reproduction ruled out. Article 5 of the statutes is explicit on the subject: 'Prints will be admitted but no reproductions.'[423] To ensure that prints were in the majority, 'paintings and drawings will be admitted only in the proportion of one quarter'. If Roger Marx's preface to the catalogue of the third exhibition in 1891 is to be believed, the aim was achieved; he states categorically 'Quite frankly, what is an original print if not "a drawing with several versions"? Like a painting or sculpture the print must be appreciated as a direct product of the artist, complete and whole in itself.'[424]

The first exhibition, held at the Durand-Ruel Gallery in January put an end to 'the era of Salons and dissidents',[425] as Philippe Burty put it in the preface to the second exhibition in 1890. This preface, the last ever written by Burty, is remarkable for having ceased to be militant and become official in tone. Virtues are extolled in it that had been forgotten by the art world for the last fifty years: the good will of the critical fraternity, the tolerance of the public, the brotherhood of artists. The word 'tranquillity' crops up several times in the text. 'The press has been generous with its publicity', writes Burty.[426] There are no criticisms of the broad spectrum of the artists on show. The rules stated that 'the Society has no jury and no prizes'. Any painter with an original

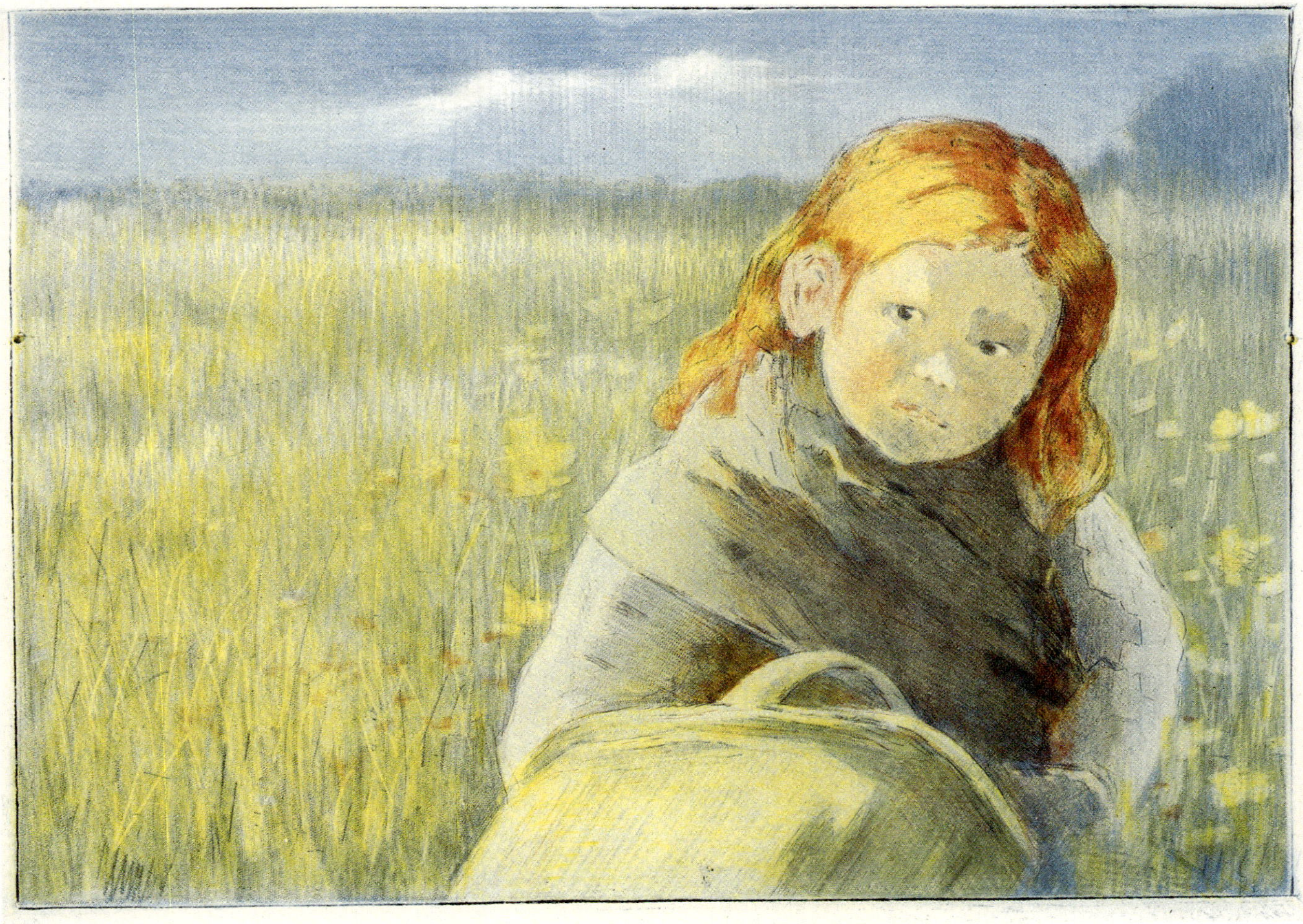

221. Henri Guerard, *In the Wheatfield*. About 1885 (?). Etching, 118 x 158 mm. Private collection, Paris.

print or two in his portfolio was up there on the walls with the rest of them, now that the skill of printmaking had come back into fashion. The old guard – Bracquemond (Fig. 222), Pissarro and Degas, Desboutin, Fantin-Latour, Legros and even real veterans of etching like Appian and Chaplin – figured beside the post-1870 generation – Guérard (Fig. 221), Goeneutte, Buhot, Somm (Fig. 220), etc. – as well as new names like Chéret, Lucien Pissarro, Redon or Rodin (Figs 223–4). The scope was very broad and this exhibition could with justification be regarded as an anthology of contemporary printmaking, particularly because it contained more works from the past than it did innovatory pieces. Such unanimity and 'tranquillity' were possible now only because the market had become conclusively free; collectors were reassured, their differences being recognised and accepted. Burty refers to this in the same preface when he writes that the exhibition of painter-printmakers would 'catch the attention of anyone with pictures to hang, corridors to fill or collections to complete in their houses.'[427] The Durand-Ruel Gallery had been renovated and now offered suitably domestic surroundings to the works. The State put in a bid for forty prints in 1890 and twenty-eight in 1892. Dealers sold and the Government bought,[428] like any other collector: the new order was established.

This comfortable state of affairs was not ultimately helpful to the development of the movement. After 1890

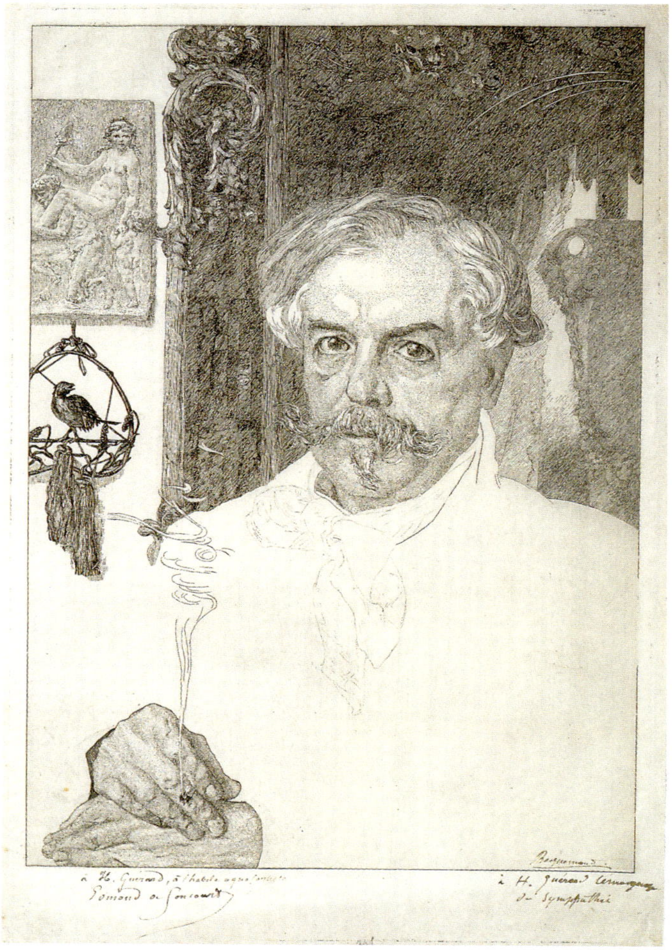

222. Félix Bracquemond,
Portrait of Edmond de Goncourt. 1881.
Etching, first state, 460 x 320 mm.
Private collection, Paris.

223. Auguste Rodin,
Portrait of Victor Hugo, full face. 1885.
Drypoint, 225 x 175 mm.
Bibliothèque nationale, Paris.

224. Auguste Rodin,
Portrait of Victor Hugo, three quarter face. 1885.
Drypoint, 229 x 178 mm.
Bibliothèque nationale, Paris.

the list of artists was augmented only by little-known academic artists who were attracted to this new kind of Salon. In February 1891, the year that Forain was elected to the committee, the general assembly voted a new article on to the statute book which stated that foreigners would no longer be full members of the Society but would have to be invited to exhibit in a separate section and would be obliged to present a copy of every work they exhibited to the Society's portfolio. The series of rough drafts of the new statute[429] give some idea of the ramifications of the proposal, which was designed to allow the Society to be re-named the 'Société des peintres-graveurs *français*' or the 'Société *française* des peintres-graveurs'. Pissarro and Mary Cassatt were appalled by this ostracism and withdrew. Pissarro scornfully dubbed members of the society 'the patriots', and wrote to his son 'they are hungry for official recognition'.[430] In 1892 the printmakers, mainly traditional, closed the Society's ranks. There was talk of an album but nothing came of it. Two years later Bracquemond remarked that it would be impossible to sell, admitting to Guérard that 'there are prints in there that wouldn't fetch 15 sous!'[431] In fact the solidarity behind the collective exhibitions concealed an absence of cohesion. Evidence of this can be discerned in the minutes of the general assembly, held once a year before the exhibition, to prepare and settle the accounts of the previous one.[432] Most of the exhibitors won a degree of success, and there was no exhibition in either 1894 or 1895. When Bracquemond and Gérard started the process up again in 1896 for a sixth exhibition, at the Galerie de La Bodinière, only thirteen artists took part and the only new recruit was Toulouse-Lautrec, who had ben invited to the previous exhibition in 1893; four others were invited but only one of them, Hermann-Paul, showed any drawings with his prints.

Vollard spotted the opportunity offered by this vacuum and the following year organised an exhibition of 'painter-printmakers'.[433] He retained the name but put forward quite a different list of artists and products: his list included Impressionists, Cézanne, Gauguin, Guillaumin and Pissarro, whose offerings were totally transformed by colour lithography, and members of the young avant-garde: Bonnard, Maurice Denis, Lautrec, Munch, Redon. Included also were some shining lights of Art Nouveau: Carrière, de Feure and de Groux. This collection of artists fulfilled the requirements that the 'French painter-printmakers' had forgotten too quickly. The Society became dormant until 1906, when it re-emerged as an association of printmakers and it has continued as such to this day.

43. *Rodin*

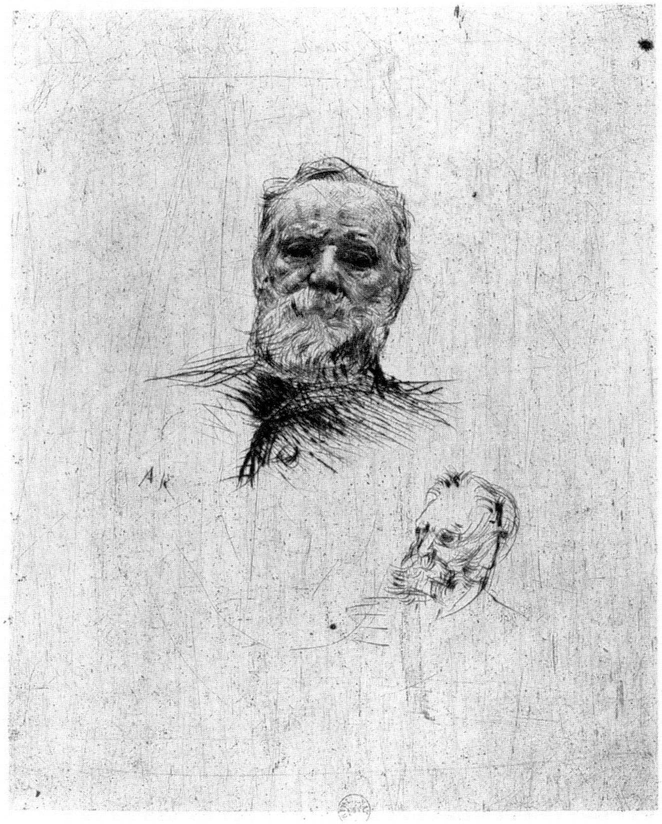

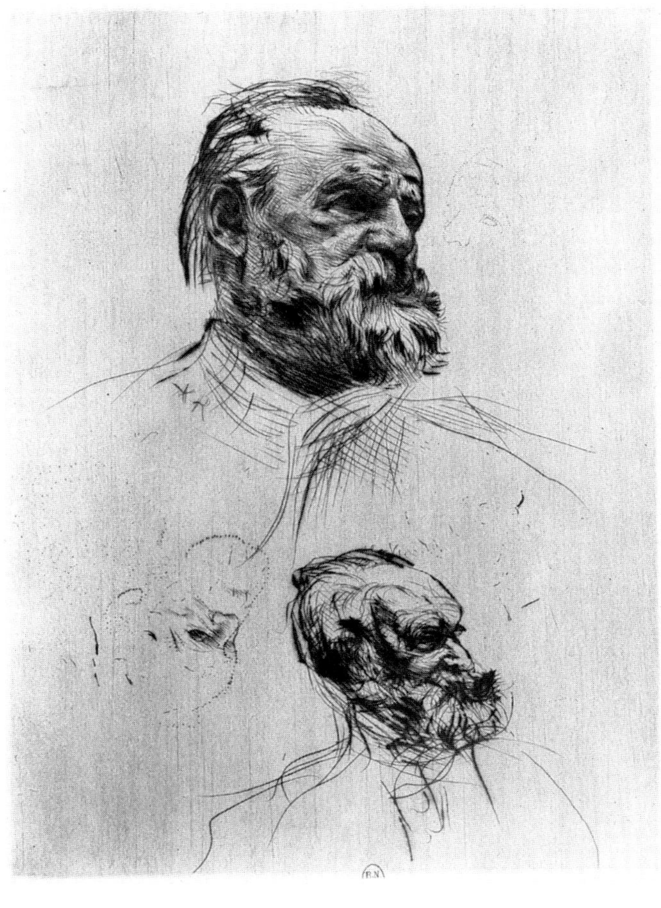

Before 1889, Rodin's prints were unknown to the general public. His two portraits of Victor Hugo (Figs 223–4) were exhibited at the Society of Painter-Printmakers and then published, one in March 1889 in the *Gazette des Beaux-Arts*[434] and the other in September in *Les Lettres et les Arts*, to illustrate an article by Gustave Geffroy.[435] In fact, the second had been published in *L'Artiste* in 1885,[436] by which date the printmaking career of Auguste Rodin, which produced only a dozen drypoint etchings, was nearly at a close. In circumstances such as these the activities of the Society of Painter-Printmakers helped to unearth prints which might have been neglected or regarded as unimportant, perhaps having been executed in that spirit, but also happening to be the work of a leading artist. The painter-printmakers showed, by including Rodin, that they were willing to extend membership to sculptor-printmakers, a daring new idea although Carpeaux had occasionally been represented among the contributors. The quality of the piece on show did not now depend on the techniques used in its execution, but on the status of the artist who signed it. For a print to be original it had to be signed by an artist, or someone regarded as such, or a painter or sculptor.

There is more plastic invention in the style of a sculptor than there is the style of a painter. Rodin's choice of an etching needle to cut directly into the metal is characteristic of a sculptor, as is the spirited, impulsive line that captures the movement on the white paper, in space. As in his sculpture, Rodin does not enclose his forms; he gives the lines their momentum and allows them to find their own end. His cut is peremptory, quite deep at the outset, creating roughnesses, even smudging; Rodin uses ink as a third dimension. The same power can be seen in some of the monotypes of Degas, where, like a sculptor he models the ink with his thumb and the palm of his hand. Degas was as much of a sculptor as Rodin.

The chronology of Rodin's twelve drypoints is difficult to establish. Rodin was an acquaintance of Legros, with whom he worked in London in 1881, and it could be assumed that he learned the rudiments of printmaking from him. At this period he was working for the potteries in Sèvres, and also knew Bracquemond, dedicating to him one of the proofs of his *Victor Hugo, full face* (Fig. 223). He was not short of instructors. But

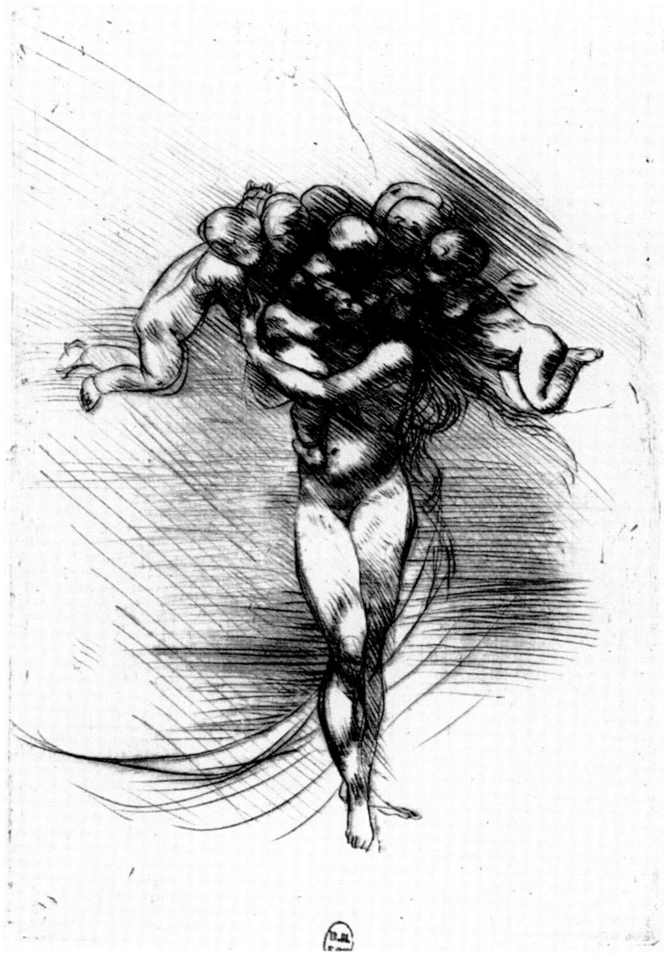

225. Auguste Rodin,
Spring. Undated.
Drypoint, 148 x 100 mm.
Bibliothèque nationale, Paris.

when he drew up a short list of his prints for the collector Gustave Bourcard in 1903,[437] he dated his first attempts at 1884, spacing his production up to 1888. This late list, in his own handwriting, should perhaps be treated with caution, because it in fact seems more logical to identify two quite separate groups of drypoints by Rodin. There is a series of sketches, in no particular order, which may date from 1881; he re-used the backs of some of the copper plates for his later works: a *Centaur*, an *Amphora* and some *Figures*, left off his list, to which could be added a more successful work, *Cupids leading the World*, sketched as if with a pair of compasses on the back of one of Legros's plates and assumed therefore to date from the same year, 1881. The other, more complete, works appear to date from 1884–5: *La Ronde*, *Spring* (Fig. 225), *Bellona*, *Victor Hugo, three-quarter face* (Fig. 224), *Victor Hugo, full face* (Fig. 223), *Antonin Proust* and *Henri Becque*, the last five being printed versions of sculptures. Finally, there are two late sketches dated 1893 and 1916. None of these was published before the death of Victor Hugo, when the opportunity was taken to extricate them from Rodin's studio (where they would have remained in perpetuity) to illustrate the event in a remarkable and original fashion.

Rodin clearly had no ambitions for his etchings. He exhibited a few at the request of the Society of Painter-Printmakers and the others did not see the light of day until they were exhibited at the Salon of the Société Nationale des Beaux-Arts in 1901.[438] No artist was as willing as he, however, to have his work reproduced. His prints were frequently reproduced during his lifetime, by a variety of processes, as the frontispiece to books or to illustrate articles about him and his work. He produced one lithograph only, as black as some of his first drawings, somewhere between the black produced by Redon and Carrière's black. In 1884 he supplied two pen and ink drawings to illustrate *Enguerrade* by Emile Bergerat and, much later, in 1902, about thirty wash drawings were carefully reproduced by lithography by the printer Clot to illustrate Octave Mirbeau's *Le Jardin des Supplices*, published by Vollard. His interest in the reproduction of drawings manifested itself also in a curious experiment, dated by Victoria Thorson to 1887 and explained by her as follows: 'Possibly in response to the excitement of multiplying his images through printmaking, Rodin took the image of *Le Printemps* and experimented with a common reproductive method, the ancestor of today's mimeograph and of the French "Reniotype" machine, commonly used for printing menus.'[439]

His most ambitious and most modern work (modern because of its relationship with current books by artists) was his series of hand drawn illustrations in the copy of the collector Paul Gallimard's *Fleurs du Mal* (Fig. 227). This work, original in the strictest sense of the word, was commissioned by Gallimard in 1887 and completed

226. Auguste Rodin,
Eternal Idol. 1896–1905.
Lithograph, 284 x 206 mm.
Musée Rodin, Paris.

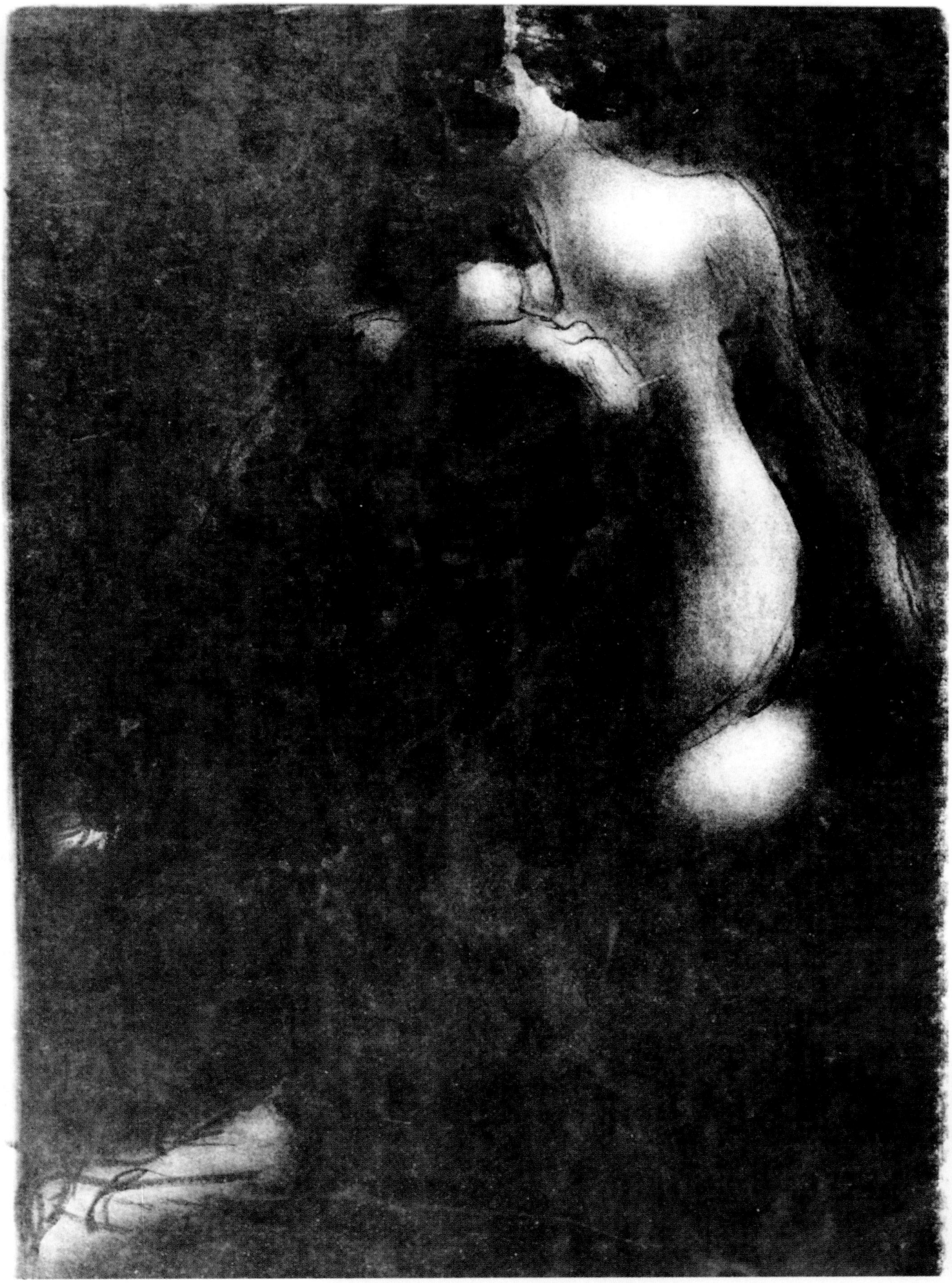

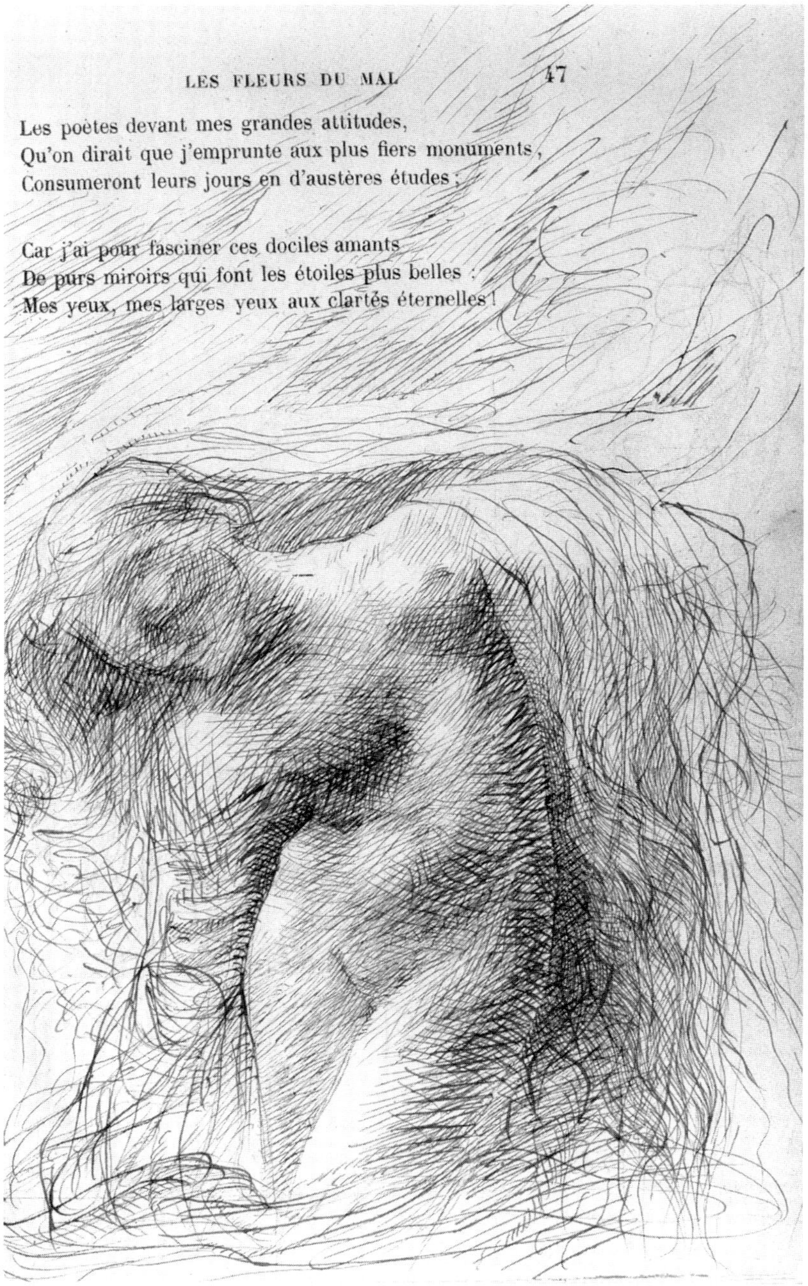

227. Auguste Rodin,
pen drawing on a copy of *Les Fleurs du Mal*, p. 47, *Beauty*. 1887.
Musée Rodin, Paris.

in 1888. His pen and wash drawings are scattered through the margins, over the headings and even over the text of Poulet-Malassis's first edition (1857) of Baudelaire's book. No painter-printmaker had ever allowed himself such licence as this.

From techniques of mechanical reproduction to the illumination of a single copy of a book, via the lithographic reproduction of watercolours and original drypoint etchings, sometimes copied from sculptures, Rodin came into contact with printmaking in all its aspects. Though he did not linger for very long over any of them, he provides excellent evidence of the way printmaking styles and techniques developed in the 1880s and 1890s, extending even as far as a sculptor's studio.

44. *Sisley*

One of the tenets of the painter-printmakers was that a good painter made a good printmaker, but not the reverse. The favourite strategy of dealers, from Cadart to Vollard, to encourage the assimilation of prints with paintings, was to urge painters to make prints. There were several key Impressionists who were still 'available': Caillebotte, Monet, Sisley, Renoir, Berthe Morisot. Caillebotte died a little too early, perhaps, and Monet, who very nearly yielded to Mallarmé's entreaties, remained uncompromising to the end. The other three allowed the movement to sweep them along and, rather late in life, tried their hand at printmaking.

Sisley's printed work consists of a modest four small etchings and was the fruit of his later period, rather as Cézanne's etchings appeared early in his career – they were circumstantial and without consequence. Apart from *The Banks of the Loing, the Cart*, (Fig. 231), of which a few further prints, now very rare, were made, Sisley's four etchings were never published. They were shrouded in mystery until the zinc plates were found in Gérard's studio and presented to the Bibliothèque Nationale in 1972. These etchings are included in the catalogue of the second exhibition of the Société des Peintres-Graveurs.[440] The fact that the plates remained in Guérard's studio (Guérard organised the exhibition and probably printed the etchings) suggests that they were executed expressly for this exhibition, at Guérard's request. Guérard may have paid a visit to Sisley who, like Monet, had withdrawn from life in Paris and was living at St-Mammès on the banks of the Loing, where he was able to find plenty of subject matter (and light) to paint. It seems that Renoir was recruited by a similar visit; perhaps the organisers were rallying those Impressionists who had not yet tried etching, in order to link the revival of printmaking quite firmly with Impressionism. A letter written by Buhot exists in which he 'recruits' the ageing Eugène Boudin (then sixty-seven) in the following terms: 'The painter-printmakers . . . have, on my recommendation, elected you a member of the aforenamed society. Have you ever made sketches on copper plates? . . . If you had anything to hand I could get it etched for you by the end of the week.'[441] In the autumn of 1888 Sisley was engaged in painting the banks of the Loing, whose charms he had depicted repeatedly in a large number of canvases in 1883, 1884 and 1885;[442] some of these were now echoed in his four etchings. He refused to exhibit his work with the last Impressionists, those close to Degas, in 1886, but in the same year, thanks to Durand-Ruel, enjoyed his first success in New York. His first one-man show was in New York, in the gallery opened by Durand-Ruel in 1887, in 1889.

The qualities shared by Impressionist painting and the Impressionist print are very pronounced in these etchings; if they had been executed in the 1860s they would have been called 'impulsive' by the critics. They appear spontaneous and may have been drawn in the open, although drawing from the motif in reverse, on dark etching ground, is very unusual. Sisley's economy with the drawn line means that light, or rather the white of the paper, plays a major role; for the artist this meant leaving the etching ground black and working as it were in white on black. In *The Cart* (Fig. 231) the lines made with the etching tool are reminiscent of Guillaumin's roughish cuts; in *Banks of the Loing, Six Moored Punts* (Fig. 229) the fluid lines resemble the lines that Manet learned from Tiepolo. The figure in *Banks of the Loing, the Riverbank* (Fig. 228) is merely a silhouette and hardly distracts the eye from the focal point – a boat seen from the stern and a tree between the sky and the water. The very ordinary zinc plates, which the printer's hand never quite manages to wipe clean, retain a thin veil of ink and cast a light mist over everything. There are scratches and stains all over the plates and the artist does not seem to mind; they give the prints the slapdash style so sought after by the Impressionists but so irritating to their critics (Fig. 230). The printing in fact adds a further layer of *Impression*, and here improvisation is difficult to distinguish from intention. Was zinc used in order to provide the misty effect or was it for lack of anything better? Given the poor quality of the plates, the latter seems likely. Was the use of subjects very similar to the subjects of Sisley's paintings just for speed and convenience, in response to an urgent request, or was it a deliberate policy? Was the restraint of the etched lines, short and allusive, the result of timidity or audacity? The hold that Impressionism still exerts on us today is embodied in these ambiguities. We can appreciate them better, perhaps, in the work of the printmakers on the eve of Impressionism like Guillaumin or Cézanne because they seem almost accidental, than in the work of those immediately following Impressionism, like Sisley or Berthe Morisot.

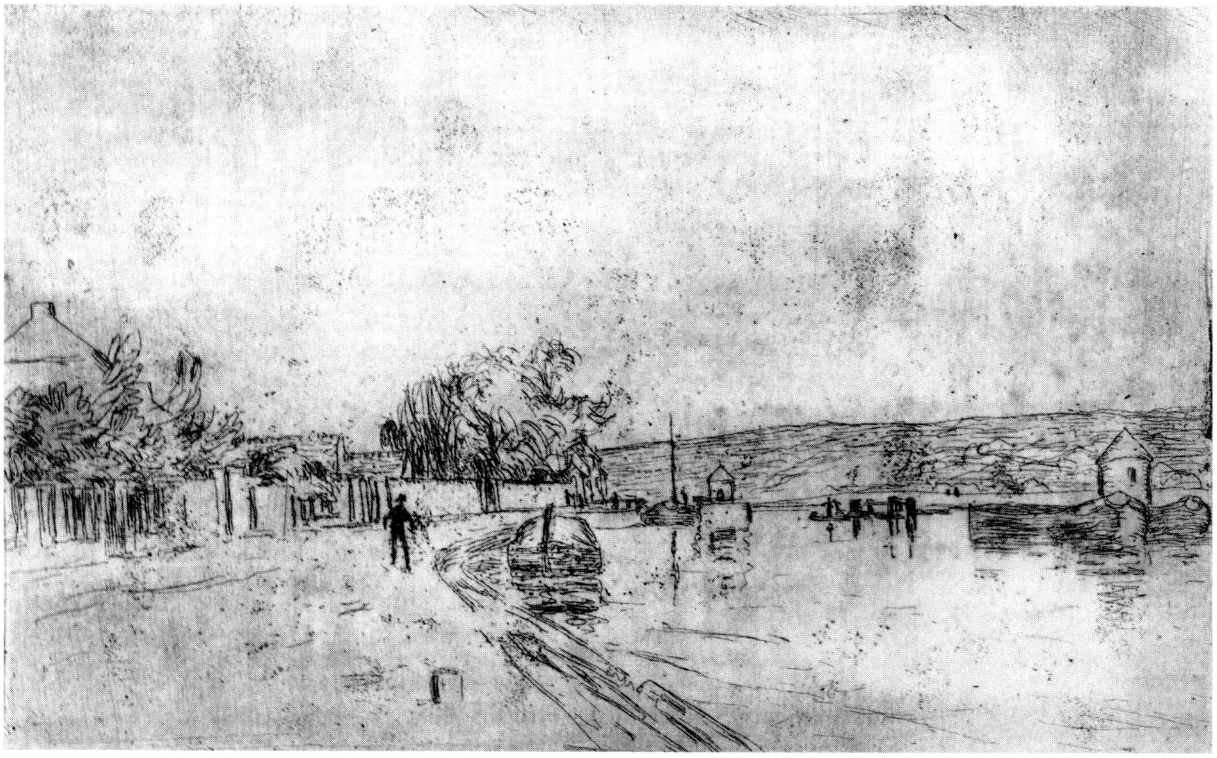

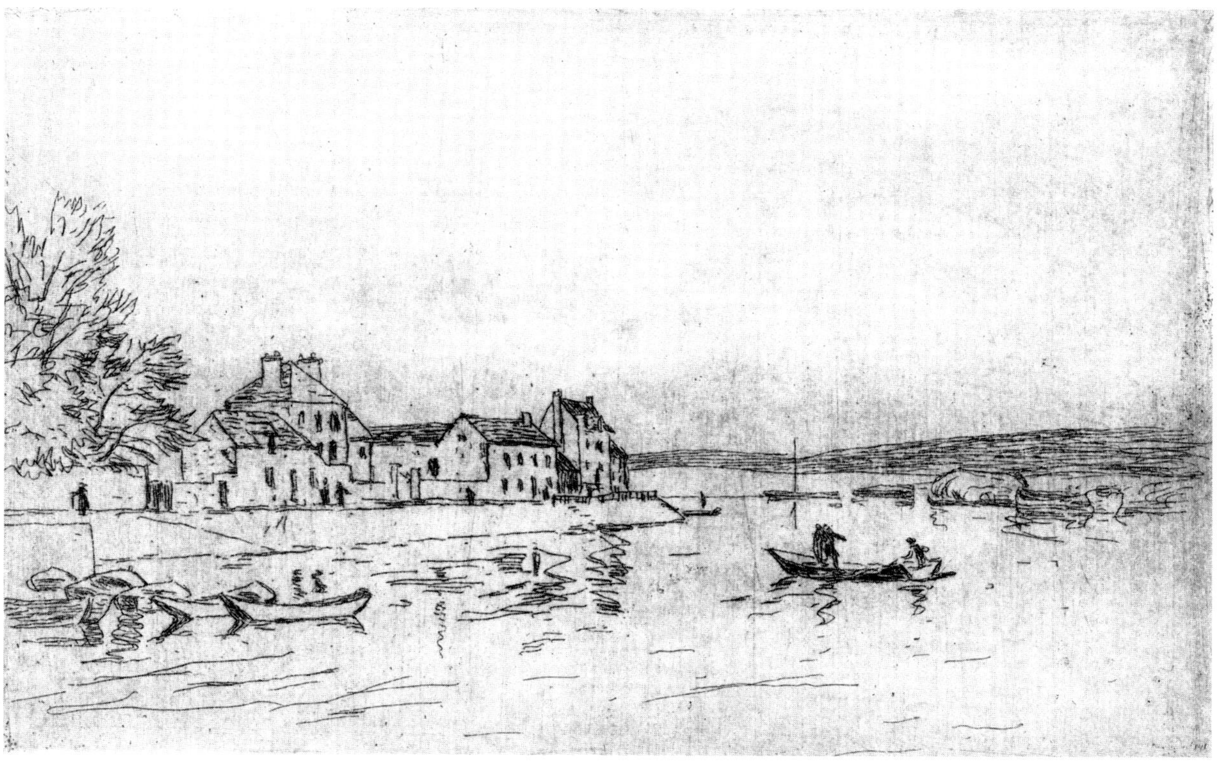

228. Alfred Sisley, *The Banks of the Loing*. 1890. Etching, 147 x 226 mm.
Bibliothèque nationale, Paris.

229. Alfred Sisley, *The Banks of the Loing, Six Moored Punts*. 1890. Etching, 147 x 224 mm.
Bibliothèque nationale, Paris.

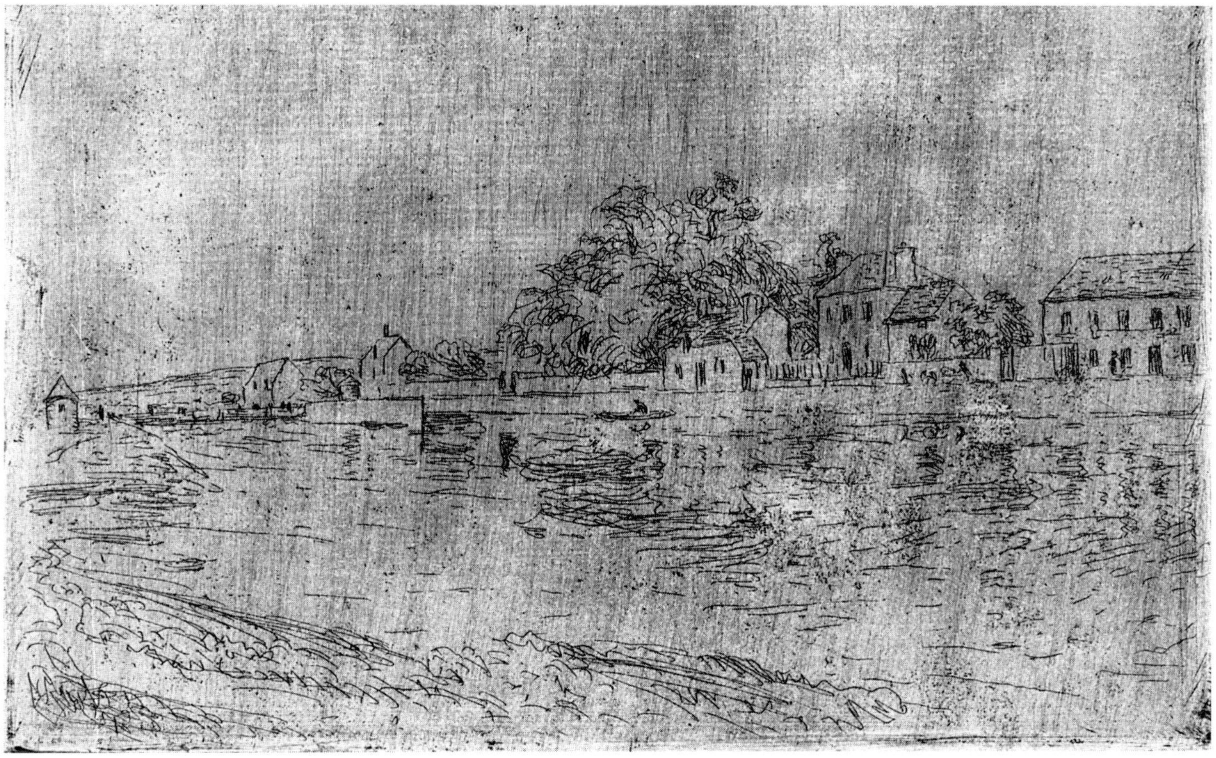

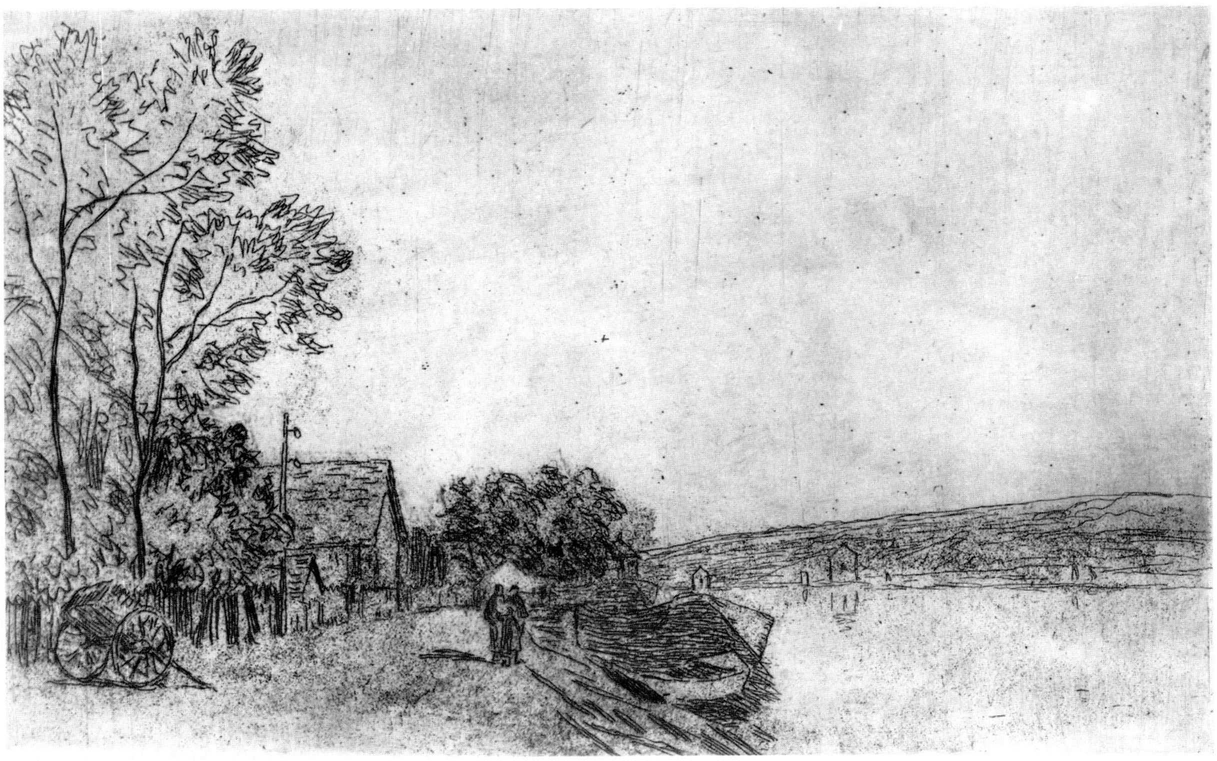

230. Alfred Sisley, *The Banks of the Loing, Houses at the Water's Edge*. 1890. Etching, 147 x 220 mm. Bibliothèque nationale, Paris.

231. Alfred Sisley, *Banks of the Loing, the Cart*. 1890. Etching, second and final state, 145 x 225 mm. Bibliothèque nationale, Paris.

45. *Berthe Morisot*

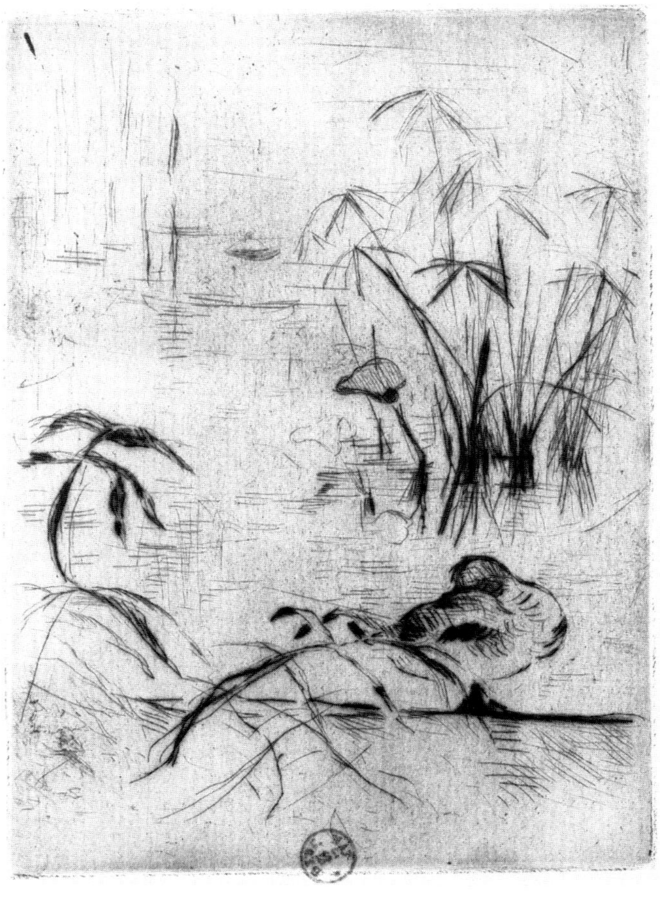

232. Berthe Morisot,
The Duck. 1888.
Drypoint, 137 x 100 mm.
Bibliothèque nationale, Paris.

After his collaboration with Manet on *The Raven* in 1875 and *L'Après-Midi d'un Faune* in 1876, Stéphane Mallarmé kept his attention firmly fixed on the Impressionists. In the same year as Duranty, 1876, he wrote an article about them for an English magazine.[443] At the end of 1887 Mallarmé had the idea of publishing his prose poems under a Japanese-sounding title, *Le Tiroir de Laque* (*The Lacquer Chest*), and collaborating with those Impressionist painters he held in greatest esteem: Renoir, Berthe Morisot and Degas, to whom he briefly added Claude Monet. He asked the lithographer John Lewis Brown to do the cover and requested illustrations from each of his four friends. *Le Tiroir de Laque* was eventually published by Deman in Brussels in 1891 as an anthology entitled *Pages* and contained only one engraving, a nude by Renoir. Monet gave up; Degas, in characteristic fashion, procrastinated indefinitely, and Berthe Morisot was probably dissatisfied with her contribution, as usual. The story is interesting because it confirms Monet's opposition to illustration, and to printmaking in particular, and his general dislike of drawing, which is the starting point for printmaking and has much in common with it: 'I am really ashamed of my behaviour and I deserve all your criticism', he wrote to Mallarmé on 12 October 1889, 'as you can imagine there is no ill-will on my part. The real truth is that I feel incapable of producing anything good enough for you. This may be an excess of pride, but truthfully, whenever I want to do anything in pencil it comes out hopeless, completely without interest, and consequently unworthy of accompanying your exquisite poetry.'[444]

Mallarmé was evidently an admirer of Degas, who always found personal relationships difficult and whose behaviour on this occasion was reminiscent of the way he allowed *Le Jour et la Nuit*, the journal he was planning to publish, to sink without trace. Degas replied to a request from Mallarmé on 29 August 1888[445] in dilatory fashion; writing from Cauterets on the following day, he said: 'My dear Mallarmé, you must not push the bear out in front. . . as they say in the Pyrenees. The quality of the paper is not as important as you think. I shall be in Paris before 20 September and will advise. . .' His lack of eagerness probably concealed a certain embarrassment because we know from Valéry that Degas preferred the man Mallarmé to his poetry.[446] 'The illustrations?

Everything's ready', Mallarmé wrote confidently to his publisher on 7 August 1888, 'except for Degas, I am going to write to that sublimely unpunctual character, and I shall ask J.L. Brown, who was so amiable as to suggest the plan, if he would supervise the printing at Lemercier's.'[447] Then, on 2 September 1888, he wrote to Berthe Morisot: 'Degas has written from Cauterets promising his drawing for the twentieth of next month. I know your punctuality and I also know something else very flattering about you from the delightful Lewis Brown; please don't gainsay me.'[448] Finally, on 8 October, to Deman: 'Saw Degas, he named the middle of the month, seriously this time. Lewis Brown and Madame Morisot are ready. I will tell you when it is time to write to Lemercier and Delâtre about the colour printing and the black and white. . .'[449]

Renoir and Morisot often worked together,[450] but neither of them had tried printmaking yet, and when Mallarmé sent his texts to them in December 1887 they were disconcerted. Berthe Morisot wrote to him: 'Please be so good as to come to dinner on Thursday. Renoir and I are stunned, we need some instructions about the illustrations.'[451] Mallarmé replied: 'I am replying to your letter because it upsets me to think that you are stunned: fortunately your smile peeps out from behind. . . I have had to wait all this time, and am still waiting, to settle the format of my book; as an instrument of torture I am sending you the page to be illustrated, the last piece of the enclosed publication.'[452] Berthe Morisot knew Mallarmé well. He had been an admirer since the article of 1876 and, like her, was a frequent visitor to the Manet household. Print was less familiar to her. They practised with a three crayon drawing (which must be lost) which made Monet envious: 'Monet, who was charmed by the white waterlily, in the notorious three crayons, is doing as you are doing and producing an illustration for my book.'[453] Two etchings by Morisot, *The Lake in the Bois de Boulogne* (Fig. 233) and *The Duck* (Fig. 232) seem to fit the first lines of Mallarmé's text, *Le Nénuphar blanc*. They are delicate sketches drawn directly on to the copper plate, almost certainly in the Bois de Boulogne which was near where she lived. The allusion to the 'three crayons', however, sows the seeds of doubt: was she not planning to produce a coloured lithograph, in the manner of John Lewis Brown from whom Mallarmé had commissioned the cover of the book?[454] Brown was ill, and died on 14 November 1890, before he could finish his project – although Mallarmé had already pronounced himself delighted with it: 'As for the illustrations, it is going to be outstanding, and one of the most beautiful women in Paris has posed for the cover; she will be 'opening' the said *tiroir* (drawer). Ah! my dear fellow, you cannot imagine the to-ing and fro-ing about the illustration! they only want to deliver works of genius, and it's so complicated. Madame Morisot (only one S) is seduced by Lewis Brown's use of colour and has learned the 'three crayon' technique; Degas himself

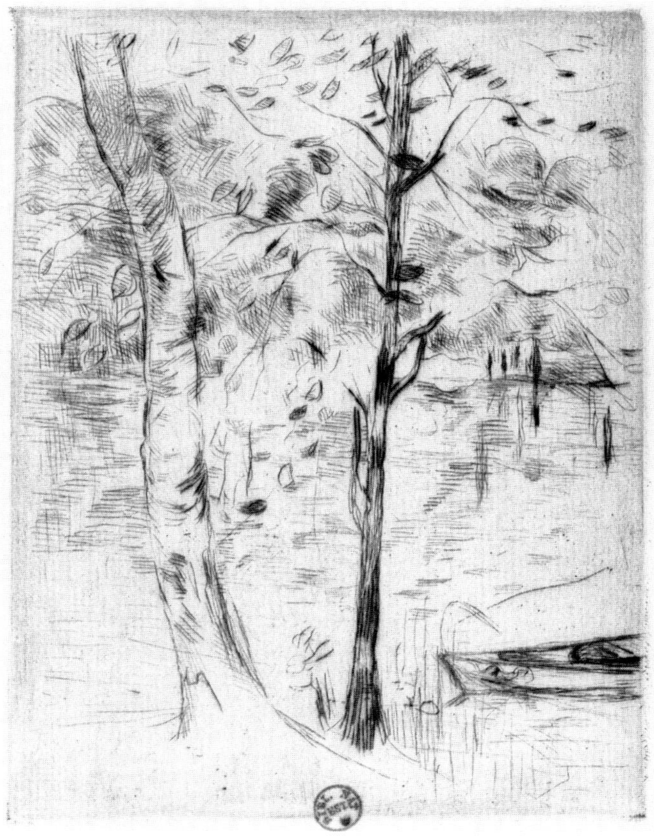

233. Berthe Morisot,
The Lake in the Bois de Boulogne. 1889.
Drypoint, 155 x 115 mm.
Bibliothèque nationale, Paris.

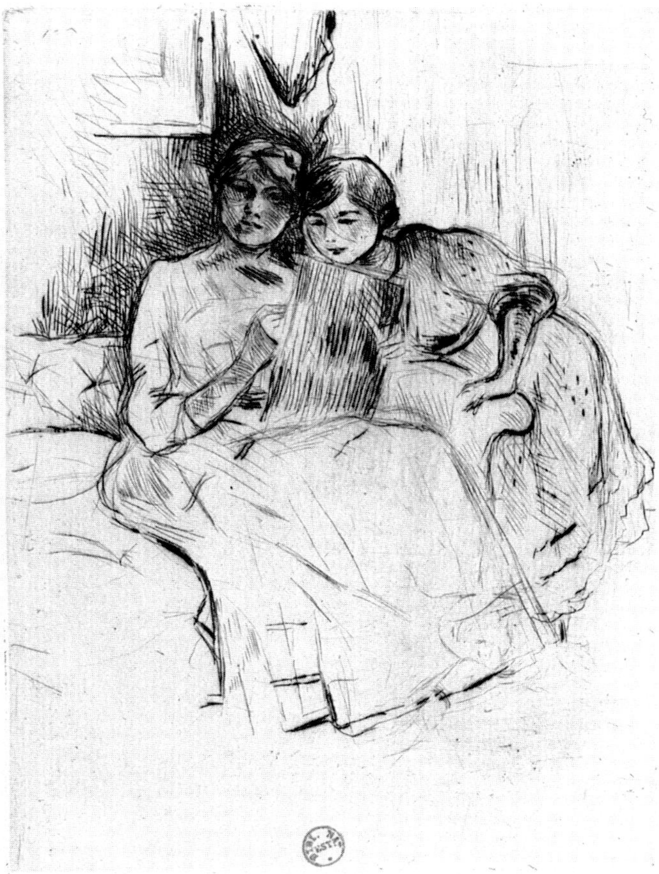

234. Berthe Morisot,
The Drawing Lesson (Berthe Morisot and her Daughter) 1889.
Drypoint, 182 x 136 mm.
Bibliothèque nationale, Paris.

is also proposing colour. It's going to be a great catch: it will all be ready at the end of the month and you could do the same! at Lemercier the lighographer's. He has trained Brown single handed to supervise the printing: we shall need Japan paper, I think we're agreed. Perhaps Renoir's etching (I will leave the plate with Dujardin while I'm away) will also be printed in Paris, unless you prefer to receive this plate in Brussels.'[455]

We know from her correspondence that at this time Berthe Morisot was planning to produce an album of coloured lithographs, based on pictures of her daughter Julie.[456] On 1 November 1888 Mallarmé asked: 'Is the little album still going strong?'[457] And in July 1890 Berthe wrote to her sister Edma: 'I am so disappointed with my attempts at making colour prints, it's all that has interested me recently. I worked all summer with the idea of publishing a series of drawings of Julie.'[458] A single example of these lithographs survives today, in the Rouart collection: Julie, seated at the foot of a tree with her hat on the grass, playing a whistle (Fig. 235). Were there any others? Was the album to consist of reproductions of her drawings, or lithographs done by herself probably with the help of John Lewis Brown? If the latter was the case this album, along with Manet's *Polichinelle,* would have been one of the key documents of the movement, in which almost all the painters of the last decade of the century were to try their hand at colour lithography. The hypothesis that it was to be an album of lithographs is endorsed by a letter from Mallarmé dated 17 February 1889: 'The good Lewis Brown is overwhelmed by the death of one of his wife's daughter's children (a girl); he is working intermittently on the printing of your and my designs. Degas, on the other hand, to whom I am about to send four lines on stamped paper, permits his editor to enjoy some leisure. His own poetry is occupying him and the most important news of this winter is that he is on his fourth sonnet.'[459] The plan for an album in colour must have some connection with Berthe Morisot's friendship with Mary Cassatt,[460] with whom she visited the exhibition of Japanese prints in 1890. The following winter Mary Cassatt produced a series of coloured aquatints which were exhibited at Durand-Ruel in 1891. The two women saw each other frequently, at least from 1879 onwards, thanks to Degas. Their friendship strengthened in 1887, and on Tuesday 29 April 1890 Mary Cassatt wrote to Berthe Morisot: '. . .we will go and see the Japanese prints at the Beaux-Arts. Seriously, they are not to be missed. You want to make coloured engravings – you can't imagine anything so beautiful. I'm dreaming of it and thinking only about colour on copper. Fantin went on the first day, and I went and came away in ecstasy. I saw M. Tissot there – he is very preoccupied with the problems of colour printing . . .'[461]

The printed work of Berthe Morisot, in spite of all this, consists of eight drypoint etchings in black and white. Bearing in mind the demands she made on herself and

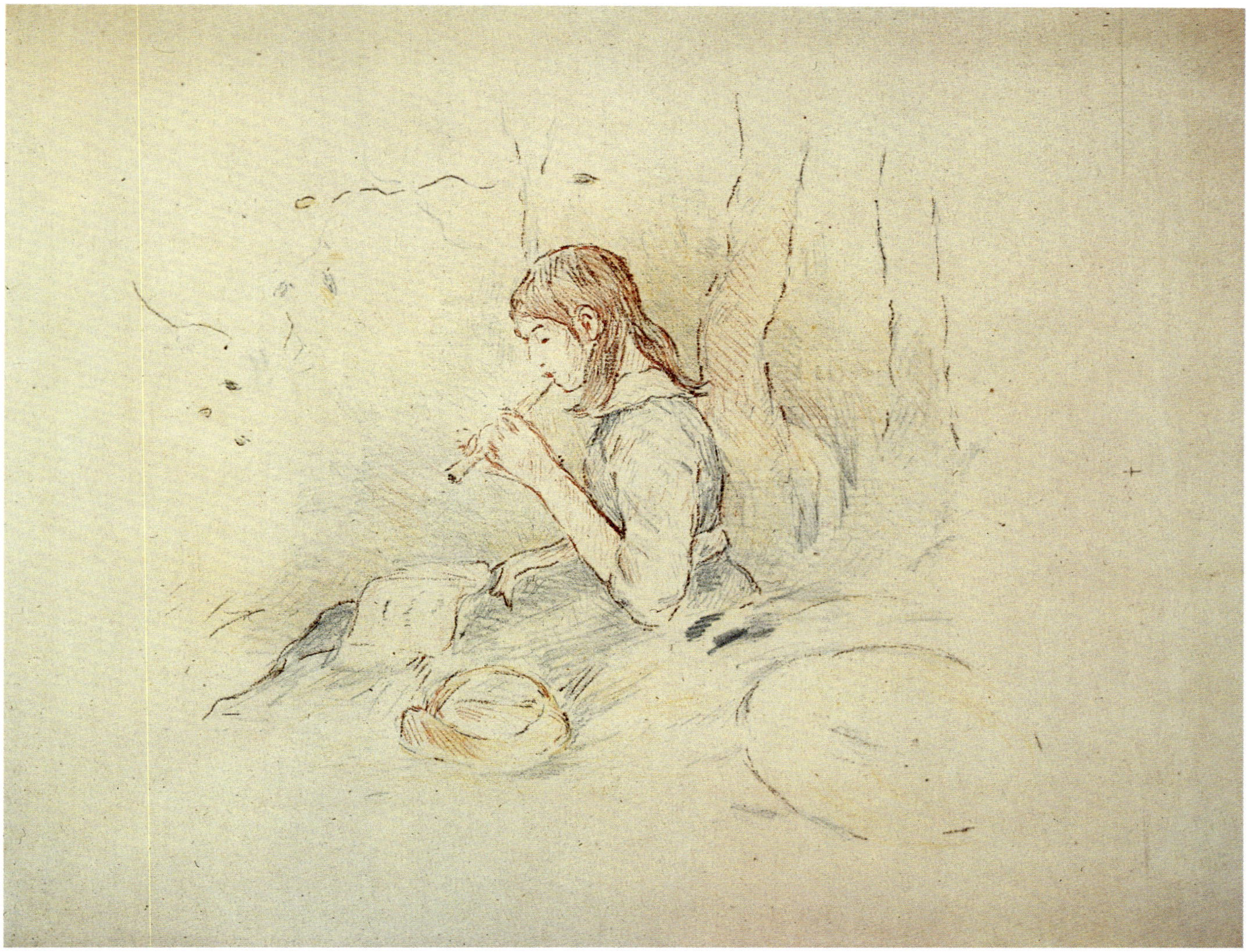

235. Berthe Morisot, *The Whistle*. 1890. Colour lithograph, 250 x 335 mm.
Private collection, Paris.

her perpetual self-doubt, it would be no surprise to learn that she had abandoned and destroyed her experiments, as she often did her other work. Janine Bailly-Herzberg reminds us perceptively of the example of Marcellin Desboutin, a friend of John Lewis-Brown.[462] His drypoint portrait of Berthe Morisot dated from 1876, although Durand-Ruel included it in a retrospective exhibition of her prints in the summer of 1889. It is also worth considering that Berthe Morisot might have taken up printmaking independently, on the invitation of Mallarmé. As a young woman she attended the classes of Guichard, the painter who taught Bracquemond, and then Corot.[463] She met Bracquemond in the Louvre in 1859. She was surrounded by references to printmaking. Her drypoints show an increasing mastery of the technique: her handling of the etching needle was still slightly unsure in the plates assumed to have been done for *Le Tiroir de Laque* and in two others, *The Goose* and *Swan and Duck*, but it is more confident in *Nude, Backview* (Fig. 236), in *The Girl with the Cat (Julie Manet)* (Fig. 237), after a painting by Renoir, and in *Girl Resting*, taken from her own painting of 1887;[464] her handling reaches its peak in *The Drawing Lesson* (Fig. 234), a self-portrait with her daughter, about which she confided to her diary that she hesitated nervously before starting work on the large copper plate.[465]

The eight etchings were not published and no-one, apart perhaps from her family and close friends, saw them until they were bought by Vollard who printed twenty-five copies (in about 1904–5), hanging them in the Salon d'Automne in 1907.[466] Berthe Morisot, her own severest critic, provided no successors. Mallarmé took it upon himself to convince her. The exhibition held by the Society of Painter-Printmakers gave him the opportunity to express his admiration in these terms, on 17 February 1889: 'The exhibition of the Painter-Printmakers, at Durand-Ruel, contains some delightful trifles and I know of two drypoints that ought to be included.'[467] It was too late for the first exhibition which opened in January, Berthe Morisot's prints were not exhibited at the second nor at those that followed, nor anywhere before the death in 1895 of the artist who had said: 'We shall all die with our secrets intact.'[468]

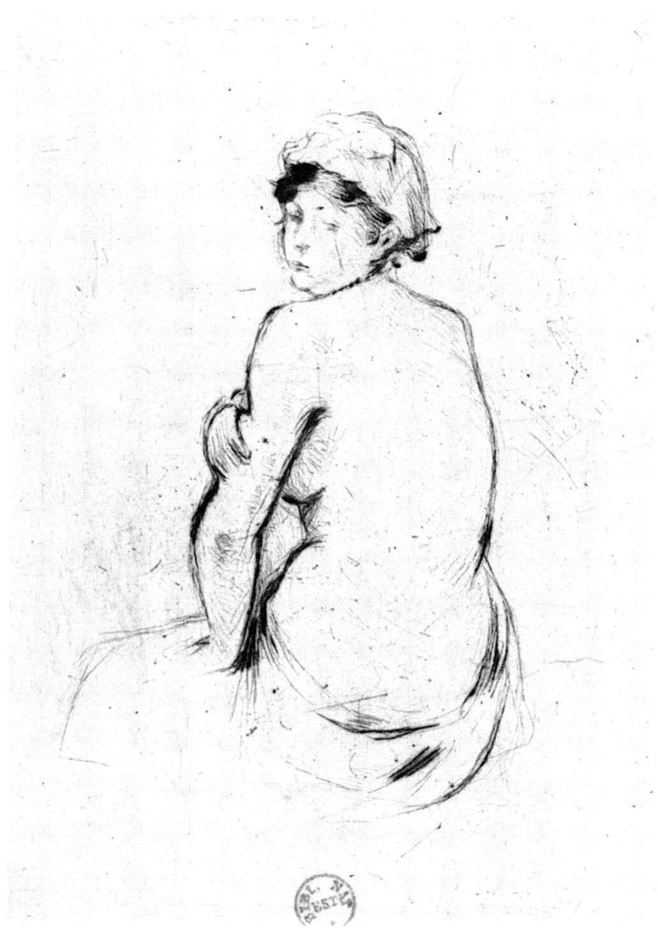

236. Berthe Morisot,
Nude from Behind. About 1889.
Drypoint, 130 x 92 mm.
Bibliothèque nationale, Paris.

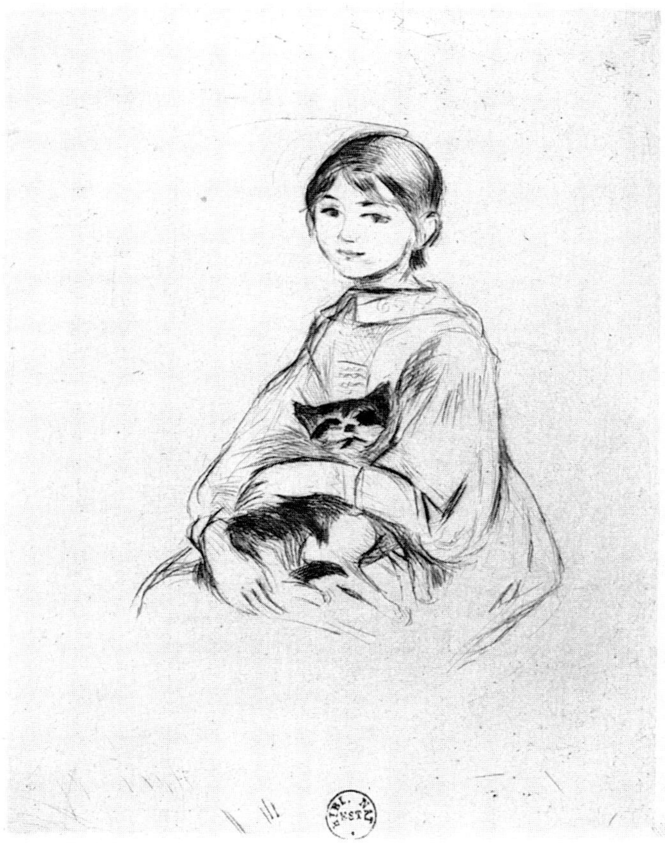

237. Berthe Morisot,
Girl with a Cat (Jule Manet). About 1889.
Drypoint, 145 x 113 mm.
Bibliothèque nationale, Paris.

46. *Renoir*

The Impressionists grew less and less interested in printmaking as the commercial demands made upon them increased. It is worth noting that printmaking grew successful at the same rate as Impressionist painting, proof (with hindsight) that both movements were borne along on the same tide. The career of Renoir, the first Impressionist to enjoy real success, demonstrates most clearly the correlation between the two phenomena. He was the first artist to return to the Salon and to find his clientèle there, the first to return to an almost classical style of drawing, the first to revive the Romantic taste for the exotic, the most regular painter of nude figures, the readiest to be seduced by the cloying attractions of decorative art. He was also the least theoretical of all the Impressionists and the last one to be drawn in to printmaking. His printed *œuvre* is nonetheless large and very varied: slightly more than fifty plates, half of them line etchings, the other half lithographs, but three-quarters of them produced for inclusion in books, after 1900 when the painter was famous and the print an art of mass production.

When he was invited to take part in the exhibition of the Society of Painter-Printmakers, Renoir replied to Durand-Ruel: 'I only have one etching and it belongs to Mallarmé: ask him for it if you like, but it's not much.'[469] Designed originally as an illustration to the poem *Le Phénomène futur*, the etching eventually became the frontispiece and only illustration to the collection entitled *Pages*, published in 1888.[470] It is the sole vestige of a project aimed at including all the poet's favourite artists: Renoir, Morisot, Degas. It was Renoir's first attempt at printmaking: a nymph whose curves obviously presage *Art Nouveau*, and whose outline betrays a return to the purest Classicism. Impressionism has completely disappeared as art enters this new era.

Impressionism survives unaltered, however, in the five small drypoints apparently executed in the wake of Berthe Morisot, with whom he worked at printmaking during the encounter with Mallarmé. One of these is a fine profile portrait of his friend, showing the proud carriage of her head and her frank gaze; her hair is already grey (Fig. 239). Another equally delicate etching shows Berthe Morisot's daughter Julie from behind, pinning flowers on her cousin Paulette's broad-brimmed hat. Renoir returned to this subject several times – three line etchings, several pastels, a painting,[471] then two litho-

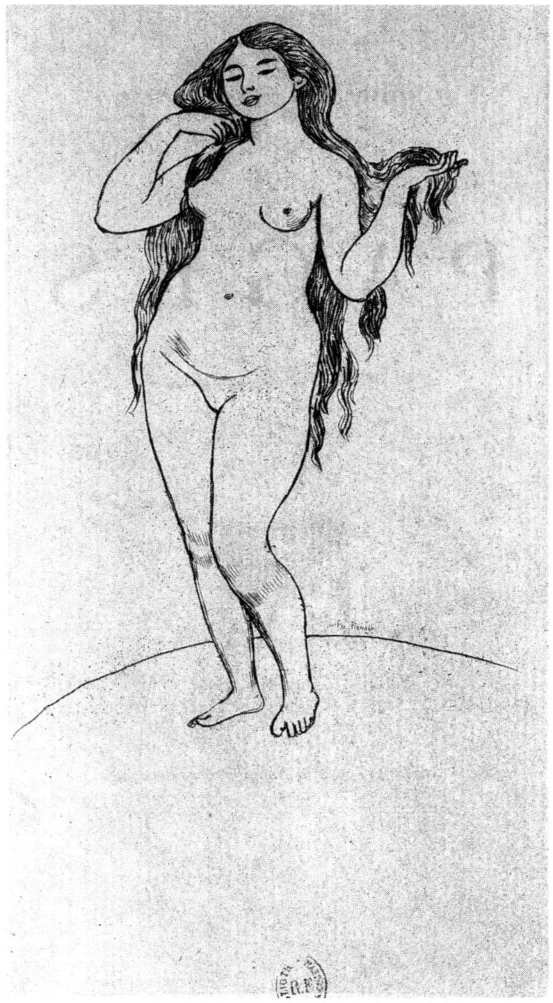

238. Pierre-Auguste Renoir, frontispiece to Mallarmés *Pages*. 1890. Etching, single state, 198 x 107 mm. Bibliothèque nationale, Paris.

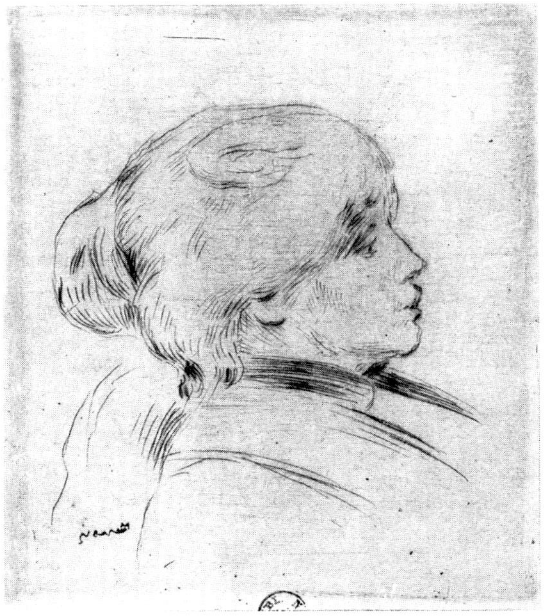

239. Pierre-Auguste Renoir,
Berthe Morisot. About 1892.
Drypoint, single state, 110 x 90 mm.
Bibliothèque nationale, Paris.

240. Pierre-Auguste Renoir,
Study of Seated Nude. 1904.
Ink wash lithograph, single state. 185 x 160 mm.
Bibliothèque nationale, Paris.

241. Pierre-Auguste Renoir,
Study of Seated Nude. 1904.
Lithograph, second and final state, 123 x 114 mm.
Bibliothèque nationale, Paris.

242. Pierre-Auguste Renoir,
Seated Bather, c. 1905.
Etching, first plate, single state, 217 x 135 mm.
Bibliothèque nationale, Paris.

243. Pierre-Auguste Renoir,
Seated Bather. 1906.
Etching, second plate, single state, 182 x 142 mm.
Bibliothèque nationale, Paris.

graphs, one in black and white (1897) published by Vollard in an edition of 200, one in colour (1898). Under the title of *Pinning the Hat* the coloured one has become the most famous and most sought-after of all Renoir's etchings (Figs 305–7), perhaps because it is the most similar to the paintings of his final period. The story of this subject illustrates the increasing importance of the print after its humble and very private beginnings; it became the means of distributing a painting to an international circle of admirers. Only the etchings done in 1888–90 retain the freshness and spontaneity of an art aiming at originality. A small etching of the same period, *On the Beach at Berneval* is like a holiday souvenir; it is a sketch of the Bérard girls, with whose family Renoir went on holiday to Wargemont, near Dieppe.[472]

Renoir did some innovatory printmaking when he experimented with a technique, soft ground etching, that was popular with the Impressionists, being particularly well-suited to imitating the spontaneity of drawing, and allowing a soft blur to develop around its contours. According to Bracquemond, Degas gave instructions on its use to Pissarro for his *Cabbage Patch* in 1880. The technique consists in drawing on a sheet of paper that has been applied to a copper plate covered in a soft wax. When the drawing has been completed and the sheet is removed (a tricky operation) the wax adheres to the back of the paper where the pencil has exerted its pressure and leaves the copper bare. The drawing is thus transferred to the plate and is carefully etched with acid. This method of printing offers a very accurate copy of the drawing; the lines are a little thickened but they are soft and if the bite of the acid has been correctly controlled the lightest strokes of the pencil are reproduced, and even the lightest creases in the paper.

Probably in response to another request for an illustration Renoir used the soft ground technique to reproduce the subject of his large painting of 1883, *The Dance in the Country*.[473] A first spoiled plate illustrates the problems inherent in the technique but the second one, a success, perfectly renders Renoir's generous style of draughtsmanship, retaining the sensuality and opulence of the figures so pleasing to his public. Later, Renoir revived a drawing done in 1881, *Seated Bather*; the soft ground process softens the lines and seems to embrace the generous charms of the model. Renoir shared the Impressionists' liking of returning repeatedly to a subject in a series of very varied works, as he did with his *Reclining Nude*: he derives continuing pleasure from her in the three small variations, each in a different style (Figs 244–6). The first plate has the very smooth line of the drypoint; the second is unadorned, like a working drawing; the third has the vibrant quality of an etching.

After these brief incursions into the field of line-etching between 1888 and 1891, which might have been his only attempts at the technique (as with Sisley or Morisot) Renoir fulfilled a number of commissions from

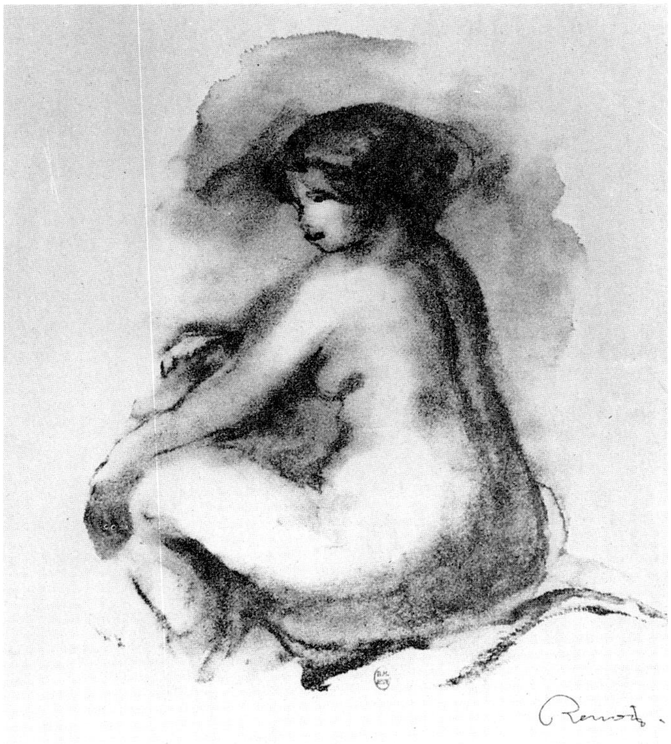

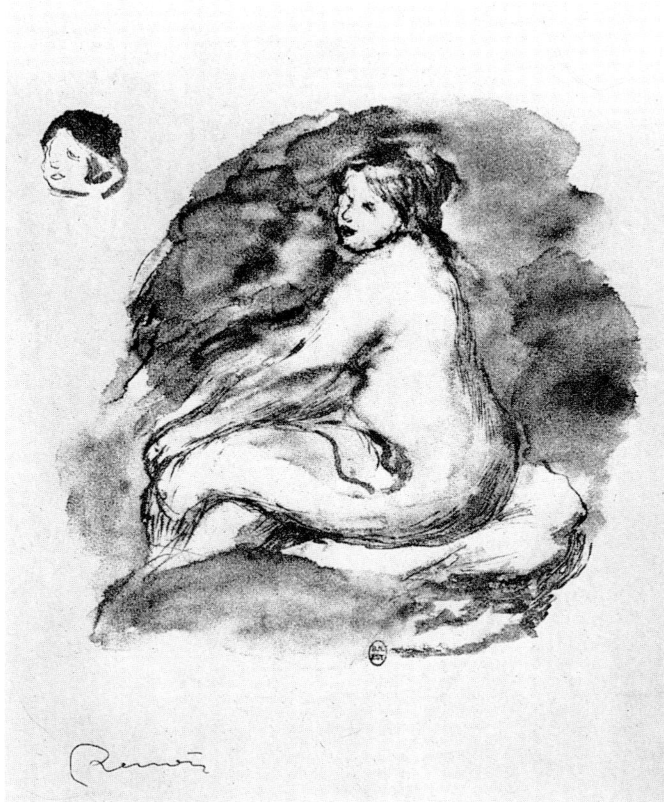

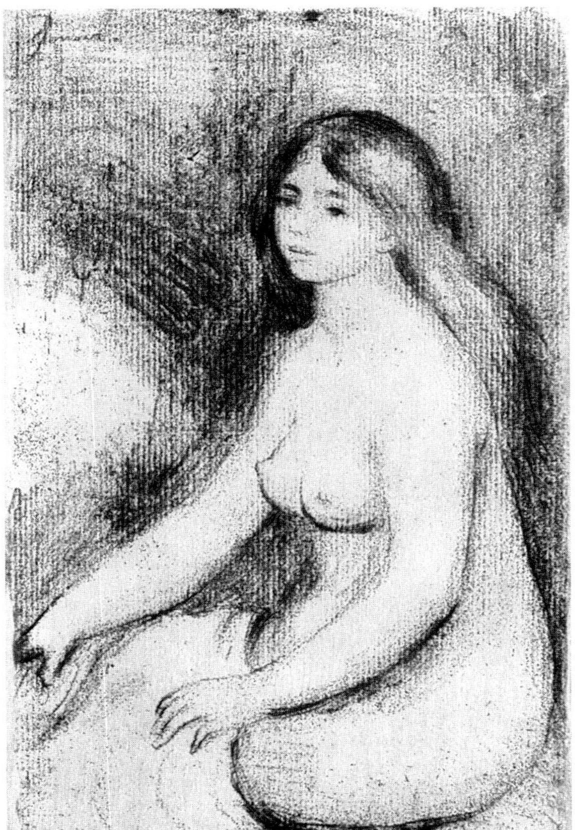

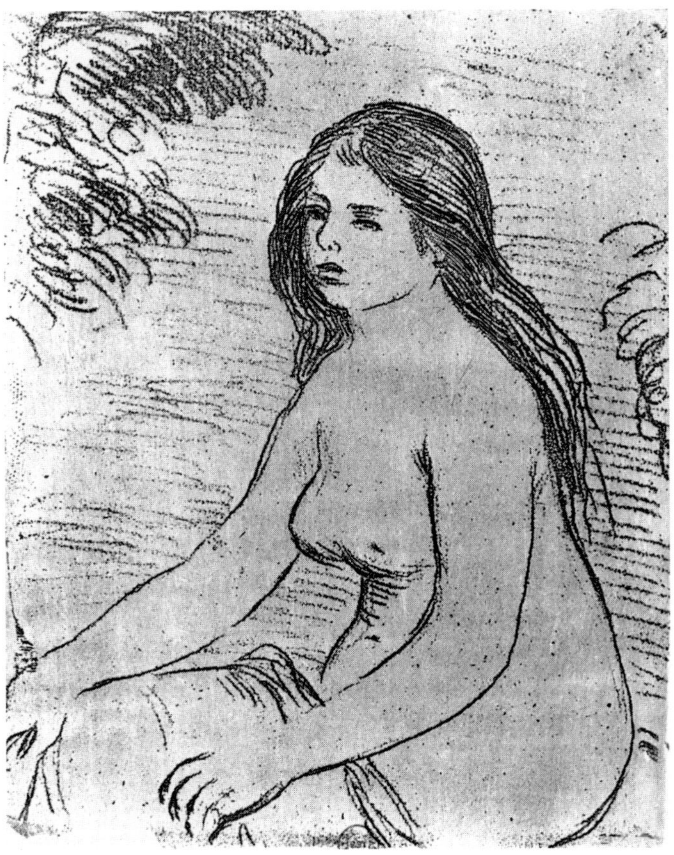

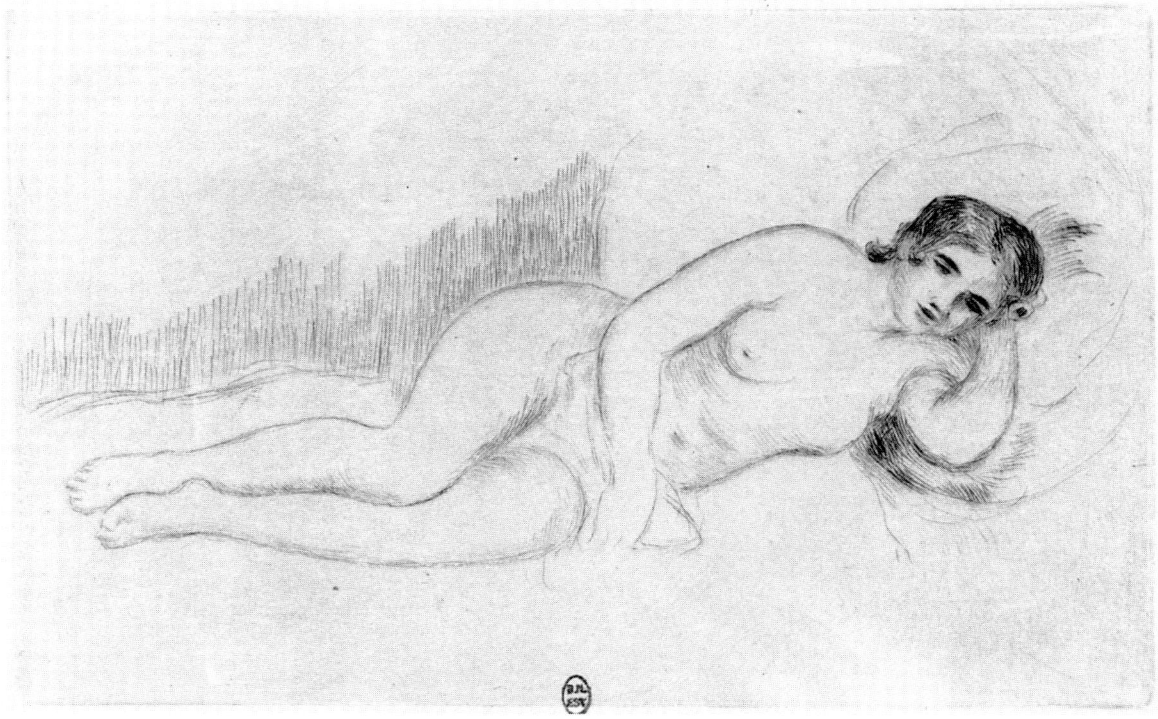

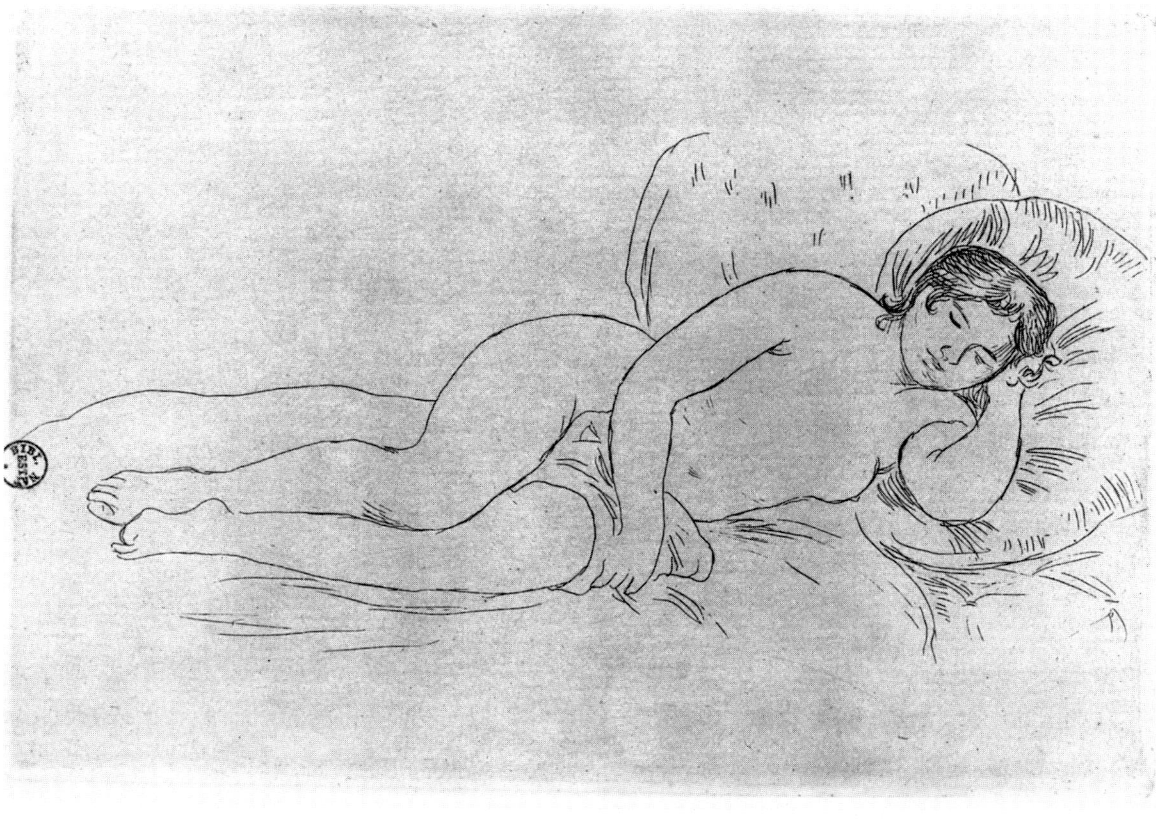

244. Pierre-Auguste Renoir, *Nude Lying, Facing Right*. 1906. Etching, first plate, single state, 122 x 192 mm. Bibliothèque nationale, Paris.

245. Pierre-Auguste Renoir, *Nude Lying, Facing Right*. 1906. Etching, second plate, single state, 137 x 192 mm. Bibliothèque nationale, Paris.

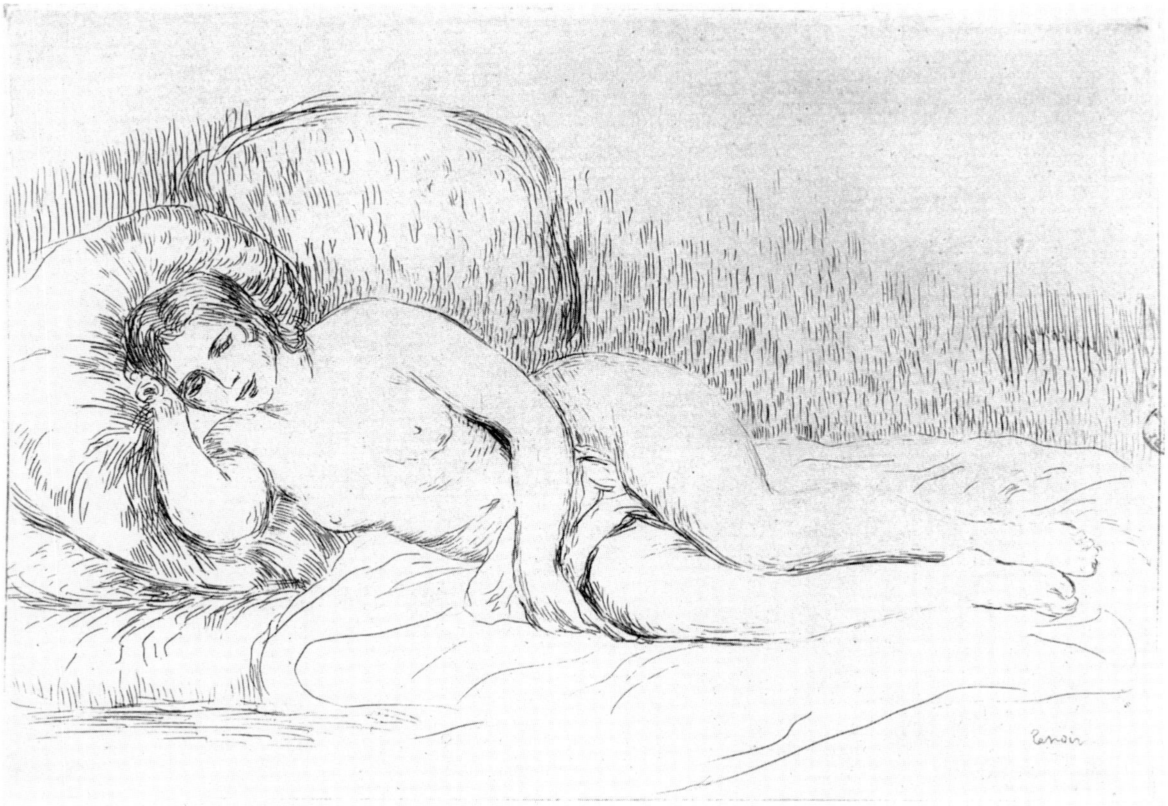

246. Pierre-Auguste Renoir, *Nude Lying, Facing Left*. 1906. Etching, single state, 137 x 192 mm. Bibliothèque nationale, Paris.

publishers, and was included in all the major albums published at the turn of the century and afterwards. First in the album brought out by Marty's *L'Estampe originale* in October 1893, with his first lithograph: *Pierre Renoir, front view* then, in 1895, an etching, *Two Women Bathing*. In Vollard's first album in 1896 he was represented by a colour etching, *Mother and Child*, (his wife and his son Jean). Two other coloured lithographs, the celebrated *Standing Female Bather* and *The Child with a Cake* appear to have been intended for Vollard's third album, which never appeared. Vollard devoted a whole album of twelve lithographs to him in 1904. With Vollard's encouragement, his output grew gradually better adapted to the new clientèle. The format was designed for framing and this predestined the prints for the walls of smart apartments: the colours were always fresh and bright, the subjects - innocent girls, nursing mothers, artless nudes - lent themselves to the creation of a modern popular imagery. There is experiment and innovation even in the *Standing Female Bather*, his first coloured lithograph, printed by Auguste Clot in 1896, in which a diluted Impressionism spreads dulcet sweet colours over a smiling subject, or in *Pinning the Hat*, a bowdlerised version of a painting, aimed at a less exacting class of buyer to match the interior décor of the family home. Just as he had found soft ground etching well-suited to his style, he practised colour wash lithography with enthusiasm and achieved the same undertones of sensuality with the sticky liquid ink spread in a cloud over the stone to add a misty veil to the motif. Examples of this are his *Study of a Seated Nude* (Figs 240, 241), his five variations of *Woman with a Vine Stock* and, once again, *Pinning the Hat*, repeated in a small format like the original etching.

As an old man in his villa in Cagnes, rich and revered, Renoir made a few more etchings with a friend, the engraver Victor-Joseph Roux-Champion. He put his signature to the last unpublished prints by the Impressionist group in 1908; these were the last made by the inner circle of Impressionists. Bracquemond, however, the first Impressionist ever to exhibit his prints, signed the very last ones of all in 1909.

47. *Degas's Women in the Bath*

The banker's son who longed for nothing more than to be one of the 'illustrious unknown' was on his way to fame and riches. He continued to experiment with techniques as vigorously as ever. After about 1876 he began to pay particular attention to the nude, devoting himself to monotype as another might devote himself to a dissolute life. His earliest experiments with lithography, his first monotypes and his first female figures getting out of the bath, in a paste of ink and pigment, all date from this period. The products of this period were endlessly re-worked and were submitted to a whole series of aesthetic modifications. The first lithographs (about 1875, when the lithograph was beginning to reappear in the studios of painters like Manet and Pissarro) arose out of the monotypes and used the same subject matter – scenes from the theatre and the bathroom. Degas only ever made one lithograph on stone, *The Singer at the Café-Concert*; the others were drawn on transfer paper or were produced by a strange process involving the transfer of a drawing on a sheet of celluloid to a stone block, like a monotype. The passage from lithograph to monotype did not particularly indicate development – the same work was produced by different methods. Degas submitted his etchings to the same process of trial and error: the theme of *Getting out of the Bath*, in 1879–80, was tackled first (before 1877) in three monotypes, two of which were coloured with pastel;[474] it was then re-used in the twenty-two successive states of a small etching, a record number for Degas. *Mary Cassatt at the Louvre: Paintings* went through 'only' twenty states (Figs 201–6).

Degas made no more distinction between etchings and monotypes than he did between etchings, monotypes and pastels. *Getting out of the Bath* (Fig. 195),[475] heightened with pastel, was exhibited at the third Impressionist exhibition in 1877. Later it became a kind of ritual to heighten etchings, lithographs and monotypes with pastel. The two etchings *At the Ambassadors* (Figs 180–1)[476] and *Mary Cassatt at the Louvre: Paintings*[477] were used as the basis of new work, some of which was faithful to the original; some had new parts added in the shape of bands of paper, completely repainted. This is how the lithograph of *Mlle Bécat at the Ambassadors* was altered (Figs 178–9).[478] Photography was included in this recycling process, for

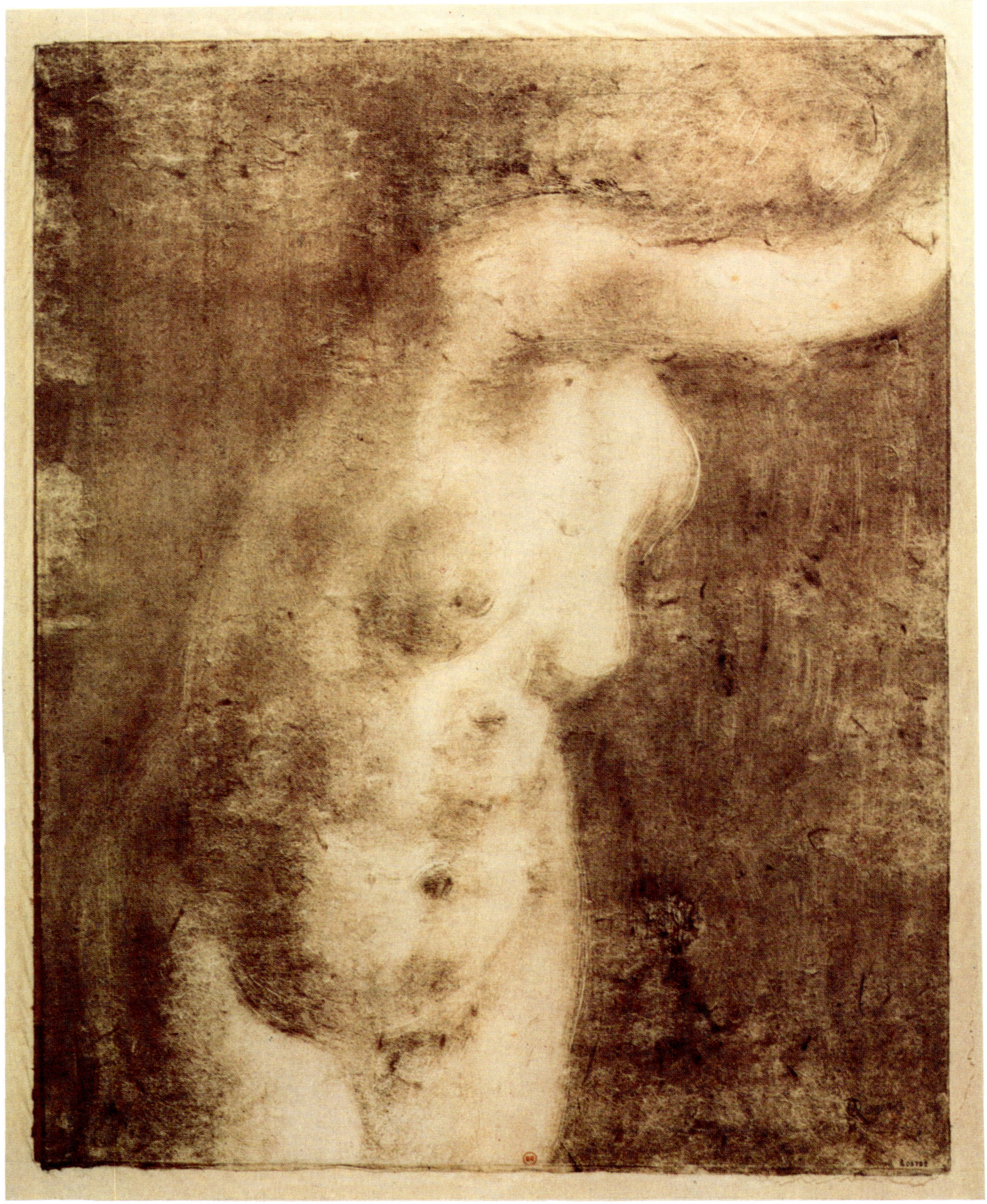

247. Edgar Degas, *Female Torso*. About 1885. Monotype, 500 x 393 mm. Bibliothèque nationale, Paris.

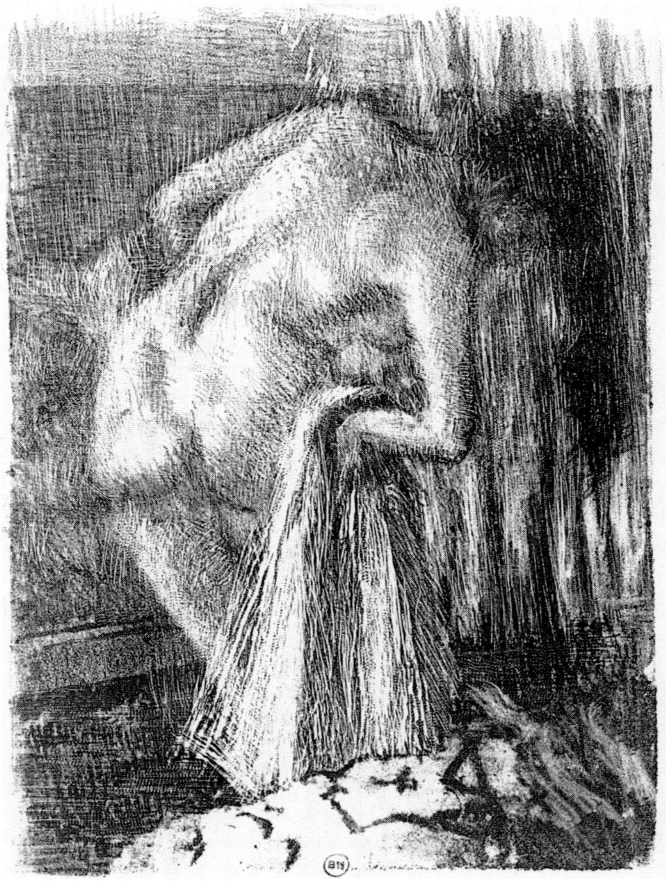

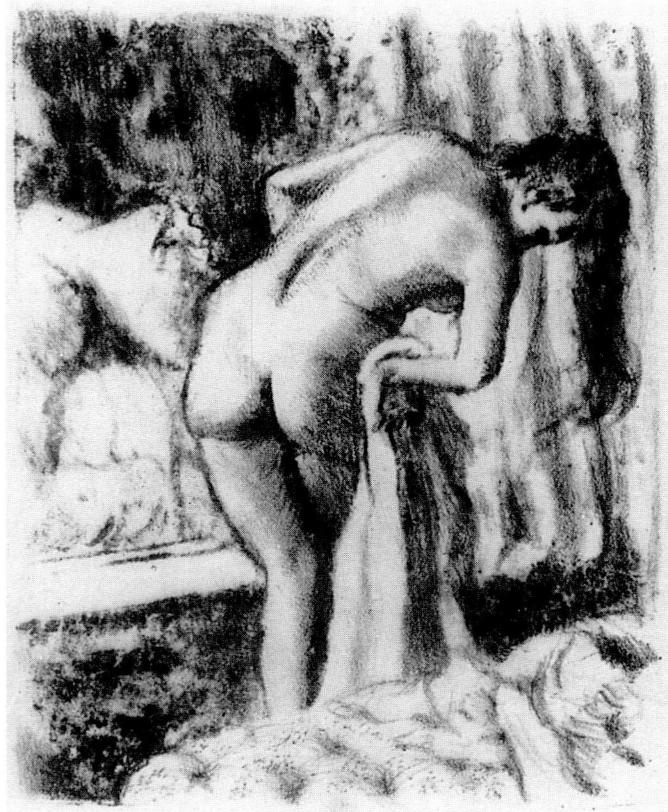

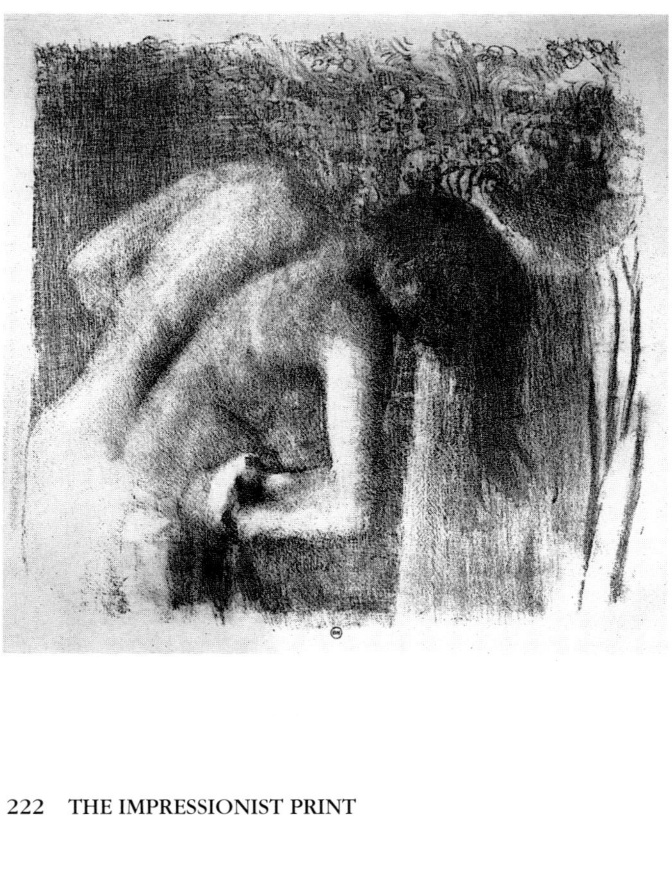

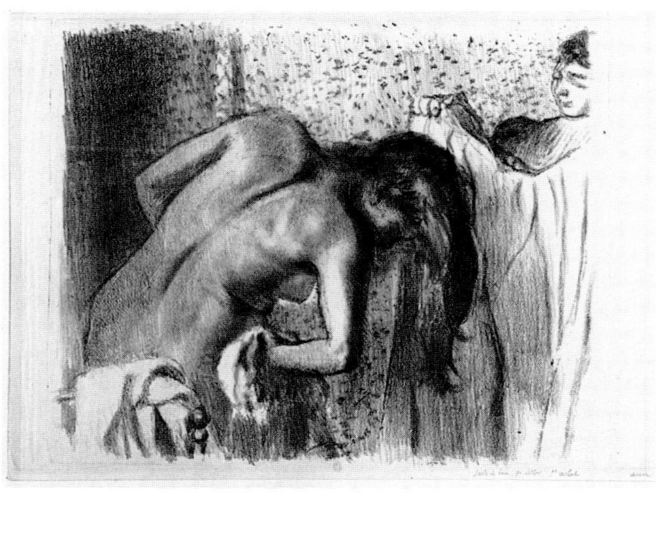

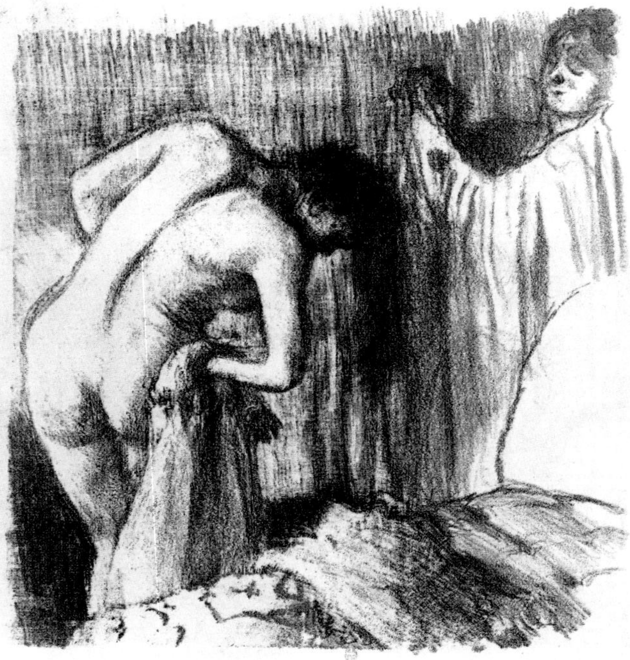

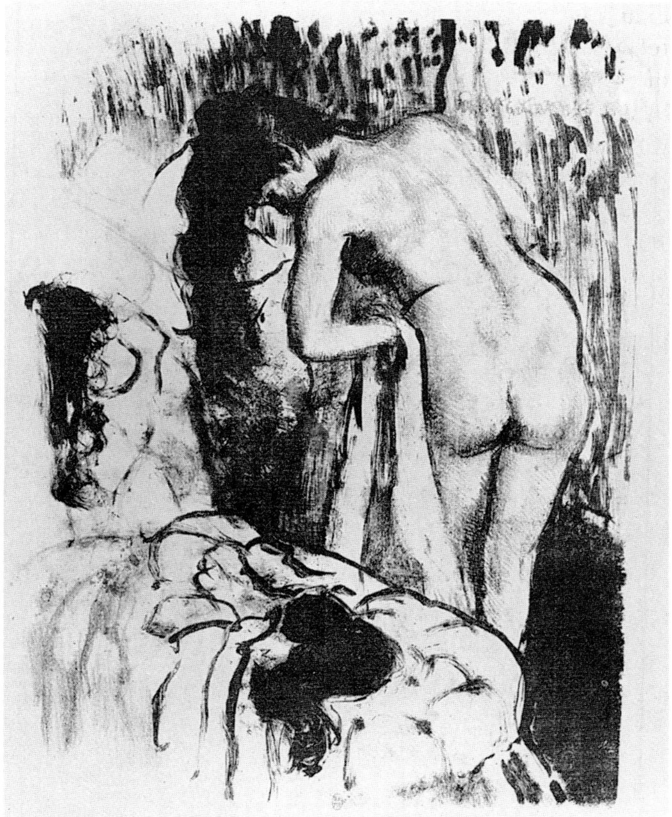

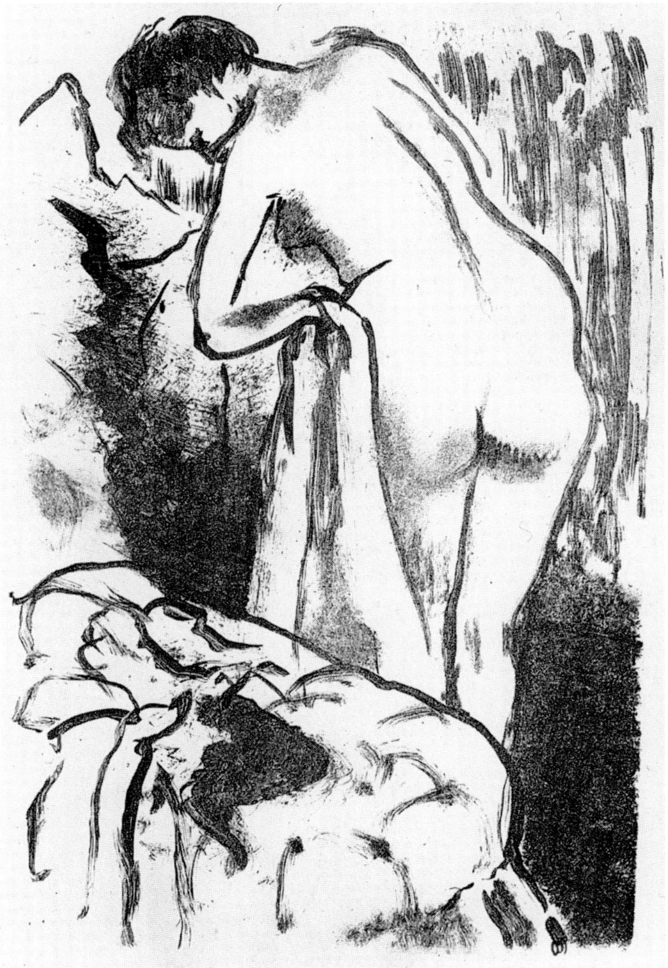

248. Edgar Degas,
After the Bath (Woman standing at her Toilette, Facing Right).
About 1891.
Lithograph, first plate, sixth state, 205 x 147 mm.
Bibliothèque nationale, Paris.

249. Edgar Degas,
After the Bath (Woman standing at her Toilette, Facing Right).
About 1891.
Lithograph, second plate (?), second state, 205 x 147 mm.
Bibliothèque d'Art et d'Archéologie, Paris.

250. Edgar Degas,
Getting out of the Bath (large plate).
Lithograph, second state, 280 x 301 mm.
Bibliothèque d'Art et d'Archéologie, Paris.

251. Edgar Degas,
Getting out of the Bath (large plate). About 1885–90.
Lithograph, fifth state, 280 x 301 mm.
Bibliothèque nationale, Paris.

252. Edgar Degas,
Getting out of the Bath (small plate). About 1890.
Lithograph, first state, 249 x 229 mm.
Bibliothèque nationale, Paris.

253, 254. Edgar Degas, *Naked Woman Standing at her Toilette, Turning Left.* About 1890.
Lithograph, 333 x 245 mm. *First* state,
Bibliothèque d'Art et d'Archéologie, Paris; *third* state,
Bibliothèque nationale, Paris.

example in *The Song of the Dog* which began as a pastel, was photographed, then the photograph was traced on to transfer paper, the transfer paper was printed as a lithograph and finished up as a monotype.[479] Degas's relentless labour over his prints came to a head in the series of nudes who first appear, plumply displayed, in his earliest monotypes of brothel scenes in about 1876–7. They return in the series of bathers in the 1880s and include the series produced for the last Impressionist exhibition in 1886, and the series begun in 1890 when, with fading eyesight, he returned more assiduously to printmaking and pastel and to his favourite fantasies of women: women contorted and caressed, women studied for hours on end.[480] Goncourt records in 1894 the astonishment of the model whom Degas painted for four hours without ever setting her in a pose. He returned to the prostitutes in Pigalle, repeatedly wetted and dried in the bathtub in his studio, to those opulent, disturbing figures described by Eugenia Parry Janis as 'faceless nudes'.[481]

In a letter to his friend Valernes, dated 6 July 1891, Degas writes: 'I am planning a series of lithographs, the first set to be nudes at their toilet (Figs 253–4) and the second nudes practising dance.'[482] On 25 April the series was advanced enough for Pissarro to comment that 'Degas is making lithographs. Mayer wants them. It's a big undertaking'.[483] This project produced eight lithographs, or eight times the same lithograph in multiple states but (for the most part) single prints (Figs 248–54); it is difficult to identify the main technique and even the tools used because the prints have been subjected to so much additional working.[484] What is the significance of this drawing printed once only on at least three different supports, or on three different sizes of paper, and achieving a final state of which only five proofs were made? A pencilled note on one of the proofs in the Doucet collection gives a clue: 'Essai chez Manzi, Degas'.[485] Adhémar points out that in the Manzi sale in 1919, number 128 is a 'drawing in thick ink on celluloid used by Degas for making a heliographic negative print on damp paper'.[486] Another proof, in the Bibliothèque Nationale, from another state or another plate, also bears the words 'Essai chez Manzi'[487] in Degas's handwriting. Michel Manzi, who was very friendly with Degas in 1892–3, worked at Goupil before setting up his own photoengraving studio in rue Forest. He printed the illustrations for *Le Figaro Illustré* between 1893 and 1896 and invented a process known as 'chrono-typo-engraving'. It was he who, in 1896, published an album containing 'Twenty drawings by Degas'. It was in his studio, with him, that Degas printed the lithographs from ink drawings on celluloid which he terms his 'experiments' (*essais*).[488] He used the same term when he presented his first 'greasy ink drawings' at the Impressionist exhibition in 1877. Relevant to this also was his plan to illustrate Ludovic Halévy's *Les Petites Cardinal*, based originally on monotype prints.[489] Reff has suggested that his monotypes of brothels may also have been the result of a plan for book illustration, this time to *La Fille Elisa*.[490] The pencil drawing for his first monotype, *The Ballet Master* was, according to Pickvance, offered to the *Illustrated London News*, which had a very large circulation at the time, but was refused.[491]

Degas never gave up the idea of publishing his prints. The *Getting out of the Bath* series, printed by lithography in 1891, may have been a final attempt at finding a satisfactory process for reproducing prints (Figs 248–52). If this was the case than the word failure has to be returned to, if a process repeated so doggedly be termed a failure. Such application within a situation deemed a failure would be astonishing, particularly when these 'experiments' are to our eyes so successful. Degas undeniably persevered most painstakingly and with some pride at his failures and these failures, by their numbers alone, transform his impotence into extreme potency. Degas seemed quite uninterested in reproduction for its own sake but was intrigued by the possible ways of making reproductions. He derided and defied reproduction, imposing such constraints on the techniques as to permit no chance of success.

Degas arranges and rearranges his women issuing from the bathtub, caressing their ample forms, drenching them, moulding them tirelessly in wax for his statuettes or in ink for his monotypes. A lithograph is fashioned in ink. The large monotype in brown ink, *Woman's Torso* (Fig. 247), is monumental in its proportions; the strong movement of the arm is modelled in the thick ink. Work stopped only when the paper was saturated, to be started again immediately on another plate. The woman stands up, half turns and dries herself again. Degas works on the woman's hair, returning to the abundant flowing hair he had given the martyred women in his *Scene of War in the Middle Ages*. He returns to the modelling of the hip, twists it a bit more but does not finish the upper body. He submits his model to torture but his inability to complete the work forces him to start again. The woman is condemned to eternal towelling; the artist to highlighting her body for a reproduction that he has rendered impossible. He is incapable of abandoning this single proof, and finds satisfaction only in repeating it again and again.

48. *Mary Cassatt*

Although her first art teacher in America was John Sartain, an engraver of reproductions celebrated for his mezzotints, Mary Cassatt was at that time interested only in painting. It was to establish a career as a painter that she came to Europe and exhibited at the Salon in 1868, under the name Mary Stevenson. She did not really discover printmaking until exposed to the work of Degas and Pissarro in 1879,[492] when she took it up in preparation for the publication of *Le Jour et la Nuit*. She is a typical example of the painter-printmaker, a painter who practised printmaking as if it were another branch of painting. She worked on her plates as an artist works on a canvas: preparing the plate, applying the aquatint then rubbing and scratching and scraping; after the first etching, she would mask certain areas of the plate with resin and apply the acid again, etching some more, adding touches of drypoint etc. She applied the 'Degas method' of working over the plate until it was either completely filled up or worn out. She moved as easily as he did between paper and copper, and copper and canvas. Most of the prints are etched versions of pastels, but she occasionally reversed the process, modelling a painting or a pastel on an engraving. In 1879 Degas wrote that 'Miss Cassatt is doing some enchanting experiments with etching',[493] and, in 1893, Pissarro enthused: 'She is decidedly very gifted'.[494]. It is no surprise that they should have been fascinated by such a brilliant and diligent student.

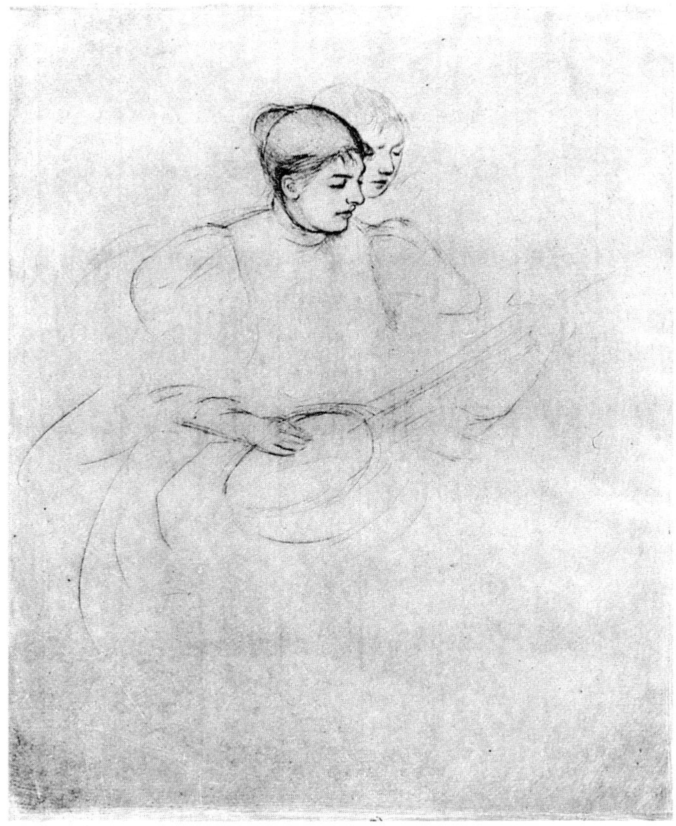

255. Mary Cassatt,
The Banjo. 1894.
Drypoint, first state before application of colour, 419 x 292 mm.
Bibliothèque d'Art et d'Archéologie, Paris.

The young American woman was unaware of the endless disputes raging between painters and etchers in Europe and threw herself into prints remarkable for their pictorial qualities, without the backward glance that a European etcher might have cast over his or her past as a craftsman. It is not really surprising that she chose colour lithography. Her first attempts at printing for *Le Jour et la Nuit* were the promising prelude to an abundant output: 250 etchings and one lithograph. She participated in the movement of painter-printmakers between 1889 and 1890, and this stimulated her interest in printmaking and helped to confirm her vocation. A letter from Cassatt to Delâtre on 10 October 1889 indicates her wish to 'take in hand' her prints and to look after the actual printing herself. She got hold of a press and asked the printer to deliver the paper he had put on one side for her.[495] The exhibition of Japanese prints at the Ecole des Beaux-Arts that opened on 15 April 1890

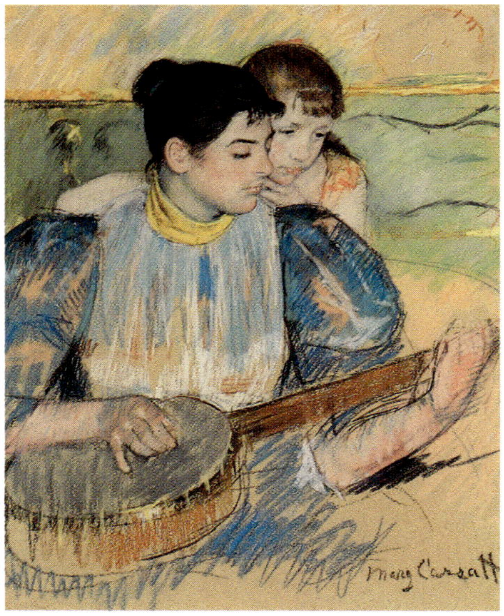

256. Mary Cassatt,
The Banjo Lesson. About 1894.
Pastel on paper, 711 x 572 mm.
Virginia Museum of Fine Arts, Richmond,
the Adolph D. and Wilkins C. Williams Fund.

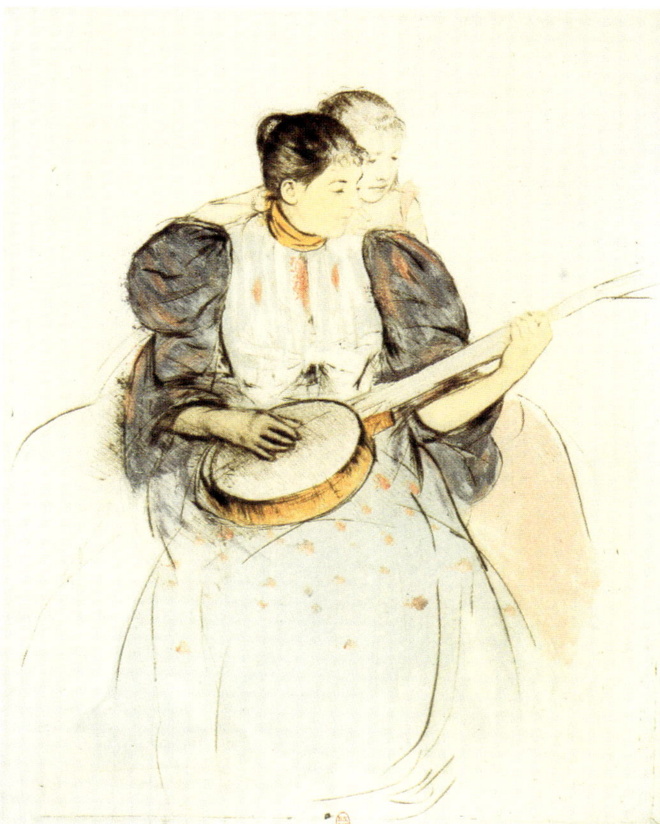

257. Mary Cassatt,
The Banjo Lesson. About 1893.
Drypoint and aquatint, 419 x 292 mm. Fourth state, Bibliothèque nationale, Paris;

next page: 258. monotype proof,
National Gallery of Art, Washington, gift of Mrs Jane C. Carey,
in addition to the Addie Burr Clark Memorial Collection.

acted as a final trigger; she began making prints that were not only representational in their drawing and inking, but were also in colour. Her letter to her friend Berthe Morisot expressed her enthusiasm for the exhibition which contained 725 prints and a large number of albums: 'Seriously, *you must not* miss it. . . You *must* see the Japanese. . . Come *as quickly as you can*.'[496] The first colour etching exhibited by her at the Durand-Ruel gallery the following year, *The Child's Bath*, bore the words: 'Print in imitation of the Japanese.' Also as a tribute to the Japanese she compiled an album consisting of a series of ten plates that were similar in format, subject matter, technique and style. The Japanese had nothing to teach her, in fact, so meticulous was her handling of the plates. She combined the techniques then in use for colour printing: plates superimposed, bearing different colours, and hand colouring, using the 'dolly' or dabber, the little wad of gauze with which touches of coloured ink are placed on the copper plate before each printing. She would first transfer a drawing on to two or three different plates using the soft ground technique. A first very light etching would outline the motif. Each plate would then be covered with a very fine aquatint, the resin being dispersed over the surface by the action of the aquatint box, the selected areas defined by stopping-out varnish. Then acid would be applied to the plates masked in resin; the grain achieved is so fine that it seems likely that the plates were exposed for only a moment to the vapours emanating from the acid, rather than being immersed. The grainy areas of the plates, superficially etched only by the acid and finished with drypoint, are then inked and colour is added in places with the 'dolly'. The printing of the plate on a carefully marked page, then the printing of the layers of coloured inks on the same page, took more than an hour. Mary Cassatt, with the aid of Leroy, an excellent printer who trained with Cadart, could print eight to ten plates a day at home.[497]

A letter from Mary's mother[498] informs us that the album of ten coloured aquatints was prepared during the winter of 1890–1, and that the artist's sights were fixed on the third exhibition of the Société des Peintres-Graveurs which opened at Durand-Ruel on 3 April. The exclusion of foreigners from the Society that year has already been mentioned; Pissarro and Mary Cassatt had their revenge, organising a small two-person show at Durand-Ruel, running parallel to the 'patriots' show. The public were able to see for the first time the ten album plates bearing Mary Cassatt's signature and a handwritten note: 'Edition de 25 épreuves imprimées par l'artiste et par M. Leroy' (Edition of 25 proofs printed by the artist and by M. Leroy). Pissarro's comments to his son Lucien were enthusiastic enough to be worth quoting in full: 'Do you remember those experiments you did at Eragny? Well! Miss Cassatt has succeeded admirably: her colours are matt, and very delicate, without any blots or drips. Her blue is adorable, her pinks fresh, etc. What

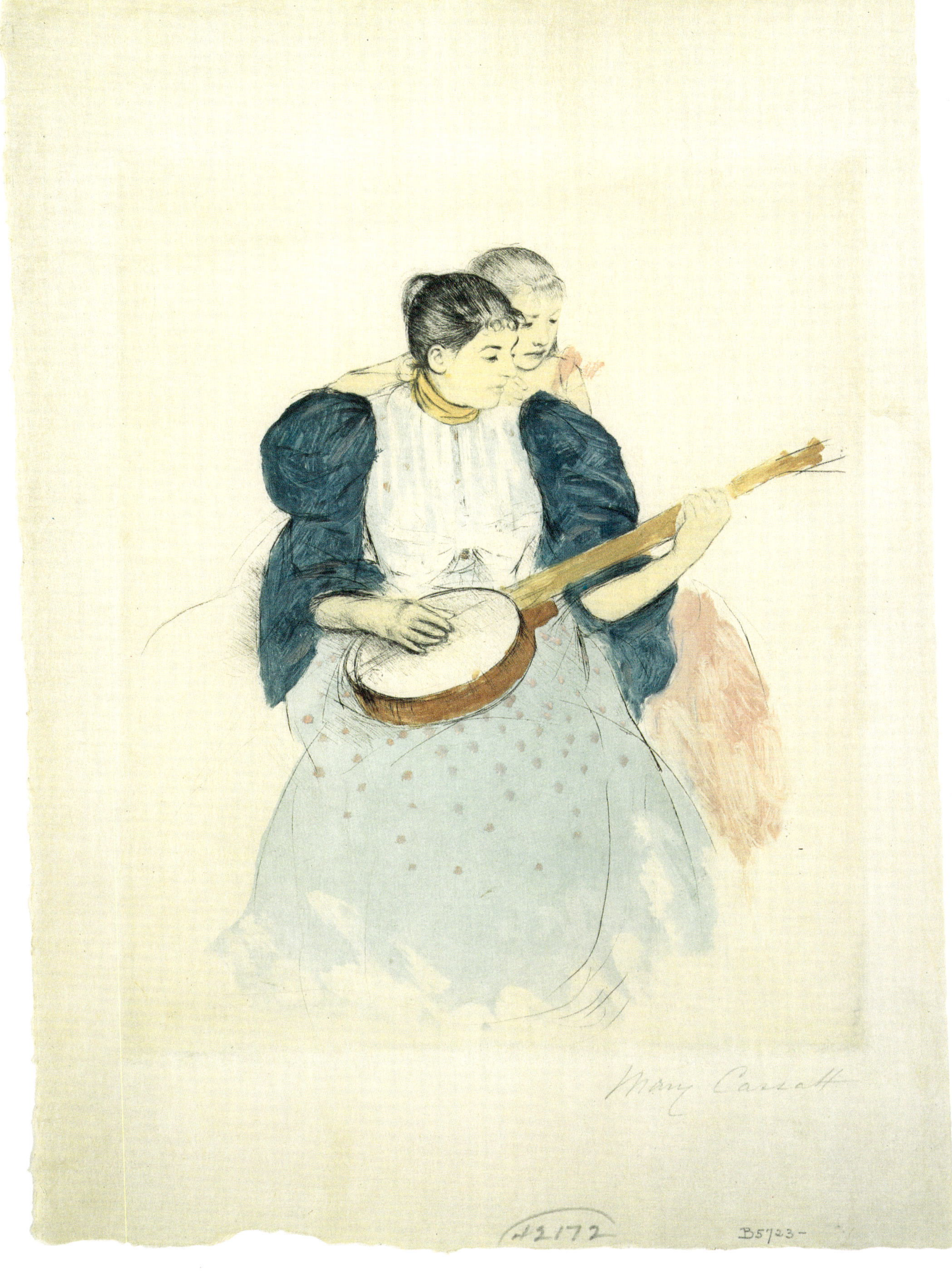
Mary Cassatt
B5723-

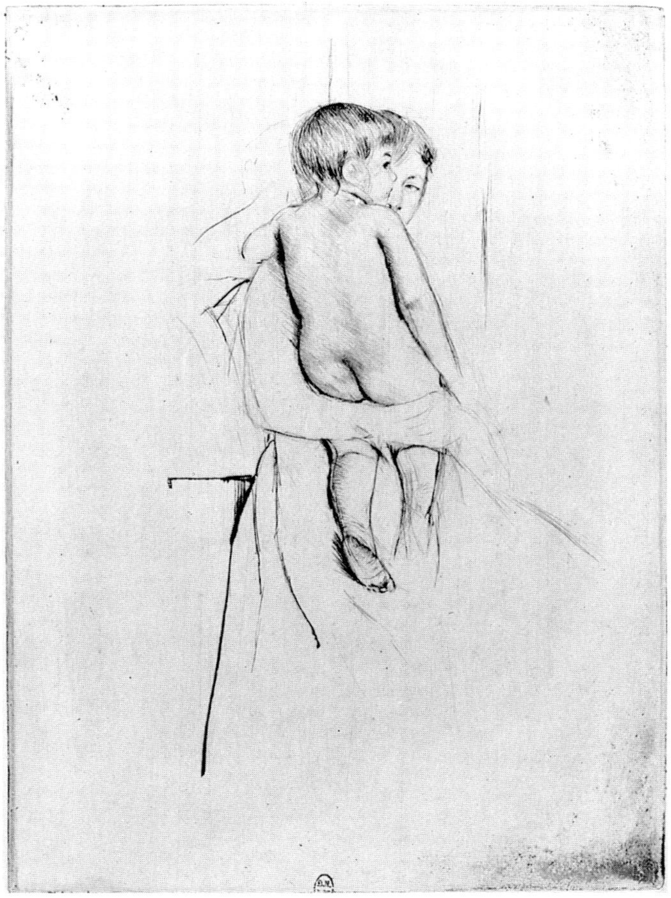

259. Mary Cassatt,
Baby's Back. 1890.
Drypoint, third state, 238 x 163 mm.
Bibliothèque nationale, Paris.

260. Mary Cassatt,
Portrait of Celeste. 1899.
Drypoint, only known proof,
275 x 390 mm.
Bibliothèque nationale, Paris.

prevented our succeeding, I wonder? Lack of money, yes, money. . . First we needed copper plates and an aquatint box – large and awkward but absolutely necessary for a smooth, uniform grain – and a good printer. But her results are admirable, just as good as the Japanese, and it's printed in colour!. . . When I have some proofs I'll send them to you. Anyway I've arranged to do a series with Mlle Cassatt, I shall do markets, women working in the fields and, wonderful idea, I could try and put in to practice some of the principles of neo-Impressionism, what do you think? If we could do really good colour etchings it would be a great plus. . . I saw some attempts at colour etchings that are supposed to be going to appear in the patriots' exhibition but they are ugly, heavy, dull and so commercial.'[499]

A few days later he visited Mary Cassatt: 'Before leaving Paris I went to see Mlle Cassatt and watched her printing her coloured aquatints. She does it just as we did except that she does not use pure colours, she mixes her tones which means that she only needs two plates. There's one drawback, the colours are not so fresh and bright – but they work and are attractive all the same.'[500] He was surprised, as was Degas, at the subtlety of the colours because he knew how heavy and sticky printer's ink was compared with the watercolours and pastels that Mary Cassatt succeeded in imitating; thanks to the delicacy of the grain and the fine texture of the etching she managed to obtain a light film of colour.

Before undertaking her series of ten plates Cassatt had practised on four colour plates that, in the light of subsequent developments, look like a trial run.[501] Once she had mastered the process, so suited to her linear style, she tried again with five plates executed in 1893–5. She was unable to achieve the coherence of her first album and they were sold separately. She produced four more prints in 1896. Durand-Ruel held another exhibition in 1893 in which she showed seventeen paintings, fourteen pastels and sixty-seven prints, some of them in several states as was the custom with the Impressionists: *The Banjo Lesson* was presented in three states, plus the final one (Figs 255–8). In April 1895 Durand-Ruel organised a big exhibition in New York for her. She returned to her home country and her prints were bought by all the important American collectors. *Under the Horse Chestnut Tree*, her last colour plate, was advertised in February 1896 and published in an album brought out by *L'Estampe Nouvelle* in October 1897.

The success of Mary Cassatt's prints was not affected by the snarls of Edmond de Goncourt at his most crotchety: 'The admiration expressed in all the newspapers for the etchings of Mlle Cassatt is enough to make one die of laughter! There may be one successful corner in one of her prints. . . hidden away in a stupid, clumsily etched drawing. Oh dear! this age makes a religion of failure, the great pontiff being Degas, the choirboy Mlle Cassatt.'[502] The reverse was true, in fact: her success was confirmed by her colour prints, even though they were aimed at

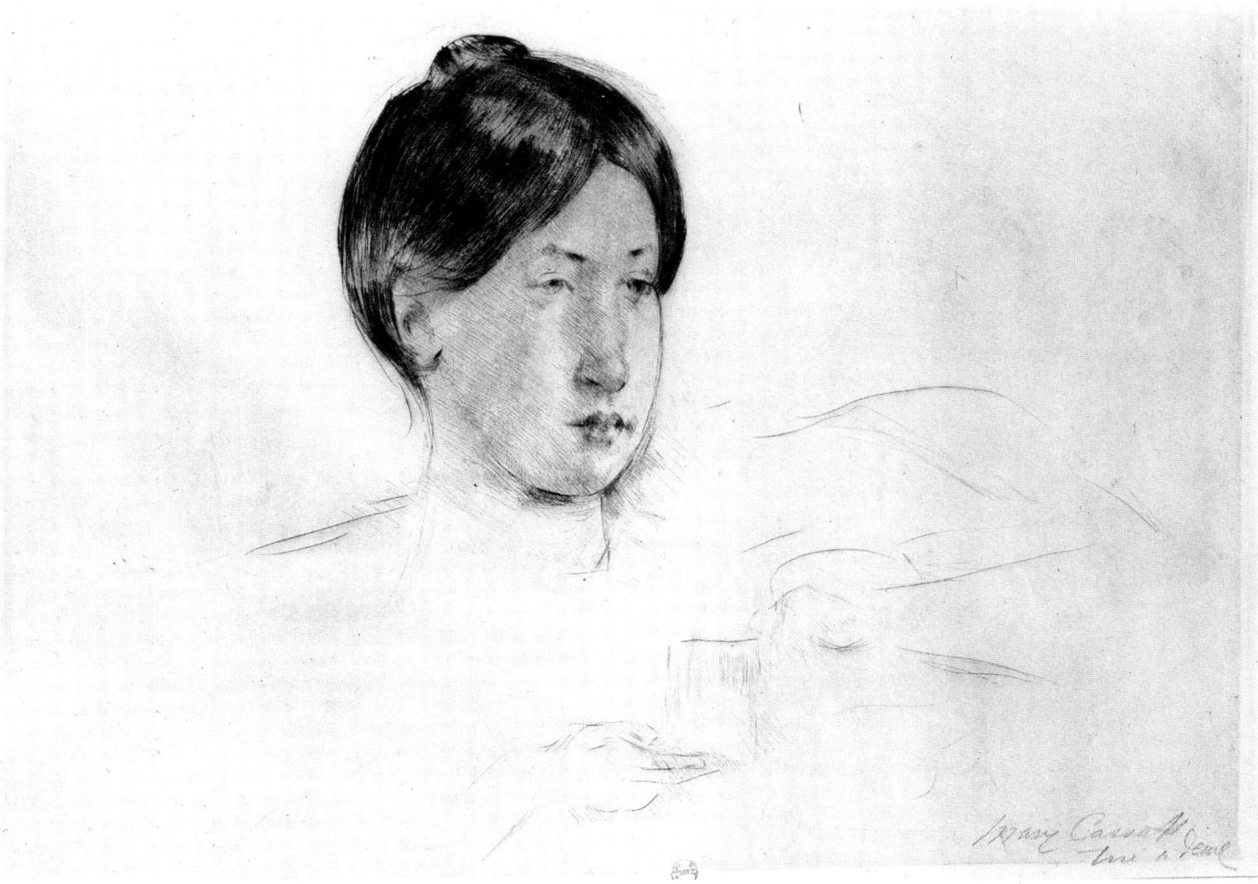

the recently established market for decorative art. Nancy Mathews states that 'Cassatt's adoption of drypoint in her prints indicates the dramatic change in attitude that had affected her paintings: she was no longer interested in the active, transitory images of the Impressionist style. She now sought a quieter, more classic art (Figs 259, 260).'[503] Admiration for Japanese art has already been cited as a popular explanation for the increasing refinement of art. Mary Cassatt's art is a good example.

Following the example of critics like Louis Gonse who promoted Japanese art as 'popular', Cassatt was mindful of the social responsibility of the printmaker. According to her friend Mrs Havemeyer she said: 'I like making colour etchings and I hope that Durand-Ruel will put mine on the market at a reasonable price because nothing, I believe, stimulates the taste for art as much as the opportunity of having it about one at home. I should like to think that American collectors can have an example of my work, a print or an etching, for a few dollars. That is what happens in France. It is not only the rich who buy works of art. Members of the public, even quite humble ones have good taste and buy what they can afford. They can always find something within their means here.'[504] This generous declaration did not prevent Cassatt producing complex and costly prints (compared with the price of pictures in the popular press), well beyond the reach of the 'poor' but accessible to a whole new middle class, who were able to collect them. For many of these purchasers colour was a stylish new attraction. Pissarro was sceptical: 'I'm sure Miss Cassatt's innovations are going to be imitated by all sorts of printmakers who will produce insipid, pretty-pretty pieces. . .'[505] The print as produced by the Painter-Printmakers was first and foremost a work of art, though remaining a print; even in its most representational form its wide circulation and large public exerted strong pressures on it, stronger than the pressures exerted on the paintings of the period.

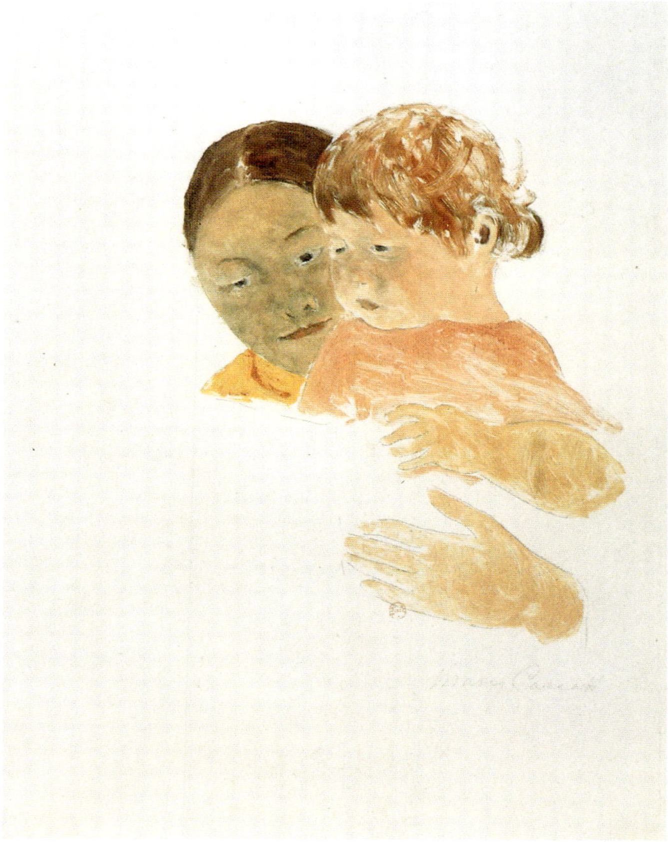

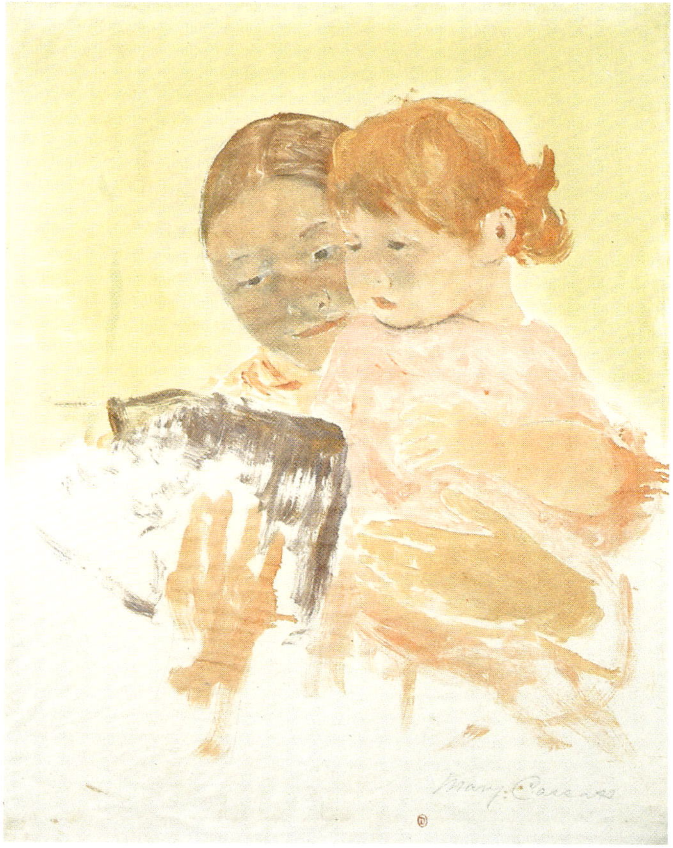

261. Mary Cassatt, *The Album*. About 1885. Monotype, 472 x 393 mm. Bibliothèque nationale, Paris.

262. Mary Cassatt, *The Album*. About 1885. Monotype, 480 x 393 mm. Bibliothèque d'Art et d'Archéologie, Paris.

49. *The Arrival of Colour*

Colour printmaking contains an inherent contradiction: while appealing to a much wider public than black and white printmaking, and while being generally easier to buy or to give as a present, or to frame and hang, it is also much more costly to reproduce. Serious collectors suspected colour printmaking of being a luxury produced to indulge popular and commercial taste. As a result, success came as late as the middle of the eighteenth century to the medium, in the West as in Japan. Colour printmaking was not revived until the last decade of the nineteenth century, thirty years after black and white etching. Once again Bracquemond deserves credit for the first attempts: his etching *In the Jardin d'Acclimatation* (Fig. 263) probably dates from 1873, although it was not exhibited until the fourth Impressionist exhibition in 1879. In lithography, although the commercial firms of Lemercier in Paris in 1837 and Hullmandel in London in 1839 introduced costly chromolithographic processes, the first printed watercolours appeared in Manet's *Polichinelle*, a page of which was exhibited at the Salon of 1874,[506] the earliest example of a colour print by an artist. Manet's print was a caricature of MacMahon and was obviously closely allied to popular political prints, but the care lavished on the colour and on the printing distinguished it as the work of an artist aimed at an educated public. Bracquemond's plates, on the other hand, are unmistakeable attempts at reviving the old colour printing techniques: several plates each carrying a basic colour and printed exactly on top of each other. These were first produced between 1730 and 1760 in response to the demands of a clientèle who regarded a print as a domestic decorative item, a substitute for a painting.

Colour printmaking, however, took time to find a public. It was too expensive to appeal to the less wealthy and too popular to appeal to collectors, except when the subject was a political or an exotic one. Everyone confused colour printmaking with hand-coloured prints, rapidly coloured in with primary colours by a workforce of women or under-paid children, punched out in series, often a cut-out design or a stencil. The charms of these popular prints had been sung by Champfleury and the realist critics; they were rehabilitated once more by the Saint-Simonians and used by Courbet, but they only appeared on the art market as objects of curiosity or folk art. Another handicap to the acceptance of the colour

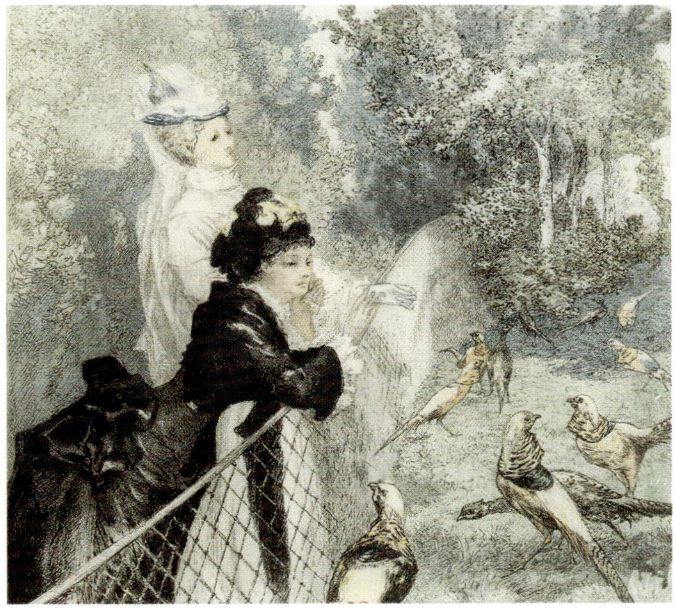

263. Félix Bracquemond,
In the Jardin d'Acclimatation. 1873.
Colour etching and aquatint, 187 x 200 mm.
Bibliothèque nationale, Paris.

print was the poster, which had invaded the larger cities to such an extent that local councils had been authorised by the department controlling the freedom of the press to limit bill-posting to certain designated walls. Jules Chéret produced his first poster in colours for Offenbach's operetta *Orpheus in the Underworld* in 1858. After a spell in England he returned to work in France in 1869. This period saw the beginning of the fashion for coloured posters, whose increasing sophistication continued nevertheless to bear the ignominious stigma of the circus poster (in the eyes of the educated public), or of advertisements for a 'good pint of beer'.

Industrial colour printing processes preceded the use of colour in printmaking, as might have been expected. Following the work done on colour photography by Ducos du Hauron and Charles Cros, the techniques of photomechanical printing were mastered and the first applications to be seen in the Christmas number of *L'Illustration* in 1881, in Ernest Hoschedé's small volume entitled *Impression de mon voyage au Salon en 1882*; it was used by Charles Cros for his reproduction of Manet's painting *Jeanne*, and for a luxurious edition of *L'Histoire des quatre fils Aymon*, illustrated by Eugène Grasset.[507] After 1882, when the victorious Republic was trying (through Daumier and Manet) to establish an aesthetic and its own range of symbols, the colour poster had its defenders and even its collectors and dealers, like Sagot, but it had its critics too. Ernest Maindron published a book on *Les Affiches illustrées* in 1886, illustrated with chromolithographs by Chéret, and was responsible for a large exhibition of posters at the Exposition Universelle in 1889. Chéret thus gained recognition as an artist and the poster as a work of art: the same year he held his first one man show of paintings, pastels and posters.

Once the relationship between popular taste and the refinement sought by the educated classes had been established there was no further reason why colour printing should not develop as an art form. The first success was achieved by the artists who had been involved in the decorative arts movement in the 1880s; they were a generation younger than the Impressionists. After Bracquemond, it was to the talent of Henri Guérard that tribute should paid: the two of them were leaders of the painter-printmakers and both were practising printmakers who could guide painters in the direction of printmaking. Guérard's small colour print, *In the Cornfield*, dated by Claudie Bertin to 1888,[508] reproduced Impressionist colour values although it is etched; the inks are lightly applied and the colours bright; the superimposition of the plates gives vitality to the atmosphere rather than deadening it. Raffaelli produced his first colour etchings in 1889 and a series of six of his plates was published by Boussod and Valodon in 1893. Henri Rivière (at the same time as Lepère) imitated Japanese colour woodcuts in a series of *Views of the Eiffel Tower*, pursuing a career as a watercolourist, pastellist and colour lithographer.[509] In 1891, Charles Maurin sought copyright on his technique of printing with oil paints.[510] Like the poster, colour became a craze in the 1890s. The pioneers of colour printmaking were not the painters – they were not interested in it because opaque printing inks have none of the qualities of oil paint, and even less of gouache or watercolour. The technique of superimposing colours one on top of the other requires the breaking down of a colour scheme into three or four primary colours and the division of these over three or four different plates; to a painter this contradicts his normal practice and can often have disappointing results. Mary Cassatt was the first painter to approach printmaking in painterly fashion and to seek comparable effects. She modelled herself on two excellent examples: Japanese woodcuts and the pastels of Degas, both of which she admired intensely. Degas himself never tried making colour prints (except as transfer prints). He used coloured inks (though in the manner of a monochrome) when printing his friend Pissarro's aquatint *Sunset with Haystacks*; Pissarro wrote 'imprimée par Degas' on some of the proofs.[511]

Pissarro was attracted by colour prints, as he was drawn to decorative and popular art, but he only dared practise them through the intermediary of his son. He realised at once that the deconstruction of a colour scheme offered opportunities to an Impressionist, to apply rigorously the theories of the colourists. After Mary Cassatt's first exhibition he wrote to Lucien: 'I could try and put some of the principles of neo-Impressionism into practice.'[512] He bought a press in 1894 and at once began experimenting with colour printing.[513] In May 1894 Mary Cassatt encouraged him to make some coloured etchings for an exhibition in New York, and a spell of bad weather did the rest: 'The weather is terrible here, cold and windy, impossible to work out of doors, so I've started work on colour etching. I'm waiting for my plates from Miss Cassatt, two weeks to make the guide holes, I would have finished the etching already if I'd had the plates. I'll do it with emery paper, I don't want to do it in the same way as Miss Cassatt, I shall just touch up the highlights; I've begun a Market.'[514] Pissarro produced five colour etchings: *Women Begging*, *The Market at Gisors* (Figs 267–9), *Peasant Women Gathering Grass* (Figs 214–18), *Goosegirls Bathing* (Figs 295–7), *Church and Farm at Eragny* from a painting dated 1895. Work on the etchings lasted until that date apparently: on 18 January 1895 he wrote: 'The steel plater has returned my plates and I shall soon be able to send you a charming proof of my peasant girls making hay and a market, in black and white heightened with colour. I think nice things can be done in this way. . . It is not like Miss Cassatt's work at all, it's just coloured in. . . I've got some good prints already, but it's difficult to find exactly the right colours'.[515] He only made a few prints, exhibiting them successfully at Vollard in June 1896.

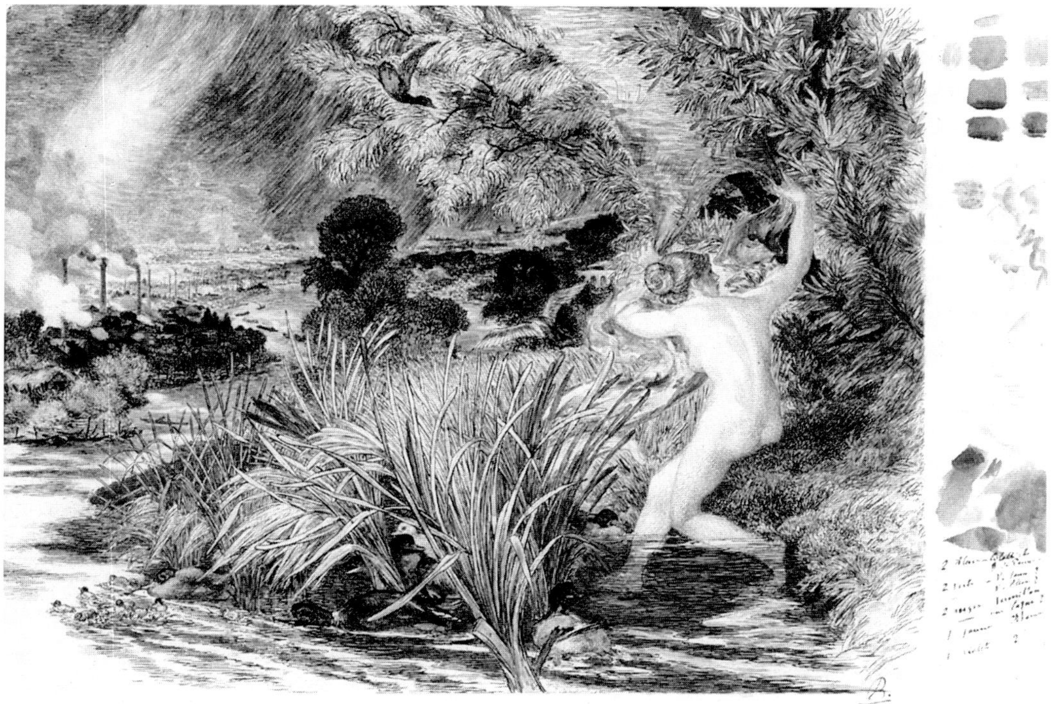

264. Félix Bracquemond, *The Rainbow*. 1893–7. Etching in black and white with watercolour, 410 x 540 mm. The State University of New Jersey, Rutgers, Zimmerli Art Museum, Friends Purchase Fund.

In his desire to be different from 'Miss Cassatt' Pissarro worked with the dabber (or 'dolly') more than she did and as a result treated some of his plates like monotypes (*Women Begging*, second state). The main difference between his work and that of Mary Cassatt (she favoured flat, even patches of colour) was his search for a blending of colours produced by the superimposition of the plates; thanks to his three-colour or four-colour etching he achieved a kind of pointillism. In the same letter written in 1895[516] he announced to his son that he was 'continuing work in the fields', referring to the drawings that were to be etched and colour printed by Lucien. These plates show the pointillist effect to the full, and come close to the four-colour effects achieved mechanically by silk-screen in the printing of colour photographs, a common procedure after 1896. In 1898 Pissarro agreed to make a coloured lithograph for his anarchist friend on *Les Temps Nouveau,*[517] instead of for Vollard who was requesting it. His lithograph *Labour or the Plough*, published by Jean Gave on the cover of a booklet by Kropotkin, was a return to campaigning lithography, in colour, in the same vein (and the same bright colours) as Manet's *Polichinelle*.

The meagre number, the lateness and relative unimportance of the colour prints produced by a movement generally defined by its use of colour may come as a surprise. The definition needs evaluating. Impressionist drawing and printmaking, whose formal characteristics are described in this book, does not have colour as a criterion. Experiments with colour were aimed at producing a new kind of object rather than any particular style. Bracquemond, whose last work bears no relation to Impressionism, never ceased to experiment. He had the last as well as the first word. Edmond de Goncourt reports that, on 10 January 1894: 'Bracquemond brought me an etching he has just finished, a cock done in flourishes rather like a Japanese cock, very stylish. He told me about a colour plate he is trying to make, a copy of one of his etchings; he wants to do it in twelve colours, with grains that are evenly coloured, making smooth areas of tone. He says that this kind of work is effective only if it is expensive, and that no corners should be cut. The colours only work if the dark and light shades of each colour are used, and he adds that the appreciation of colour is a new sensation for Western eyes, one that has not yet been analysed.'[518]

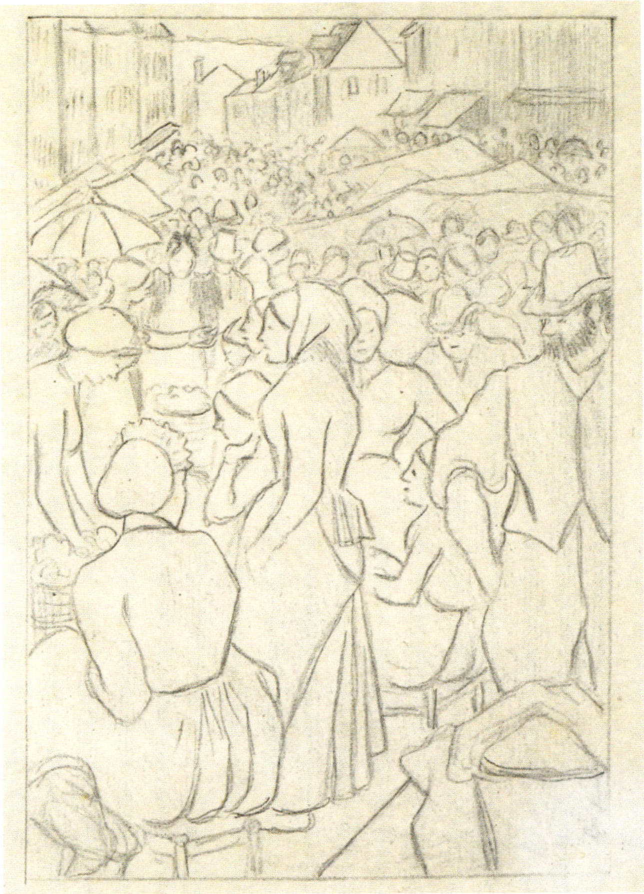
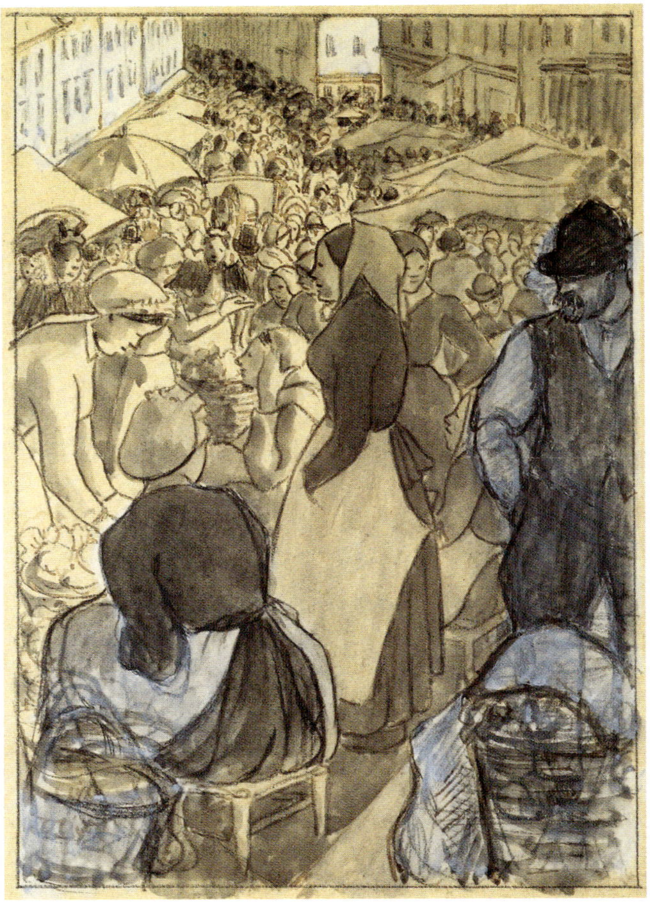
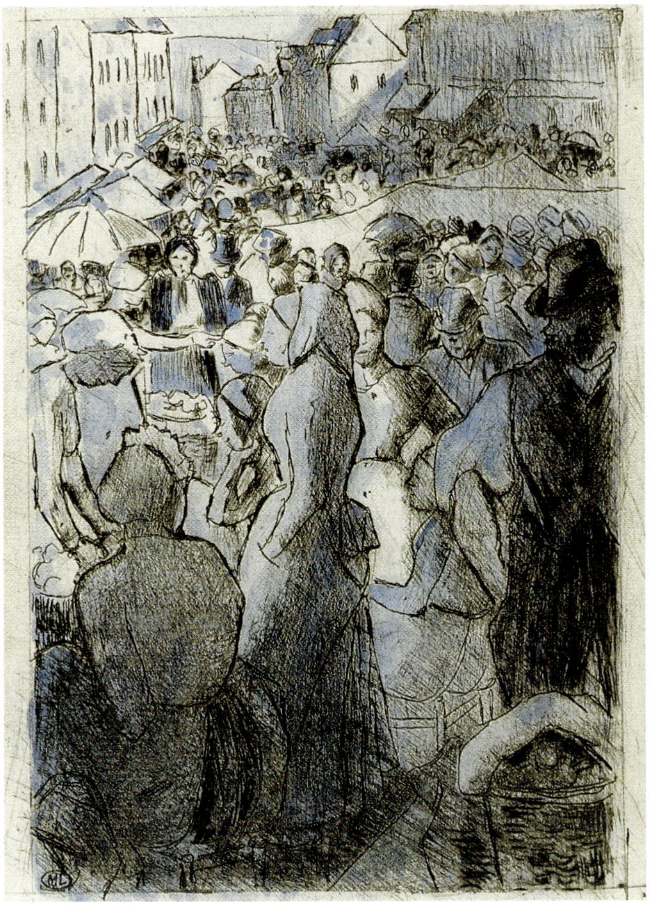
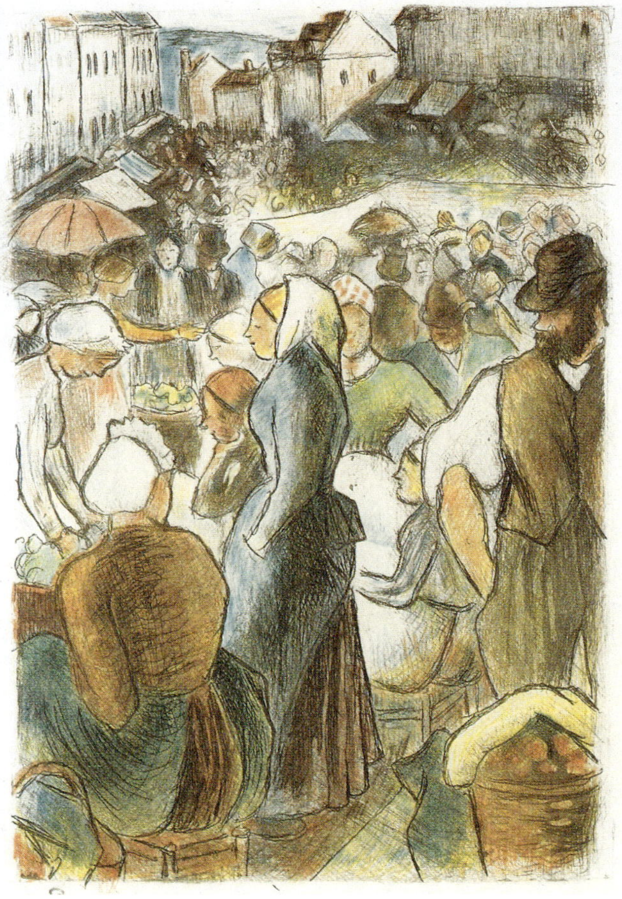

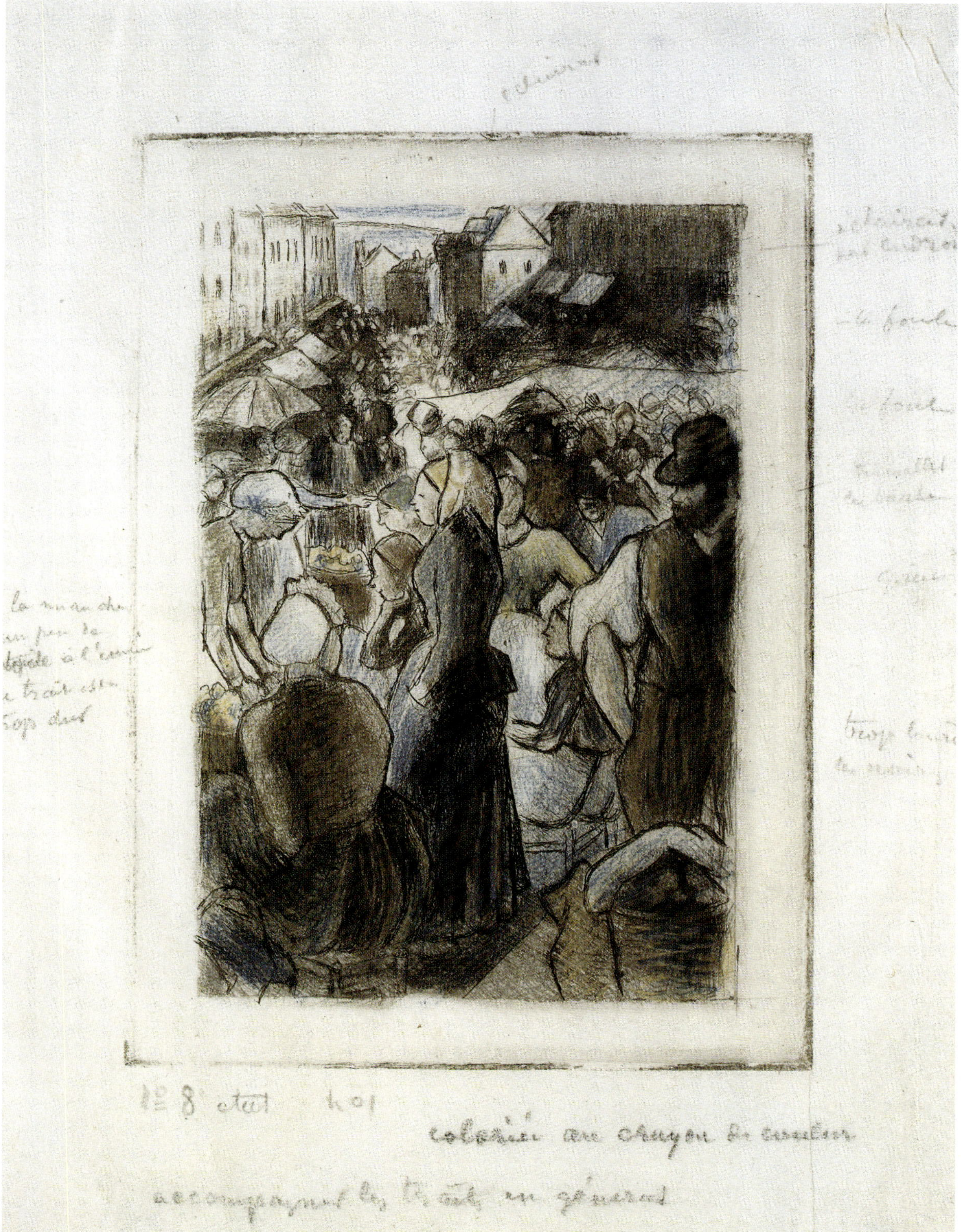

265, 266, 267, 268. Camille Pissaro,
Market at Gisors, Rue Cappeville. 1894–5.
Pencil drawing, pen and ink drawing, 170 x 110 mm.
Ashmolean Museum, Oxford. Etching touched up,
Musée du Louvre, Paris, Département des Arts
Graphiques. Etching printed in colour.
Bibliothèque nationale, Paris.

269. Camille Pissarro,
Market at Gisors, Rue Cappeville. 1894–5.
Etching and coloured pencils, 170 x 110 mm.
Ashmolean Museum, Oxford.

50. *The Monotypes of Degas*

The monotype technique is simple but its results unpredictable, two attributes that might tax the patience of an artist with perfectionist leanings. Series of monotypes are rare, in fact, and experiments generally short-lived. Degas was the only artist to use monotype creatively, re-working his monotype backgrounds in pastel.[519] About 450 monotypes by this steadfast producer survive, about eighty of them re-worked in pastel; the low proportion of re-worked monotypes should not be taken to indicate that Degas regarded the technique as a goal in itself. Long series such as the one illustrating the first stories about *La Famille Cardinal*, by his friend Ludovic Halévy, and the brothel series, were produced in the hope of printing illustrations by some ill-defined process of transfer lithography or heliography done with greasy ink, the ink being spread over a transparent sheet of celluloid.[520] Dozens of abandoned monotypes appeared among Degas's effects when his studio was sold in 1918; these were either unfinished sketches put to one side until the final pastel treatment was applied, or they were rejects (Fig. 273). It is said that René de Gas, the painter's brother, threw away about seventy monotypes while sorting through his brother's papers, considering them (perhaps rightly) to be just smudges of ink.[521]

Degas worked at his monotypes with his friend Lepic, who was engaged at the time in preparing his collection for *L'Eau-forte mobile*, published in 1876. One of the monotypes, which may be Degas' first, on the same subject as his painting *The Ballet Master* is signed with both their names (Figs 271–2).[522] Degas made a great many black and white monotypes between 1876 and 1880 (Fig. 270). His series of brothel scenes is made more mysterious by the fact that he never tackled the subject in any other medium. His more 'respectable' series, the *Dancers* and the *Café-concert Singers* were carefully worked over in pastel. They were probably among the 'articles' produced by Degas to earn a living when he was facing bankruptcy. The rich effect produced by the pigments laid one on top of the other, printer's ink with solid pastel on top, the matt texture of the ink being set off by the sparkle of the pastel, make these the most sophisticated and perhaps the most representative examples of the Impressionism of Degas. Eugenia Parry Janis shows perceptively how they resolve the contradiction between line and colour, treating light separately from drawing; Degas was continually torn between his profound classicism and a strong desire to be modern, and the handling of light was one of his obsessions. He only used pastel on monotypes in black ink.[523]

The marriage of colour and the monotype was consummated by Degas in the autumn of 1890, during a trip well-known to us through the letters he sent to Halévy and the description of it by his host, the painter Georges Jeanniot, in whose large house in Burgundy, at Diénay, Degas stayed. Degas and his friend Bartholomé, the sculptor, left Paris like two students on vacation in a tilbury drawn by a white horse. During the journey they ate well and enjoyed the autumn tints. When he got to Diénay Degas discovered an etching press and all the equipment for printmaking in Jeanniot's studio.

'"Good!", he cried, "we shall be able to work in your 'Swiss watchmaker's' studio, you've got paper, ink, a printer's brush with your initials on it! Dammit! This is serious stuff. Here's a really well-maintained dabber. Let's start. . . Have you got an overall?"

'. . . I put the apron on him. He had taken off his jacket and rolled up his shirt sleeves.

'"Have you any copper or zinc plates?. . . That's just the job. I'd like a piece of cloth to make a dabber for my own use. I've been wanting to make a series of monotypes for such a long time!. . ."

'As soon as everything was assembled, without stopping to look round, he started work. Bartholomé was astounded to see him drawing landscapes as if they were still before his eyes:

'"And mark you," he said, "he did not stop once to inspect them at greater length!"

'. . . Gradually we saw a valley appearing on the metal surface, then the sky, some white houses, some fruit trees with dark branches, some birches and oaks, ruts on the ground filled with water from a recent shower, orangey clouds crossing a stormy sky above the red and green earth. . . Bartholomé recognised scenery that they had passed in their tilbury, at the pace of the trotting white horse.

'After half an hour, no more, Degas suggested: "If you like, we'll print this. Is the paper damp? Have you got the sponge?. . ." When the plate had been printed the proof was hung on a line to dry. We made two or three each morning. Then he asked for pastels to finish the monotypes.'[524]

This charming story is informative, even though does not tell us exactly which of his colour monotypes Degas executed while at Diénay. He must have produced other landscapes during other journeys. In fact he mentions other monotypes to Halévy after the summer of 1892: 'I stayed by the door of the wagon and looked vaguely around. It gave me an idea for some landscapes. . .

'"What?" replied Halévy, "something very vague?"

'"Perhaps".

'"States of the soul? Amiel has said "A landscape is a state of the soul. Do you like the word?"

'"State of the eyes. We do not use such pretentious language."'[525]

About twenty of these landscapes were exhibited at Durand-Ruel in 1892 and 1894.[526] Degas was so fearful of publicity that the exhibition was almost held in secret. Nevertheless the critics' descriptions have made it possible to identify one or two of the landscapes on show from among the known pastel-on-monotypes surviving (Fig. 273). Arsène Alexandre defines them as 'recollections of feelings about nature' rather than 'landscapes', and gives the formula: 'watercolour handled and brushed like oil paint, then mixed with gouache, reworked and highlighted with pastel; sometimes buffed and rubbed with a cloth or with the tips of the fingers – as a child daubs for fun.'[527]

The difference between Jeanniot's view of the monotype and the view expressed by Degas is crucial. Jeanniot is talking about representational works, although this is gainsaid by the monotypes themselves, particularly those that survive without having been highlighted with pastel; in these it is frequently difficult to see any resemblance to a landscape. Degas's words, on the other hand, could stand as one of the earliest descriptions of abstract art foreshadowing those other 'states of eyes', Monet's series of *Nymphéas*. Degas monotypes mark a conclusive step towards pure abstraction. We do not know, however, the extent to which Degas regarded these early, uncoloured versions of his monotypes as finished works; do we, brought up on abstraction, mentally complete them and appreciate them from a twentieth-century view point? A number of black and white monotypes were regarded as finished works by Degas, who signed them and presented them to his friends. The colour monotypes which remained among his papers only gained their reputation in the 1950s:[528] it was art historians and critics then who heaped retrospective (and almost prophetic) value upon them.

The black and white monotypes of Degas have often been compared with the heavily-inked prints of the School of Rembrandt, or to the monotypes of Castiglione.[529] His colour monotypes could also be compared with the strange prints (in coloured inks) of Hercules Seghers, who also flourished in the 1630s. These were admired in the twentieth century as the works of a visionary, but we know in fact that they were unsuccessful attempts at 'printing coloured paintings',

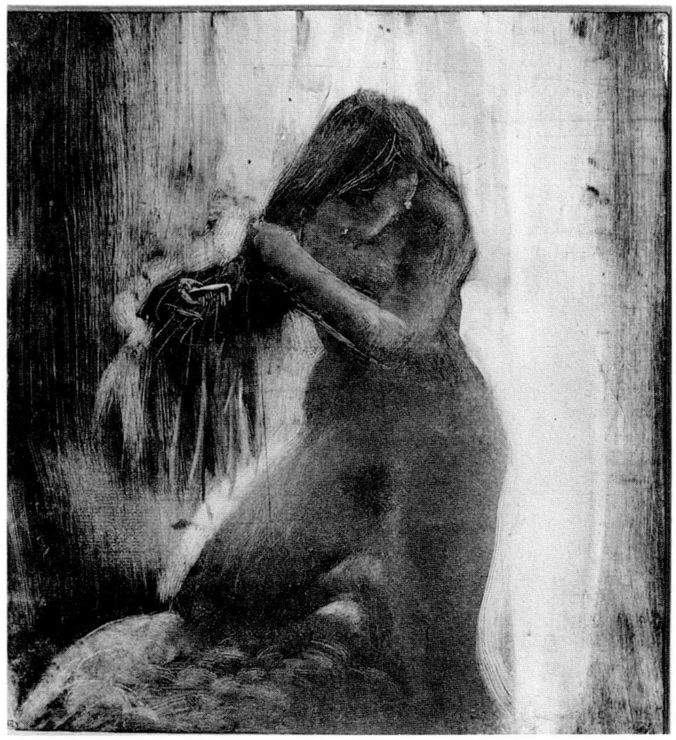

270. Edgar Degas,
Woman Brushing her Hair (The Head of Hair). 1880–5.
Monotype, 313 x 279 mm.
Musée du Louvre, Paris, Département des Arts Graphiques.

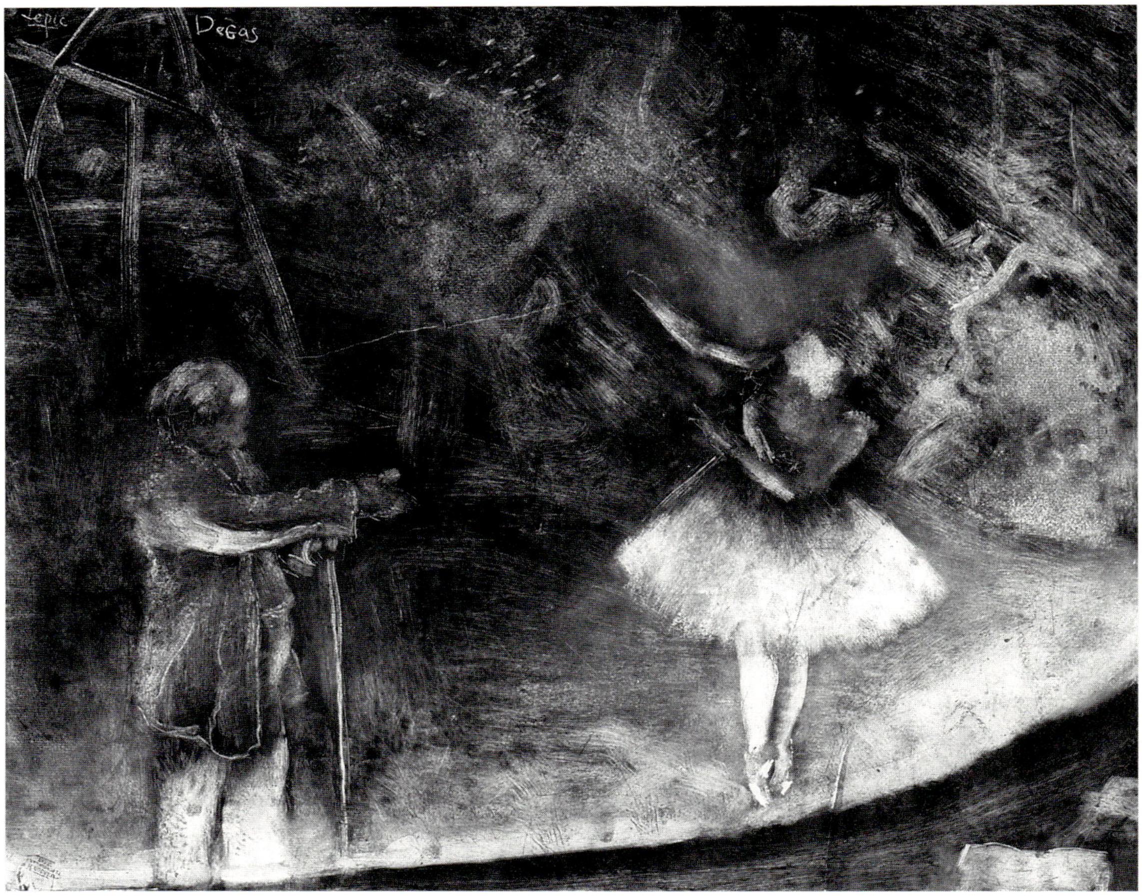
Lepic
Degas

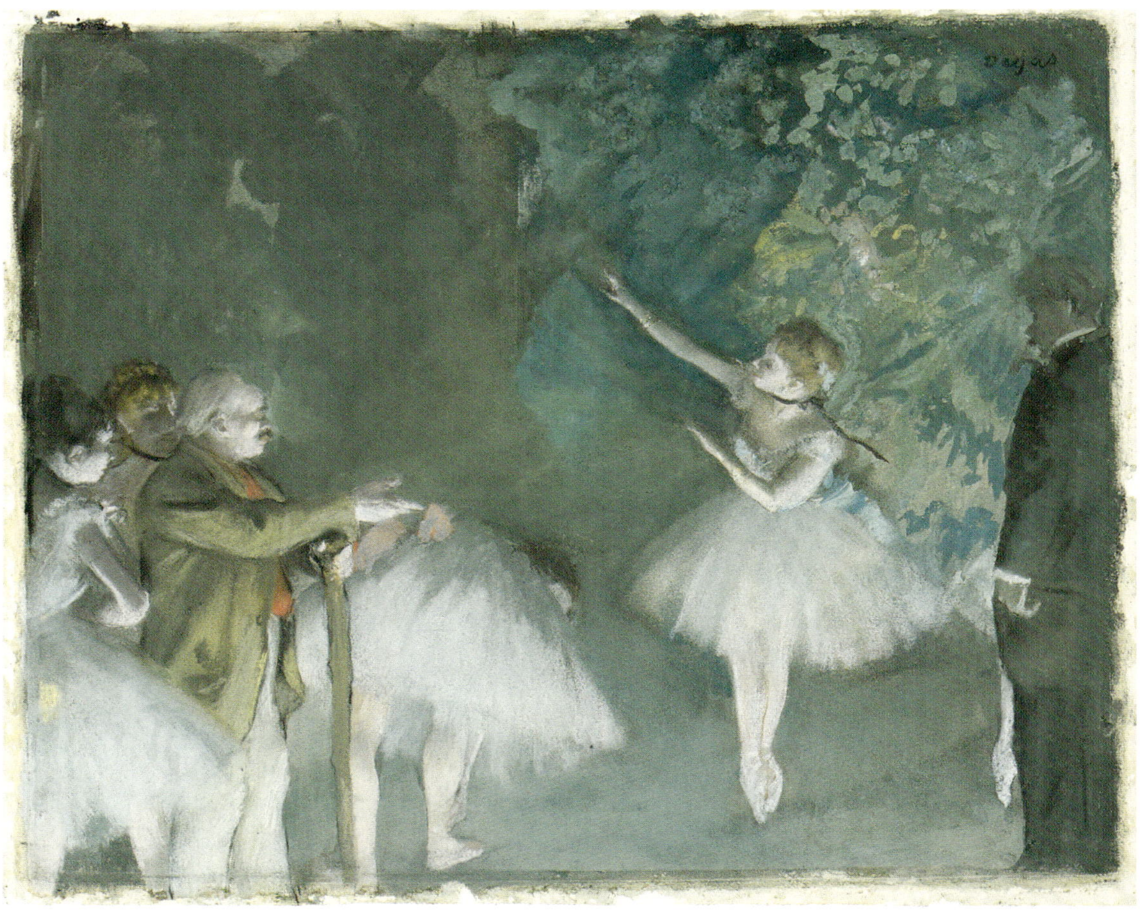
Degas

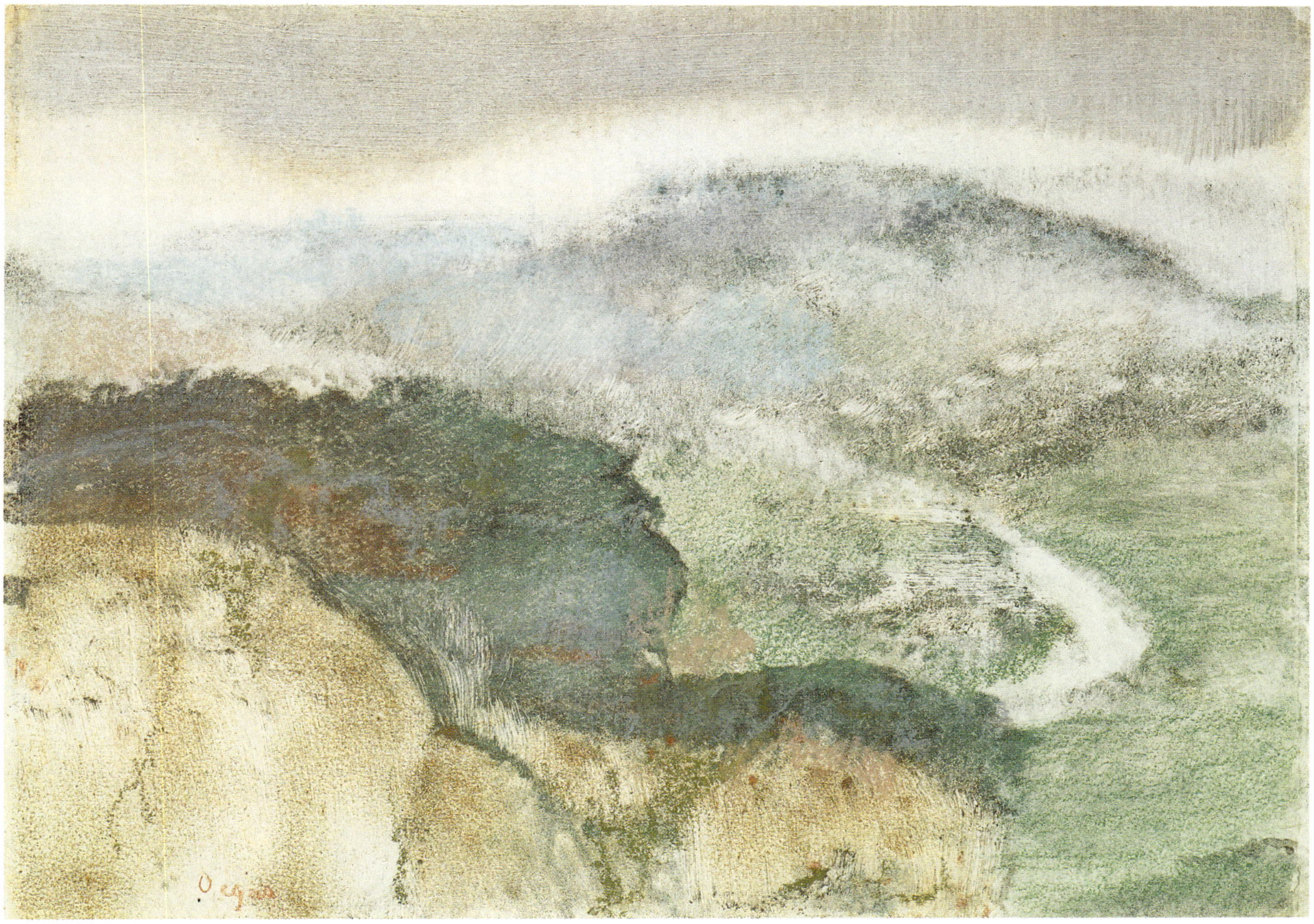

and were probably regarded as failures by Seghers himself, judging by the very few copies that survive.[530] There are two ways of seeing these monotypes: Degas probably regarded them simply as preparatory backgrounds for his pastels but we, fifty years on, see them as masterpieces in their own right. The relationship between these two ways of seeing is beyond the control of both the artist and the spectator.

273. Edgar Degas,
Landscape. About 1890–3.
Monotype touched up with pastel and oil. Metropolitan Museum of Art, New York, donation of Mr and Mrs Richard J. Bernhard.

271, 272. Edgar Degas,
The Ballet Master. About 1874.
Monotype, 560 x 700 mm. National Gallery of Art, Washington, Rosenwald Collection. Proof touched up with gouache and pastel, Nelson-Atkins Museum of Art, Kansas City.

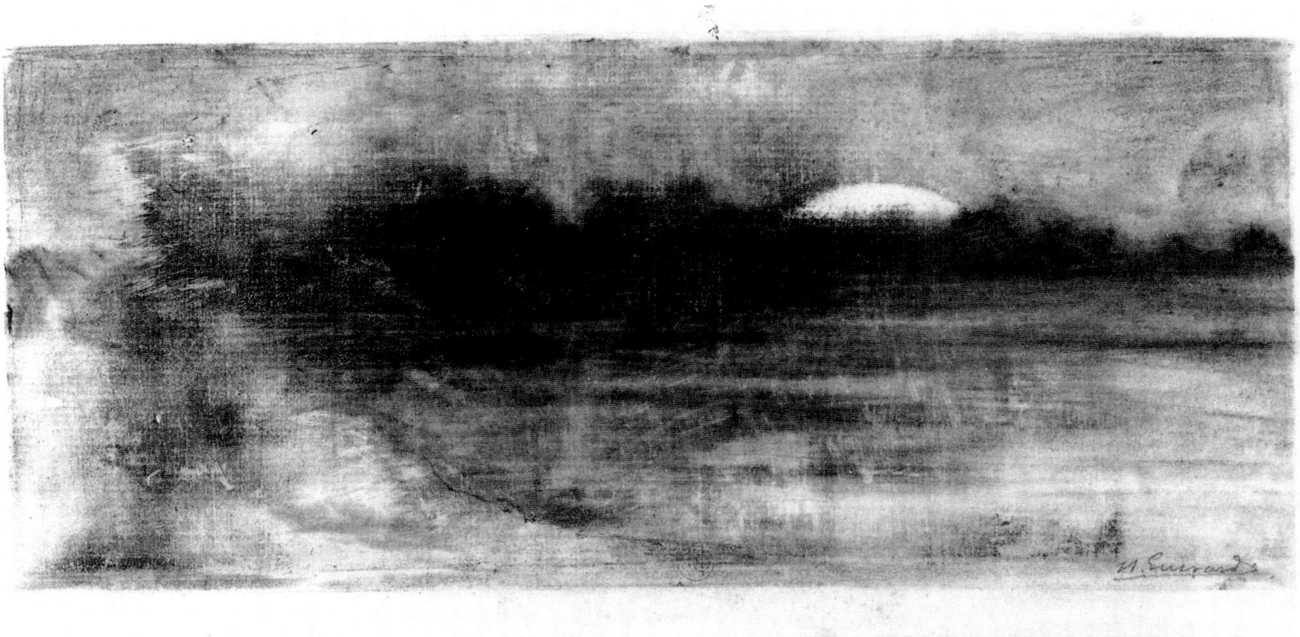

51. *Other Monotype Artists: Pissarro and Gauguin*

274. Henri Guerard,
Setting sun. Undated.
Monotype, 113 x 252 mm.
Bibliothèque nationale, Paris.

275. Camille Pissarro,
Naked Peasant Women in the Grass. About 1895.
Monotype, 128 x 179 mm.
California Palace of the Legion of Honour, San Francisco,
Achenbach Foundation for Graphic Arts.

276. Edgar Degas,
Two Women. About 1879.
Monotype, 214 x 283 mm.
Museum of Fine Arts, Boston, Katherine Bullard Fund.

The monotype print was a natural sequel to the inking techniques developed by the Impressionist printmakers and was practised by many artists almost unintentionally: Mary Cassatt in *The Banjo Lesson* (Fig. 258)[532] and Camille Pissarro in a second state of his *Women Begging*[533] produced monotype proofs, prints in which the ink overflows and establishes its own outlines. Manet, Charles Jacque and Paul Huet had already experimented with the technique. Whistler used it systematically, and making monotype prints had become something of a game in the community of American artists gathered around Whistler's close friend Frank Duveneck, with quantifiable long-term effects on American art. Delâtre's technique was based almost entirely on an over-generous application of ink which, when carefully managed by the printer, produced unique results. He declared himself a 'printer-artist', producing as evidence some small monotypes, *Effects of Moonlight*, evidently late works.[534] It is difficult to date Henri Guérard's monotypes, the *Sunset* (Fig. 274) and *Interior in the Auvergne*, unearthed in his studio.[535] These experiments with ink, usually unsaleable and not belonging to any category, were generally not followed up. Most printmakers were tempted to try monotypes at some stage; Bracquemond, who was eager to try every

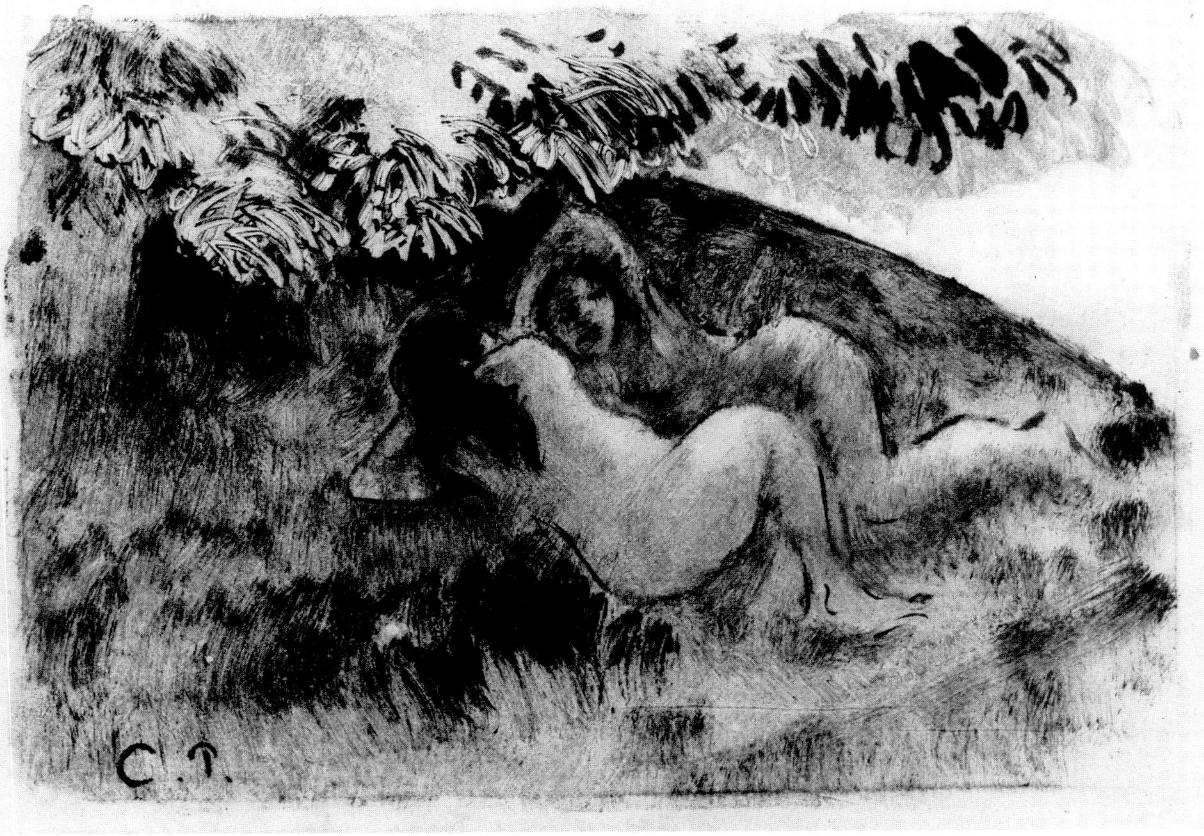

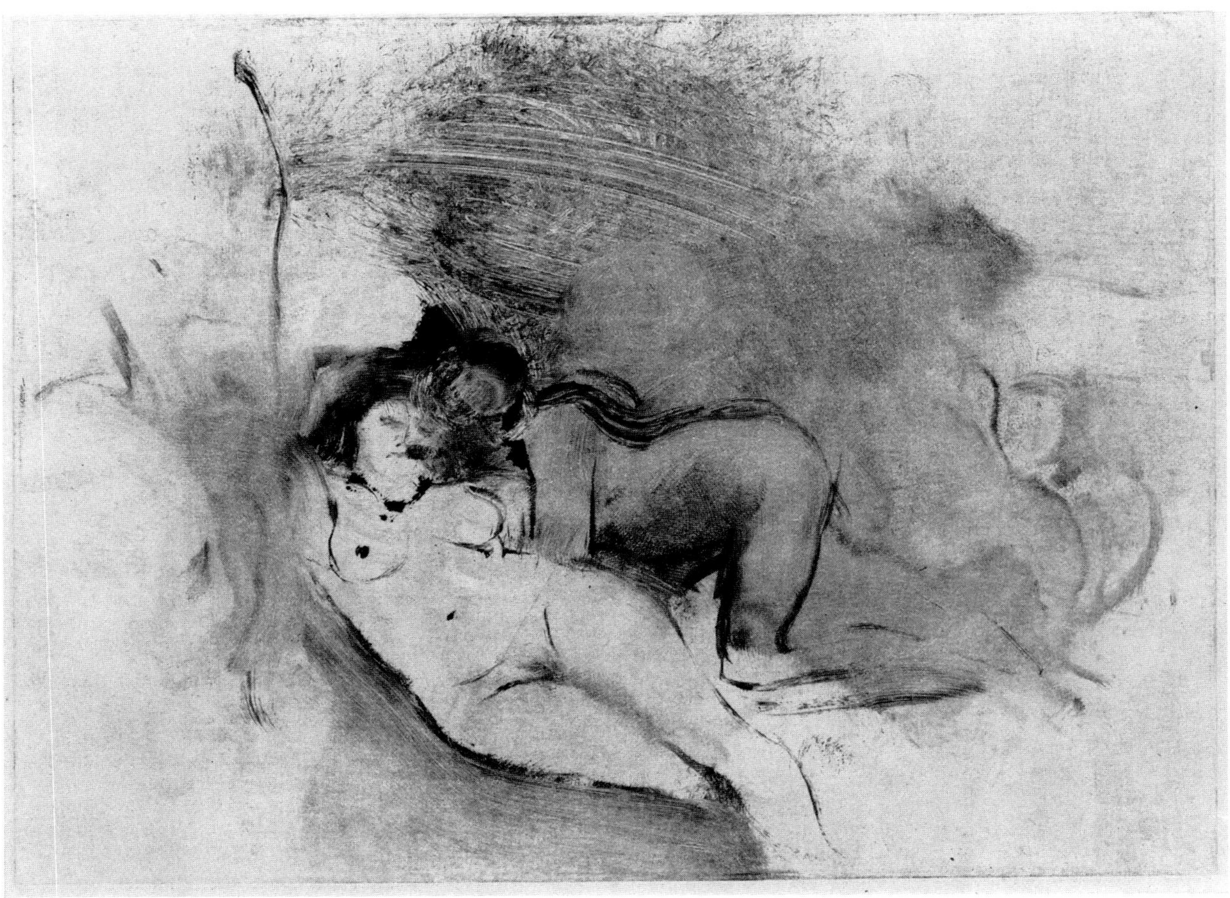

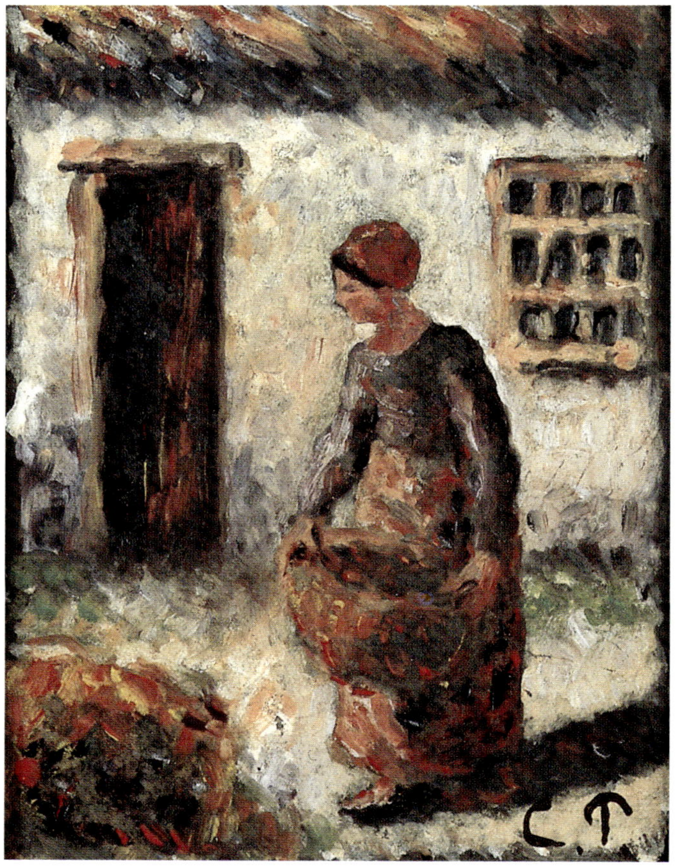

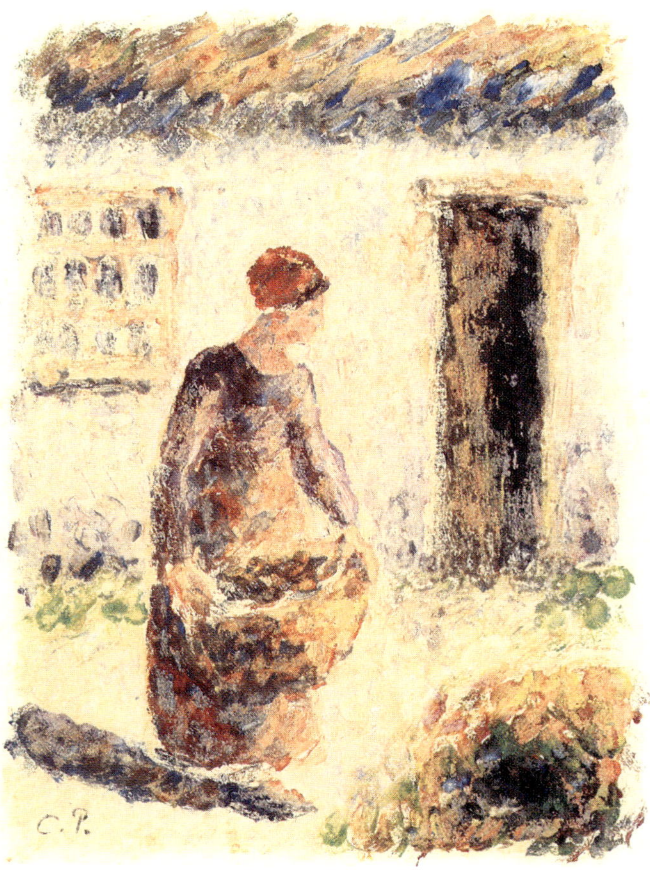

new experience, left only one monotype, a late piece (1906) depicting a *Woman in a Pink Dress* half lying on a sofa.[536] We know of two monotypes by Toulouse-Lautrec; one by Buhot, an illustration to Barbey d'Aurevilly's *Une vieille maîtresse* (about 1884);[537] others by Forain, Louis Legrand, Steinlen and, later, Picasso and other painter-engravers, particularly the Americans. In the case of the Americans theirs were almost without exception one-off pieces.

Pissarro and Gauguin were more systematic in their approach. Although experimenting at exactly the same time, there was apparently no contact between the two. The confusion between printmaking and painting reached a climax here: the plates bear no engraved lines, printer's ink is replaced by paint – watercolour, gouache or oil-paint – and, in Gauguin's case, the celluloid or metal plate is replaced by paper. The taking of an Impression is the only feature of the printing process that remains, but it is a fundamental feature (and gives the process its name). Pissarro's monotypes have never been formally inventoried.[538] About twenty of them are known and, thanks to his correspondence, we know of the circumstances in which they were made. During the winter of 1894, when the printing press he had bought from Delâtre arrived and he was waiting impatiently for the printer's ink to be delivered, he wrote on 3 January: 'I'm waiting for the ink to start printing. We've tried with oil paints, it's going to be marvellous. I'm getting a taste for it.'[539] He may also be referring to monotypes in a letter of 8 April 1895: 'I've made some amusing prints from plates and I've decided to do a series on zinc (it's more convenient). I shall do them in two or three colours with a few embellishments – nothing really! – it will be fun. What a pity nobody wants my prints. To me they are just as interesting as the painting everyone is doing. . .'[540]

Pissarro's monotypes are finished works of art, usually in black and white, occasionally in colour, using the same themes that he was using in his etchings (bathers on wooded river banks) or had used before (landscapes, markets, a woman picking cabbages). They convey a sense of returning to a less sophisticated, more natural era when art was in its infancy. Because the mnotype is without market value, it combines simplicity with extreme sophistication: paradoxically, the most elementary reproductive technique produces a work that cannot itself be reproduced. One of Pissarro's monotypes, *Peasant Women Lying Naked in the Grass* (Fig. 275) bears a striking resemblance both to Degas's brothel scenes and to Gauguin's prints on the same theme: the composition and exaggerated curves are very similar, as are the exotic female figures. The most unusual of Pissarro's monotypes is the reverse print of a painting in gouache done on a small zinc plate, *Woman carrying a Large Wicker Basket* printed on to a piece of paper and then touched up with gouache (Figs 277–8).[541] This pair of symmetrical pictures, the painting on zinc and the touched-up print, with the subject facing in different directions, are the final manifestations of the Impressionist print.

Gauguin's many monotypes, produced at more or less the same time, display the same calculated combination of simplicity and sophistication. His first series dates from a little earlier than Pissarro's first attempts. At the beginning of 1894 he made about thirty watercolours transferred to paper, applied to the paint when it was still wet; these were produced during the unhappy period he spent in France after his first trip to Tahiti.[542] He used subjects from Tahiti and from Brittany, two places strikingly similar in their primitivism. The watercolour paint, made even paler by being transferred on to other paper, distinguishes these duplicated prints from anything else produced to date. They do not belong in the traditional domain of the print, nor do the exotic iconography and deliberately unrealistic style fit the usual criteria of the Impressionist aesthetic. Were Pissarro and Gauguin, who had been friends, now, when their output was so similar, showing distrust and a growing failure to understand one another? In 1887 Pissarro described Gauguin's art as 'anti-art' and 'trifling';[543] he was critical of his work again in 1893, when he remarked that 'only Degas admires him. . .'[544] Degas had proved receptive to Gauguin's art, buying several of his monotypes and recommending him to Durand-Ruel.[545]

After his return to Polynesia in July 1895 Gauguin made a number of monotypes by a different method (Fig. 279): drawings were printed from an outline on a sheet of paper placed on top of another sheet covered with a layer of paint (like carbon paper). The simplicity of the technique suited the conditions of his new studio in which he had neither plates nor a press. He may have wished to use this rustic method of printing to illustrate the books he was producing – his journal, *Le Sourire*, some humorous pictures or the manuscript of *Avant et après*. He extended the technique he had used for transfer watercolours to gouache, echoing Pissarro's experiments (albeit unconsciously). One of his transfer gouaches was used as a frontispiece to the manuscript of *Noa Noa*.[546] A letter written to Vollard in January 1900 suggests that he hoped to be able to sell these 'experimental designs'.[547] About a hundred 'pencil' monotypes survive, produced between 1899 and 1903; dozens must have been lost or destroyed. Gauguin explained how he made them to his friend Gustave Fayet in March 1902.[548] On the back of the monotypes produced by this method the original drawing survives, often very rough and ready, but occasionally much more careful. The technique is similar to soft ground etching when the artist draws on the back of a sheet of paper in order to transfer the drawing on to the plate. These works are all double, with the drawing on one side of the sheet and the Impression (in paint) on the other. Do these constitute paintings, drawings or prints? And which is on the back, the print or the drawing?

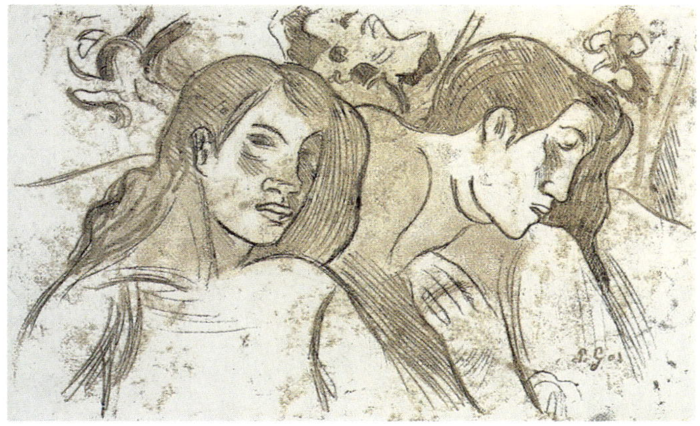

279. Paul Gauguin,
Heads of Two Tahitian Women. About 1902.
Monotype executed with a point, 321 x 510 mm.
British Museum, London.

previous page:
277. Camille Pissarro,
Woman Carrying a Large Basket. About 1889.
Oil on zinc, 155 x 48 mm.
Musée Faure, Aix-les-Bains.

278. Camille Pissarro,
Woman Carrying a Large Basket. About 1889.
Monotype, 155 x 48 mm.
Private collection, Paris.

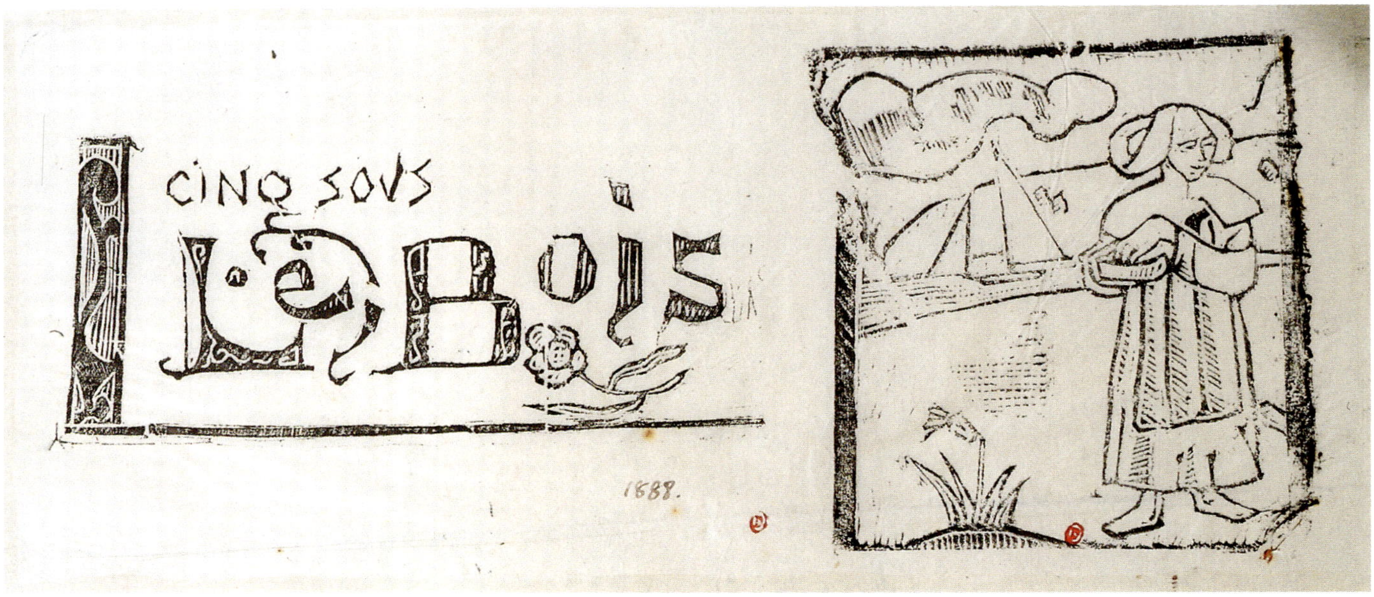

52. *Gauguin and Primitivism*

280. Emile Bernard,
Le Bois, title of review. 1888.
Wood engraving, 151 x 359 mm.
Bibliothèque d'Art et d'Archéologie, Paris.

Paul Gauguin's first painting, executed in 1873 when he was twenty-five, was inspired by Pissarro. Pissarro was then forty-three, and it was from the older painter that the young amateur, then employed in the Bourse in Paris, received advice and his first lessons. As Françoise Cachin points out, Gauguin spent the early part of his career as a painter vacillating between Pissarro and Degas.[549] Unlike Pissarro, Degas never repudiated him, but it was Pissarro who encouraged him to take part in the fourth Impressionist exhibition in 1879. In 1882 the economic crisis caused the young stockbroker to lose his job at the Bourse, and as a result he was able to turn his attention wholly to art. Two strong obsessions guided his progress: the first was to restore to art its primitive, natural strength and the second to diversify the range of non-industrial artistic products. In 1884 he took up sculpture, under the influence of Japan, then pottery, with the assistance of Bracquemond who introduced him to the potter Ernest Chaplet during the winter of 1886–7. He talked of trying his hand at Impressionist tapestry.[550] Printmaking was also to play a rôle in his output of *bibelots* (knick-knacks). The English Arts and Crafts movement, whose aim was to socialise art, arrived in France somewhat late in the day; the movement promoted a return to craft practises as well as the use of industrial processes, and aimed to meet the needs of a very diverse clientèle that was by now relatively comfortably off. The myths and legends of this secular, materialistic and international society needed to

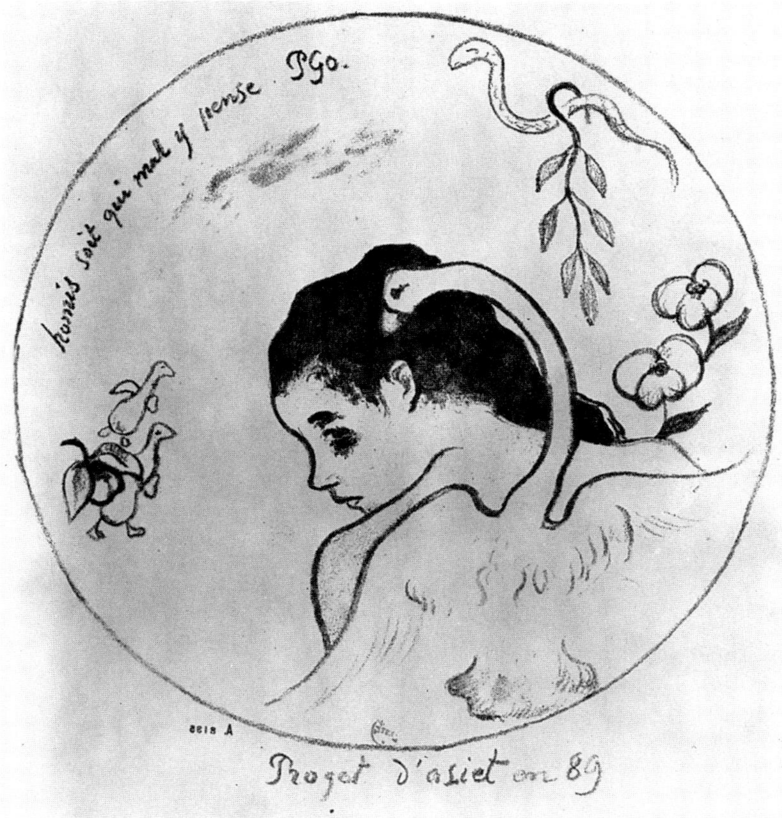

281. Paul Gauguin, *Leda*, design for a plate. 1889. Lithograph, 221 x 204 mm. Bibliothèque nationale, Paris.

be renewed. A return to the past was on the agenda, and a new publication, *L'Ymagier*[551] championed the revival of Gothic art and of endgrain wood engraving, a tradition that Millet had already tried to revive.[552]

The symbolic search for archaism had its headquarters in Brittany. When Gauguin and his friends moved there in the summer of 1886, Pont-Aven was already home to a group of American painters, who had been there since 1865, and a sprinkling of French artists including the engraver Henri Delavallée, who had arrived in 1881.[553] Gauguin went to Martinique in 1887, back to Pont-Aven in 1888 and then on to Arles. Emile Bernard, before Gauguin, had adopted the wood-cut, where the roughness is used to add piquancy to the effect. Emile Bernard wanted to start 'a journal devoted entirely to woodcuts and costing 5 sous'; the first rough sketches date from 1888 (Fig. 280),[554] and his *Bretonneries* belong to this period as well. In this series of lithographs on zinc, flourishes, smooth areas and patches of texture combine to display the artist's sinuous, sometimes violent draughtsmanship. In 1889 Gauguin also produced an album of zinc etchings, all based on earlier work and synthesising his previous experience: there are Breton motifs and themes from Martinique and Arles, the search for primitivism being the common denominator. These eleven zinc etchings, ten plates and a cover which is a 'design for a plate' (Fig. 279) were exhibited in June 1889 at the 'first exhibition of the Synthetist and Impressionist Group, on premises belonging to M. Volpini in the Champ-de-Mars' i.e. on the fringes of the Exposition Universelle, which opened in May and celebrated the triumph of colonialism, Javanese dancing girls and the Temple of Angkor Wat. Mallarmé presided over the farewell dinner held for Gauguin on 23 March 1891 at the Café Voltaire, before Gauguin's departure for Tahiti. Mallarmé spoke of 'the admirable conscience which exiles him, as his talent explodes, to re-immerse himself in far off countries and in himself'. In January 1891, with the assistance of Eugène Carrière, Gauguin had presented Mallarmé with an etched portrait bearing the words 'To the poet Mallarmé, a token of my great admiration'. In a kind of double homage, the poet bore above his head the *Raven*, borrowed from Manet. Mallarmé showed profound understanding of the painter who had written to Emile Bernard in November 1889: 'What I long for is to find a still undiscovered corner of myself.'[555]

During Gauguin's stay in Polynesia the wood-cut gained new credibility, quite independently of the printmaking of the Gothic revival. The need for new mythologies was answered. On his first return from Tahiti, Gauguin was still approaching the wood-cut as an illustrator: in August 1893 he prepared a book with ten chapters and ten woodcuts, in collaboration with Charles Morice, for an exhibition at Durand-Ruel. He wrote to Morice in May 1894: 'I have just finished my work (woodcuts) on Noa Noa, and I think it will contribute a lot to the success of the book.' In January 1985 the second number of *L'Ymagier* mentions a presentation of woodcuts by Gauguin in his studio in December. 'It is both classical and barbaric, deliberate yet savage.'[556] The naturalism of the Impressionists is wholly absent from this work, hacked out with gouges and chisels, as sharply contrasted as heaven and hell (Fig. 282). On the other hand many of their more extreme printmaking techniques can be found in it: the prints are brightly coloured with printer's ink, each one different from the next; the printing press adds ambiguity to the proofs, the ambiguity being enhanced by the inking of some of the cuts made in the wood as well as the relief areas, by applying more or less pressure with the press or by deliberately slightly misprinting the different overlays. Gauguin continued to work phenomenally hard in Paris, from 1893 to 1895, and back in Tahiti from 1896. He sent his woodcuts from Papeete to Vollard: 'Next month I am sending you about 475 proofs with someone who is going to France.' Primitive methods of production did not prevent the product from being highly sophisticated: 'Each plate produces 25 to 30 numbered proofs, then the plate is destroyed. Half of them anyway have been used before, and I am the only person able to print in this way.'[557]

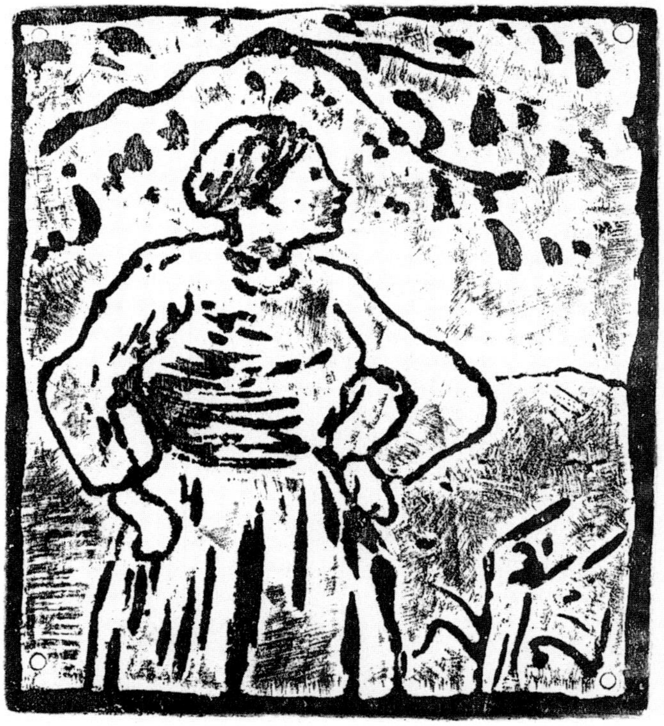

282. Camille Pissarro,
Peasant under a Tree, Hands on Hips. About 1900 (?).
Relief engraving on metal, 125 x 142 mm.
Bibliothèque nationale, Paris.

In the same backward-looking spirit, Pissarro spontaneously revived one of the techniques of the prints of the Gothic period. They had tried to make relief etchings on metal plates. Pissarro obtained a rustic-looking plate[558] which could be printed either with the dotted effect of fifteenth-century engraving, or (by inking the hollow parts) as a line engraving, or (by inking the relief parts) as a woodcut (Fig. 281). As in the fifteenth century, this mongrel technique was not pursued further. Although Pissarro was disturbed by his former pupil Gauguin's drift towards decorative, anti-realist art, he and his son Lucien followed (with great interest) developments in England, where a decorative art laden with archaism and symbols was appearing. In 1893 Camille completed his series of idyllic scenes, *Labour in the Fields*, to be engraved by Lucien on endgrain blocks, before starting another set of bucolic illustrations, this time for *Daphnis and Chloë*. His civilised archaism, firmly rooted in the courtly tradition, had none of the bracing savagery of Gauguin's archaism; it was the latter finally that was to influence the course of modern art. Pissarro tore his hair at the activities of this 'hack. . . to hear him, you'd think that drawing and painting were superfluous to art, that ideas sufficed, expressed by some random signs'; he grumbled at this 'need to return peoples to superstition . . . Gauguin was aware of the movement and had to do his utmost to turn it into a death rattle, the last one of all!'[559]

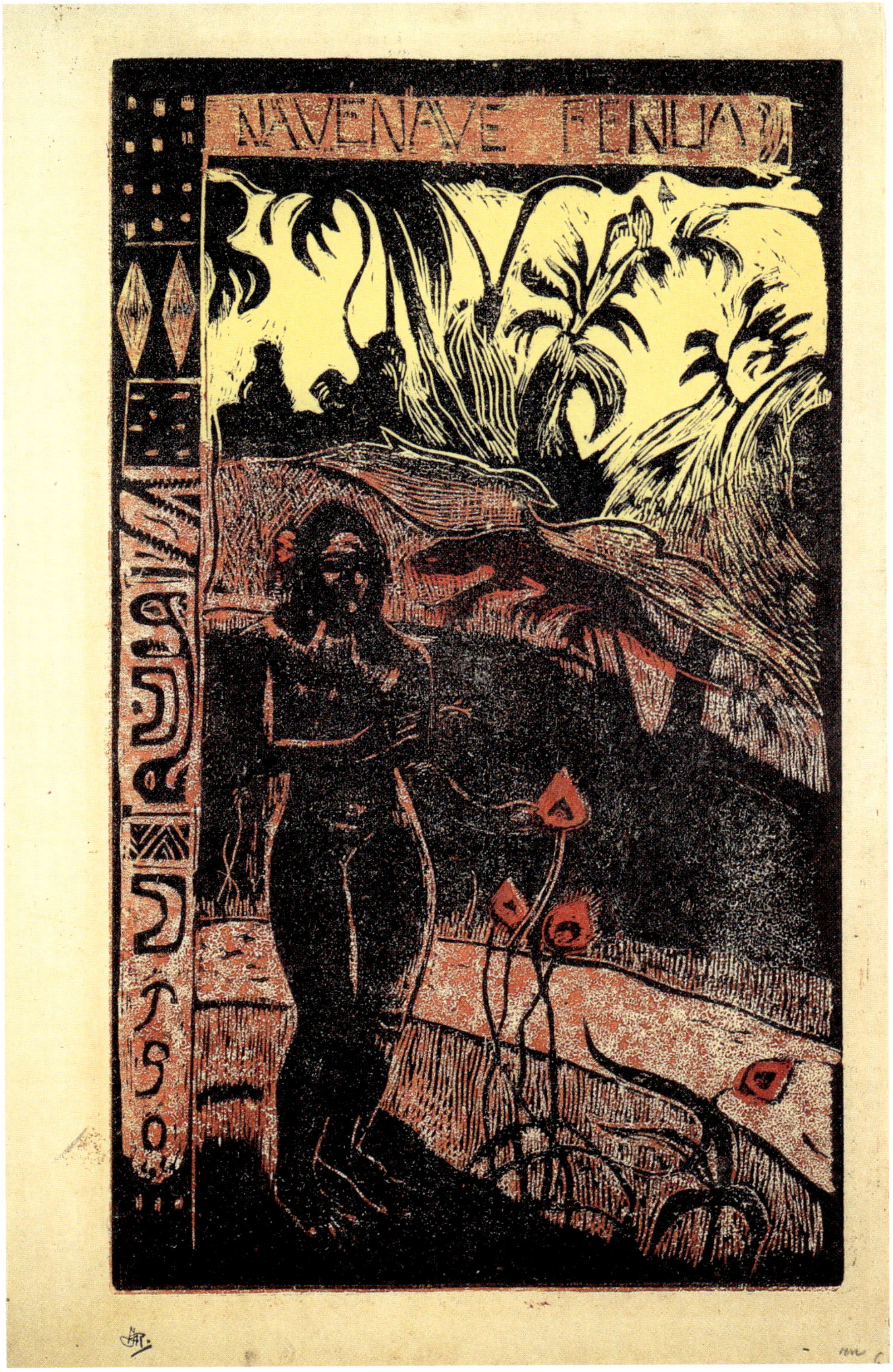

283. Paul Gauguin, *Nave Nave Fenua*. 1896. Watercolour monotype print, 397 x 242 mm. Museum of Fine Arts, Boston, gift of W.G. Russell Allen.

53. *Van Gogh*

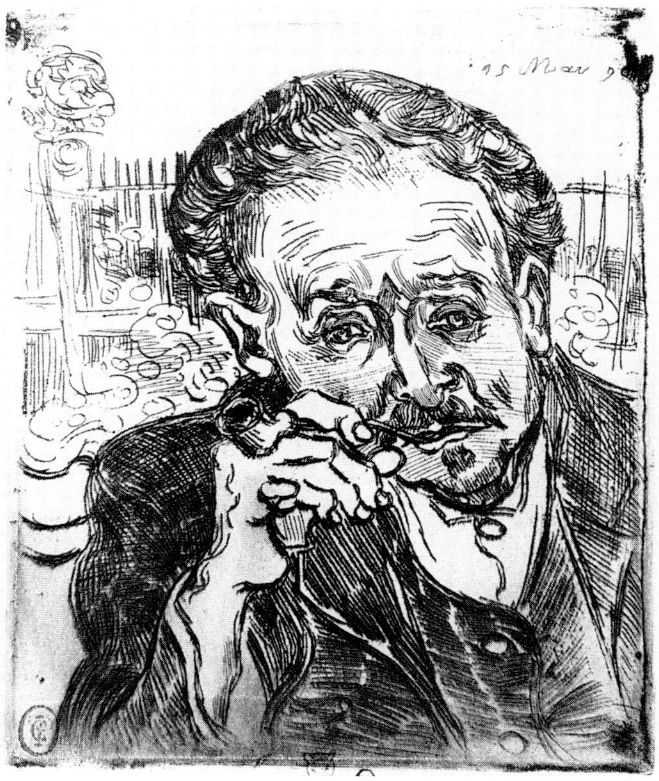

283. Vincent Van Gogh, *Portrait of Dr Gachet*. 1890. Etching, 182 x 150 mm. Bibliothèque nationale, Paris.

When Vincent van Gogh came out of hospital in Arles on 16 May 1890, he went straight to the house of Dr Gachet in Auvers-sur-Oise, arriving there on 20 May. The press used to print the early etchings of Cézanne, Guillaumin and Pissarro was still there. In the frenetic bout of work he then began, Van Gogh decided to try his hand at printmaking: 'I am hoping to make some etchings on themes from the South of France, about six perhaps; I can have them printed at Dr Gachet's house, and he has offered to print them for nothing if I produce them. . . And Gauguin will probably do prints of some of his pictures along with me.'[560] A few days later he took a small copper plate and sketched a portrait of his host (Fig. 283). The very intense drawing distorts and tilts the face. With its eyes staring blindly forwards, it could almost be a self-portrait of the artist. Once the drawing had been etched it was printed several times (about twenty copies are known);[561] there Van Gogh's printmaking, just begun, came to a halt.

Van Gogh had always dreamed of another kind of printmaking. In his youth his greatest ambition was to use the powerful images being published in the newspapers in the service of the ministry to which he felt called; to combine his passion for drawing with his evangelism. When he went as a lay evangelist to the Borinage in Mons, in 1878 at the age of twenty-five, he nurtured his mission with pictures cut from magazines: 'You will know what I need', he wrote to his brother, . . . 'Figure studies in particular, like Millet's Labourers, or the lithograph of the painting.'[562] he gave up his mission but he did not give up his drawing. '. . . By carrying on with my drawings of workers I hope to be able to work as an illustrator of books and magazines.'[563]

The two most vivid mental pictures he took away with him from London, where he worked for Goupil in 1873, were the poverty of the slum areas, and the amazing illustrations in the big news magazines, *The Illustrated London News* and especially *The Graphic*. He wrote again to Van Rappard in 1883: 'I can tell you that my engravings from the Graphic are prodigiously interesting. More than ten years ago, when I was in London, I used to go every week to look at the pictures displayed at the printworks of the Graphic and the London News. The impressions I received were so powerful that I have retained the clearest memory of these drawings, in spite of everything that has gone through my head since then . . . the enthusiasm I felt for those illustrations is if possible even stronger now than it was then.'[564] Later, in The Hague, he bought a collection of twenty-one volumes of *The Graphic*. 'I hope that these Graphics will teach me a lot about the virtues of black and white. . .'[565] With the assistance of his brother Theo he made a collection of woodcuts and prints from the English and French press, and the Dutch *De Zwaluw* (to which he offered his drawings); he stuck them carefully on to thick grey paper to stock his make-believe museum.[566]

Van Gogh's example brings us back to an important aspect of the history of Impressionism. His involvement with the style and iconography of the flood of cheap illustrations must surely at that period have contributed in no small measure to his lack of success. Gauguin also, when he left for the Antipodes, took with him a whole collection of photographs, reproductions and cut outs to help him with his work. The etchings as well as the press illustrations by the English illustrator Charles Keene were greatly admired by Bracquemond, Degas and Pissarro; Pissarro offered Keene as an example to his son Lucien and Bracquemond organised an exhibition in his honour under the aegis of the Société des Peintres-Graveurs Français, with works from his own collection. Van Gogh's heroes were not Rembrandt or Goya, but Herkomer, the leading illustrator of the *Illustrated London News* and the *Graphic*, whose spectacular drawings were admired by a readership of thousands. He admired the Frenchman, Paul Renouard, who worked for the *Graphic* as well.[567]

Paul Renouard was to some extent the heir to Constantin Guys. Van Gogh was not his only admirer. Vollard describes how, one day in 1910, the collector Isaac de Camondo refused to buy a Renoir, protesting that 'He's not like his namesake, the draughtsman Renouard, whom I met the other day in the museum in silent contemplation before a Holbein.' Vollard subsequently presented him with a drawing by Renouard which Camondo mistook for a Degas.[568] In the engraving section of the Salon of 1879 Huysmans had eyes only for 'the wonderful ballet dancers of M. Renouard, previously seen in L'Illustration.'[569] Pissarro reports that, in an interview in *L'Eclair*, Gérôme requested that Renoir and Renouard should not be confused because, unlike the former, the latter, 'Renoir-nouard' knew how to hold a pencil.[570] Paul Renouard, along with Herkomer and other newspaper illustrators like Keene, Du Maurier, Luke Fields and Eugène Burnand had, after Millet, the greatest influence of anyone on Van Gogh's drawings, teaching him naked realism, vigorous draughtsmanship and an absence of any prejudice about methods of reproduction.[571]

In November 1882 Van Gogh, who had heard rumours of the transfer technique used for the illustrations of *La Vie moderne*, decided with his friend Van Rappard to found a popular illustrated journal: 'The

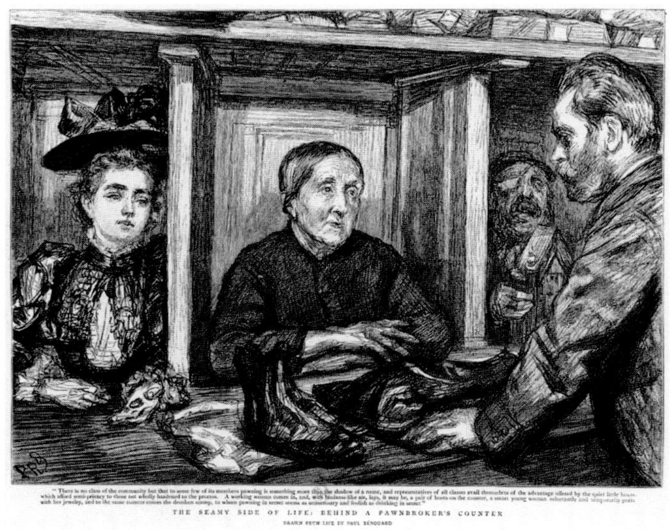

284. Paul Renouard,
The Seamy Side of Life (behind a pawnbroker's counter).
Plate for *The Graphic*, 350 x 230 mm.
Bibliothèque nationale, Paris.

need for a popular newspaper is felt, in fact is strongly felt and especially in Holland. Such an undertaking would involve producing a series of thirty drawings and making reproductions of them; the subjects would be, for instance, different types of labourers, someone sowing or digging, a woodcutter, a washerwoman. . . It has always been said that Holland could not produce prints for the working classes. I have never been convinced and now I can see it clearly . . . we need to set up a printmaking business for them . . . to donate not sell our work . . . since it is useful and necessary to produce, reproduce and circulate Dutch drawings aimed at the homes of the poor and of farmers, in sum, to the entire labouring class. . . . The promoters of this enterprise consider that they are fulfilling a social duty,'[572] The publication never appeared but six lithographs survive, executed by Van Gogh on transfer paper he had had sent from Germany. As he had announced, the subjects depicted are simple: an old man, a man digging (Figs 286–7), someone drinking coffee, a young labourer cutting a loaf of bread, an old man with his head in his hands and *Sorrow*, a naked woman seen in profile, her body and breasts exhausted, her face hidden in her arms, her hair dishevelled: she is the image of distress. The line is fixed then scratched, and the placing of the figure in the void recalls the stark, black images produced by the Expressionists.

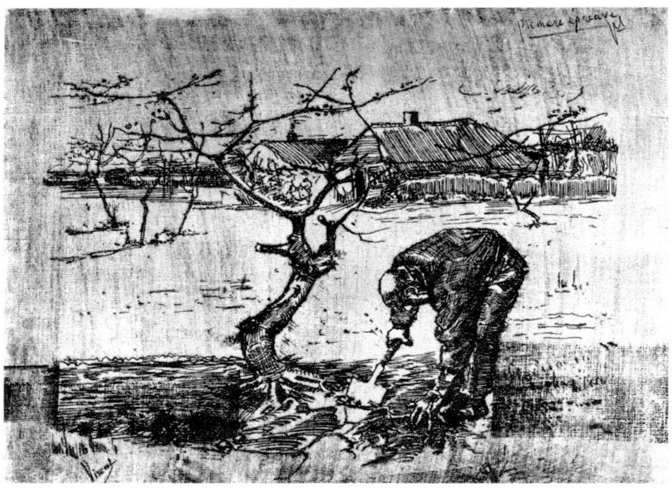

285. Vincent Van Gogh,
In the Orchard. 1883.
Lithograph on transfer paper and zinc, 325 x 249 mm.
Bibliothèque nationale, Paris.

The following year, in July 1883, Van Gogh obtained some more transfer paper and, through his brother, received advice from Felix Buhot. 'I have already received the paper samples and I have had a few tips about the virtues of black and white and on ways of proceeding.'[573] He made two new prints but was not satisfied with them (Fig. 285): 'I have arrived at a crossroads . . . I must alter my technique . . . I must overcome that spareness which is seen as harshness.'[574] In April 1885 his wish was granted: 'I'd like to make lithographs myself one day, without using special paper or anything like that; I'd like to draw straight on to the stone. However attractive the pages of the Christmas number of *Harpers*, for example, or *La Vie moderne*, there is always something mechanical about these reproductions all the same . . . something to remind one of photography or photogravure; a lithograph by Daumier or Gavarni or Lemud seems preferable to me . . . . I'm afraid that the modern process is one of those things that is never wholly satisfactory because it's really a bit too bland. To me an ordinary etching, a simple wood engraving or lithograph has an original and natural charm that nothing mechanical can replace.'[575] Like his fellow artists, Van Gogh, the missionary, was struck in 1885 by the advantages of the original print and learned to distinguish the different varieties. In the printing shop of Dimmen Gestel, in Eindhoven, he drew a reproduction of his painting *The Potato Eaters*[576] on to a stone block and made thirty prints. Neither Theo nor Rappard was convinced by the quality of the outcome and their criti-

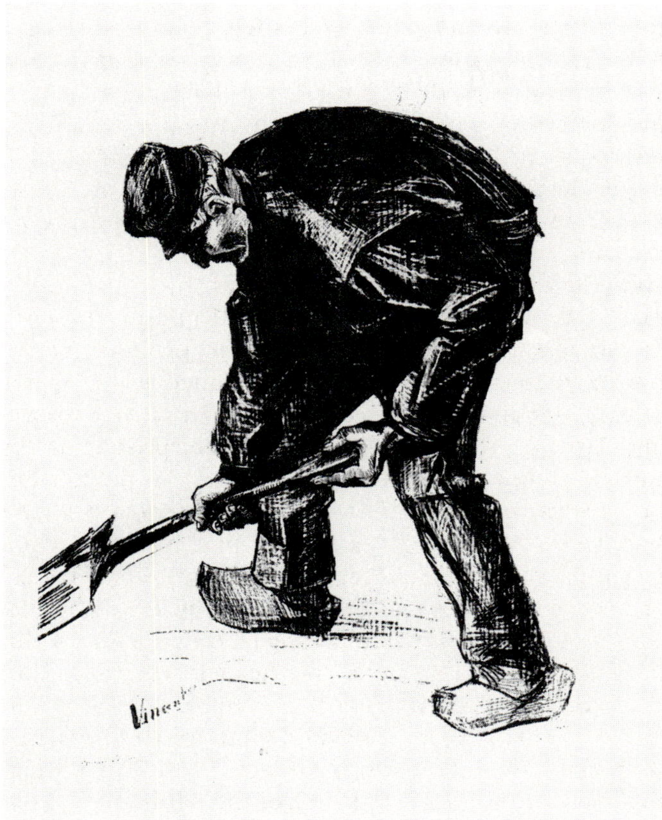

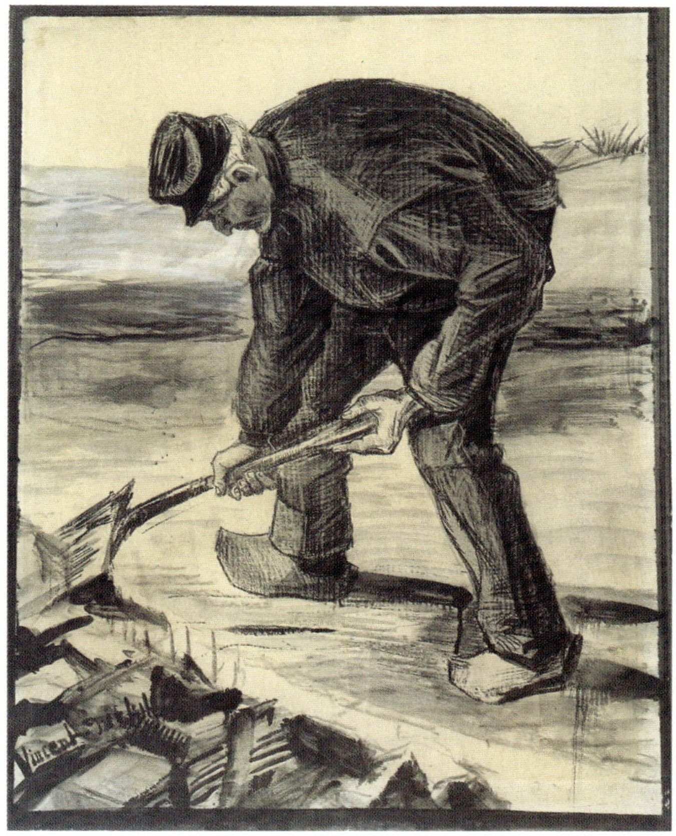

cism provoked a quarrel with Rappard which put an end to any hope of publication, assuming that Van Gogh's new technique was still compatible with the social programme outlined at the beginning of the project.

It remained now for Van Gogh to jump on the bandwagon of original printmaking, with no particular aim or subject matter in view. At the end of May 1890 he was invited to join Dr Gachet, seventeen years after his friends Pissarro, Cézanne and Guillaumin had done the same. It was late in life to start a series of etchings. Van Gogh hoped that Gauguin would associate himself with the project, but he refused. On 29 July Vincent died from the effects of a self-inflicted gunshot wound in the chest.[577]

286, 287. Vincent Van Gogh,
Man Digging. 1882.
Lithograph, 520 x 370 mm.
Bibliothèque d'Art et d'Archéologie, Paris; proof touched up with wash and white chalk, Vincent van Gogh Foundation/ Van Gogh Museum, Amsterdam.

54. *Toulouse-Lautrec*

The direct heir to the Impressionists (if such a concept can be said to exist) was Toulouse-Lautrec, through Degas. The characteristic features of the work of Degas – the representation of transient, ephemeral subjects, his passion for movement, the stark realism of his chosen themes and the variety of 'articles' produced by him – became widespread features of the art of the 1890s. Toulouse-Lautrec provides a link between the art of Degas, of whom he was an early admirer, and Picasso, who in turn admired him. In September 1891 Toulouse-Lautrec wrote to his mother: 'Degas encouraged me, telling me that the work I had done this summer was not too bad. I would like to believe him.'[578] Picasso might have encountered Lautrec, who died in 1901, the year of his second visit to Paris; Picasso was imitating Lautrec's drawings for the magazine *Frou-frou*, using the tragic but informal style since nicknamed 'Montmartre Expressionism.'[579] The work of Toulouse-Lautrec first attracted attention in the gallery of his friend Maurice Joyant and at the Salon des Indépendants in 1893. An exhibition at Durand-Ruel in 1894 began to help him make his name; he was thirty years old and, having started painting at the age of fifteen, had already produced a considerable body of work. In 1895 he took part in the first Salon de l'Art Nouveau, and in the large exhibition organised to celebrate the centenary of lithography; the centenary arrived just in time to sanction the new interest being taken in lithography by collectors of fine prints. In the same year a young publisher, Gustave Pellet, whose premises were at 9 quai Voltaire and who, in 1893, had published a series of thirteen etchings by Louis Legrand entitled *Petites Filles du ballet* (*Little Girls of the Ballet*), published Toulouse-Lautrec's series of colour lithographs entitled *Elles* (*Women*), depicting scenes from the daily life of the residents of the brothel within whose walls Toulouse-Lautrec had been cloistered since 1890. The album contained eleven colour lithographs, and probably a twelfth was intended. Pellet exhibited the album at 31 Rue Bonaparte, the headquarters of *La Plume*, a somewhat anarchical newspaper which provided a forum for aesthetes, and then at the Salon des Cent, one of the many locations that would nowadays be termed 'alternative'. It won praise from the critics but did not sell.[580] The publisher was not discouraged and proceeded to publish two new lithographs by Lautrec, *Elsa the Viennese* and *The Female Clown Cha-U-Kao*. The influence of Japan reached its peak in this series of brilliant arabesques with their false perspectives and muted colours; the subjects (scenes from the daily life of prostitutes), the form (an album of twelve prints, traditional in Japan), were produced for the same kind of clientèle (a recently enriched middle class, pursuing refinement as well as the pleasures of the flesh) as the works of Utamaro; Toulouse-Lautrec had made a catalogue of the Utamaro prints in the collection of Théodore Duret.[581]

Whereas Degas's brothel pictures were private monotypes, Lautrec followed the dictates of current fashion; the theme was almost compulsory for any writer or painter with aspirations towards realism. Unlike Degas and his colleagues including Louis Legrand, Félicien Rops, Henri Bouter, Charles Maurin, all more famous than he at the time, Lautrec never painted erotic scenes, refraining from any connivance or complicity. In the circumstances Renoir's comment, when Vollard asked him to compare Degas with Lautrec, seems lacking in sensitivity: 'Both did brothel scenes but they are worlds apart. Lautrec depicted a woman in a brothel, Degas all the women in the brothel rolled into one. And besides, Lautrec's are dissolute in a way that Degas's never are.'[582] In *Elles*, perhaps the most accomplished of all his work, Toulouse-Lautrec ignored the fact that his subjects were prostitutes (thereby disappointing some of his clientèle, no doubt); with total naturalism he produced completely honest, immortal portraits (Fig. 288). Moreover, unlike the women of Degas, his women have faces. Disappointing too to masculine expectations, which were not attuned to dramatic realism or idealism, even less to social and moral implications, Lautrec's lithographs were of no significance at all to most of his contemporaries. Other artists made a fortune exploiting the taste for erotic prints. Félicien Rops had already (in 1888) been awarded the Légion d'Honneur. Erasthène Ramiro – pseudonym of the lawyer and keen collector Maître Rodriguez – published a catalogue of his work in 1895 at great expense, and of the work of Louis Legrand in the following year.[583]

The relationship with his period expressed by Toulouse-Lautrec in these lithographs foreshadows the writing of Marcel Proust, with its subtle, fragile layers of meaning. Lautrec borrowed from photography the charm and originality of the 'snapshot', a word that was

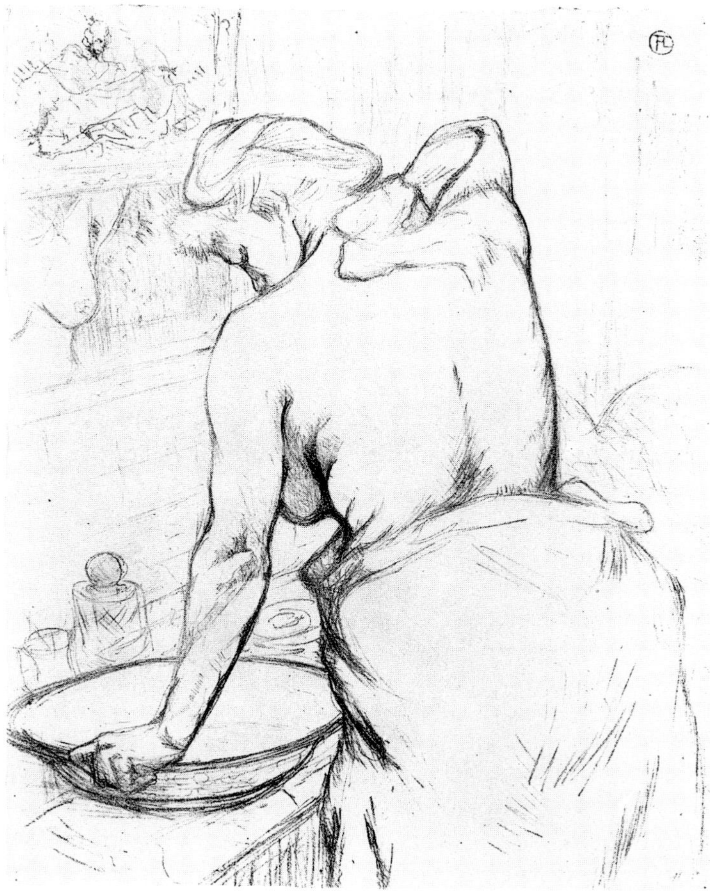

288. Henri de Toulouse-Lautrec, *Woman Washing Herself*, from the series *Elles* (*Women*). 1896.
Lithograph in two colours, 540 x 445 mm.
Bibliothèque nationale, Paris.

beginning to be fashionable: 'No, I can think of no better name to give to these etchings than "snapshots" of woman's elegance', wrote Edmond de Goncourt in the preface to an exhibition of the work of Helleu in 1894.[584] Lack of success was the price that Toulouse-Lautrec had to pay for his unconventionality.[585]

Lautrec inherited his freedom with printmaking techniques from Impressionism; his freedom from preconceived ideas meant that he could express himself in any genre, from newspaper illustrations to the mechanical reproduction of pictures from the press, provided that such 'articles' did not compete with original works of art. He developed his important sideline as a designer of posters and illustrator without any thought of abandoning his painting. Lautrec's silhouettes and his lively line, bordering on caricature, are reminiscent of Manet, and his passion for scenes from the cabaret of Degas; his Nabi friends, by contrast, translated the violent instability of the nineteenth-century into the tranquil colour schemes and comfortable interiors appropriate to a wealthy and stable society. It was Lautrec not the Nabis, however, who heralded the innovations of the twentieth century. Lautrec shared Degas' fascination with the effect of footlights, which lengthen chins and make cheekbones and eyes stand out, bathing the painted faces of the actresses and singers in a mask of light; Degas and he were the first painter of electric light (Figs 289–91). His lithograph of *Loïe Fuller* is typical of the artistic situation of the period; the colours are fractured (Lautrec even uses gilt powder on some of the proofs), and the drawing borders on abstraction. Theatres, cabarets and music halls were like studios to Manet, Degas and Toulouse-Lautrec. They shared a propensity for mixing genres as they shared a fascination for the shady world where all the different social classes mingle: race courses, café-concerts, circuses. The vitality of their style expresses their profound enjoyment of this diversity.

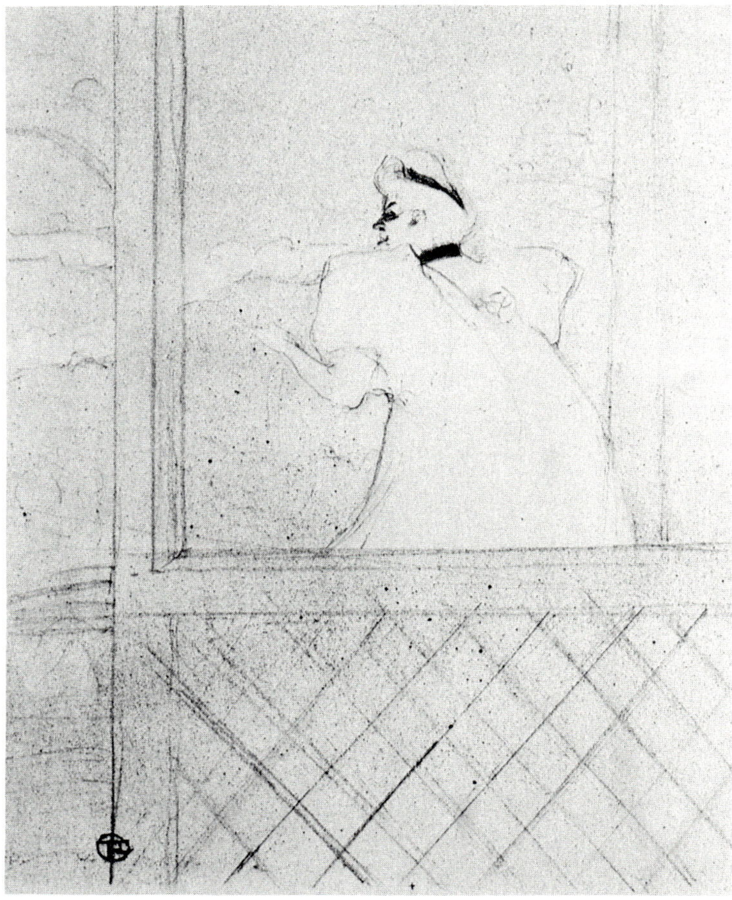

289, 290. Henri de Toulouse-Lautrec, *At the Ambassadors.* 1894.
Lithograph, 305 x 247mm.
Line proof and colour lithograph,
Bibliothèque nationale, Paris.

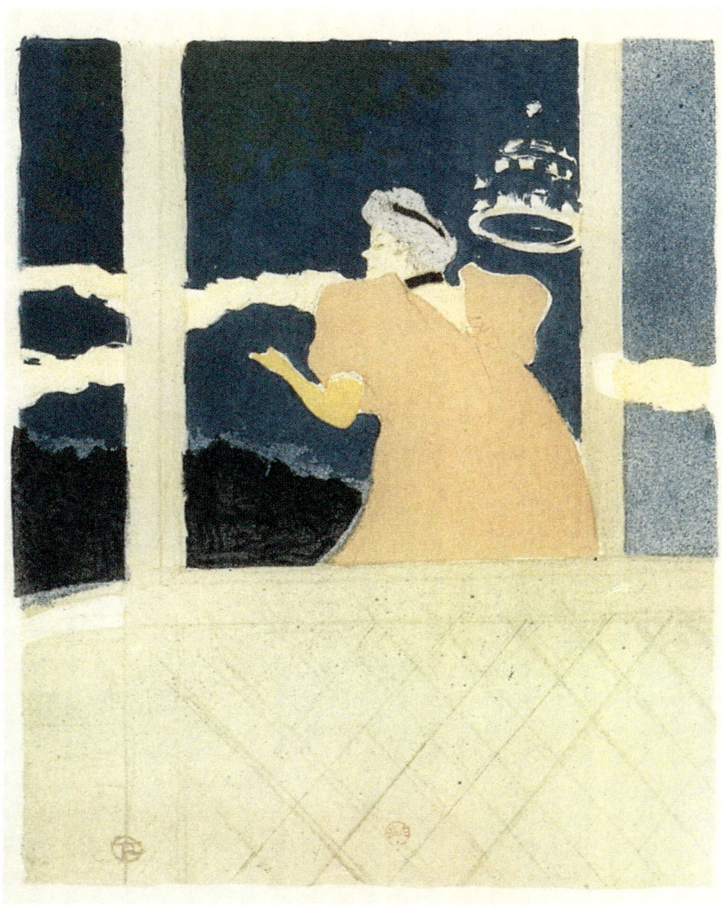

291.
Henri de Toulouse-Lautrec,
Princely Idyll. 1897.
Lithograph, 380 x 285 mm.
Bibliothèque nationale, Paris.

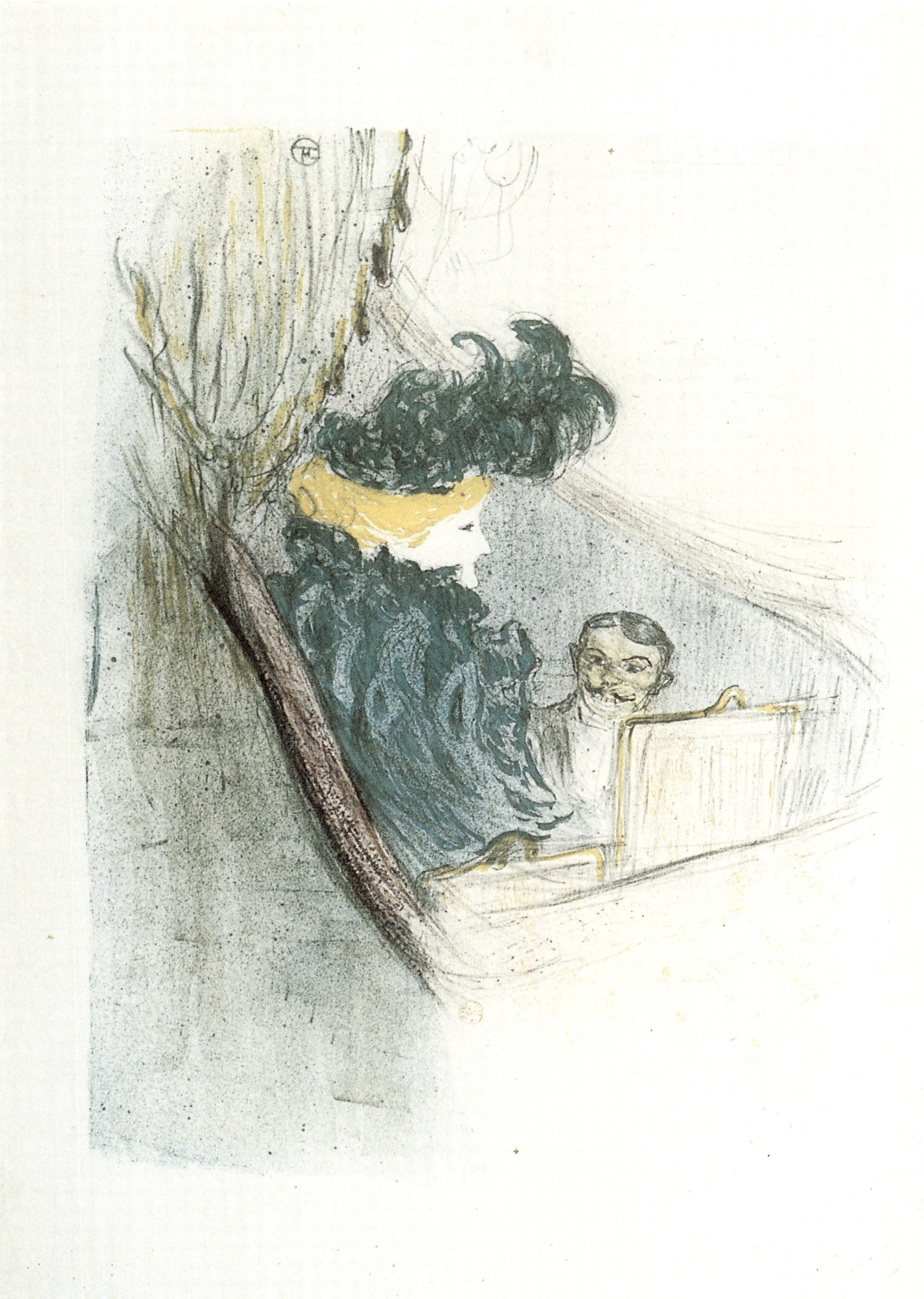

55. *Pissarro's Bathers*

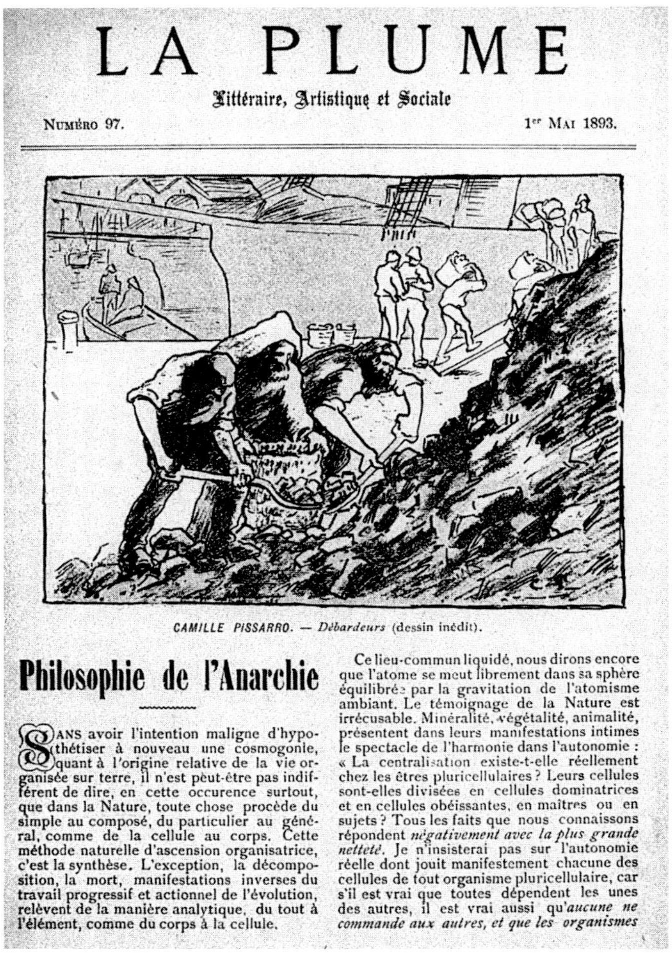

LA PLUME

Littéraire, Artistique et Sociale

NUMÉRO 97. 1er MAI 1893.

CAMILLE PISSARRO. — *Débardeurs* (dessin inédit).

Philosophie de l'Anarchie

SANS avoir l'intention maligne d'hypothétiser à nouveau une cosmogonie, quant à l'origine relative de la vie organisée sur terre, il n'est peut-être pas indifférent de dire, en cette occurence surtout, que dans la Nature, toute chose procède du simple au composé, du particulier au général, comme de la cellule au corps. Cette méthode naturelle d'ascension organisatrice, c'est la synthèse. L'exception, la décomposition, la mort, manifestations inverses du travail progressif et actionnel de l'évolution, relèvent de la manière analytique, du tout à l'élément, comme du corps à la cellule.

Ce lieu-commun liquidé, nous dirons encore que l'atome se meut librement dans sa sphère équilibrée par la gravitation de l'atomisme ambiant. Le témoignage de la Nature est irrécusable. Minéralité, végétalité, animalité, présentent dans leurs manifestations intimes le spectacle de l'harmonie dans l'autonomie : « La centralisation existe-t-elle réellement chez les êtres pluricellulaires ? Leurs cellules sont-elles divisées en cellules dominatrices et en cellules obéissantes, en maîtres ou en sujets ? Tous les faits que nous connaissons répondent *négativement avec la plus grande netteté*. Je n'insisterai pas sur l'autonomie réelle dont jouit manifestement chacune des cellules de tout organisme pluricellulaire, car s'il est vrai que toutes dépendent les unes des autres, il est vrai aussi qu'*aucune ne commande aux autres, et que les organismes*

292. Camille Pissarro,
Unloading Coal in Rouen Harbour.
Drawing published in *La Plume*, no. 97, 1 May, 1893.
Bibliothèque nationale, Paris.

Pissarro's commission in April 1888 for a selected series of etchings for the collection of Samuel Avery in New York, sent off by him carefully numbered and dated, must have encouraged him to carry on with printmaking From that time forward he produced and exhibited prints continuously, and little by little began to sell them. He took part in the first two exhibitions held by the Société des Peintres-Graveurs, in 1889 and 1890. From 1890 his etchings were stocked at Durand-Ruel[586] then, from 1892, at Boussod and Valadon who had about forty of his prints in their possession.[587] In 1891 his son Lucien suggested that he exhibit in London and, at the same time, on 3 April, he opened his own first exhibition at Durand-Ruel: 'I'm having a small exhibition with Miss Cassatt at Durand-Ruel, a small room for each of us. I shall just hang some proofs of different states of new etchings, some pastels and drawings, twenty-four items in all.'[588] With the encouragement of 'Miss Cassatt' he set to work on some etchings in June 1891, declaring it his intention to 'do a series of markets'. He used his trips to London and Bruges to enlarge his repertoire, and produced more family portraits. His labouring peasant women (*Women Cutting Hay* (Fig. 214), *Woman Carrying Buckets*, *Peasant Woman Digging*) were succeeded by *Shepherdesses* who grew more and more idealised, almost becoming mythological figures; naked young women playing happily on the shady river bank, with opulent figures and rich effects of light and shade (Figs 294–7).[589]

In 1894 the German dealer Gutbier from Dresden joined Pissarro's American, English and French dealers.[590] Pissarro bought a printing press from Delâtre: 'Since I've had the press I've been doing Women Bathing; all was going well when I had to stop. The press that I bought with accessories from Delâtre for three hundred francs broke. . .'[591] Pissarro's change of repertoire is surprising; the strict, almost dogmatic realist suddenly became passionate about nymphs. In his own way the unreconstructed Impressionist was paying tribute to Art Nouveau. The novelty should be seen in context, however; Pissarro had always dreamed of a simple art whose innocence would be expressed through simple subjects rather than through the immediacy of any emotional content. He achieved this by encouraging his son to produce the kind of decorative

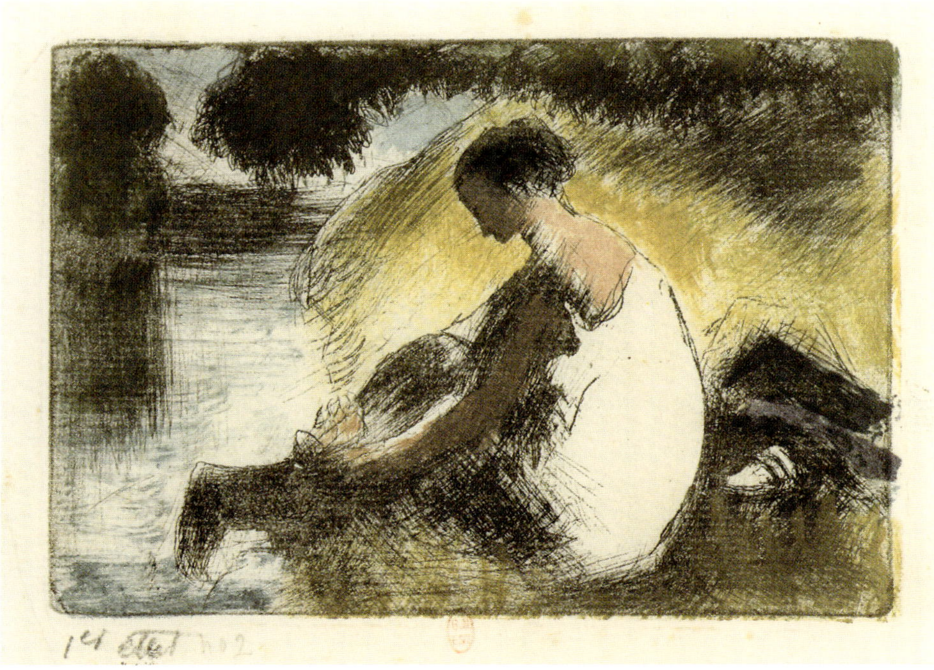

293. Camille Pissarro, *Woman Putting on her Stockings*. 1895. Monotype etching, 80 x 114 mm. Bibliothèque nationale, Paris.

art that he refrained from producing himself. His young women are not the pure spirits beloved of the Symbolists (Fig. 293). The intensity with which he depicts their forms rivals the intensity Degas brought to his prostitutes. For once he was delighted with his work: 'I've just printed two etched plates of women bathing and they're marvellous, you'll see. They might almost be too lifelike, they are plump peasant women with firm flesh!. . . They may offend my daintier admirers I'm afraid, but I think they are my best work, unless I'm much deceived. . .'[592]

To liven up his work he asked the publisher Marty to provide him with a lithographic stone – real stone and not zinc. In early 1895 he wrote to Lucien: 'I'm doing a lithograph on stone for Marty's latest number. I hope he's going to keep me a dozen proofs. I am also having some zinc plates printed by Tailliardat, the first proofs of lithographs of Women playing about in the water.'[593] But to Georges on 9 February: 'I don't like my stone litho. It's thin and ineffectual; if I were more familiar with the medium I would have done it again but I'm not sure if that's possible.'[594] To Lucien on 14 February: 'In fact I've had a stone but what I did on it disgusted me mightily, so they are going to send it back for me to rework it. I did not dare wash it over for emphasis, so it's empty and white with no colour contrasts. However much I pencil it over it stays pale. I must find a way, by scraping or scratching, but how can I get blacks??'[595] As he had promised 'Miss Cassatt', he set about producing a *Market* on stone (almost certainly *Le Marché de Gisors*), but he was still thinking about the *Women Bathing*: 'I've got a big stone lithograph on the go, a Market. I'm working on it here in Paris. I've messed around with wash, scratched it and rubbed it with emery paper. I don't know how it will turn out, but I was stupid to do a Market, I should have done Women Bathing.'[596] This iconographic transformation, with the themes of *Markets* and *Women Bathing* jockeying for pre-eminence,[597] took place at a time when his militant anarchy was as strong as ever. He continued his financial support for Jean Grave's publications, *La Révolte* and *Les Temps nouveaux*, but his art did not involve itself with his politics. 'I was wondering what a man of letters means by anarchist art?', he wrote to Octave Mirbeau on 30 September 1892, '. . . Forain? I guess so? . . . Is there such a thing as anarchist art? What?? . . . They certainly don't understand! All the arts are anarchical! When they are beautiful and well-executed! That's what I think.'[598]

He preferred donating paintings to lotteries organised by the cause[599] to providing lithographs for militant magazines – as was the practice of Signac, Luce, Van Rysselberghe and other artists of the younger generation. He only agreed to contribute lithographs to *Les Temps Nouveaux* on three occasions: *Woman Carrying Firewood*, *The Tramps* and, in colour, *Labour*.[600] His only political illustrations were the series of caricatures gathered in an album under the title of *Social Turpitudes*, sent (with captions by himself) to his nieces in London, but this was a private fantasy for the family only.[601] In 1802 he kept his promise to Mirbeau and produced a drawing depicting the coal heavers in the docks at Rouen, reproduced in *La Plume* (Fig. 292).[602] In 1893, however, he returned an illustration to Charles Châtel, editor of *La Revue anarchiste* with a polite refusal to interpret it, 'because it would be difficult, I think, to produce an artistic picture from a very run-of-the-mill print'.[603] His desire to protect his art from social involvement was not a betrayal of his anarchism; it represented his own feelings and the feelings of his class, which were really no different from those of Degas. In 1887 Berthe Morisot expressed her astonishment at Pissarro's exhibiting at Petit: 'He is not afraid of appearing in such bad company. His convictions are short-lived. I would not expect such a thing from Degas, unfortunately.'[604] Pissarro confused quality with rarity, and rarity with inflated prices, seeking the latter whether his work was successful or not: 'I have raised the price of all my etchings, in proportion; I don't see why I should not ask the same prices as Legros, but I have so little chance of selling anything!'[605] In this his art was similar to the art of the other Impressionists, and could not (with sincerity) have been any different. Like them, Pissarro eventually came round to the appeal of the academies, creating nudes bathed in light in classical vein and calling them shepherdesses.

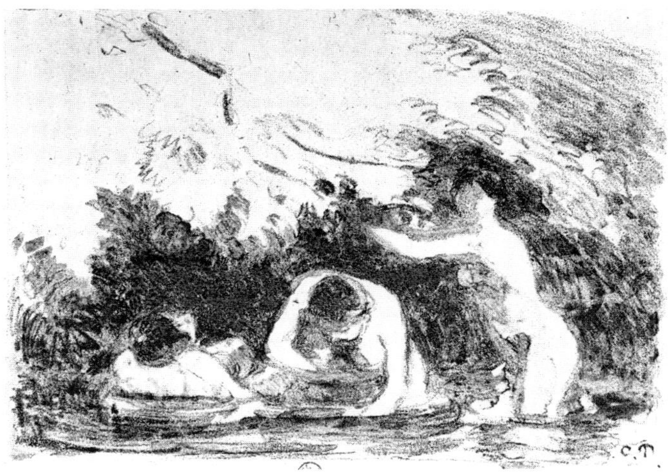

294. Camille Pissarro,
Women Bathing in the Shade of the Wooded River Bank. 1894.
Lithograph, second and final state, 159 x 217 mm.
Bibliothèque nationale, Paris.

Pissarro's politics are not reflected in the content of his work. He was always deeply suspicious of any suggestion that, because of the militant milieu in which he lived, he might produce some political prints. After 1890 he allowed his son Lucien to persuade him to design some woodcuts, to be engraved and printed by Lucien for the rare book business he had established in England. This was the origin of the album entitled *Travaux des Champs* (*Farm Labour*).[606] Another project, even more reluctantly undertaken by Pissarro, was *Daphnis and Chloë*; this was begun too close to the artist's death on 13 November 1903 and remained at the trial stage. His final work, beginning with the *Women Bathing* of 1894, bears little connection with the realism of his early days. Pissarro, we know, although intransigent in matters of technique, was the most open to the new styles that succeeded Impressionism of all the Impressionists, and was among the first, if not the first, to recognise the talents of Cézanne, Gauguin and Van Gogh. His own aesthetic developed latterly in the direction of simple design and idyllic subjects, as if the influence of his son, the press illustrator and publisher of fine books who became for Pissarro (as his letters prove) a kind of *alter ego*, had prevailed.

295, 296, 297. Camille Pissarro,
Woman Bathing with Geese. 1895.
Reverse drawing on limestone, 127 x 173 mm.,
Ashmolean Museum, Oxford; wash and gouache,
Ashmolean Museum, Oxford; etching and soft ground etching,
British Museum, London.

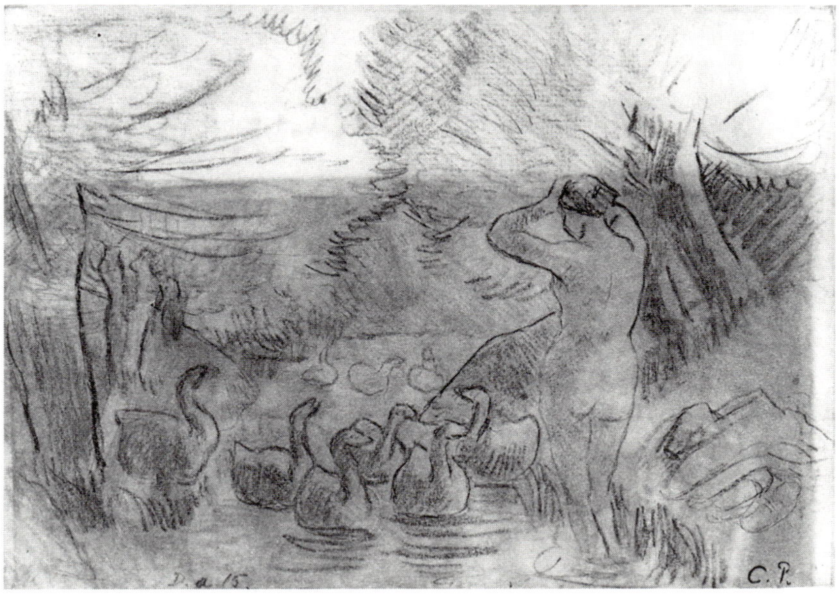
C.P.

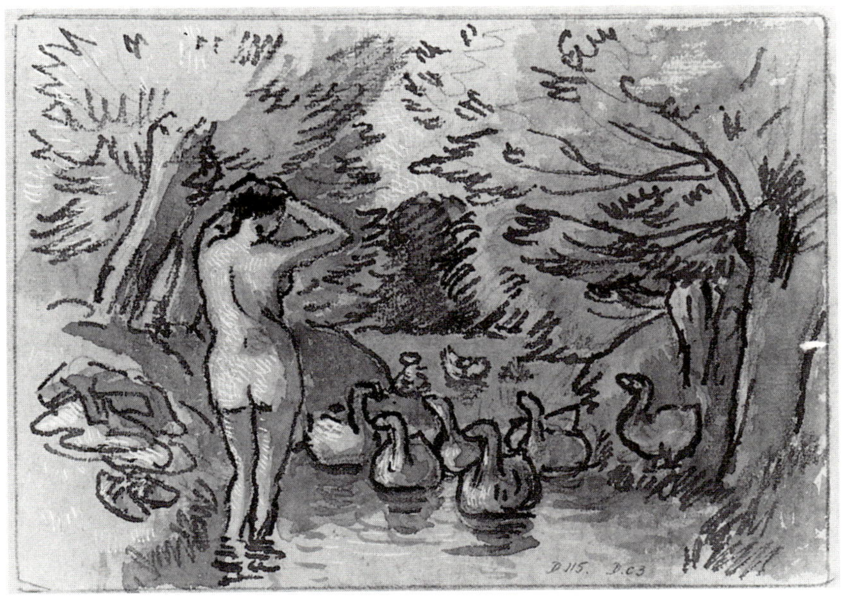

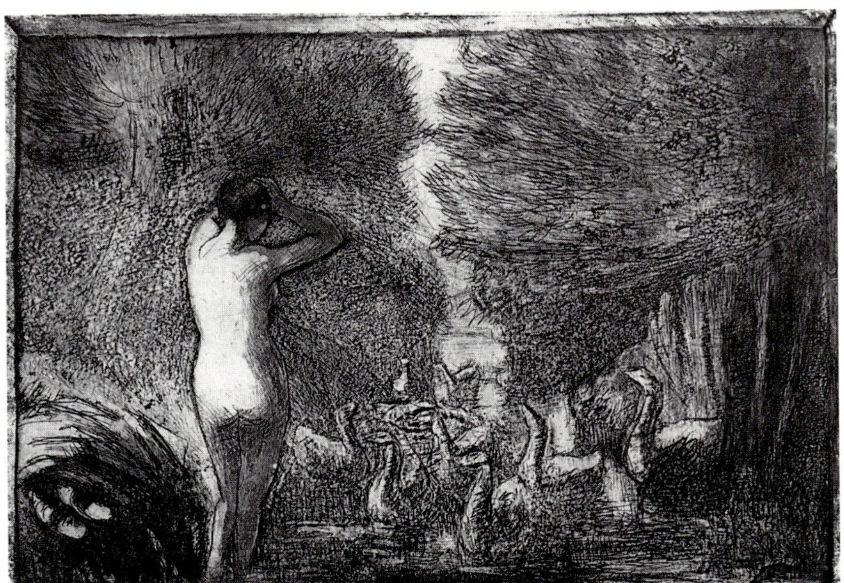

56. *The Success of the Original Print*

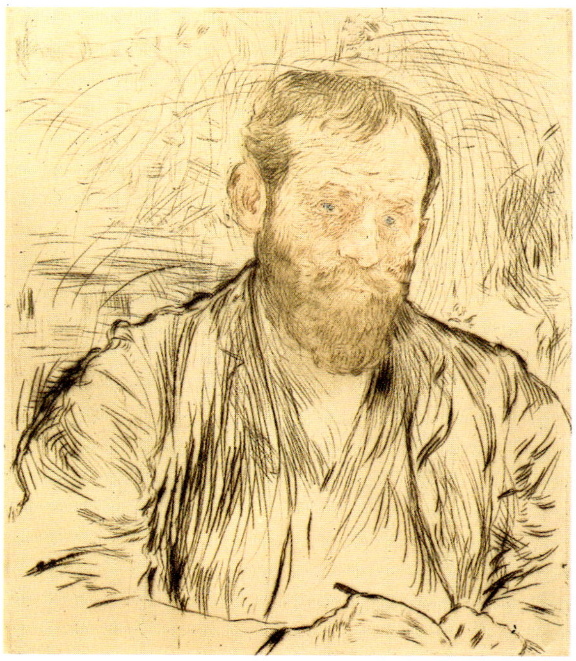

298. Jean-François Raffaëlli, *Self Portrait*. 1893. Drypoint, touched up, 184 x 158 mm. Bibliothèque nationale, Paris.

The great change that came over Pissarro's subject matter occurred at the same time as the spectacular expansion of the print market in the last ten years of the nineteenth century. *Women Bathing* was the second plate contributed by Pissarro to *L'Estampe originale*, the publication launched by the publisher André Marty, editor of the contemporary *Journal des artistes*. Pissarro was introduced to him on 3 March 1893 by Toulouse-Lautrec.[607] He replied to Marty on 6 January 1894: 'I know nothing about your publication, I don't know its format and I have not yet seen the work of the artists who are to appear in it, at least not that I can remember. I ask for nothing better, but what?. . . All I've got here is a stippled zinc plate, do you want something like that? Send me a copy of the magazine so that I can at least find out the format. . . How do you publish your journal? Do you print many copies? Forgive these questions, but it is necessary to know if an etching can be printed in the required quantity etc. etc.'[608] Quite clearly, Marty had no preconceptions about techniques, the essential thing now being originality. Pissarro too was hesitating between zinc lithography (which he had practised in 1874) and line etching, but was worrying about the printing. His first proposal to Marty was an etching. It was a zinc lithograph, however, that he had printed for *L'Estampe originale*[609] (through the good offices of Luce) by Tailliardat, the printer. Alas, on 9 March he warned Marty of the 'absolutely disastrous printing of my lithograph; it is too poor to appear in the state it's in now. I will send something else, a copper plate etching, my *Two Women Bathing* for instance, to be sent from Eragny. My son will supervise the printing by Delâtre'. It was *Landscape at Osny* that was finally selected. Only seven proofs had been made of it previously; one hundred copies were published in Number V, January-March 1894.[610]

Pissarro's dithering, his veering from one technique and from one subject to another, were the symptoms of his predicament. What can a person who has always struggled against the tide do when, in spite of everything, the tide turns, taking him with it? *L'Estampe originale* was a success and ran to ten numbers, each containing ten prints, between March 1893 and 1895. The presentation was luxurious and the choice eclectic; the very varied techniques and trends of modern art were all represented. The first issue, published in March

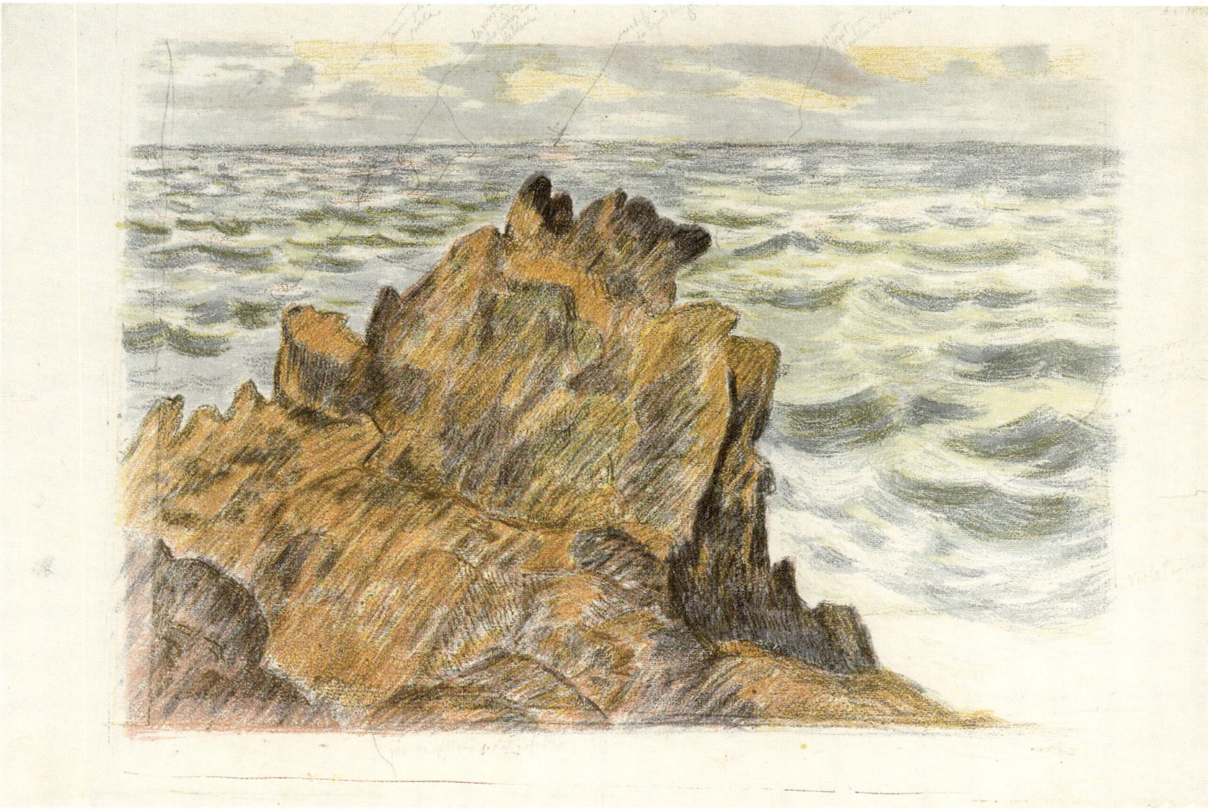

299. Armand Guillaumin, *The Red Rocks*. 1896. Lithograph, trial proof, 395 x 540 mm. Bibliothèque nationale, Paris.

1893, contained nothing but 'Neo-Impressionists' and 'Nabis': Anquetin, Bonnard, Denis, Ibels, Roussel, Vallotton, Vuillard, etc. The second, however, contained more by the printmakers of the older generation who had been through Impressionism: Henri Guérard was represented by a wood engraving, and Raffaëlli by a colour etching (Fig. 298). The veterans of Impressionism obviously included Bracquemond, who published *Long Live the Tsar!*, an etching, in the fourth issue in October 1893; this also contained a lithograph by Whistler, *The Dancer*, and another by Renoir, his *Head of a Child* (Pierre Renoir, the artist's son). Pissarro's etching appeared in the fifth issue, with another by Henri Somm, *Head of a Parisian Woman*. In the sixth there appeared a lithograph by Gauguin, *Manao Tupapu*, plus Pissarro again, Guérard and, in the following issue, Renoir.

L'Estampe originale was not the only successful publication. Younger artists published their prints in *L'Album de la Revue Blanche* (July 1893–December 1894); eclecticism became a necessity even for the avant-garde, since they were diversifying as fast as the preferences of their clientèle. Impressionism was the last 'unified' avant-garde movement (if it can be termed as such); subsequently the word avant-garde had to be used in the plural: movements multiplied without cancelling each other out. *L'Epreuve* (December 1894–December 1895) published Guérard and Gauguin. *L'Estampe moderne* (October 1895–April 1899) was more traditional. *L'Image* (December 1896–November 1897) published Lucien Pissarro, Jeanniot and Bracquemond (*Portrait of Blanqui*). *L'Estampe nouvelle* published Mary Cassatt's last two colour etchings: *Woman and Child on the Grass* (October 1897) and *Woman Knitting with a Child* (February 1904); the 'Exposition Nationale de l'eau-forte moderne' in May 1896 at the Ecole des Beaux-Arts assembled 850 prints by 200 artists; visitors were greeted by the *Portrait of Monseigneur de Pressigny*, Ingres's only etching. In the preface to the first issue of *L'Estampe moderne*, a monthly album containing four original, unpublished prints, Léonce Bénédite proclaimed: 'The original print has been revived. . . there are societies now to exploit it, disseminate it, support and point it in the right direction: the *société des peintres-lithographes*, the *lithographes français*, *l'estampe originale*, *l'estampe nouvelle*, and the society of wood engravers publishing their remarkable series of twelve issues of *L'Image*. Publications are spawning too: *L'Estampe originale*, *L'Epreuve*, *L'Album des peintres lithographes*, *Les Maîtres de l'affiche*, *Le Japon*. . .'[611] In 1897 Pissarro wrote to his son: 'No-one does anything but printmaking here, it's the great rage, the young do nothing else.'[612]

In this great wave of elegant publications the work of Roger Milès should not be forgotten. In 1889 he had published a fine collection of poetry, *Les Veillées noires*, peppered with prints printed by Delâtre; in the first batch of copies there are monotype prints and a series of proofs printed in different colours. In 1897, in the same vein, he published a collection entitled *Art et nature, études brèves sur quelques artistes d'hier et d'aujourd'hui*, with engravings by Pissarro (*Women Making Hay at Eragny*), Renoir (*Study in soft ground etching*), Sisley's only black and white etching (*The Loing near Saint-Mammès*), a lithograph sketch by Forain, a heliogravure by Rodin.[613] The collection contains one great curiosity, a small lithograph by Eugène Boudin, one of the fathers of Impressionism. As a young man in Le Havre, Boudin worked for a lithographer and had made one small poster. His picture of the *Mathurins* (Fig. 301), the sailors on the harbour wall, is Boudin's only contribution to printmaking, plus a small etching, a *Marine* (Fig. 300) which was not published until the last issue of *L'Estampe et l'affice* (December 1899), just after the artist's death in 1898.[614] This print appeared as a free gift in the de luxe editions, with the following commentary: 'The etching by Boudin which we are giving away with this issue is the only one of its kind. Boudin confined himself to painting and only once attempted to translate his vision into black and white; the plate we are including today was the result. Other work was in preparation. This master of harmony must have felt at ease with printmaking, but of the two plates on which he tried out his talent, only one was submitted to the etching process. This is the *Marine* that we are publishing today. We have left this sketch with all the character and flavour of a first state etching, including its holes and acid burns. Even in this state it is obviously a Boudin, and it is much more than just a curiosity, it is a work of art that we take pride in presenting. . .'

At this time magazines containing prints were multiplying. *La Plume* (1889–1914) was joined by *L'Ymagier* (1894–6) by Rémy de Goncourt and Alfred Jarry, then *L'Estampe et l'affiche*, by Clément Janin (March 1897–December 1899). This wave of prints burned itself out spontaneously at the end of the century. In its farewell number in December 1899 *L'Estampe et l'affiche* drew attention to the demise of the poster, whose most extreme supporters had tried to promote it as an art form worthy of inclusions in collections: 'Our work on behalf of the poster seems to be at an end. Collectors are no longer interested and, for one artistic item, a hundred duds are produced . . . Photographic processes offer enormous competition which, in spite of their high quality, we find most regrettable. As for the original print, the future belongs to it.'

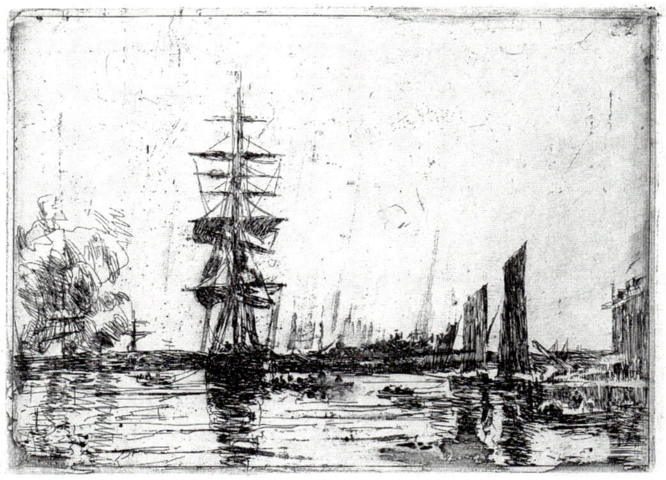

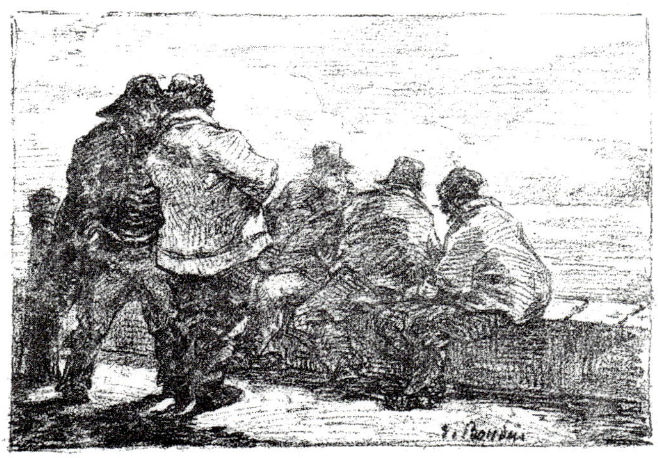

300. Eugène Boudin, *Marine*, 1891 (?). Etching, published in 1899, 102 x 162 mm. Private collection, Paris.

301. Eugène Boudin, *The Deep Sea Fishermen*. Lithograph published in 1897 in *Art et Nature*, 157 x 112 mm. Private collection, Paris.

57. *Vollard and the Impressionists*

At the beginning of 1894, when the artist was at his most preoccupied with lithography, Pissarro's attention was caught by the opening of premises belonging to a new dealer: 'A young man whom I met at John Lewis Brown's, and who has been warmly recommended to me by M. Viau, has opened a little shop in Rue Laffitte. He has canvases by young artists only: there are some early Gauguins, very beautiful, and exceptional items by Guillaumin, Sisley, Redon, Raffaëlli, de Groux, the last something really lovely. I talked to him about you and Georges.'[615] This letter proves that when still a law student Vollard frequented the studios of lithographers, in particular the studio of John Lewis Brown who died in 1890. He himself recalls how, in his student lodgings, he began 'to make money from drawings and etchings, having saved to build up a small collection.'[616] Prints were the stimulus to the vocation of the young man who arrived from the island of Réunion in 1890, at the age of twenty-three, and, more precisely, to the trade that had been almost forgotten since Cadart but which was gradually reviving: publishing artists' prints. In his *Souvenirs*, Vollard relates how he 'was always fond of prints. In about 1895, when I had just set up shop in Rue Laffitte, my greatest wish was to publish prints that I had commissioned personally from painters. The term 'painter-printmaker has been misused by being applied to professional printmakers who were by no means painters. My idea was to commission prints from artists who were not printmakers by profession.'[617]

Two years after opening his shop in Rue Laffitte, Vollard organised the first retrospective exhibition of the works of Cézanne. Over the previous thirty years the situation had changed quite dramatically. Cadart's failed attempt at publishing lithographs by bringing young painters – Manet, Legros, Ribot and Fantin-Latour – directly into contact with the lithographic stone could be repeated: the public was now ready for it. The first painter commissioned by Vollard to produce an album of lithographs was Bonnard; the work was finished in 1895 but was not exhibited in the gallery until 1899 and it did not sell.[618] Two recent examples, however, acted as inspiration for Vollard: Marty's success, interrupted in 1894 by his departure, and the exhibitions of the Société des Peintres-Graveurs Français, kept going by Bracquemond and Guérin until 1896. He took both these over and in June 1896 published his first album, *Les Peintres-Graveurs*, accompanying its appearance with an exhibition with the same title (15 June–20 July); the poster was designed by Bonnard. The twenty-two artists represented in the album and the twenty-nine in the exhibition included famous Impressionists whom Vollard had persuaded to take part – Cézanne, of course, over whom he had exclusive rights, Gauguin, Guillaumin and Pissarro; young lithographers like Redon, Bonnard, Denis, Toulouse-Lautrec rubbed shoulders with veterans like Buhot and Fantin-Latour. Vollard's eclectic selection also included representatives of Art Nouveau like De Feure, de Groux, Lunois and the Norwegian, Edvard Munch. His panorama of modern art was almost complete, even though Pissarro made a rough note of 'some names missing' in his copy of the catalogue; he thought the inclusion of Jeanniot and Guérard indispensable.[619] For once Bracquemond did not appear. Vollard realised that lithographs were the fashion: twelve of the twenty-two prints in the album are lithographs, ten of them in colour, not counting Bonnard's cover. He had persuaded Guillaumin, who had had no contact with printmaking since his vignettes for *Paris à l'eau-forte* in 1873, to reproduce his painting *The Red Rocks* as a colour lithograph. Like *L'Estampe originale* Vollard's album contained examples of all the techniques: Renoir provided an etching printed in colour, *Mother and Child*, Vallotton a wood cut and even a *gaufrage*.

The failure of the first album did not prevent Vollard publishing a second, even larger one at the end of 1897, *L'Album d'estampes originales de la Galerie Vollard*: thirty-one artists and thirty-two prints, thirty of which were lithographs, twenty-four of them in colour. The younger artists including Vuillard, Cross, Roussel, Toulouse-Lautrec etc.[620] were joined by Whistler, with a lithograph *Conversation, Afternoon Tea*, Forain, Lucien Pissarro, Rodin, Sisley, Cézanne and others. Apart from this brief incursion into the Painter-Printmakers, Sisley had been no more interested in printmaking than Cézanne or Guillaumin. Vollard persuaded him to provide a pastel, *The River Bank* (also known as *The Geese*), to be transformed into a lithograph by the printer Auguste Clot. The critic André Mellerio's immediate comment on this transposition, and the transposition of a watercolour by Rodin, was that it was 'an extraordinarily professional job by Clot, taken from a

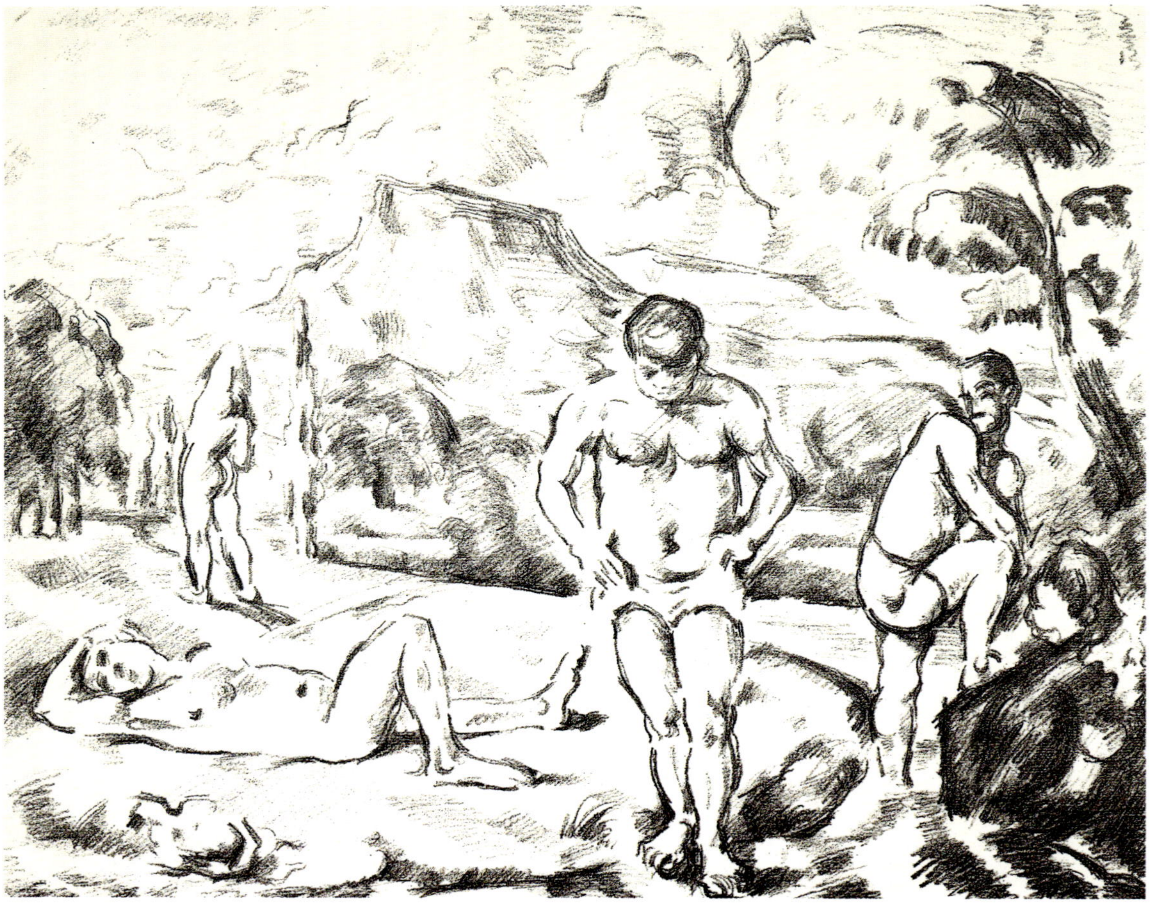

302. Paul Cézanne, *The Large Bathers, c.* 1890. Lithograph before the application of blue, 414 x 513 mm. Private collection, Paris.

303. Paul Cézanne, *The Large Bathers*. About 1890. Lithograph printed before the application of colour, 410 x 500 mm. Private collection, Paris.

304. Paul Cézanne, *The Small Bathers*. Colour lithograph, 216 x 266 mm. Private collection, Paris.

pale and luminous pastel by Sisley'. Redon's colour lithograph *Beatrice* was also produced by Clot from a pastel.[621] A third album was begun for 1898 but the failure of the second one halted publication. The cover, by Vuillard, only reached proof stage, but several lithographs were produced, including Cézanne's *Standing Woman Bather* and Renoir's *Child with a Biscuit*.

Pissarro and Degas followed the development of Vollard's business with close attention. They seem to have advised him on the choice of Cézanne and Gauguin, whose work he bought from 1896, and also to have encouraged him into publishing original prints. Neither of them, however, would submit to being employed by the young dealer. Pissarro refused to accept his conditions: 'This confounded Vollard has big ideas, he wants to go into print dealing; all the other dealers, Sagot, Dumont etc. are waging bitter war against him because he's upsetting their businesses. He talks to me endlessly about books he wants you to do. I told him to write to you, but he's a real butterfly, I'm afraid he'll burn his wings!! . . . at any rate, we must not delude our-

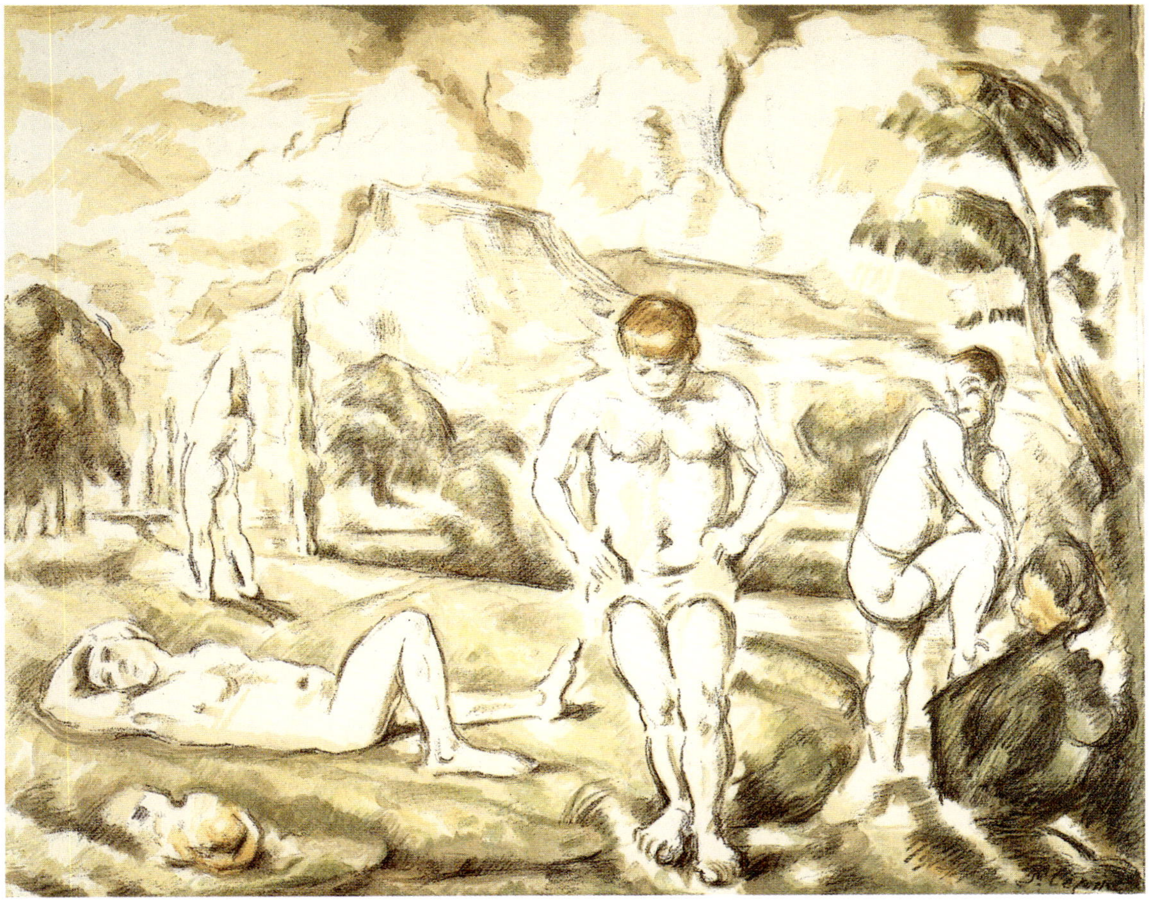

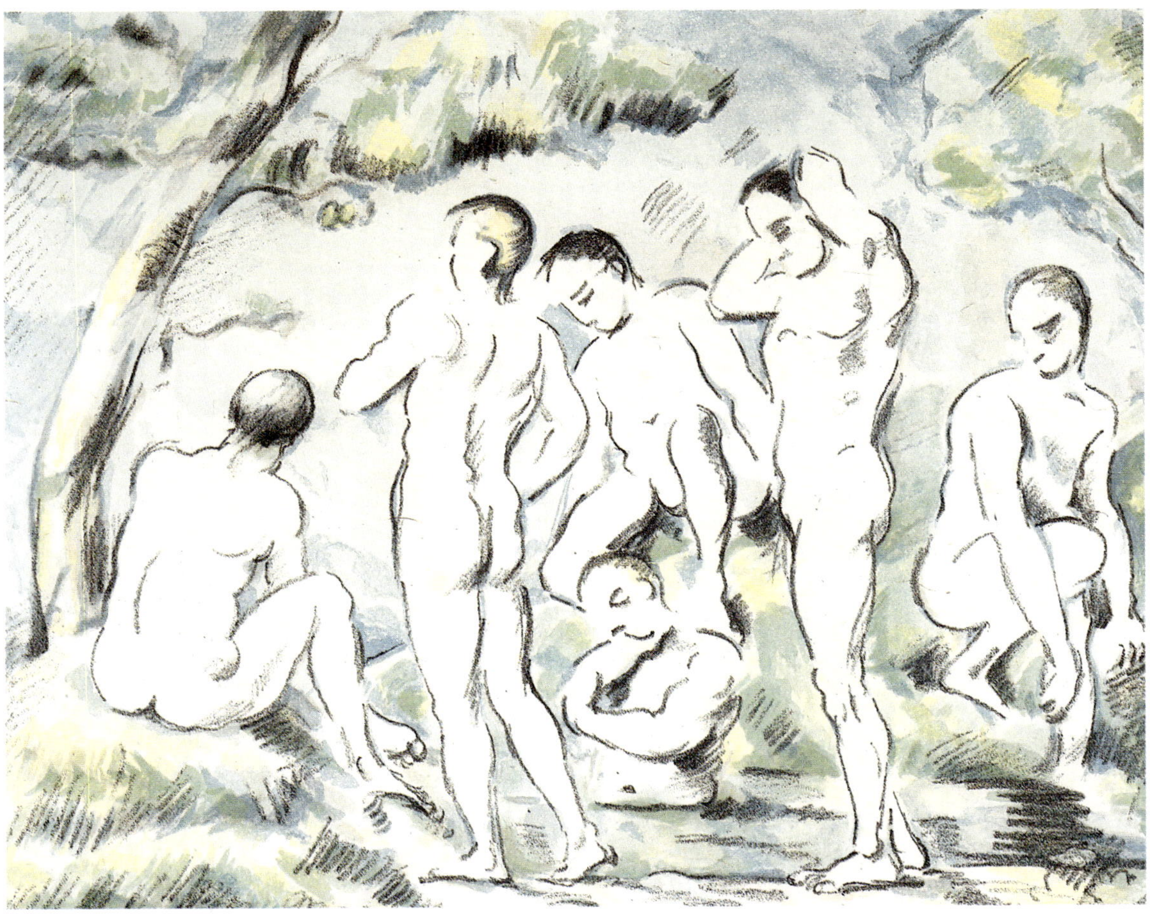

selves!!'[622] Things collapsed after a few days. 'I popped in on Vollard, we discussed prices for the colour lithography, I had difficulty getting any sense out of him, you'll never believe what he suggested, no really, he wants us to be his lackeys! Keep your nose to the grindstone, old thing, keep on trying and I'll look after earning the money!! . . . Under the pretext that Fantin-Latour sells his lithos at a hundred francs a plate, he proposed five hundred francs for a hundred copies and the plate destroyed; of course I did not accept and he said: 'All right! We'll do it another way, you print a hundred copies at your own expense, give them to me to sell and then give me a percentage of sales as my commission'. If he thinks I'll do as he suggests he's mistaken. I'll do my plate and then decide what to do . . . There's no way of dealing with Vollard or Bing, or Sagot and the rest without getting fleeced. I told Vollard he should make Degas an offer for his lithos . . . no chance.'[623]

On 4 September Pissarro noted: 'Vollard is going to have a lithographic press in Rue Lafitte. This brave Creole is astonishing, he hops from one thing to another with astonishing ease. He and his wife have been nagging me recently to do a bit of business with them, gouaches or lithos; the day before yesterday I showed him three things I was working on and he didn't even glance at them. He dashed off leaving me stranded to show me a Cézanne and took no more notice of my work; it will be a long time before I show him anything again.'[624] The epilogue to this exchange can be found in a letter of 18 September 1896: 'Poor Vollard! . . . I told him he was embarking on a project which required some expertise, and that prints did not sell, that dealers did not know a great deal about it and only survived by using gimmicks like posters, colour prints, etc.'[625] Camille dissuaded his son Lucien from making any commitment to Vollard for the same financial reasons; Vollard had suggested that Lucien illustrate the first book he planned to publish – Verlaine's *Parallèlement* – eventually entrusted to Bonnard.

Vollard used other methods to encourage Cézanne to produce a few colour lithographs, in spite of the scant interest he had shown in printmaking; he had done nothing since the small prints he made in Auvers in the summer of 1873. Douglas Druick has attempted to disentangle their complicated relationship, which eventually produced three lithographs, only one of which was published, *The Small Bathers* (Fig. 304) published in Vollard's second album in 1897.[626] These late works are interesting because of the way they were executed: Cézanne found breaking up the plate into different colours a problem and transfer of the image on to stone was therefore entrusted to the printer, Auguste Clot, Cézanne working in water-colour on a black-and-white proof (Figs 302–3). It might be justifiable to wonder whether these were preparatory sketches for the printer who was charged with preparing four blocks for the colours, or exercises that were an end in themselves – for the artist, basically not much interested in lithography, or for the dealer, who regarded the results as attractive and saleable.[627] The final edition of *The Small Bathers* ran to one hundred copies, published in Vollard's second album on thick paper; it is very far removed from the wild, intimate prints produced by Cézanne in 1873. With some justification, Druick emphasises that something private has become public; twenty years on, the print has returned to its original sphere, the sphere of publishing.

Discouraged by the lack of success of his mixed albums, Vollard turned to publishing albums and illustrated books devoted to a single painter: Redon, Bonnard, Vuillard, Emile Bernard, Maurice Denis, Armand Seguin etc. In 1894 he republished Gauguin's zinc prints, having managed to acquire the plates, and in 1900 the etchings of Berthe Morisot. He had no qualms about reprinting old plates or reproducing pictures posthumously: he had a hundred pictures by Van Gogh reproduced as woodcuts to illustrate Van Gogh's correspondence with Emile Bernard. In 1906 he commissioned Clot to make a colour lithograph of Cézanne's *Déjeuner sur l'herbe*, six years after the painter's death. The question of authenticity was swept aside, forgotten. It was the high reputation of the Impressionist painters that caused their inclusion in the repertory of reproduction prints.

58. *The Vogue for Colour Lithography*

Artists won acclaim now through the reproduction of their work. After 1886 the Impressionists were lithographers, whose work appeared reproduced as lithographs. In 1887 a young Englishman, William Thornley, a great admirer of Degas, made a series of reproductive prints of his drawings: fifteen lithographs in black and white, sepia or bistre, published in 1888 by Boussod and Valadon.[628] Can such faithful and lively reproductions of the work of Degas be termed 'Impressionist prints'? The divide between the old types of reproduction and the new was not so self-evident that the question could be brushed aside; it was posed at the time. Degas himself made no distinction. He was so excited by Thornley's talent that he started working with him, and was always full of enthusiasm for printing: 'I told them to stop the print run', he wrote to Thornley, 'and said I would be going to the print works. It was not possible for me to get there, nor was I able to meet you at Rouart with the drawing on transfer paper. I wanted to make some alterations and I have no regrets about not making them because you weren't there. I shall be in Paris about 15 September and we will finish it off then.'[629]

The art world was receptive to these reproductions, and even the most passionate admirers of the original print rallied to promote them. Gustave Kahn, editor of *La Vogue*, claimed to prefer 'a lithograph by Thornley designed by Degas to any of Buhot's tricks',[630] and Fénéon compared them to artist's prints: 'To a far greater degree than the obsequious antics of the painters, such engravings will be works of art in their own right; take for example the subtly expressive lithographs made by Mr G. W. Thornley after Degas, which can be found in the album published last winter by Boussod and Valadon.'[631] Because Degas had not previously published any of his prints, his own lithographs could not be compared with those of William Thornley. The same could not be said however of Pissarro, also reproduced in lithograph by Thornley in an album prefaced by Gustave Geffroy: 'Mr Thornley, an artist who is well-known for his lithographic transcriptions, already having translated from one art form to another the works of Puvis de Chavannes, Claude Monet, Degas, today presents to amateurs of the print a collection of 25 images after the paintings of Camille Pissarro.'[632] This album followed the same pattern as the albums of artists' prints: the edition was limited to one hundred copies, each numbered and personally signed by Thornley and Pissarro, the plate being then destroyed. In a second album of twenty reproductions of drawings after Degas (1861–96), published by Goupil, Boussod, Manzi, Joyant et Cie, the title page bears the words: 'One hundred copies of these twenty facsimile prints of drawings by Degas have been printed, each copy is signed by the artist'.[633] Degas also put his signature to an album of ninety-eight photomechanical reproductions of his work, published in 1914 by Vollard, although he had never published any original lithographs and although Pissarro had predicted that 'there was no danger' of Degas's being persuaded by a publisher.[634] Bearing in mind the intransigence shown by Degas towards reproduction it would be inconsistent to suspect him of being commercially motivated; on the contrary, the opposite conclusion must be correct: that he was satisfying his old ambition to publish mechanical reproductions, albeit at a time when he was experiencing more and more difficulty with his work but had lost none of his professional rigour. The late reproductions of Degas's drawings were the outcome of what should still be called his art (whatever critical opinion may call it today), not just a concession.

The most ardent champions of the original print, André Mellerio, Roger Marx and Léonce Bénédite, were well aware of the threat posed by publication to the idea of the original print, based initially on the notion of rarity. They were in favour of the democratisation of art in the expanding market but refused any return to the erstwhile state of confusion between artists' prints and reproductions. This state of affairs lasted for a whole century, becoming accentuated whenever the print market, created to encourage collectors to buy, grew too quickly. The original print was then in the difficult position of having to respond to its own success with loud protests. First in the review *L'Estampe et l'affiche*,[635] managed and edited by Clément Janin, then in a manifesto in book form, *La Lithographie originale en couleurs* (1898), André Mellerio discusses the art market and the definitions and distinctions there holding sway, with particular reference to the power struggles dividing different sections of a European bourgeoisie in ferment. In a modest way, the lithograph was the subject of the kind of misunderstanding that arises when a power

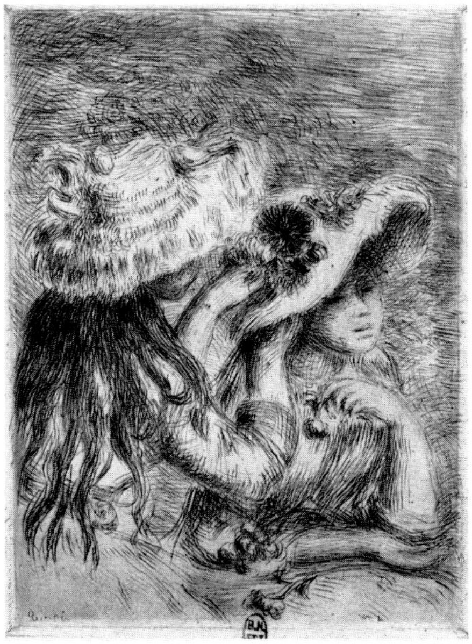

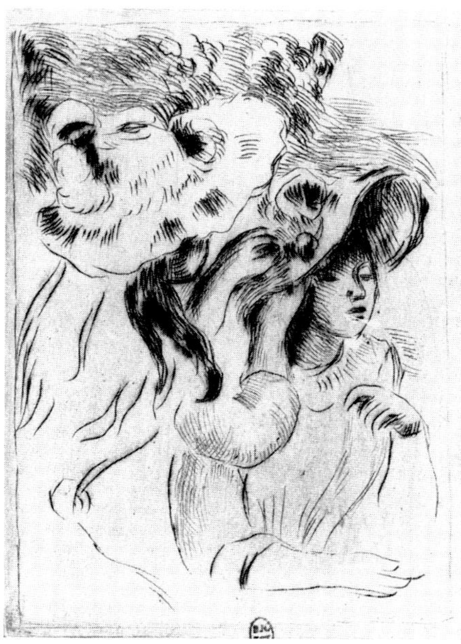

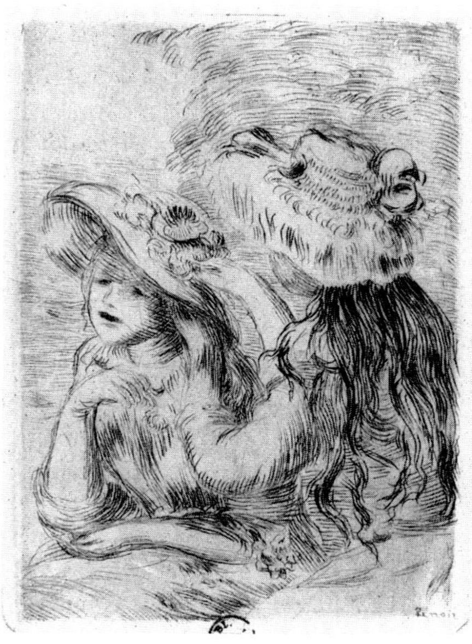

structure is being set up, when arguments can be solved only by the collapse of one party and the rise to dominance of the other. At least four such arguments can be identified.

The first concerns the lithograph as such, unacceptable to many because of its commercial and utilitarian image. Yet Mallarmé told his publisher in 1889 that the colour lithographs he wanted to have printed by Lemercier would cost more to print than line etchings;[636] nothing, however, could erase the trivial way the process had developed since 1830. The second argument concerns whether or not artists had a right to use transfer paper. The obligation to draw directly on to stone would have disqualified a large number of them. The trial still continues today, even though the verdict has been pronounced and the use of stone is one of the criteria for evaluating lithographs; transfer paper has nevertheless had many advocates among the most celebrated lithographers. Without it we should have almost no lithographs by Bresdin, Whistler, Pissarro, Degas, Fantin-Latour, Van Gogh, or Odilon Redon. Whistler gave evidence successfully in favour of his friend Joseph Pennell when he brought an action for slander against the painter Sickert who, in 1897 in the *Saturday Review*, accused him of deceiving collectors by confusing lithographs drawn on transfer paper with lithographs drawn directly on to stone. Sickert asserted that 'to pass off drawings on paper as lithographs is as misleading to the purchaser, as far as commercial value is concerned, as to sell photogravures as etchings'.[637] In 1890, when the battle was at its height, the most zealous defender of transfer paper was the most innovatory of lithographers, Odilon Redon, who had learnt his art from Bresdin and Fantin-Latour and who indicted stone as 'surly and unco-operative', proclaiming that 'the whole future of lithography (if it has a future) lies in the as yet undeveloped possibilities of the paper that can transfer the most delicate inflexions of hand and mind on to the stone so perfectly. The stone will assume a passive rôle'.[638] Léonce Bénédite, the curator of the Musée du Luxembourg, came to the rescue of Fantin-Latour: 'M. Fantin has strongly defended his position as a lithographer while those working on stone have distanced themselves from him, considering him only to be a draughtsman producing drawings on transfer paper. All these arguments between people throwing brickbats at one another are, it must be said, ancient history. To distinguish between different arts or processes according to types of pencil, the shape of instruments etc. is just hair-splitting, and could easily be carried on *ad infinitum*.'[639] The third argument concerned colour, which was also tainted by charges of vulgarity. The colour lithograph was suspected of being aimed at an easy-to-please public looking for a 'wall print', something decorative to hang between two pairs of matching curtains; Théodore de Banville denounced this kind of picture, comparing it unfavourably with the 'boxed'

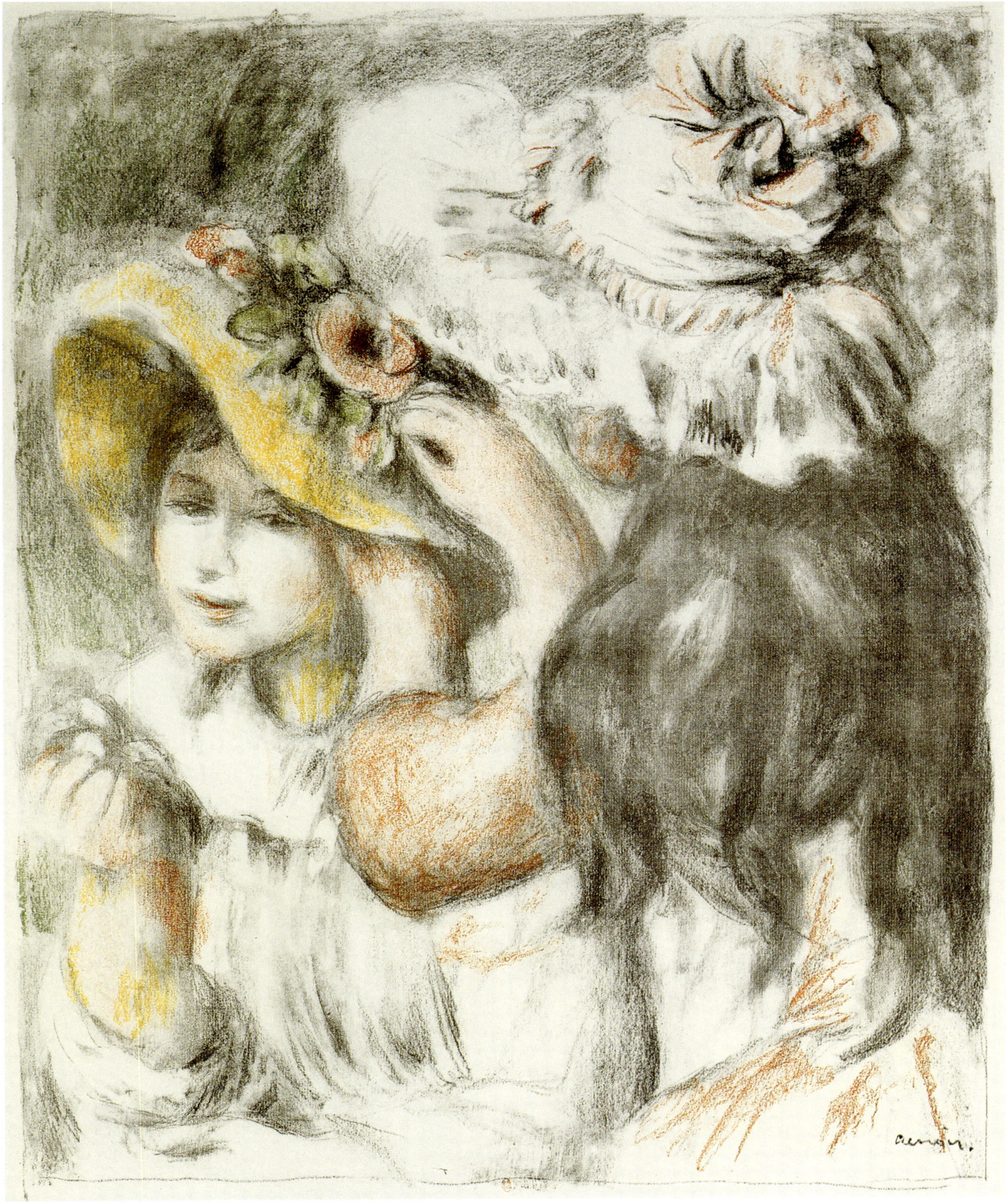

Previous page:
305, 306, 307. Pierre-August Renoir, *Pinning the Hat*. About 1894. (first plate). Drypoint, single state, 116 x 82 mm. (second plate). Drypoint, second and final state, 131 x 92 mm. (third plate). Drypoint, second and final state, 115 x 80 mm. Bibliothèque nationale, Paris.

308. Pierre-Auguste Renoir, *Pinning the Hat* (second plate). About 1898. Lithograph, single state, 600 x 488 mm. Bibliothèque nationale, Paris.

prints favoured by collectors. The critic Thiébault-Sisson spoke of 'a search for effects that are not within the realm of lithography'.

Henri Lefort, who was president of the engraving and lithographic section of the Société des Artistes Français condemned what he called the 'coloured image', reminding that 'in principle, in origin and by tradition the art of printmaking is incontrovertibly a black and white art form'. Charles Maurin, feeling himself under attack, rejoindered and the critic Roger Marx wrote *Pour la gravure en couleurs*[640] in defence of colour. The argument about colour prints did not arise over Impressionism, as we have seen; the later use of colour by the Impressionist printmakers and lithographers merged completely into the' groundswell of Art Nouveau.

The fourth and last grievance levelled against colour lithography was that it threatened the principle of the non-division of artistic labour, the touchstone of the modern definition of a work of art. In the printmaker's studio the printer stays at a respectful distance; if the printer's contribution is too visible (like Delâtre's inking) it is reckoned to be overzealous. The colour print, paradoxically, causes problems to the painter: it requires the colours to be broken in to component parts, the reverse of the painter's normal practice. To produce coloured lithographs, the painter needs training and quite frequently specialised assistance. André Mellerio, the fiercest champion of colour lithography, justified his stance: 'The word "printer" in fact designates a highly skilled technician who is responsible for overseeing the printing of the plate, from trial runs to the final proofs. When a large number of proofs is required, the job is finished by ordinary workmen, or by machine.'[641] Duchâtel, who worked for Lemercier and was the author of a treatise on the lithograph as art, Stern for Toulouse-Lautrec and especially Auguste Clot for Sisley, Cézanne and Rodin played this indispensable (if controversial) role. Mellerio's justification of the need for a 'stone compositor' opened the way for the reproduction considered as a work of art in its own right. The dealer Rochoux's quarrel with the artist-printmakers in the 1860s, when the market for prints first began to grow, was renewed during the second expansion in the 1890s and was revived again, virtually intact, in the 1970s.[642]

One last large album, published in 1899 by the German critic Julius Meier-Graefe with the title *Germinal*, illustrates the way this mix-up between originals and reproductions was fostered. The luxurious cover contains twenty prints on large paper. All the different techniques are represented, with the lithograph in the lead - there are fourteen, nine in colour. To Gauguin's long-disputed etching *Woman with Figs*, and lithographs by Vuillard, Bonnard and Toulouse-Lautrec are added a facsimile by Clot (named as such in the contents list) of one of Degas's dancers, another (unattributed) after Rodin and a reproduction by someone named Weiss of a painting by Van Gogh, *Landscape at Auvers*. The mix is so total that it is impossible to guarantee the authenticity of any of the contents. In his preface to *Germinal*, Gustave Geffroy draws attention to the 'outline of a European movement in the arts' represented in the selection: Max Liebermann, Georges Minne, Jan Toorop also appear. The growing internationalism of the clientèle (in addition to that of the artists) provoked an expansion of the market, and a simultaneous sanctioning and debunking of the principle of rarity, at the root of the monetary value of the print as a work of art.

next page:
309. Jean-Louis Forain, rejected frontispiece for *Marthe* by J.-K Huysmans. 1879. Etching, 149 x 99 mm. Bibliothèque nationale, Paris.

310. Jean-Louis Forain, accepted frontispiece for *Marthe* by J.-K Huysmans. 1879. Etching, 130 x 103 mm. Bibliothèque nationale, Paris.

59. *Forain, the Last of the Impressionists*

Jean-Louis Forain, who died in 1931, was the longest surviving printmaker of the Impressionist period. His last illustration is dated 1925, and his last etching, *Rest on the Flight into Egypt*, 1923.[644] He had long since abandoned subjects from everyday life for devotional themes. The man who shared the bohemian existence of Verlaine and Rimbaud in 1871 had now taken up religion. The second generation of painter-printmakers was not around at the height of the struggle to establish the artist's print. When Forain started work in about 1870 all the different outlets were already in place – newspapers, exhibitions, collectors. Jean-Louis Forain pursued a glittering career, deprived of that rich vein of anxiety and uncertainty that had nourished his predecessors.

He saw Goya's prints in the Bibliothèque Impériale in 1869 and was won over to printmaking. He studied with Gérôme, then with André Gill – an interesting succession of a genre painter and a caricaturist. In April 1876 he produced the cover of the illustrated magazine *Le Scapin*, tried to become a contributor to *Le Charivari* and, at the end of the year, published two of his early etchings in *Paris à l'eau-forte*.[645] Three careers were open to him: painting small genre paintings, press illustration and printmaking. In 1879 Degas, whom he greatly admired (and who admired him in return) involved him in the fourth Impressionist exhibition, where he showed paintings only, twenty-five in number. This was the most lucrative of all the Impressionist exhibitions, making a profit of 6000 francs.[646] Huysmans had spotted Forain. They became firm friends and later made the pilgrimage to Lourdes together. Huysmans suggested that Forain illustrate his *Marthe*, to which Forain's response was a picture of a hoydenish girl with plaits, naked except for a pair of striped stockings; the writer turned it down (Fig. 309). In his second attempt the girl was in a ball gown, leering impudently and holding a bottle; the figure is seated with the light behind her, with three large lights round her head in the manner of Degas (Fig. 310). In the same year, 1879, Forain was recommended to Charpentier by Degas and De Nittis to do illustrations for *La Vie Moderne*. The following year Forain produced some vignettes for Huysmans's *Croquis parisiens* and exhibited two etchings (it is not known which ones) at the fifth Impressionist exhibition, which contained the largest number of prints. In 1881 he entered oil paintings, watercolours and pastels in the

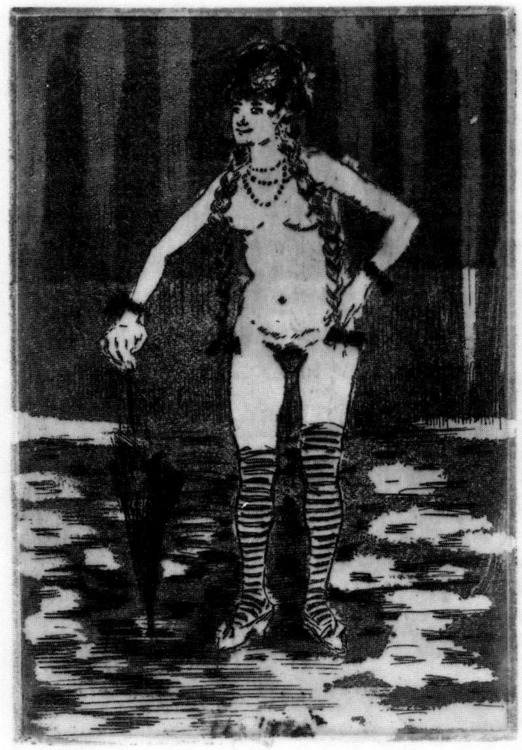

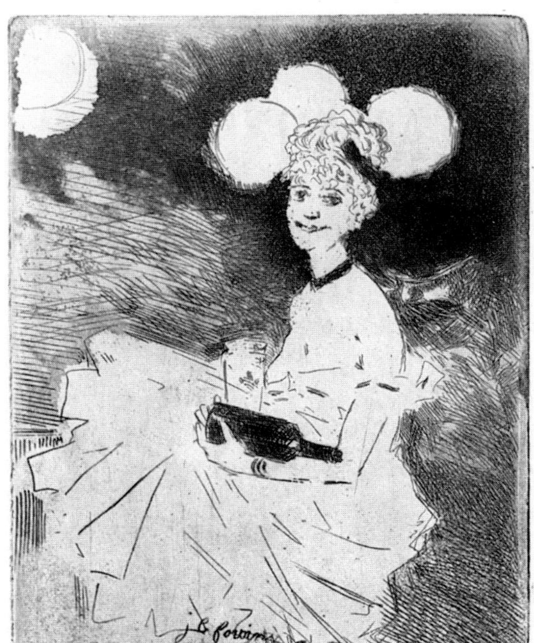

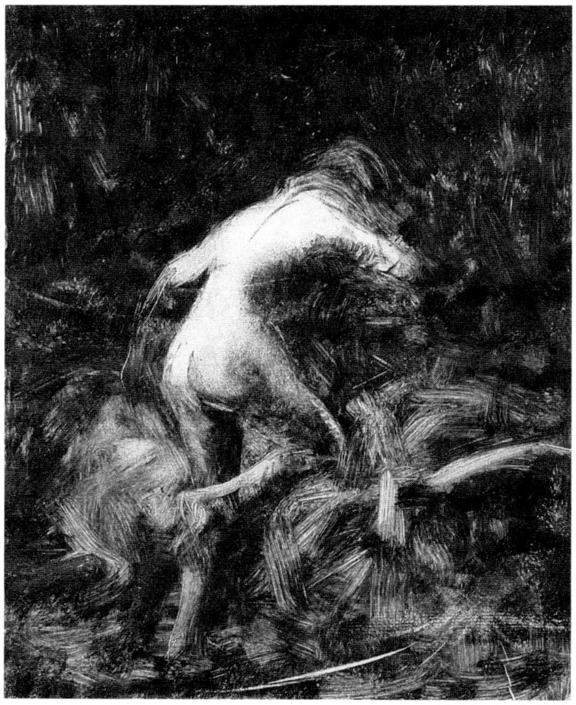

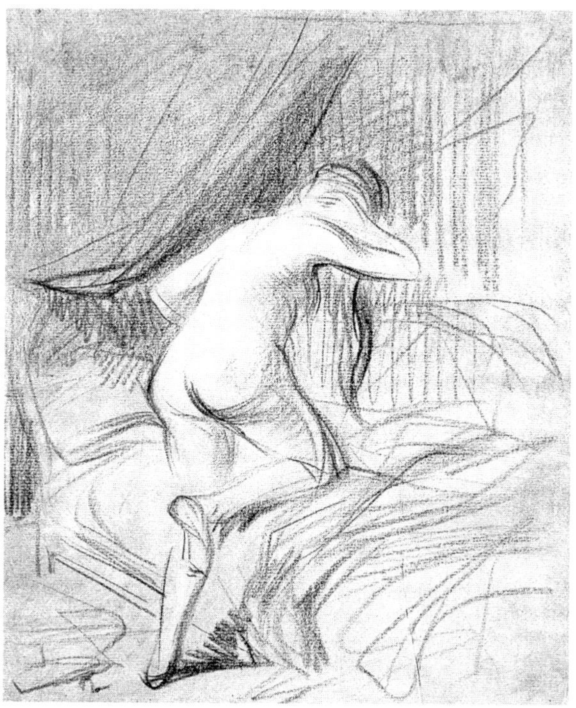

311, 312. Jean-Louis Forain,
Female Nude with one Knee on the Bed. 1908.
Pencil after the monotype, 300 x 243 mm.
Bibliothèque d'Art et d'Archéologie, Paris.

sixth, selected by Degas, and withdrew, with Degas and his friends, from the seventh. He exhibited thirteen works at the eighth and last exhibition in 1886 and was invited to show at the Salon des XX in Brussels in the same year. He was an illustrator by inclination, always more interested in a straightforward moral message than in complex composition, and he earned a reputation as a polemicist in the Third Republic. His work was spread through the press of the period: *La Revue illustrée*, *Le Monde parisien*, *Le Chat noir*, *Le Gil Blas*, *L'Echo de Paris*, *Le Journal*, *Le Courrier français*, *Le Rire* and dozens of other titles, before he was taken on permanently by *Le Figaro* in 1902. His success encouraged him to publish albums of his own: *La Comédie parisienne* (1892), *Album Forain* (1893), *Nous, Vous, Eux* (1893), *Doux pays* (1897) etc. he followed the traditional conservative path of the self-made man, encouraging anti-semitism and heedless nationalism.[647] In 1893 he was awarded the Légion d'Honneur.

The career of Raffaëlli, the other remaining 'impure' Impressionist, followed a similar pattern. His early days as a painter-printmaker with Degas, who involved him in the experiment with *le Jour et la Nuit* and with Huysmans, whose *Croquis parisiens* he illustrated in 1880, seemed to lead him nowhere; he was completely absorbed in publishing albums and illustrating weekly magazines. Success came more easily to him in the 1890s and from 1893 he produced numerous colour engravings, becoming president of the Société de la Gravure Originale en Couleurs, which he founded in 1904. The relationship of the print to fine art and industrial art remained ambiguous. Edmond de Goncourt wrote in 1896: 'I met Raffaëlli who told me that he only likes industrial art when it betrays the hand of man, and he therefore detests English industrial art which is smoothed and buffed to such a degree that every object appears to have been produced by a mechanic.'[648]

The years 1889–90, so important in the history of the print, also marked a turning point in the career of Forain. In 1889 he tried to start his own review, *Le Fifre*, which ceased publication after five issues, on 1 June, and he tried again in 1898–9, bringing out an anti-Dreyfusard broadsheet entitled *Psst*. . . . In 1890 he had his first one-man show, not at Durand-Ruel but at the more traditionalist Boussod et Valadon, and at this time began producing artist's lithographs. Forain had never tried lithography before. For him it was a way of producing expensive items for sale, pursued quite separately from his press illustrations, and the debate about the distinction between lithography and ordinary reproductive techniques appears not to have bothered him at all. In 1890 his first lithograph, *At the Restaurant*, based on his painting *At the Café Riche*, was given to the printer Belfond to be printed on handsome, lightly tinted paper; the fifty copies were signed and numbered by the artist. The style is only marginally more refined than the style of his newspaper illustrations; the picture was published

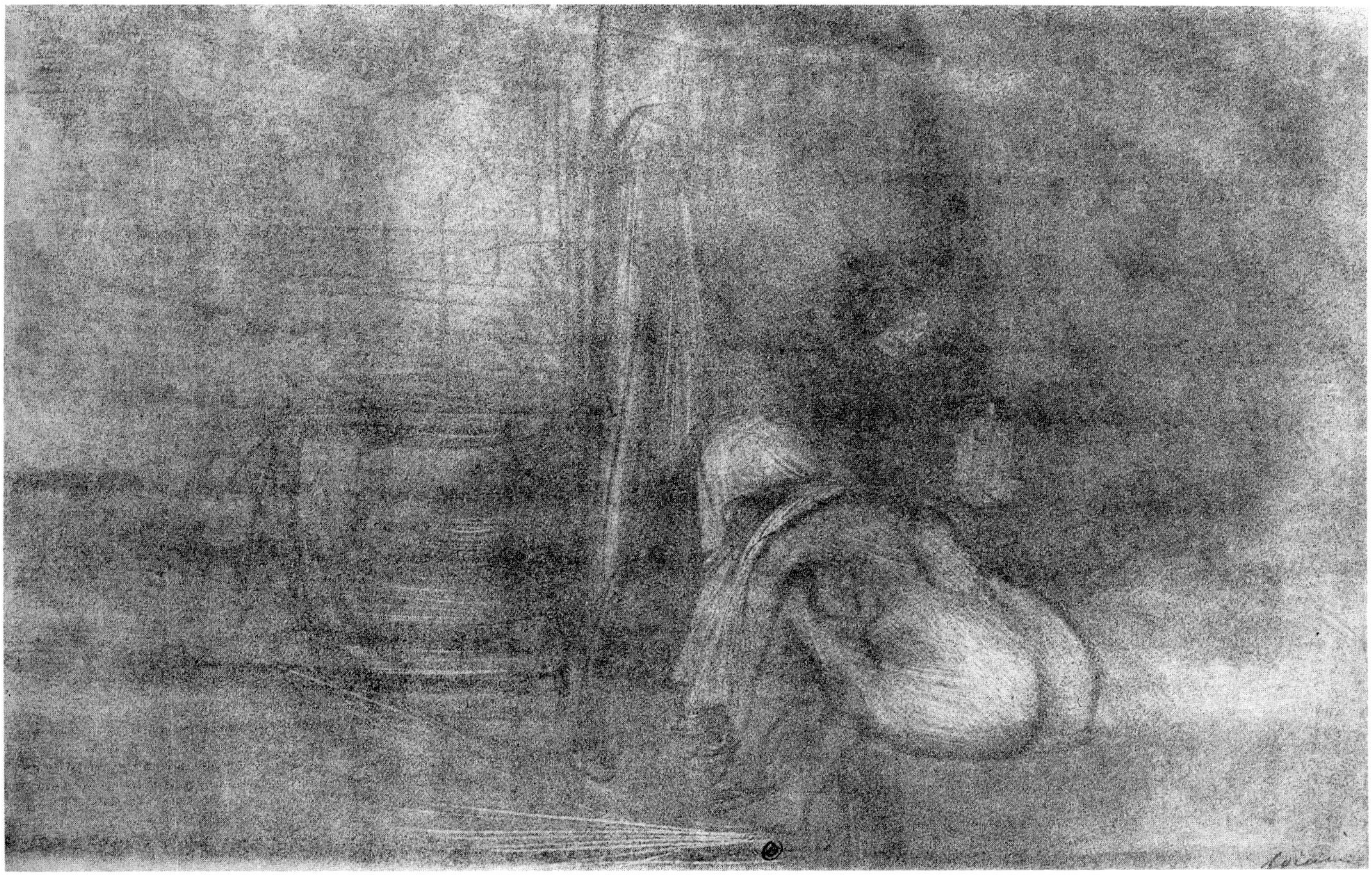

313. Jean-Louis Forain, *Rubbing down after the Bath*. Undated. Lithograph, first plate, 243 x 390 mm. Bibliothèque d'Art et d'Archéologie, Paris.

anyway as an illustration in *Le Courrier français* on 3 May 1896. His other lithographs, mainly based on subjects from his paintings and limited to around a dozen copies, were also reprinted in the newspapers. Fine art covered a huge spectrum henceforth, from oil paintings to press cuttings, demonstrating the diversity of the clientèle and the interaction between them and the artists. In 1891 Forain exhibited five paintings and five drawings at the painter-printmakers, but no prints. In 1892 he showed his lithographs at the Galerie Georges Petit, transforming them into posters in 1893. An artist can embrace a number of registers with a single theme, but the ambition to be versatile will tend to disaggregate his style, and to predetermine his choice of subject. An anecdotal press illustration will not make a genre painting, nor can a very finished painting be turned into a caricature. Forain was careful in his handling of these discrepancies, in order that his fame should enhance his reputation as an illustrator, and the popularity of the journalist be of profit to the painter.

Forain was no mean draughtsman. He embellished his lithographs with the same bold Indian ink lines that he used in his newspaper illustrations. For instance, in his *Women at their toilette*, with their clouds of vapour, the weight of the torsos is enhanced by modelling; the figures have no faces (like Degas' figures) but their buttocks are cheerfully exposed to view (Figs 311–13). Forain was the first of any of the printmakers discussed here to have an inventory of his work published (in 1910).[649] From the moment he began making lithographs he abandoned etching having produced about thirty etchings with all the brutality (the hasty drawing, the deeply etched lines, the light provided by white paper) of the early Impressionists. Manet's shadow hovers over a provocative kind of *Nana*, as it does over *Dancers in their Dressing Room* (1876) or *The Bar at the Folies-Bergère*. He began making etchings again in 1902, producing about 150 before 1923; they hark back to his early works but their effect is dulled by the passage of time.

60. *Conclusion*

Although at the time of the Empire in France competition between Paris and London entailed continual exchanges of artists between the two cities, it is nonetheless appropriate to have concentrated here on France. The period dealt with spans the years 1855 to 1889, between the two Expositions Universelles in Paris which, following the Great Exhibition of 1851 in London, covered a period of French supremacy in the arts. Not to be forgotten either is the fact that Impressionism took a hold in other industrialised countries from then on, and it was the Americans who first helped the Impressionists to make their name. The first pastel monotype print ever sold by Degas was sold in 1875 to Louisine Elder, the future Mrs Havemayer.[650] The first collection of etchings sold by Pissarro was sold to Samuel Avery.[651] It was an American, Keppel, who extolled Millet's etchings,[652] and an American, Lucas, who bought works as eccentric as Lepic's 'mobile' etchings,[653] or as the tentative experiments of Degas, termed by Edmond de Goncourt 'the religion of failure'.[654] If the American contribution to the literature on Impressionism, to exhibitions and catalogues of Impressionist work were excluded only about a third of the volume would remain, and that third, it has to be said, not always the best. American taste was built upon Realism. In London in 1844, Maberly published a guide for collectors of artists' prints, republished in New York in 1880 (Beraldi only brought his out in 1885) with an additional article on the superiority of the French School of etchers. The modern school was immediately accepted in the United States. Where Beraldi had only seen *griffonis* (scribbles), Maberly admired 'Corot's etchings echoing his paintings most agreeably . . . they are hard to come by and do not cost much, but they are nonetheless remarkable as etchings.' He is of the opinion that 'the American mind is particularly adapted to the expression of art in this form, and, with the encouragement offered by the constantly increasing numbers of collectors and purchasers, it will no doubt attain to a development at once rapid and vigorous.'[655]

To an even greater extent than Europeans, Americans expected the *objets d'art* that they bought to symbolise the values and customs that had grown from their newly-acquired wealth. International relations were re-established as the Republic gained control. The only French painter to win American sympathy before that was Manet, the scourge of the government, with his *Execution of Maximilian*, exhibited in New York in 1879. In 1883, the year in which France presented the Statue of Liberty to the United States, a large international exhibition of modern art opened in Boston, with support from the French government.[656] In 1883 also Durand-Ruel did business with his first German customer. The triumph of capitalism had reached the West. Other Western capitals were born. Societies of Etchers were established in Cincinnati and Philadelphia in 1880, in Boston in 1881, in Brooklyn in 1882, as well as the Society of American Etchers.[657] In 1869 a society of Italian artists, L'Acquaforte, was founded, publishing its first album of forty etchings in 1870 and its second in 1871. Signorini and Fattori took up printmaking.[658] By this time the Prussian printmaker Menzel, who belonged to the previous generation, had completed his work;[659] neither he nor Fattori went as far in the art of printmaking as Seymour Haden. Anders Zorn, the Swedish artist, made his first print in London in 1882.[660] In 1881 Louis Gonse rewarded Tadamasa Hayashi for his help with his book on Japanese Art with a drawing by Paul Renouard. Hayashi presented a complete collection of the works of Renouard to the Museum of European Art in Tokyo, where a special room was devoted to it.[661] After the American dealers, the Germans built up collections of Pissarro's prints in Bremen, Dresden and Munich. Paul Cassirer, the Berlin publisher and dealer, visited him in February 1903,[662] and at the same time the English magazine *The Studio* was preparing a first article on his etchings;[663] it was an English scholar, Arthur Hind, who published the first study of Pissarro's prints in a German magazine in 1908.[664] An international Society of Etchers was established in Brussels in 1874.[665] Impressionism was spreading its net internationally at the same pace as the newly-acquired wealth of its contemporaries; the relationship between craft, art and industry was being redefined and artistic hierarchies reordered.

The print as an independent entity comes into the story in a variety of guises. Van Gogh's lithographs on the poverty of the working classes were designed as propaganda (Fig. 287) and bear little relationship to his *Portrait of Dr Gachet* (Fig. 283), an etching made for himself and a few friends. Conversely, Cézanne's first etchings, designed to please Dr Gachet, bear only a distant connection with his lithographs of 1896, designed to please Vollard who was hoping to appeal to a hundred as yet unknown collectors. In both cases, however, a group arose who shared a taste for a particular work of art and a desire to possess it; in this way bonds were created between a scattered network of people who had no need to communicate with one another but who could recognise one another through the possession of this one symbolic object. Subscribers to a magazine, readers of a certain book, visitors to the Salon, customers in a café, theatre-goers, strollers in the street all constituted fluid groups which, together, added up to the new pattern of society.[666] The execution of a work of art, of whatever kind, marks the phase immediately preceding these moments of recognition, when spectators or collectors are momentarily linked by appreciation of the same piece. This is how different styles come into being. Besides its actual execution, each style embraces the institutions championing it and the networks supporting its creation.

The print is versatile and finds its own public, conferring membership of an association of owners on its admirers. Prints are renowned for attracting new buyers, to the disappointment of longstanding collectors who sometimes see their collections decreasing in value. Democracy rules, and poor Millet, who grumbled about commercialisation and refused to have his plates destroyed, became the most hackneyed artist of all in the chromolithography of the Third Republic. The register of the print is a very broad one: the class struggle and social rivalries can be read in it as in a history book. The incessant border disputes, the populist claims, the protestations of good taste, the obsession with exclusivity and distinctions, the technical tricks are all there. The artist becomes a printer and sometimes a publisher, if the word publisher has any meaning in an artist's studio. The artist has to choose between unearthing a hitherto unknown clientèle, and satisfying an existing one. Bracquemond's prolific and untidy output vacillated between these two choices and did not as a result attract any loyal or lasting followers; his work survived the century far less well than did the dogged and sometimes desperate search for a new kind of clientèle pursued by Degas and Pissarro.

The print as an 'averagely priced' investment fluctuated in a new kind of market. A print is a work that evolves over the years and, according to its location and period, may or may not be a work of art, or may be 'more or less' a work of art (as analysed in great detail by Marcel Proust;[667] it has constantly to justify its status as art, independently of its inherent quality.[668] The print was the product of a period of middle-men and mediators, when society had been blown apart and then, when reassembled, was held together by the invisible bonds of a more evenly distributed economy; the print played an essential rôle in the diversification and internationalisation of the art market, being loosely connected with the politics of a democracy that pushed the privatisation of art to its limits. The print bridges the gap bewteen literature and the visual arts, yet suddenly rejected the writing in the margins, dismissing script engravers to leave space for the painter's handwritten signature, abandoned the bookshops in favour of picture galleries and the libraries in favour of museums. Language was foiled on its own terrain, as it was in the philosophy of Bergson, so convincingly exemplified by Impressionism.

The print is mutable and could therefore represent the relativity that had appeared along with the new ways of viewing the world; it is fragile and can express the changes wrought by time. For a public accustomed to a stationary world with well-defined boundaries, and whose wealth was based on fixed incomes and immutable values it was difficult to come to terms with the work of artists who extolled the obsolescence and instability of the real world. The Impressionism that was shared by painters and printmakers alike defines a moment in history when time had eroded the value of objects. Bergson, who presented his thesis on *Time and Free Will* in the year that saw the final Impressionist exhibition, summed up his philosophy in challenging terms: 'I said that time existed and that it was not space.'[669] Although such a thesis was difficult to express in visual terms, the Impressionists come near to success. The print helped them then and helps us to understand them today. Public resistance to such novel ideas was expressed in economic terms by a crisis that accompanied, and to some extent explains, the crisis affecting Impressionism between 1874 and 1886. The aesthetic and economic crises were so bound together that Impressionism might almost be termed the original art of monetary capitalism. Stocks and shares, almost unknown to the general public before 1848, continued to intimidate people for a while but eventually gained ground as government stocks and bonds took off. The value of the print, an intermediate agent, grew as public confidence in it grew, and gradually allowed print as a medium to be accepted into the French heritage. The symbolic value of an object is not based solely on its public face.[670] The success of Impressionism was linked to the emergence of new political powers and also undeniably to the doubling of the value of investments between 1855 and 1889. In 1890 investments outstripped savings in France,[671] and the rise of capitalism came about even more rapidly in the United States. The Impressionist vision was no longer in dispute.

NOTES

1. Théodore Duret, *Les Peintres Impressionistes*, 1878 (for the various editions see Zola, 1974, p.202 and note); his point was reiterated at once by Emile Zola. 'L'Ecole française de peinture à l'Exposition universelle de 1878', in Zola, 1991, p.393.
2. On criticism before 1870 see Parsons and Ward, 1986, and for the period in general: Lethère, 1959, Riout, 1989, in *La Promenade du critique influent*, 1990, with the minutes of the conference organised by the same team: *La Critique d'Art en France, 1850–1900*, 1989.
3. Distel, 1989. See also Pierre Angrand, 'Les commandes des gravures d'Etat sous le Second Empire', in *Nouvelles de l'estampe*, 1966, no. 8, pp.375–7, and 'L'Etat mécène, période autoritaire du Second Empire', in *Gazette des Beaux-Arts*, May–June 1969, pp.303–48.
4. For a general survey and bibliography, see Mayeur, 1973; Rioux, 1989 (on economic expansion, pp.196 ff.); Sorlin, 1969; Hobsbawm, 1975; Braudel and Labrousse, 1976; Bouvier, Furet and Gilet, 1965.
5. Weisberg, 1967.
6. *Portrait of Paul Hugot*. See Berhaut, 1977, no.81 for the painting, dated 1878, and 81a for the engraving. Paul Hugot was a friend of Caillebotte, which might explain why the painting was done from a photograph, as Peter Galassi suggests in 'La Méthode de Caillebotte' in Varnadoe, 1987, pp.27–40; and also why he made an engraving as well, and may have presented it to his friend as a gift. It was not published. In his *Dictionnaire de l'estampe*. 1985, p.368, J. Bailly-Herzog mentions an etching by Caillebotte apparently published by Moline, *Old Woman Sewing*, possibly after a painting (Berhaut, no. 53, 1877).
7. Isaacson, 1980. The question of the generations is also dealt with by Renato Barilli, 'L'Impressionismo e la stampa: una fiore con molte spine' (text in Italian and French) in Fossier, 1990. For a more theoretical approach, see Karl Mannheim, 'Le Problème des générations' (French edition, with an introduction by Gérard Mauger), Paris, 1990.
8. Pierre Dupont-Ferrier, *Le Marché financier de Paris sous le Second Empire*, F. Alcan, Paris, undated, pp.2–6, emphasises the fact that during the thirty years of peace 1830–60, capital had accumulated but there were no systems in place to make it yield. These began to appear gradually during the Second Empire and were firmly established by the beginning of the Third Republic, mirroring what was taking place in the art market at the same time: 'On the eve of the revolution of 1848 the public, who had been quietly saving during the preceding period of peace, left their savings almost untouched in spite of the example of England. Landowning retained its prestige, but transferable securities were virtually unknown to the general public . . . During the years that followed a huge number of securities were created by the state, by finance companies and by foreign governments . . . The economic activity that resulted was of a vigour rarely witnessed before or since.'
9. On the condition of art in general, see White, 1991; Rosenthal, 1910; Sloane, 1951; Genêt-Delacroix, 1987.
10. Sensier, 1881, pp.44–5.
11. See for example Beth S. Wright, 'Henri Gauguin et le musée Colbert', in *Nouvelles de l'estampe*, no.114, December 1990, pp.24–31.
12. Jeff Rozen, *Lemercier et Cie, The Advent of Photo-Lithography and the Transformation of Print Production during the Second Empire*, Ph.D., Northwestern University, Evanston, USA, 1985, p.20. Summarised in 'La Photographie et l'estampe industrielle en France dans les années 1840', in *Nouvelles de l'estampe*, no. 92, May 1987, pp.4–15.
13. Corinne Bouquin, *Recherches sur la lithographie à Paris au XIXe siècle: l'imprimerie Lemercier*, DEA of the Université de Paris I, 1987.
14. Rozen, *op. cit.*, note 12, p.8.
15. Pierre Miquel, *Paul Huet de l'aube romantique à l'aube impressioniste*, Sceaux, 1962, p.152. The Société Schongauer had already set up a museum in Colmar in 1847 designed to 'propagate knowledge of works of art, facilitate their study and develop the appreciation of beauty.'
16. Raoul de Croy, 'Les Magasins pittoresques à deux sous', in *Journal des artistes et des amateurs*, 3 November 1833, p.1.
17. Hippolyte Castille, *Les Hommes et les moeurs en France sous le régime de Louis-Philippe*, Paris, 1853, Chap. XII, 'De l'industrie intellectuelle', p.395 ff.
18. Published in Rouillé, 1989, pp.35–43.
19. Théodore de Banville, *Odes funambulesques*, Paris 1878, pp.179–80.
20. Hippolyte Castille, *op. cit.*, p.337.
21. Laborde, 1856, p.451.
22. *Ibid.*, p.465.
23. Jacques de Caso, 'Serial sculpture in Nineteenth-Century France', in J. Wasserman, *Metamorphosis in Nineteenth-Century Sculpture*, Cambridge, 1975, pp.1–27.
24. Victor Ladet, 'De la propriété en matière d'art', in *L'Artiste*, 1841, Vol. 7, pp.71–4.
25. Baudelaire, *Le Peintre de la vie moderne, Oeuvres complètes*, p.881. On the rise of the reproduction, see Farwell, 1977.
26. Frédéric Villot, 'De la gravure à l'eau-forte', in *L'Artiste*, December 1834, pp.301–3.
27. Marie-Madeleine Rousseau, *Jeanron, peintre, écrivain, directeur des musées nationaux, 1808–1877*, Paris 1935.
28. Lugt, no. 1944, and Paul Mantz, announcement at the begining of the catalogue to the sale held on 18–19 March 1873, reproduced in *Nouvelles de l'estampe*, 1971, no. 2 (March-April), pp.564–8: 'Jules Niel (1800–1872)'. Pierre Angrand, 'Lettre inédite de Meryon à Jules Niel', in *Nouvelles de l'estampe*, 1969, no.8, pp.357–62. This enlightened antique dealer enjoyed sixteenth century drawings as much as he did Meryon's prints. He supported Meryon, encouraging collectors like the Duc d'Arenberg, from Brussels, to appreciate and buy his work, and also entrusted to him his daughter Gabrielle as his apprentice.
29. Written up by Philippe Burty, 'Paul Huet', in *Gazette des Beaux-Arts*, April 1869, pp.297–315. Paul Huet left seventeen unpublished prints when he died; they were published in 1869 by his son, and proved more successful than his first album.
30. Guiffrey, 1866. A more complete catalogue was published using Paul Prouté's entries in *L'Inventaire du fonds français* by the Département des Estampes in the Bibliothèque Nationale, Paris, vol. XI, pp.99–134. See also the article on Jacque by Robert J. Wickenden in *Print Collector's Quarterly*, 1912, vol.II, pp.74–101.
31. Pissarro, *Correspondance*, Vol. III, p.100, 28 June 1891: 'This terrible painter, Charles Jacque. . .', and also Vol.IV, p.77, 30 March 1895.
32. On relations between Charles Jacque and Millet, see Melot, 1978, p.286. The Lebrun catalogue was published after the publication of Alfred Sensier's book in 1881.
33. On Hervier (1821–79), see Franz Weitenkampf in *Print Collector's Quarterly*, vol.XII, April 1925, pp.205–3, and Raymond Bouyer, 'Les Petits Maîtres oubliés: Adolphe Hervier', in *Gazette des Beaux-Arts*, July 1896, pp.61–72.
34. Melot, 1978, p.251.
35. Bailly-Herzberg, 1975. On Corot, see Melot, 1978, pp.257–9.
36. Fidell-Beaufort and Bailly-Herzberg, 1975, p.60. See also Etienne Moreau-Nélaton, *Daubigny raconté par lui-même*, Paris 1925.
37. Castagnary, *Salons*, Paris, 1892, vol.I, p.254.
38. Théodore Pelloquet, *Dictionnaire de poche des artistes contemporains*, Paris, 1858.
39. Frédéric Henriet, 'Les paysagistes contemporains: Daubigny', in *Gazette des Beaux-Arts*,

May 1874, pp.464–75, and, more importantly, *Charles-François Daubigny et son œuvre gravé*, Paris, 1875, p.464. On Daubigny as an illustrator, see Fidell-Beaufort, 1974.
40. Quoted in Melot, 1978, p.272.
41. Fidell-Beaufort, 1974, p.78.
42. Bouillon, 1979, p.275 ff.
43. Melot, 1978, p.275, no. 66.
44. Alfred de Lostalot, obituary in *Gazette des Beaux-Arts*, 1878, pp.346–7.
45. Georgel, 1973, p.11.
46. Isabelle James, *Blanquart-Evrard et les origines de l'édition photographique française*, Geneva, 1981.
47. This question is dealt with very thoroughly in Rouillé, 1982.
48. E. de Valicourt, *Galvanoplastie, Daguerréotype. Nouveau manuel complet de galvanoplastie. . ., suivi d'un traité de Daguerréotypie*, Paris, 1945 (reprinted by Laget, Paris, 1976). Gillotage was invented by Spencer and Jacobi and was imported into France in 1836 by Boquillon.
49. There is as yet no comprehensive study of the industrial techniques of reproduction developed in the nineteenth century. The following can be consulted: Fawcett, 1986; Adeline [1984], and by the same author, *L'Illustration photographique*, Paris, 1896; Eugène Ostroff, 'History of photomechanical reproduction', in *Journal of Photographic Science*, 1969, no.3, pp.65–80, and no.4, pp.101–15; Otto M. Lilien, *History of industrial gravure printing up to 1900*, London, 1972; and the catalogue to the exhibition *De Niepce à Stieglitz, la photographie en taille-douce*, Musée de l'Elysée, Lausanne, 1982. For a comprehensive survey, see Melot, 1990, pp.329–55.
50. On 'clichés-verre' see 'Note sur le cliché-verre', in Melot, 1978, pp.21–4, and the catalogue to the exhibition *Cliché-verre. . .*, 1980. Two other exhibition catalogues on the same subject are: *Malerei und Photographie im Dialog von 1840 bis heute*, Kunsthaus, Zurich, 1977, and *Le Cliché-verre: Corot et la gravure diaphane*, Musée d'Art et d'Histoire, Geneva, Department of Prints, 1982.
51. Gustave Bourcard, *La Cote des estampes des differentes écoles. . .*, Paris, 1912, p.157.
52. *Auguste Delâtre imprimeur-artiste raconté par lui-même*, unpublished lecture, typescript in B.N. Est: S.n.r. 4, Delâtre.
53. On Meryon see Stuffmann, 1975, and Burke, 1974–5. See also Weisberg, 1972.
54. E. and J. Goncourt, 'Feu M. Thomas', in *L'Artiste*, 28 December 1856, pp.253–9.
55. E. and J. Goncourt, *Journal*, 19 October 1856.
56. *Id., Manette Salomon*, p.380. This novel was published in 1865.
57. Beraldi, Vol. x, 1890, pp.37–8.
58. Burty in *Gazette des Beaux-Arts*, June 1863, p.521, note 2, and Loÿs Delteil in the preface to his catalogue, 1927, p.9; more recently, see: Philippe Néagu: 'Lettres de Meryon à l'administration des Beaux-Arts concernant la publication de son "Voyage en Océanie",' in *Nouvelles de l'estampe*, no.58–9, July–October 1981, pp.12–23, and R. D. J. Collins, 'Les "Projets" de Charles Meryon', in *Nouvelles de l'estampe*, no.110, May–June 1990, pp.5–12. According to Ducros, it was Bléry who encouraged Meryon, see the catalogue to the exhibition *Meryon peintre de marine*, Musée de la Marine, 1968–9, notice no. 398. For the relationship between Meryon and Millet, to whom he was apparently mentor, see Moreau-Nélaton, *Millet raconté par lui-même*, Paris 1921, vol.II, p.100.
59. *Le Magasin pittoresque*, vol.xx, pp.188, 236, 292, 331 and 372.
60. On the lithographs of Dupré, see Melot, 1978, pp.238–4.
61. Charles Chaplin (1825–91) made etchings from 1848 onward in the tradition of Decamps and Millet, publishing his first plate in *L'Artiste* in 1848; he later produced some original landscapes (*November, Aunay*, 1856, *Farm Interior*, 1858), publishing an album in 1860, after which he became a member of the Société d'Aquafortistes and began pouring out the genre scenes that made him a household name.
62. Laurens, 1901, pp.449–50, quoted in Georgel, 1973, p.24. Laurens quotes his friends Chauvel, Bracquemond, Saint-Etienne, Jules Didier, de Curzon, Peigné. Georgel, 1973, also mentions that *La Revue fantaisiste*, published by Catulle Mendès from February to November 1861, contained an etching by Bresdin in each number; he reminds us that the efforts of Paul Chenay to introduce Victor Hugo to original printmaking, which would have suited his 'temperament' so well and would have been an undoubted commercial success as well, date also from 1860.
63. Bouillon, 1979, p.246.
64. Bouillon, 1987; Getscher, 1974.
65. Bouillon, 1978, pp.4–10.
66. Bouillon, 1987, pp.53–4.
67. *Ibid*, p.73.
68. *Eight Subjects from the Fables of La Fontaine*, 1852; *Etchings by Bracquemond*, 1844. In 1855 Bracquemond was able to exhibit at the Salon his *Self Portrait* as an etcher, painted in 1853, and four etchings including *The Top of a Door Frame* of 1852. His lack of success forced him to sell his three best plates for 45 francs. See Bouillon, 1979, p.242ff.
69. *Ibid*, 1979, p.247.
70. *Ibid*, 1979, p.774.
71. *Ibid*, 1979, p.777.
72. Beraldi, vol. III, 1885, p.15.
73. On Millet's early work see Melot, 1978, pp.286–7: Sensier reports that 'it was in 1855, when he had finished his painting for the Exposition Universelle, that Millet made five etched engravings of rural subjects and was soon able to sell them. Two others were made but he was unhappy with the etching and did not publish them. A little while earlier he had tried some copper and zinc engravings, but these were too small to be exhibited.' (c.f. *La Vie et l'œuvre de J.-F. Millet. . .* Paris 1881, p.162). This is confirmed by the American painter Edward Wheelwright who, in his memories of Millet and Barbizon (*Atlantic Monthly*, September 1876, pp.257–76), writes that Millet finished four or five plates between October 1855 and June 1856. See also Philippe Burty, 'Les eaux-fortes de J.-F. Millet', in *Gazette des Beaux-Arts*, vol. IX, September 1861, pp.262–6.
74. On *The Gleaners*, see Herbert, 1975, pp.143–9.
75. Sensier, *op. cit.*, Paris, 1881, p.162, note 1. The idea of publishing the plates was abandoned; they were bundled up and forgotten until Millet again thought of publication and asked Sensier to contact Delâtre. Sensier wrote to Millet on 8 February 1858: 'Let's discuss Delâtre. I wrote to him and the letter eventually found him. He came and I spoke to him of your intentions. He then requested money for the paper. I gave him an advance of ten francs. He asked to take the plates away, but I postponed handing them over. He's sent for the plates again this morning and I sent a message to say one was missing (this is just an excuse, because in fact I have found all five. They were so tightly tied up that the smallest one disappeared under the others). Delâtre's reply was immediate!! I'll take the plates to him on Friday, the day he has named, but I shall think of pretexts for further delay; it's difficult and awkward to act so suspiciously, but what can I do.' Millet's letters to Alfred Sensier are in the Cabinet des Dessins in the Musée du Louvre.
76. Letter from Sensier to Millet, 21 November 1860, which also contains the following: 'As for Meryon, he's a smoky glass, a fakir living on tea and raisins; it would only take a smile from your excellency and a proof of your *Men Digging* inscribed: Millet to Meryon. He would be perfectly satisfied. You have become a prince. M. Niel is sure that Meryon would be delighted. Should I publish?'
77. On Legros, see Wedmore, 1883; Soulier, 1904; Geiger, 1957. On the realists, see Weisberg, 1980.
78. Baudelaire: 'L'Eau-forte est à la mode', in *La Revue anecdotique*, 15 April 1862 (reprinted in *Le Boulevard*, 14 September) in *Œuvres complètes*, p.849.
79. Poulet-Malassis and Thibaudeau, 1877. Delâtre remembers having printed Legros's first etchings; 'from one to ten proofs, never more'. The Bibliothèque Nationale has a proof of Legros's dry point portrait of Delâtre, dedicated: 'A son confrère Delâtre le typographe'.
80. Dodgson, 1922, with reference to the catalogue of Poulet-Malassis and Thibaudeau. In particular nos.144 and 146 (retouched proofs). In the Bibliothèque Nationale there is also a proof of *Communion at Saint-Médard*, touched up with gouache (former collection of Moreau Nélaton).
81. Exposition Universelle 1855, English section, no.1225.
82. Gustav Kobbé, 'Whistler in the U.S. Coasts Survey', in *The Chap Book*, 1898, pp.479–80. On Whistler, see Pennell, 1913 and Lochnan, 1984. For a general biography, See Sutton, 1966. For the lithographs, see Way and Dennis, 1903 and for a catalogue of the lithographic work, MacDonald, 1988.
83. Schneiderman, 1983, reported by John Klein in *Print Quarterly*, December 1984, vol.1, no.4, pp.291–3.
84. *Etudes à l'eau-forte par Francis Seymour Haden*, note and description by Philippe Burty, Paris, 1866, in-fol, 43 pp., 25 pl. See also Philippe Burty, 'L'oeuvre de M. Francis Seymour-Haden', in *Gazette des Beaux-Arts*, September 1864, pp.271–87, and October 1864, pp.356–66.
85. Schneiderman, 1983, p.26.
86. William R. Drake, *A Descriptive Catalogue of the Etched Work of Francis Seymour Haden*, London, 1880, completed by H. Naseby Harrington, *A Supplement to Sir William Drake's Catalogue of the Etched Work of Sir Francis Seymour Haden*, London, 1903.
87. The first article is accompanied by a 'letter on etching', by Seymour Haden, pp.277–9; the part entitled 'printing' contains the words: 'I think that every etcher needs to be his own printer', and a eulogy of Delâtre.
88. Seymour Haden's 'About etching' was published in *The Fine Art Quarterly Review* in June 1866 (pp.145–60). The speeches of Seymour Haden contain other declarations in support of the art of the painter-engravers: in the *Presidential Address to the Royal Society*

of Painters-Etchers, London, 1890 and 1891 and also in *The Relative Claims of Etchings and Engraving to Rank as Finer Arts and to be presented as such in the Royal Academy of Arts*, London, 1890.
89. Valéry, 1938, p.10 (the first edition dates from 1936).
90. According to Jean Sutherland Boggs, in *Degas*, 1989, pp.34–45, Degas venerated his mother. The story about the wedding dress was recounted by Louisine Havemeyer in 1961 and reproduced by Nathalie Reymond in *Degas illustre et inconnu*, Paris, 1988, p.14. See also Thomson, 1987.
91. Carnet 5, p.33 (18 January 1856). See Reff, 1985, vol.1, p.49.
92. The plate, now scratched and in the Los Angeles County Museum, was printed in five states. Two examples of the first state exist (Bibliothèque Nationale, Paris and Metropolitan Museum, New York), and two of the second (Bibliothèque Nationale, Paris, Curtis collection, and Metropolitan Museum, New York). There is one proof of the third state in the Art Institute, Chicago and one of the fifth in the Bibliothèque d'Art et d'Archéologie (Strölin, Roger Marx and Doucet collection); both are marked in pencil, in handwriting not belonging to Degas, the first one 'Degas, 1857', the second 'planche après essuyage, dernier état', with the note 'Florence, 1857', in the same handwriting but evidently added later.
These notes may have been added later and do not necessarily refer to the print of 1857 (after 1 November), as Moses thought; the portrait of Tourny clearly bears this date.
There is no evidence to show that Degas was in Florence at the end of 1857. He was in Rome in November. He was in Florence at the beginning of the following year and returned there for a long stay in August 1858. There is a preparatory drawing in a notebook (Reff, Nb7, p.22) used in Italy from July to October 1856 (Reff, vol.1, p.55) now in the Louvre.
93. Editorial of the first issue of the *Gazette des Beaux-Arts*, January 1859. Law was a Scottish banker who enjoyed considerable success as Controller General of Finances in France in the early eighteenth century.
94. Bouillon, 1982.
95. *Gazette des Beaux-Arts*, 1863, p.148.
96. Emile Zola, 'Edouard Manet', in *Revue du XXe siècle*, 1 January 1867, in Zola, 1991, p.167.
97. In his first 'Salon', Emile Zola made a similar observation: 'Distemper is fine for the badly off, but the rich need paintings on their walls. Now a whole team of workmen has emerged to finish the work begun by the bricklayers.' Emile Zola, *Mon Salon, Le Moment artistique*, Paris, 4 May 1866, In Zola, 1991, p.110.
The same observation could be made about prints except that they are frequently not hung on the walls but are 'consumed' by individuals, are bought for private indulgence in this society where capital is beginning to make its way into private life, and public life is broken up into smaller and smaller units by the growth of the cities.
98. 'Private work gave the green light to the kind of subjects ("of no interest") that began to appear in Villers-Cotteret's series of 1853: dark, dull landscapes without picturesque features, or subjects that might strike the public as "aggressive" – like *The Plucked Chicken*. At the same time it also encouraged 'pure' experiments, quick sketches or the use of different processes, which were not always successful'. Bouillon, 1979, p.771.
99. *Ibid*, p.247.
100. Georgel, 1973, p.15.
101. Louis Figuier, *La Photographie au Salon de 1859*, Paris, 1860, p.1. This can be read, with texts by Nadar and Burty, In Rouillé, 1989, pp.319–24.
On the conflict between engraving and photography, see Henri Delaborde, 'La Photographie et la gravure', in *Revue des Deux Mondes*, 1 April 1856, published in Rouillé, 1989, p.228.
102. Copyright 20 May 1859, see Bailly-Herzberg, 1972, vol.1, p.15. On Chifflart, see: Sueur, 1993; the publication of her thesis (1992) written for the Ecole du Louvre, is expected soon.
103. Lugt, Suppl., 1956. Arozarena, no. 109. The Arozarena Sales: 11 March, 10 April, 27 and 28 May 1861. There was a fifth sale on 29 May, of drawings.
104. Introduction to the catalogue of the Arozarena Sale [by Clément], 11 March 1861.
105. A. Rochoux, *Observations sur l'introduction au catalogue de M.D.G.D.A., curiosité littéraire et artistique par A. Rochoux*, Paris, March 1861.
106. Anonyme [Rochoux], *Les Moutons de panurge, chapitres émouvants et drôlatiques sur les estampes, les experts, les catalogues et les collectionneurs*, Paris 1861.
107. *Gazette des Beaux-Arts*, 1863, p.148.
108. Philippe Burty, 'Le Belle épreuve', préface à l'album *L'Eau'forte en 1875*, Paris, Cadart 1875.
109. Bailly-Herzberg, 1972.
110. Théophile Gautier, 'Un mot sur l'eau-forte', preface to the first album published by the Société des Aquafortistes (1863). reprinted in Bailly-Herzberg, 1972, vol.I, pp.266–7.
111. Jules Janin, 'L'eau-forte, le soleil et le crayon', preface to the second album (1864), *ibid.*, pp.268–9.
112. Beraldi, vol.V, 1886, p.92.
113. On Chaigneau, 1830–1906, see Bailly-Herzberg, 1972, vol.II, pp.36–7.
114. On Xavier de Dananche (1828–1894), *ibid.*, pp.55–9.
115. On Michelin (1815–1870), *ibid*, p.53; on Vollon (1833–1900), vol,II, pp.177–8.
116. Bailly-Herzberg, 1972, vol.I, p.255, note 83, suggests that the cause may have been the Republican vote against President Johnson, or, more likely, the cooling of relations between France and America.
117. Bailly-Herzberg, 1985, p.22. No contemporary print of this etching is known. The plate resurfaced in 1978 and fifty copies were then printed.
See *Frédéric Bazille and Early Impressionism*, 1978, no. 31, and Daulte, 1992, no. 39, p.170. The painting of *View of a Village* (Musée Fabre, Montpellier) is signed and dated 1868. There are various charcoal sketches for the painting (Musée du Louvre, RF 5259, fol., 52, 53, 55). See also Champa, 1973, pp.88–9, fig. 125.
118. Baudelaire, *Œuvres complètes*, p.892.
119. For a general survey of Manet's work, see Clark, 1985; Hanson, 1977; Tabarant, 1947 and Darragon, 1989.
120. Manet's engraved work has been catalogued several times. Better than the early catalogues by Moreau-Nélaton (1906) and Marcel Guérin (1944), or the more recent Harris, 1970, (see our revue in *Nouvelles de l'estampe*, no. 4, summer 1972, pp.11–13), even in the revised edition (by Joël M. Smith, San Francisco, A. Wofsy Fine Arts, 1990, see the review by Juliet Wilson-Bareau in *Print Quarterly*, Vol. IX, September 1992, pp.301–2), are the meticulous studies by Juliet Wilson-Bareau, author of the catalogue entries to the exhibition in 1983, see Bareau, 1977 and 1978. See also Melot, 1983, and the review by Henri Zerner in *Print Quarterly*, vol.I, no. 1, March 1984, pp.71–2, and Fisher, 1985. An overview of the different catalogues can be found in our entry on Manet in *Inventaire du fonds français après 1800*, Paris, Bibliothèque Nationale, Département des Estampes, vol.XV, 1985, pp.96–7.
121. Adhémar, 1967, commented by Bruce, 1983, pp.47–8.
122. On *The Little Horsemen*, see Harris, no.5, and Fisher, 1985, no.6, p.37.
This print, like most of the prints that followed, produced a storm of reaction from critics and historians alike. Rosenthal commented that 'the figures are bathed in light and air to the point almost of dissolution'.
Harris remarks that 'it is certainly the most accomplished of Manet's early etchings because of its complexity and the mastery with which the complexity is handled' Philippe Burty, curiously enough, was more reserved – at any rate if he was thinking of Manet when he warned collectors against 'brutal' etchings and 'excessive' etchers. Rosenthal, 1925; Harris, 1970.
123. Fisher, 1985, p.51.
124. Rosenthal, 1925, quotes the influence of Chardin on Manet (p.35), then of Ribera, Tiepolo and Delacroix (p.36), before recalling (p.43) that Duret, 1902, tells us that Manet had special regard for Canaletto's etchings: he admired the airy, brilliant, busy manner that carries over from the Venetians to the Realists via the Spanish painters.
125. On his relationship with Goya, see Nigel Glendinning, *Goya and his Critics*, New Haven and Londons, 1977, pp.119ff., and Isaacson's exhibition catalogue, 1969.
126. The *Tauromachia* was reprinted in 1855, the *Disasters of War* in 1863, the *Proverbs* in 1864, the *Caprices* in 1855 and 1868. *Exotic Bloom* is a pastiche by Manet of one of the *Caprices*, which Manet must have known through the Lumley edition and the reproduction of *Bellos consejos* that appeared in the *Gazette des Beaux-Arts* in 1860. The *Caprices* were reprinted in Madrid by the chalcographic process in the same year. Mariel Frèrebeau has shown that the Spanish painter-engraver Ricardo do Los Rios imported the plates of the *Tauromachia* into France before 1876; they were printed by Porcabeuf: 'Une édition inconnue de la Tauromachie de Goya', in *Nouvelles de l'estampe* no. 10, July–August 1973, pp.5–7.
127. On relations between Bracquemond and Manet, see Bouillon, 1983, and 1974.
128. Fisher, 1985, p.16.
129. On the Parguez sale, *Catalogue de lithographies, oeuvres de Bonington, Charlet, Decamps, Delacroix, Devéria, Géricault, Ingres, Prud'hon, Horace Vernet, d'Amateurs tels que la duchesse de Berry, Princesse de Chimay, baron Denon etc. etc. et livres à figures [. . .], lundi 22, mardi 23 et mercredi 24 avril 1861. Préface de Ph. Burty, pp.VII–XIV.* Lugt, no.2071 (article 'Burty').
130. On the contest organised by the Duc de Luynes, see Bernard Marbot, *Une invention du XIXe siècle: la photographie*, Bibliothèque Nationale, Paris, 1976, p.82, and Rouillé's collection of texts, 1985, p.201.
131. Pissarro, *Correspondance*, vol.I, p.274, 2 January 1884.
132. For example: Bonington, Curtis no.66,

the only known proof in the British Museum. Pierre Georgel says of Bonington (in my opinion correctly) 'Baudelaire was thinking of Bonington when he spoke of the magic of the English. . . It was Baudelaire who discovered Boudin and Jongkind, who are really the descendants of Bonington.' Pierre George, *Bonington, un romantique anglais à Paris*, Musée Jacquemart-André, 1966, no.28b.
133. Pissarro, *Correspondance*, vol.I, p.284, 17 February 1884, 'These are marvellous from all points of view . . . particularly because the composition is admirable.'
134. *The Academy*, 22 July 1876, quoted by Bailly-Herzberg, 1972, vol.II, p.138, note 50.
135. On the lithography movement see Druick and Zegers, 1981; Carey and Griffiths, 1978.
136. Druick and Zegers, 1983. On the 'balloon' as a symbol of progress in the Second Empire, see Bradford R. Collins, 'Manet's "Rue Mosnier decked with flags" and the flâneur concept', in *Burlington Magazine*, 1975, pp.709–14, with reference to Daumier's lithograph of 30 May 1868 (L.D. 3643, reproduced fig. 29).
137. Darragon, 1989, p.26 and Baudelaire, letter to Edouard Manet of 11 May 1865, edited by Yves Florenne, in *Ecrits sur l'art*, Livre de poche, vol.II, Paris, p.351.
138. 'Chronique des arts et de la curiosité', in *Gazette des Beaux-Arts*, 7 Febraury 1869, quoted by Antony Griffiths, 'L'Exécution de Maximilien', in *Burlington Magazine*, November 1977, p.777, following up L. Johnson's article 'A New Source for Manet's Execution of Maximilian' in *Burlington Magazine*, August 1977, pp.560–4. See also *Edouard Manet and the Execution of Maximilian*, Bell Gallery, Brown University, Dept. of Art, Providence, Rhode Island, 1981, and *Manet, the Execution of Maximilian*, National Gallery, London, 1992.
139. The *Portrait of Monet* by Manet appeared in *La Vie moderne*, 12 June 1880, illustrating an article on Monet by E. Taboureur. See Melot, 1977.
140. Carl Chiarenza, 'Manet's use of photography in the creation of a drawing', in *Master Drawings*, vol.7, no.1, 1969, pp.38–45, and Ariane Isler de Jongh, 'Manet, Charles Cros et la photogravure en couleurs', in *Nouvelles de l'estampe*, no. 68, March-April 1983, pp.6–12; Leiris, 1969, p.10 and p.28; Sharf, 1968, pp.40ff.
141. Antonin Proust, 'Le Salon de 1882', in *Gazette des Beaux'Arts*, June 1882, pp.531–54.
142. Letter from Manet to Guérard published by Adhémar, 1965. Manet died on 30 April 1883: 'On the day of his death, Paris rang with news of the event.' (La Liberté, 2 May 1883). On critical opinions of Manet after his death, see the recent study by Shigemi Inaga, 'Manet en 1883: un supplément au bilan critique d'après le dépouillement des articles nécrologiques', in *Jinbun Ronso*, Mie University, no. 12, 1995, pp.55–88.
143. 'Le Salon des Refusés de 1863, étude et documents publiés sous la direction de Daniel Wildenstein', in *Gazette des Beaux-Arts*, September 1965, pp.125–52. See Albert Boime, 'The Salon des refusés and the Evolution of Modern Art', in *Art Quarterly*, vol.XXXII, 1969, pp.411–26.
144. François Forster, in the Bibliothèque Nationale, *Inventaire des fonds français*, vol.VIII, pp.114–16.
145. Henriquel-Dupont, *ibid*, vol.X, pp.281–92.
146. Jacques Eouard Gatteaux, *ibid*, vol.VIII, p.425.
147. Philippe Burty, 'Le Salon de 1863', in *Gazette des Beaux'Arts*, 1863, p.152, note 1. On Edouard Girardet, *Inventaire du fonds français*, vol.IX, p.157.
148. Jean-Paul Bouillon, 'Degas, Bracquemond, Mary Cassatt. Actualité de l'ingrisme autour de 1880', in *Gazette des Beaux'Arts*, January-February 1988, pp.125–7.
149. Gabriel Laviron, *Le Salon de 1834*, Paris 1834, p.369.
150. Dubufe, in Bibliothèque Nationale, *Inventaire du fonds français*, vol.VII, p.126.
151. Couture, *ibid.*, vol.V, p.298.
152. Carolus Duran, *ibid.*, vol.IV, p.110.
153. Bouguereau, *ibid.*, vol.III, p.209.
154. Gérôme, *ibid.*, vol.IX, p.63.
155. Emile Zola, *Nos peintres au Champs de Mars*, 1867, in Zola, 1991, p.84.
156. Bailly-Herzberg, 1972, vol.I, p.219. Courbet's etching was published in *La Société des aquafortistes* in September 1866.
157. The term is White's, cf. note 9. On relations between critics and painters, see Gamboni's detailed study, 1989.
158. Cassagne, 1959.
159. 'Le Salon des Refusés', in *L'Artiste*, 15 August, 1863, p.75.
160. Jongkind's letters were deposited in the Bibliothèque des Musées Nationaux in 1972 and published by J. Bailly-Herzberg, 1974, pp.14–16; Hefting, 1975 (with a *catalogue raisonné* of 820 representative works).
161. Melot, 1978, pp.205–24.
162. Philippe Burty, *Chronique des arts et de la curiosité*, no. 17, 23 March 1862.
163. Baudelaire, 'L'Eau-forte est à la mode', in *La Revue anecdotique*, 2 April 1862; in *Œuvres complètes*, p.849.
164. Jongkind wrote to Burty on 15 March: 'I must tell you also that your friend Poulet-Malassis came to see me this morning just popped in as he was passing to offer me half as an advance. . .' Then, on 28 April, to Poulet-Malassis: 'I'll tell you also that so far I have not even recovered the expenses of my etchings, although I've had quite a lot of praise – so called. The printer made 150 copies and I took the plates back. If this work is satisfactory, I suggest that I make two more books just of views of Holland and you could be the sole publisher; when I eventually earn some money from my work it would not be in my interest for you to lose.' Poulet-Malassis turned down his proposal, but bought a painting from him; Jongkind replied 'Please be so good as to keep a copy of that paper in which my etchings are discussed [Baudelaire's article]. I am really sorry that my proposals for paintings to you as a collector are not acceptable at the present time, and neither are my etchings.'
165. Edmond and Jules de Goncourt, *Journal*, 17 June, 1876.
166. Hamerton, 'Modern Etchings in France', in *Fine Arts Quarterly Review*, January-May 1864, II, pp.87–8, quoted (in translation) in Bailly-Herzberg, 1972, vol.II, p.123; reprinted in *Etchings and Etchers*, 1868, p.224.
167. Marie-Félicie Pérez, 'La Diffusion en Allemagne des gravures de Jean-Jacques de Boissieu d'après sa correspondance', in *Nouvelles de l'estampe*, no.57, May-June 1981, pp.4–13.
168. Colette E. Bidon and Paul Prouté, 'Louis-Hector Allemand, peintre-graveur lyonnais (1809–1886)', in *Nouvelles de l'estampe*, no. 33, May-June 1977, pp.5–22. 'The museums of Dresden, Munich and Bremen received collections of his engravings', writes Colette Bidon, '. . .he preferred the banks of the Saône to the banks of the Seine . . . It was at Ravier's house in Crémieu that he met Harpignies and Achard, the inseparable pair.'
169. Reproduced in the 'Supplément au catalogue des eaux-fortes d'Adolphe Appian', by Paul Prouté, in *Nouvelles de l'estampe*, no. 25, January-February 1976, p.9. This supplement is extremely thorough, thanks to the contribution of Jacques Gruyer, a descendant of the artist; it follows and complements the catalogue by P. Prouté, published by Atherton Curtis in 1968. See also Bailly-Herzberg, 1972, vol.II, pp.2–6.
170. Colette E. Bidon, 'Paul Borel, peintre-graveur lyonnais', in *Nouvelles de l'estampe*, no. 60, November-December 1981, p.6. A supplement to the catalogue of Borel's engraved work was published by Colette E. Bidon in the same journal in July 1985, no. 81, pp.4–35.
171. Bailly-Herzberg, 1972, vol.II, p.4.
172. Philippe Burty praises Allemand and Appian in his review of the exhibition of the Société des Amis des Arts de Lyon, in *Gazette des Beaux-Arts*, March 1862, p.284.
173. Curtis and Prouté, 1968.
174. Melot, 1974, no. 62.
175. Baudelaire, 'Quelques caricaturistes français', in *Œuvres complètes*, p.729.
176. David Kunzle, 'L'Illustration', in *Nouvelles de l'estampe*, no. 43, January-February 1979, pp.8–19.
177. Duflo, 1988.
178. Isaacson, 1982, pp.95–115.
This study contains a very full bibliography, evidence of the interest the question holds for the study of Realist painters. On Courbet, see the works of Meyer Shapiro, Linda Nochlin, Beatrice Farwell, Klaus Herding etc, and on Manet, Ann Coffin Hanson, Theodore Reff, Timothy Clark, etc. See in particular Ann Coffin Hanson's 'Manet's Subject Matter and a Source of Popular Imagery', in *Museum Studies*, Art Institute of Chicago, vol.III, (1968), pp.63–80. See also Madeleine Fidell-Beaufort, 'L'Imagerie populaire et l'iconographie impressioniste', in *Nouvelles de l'estampe*, no. 18, November-December 1974, pp.17–20, and Farwell, 1977.
179. This example is illustrated in the article by Fidell'Beaufort, *op. cit.*, note 178.
180. Isaacson, 1982, p.108.
181. Quoted by Duflo, 1988, p.53.
182. *Ibid.*, p.58.
183. 'Le Peintre de la vie moderne', by Baudelaire, was submitted to the newspaper *La Presse* on 4 February 1860, but was published (by *Le Figaro*) only on 26, 29 November and 3 December 1863.
184. Nadar, 'Le Peintre de la vie moderne', in *Le Figaro*, 15 March 1892. The article is reproduced with Baudelaire's article in P. Duflo, 1988.
185. Correspondence between Sensier and Millet (Cabinet des Dessins, Musée du Louvre). The letter of 16 May 1863 also informs us that an old lady wishes to buy two engravings, 100 francs each, a high price for an etching.
186. Then, a few days later on 14 July: 'M. Chassaing came for the etchings this morning, he's going to make arrangements to take two or three collections, or more if he can. M. Moureau, two, and when I have 200 francs capital I shall go and get them printed under my own eyes by Delâtre. . .'
187. Jean-Claude Chamboredon, 'Peinture des rapports sociaux et invention de l'éternel paysan: les deux manières de Jean-François Millet', in *Actes de la recherche en sciences*

sociales, no. 17–18, November 1977, p.6–28.
188. *L'Artiste*, 15 March 1864, p.144. The article recalls how a proof from the plate earned 10–21 francs at the Delacroix sale, 'so curious were the public to possess it'.
189. Pierre Casselle, 'Le Commerce des estampes à Paris dans la seconde moitié du XVIIIe siècle', thesis written for the Ecole des Chartes, under the supervision of Henri-Jean Martin, 1976, unpublished, pp.38–40.
190. Claudette Hould, 'La Gravure en révolution', in *L'Image de la Révolution française*, Musée de Quebec, Quebec, 1989, p.80.
191. *Ibid.*
192. Nostalgia for the eighteenth century is one of the important features of taste under the Second Empire. It is evident in the elegant objects made for high society, and also in Manet's sources: he borrows the spirit of some of his paintings from Watteau (one of the theses of Michael Fried, 1969), and, from Canaletto, a new engraving technique. Nostalgia for 18th century life also manifested itself in the appearance of book-buying bibliophiles, eager to get their hands on fine books of the late eighteenth century (Bouillon, 1982, pp.247–88). The Goncourts' studies of eighteenth century art began to appear in 1859 (see the introduction by Jean-Paul Bouillon to the volume of extracts from these studies: *Goncourt, l'art du dix-huitième siècle*, Paris, 1967).
193. Bouillon, 1975 and 1976, vol.IV, p.394 and note 82.
194. The numbering of books, like the numbering of prints, began at the end of the eighteenth century, to protect against copyists. Copies of Latude's *Mémoires*, Paris, 1793, bear the following hand-written note: 'Nota: pour éviter la contrefaction, tous les exemplaires seront signeés de la main de l'auteur' (Note: to avoid counterfeit, all copies will be signed by the author).
195. Baudelaire, 'Le Peintre de la vie moderne', in *Œuvres complètes*, p.892. On Japonism, see Ives, 1974; *Le Japonisme*, 1988; Wichmann, 1980; Berger, 1980.
196. Weisberg, 1975, p.4 and note 28.
197. Janine Bailly-Herzberg, 'Georges Duseigneur, peintre-graveur lyonnais', in *Nouvelles de l'estampe*, no. 9, 1973, pp.15–17. See also Suzanne Esmein, 'Une Bibliothèque japonisante en France au milieu du XIXe siècle: celle de Léon de Rosny', in *Nouvelles de l'estampe*, no. 85, March-April, 1986, pp.4–15.
198. Phyllis Floyd, 'Documentary Evidence for the Availability of Japanese Imagery in Europe in Nineteenth-Century Public Collections', in *The Art Bulletin*, March 1986, pp.105–41, shows that the collections of Japanese prints in the Bibliothèque Nationale date from 1795 (collection of Bertin, Secretary of State to Louis XV), and that two large collections were acquired in 1843 and 1855. Martin Eidelberg (*Art News*, October 1975, pp.44–7) dates the first reproduction of a Japanese print in France to an etching by Eugène Collinot for *Le Recueil des dessins pour l'art et l'industrie* by Adalbert de Beaumont, 1859. On Bracquemond's discovery of Japan, see Bouillon, 1980, a critical survey. See also Jacques de Caso, '1861: Hokusai, rue Jacob', in *Burlington Magazine*, no. 111, September 1969, pp.562–3.
199. Geneviève Lacambre, 'La découverte de l'art japonais à travers les expositions universelles de Paris, 1867, 1878, 1889, 1900', in *L'Age du japonisme. La France et le Japon dans la deuxième moitié du XIXe siècle*, Société Franco-Japonaise d'Art et d'Archéologie, Tokyo, 1983, pp.33–46.
200. Ernest Chesneau, chapter on Japanese art in *Les Nations rivales dans l'art*, Paris, 1868, pp.414–54; C.-Y. [pseudonym of Champfleury], 'La mode des japoniaiseries', in *La Vie parisienne*, 21 November 1868; Philippe Burty, 'Le mobilier moderne', in *Gazette des Beaux-Arts*, 1868, vol.I, p.28. See also the passage on Japanese albums in *Manette Salomon*, by the brothers Goncourt, 1865, pp.188–9.
201. Bernard Franck, 'L'intérêt pour les religions japonaises dans la France du XIXe siècle et les collections d'Emile Guimet', in *L'Age du japonisme: La France et le Japon dans la deuxième moitié du XIXe siècle*, Société Franco-Japonaise d'Art et d'Archéologie, Tokyo, 1983, pp.1–18.
202. Pissarro, *Correspondance*, vol.II, p.224, 25 June 1883. The relationship between 'Japonism' and 'Primitivism' in the early twentieth century is mentioned, but not analysed as clearly as it deserves, in the catalogue to the exhibition *Primitivism*, edited by William Rubin, Museum of Modern Art, New York (1984). See also Martin Eidelberg, 'Japonsime, historicism, modernism', in *Art News*, October 1975, pp.44–7.
203. Michel Revon, in the Introduction to his *Histoire de la Civilisation japonaise*, Paris, 1900. On relations with other civilisations, see also Melot, 1980.
204. Bouillon, 1980, pp.83ff.
205. Edmond and Jules de Goncourt, *Outamaro*, Paris, 1891, p.53.
206. *Id., Journal*, 13 May 1892.
207. Karin van Maur, 'Edmond de Goncourt et les artistes de la fin du XIXe siècle', in *Gazette des Beaux-Arts*, November 1968, p.226. This phrase summarises one of the most perspicacious accounts of the relationship between Japonism and Western art: Ernst Scheyer, 'Far Eastern Art and French Impressionism', in *Art Quarterly*, vol.VI, 1943, pp.117–42.
208. Richard Lane, *L'Estampe japonaise*, Fribourg, 1979. See also Shigemi Inaga, 'La transtextualité dans l'image "populaire" au Japon. L'iconographie de l'ukiyo-e et sa fonction sociale', in *L'Ecrit-Voir. Revue d'histoire des arts*, no. 6, 1985, pp.123–38.
209. Bouillon, 1978.
210. Darragon, 1989, p.142.
211. On Edwards, see Edmond Duranty, 'Edwin Edwards, peintre et aquafortiste', in *Gazette des Beaux-Arts*, no. 5, 1879, pp.438–42. On Ionides, see Luke Ionides, *Memories*, Paris 1925, and Alexander C. Ionides, *A Grandfather's Tale*, Dublin, 1927. See in particular, Hamerton, 1868.
212. Raymonde Moulin, *L'Artiste, l'institution et le marché*, Paris, 1992, p.345. 'Crises in the art market, plus the general economic climate, did not affect all sectors of the market with the same intensity. The sector least able to survive was the least settled sector, i.e. the contemporary sector. The Impressionist painters felt the backlash of the economic disaster of 1882.' See Rioux, 1989, p.148. For a fuller survey, see Braudel and Labrousse, 1976, and Bouvier, Furet and Gillet, 1965. For a more synthetic approach see F. Caron, *Histoire économique et sociale de la France XIXe – XXe siècles*, Paris, 1981.
213. Bailly-Herzberg, 1972, Vol. I, p.32.
214. Rewald, 1965, Vol.III, pp.113 and 138. Charles Kunstler's *Pissarro*, 1971, contains a reproduction (p.49) of an illustration dating from February 1882 showing the arrest of Feder. On the collapse of the Union Générale, see Bouvier, 1960.
215. Loyrette, 1991, pp.316–7.
216. Bailly-Herzberg, 1972 (2). See also the Goncourts' *Journal*, 6 February 1975.
217. Harper and Shikes, p.117.
218. Paul Gachet, *Cézanne à Auvers, Cézanne graveur*, Les Beaux'Arts, Paris, undated.
219. *Paris à l'eau-forte*, no. 40, 28 December 1873, p.77.
220. *Ibid.*, no. 22, 24 August 1873, pp.42–4. For Guillaumin's letter, see Paul Gachet, *Lettres impressionistes. . .*, Paris, 1957, p.66. Van Ryssel's (Gachet's) seven etchings appeared in the third volume of the first year (1873) of *Paris à l'eau-forte*.
221. *Ibid.*, no. 23. There are engravings by Guillaumin on pp.51, 55, 59, 61 then in no.27, 28 September 1873 and in no. 32, 2 November 1873, p.199. Guillaumin's prints have recently been the subject of an exhibition, whose catalogue constitutes the first *catalogue raisonné* of his work. It contains thirty etchings and seven lithographs: Gilles Kraemer, *Armand Guillaumin 1841–1927, gravures et lithographies*, Musée des beaux-Arts, Clermont'Ferrand, 17 February – 11 June 1995.
222. *Ibid.*, no. 40, 28 December 1873, p.65.
223. *Ibid*, p.77.
224. *Ibid.*, no. 18, 27 July 1873, p.285.
225. *Ibid*, specimen, March 1873, p.285.
226. Melot, 1972.
227. Bailly-Herzberg, 1972, Vol. II, p.159.
228. Herbert, 1970; Thomson, 1990.
229. Bibliothèque Nationale, Département des Estampes, Dc614 Fol., 2 vols.
230. On this period, see Aflred Darcel, 'Les Arts et les musées pendant le siège', in *Gazette des Beaux-Arts*, 1 October 1871, pp.285–306, and 1 November 1871, pp.414–29, and 'Les Musées, les arts et les artistes pendant la Commune', in *Gazette des Beaux'Arts*, 1872, p.51. There is a more recent study by Kaplow, 1971.
231. M. Courmont, *La Photogravure, histoire et technique*. Paris, edited by Colbert, 1942. On Gillot's process see B. Denis, 'Le Procédé Gillot', in *L'Imprimerie*, no. 222, May 1883, pp.811–12. See also Paul Prouté's note in the catalogue to the *Daumier* exhibition, Ingelheim-am-Rhein, 1971.
232. Moreau-Nélaton, *Histoire de Corot*, p.280. See Melot, 1972, pp.260–1.
233. Druick and Hoog, 1983, pp.215–30.
234. Harper and Shikes, 1981, pp.150–1.
235. Pennel, 1911, pp.155–6.
236. Van Gelder, 1976, Vol.I, pp.173–82.
237. Redon, 1921, p.124.
238. Melot, 1988. See also Philippe Roberts-Jones, 'Daumier précurseur de l'impressionisme', in *Gazette des Beaux-Arts*, April 1960, P. 247–50.
239. Documentary retrospective of the 1874 exhibition in the catalogue to the exhibition *Centenaire de l'Impressionisme*, pp.223–77 and, more recently, *The New Painting*, 1986. A critical bibliography has been drawn up recently by Bouillon, 1981 and 1989 (2).
240. Bouillon, 1986, pp.89–113. See also Genêt-Delacroix 1986; Heinich, 1991, p.62.
241. On Ottin, see Monneret, 1978, Vol. II, p.110 and Reuterswärd, 1952, pp.19–20: 'The first exhibition was a gathering of various heterogeneous movements: as well as the 'Révoltés', centred around Monet, the nucleus of the Impressionist groups, there were also the 'Intransigeants du pinceau' (Auguste and Léon Ottin, Lepic, Tillot and Béliard) and the 'Refusés de 1873' (Bureau, Attendu, Renoir and

Rouart'. Add to these the 'invités', Bracquemond and De Nittis, who were the guarantors of the respectability of the whole operation. Bracquemond, like Brandon, Lépine and Colin, had not joined the 'Révoltés' with any enthusiasm. The 'invités' did not appear in the second exhibition.' (Reutersward, p.21ff.). After the second exhibition, when Auguste Ottin had defected, the offices were moved to the dealer Alphonse Legrand's premises in the Rue Laffitte; his shop became the headquarters of the Impressionist movement (*Ibid.*, p.61).

242. It appears that Stanislas-Henri Rouart, the industrialist and friend of Degas, made only these ten or so etchings, at a date before 1874. He exhibited paintings, drawings and water-colours regularly in all the Impressionist exhibitions except for the seventh, from which Degas and his friends withdrew. 'His modesty meant that his oddly precise work has remained almost unknown and belongs entirely to his children', wrote Paul Valéry (preface to a retrospective exhibition of Rouart, Paris, Durand-Ruel, 1912).

243. Bibliothèque Nationale, Cals, Vol. IV, p.22.

244. Bertin, 1977, p.5. For more detail, see Bertin, 1975.

245. Beraldi, Vol. VIII, 1888, p.263.

246. Richard Lesclide, 'Silhouette', in *Paris à l'eau-forte*, 4 October, 1875.

247. Beraldi, Vol. VII, 1888, p.192.

248. *Ibid.*, p.197.

249. Beraldi, Vol. VII, 1888, p.265.

250. Respectively, Bertin no. 231 (*Moulin de la Galette*), 185 (*Return from the Fishing Grounds, Honfleur*), 199 (*Leaving the Port, Le Havre*), 179 (*Lines of Boats*), 123 (*Interior in the Auvergne*), 96 (*In the Corn*).

251. Guérard's hundred or so 'marines' present an almost complete anthology of Impressionist engraving, from quick 'griffonis' (*The Port at Le Havre*), to the tortured lines made by neat acid (*Return from the Fishing Grounds*). *Effect of Morning, Calais* exists in a heavily inked first state, exaggerating all the 'whiskers' of the dry point, and in a 'whiskerless' second state, with a sky produced by scraping with glass paper, mists created with a roulette, in a copy printed very clearly in brownish ink, and in a third state which is very pale, with an almost white sky, with a note in pencil, 'Effet de matin, tiré par l'auteur' (Effect of morning, printed by the artist). *Return from the Fishing Grounds, Honfleur* is printed once with a misty effect, once with a moonlit effect. See Bertin, no. 174 (*Port at le Havre*), 187 (*Return from the Fishing Grounds*), 175 (*Effect of Morning, Calais*), 185 (*Return from the Fishing Grounds, Honfleur*).

252. Article by Félix Fénéon, in *La Revue indépendante*, reprinted in Fénéon, 1970, Vol. I, p.79.

253. Bertin, 1977, pp.7-8.

254. *Ibid.*

255. Goeneutte exhibited in the Salon of 1876; he had specialised in female figures, dear to the illustrators of fashion magazines (he worked on *La Vie parisienne* for a while), giving them the freedom and spontaneity as well as the velvety shades of the dry point etching. See Beraldi, Vol. VII, 1888, p.170, and de Knyff, 1978.

256. Bertin, no. 240.

257. Ducros, 1974 and 1975.

258. *Ludovic Lepic and his Daughters*, L. 272, *Ballet of Robert le Diable*, L. 294 and L. 391, *Place de la Concorde*, *Ludovic Lepic and his Daughters*, L. 368, *Ludovic Lepic holding his Dog*, L. 950.

259. 'Comment je divins graveur à l'eau-forte' ('How I became an etcher'), by Comte Lepic, with a historical essay by Raoul de Saint-Arroman, *La Gravure à l'eau-forte*, Cadart, 'L'Eau-forte mobile collection', Paris 1876.

260. Loyrette, 1991, pp.397-8. See also pp.447-9.

261. See the reproduction of nine different states (of sixteen in the collection of the Baltimore Museum of Art) in the catalogue to the exhibition *The Painterly Print*, 1980, pp.20-1 and 94-5.

262. The work by Van Ryssel (alias Dr Gachet) in the Bibliothèque Nationale includes two monotypes classified by his son Paul Gachet (P. Gachet, no. 27, dated 1876), one of them after a picture by Amand Gautier (P. Gachet no. 13, dated 1873).

263. *Paris à l'eau-forte*, 28 November 1875.

264. Text of an autobiographical talk by Delâtre, Delâtre Archives, Bibliothèque Nationale, Département des Estampes, S.N.R Quarto, Delâtre.

265. Herbert, 1975, p.167.

266. Hamerton, 1868, p.249.

267. Wentworth, 1978, on Delâtre, p.13.

268. On Whistler's complaints about Delâtre's inking, see Pennel, 1911, pp.197-8, and Mortimer Mempes, *Whistler as I knew him*, London 1904, p.92.

269. Bailly-Herberg, 1972 (2).

270. Clément-Janin, 1922. His archetypal aspect made him a popular artists' model: Manet's *Portrait of an Artist* (1876), Degas *Absinthe Drinker* (1877) and *Desboutin etching with Comte Lepic*. He posed for his friend De Nittis in 1873.

271. Clément-Janin nos 66, 67, 68, 78 and 73.

272. Clément-Janin no. 238.

273. A special edition of *La Plume*, no. 138, 15-31, January 1895, was devoted to Puvis de Chavannes. The title page bears the words: 'Unpublished portrait of Puvis engraved in dry-point by Marcellin Desboutin'; this is followed by 'Supplement to the de luxe edition: Pierre Puvis de Chavannes in 1875, dry point of the same'. Clément-Janin nos 203 and 204.

274. Pittaluga and Piceni, 1963, p.359. Letter from Marcellin Desboutin to De Nittis, 13 April 1875, pp.353-4.

275. *Ibid.*, 20 April 1876, p.355.

276. *Ibid*, 17 July 1876, p.359.

277. Melot 1874, pp.103-4 (Portrait of de Gas 20 February by Desboutin, Bibliothèque Nationale, Moreau-Nélaton collection).

278. Pittaluga and Piceni, 1963, letter of 5 April 1874 to Enrico Cecioni, *op.cit.*, p.302.

279. Hoschede, *Brelan de Salons*, Paris, 1889.

280. Louis Gonse, *L'Art*, weekly magazine published from 1875.

281. Philippe Burty, 'La Belle épreuve', preface to the album *L'Eau-forte en 1875*, published by Cadart. On the papers used by Buhot, see also Baxter, 1980.

282. Gustave Kahn writes that 'Buhot's sleight of hand leaves him cold', in *La Vogue*, July-August 1889, II, 2, p.237, but in the sprinkling of articles following the exhibition of Painter-Engravers in 1889 it is the name of Buhot that recurs most frequently. His talent and skill are admired, as well as his virtuoso technique etc. See *L'Art français*, 2nd year, no. 93, 2 February 1889, or *L'Art*, Vol. 46, 1889, pp.91-2.

283. Monique Bacquier, preface to the catalogue to the exhibition *Félix Buhot, le travail d'un peintre-graveur*. On Buhot's papers, see also Baxter, 1980, and Philip Dennis-Cate, 'Félix Buhot and Japonism' in *The Print Collector's Newsletter*, Vol. VI, no. 3, July-August 1975, pp.64-7.

284. *Journal des arts*, 3 February 1888. See also *Catalogue of an exhibition of the etched work of Felix Buhot with an introduction by Philippe Burty*, 1888.

285. 'Le Whistlérisme et le pissarrisme', article signed 'Pointe-sèche', Buhot's pseudonym in *Journal des arts*, 3 February 1888.

286. Bouillon, 1975 and 1976.

287. Le Men and Scott, 1990, pp.39-58 (for more about this success, see p.56, note 4, according to Lemerre's catalogue of 1874 now in the Bibliothèque Nationale).

288. Gustave Doré, 1983.

289. Letter from Charles Cros to Richard Lesclide (Doucet collection) in the catalogue to the exhibition *De Fil en aiguille, Charles Cros et les autres*, Bibliothèque Nationale, 1988-9, no. 22.

290. Zola, 1974, p.305 (8 May 1867). On relations between Zola and Manet, see Bouillon, 1989.

291. Wilson-Bareau and Mitchell, 1989, p.263, notes 15 and 16.

292. The publication of the thesis of Mrs Anna Sigridur Arnar, of the University of Chicago, is eagerly awaited; she shows how Mallarmé's strategy of turning poetry into a work of art by presenting it as an illustrated book uses the way already paved by that other product of the printing press - the print.

293. Le Men, 1984.

294. Etienne Moreau-Nélaton's preface to his *Catalogue de l'oeuvre gravé de Manet*, Paris 1906. The debate is of interest because it illustrates how particular market forces determine the work of art historians; on the reproductive techniques used in Manet's *Raven* see the complete bibliography in Wilson-Bareau and Mitchell's article, p.258. note 1.

295. Leiris 1969, no. 595.

296. Jean-Michel Nectoux, *L'Après-Midi d'un Faune: Mallarmé, Debussy, Nijinsky*, Musée d'Orsay, 1989.

297. Félix Buhot's reflections on *The River* by Manet can be found in Fontaine p.76ff. (The manuscript of Fontaine's thesis on *The Doctrines of art in France* was not published until 1982).

298. Melot, 1984, pp.202-3; Antoine Coron, 'Aux origines du livre d'artiste en France', in *Impressions, bulletin de l'Imprimerie nationale*, no. 10, December 1978, pp.9-15.

299. Lemoisne, 1946, Vol. I, pp.92-3.

300. Loyrette, 1991, p.381.

301. Edmond Duranty, *La Nouvelle Peinture*, Paris, 1876, p.30.

302. Isaacson, 1980, p.148, Shikes and Harper, p.117.

303. Druick and Zegers, 1984, p. XLIII.

304. Druick and Zegers, 1988, pp.197-211, based on the article by C. M. Gariel in *La Nature*, no. 306, 12 April 1879, pp.289-91.

305. It says: 'On to a zinc plate, transfer an engraving impregnated with copper sulphate; by placing it in a bath of dilute nitric acid you get a soft ground etching . . . . On a plate, covered in 'daguerre's' silver, place an engraving impregnated (and wiped) with chlorate of gold. . . put it in the press - a negative plate with damasked surface will result. If you want a soft-ground etching, use dilute nitric acid (10:100).' Or: 'Recipes: oil the plate lightly, sprinkle with powdered copal; this gives an interesting grain. Heat it to quite a high heat, soap the plate and rinse well. Acid can be painted on without dripping too much. I've

heard that if you leave whiting in the holes it can blow out the etching ground and etch the grains a bit more deeply.' Degas, Carnet 30 (1877–83), p.22 and p.89 (Reff, 1985, Vol. I, p.134).
306. Pittaluga and Piceni, 1963, p.359.
307. Menon, 1992. Henri Somm has recently been the subject of a comprehensive thesis by Elizabeth K. Menon, under the supervision of Gabriel P. Weisberg. Also by the same author, 'Henry Somm: Impressionist, Japoniste or Symbolist?', in *Master Drawings*, Vol. 33, no. 1, Spring 1995, pp.3–28.
308. Isaacson, 1980, p.101.
309. On the development of the illustrated press, see Philippe Roberts-Jones, 'La presse satirique illustrée entre 1860 and 1890', in *Etudes de presse*, new series, Vol. VIII, no. 14, 1956, p.111, and 'La Liberté de la caricature en France au XIXe siècle', in *Synthese*, no. 165, February 1960, p.11.
310. The original edition contained sixty original etchings including one by Desboutin. See Druick and Zegers, 1984, XLIII.
311. *Les Beaux-Arts illustrés*, weekly, began publication in May 1876.
312. *L'Art de la mode*, monthly, began publication in August 1880 and became *L'Art et la mode*.
313. Emile Bergerat, 'Notre programme', in *La Vie moderne*, no. 1, Thursday 10 April 1879, pp.2–3.
314. The 'Carnets de Ludovic Halévy' in *Revue des deux Mondes*, 15 December 1937, p.826.
315. 'La Journée parisienne: impressions d'un impressioniste', was published by Charles Stuckey, using the pseudonym 'Le Tout'Paris'; in 'Recent Degas publications', in *Burlington Magazine*, Vol. CXXXVII, July 1985, p.466, reprinted in the catalogue to the *Degas* exhibition, 1988, p.305. Cf. Druick and Zegers, 1984, pp.XXIX–LI and Degas, *Letters*, 1945, no. XVIII, p.45, no. XIX, pp.46–7, no. XXI, pp.48–9, and no. XXII, pp.49–50; see also Loyrette, 1991, p.373.
316. Bouillon, 1989, pp.251–9 and in *Revue de l'art*, 1975, no. 45.
317. Bouillon, 1975, Vol. III, p.284: 'A publication on etchings to be directed by your humble servant is mooted; either it will be good, or it won't exist.'
318. Degas, *Letters*, CCXXXIII, p.235, undated [30 December, 1905].
319. *Le Gaulois*, *op. cit.*, note 315.
320. Letter from Mrs Cassatt to her son Alexander, in Matthews, 1984, p.151.
321. Degas, *Letters*, 1945, no. XXI, undated, pp.48–9.
322. *Ibid.*, no. XXII, undated, p.49.
323. *Ibid.*, no. XXIII, undated, p.50.
324. *Ibid.*, no. XXVI, undated, p.55.
325. Michel Melot, 'Raffaëlli l'oublié', in *Nouvelles de l'estampe*, May 1993, no. 128, p.23.
326. All the prints mentioned are almost square in format, or slightly rectangular, with sides measuring between 20 and 29 cm.
327. This is what their junior, Renoir, did, producing the comfortable *Portrait of Mme Charpentier*, success of the Salon of 1879.
328. Pissarro, *Correspondance*, Vol. I, p.126, to Murer, undated [end August 1878]. There are other letters similar in tone on p.129 and p.131 (25 November 1878): 'Bad news from America. Legrand wrote to say that they find my paintings so bad that they are sending back all the Impressionists with hoots of derision.' Pissarro was then living on a couple of advances from Murer and the hope of selling a painting to Victor Choquet, a customs inspector, and to Diego Martelli, an Italian art critic introduced to him by Marcellin Desboutin, and finally to Louisine Elder, later to become Mrs Havemeyer, Mary Cassatt's friend.
329. Druick and Zegers, 1984, p. XXXIII. The problems arising from this are discussed in Melot, 1977, and the article developed by Lant, 1979 and 1986, pp.18–29. The questions were further developed and broadened by Druick and Zegers, 1984 (with regard to Degas) and by Rittmann, 1992 (with regard to Pissarro, see especially the introduction).
330. Degas, *Letters*, 1945, no. XXVI, undated, p.55.
331. Degas, *Letters*, 1945, 13 May 1879, p.45.
332. Druick and Zegers, 1984, p. XLIV.
333. Portrait of Riesener by Renoir, on the cover of no. 2, 17 April 1879 of *La Vie moderne*.
334. Degas published a *Dancer* in *La Vie moderne* of 8 May, 1879, no.5 , p.71, then another on 29 May 1879. Mary Cassatt published a reproduction of her drawing *A Box at the Theatre* in the same journal, 9 August, 1879, p.283. There is another reproduction of a picture by Degas in *L'Impressioniste*; the Devaux negative process was used.
335. Druick and Zegers, 1984, pp.XXXVII–XXXVIII.
336. *Ibid.*, p.XXXIX.
337. On the subject of Degas, Druick and Zegers, 1984, p.XXXIII, explain that 'his fascination with lithographic transfer and other new industrial transfer techniques shows his wish to move away from the idea of exclusivity inherent in the techniques he had been using, to serve up his 'cookery' to a wider audience'. From a biographical point of view, it is reasonably accurate to state: 'It was at that moment that Degas might have been (incorrectly) thought of as a living stereotype of a printmaker willing to sacrifice all else to 'rarity'. In fact, however, this aspect of his printmaking was purely circumstantial' (p.LVI). From a historical point of view, on the other hand, we cannot consider Degas' prints as 'circumstantial' because it was this aspect of his art that brought him recognition and won acceptance for the original print, as Druick and Zegers point out: 'It was evident that the original print was firmly established and that such processes posed no threat to its position' (p.LXX). The question is to find out the extent to which a 'circumstantial' practice by an artist is the result of an historical situation.
338. Degas, *Letters*, 1945, no. XXV, undated, p.52.
339. *Ibid.*, p.54.
340. Pissarro, *Correspondance*, Vol. I, p.274; p.284, 17 February 1884.
341. *Ibid.*, undated, p.292 (beginning of March 1884).
342. *Ibid.*, p.289, 19 February 1884.
343. *Ibid.*, p.278, 29 January 1884. It is interesting to note that Pissarro compares Degas and Keene, two artists who accepted (to differing degrees) the reproduction of their drawings. Later (10 December 1886) he censures the illustrated magazines: 'Dumas (or the *Revue illustrée*) pleases neither people with taste nor people without. He wishes to create a publication that will survive and will flatter neither the very good nor the very bad. One or the other. He should aim to be as dull as the Figaro illustré or even duller!!! A wind of change is blowing through the world of illustration, we should put a tinder to it and let the wind fan the flames.' In 1890 he was railing against the 'garbage' coming from the house of Goupil (Vol. II, p.380, 26 December 1890) and against the 'convenient expedient of "gillotage" which does such a grand service to the commercial world' (Vol. II, p.23, 15 January 1891).
344. *Ibid.*, p.282, 10 Febraury 1884.
345. *La Vie moderne*, no. 10, 1880, p.158.
346. Degas, *Letters*, 1945, no. XXV, undated [1880].
347. *Ibid.*
348. Druick and Zegers, 1984, p. L.
349. Delteil 20 and 34. On these questions, see Théodore Reff, 1976, pp.270–303, and Rouart, 1945.
350. Pissarro, *Correspondance*, Vol. III, p.38, I March 1891.
351. *Ibid.*
352. *Ibid.*, p.57, 8 April 1891. The ones in question are Delteil 16 to 23, Delteil 25 and 39. See Melot, 1977. See also Rittmann, 1992, p.95ff. Several proofs were sold when Degas' studio was sold in 1918; this proves that the few prints made in the winter of 1879–80 were neither used nor sold but were forgotten in their boxes (*Village seen through Trees*, second state, 3 proofs, 1 signed, *The Peasant Woman with a Wheelbarrow*, 8 proofs, trials and states, *The Cottage*, *The Haystacks*, Degas sale, 1918).
353. Private collection. *Degas*, 1988, no. 175.
354. *Degas*, 1988, no. 190, Musée d'Orsay, RF 12255, shown at the third Impressionist exhibition in 1877, part of the Caillebotte bequest in 1894. The other pastel on monotype of the same subject is in the Norton Simon Museum, Pasadena.
355. Reff, 1976, pp.282–4.
356. Delteil 36, Rhode Island Museum.
357. *Woman Carrying a Wide Basket*, Museum of Aix-les-Bains. See Melot, 1974, no. 264.
358. Pissarro, Correspondance, Vol. II, p.255, 13 December 1888.
359. *Ibid.*, p.265, 20 February 1889.
360. *Ibid.*, Vol. III, p.38, 1 March 1891. Later, (p.42, 9 March 1891): 'I refused (to exhibit with the 'Painter-Engravers') for a number of reasons; among others, that the artist is required to give to the Society a proof of each print hung in the show. I can understand it for someone who prints three or four hundred, but for someone who only prints three or four copies it would mean I was giving them all my stock.'
361. E. and J. de Goncourt, *Journal*, 24 Febraury 1874.
362. For a resolution of the apparent contradiction between subjectivity and realism, see the excellent analyses by Shiff, 1978.
363. Pissarro, *Correspondance*, Vol. III, p.31, 10 February 1891.
364. Huyghe, 1974, pp.11–27, develops the idea of 'the death of matter' (pp.15–19), and of a 'time of renewed power' (pp.24–7), and their relationship with 'data directly from consciousness' (pp.23–4). See also Lionello Venturi, 'The Aesthetic idea of Impressionism', in the *Journal of Aesthetics and Art Criticism*, 1941, no. 1, pp.35–6.
365. On Darwin and Degas, see Druick and Zegers, 1988, pp.205–7.
366. Pissarro, *Correspondance*, Vol. I, p.274, 21 January 1884.
367. Pissarro, *Letters to his Son Lucien*, edited by John Rewald, Paris 1950, p.193 [November 1890] and 223 [March 1891].
368. Breeskin nos 30, 68–9, 71, 64 etc.
369. Weitzenhoffer, 1986, pp.20–1, and

Breeskin, 1967, p.12.
370. Reff, 1985, Carnet 30, p.208; see also pp.202, 204, 206.
371. Degas sale, 1918, no. 96. For the 'crayon électrique' which Degas is said to have used, See Druick and Zegers, 1984, p.L.
372. This comparison already irritated Pissarro: 'I'm the one who's Jewish, he's the biblical one'; Degas analysed the contrast accurately: 'Millet's sower is sowing for eternity, Pissarro's to earn his living.'
373. Breeskin, no. 172.
374. Monique Lepelley-Fonteny, no. 45 in the catalogue of the engravings of Léon Lhermitte in *Nouvelles de l'estampe*, no. 117, July 1991, p.21.
375. On this problem see Isaacson, 1980, and on the conflict introduced by the presence of Raffaëlli, Loyrette, pp.397-8 and 447-55. On Raffaëlli, Loys Delteil, *Le Peintre-graveur illustré*, Vol. XVI, Paris, 1923 and Alexander, 1909.
376. On Lhermitte's admission see Rewald (ed.) 1965, Vol. II, p.110, note 29 (based on a list in one of Degas' notebooks).
377. Huysmans praises Raffaëlli in his *Salon de 1879*, p.71.
378. J.K. Huysmans, 'Exposition des Indépendants', 1880, in *L'Art moderne*, p.91. On the development of criticism, see Rewald, ed., 1965, Vol. II, p.99.
379. Bouvier, 1960.
380. Bouillon, 1972, p.5.
381. Emile Zola, *Le Naturalisme au Salon*, 1880, in Zola, 1991, p.418.
Philippe Burty, 'L'Exposition des artistes indépendants', in *La République française*, 16 April 1879.
382. Letter to Pennell (Pennell collection, Library of Congress), in Lochnan, 1984, p.223.
383. On Whistler in Venice, see Bacher, 1908.
384. Lochnan, 1984-5, p.266.
385. According to a reminiscence of Hyatt Mayor, Lochnan, 1984-5, p.266.
386. Duret, 1914 (on Venice, p.64).
387. Pissarro, *Correspondance*, Vol. II, p.177, 28 February 1883.
388. Pissarro, *Correspondance*, Vol. I, p.141, 23 December 1880.
389. *Ibid.*, p.142, 4 January 1881.
390. *Ibid.*, p.144, note 1, 14 January 1881.
391. *Ibid.*, p.144-5, 17 January 1881.
392. Loyrette, 1991, p.458.
393. Pissarro, *Correspondance*, Vol. I, p.186, 29 March 1883.
394. Bailly-Herzberg, 1981, pp.53-9.
395. Beraldi, 1885, Vol. III, p.9.
396. Melot, 1986, pp.117-22.
397. Bailly-Herzberg and Dardel, 1980, p.8.
398. On Lepère, see Baas, 1982.
399. Letter from Lucien Pissarro to Clément-Janin, October 1919 (Bibliothèque d'Art et d'Archéologie, box 24) published by Bailly-Herzberg, in Pissarro, *Correspondance*, Vol. I, p.370, note 7: 'It was at this period that M.F.G. Dumas, the then director of an illustrated magazine, gave me a short story by Octave Mirbeau to illustrate, Maït' Liziard [15 June 1886]. The wood engravings appeared and caused howls of protest, and this put an end to my collaboration.'
400. Pissarro, *Correspondance*, Vol. II, p.106, 12 January 1887.
401. *Ibid.*, Vol. II, p.85, 10 December 1886.
402. *Ibid.*, Vol. II, p.87, note 2.
403. *Conférence faite par M. J.-F. Raffaëlli au Palais des Beaux-Arts de Bruxelles au salon annuel des XX, le 7 février 1885*, p.33. To make these popular illustrations, Raffaëlli requests a book '14-18 with *yellow cover*, and *ordinary paper*, de luxe paper for the elegant ones, the ordinary selling at whatever price books sell at today, 3f50, the de luxe edition at a higher price.' See Melot, 1993, p.26.
404. Beraldi, 1891, Vol. IX, article 'Raffaëlli'. Beraldi mentions four copies of *Germinie Lacerteux*, the Goncourts three, *Journal*, 1 December 1888 and 21 June 1889.
405. The first French book to be illustrated with screen printed photographs, *La Civilisation des Arabes* by Dr Gustave Lebon, appeared in 1884, published by Firmin-Didot. On 5 September 1886 *Le Journal illustré* was the first French daily newspaper to use the process to reproduce Nadar's interview with Chevreul, on the occasion of his centenary.
406. Durand-Ruel wrote to him: 'For this campaign it would be a good thing to have some etchings taken from some of your paintings. Would you agree to making some? You would do them better than anyone else and it would lend the paintings added weight. I am also planning to have etchings interspersed through the exhibition catalogue' (Durand-Ruel Archive, quoted by Bailly-Herzberg in Pissarro, *Correspondance*, Vol. I, p.346, note 2, 16 September 1885). In Durand-Ruel's catalogue of 1873 six paintings by Pissarro had been reproduced by different engravers.
407. The first mention of Proud'hon occurs in his Correspondance in December 1883, while he was reading *Le Prolétaire*. When he had finished reading Kropotkin's work Pissarro exposed his anarchist convictions in two passionate letters sent to his niece Esther Isaacson in December 1885. See *Correspondance*, Vol. I, pp.359 and 368. On the relationship of the anarchist movement to the arts, see Herbert, 1961. See also Egbert, 1970, and Reszler, 1973.
408. Although Fénéon mentions only about fifteen 'drawings' ('Les impressionistes en 1886', in *Oeuvres plus que complètes*, Vol. I, p.32), Bailly-Herzberg has shown that the works in question were lithographs (Pissarro, *Correspondance*, Vol. II, p.48); this is based on an anonymous article [Louis Ganderax] in *La République française* of 17 May 1886. On Odilon Redon, see Gott, 1990.
409. Pissarro, *Correspondance*, Vol. II, p.54 [June 1886].
410. Pissarro, *Correspondance*, Vol. I, p.346, note 2 (see note 406).
411. Pissarro, *Correspondance*, Vol. II, p.269, to Durand-Ruel, 29 March 1889: 'Of course it would be a net price, with no commission, if your friend wants to buy them. The collection is of such importance that I would give it him for one thousand three hundred francs instead of one thousand six hundred and thirty - that's my last price.' Bailly-Herzberg thinks the buyer may have been Mrs Havemeyer (Vol. II, p.269, note 1).
412. *Ibid.*, Vol. IV, p.438, 22 January 1898.
413. *Ibid.*, Vol. II, p.224, 26 April 1888.
414. On the conduct of the relationship between Portier and Avery, see Avery 1979.
415. Henri Beraldi, *Les Graveurs du XIXe siècle*, Paris 1885-92, 12 vols.
416. Pissarro, *Correspondance*, Vol. II, pp.280-5, to Beraldi, 27 July 1889.
417. On Childs see Bailly-Herzberg in Pissarro, *Correspondance*, Vol. II, p.287, note 1.
418. On Lucas, see *The George A. Lucas Collection of the Maryland Institute*, Baltimore Museum of Art, 1965, in particular Victor Carlson, 'A Note on the Lucas print collection', pp.20-1. Like Avery, Lucas left a diary: Lucas, 1979.
419. Pissarro, *Correspondance*, Vol. III, p.87, 21 May 1891, and p.97, 23 June 1891.
420. Félix Bracquemond, *Du dessin et de la couleur*, Paris, Charpentier, 1885, XIV-284 pages. Bracquemond later published another essay, ninety-six pages long: *Etude sur la gravure sur bois et de la lithographie*, Paris, Beraldi, 1897.
421. Félix Fénéon, in *La Revue indépendante*, January 1888, published in Fénéon, 1970, Vol. I, p.92.
422. Laforgue, 1988, in particular *L'Impressionisme*, pp.167-75.
423. The archives of the Société des Peintres-graveurs can be reconstituted from Guérard's papers, now in the Bibliothèque Nationale, Département des Estampes (Yb3 4158, Quarto) and from Bracquemond's letters to Guérard, in the manuscript department (see the inventory published by Bouillon, 1973, pp.351-86, nos 362-84).
424. *Société des Peintres graveurs français. Troisième exposition. 4-30 avril 1891.* Preface by Roger Marx, p.8.
425. Galerie Durand-Ruel, *Deuxième exposition de Peintres'graveurs, 6-26 March 1890.* Preface by Philippe Burty, p.10.
426. On reactions to the first exhibition, see Druick and Zegers, 1984, p. LXXXI, note 28.
427. *Op. cit.*, pp.6-7, note 425.
428. Distel, 1984, pp.8-13.
429. Bibliothèque Nationale, Département des Estampes, Guérard papers.
430. Pissarro, *Correspondance*, Vol. III, p.13, 10 January 1891.
431. Bibliothèque Nationale, Département des Estampes, Guérard papers.
432. *Ibid.*
433. The catalogue consists of a single sheet of paper; a copy with Pissarro's notes on it can be found in the Bibliothèque Nationale, Département des Estampes, serial number Yb3 1338, Octavo.
434. *Gazette des Beaux-Arts*, March 1889, p.238.
435. Gustave Geffroy, 'Le Statuaire Rodin', Boussod and Valadon, 1889, and in *Les Lettres et les Arts*, September 1889, pp.289-304.
436. *L'Artiste*, February 1885, p.156.
437. List drawn up by Rodin for Bourcard, in Thorson, 1974 and 1976.
438. Roger Marx, 'Les pointes-sèches de Rodin', in *Gazette des Beaux-Arts*, March 1902.
439. Thorson, 1975, p.28, and illustrations p.17.
440. Leymarie and Melot, 1970, contains the illustrated catalogue of Sisley's six prints. See also Melot, 1974, pp.303-6.
441. Melot, 1978, p.257.
442. François Daulte, Alfred Sisley, *Catalogue raisonné de l'œuvre peint*, Paris 1959, and *Sisley*, Paris, Réunion des Musées Nationaux, 1992.
443. Stéphane Mallarmé, 'The Impressionists and Edouard Manet', in *Art Monthly Review*, 30 September 1876, pp.117-22. See also Henri de Regnier, 'Mallarmé et les peintres', in *L'Art Vivant*, Vol. VI, nos 127-8, April 1930, and Mondor, 1941, pp.543-50.
444. Mallarmé, *Correspondance*, 1969, 3 vols, Vol. III, p.363, note I. Monet illustrated *La Gloire*, see Vol. III, p.151, note 2.
445. Not found. Mallarmé, *Correspondance*, Vol. III, p.254, notes 1 and 2.
446. Paul Valéry, *Degas, danse, dessin*, in *Œuvres*, Vol. II, La Pléiade collection, p.1182.
447. Mallarmé, *Correspondance*, Vol. III, pp.237-8, 7 August 1888.
448. *Ibid.*, pp.256-7, 2 September 1888.

449. *Ibid.*, p.265, 8 October 1888, to Deman. According to Adhémar, 1973, no. 60, for reasons of format and date the plate selected by Degas may have been *Dancer Tying her Shoe*, but it was not published in *Pages* in 1891.
450. Renoir was almost a member of the Manet-Morisot households, see Higonnet, 1989, p.186.
451. Berthe Morisot, *Correspondance*, 1950, p.133.
452. Mallarmé, *Correspondance*, Vol. III, p.151, December 1887.
453. *Ibid.*, p.290, 17 February, 1889. According to Mondor (note 3), Mallarmé is putting his own reading on the letter from Monet of 15 February, thanking him warmly for sending a copy of his translation of Poe's *Poems* and ending thus: 'I shall not forget your drawings, but I still have no time.'
454. Bailly-Herzberg, 1979.
455. Mallarmé, *Correspondance*, Vol. III, p.274. 1 November 1888.
456. Morisot, *Correspondance*, December 1888, p.141.
457. Mallarmé, *Correspondance*, Vol. III, p.274, 1 November 1888.
458. Morisot, *Correspondance*, to Edma, July 1890.
459. Mallarmé, *Correspondance*, Vol. III, p.290, 17 February 1889.
460. On the friendship between Berthe Morisot and Mary Cassatt, see Higonnet, 1989, p.209.
461. *Ibid.*, p.157.
462. Bailly-Herzberg, 1979, p.218.
463. Higonnet, 1989, p.30.
464. Bataille and Wildenstein, 1961, no. 213 (1887). For other comparisons with the drawings of Berthe Morisot, see Melot, 1974, p.164.
465. Bailly-Herzberg, 1979, p.224.
466. Johnson, p.137, gives a list of twelve dry point etchings, eight of which are known and four in the Vollard Archives in Winterthur (Winterthur Kunstmuseum, Schenkung Vollard, Catalogue by Heinz Keller, Winterthur, 1949, nos 88–91). The list in question probably contains duplicates, and Winterthur does not possess the plates. This information was provided by J. Bailly-Herzberg.
467. Mallarmé, *Correspondance*, Vol. III, p.290.
468. Higonnet, 1989, p.226.
469. Lionello Venturi, *Les Archives de l'impressionisme*, Paris, New York, 1939, Vol. I, p.141. Postscript to a letter to Durand-Ruel written in February 1890, probably on the subject of the second exhibition of the Painter-Engravers: 'Dear M. Durand-Ruel, Received your letter and enclosures, many thanks. I'll send the measurements as soon as possible. I've got the names on your exhibition list. It would be excellent if all of them contributed paintings. It would be less of a clique and draw a wider public. I can't think of any other names. I'm a bit far off for that. At any rate, if it turns out well, others will come.'
470. On the publication of *Pages* in 1888, see Mallarmé, *Oeuvres complètes*, Paris, 1961, La Pléiade collection, *Poèmes en prose*, p.167ff.
471. Vollard, 1918, Vol. II, p.64, nos 76, 79, 87.
472. [Maurice Bérard], *Renoir à Wargemont*, Paris 1938.
473. There are two paintings of the subject, both 1883, and a number of drawings (John Rewald, *Renoir Drawings*, New York and London, 1958, nos 13, 15, 16, 17, 18, and Vollard, 1918, nos. 53 and 77, all 1883).
474. Degas, 1988, nos 190–4, pp.303–5.
475. *Ibid.*, no. 190.
476. *Ibid.*, no. 265.
477. *Ibid.*, no. 266.
478. *Ibid.*, no 264.
479. Douglas and Zegers, 1984, p.XXXVII, and Reff, 1976, p.270ff., particularly on the mixing of techniques, pp.282–4.
480. E. de Goncourt, *Journal*, 2 December 1894.
481. Janis, 1984, p.399. See also Lipton, 1987, chapter 'The Bathers, modernity and prostitution', pp.151–186.
482. Degas, *Letters*, no. CLIX, p.182. On de Valernes, *Degas*, 1988, no. 58.
483. Pissarro, *Correspondance*, Vol. III, p.68, 25 April 1891. The dealer in question was Salvator Mayer, 5 Rue Laffitte.
484. Kornfeld, 1965. For a discussion of the distinction to be made between different plates and states of this subject, see Melot, 1974, nos 201–8 (reproduced).
485. Adhémar, 1973, no. 64, second state.
486. Adhémar, 1973, no. 64, p.XLIX.
487. Adhémar, 1973, no. 66, p.XLIX.
488. Melot, 1974, p.90.
489. *Degas*, 1988, no. 168–70 and pp.280–1. According to Cachin, 1973, p.XXXII, these monotypes were to have been reproduced by the heliogravure printer Dujardin.
490. Reff, 1976, pp.172–3.
491. Pickvance, 1963, p.260, based on an article by George Moore in *The Speaker*, 5 December 1891, which notes that *The Illustrated London News* used to reproduce the work of French artists.
492. 'How well I remember seeing Degas's pastels for the first time in the window of an art dealer in the Boulevard Haussmann. I used often to go and press my nose to the window, trying to absorb all I could of his art. It changed my life. I saw art as I wanted to see it.' Letter to Mrs Havemeyer, quoted in Breeskin, 1967, p.12. See Mathews, 1982, and Weitzenhoffer, 1986, p.121. Cassatt's interest in Degas's techniques is further proved by her handwritten note on Degas's *Head of a Woman* in the Metropolitan Museum, the only known copy: 'proof using solvent, liquid grain' (cf. Mose, 1964, no. 29, not reproduced).
493. Degas, *Letters*, XXVI, p.55, to Pissarro, undated [1880]. See also Fuller, 1950.
494. Pissarro, *Correspondance*, Vol. III, p.403, 5 December 1893.
495. Delâtre Archive.
496. Higonnet, 1989, p.209.
497. See the introduction to Breeskin, 1967.
498. Shapiro, 1989, p.68 (letter to the mother of Mary Cassatt of 23 January, 1891).
499. Pissarro, *Correspondance*, Vol. III, p.55, 3 April 1891.
500. *Ibid.*, p.68, 25 April.
501. Breeskin, 1948, nos 108, 109, 126 and 122 (Shapiro, 1989, nos 1–4).
502. E. de Goncourt, *Journal*, 13 March 1890.
503. Mathews, 1989, p.33.
504. *Ibid.*, p.39, based on an unpublished passage in the *Memoirs* of Mrs Havemeyer.
505. Pissarro, *Correspondance*, Vol. III, p.55, 3 April 1891.
506. Leiris, no. 416.
507. Cate and Hitchings, 1978, pp.2–3 and Cate, 1992. See also Cate's 'The Artists and new techniques', in *Gazette of the Grolier Club*, nos 28–9, June-December 1978, pp.57–73, and Roger Portalis, 'La Gravure en couleurs', in *Gazette des Beaux-Arts*, December 1888, pp.441–57, January 1889, pp.29–41, March 1889, pp.196–212, and April 1889, pp.322–38; on the early days of colour lithography, see Gustave von Groschwitz, 'The Significance of XIX-Century color lithography', in *Gazette des Beaux-Arts*, November 1954, pp.243–66.
508. Bertin, 1977, pp.5–11.
509. *The 36 Views of the Eiffel Tower*, begun in 1888 as woodcuts, were finally published in 1902 as lithographs. See Armond Fields, *Henri Rivière, graveur, lithographe et photographe*, Réunion des Musées Nationaux, Paris 1988.
510. Shapiro, 1989, p.76. Shapiro also quotes Richard Ranft, Emile and Alfred Dezannay, Louis Legrand, Charles Houdard, Lepère and Henri Detouche (*Au Théâtre*), as well as Guérard's *Polichinelle*, 1881.
511. On Degas' dreams in colour, see Degas, *Letters*, XXV, pp.53–4, and Georges Rivière, *M. Degas, bourgeois de Paris*, Paris, 1938, p.68. At the same date, the summer of 1879, Hoschedé was apparently planning coloured reproductions for his magazine, *L'Art et la mode*: see Druick and Zegers, 1984–5, p.LI.
512. Pissarro, *Correspondance*, Vol. III, p.55, 3 April 1891.
513. *Ibid.*, p.416, 3 January 1894.
514. *Ibid.*, p.451. 9 May 1894.
515. Delteil, no. 112; Pissarro, *Correspondance*, Vol. III, p.454, 26 May 1894.
516. Pissarro, *Correspondance*, Vol. IV, p.19, 18 January 1895.
517. Dardel, 1987. See also Dardel, 1980 and Herbert, 1961.
518. E. de Goncourt, *Journal*, 10 January 1894.
519. Janis, 1968; Guérin, 1924, p.77; Green, 1985; Jean Adhémar, 'Un Monotype de Degas au Cabinete des estampes', in *Gazette des Beaux-Arts*, 1964, II. pp.374–7.
520. On the two experimental reproductions of a reduced monotype, *In the Garden*, by the heliogravure printer Dujardin, see Janis, 1968, no. 223, Cachin 1973, no. 69, and *Degas*, 1988, p.281, note 7.
521. Janis, 1967. On the destruction of the plates by his brother René, see I, p.21, note 11. See also Janis, 1984. p.401.
522. The painting of *The Dancing Class* (*The Ballet Master* repeats the motif, reversed), now in the Musée d'Orsay, begun in 1873, was finished only in 1876. See *Degas*, 1988, no. 129, p.234ff.
523. Theodore Reff in 'Some aspects of Degas' technique', in *Metropolitan Museum Journal*, Vol. IV, 1971, p.152 (reiterated in Reff, 1976, p.287) speaks of 'rembrandtesque chiaroscuro'.
524. Georges Jeanniot, 'Souvenirs sur Degas', in *La Revue universelle*, 15 October 1933, pp.152–74, and 1 November 1933, pp.280–304. On the colour monotypes, *Degas*, 1988, pp.502–6, nos. 298–301. The engravings of Jeanniot in the Département des Estampes in the Bibliothèque Nationale show aquatints in colour that seem to partake of the secrets of Mary Cassatt: *At the Seaside* (1900), *The Edge*, two states, one of them a proof 'made under the guidance of Degas', *Place de Pontorson*, (monotype?), and two monotypes, one of which, *The Butcher*, done as a study from life of how bulls are slaughtered with a view to an illustration of Zola's *La Débâcle*.
525. Loyrette, 1991, pp.564–5.
526. Howard G. Lay, 'Degas and Durand-Ruel 1892. The Landscape Monotypes', in *The Print Collector's Newsletter*, Vol. IX, no. 5, November-December 1978, pp.145–6.
527. Arsène Alexandre, in *Paris*, 9 November 1892.
528. Denis Rouart, 'Paysages en monotypes', in *L'Œil*, no. 117, September 1964, pp.10–15.

At the height of the 'lyrical abstraction' period, Degas' monotypes were exhibited at the Lefebvre Gallery (1958), and at the Galerie L'Oeil in 1964, before the 'scientific' exhibition by Eugenia P. Janis at the Fogg Art Museum in 1968.
529. Antony Griffiths, 'Monotypes', in *Print Quarterly*, March 1988, pp.56–60. On Castiglione, see Ann Percy, *Giovanni Benedetto Castiglione, Master Draughtsman of the Italian Baroque*, Philadelphia Museum of Art, 1971.
530. On Hercules Seghers, see E. Haverkamp Begeman, *Hercules Seghers, the Complete Etchings*, Introduction by Karl G. Boon, Scheltema and Holkema, Amsterdam, Martinus Nijhoff, The Hague, 1973.
531. *The Painterly Print*, 1980 (especially Shapiro, pp.29–39 and Janis, pp.9–28).
532. Shapiro, 1989, no. 16, pp.164–6.
533. Leymarie and Melot, 1971, no. 111.
534. Bibliothèque Nationale, Département des Estampes, oeuvre Auguste Delâtre, Ef 542. Delâtre's monotypes are certainly late works: they are in colour and some are repeated by his son Eugène.
535. Bertin no. 123.
536. Bibliothèque Nationale, Département des Estampes, oeuvre de Félix Bracquemond, Ef 411, Vol. I.
537. Baxter, 1980.
538. Shapiro and Melot, 1975, pp.16–23. See also the chapter on Pissarro's monotypes in Rittmann, 1992, p.252ff.
539. Pissarro, *Correspondance*, Vol. III, p.416, 3 January 1894.
540. *Ibid.*, Vol. IV, p.55, 8 April 1895.
541. Melot, 1974, no. 264. The original, an oil painting on zinc, is in the Museum of Aix-les-Bains, whose founder was none other than Vicomte Lepic, who died in 1889. The painting is from the collection of Dr Jean Faure, who bequeathed his collection of Impressionists, acquired between the Wars, to the museum.
542. Field, 1973.
543. Pissarro, *Correspondance*, Vol. II, p.121, 23 January 1887.
544. *Ibid.*, Vol. III, p.400, 23 November 1893.
545. Cachin, 1968, p.260.
546. Field, 1973, p.134.
547. Gauguin, 1943, pp.31–2.
548. Field, 1973, p.21.
549. Cachin, 1968, p.50.
550. *Ibid.*, p.6. On Gauguin's 'decorative art', see Christopher Gray, *Sculpture and Ceramics by Paul Gauguin*, Baltimore, 1963; Merete Bodelsen, *Gauguin's Ceramics. A Study in the development of his Art*, London, 1964.
551. *L'Ymagier* appeared from October 1894 to 1896.
552. Melot, 1978, pp.290–1.
553. Boyle-Turner, 1986 (Preface by Douglas Druick).
554. Grivel, 1989, p.39, no. 18. On the engravings of Emile Bernard, see also the catalogue *Pont-Aven* from the Maison Paul Prouté, Paris, 1989.
555. Gauguin, 1946, p.172.
556. Mongan, Kornfeld and Joachim, 1988, p.138 (see the review by Richard S. Field, in *Print Quarterly*, June 1989, no. 2, p.197, for the bibliography lacking in the *catalogue raisonné*). See also *Paul Gauguin, das Druckgraphische Werk*, Wolfgang Wittrock, Düsseldorf, 1979.
557. Letter to Vollard, July 1900, in Mongan, p.155.
558. Melot, 1974, no. 263. The metal plate hollowed out with a gouge is in the Bibliothèque Nationale, Département des Estampes. No former print of it is known. Posthumous proofs are mentioned in Cailac, 1932, pp.75–86.
559. Pissarro, *Correspondance*, Vol. III, p.65, 20 April 1891, and p.82, 13 May 1891.
560. Van Gogh, *Correspondance*, 642F, Vol. III, p.474, 17 June 1890.
561. Montfort, 1972, pp.5–13.
562. Van Gogh, *Correspondance*, 134F, Vol. I, p.195, 20 August 1880.
563. *Ibid.*, 140F, Vol. I, p.208, January 1881.
564. *Ibid.*, R20N, Vol. I, p.560, early February 1883.
565. *Ibid.*, R22, Vol. I, p.574, 1883.
566. This collection is now in the Van Gogh Museum, Amsterdam. See Chetham, 1976; Pickvance, 1974; Werners, 1980, pp.5–15; *Les Sources d'inspiration de Vincent Van Gogh*, Institut Néerlandais, Paris, 1972. See also Lili Jampoller, 'Theo and Vincent as art collectors', in *The Rijksmuseum Vincent Van Gogh*, Amsterdam, 1988, and 'Theo Van Gogh and Camille Pissarro: correspondence and an exhibition', in *Simiolus*, 6, 1986, pp.50–61; John Rewald, 'Theo Van Gogh, Goupil and the Impressionists,' in *Gazette des Beaux-Arts*, 1973, no. I, pp.1–64 and 65–108.
567. On Paul Renouard, see Melot, 1971; Loys Delteil, 'Paul Renouard illustrateur', in *Byblis*, 1925, pp.82–4; 'L'oeuvre de Paul Renouard', in *L'Estampe et l'affiche*, 1898, p.95; Louis Vaunois, *Paul Renouard*, Blois, 1922.
568. Vollard, 1919, p.204.
569. J. K. Huysmans, 'Salon de 1879', in *L'Art moderne*, pp.73–4.
570. The interview is quoted in the margin to the *Correspondance*, Vol. IV, p.333, 9 March 1897. Pissarro adds: 'It was a long way off Degas, but it was good anyway; it was lacking style but it was energetic; it was not the first, but it made its mark'. *Correspondance*, Vol. II, p.233, 13 May 1888.
571. Linda Nochlin, 'Van Gogh, Renouard and the Weaver's Crisis in Lyon: the Status of a Social Issue in the Art of the later Nineteenth Century', in *The Ape of Nature, studies in honor of H. W. Janson*, New York, Moshe Barasch and Lucy Freeman Sandler, 1981, pp.669–88, reprinted in Nochlin, 1989, pp.95–119.
572. *Correspondance*, 249N, Vol. I, p.522, November 1882.
573. *Ibid*, R21N, Vol. I, p.569, February 1883.
574. *Ibid.*, 303N, Vol. II, p.132, July 1883.
575. *Ibid.*, 254N, Vol. I, p.540, about December 1882.
576. De La Faille, no. 78, *Mangeurs de pommes de terre*.
577. Alain Mothe, *Vincent van Gogh à Auvers-sur-Oise*, 30 May – 29 July 1890, Paris 1987. For the remainder, see Nathalie Heinich, *La Gloire de van Gogh*,
578. Toulouse-Lautrec, *Unpublished correspondence*, 1969, p.272.
579. Pierre Daix, 'Quand Picasso dessinait pour la presse parisienne', in *Les Lettres françaises*, 3 March 1971, pp.24–5, and Michel Melot, 'Le Modèle impossible. Comment le jeune Pablo Ruic abolit la caricature', in *Picasso, jeunesse et genèse, dessins, 1893–1905*, Musée Picasso, Paris, 1991, p.68, in particular, fig. 37, p.75 and fig. 48, p.83. Picasso arrived in Paris in the spring, when Toulouse-Lautrec was leaving; he returned to Bordeaux and died in September at Malromé.
580. *Elles* (*Women*, Wittrock nos 155–65) was exhibited at Vollard then, 1897, at the Salon de la Libre Esthétique, which had taken over from the Groupe des XX in Brussels. Three plates were presented in the same year at the Indépendants, and some others at the sixth exhibition of the Société des peintres graveurs français. There were some good reviews, later, in *L'Aube* (April 1896), and *La Revue Blanche* (April–May 1896), in *Le Courrier français* and, of course, in *La Plume*. On *Elles*, see Michel Melot, preface to the facsimile edition, Tchou and Bibliothèque Nationale, Paris, 1990; and, also by Melot, *Les Femmes de Toulouse-Lautrec*, Paris, 1984.
581. For the Japonism of Toulouse-Lautrec, see Theodore Reff, 'Degas, Lautrec and Japanese Art', in *Japonism in Art*, 1980, pp.189–213, and Melot, *ibid.*, pp.239–60.
582. Vollard, 1919, pp.85–6.
583. Erasthème Ramiro, *Catalogue descriptif et analytique de l'oeuvre gravé de Félicien Rops*, Paris, 1887; with a supplement, 1985; *idem., Louis Legrand, catalogue de son œuvre gravé et lithographié*, Paris, 1896. Also on the same topic see Léon Maillard, *Henri Boutet, graveur et pastelliste*, Paris 1894. In the same year as *Elles*, Boutet produced *Parisiennes d'à présent*, Paris 1896, and *Levers et couchées des Parisiennes*, then *Autour d'Elles*, which appeared in 1898, and *Ces Dames*, fifty original lithographs, Paris 1912, and also *Les Filles de joie et de misère*, 1913 etc. Also worth mentioning are albums by Guillaume (*Mémoires d'une glace*), *Les Parisiennes* by Cham and *Les Jolies Parisiennes* by Grevin.
Not to be forgotten either are Roubille and Bottini for their picturesque *petit bourgeois*, Forain and Steinlen for the social commentary, Guillaume and Bac for smuttiness, and other entrants in the field, sharing an eager public, and catering for all tastes. In the same year as *Elles* an album of *Studies of Women* by Hermann-Paul, Toulouse-Lautrec and Willette also made its appearance.
584. The word had already been spoken in an undertone by Helleu himself: 'He also told me about attempts to achieve 'instant' pictures. . .' Edmond de Goncourt, *Journal*, 9 January 1894.
585. See the letters to G. Pellet of 15 and 30 November 1898 in which he requests the unsold copies left in the stock room, in *Unpublished correspondence, op.cit.*
586. Pissarro, *Correspondance*, Vol. III, p.20, 14 January 1891. See the lists drawn up by Rittmann, 1992, for the prints exhibited (p.283), sold (p.286), with prices (p.288).
587. 15 May 1892, about forty etchings were deposited with Boussod and Valadon (list in *Correspondance*, Vol. III, p.230).
588. *Ibid.*, to Monet, Vol. III, p.52, 1 April 1891.
589. Rittmann, 1992, pp.201–13.
590. On holiday by the sea in Knokke, Belgium, in August 1894, he made the acquaintance of some German artists, including the painter Max Stremel (*Correspondance*, Vol. III, p.471, note 3): 'I'll think about the dealer in London you told me about, I spoke to you about Munich; I have supporters and a few collectors there' (9 August, 1894, to Lucien, Vol. III, p.95) gives the names of the twenty or so proofs held by Gutbier, director of Arnolds, Dresden.
591. Pissarro, *Correspondance*, Vol. III, p.415 and p.418.
592. *Ibid.*, Vol. III, p.419, to Lucien, 21 January, 1894. He is taking about Delteil nos 116–7.
593. *Ibid.*, Vol. IV, p.25, to Lucien, 28 January 1895.

594. *Ibid.*, Vol. IV, p.29, to Georges, 9 February 1895.
595. *Ibid.*, Vol. IV, p.31, to Lucien, 14 February, 1895.
596. *Ibid.*, Vol. IV, p.54, to Lucien, 8 April 1895.
597. On the subject of 'markets', see MacDuffee, 1897; Rittmann, 1992, p.214ff., and, more generally, Herbert, 1970.
598. Pissarro, *Correspondance*, Vol. III, p.260, to Mirbeau, 30 September 1892.
599. Claude Chambelland, 'Correspondance de Jean Grave', in *L'Actualité de l'histoire, bulletin trimestuel de l'Institut français d'histoire sociale*, no. 27, April-June, 1959, pp.38–43.
600. He is referring to Delteil, no. 153, *Women Carrying Sticks*, 154, *The Vagabonds*, and 194, *Labour* (in colour). See Aline Dardel, 1980.
601. *Social Turpitudes* [1890], facsimile, Geneva, 1972, with text by André Fermigier. See also Thomson, 1982.
602. Pissarro published his drawing of *Dockers loading Coal in Rouen Harbour* in an issue of *La Plume* on anarchy, 1 May, 1893.
603. Pissarro, *Correspondance*, Vol. III, p.395, to M. Chatel, 9 November 1893.
604. Higonnet, 1989, p.199, and Pissarro, *Correspondance*, Vol. II., p.138, 4 March 1887.
605. Pissarro, *Correspondance*, Vol. IV, p.26, 28 January 1895.
606. On *Agricultural Labour* (*Travaux des Champs*), see the detailed history of its publication in Bretell and Lloyd, 1980.
607. 'I saw Lautrec yesterday and he introduced me to M. Marty, editor of a review of prints; he requested something for his forthcoming issue, the second, and would like something from you as well. It needs to be something very straightforward. I don't know what I could provide; a lithograph perhaps?' Pissarro, *Correspondance*, Vol. III, p.318, 3 March 1893.
608. *Ibid.*, p.417.
609. *Ibid.*, to Lucien, 14 January 1894, p.418, 'I was planning to give Marty an etching, but it will not be possible unless what I'm doing comes out well.' According to Janine Bailly-Herzberg (p.420, note 3) he was already thinking of *Women Bathing in the Shade of a Wooded Riverbank* (Delteil 144); the proof of the second and last state bears the note '24 Janvier 1894', but it was not published until the seventh delivery, in 1895, instead of a lithograph on stone (most likely the *Market at Gisors*) which he had spoiled.
610. *Ibid.*, Vol. III, p.538, note 1.
611. Leonce Bénédite, preface to the first annual anthology of the albums of 1896, *L'Estampe moderne*, p.8.
612. Pissarro, *Correspondance*, Vol. IV, p.346, 13 April 1897.
613. Roger Milès, *Les Veillées noires*, Paris, undated [1889], and *Art et Nature*, Paris, 1897.
614. On Eugène Boudin's contribution, see Melot, 1972, p.257. It may refer to Boudin's response to Buhot's request for the Peintres-Graveurs, cf. *supra*, note 441.
615. Pissarro, *Correspondance*, Vol. III, p.420, 21 January 1894, and note 1.
616. Vollard, 1937, p.55.
617. *Ibid.*, p.298.
618. Johnson, 1977.
619. 'Received catalogue yesterday evening, my letter already sealed and about to be posted. I can see a few of the most vital names that I had particularly singled out and recommended to M. Vollard, including the name of Jeanniot. I had also particularly emphasised that he should go and see M. Guérard and enlist his participation.' Bibliothèque Nationale, Departement des Estampes, Yb3 1338, Octavo.
620. Druick, 1977, p.120.
621. Mellerio, 1898, p.19.
622. Pissarro, *Correspondance*, Vol. IV, p.222, to Lucien, 3 July 1896. The same letter also says: 'I'm sending you the Vollard catalogue. . . There are some nice things as well as some atrocities. . . Vollard has ordered a colour lithograph from me, a large plate, he'd like a market scene, he's asked my price. I've told him I'd think about it, what do you think I can ask?. . . I haven't a clue.'
623. *Ibid.*, p.231, 16 July 1896.
624, *Ibid.*, p.245, 4 September 1896.
625. *Ibid.*, p.255, 18 September 1896.
626. Druick, 1972. On the *Bathers* lithographs, see also Jean Goriany, 'Notes on prints: Cézanne lithograph 'The Bathers'', in *Gazette des Beaux-Arts*, Vol. 23, 1943, pp.123–4, and Harry Salamon, 'Paul Cézanne, critical notes and catalogue of his engravings,' in *Print Collector*, no. 4, September-October 1973, pp.36–45.
627. Druick, 1977, p.129. There are also proofs of Renoir's *Pinning the Hat* touched up with pastel, or another with watercolour (according to the catalogue by Claude-Roger Marx). Only one watercolour on a black and white print of the *Little Bathers* is known; there is another one for the *Self Portrait*, designed to be a second colour lithograph for the third album which in the end was printed only in black and white. Three of these preliminary workings exist for *The Large Bathers*. Druick is sure that this was the first lithograph commissioned by Vollard from Cézanne: the painting, *The Large Bathers*, from which the print is taken, was exhibited at the third Impressionist exhibition in 1877, and was part of the Caillebotte bequest to the government in 1893: Vollard chose it for his shop window during the 1895 exhibition.
628. *15 lithographies d'après Degas*, by G.W. Thornley, undated [copyright 1889], Boussod, Valadon et Cie.
629. Degas, *Lettres*, CXXI, p.153, 28 April [1887].
630. *La Vogue*, July-August 1889, II, 2, p.237.
631. Félix Fénéon, in *La Revue Indépendante*, June 1889, in *Oeuvres plus que complètes*, Vol. I, p.153.
632. Gustave Geffroy, preface to the album *25 lithographies d'après Pissarro*, by Thornley, undated. The title page bears the legend: '108 copies of this series of lithographs were printed and the plates destroyed'. Each cover page bears the handwritten signatures of Pissarro and Thornley.
633. *Degas. Vingt dessins. 1861–1896.* Goupil et Cie, Boussod, Manzi, Joyant et Cie, undated [1896].
634. *Degas. Quatre-vingt dix-huit reproductions signées par Degas (peintures, pastels, dessins et estampes)*, Vollard, undated, edition of 800 numbered albums. Republished by Bernheim in 1918.
635. André Mellerio, 'La rénovation de l'estampe', in *L'Estampe et l'affiche*, no. 1, March 1897, p.5.
636. Mallarmé, *Correspondance*, Vol. III, pp.237–8, to Deman, 7 August 1888: 'I know nothing of prices except that they are only slightly higher than the price of a good etching.'
637. Lochnan, 1981.
638. Odilon Redon, *A soi-même*, p.125.
639. Léonce Bénédite, *Exposition des lithographies originale de Fantin-Latour*, Paris, Musée du Luxembourg, 1 June, 1899.
640. Thiébault-Sisson in *Le Temps*, 5 November 1897; Henri Lefort, president of the engravers' and lithographers' section of the Société des artistes français; Charles Maurin in *Le Journal des artistes*, 20 March 1898 (quoted by André Mellerio, 1898, pp.4–5, and note 1).
641. Mellerio, 1898, p.24.
642. See the collected files in *Nouvelles de l'estampe*, no. 13, January-February 1974.
643. *Germinal, album de XX estampes originales*, published by La Maison Modern, 82, Rue des Petits-Champs, in an edition of 100 copies with a preface by Gustave Geffroy.
644. Faxon, 1982, no. 7 and no. 9.
645. *Paris à l'eau-forte*, 15 October and 5 November 1876.
646. Rewald, editor, 1965, Vol. II, p.93.
647. Jacqueline Magne, *Forain témoin de son temps*, University of Aix-Marseille, thesis, third cycle, [1973], typescript. (Bibl. Nat., Dép. des Estampes, Yb3 3778). See, by the same author, 'Forain et l'affaire Dreyfus', in *Nouvelles de l'estampe*, no. 8, March-April 1973, pp.9–14, and 'Forain témoin de son temps: la satire sociale et morale', in *Gazette des Beaux-Arts*, no. 81, 1973, pp.241–51.
648. On Raffaëlli, see Melot, 1993. E. de Goncourt, *Journal*, 8 June 1896.
649. Guérin, 1910 and 1912.
650. Weitzenhoffer, 1986, p.21. It was Mary Cassatt who urged her friend to buy the pastel by Degas in Père Tanguy's shop, in Rue Clauzel: 'And I bought it upon her advice', wrote Louisine in *Sixteen to Sixty, Memoirs*, pp.249–50. The pastel cost 500 francs.
651. Pissarro, *Correspondance*, Vol. II, pp.223–6 (26 April 1888) and, for the first contacts with Germany, which increased after 1900 with the dealer Julius Elias: Vol. IV, p.438 (22 January 1898).
652. *The Golden Age of Engraving, a specialist's story about fine prints*, by Fr. Keppel, New York, 1910, pp.120–3.
653. Victor Carlson, 'A Note on the Lucas Print Collection', in the George A. Lucas Collection of the Maryland Institute, Baltimore Museum of Art, 1965.
654. E. de Goncourt, *Journal*, 13 March 1890.
655. Maberly, 1844. New edition, 1880. The introduction asserts: 'The American mind is especially adapted to the expression of art in this form, and, with the encouragement offered by the constantly increasing numbers of collectors and purchasers, it will no doubt attain to a development at once rapid and vigorous.'
656. Hut, 1946, pp.235–56. See René Brimo, *L'Evolution du goût aux Etats-Unis*, Paris, 1938, p.48ff., Fink, 1978, and 'American Artists in France 1850–1870', in *American Art Journal*, November 1973, pp.32–49: see also *French Impressionists' influence on American Artists*, Lowe Art Museum, University of Miami, Coral Gables, Florida, 1971.
657. Weitzenhoffer, 1976, pp.7–14. See also in the same number, Madeleine Barbin, 'Des Américaines à Paris', pp.16–19.
658. The *catalogue raisonné* of the engravings of Fattori was published by Andrea Baboni with an introduction by Anna Allegranza Malesci (Milan, 1983, 2 Vols.) See also Dario Durbe, 'Fattori incisore', in *Rivista di Livorno*, nos. 5–6, 1959, pp.29–32; Lamberto Vitali, 'Les gravures de Fattori', and Maria Cristina

Bonaguia, 'Fattori graveur', in *Giovanni Fattori, eaux-fortes*, Centre Culturel Italien, Paris, 1978.
659. Lucius Grisebach, Sigrid Achenbach, Ingeborg Becker and Susanne von Falkenhausen, *Adolph Menzel, Zeichnungen, Druckgraphik und illustrierte Bücher: ein Bestenkatalog der Nationalgalerie, des Kupferstichkabinetts und der Kunstbibliothek*, Berlin, 1984.
660. Karl Asplund, *Zorn's engraved work. Descriptive catalog*, Stockholm, 1920. See also: Rainer Michael Mason, *Eugène Carrière, Anders Zorn, estampes*, Musée d'Art et d'Histoire, Geneva, Cabinet des Estampes, 1983. On the development of printmaking in Sweden, see Per Bjurström, 'La gravure en Suède', in *Nouvelles de l'estampe*, no. 51, May-June 1980, pp.9-18.
661. Paul Renouard, *Catalogue d'une collection de dessins et d'eau-fortes*, La Bodinière, Paris, 17-31 May 1894. On the gradual acceptance of the Western concept of the original print in Japan at the end of the nineteenth century, see Inaga, 1984.
662. Pissarro, *Correspondance*, Vol. v, p.323, 26 Febraury 1903. On Paul Cassirer, see p.276, note 2.
663. The article in *The Studio* signed by the Comte de Soissons (see Pissarro, *Correspondance*, Vol. v, p.323, note 1) appeared in October 1903, pp.59-60, a few days before Pissarro's death on 13 November.
664. Hind, 1908.
665. *Société internationale des aquafortistes sous la présidence d'honneur de S.A.R. Madame la Comtess de Flandre. Statuts*, Brussels, 1874. After 1885 German and American collectors guaranteed the success of Durand-Ruel, and the International Exhibitions held by his rival, Georges Petit, lived up to their name. According to Reutersward, 1952, p.171, there were nineteen painters of nine nationalities in the fourth exhibition in 1885.
666. This question is tackled by Clark, 1985, for example on p.147, with reference to the outskirts of Paris, and 'the classes who come to stake their claim to this new land', p.202, or again on p.235, where he proposes 'new layers of society' distinct from the working classes.
667. Marcel Proust, 'Du côté de chez Swann', in *A la recherche du temps perdu*, La Pléiade, p.40.
668. On the question of originality, see Moulin, 1978, and Melot, 1986. See also Baudrillard, 1968, especially the chapters on 'La Collection' and 'Systèmes et séries'; and Benjamin, 1936.
669. Gérard Chomienne, *Bergson, la conscience et la vie, le possible et le réel*, Paris, 1985, p.6.
670. See recent steps forward in the history of the printed book, through the research of Roger Chartier, or D.F. MacKenzie, *La Bibliographie et la sociologie des textes*, Paris, 1991, French translation of the *Bibliography and the Sociology of Texts*, 1986. The history of the print, because of its intermediate status, benefits from these new approaches to the history of the book, enriching the history of art.
671. Mayeur, 1973, p.62: 'We are witnessing the blossoming of capitalist economics. Money dealing is easier. In December 1877, the fixed rate of the banknote established in 1870 was abandoned and convertibilty re-established'; and p.63: 'If land and mortgages retained their prestige, fixed rate securities and government stocks (at the outset) attracted the small saver. Government bonds were widely available thanks to the savings banks. The canniest capitalist turned now to investments with a variable return.'

BIBLIOGRAPHY

Adeline, Jules, *Les Arts de reproduction vulgarisés*, Paris, [1894].

Alexandre, Arsène, *Jean-François Raffaëlli, peintre, graveur et sculpteur*, Paris, 1909.

Avery, Samuel P., *The Diaries 1871-1882 of Samuel P. Avery, Art Dealer*, ed. Madeleine Fidell-Beaufort, Herbert L. Kleinfield and Jeanne K. Welcher, Arno Press, New York, 1979.

Adhémar, Jean, 'Les portraits de Baudelaire par Manet', in *Revue des arts*, n° 4, 1952, p. 240-242.

'Manet et l'estampe', in *Nouvelles de l'estampe*, n° 7, 1965, p. 230-235.

Adhémar, Jean, and Cachin, Françoise, *Degas, gravures et monotypes*, Paris, Arts et métiers graphiques, 1973. (English trans. : *Degas. The Complete Etchings, Lithographs and Monotypes*, Viking Press, New York, 1974).

Baas, Jacqueline, *Auguste Lepère, 1875-1895*, thesis typescript, University of Michigan, 1982.

Bacher, Otto, *With Whistler in Venice*, New York, 1908.

Bailly-Herzberg, Janine, *L'Eau-forte de peintre au XIXe siècle : la Société des aquafortistes*, 2 vol., Laget, Paris, 1972.

1972 (2) 'Marcellin Desboutin and his world', in *Apollo Magazine*, n° 65, June 1972, p. 496-500.

1974 'Lettres inédites de J.-B. Jongkind', in *Nouvelles de l'estampe*, n° 18, November–December 1974, p. 13-16.

1975 'L'école de Barbizon : Corot, les eaux-fortes', in *Connaissance des arts*, February 1975.

1979 'Les estampes de Berthe Morisot', in *Gazette des Beaux-Arts*, 1979, p. 215-227.

1981 'Pissarro à Rouen', in *L'Œil*, n° 312-313, July–August 1981, p. 53-59.

1985 *Dictionnaire de l'estampe, 1830-1950*, Arts et métiers graphiques, Paris, 1985.

Bailly-Herzberg, Janine, and Dardel, Aline, 'Les illustrations de Lucien Pissarro', in *Nouvelles de l'estampe*, n° 54, November–December 1980, p. 8-16.

Bareau, Juliet, *Édouard Manet, l'Œuvre gravé, chefs-d'œuvre du département des estampes de la Bibliothèque nationale*, Stadtverwaltung Ingelheim, Ingelheim-am-Rhein, 1977.

1978 *Manet : dessins, aquarelles, eaux-fortes, lithographies, correspondance*, galerie Huguette Bérès, Paris, 1978.

1983 'Documents concernant l'Exécution de Maximilien', in *Manet*, Réunion des musées nationaux, Paris, 1983, p. 529-531.

Bareau, Juliet, and Mitchell, Breon, 'Tales of a raven, the origins and fate of Le Corbeau by Mallarmé and Manet', in *Print Quarterly*, vol. VI, n° 3, September 1989, p. 258-301.

Bataille, Marie-Louise, and Wildenstein, Georges, *Berthe Morisot, Catalogue des peintures, dessins et aquarelles*, Les Beaux-Arts, Paris, 1961.

Baudelaire, Charles, *Œuvres complètes*, N.R.F. (coll. 'La Pléiade'), Paris, 1958.

Baudrillard, Jean, *Le Système des objets*, Gallimard, Paris, 1968.

Baxter, Colles, 'Les dessins et gravures de Félix Buhot, une donation importante à la Bibliothèque nationale', in *Félix Buhot, 1847-1898, le travail d'un graveur*, Paris, Nouvelles de l'estampe, 1980.

Bazille, *Frédéric Bazille and Early Impressionism*, The Art Institute of Chicago, 1978.

Bazille, Montpellier, musée Fabre, 1992.

Benjamin, Walter, 'L'œuvre d'art à l'ère de sa reproductibilité technique', 1936 (reprinted in *Poésie et révolution*, Lettres nouvelles, Paris, 1971).

Beraldi, Henri, *Les Graveurs du XIXe siècle*, Paris, 12 vol., 1885-1892.

Berhaut, Marie, *Caillebotte, sa vie et son œuvre, Catalogue raisonné de ses peintures et pastels*, Bibliothèque des arts, Paris, 1977.

Berger, Klaus, *Japonismus in der Westliche Malerei, 1860-1920*, Prestel Verlag, Munich,1980. (English translation: *Japonism in Western Painting from Whistler to Matisse*, Cambridge, 1980.)

Bertin, Claudie, *Henri Guérard, 1846-1897*, typewritten memoir from the Louvre, 3 vol., 1975 (can be consulted in the Bibliothèque nationale, département des etampes).

'Henri Guérard, peintre-graveur', in *Nouvelles de l'estampe*, n° 31, January–February 1977, p. 5-10.

Inventaire du fonds français après 18..., 15 vol. published (to letter M), Bibliothèque nationale, département des estampes et de la photographie.

Bouillon, Jean-Paul, *Félix et Marie Bracquemond*, Mortagne, Chartres, Association Échanges et rencontres au pays percheron, 1972.

1973 'La correspondance de Félix Bracquemond', in *Gazette des Beaux-Arts*, December 1973, p. 351-386.

1974 'Bracquemond, Rops et Manet et le procédé à la plume', in *Nouvelles de l'estampe*, n° 14, March–April 1974, p. 3-11.

1975 '"À gauche" : Note sur la société du Jing Lar et sa signification', in *Gazette des Beaux-Arts*, March 1978, p. 107-118.

1975-76 'Artiste et éditeur : correspondance de Bracquemond et de Poulet-Malassis', in *Bulletin du bibliophile*, vol. I, Paris, 1975, p. 49-66 and p. 193-201 ; vol. III, p. 276-287 ; et t. IV, 1976, p. 371-404 et p. 383-396.

1978 'Les portraits à l'eau-forte de Bracquemond et leurs sources photographiques', in *Nouvelles de l'estampe*, n° 38, March–April 1978, p. 4-10.

1979 *Félix Bracquemond, les années d'apprentissage*, Didier érudition, Paris, 1979 (on microfiche).

1980 'Remarques sur le japonisme de Bracquemond', in *Japonism in Art, an International Symposium Edited by the Society for the Study of Japonism*, Committee for the Year 2001, Tokyo, 1980, p. 83-108.

1981 'L'impressionnisme', in *Revue de l'art*, n° 51, 1981, p. 75-85.

1982 'La vogue du livre à gravures du XVIIIe siècle sous le Second Empire et au début de la IIIe République', in *L'Illustration du livre et la littérature au XVIIe siècle en France et en Pologne, Cahiers de Varsovie*, vol. 9, 1982, p. 247-288.

1983 'Lettres de Manet à Bracquemond', ed. Jean-Paul Bouillon, in *Gazette des Beaux-Arts*, avril 1983, p. 145-158.

1986 'Sociétés d'artistes et institutions officielles in la seconde moitié du XIXe siècle', in *Romantisme*, n° 54, 1986, p. 89-113.

1987 *Félix Bracquemond, le réalisme absolu*, Skira, Genève, 1987.

1988 'Bracquemond : Le Jour et la Nuit', in *Degas inédit*, in proceedings of the conference on Degas, musée d'Orsay, April 1988, Paris, La Documentation française, 1988, p. 251-259.

1989 'Manet 1884 : un bilan critique', in *La Critique d'art en France 1850-1900*, Université de Saint-Étienne, CIEREC, 1989, p. 159-175.

1989 (2) 'L'estampe impressionniste, chronique bibliographique', in *Revue de l'art*, 1989, n° 86, p. 65-81.

Bouvier, Jean, *Études sur le krach de l'Union générale*, P.U.F., Paris, 1960.

Bouvier, Jean, Furet, François, and Gillet, Marcel, *Le Mouvement du profit en France au XIXe siècle; matériaux et études*, Mouton, Paris, 1965.

Boyle-Turner, *The Prints of the Pont-Aven*

School, Abbeville Press, New York, 1986.

Braudel, Fernand, and Labrousse, Ernest, *Histoire économique et sociale de la France*, 5 vol., Paris, P.U.F., 1976, especially vol. III, 1789-1880, book I, ch. VI by Maurice Levy-Leboyer, 'Les nouveaux krachs bancaires, 1877-1882', p. 448 sq., and 'Les nouveaux principes : liquidité et division des risques', p. 458.

Breeskin, Adelyn D., *The Graphic Art of Mary Cassatt, a Catalogue Raisonné*, New York, 1948.

1967 *The Graphic Art of Mary Cassatt*, The Smithsonian Institution Press, Washington, 1967.

Bretell, Richard, *Degas in the Art Institute of Chicago*, Abrams, New York, 1984.

Bretell, Richard, and Lloyd, Christopher, *A Catalogue of the Drawings by Camille Pissarro in the Ashmolean Museum*, The Clarendon Press, Oxford, 1980.

Bruce, David, 'Manet's two portraits of Charles Baudelaire', in *The Print Collector's Newsletter*, n° 14, May–June 1983, p. 47-48.

Burke, James.D., Charles Meryon, *Prints and Drawings*, Yale University Art Gallery, New Haven, 1974.

Cachin, Françoise, *Gauguin*, Le Livre de poche, Paris, 1968.

Cailac, Jean, 'The prints of Camille Pissarro. A supplement to the catalogue by Loys Delteil', in *The Print Collector's Quarterly*, vol. XIX, 1932, p. 75-86.

Carey, Frances, and Griffiths, Antony, *From Manet to Toulouse-Lautrec, French Lithographs, 1860-1900*, British Museum, London, 1978.

Cassagne, Albert, *La Théorie de l'art pour l'art en France chez les derniers romantiques et les premiers réalistes*, Paris, 1959.

Cate, Philip Dennis and Hitchings, Sinclair Hamilton, *The Color Revolution, Color Lithography in France, 1890-1900*, Rutgers University Art Gallery, 1978.

Cate, Philip Dennis and Grivel, Marianne, *De Pissarro à Picasso, l'eau-forte en couleurs*, Flammarion, Paris, 1992.

Centenaire de l'impressionnisme, Paris, Réunion des musées nationaux, 1974.

Chabert, Philippe-Gérard, *François-Nicolas Chifflart, 1825-1901*, Saint-Omer, musée de l'hôtel Gaudelin, 1972.

Champa, Kermit Swiler, *Studies in Early Impressionism*, Yale University Press, New Haven, 1973.

Chase, Edward T., *Etchings of the French Impressionists and their Contemporaries*, Hyperion Press, Paris & New York, 1946.

Chetham, Charles, *The Role of Vincent Van Gogh's Copies in the Development of his Art*, New York & London, 1976.

Clark, Timothy J., *The Painting of Modern Life. Paris in the Art of Manet and his Followers*, Knopf, New York, 1985.

Clay, Jean, *L'Impressionnisme*, Hachette, Paris, 1971.

Clément-Janin, Michel-Hilaire, *La Curieuse vie de Marcellin Desboutin, 1823-1901*, Paris, 1922.

La Critique d'art en France, 1850-1900, Université de Saint-Étienne, CIEREC, 1989.

Curtis, Atherton and Prouté, Paul, *Adolphe Appian, son œuvre gravé et lithographié*, Paul Prouté, Paris, 1968.

Dardel, Aline, *Catalogue des dessins et publications illustrées du journal anarchiste Les Temps nouveaux, 1895-1914*, Paris, typewritten thesis, third cycle for the V de P, l'Université de Paris VIII (can be consulted in the Bibliothèque Nationale, département des estampes).

Les Temps nouveaux, 1895-1914, un hebdomadaire anarchiste et la propagande par l'image, Paris, Réunion des musées nationaux, 1987.

Darragon, Éric, *Manet*, Fayard, Paris, 1989.

Daulte, François, Alfred Sisley, *Catalogue raisonné de l'œuvre peint*, Paris, 1959.

Frédéric Bazille et les débuts de l'impressionnisme. Catalogue raisonné de l'œuvre peint, Bibliothèque des arts, Paris, 1992.

Degas 1984, *Edgar Degas. The Painter as Printmaker*, catalogue by Sue Welsh Reed and Barbara Shapiro, essay by Douglas W. Druick and Peter Zegers, Boston Museum of Fine Arts, 1984.

Degas 1988, *Degas*, Réunion des musées nationaux, Paris, 1988.

Degas 1988, *Degas inédit,* proccedings of the conference at the *musée d'Orsay*, 18-21 April 1988, La Documentation française, Paris, 1989.

Degas, Edgar, *Lettres de Degas*, ed. by Marcel Guérin, Paris, 1945.

De Knyff, Gilbert, *L'Art libre au XIXe siècle ou la vie de Norbert Goeneutte*, Mayer, Paris, 1978.

Delteil, Loys, *Le Peintre graveur illustré*, Paris, vol. IX, 1919, *Degas*; vol. XVI, 1922, *Raffaëlli* ; vol. XVII, 1923, *Pissarro, Sisley, Renoir*.

Distel, Anne, 'Un achat par l'État d'estampes de Camille Pissarro en 1890 et les débuts d'un cabinet des estampes au musée du Luxembourg', in *Nouvelles de l'estampe*, n° 74, March–April 1984, p. 8-13.

Les Collectionneurs des impressionnistes, Bibliothèque des arts, Paris, 1989.

Dodgson, Campbell, *A Catalogue of Paintings, Drawings, Etchings and Lithographs (1837-1911)* by Professor Alphonse Legros, from the Collection of Franck E. Bliss, with an appreciation of the paintings and drawings by Charles Ricketts and a preface to the Etchings and Lithographs by Campbell Dodgson, London, 1922.

Doré 1983 *Gustave Doré, 1832-1883*, Strasbourg, Musée d'art moderne, cabinet des estampes, 1983.

Druick, Douglas, 'Cezanne, Vollard and lithography', *Bulletin n° 19*, National Gallery of Canada, Ottawa, 1972.

1977 'Cezanne's Lithographs', in William Rubin, *Cezanne, The Late Work*, Museum of Modern Art, New York,1977, p. 119-137.

Druick, Douglas, and Hoog, Michel, *Fantin-Latour*, Paris, Réunion des musées nationaux, 1983.

Druick, Douglas, and Zegers, Peter, *La Pierre parle, Lithography in France, 1848-1900*, National Gallery of Canada, Ottawa, 1981.

1983 'Manet's "Balloon", French Diversion, the Fête de l'Empereur', 1862, in *The Print Collector's Newsletter*, vol. XIV, n° 2, May–June 1983, p. 38-46.

1984 'Degas and the printed image, 1856-1914', in *Degas, the Painter as a Printmaker*, Boston Museum of Fine Arts, 1984, p. XV-LXX.

1988 'Le réalisme scientifique', 1874-1881, in *Degas*, 1988, p. 197-211.

Ducros, Jean, 'Le comte Lepic, 1839-1883, peintre de la marine', in *L'Art et la mer*, n° 3, 15 October 1974, p. 23-26 and n° 4, 15 February 1975, p. 27-30.

Duflo, Pierre, *Constantin Guys, fou de dessin et grand reporter, 1802-1892*, Arnaud Seydoux, Paris, 1988.

Duret, Théodore, *Les Peintres impressionnistes*, Paris, 1878.

Histoire d'Édouard Manet et de son œuvre, Paris, 1902.

Histoire de James McNeill Whistler et de son œuvre, Paris, 1914.

Egbert, Donald D., *Social Radicalism and the Arts*. Western Europe, New York, 1970.

Esposito, Carla, 'Note sur la collection d'un excentrique : les estampes du Dr Gachet', in *Nouvelles de l'estampe*, n° 121, November–December 1992, p. 4-8.

Farwell, Beatrice, *The Cult of Images, Baudelaire and the Nineteenth Century Media Explosion*, University of California, Santa Barbara, 1977.

Fawcett, Trevor, 'Graphic versus photographic in the Nineteenth Century reproduction', in *Art History*, 1986, n° 2, p. 185-212.

Faxon, Alicia Craig, *Jean-Louis Forain, a Catalogue Raisonné of his Prints*, Garland, New York & London, 1982.

Fénéon, Félix, *Œuvres plus que complètes*, éd. par Joan U. Halperin, 2 vol., Droz, Genève, 1970.

Fern, Alan M., *The Wood-engravings of Lucien Pissarro, with Catalogue Raisonné*, thèse typewritten thesis, University of Chicago, 1960 (on microfilm).

Fidell-Beaufort, Madeleine, *The Graphic Art of Charles-François Daubigny*, typewritten thesis, New York University, 1974 (on microfilm).

Fidell-Beaufort, Madeleine, and Bailly-Herzberg, Janine, *Daubigny*, Geoffroy-Dechaume, Paris, 1975.

Field, Richard S., Paul Gauguin : Monotypes, Philadelphia Museum of Art, 1973.

Fink, Lois Marie, 'French art in the United States, 1850-1870, three dealers and collectors', in *Gazette des Beaux-Arts*, September 1978, p. 87-100.

Fisher, Jay McKean, *The Prints of Édouard Manet*, Washington, International Exhibition Foundation, 1985.

Fitzgerald, Fiona, *The Prints of Lucien Pissarro from 1886 to 1896*, typewritten thesis, University of East Anglia, 1981.

Flescher, Sharon, *Zacharie Astruc : Critic, Artist and Japonist (1833-1907)*, Garland, New York, 1978.

Focillon, Henri, 'Manet en noir et blanc', in *Maîtres de l'estampe*, Paris, 1930.

Fontaine, André, *Félix Buhot peintre-graveur, 1847-1898*, Lafont, Paris, undated.

Fossier, François, *Il Fiore del impressionismo, opere grafiche della Bibliothèque nationale di Parigi*, Fabbri, Aosta, 1990.

Fried, Michael, 'Manet's sources, aspects of his art', 1859-1865, in *Artforum*, vol. VII, n° 7, March 1969 (special edition).

Fuller, Sue, 'Mary Cassatt use of soft-ground etching', in *Magazine of Arts*, February 1950.

Gachet, Paul, *Cézanne à Auvers, Cézanne graveur*, Les Beaux-Arts, Paris, undated

Gamboni, Dario, *La Plume et le pinceau : Odilon Redon et la littérature*, Minuit, Paris,

1989.

Gauguin, Paul, *Letters to Ambroise Vollard and André Fontainas*, ed. John Rewald, San Francisco, 1943 (reprinted in *Studies in Post-Impressionism*, London, 1986).

Lettres de Gauguin à sa femme et à ses amis, ed. Maurice Malingue, Paris, 1946.

Correspondance de Paul Gauguin, ed. Paul Merlhès, Fondation Singer-Polignac, Paris, vol. I, 1984.

Geiger, Monique, *Alphonse Legros, peintre-graveur*, musée des Beaux-Arts, Dijon, 1957.

Genêt-Delacroix, Marie-Claude, 'Esthétique officielle et art national sous la Troisième République', in *Le Mouvement social*, n° 131, April–June 1985, p. 105-120.

1987 'Le statut social de l'artiste professionnel aux XIXe et XXe siècles', in *La Condition sociale de l'artiste*, Université de Saint-Étienne, CIEREC, 1987, p. 87-104.

1988 'Vies d'artistes : art académique, art officiel et art libre en France à la fin du XIXe siècle', in *Revue d'histoire moderne et contemporaine*, January–March 1988, p. 40-73.

1992 *Art et État sous la IIIe République. Le système des Beaux-Arts. 1870-1940.*, Publications de la Sorbonne, Paris, 1992.

Georgel, Pierre, 'Le romantisme des années 1860. Correspondance Victor Hugo-Philippe Burty', in *Revue de l'art*, n° 20, 1973, p. 9-64.

Getscher, Robert H., *Félix Bracquemond and the Etching Process*, John Carroll University, 1974.

Glassman, Elizabeth, and Symmes, Marilyn, *Cliché-verre : Hand-Drawn, Light-Printed. A Survey of the Medium from 1839 to the Present*, The Detroit Institute of Arts, 1980.

Goncourt, Edmond et Jules de, *Journal, mémoires de la vie littéraire*, Paris, 1887-1896.

Gott, Ted, *The Enchanted Stone: The Graphic Worlds of Odilon Redon*, National Gallery of Victoria, Melbourne, 1990.

Green, Lyne, *Degas Monotypes*, Hayward Gallery, London, 1985.

Green, Nicholas, *The Nature of the Bourgeoisie. Nature, Art and Cultural Formation*, typewritten thesis, Portsmouth Polytechnic and Leeds University, 1986.

'All the flowers of the fields : the State, Liberalism and Art in France under the Early Third Republic', in *Oxford Art Journal*, vol. X, n° 1, 1987.

'Dealing in temperaments : Economic Transformation of the Artistic Field in France during the Second Half of the Nineteenth Century', in *Art History*, March 1987, p. 59-78.

Grivel, Marianne, *Gauguin et l'école de Pont-Aven*, Bibliothèque nationale, Paris, 1989.

Guérin, Marcel, *Jean-Louis Forain lithographe*, Paris, Floury, 1910 (reprinted Alan Wofsy, San Francisco, 1980).

Jean-Louis Forain aquafortiste, Floury, Paris, 1912 (reprinted Alan Wofsy, San Francisco, 1980).

'Note sur les monotypes de Degas', in *L'Amour de l'art*, n° 5, 1924, p. 77.

Guiffrey, Jean-Jacques, *L'Œuvre de Charles Jacque. Catalogue de ses eaux-fortes et pointes-sèches*, Paris, 1866.

Hamerton, Philip Gilbert, *Etchings and Etchers*, London, 1868.

Hanson, Ann Coffin, *Manet and the Modern Tradition*, Yale University Press, New Haven, 1977.

Harris, Jean C., Édouard Manet, *Graphic Works, A Definitive Catalogue Raisonné*, New York, Collector's ed., 1970 (re-edited and revised by Joël M. Smith, Alan Wofsy Fine Arts, San Francisco, 1990).

Havemayer, Louisine, *Sixteen to Sixty, Memoirs of a Collector, private print for the family of Mrs Havemayer and the Metropolitan Museum of Art*, 1961.

Hefting, Victorine, *Jongkind, sa vie, son œuvre, son époque*, Arts et métiers graphiques, Paris, 1975.

Heinich, Nathalie, *La Gloire de Van Gogh*, Minuit, Paris, 1991.

Herbert, Robert, 'City versus country, the rural image in French painting from Millet to Gauguin', in *Art Forum*, vol. VII, February 1970, p. 44-55.

1975 *Jean-François Millet*, Paris, Réunion des musées nationaux, 1975.

1988 *Les Plaisirs et les jours. L'Impressionnisme*, Flammarion, Paris, 1988 (translated from American English).

Herbert, Eugenia and Robert, *The Artist and Social Reform. France and Belgium, 1885-1898*, Yale University Press, New Haven, 1961.

Higonnet, Anne, *Berthe Morisot, une biographie*, Adam Biro, Paris, 1989.

Hind, Arthur, 'Camille Pissarro Graphische Arbeiten', in *Die Graphischen Kunst*, vol. XXXI, 1908, p. 34-48.

Hobsbawm, Eric-John, *The Age of Capital, 1848-1875*, New York, 1975.

Hut, Hans, 'Impressionism comes to America', in *Gazette des Beaux-Arts*, April 1946, p. 235-256.

Huygue, René, 'L'impressionnisme et la pensée de son temps', in *Centenaire de l'Impressionnisme*, Réunion des musées nationaux, Paris, 1974, p. 11-27.

Huysmans, Joris-Karl, *L'Art moderne*, Paris, 1883.

Inaga, Shigemi, 'À la redécouverte de l'ukiyo-e: les graveurs sur bois à la recherche d'un statut d'artiste au Japon in la seconde moitié du XIXe siècle et au début du XXe siècle', in *Nouvelles de l'estampe*, n° 73, January–February 1984, p. 4-14.

Isaacson, Joel, *Manet and Spain : Prints and Drawings*, Ann Arbor, University of Michigan Museum of Art, 1969.

1980 *The Crisis of Impressionism, 1878-1882*, Ann Arbor, University of Michigan Museum of Art, 1980.

1982 'Impressionism and Journalistic Illustration', in *Arts Magazine*, vol. LVI, June 1982, p. 95-115.

Ives, Colta, *The Great Wave*, Metropolitan Museum of Art, New York, 1974.

Jampoller, Lili, 'Theo and Vincent van Gogh as art collectors', in *Art Treasures in Holland. The Rijksmuseum Vincent van Gogh*, edited by E. van Witert and M. Hoyle, Amsterdam, 1987.

Janis, Eugenia Parry, 'The role of the monotypes in the working method of Degas', in *Burlington Magazine*, vol. CIX, January 1967, p. 20-27 and February 1967, p. 71-81.

1968 *Degas Monotypes*, Cambridge, Fogg Art Museum, 1968.

1980 'Setting the tone, the revival of etching, the importance of ink', in *The Painterly Print*, 1980, p. 9-28.

1984 'Les Monotypes', in Guillaud, Jacqueline and Maurice, Degas, *le modèle et l'espace*, Centre culturel du Marais, Paris, 1984.

Japonism. Japanese Influence on French Art, 1854-1910, Cleveland Museum of Art, 1975.

Japonism in Art, an International Symposium edited by the Society for the Study of Japonism, Committee for the Year 2001, Tokyo, 1980.

Le Japonisme, Paris, Réunion des musées nationaux, 1988.

Johnson, Una E., *Ambroise Vollard éditeur Prints, Books, Bronzes*, Museum of Modern Art, New York, 1977.

Kaplow, Jeffry, 'The Paris Commune and the Artists', in *Revolution and Reaction: The Paris Commune*, ed. John Hicks et Robert Tucker, in The Massachusetts Review, vol. XII, n° 3, summer 1971, p. 144-167.

Keppel, Frederic, *The Golden Age of Engraving. A Specialist's Story About the Prints*, New York, 1910.

Kornfeld, Eberhard W., *Edgar Degas, Beilage zum Verzeichnis des graphischen Werkes von Loys Delteil. Vorschläge zur Ergänzung und Abänderung der Nummen D.62 bis 65*, Kornfeld and Klipstein, Berne, 1965.

Laborde, Léon de, *Exposition universelle de 1851. Travaux de la commission française sur l'industrie des nations*, vol. VIII (VIe groupe, XXXe jury : applications de l'art à l'industrie), Paris, 1856.

La Faille, Jean-Baptiste de, *The Works of Vincent Van Gogh*, Reyal & Co, New York, Amsterdam, 1970.

Laforgue, Jules, *Textes de critiques d'art*, collected and introduced by Mireille Dotin, Presses universitaires de Lille, 1988.

Lant, Antonia, 'Purpose and Practice in French Avant-Garde', in *Oxford Art Journal*, vol. I, n° 1, 1986, p. 18-29 (a précis of her thesis Pissarro, Degas and Cassatt as Printmakers in 1880, 1979).

Laurens, Jules, *La Légende des ateliers*, Carpentras, 1901.

Laurent, Jeanne, *La République et les beaux-arts*, Paris, 1955.

Arts et pouvoirs en France de 1793 à 1981, Saint-Étienne, 1983.

Leiris, Alain de, *The Drawings of Édouard Manet*, University of California Press, Berkeley & Los Angeles, 1969.

Le Men, Ségolène, 'Manet et Doré : l'illustration du Corbeau de Poe', in *Nouvelles de l'estampe*, n° 78, December 1984, p. 4-21.

Le Men, Ségolène, and Scott, David, 'Philippe Burty et la genèse du livre de peintre : Sonnets et eaux-fortes', in *Iconotexte*, Ophrys, Paris, 1990, p. 39-58.

Lemoisne, Paul-André, *Degas et son œuvre*, 4 vol., Paris, 1946.

Lethève, Jacques, *Symbolistes et impressionnistes devant la presse*, Paris, 1959.

Levin, Miriam R., *Republican Art and Ideology in Late Nineteenth Century France*, Ann Arbor, University of Michigan, 1986.

Levy, Mervyn, *Whistler Lithographs, an illustrated Catalogue raisonné...*, London, 1975.

Liebermann, Max, 'Zwei original-Holzschnitte von Manet', in *Kunst und Kunstler*, 1905, book 4, p. 140-144.

Ligo, Larry L., 'Manet's frontispiece etchings : his symbolic self-portrait, acknowledging the influences of Baudelaire and photography upon his work', in *Gazette des Beaux-Arts*, September 1986, p. 66-74.

Lipton, Eunice, *Looking into Degas*, Berkeley, University of California Press, 1986.

'Degas' friends and a question of stylistic choice' in *La Condition sociale de l'artiste*, Université de Saint-Étienne, CIEREC, 1987, p. 75-85.

Leymarie, Jean, and Melot, Michel, *Les Gravures des impressionnistes : Manet, Pissarro, Renoir, Cézanne, Sisley, Paris, Arts et métiers graphiques*, 1971. (English translation : *The Graphic Works of the Impressionists*, New York, 1972.)

Lochnan, Katharine A., 'Whistler and the transfer lithograph : a lithograph with a verdict', in *The Print Collector's Newsletter*, November–December 1981, p. 133-137.

The Etchings of James McNeill Whistler, Yale University Press, New Haven and London, 1984.

Loyrette, Henri, *Degas*, Fayard, Paris, 1991.

Lucas, George A., *The Diary of George A. Lucas : an American Art Agent in Paris, 1857-1909*, ed. Lilian M. C. Randall, Princeton University Press, 1979.

Lugt, Frits, *Marques de collectionneurs*, Amsterdam, 1921.

Maberly, Joseph, *The Print Collector*, London, 1844. New edition, New York, 1880.

MacDonald, Margaret F., 'Whistler's Lithographs', in *Print Quarterly*, vol. V, n° 1, March 1988, p. 20-55.

MacDuffee, Allison Jane, *Camille Pissarro's Market and Fair Scenes, 1881-1895*, typewritten thesis, Queen's University, Kingston, 1987.

Magne, Jacqueline, *Forain témoin de son temps*, thesis, third cycle, Université d'Aix-Marseille, 1973 (can be consulted in the Bibliothèque Natioanal de . . .).

Mallarmé, Stéphane, *Œuvres complètes*, N.R.F., coll. «La Pléiade», Paris, 1961.

Mallarmé, Stéphane, *Correspondance*, collected, arranged and annotated by Henri Mondor and Lloyd James Austin, 3 vol., Gallimard, Paris, 1969.

Manet 1983, *Manet*, Paris, Réunion des musées natonaux, 1983 (catalogue of prints by Juliet Wilson-Bareau).

Manet, *The Execution of Maximilian*, National Gallery, London, 1992.

Mary Cassatt : The Color Prints, Abrams, New York, 1989.

Mathews, Nancy Mowll, *Cassatt and Edgar Degas*, San Jose Museum of Art, 1982.

1984 *Cassatt and her Circle. Selected Letters*, Abbeville Press, New York, 1984.

1989 'The color prints in the context of Mary Cassatt's art', in *Mary Cassatt : the Color Prints*, Abrams, New York, 1989.

Mayeur, Jean-Marie, *Les Débuts de la Troisième République*, Le Seuil, coll. 'Nouvelle Histoire de France', Paris, 1973.

Mellerio, André, *La Lithographie originale en couleurs*, Paris, 1898.

Melot, Michel, 'Paul Renouard illustrateur', in *Nouvelles de l'estampe*, n° 2, 1971, p. 69-71.

1972 *Cézanne, l'œuvre gravé*, Pavillon de Vendôme, Aix-en Provence, 1972.

1974 *L'Estampe impressionniste*, Bibliothèque nationale, Paris, 1974.

1975 'L'estampe impressionniste et sa réduction au dessin', in *Nouvelles de l'estampe*, n° 16, January–February 1975, p. 11-15.

1976 'Les Monotypes d'Appian', in *Nouvelles de l'estampe*, n° 25, janvier-février 1976, p. 13-17.

1977 'Introduction à l'œuvre gravé de Manet', in *Édouard Manet, l'œuvre gravé*, Stadtverwaltung Ingelheim Weiterbildungszentrum C.H. Boehringer Sohn, Ingelheim-am-Rhein, 1977, p. 15-20.

1977 (2) 'La pratique d'un artiste : Pissarro graveur en 1880', in *Histoire et critique des arts*, n° 2, June 1977, p. 14-38. (English translation: 'Camille Pissarro, an anarchistic artist in bourgeois society', in *Marxists perspectives*, vol. II, winter 1979-1980, p. 22-54.)

1978 *L'Œuvre gravé de Boudin, Corot, Daubigny, Dupré, Jongkind, Millet, Théodore Rousseau*, Paris, Arts et métiers graphiques, 1978 (English translation: *Graphic Art of the Pré-Impressionists*, Abrams, New York,1980.)

1980 'Questions au japonisme', in *Japonism in Art, an International Symposium Edited by the Society for the Study of Japonism*, Committe for the Year 2001, Tokyo, 1980, p. 239-260.

1983 'Manet et l'estampe', in *Manet, Réunion des musées nationaux*, Paris, 1983, p. 35-39.

1984 *L'Illustration, histoire d'un art*, Geneva, Skira, 1984.

1986 'A rebel's role: Concerning the prints of Camille Pissarro', in *Studies on Camille Pissarro*, ed. Christopher Lloyd, Routledge & Kegan Paul, London & New York, 1986.

1986 (2) 'La Notion d'originalité et son importance in la définition des objets d'art', in *Sociologie de l'art*, edited by Raymonde Moulin, La Documentation française, 1986, p. 191-202.

1988 'Daumier and Art History: Aesthetic Judgement/Political Judgement', in *Oxford Art Journal*, vol. XI, n° 1, 1988, p. 3-24.

1990 'Le texte et l'image', in *Histoire de l'édition française*, edited by Roger Chartier and Henri-Jean Martin, vol. III, second edition, Fayard-Cercle de la librairie, Paris, 1990, p. 329-355.

1993 'Raffaëlli l'oublié', in *Nouvelles de l'estampe*, n° 128, May 1993, p. 19-30.

Melot, Michel, Griffiths, Antony, Field, Richard and Béguin, André, *L'Estampe, histoire d'un art*, Skira, Genève, 1981.

Menon, Elizabeth K., 'Henry Somm's Japonism, 1881 in context', in *Gazette des Beaux-Arts*, February 1992, p. 89-98.

Mongan, Elizabeth, Kornfeld, Eberhard et Joachim, Harold, *Paul Gauguin, Catalogue Raisonné of his Prints*, Kornfeld, Berne, 1988.

Mondor, Henri, *Vie de Mallarmé*, Paris, 1941.

Monneret, Sophie, *L'Impressionnisme et son époque. Dictionnaire international illustré*, 4 vol., Denoël, Paris, 1978-1981.

Montfort, Juliana, 'Van Gogh et la gravure', in *Nouvelles de l'estampe*, n° 2, March–April 1972, p. 5-13.

Moreau-Nélaton, Étienne, *Catalogue de l'œuvre gravé de Manet*, Paris, 1906.

Morisot, Berthe, *Correspondance de Berthe Morisot avec sa famille et ses amis*, documents collected and introduced by Denis Rouart, Paris, 1950.

Mose, Paul, *An Exhibition of Etchings by Edgar Degas*, University of Chicago, 1964.

Moulin, Raymonde, 'La genèse de la rareté artistique', in *Ethnologie française*, vol. VIII, n° 2-3, March–September 1978, p. 241-258.

The New Painting, Impressionism 1874-1886, The Fine Arts Museum of San Francisco & National Gallery of Art, Washington, 1986.

Nochlin, Linda, *Impressionism and Post-Impressionism, 1874-1904, Sources and Documents*, Prentice Hall, Englewood Cliffs, 1966.

The Politics of Vision, Essays on Nineteenth Century Art and Society, Thames & Hudson, London, 1989.

Orwicz, Michael R., 'Anti-academism and State power in the early Third Republic', in *Art History*, vol. XIV, n° 4, December 1991, p. 571-592.

The Painterly Print, Monotypes from the Seventeenth to the Twentieth Century, Metropolitan Museum of Art, New York, 1980.

Parsons, Christopher, and Ward, Martha, *A Bibliography of Salon Criticism in Second Empire*, Paris, Cambridge University Press, 1986.

Passeron, Roger, *La Gravure impressionniste, origine et développement*, Bibliothèque des arts, Paris, 1974 (English translation: Impressionist Prints, Dutton, New York, 1974.)

Pennell, Joseph, *James McNeill Whistler, sa vie, son œuvre*, 1913.

Pickvance, Ronald, 'Degas's Dancers 1872-1876' in *Burlington Magazine*, June 1963, n°105, p. 259-263.

English Influences on Vincent Van Gogh, Nottingham, 1974.

Pissarro, Paris, Réunion des musées nationaux, 1981 (English translation, London, Hayward Gallery, 1980, Boston Museum of Fine Arts, 1981.)

Pissarro, Camille, *Correspondance* , ed. Janine Bailly-Herzberg, vol. I (1865-1885), Paris, P.U.F., 1980 ; vol. II (1886-1890), vol. III (1891-1894), vol. IV (1895-1898), vol. V (1899-1903), Saint-Ouen-L'Aumône, éditions du Valhermeil, 1985-1988.

Pissarro, Ludovic-Rodo, 'The etched and lithographied work of Camille Pissarro', in *The Print Collector's Quarterly*, vol. IX, 1922, p. 275-301.

Poulet-Malassis, Auguste, and Thibaudeau, Alphonse W., *Catalogue raisonné de l'œuvre gravé de M. Alphonse Legros*, Paris, 1877.

La Promenade du critique influent, anthologie de la critique d'art en France, 1850-1900, texts collected and introduced by Jean-Paul Bouillon, Nicole Dubreuil-Blondin, Antoinette Erhard, Constance Naubert-Riser, Hazan, Paris, 1990.

Redon, Odilon, *À soi-même*, Paris, 1921.

Reff, Theodore, 'The symbolism of Manet frontispiece etching', in *The Burlington Magazine*, vol. CIV, 1962, p. 182-186.

1962 'Manet's frontispiece etching', in *Bulletin of the New York Public Library*, 1962, p. 143-148.

1976 *Degas, The Artist's mind*, The Metropolitan Museum of Art, New York, 1976.

1985 *The Notebooks of Edgar Degas, a Catalogue of the Thirty-Eight Notebooks in the Bibliothèque nationale and Other*

Collections, Oxford, Clarendon Press, second revised edition, 1985 (first edition, 1976).

Reszler, André, *L'Esthétique anarchiste*, Paris, P.U.F., 1973.

Reuterswärd, Oscar, *Impressionisterna, inför public och Kritik*, Bonnier, Stockholm, 1952.

'1881, la sixième exposition des Impressionnistes, dite des artistes indépendants, vue par la presse et l'opinion', in *Gazette des Beaux-Arts*, November 1979, p. 183-192.

Rewald, John, *Histoire de l'impressionnisme*, Albin Michel, Paris, 1955. Nouvelle éd., Paris, Le Livre de poche, 1965.

Riout, Denys, *Les Écrivains devant l'impressionnisme*, Macula, Paris, 1989.

Rioux, Jean-Pierre, *La Révolution industrielle, 1780-1914*, Le Seuil, Paris, 1989.

Rittmann, Annegret, *Die Druckgraphik Camille Pissarro*, Peter Lang, Francfort, 1992.

Roger-Marx, Claude, 'Manet etcher, lithographer and illustrator', in *Print Collector's Quarterly*, vol. XXIII, n° 4, October 1936, p. 303-322.

L'Œuvre gravé de Renoir, Sauret, Monte Carlo, 1952.

Rosenthal, Léon, 'Les conditions sociales de la peinture sous la monarchie de Juillet', in *Gazette des Beaux-Arts*, February 1910, p. 93-114 et March 1910, p. 217-241.

1925 *Manet aquafortiste et lithographe*, Paris, 1925.

Du romantisme au réalisme, essai sur l'évolution de la peinture française, Paris, 1914 (republished, Paris, Macula, 1987).

Rouart, Denis, *Degas à la recherche de sa technique*, Paris, 1945 (repub., Skira, Geneva, 1985.)

Rouillé, André, *L'Empire de la photographie*, Le Sycomore, Paris, 1982.

La Photographie en France, textes et controverses, une anthologie, 1816-1871, Macula, Paris, 1989.

Röver, Anne, *Camille Pissarro, Radierungen, Lithographien, Monotypien aus deutschen österreichischen Sammlungen*, Kunsthalle, Bremen, 1990.

Schneiderman, Richard S., *A Catalogue Raisonné of the Prints of Sir Francis Seymour Haden*, Robin Garton, London, 1983.

Sensier, Alfred, *La Vie et l'Œuvre de J.-F. Millet*, manuscript published by Paul Mantz, followed by the first complete catalogue of Millet's prints by Alfred Lebrun, Paris, 1881.

Shapiro, Barbara, 'Four intaglio prints by Camille Pissarro', in *Boston Museum Bulletin*, vol. LXIX, 1971, n° 357, p. 131-141.

1973 *Camille Pissarro, the impressionist printmaker*, Boston Museum of Fine Arts, 1973.

1980 'Nineteenth-century masters of the painterly print', in *The Painterly Print*, 1980, p. 29-39.

1981 'Pissarro graveur', in *Pissarro*, 1981, p. 191-196.

1989 'Mary Cassatt's color prints and contemporary French printmaking', in *Mary Cassatt: The Color Prints*, Abrams, New York, 1989.

Shapiro, Barbara, and Melot, Michel, 'Les monotypes de Camille Pissarro', in *Nouvelles de l'estampe*, n° 16, January-February 1975, p. 16-23.

Shiff, Richard, 'Seeing Cezanne', in *Critical Inquiry*, vol. IV, n° 4, été 1978, p. 769-808.

'The end of impressionism, a study in the theory of artistic expression', in *The Art Quarterly*, vol. I, n° 4, automne 1978, p. 338-378 (Translation of: *Cézanne et la fin de l'impressionnisme*, Flammarion, Paris, 1995).

Shikes, Ralph, and Harper, Paula, *Pissarro*, Flammarion, Paris, 1985 (Trans. of *Pissarro, his Life and Work*, New York, 1980.)

Sloane, Joseph C., *French Painting between the Past and the Present: Artists, Critics and Traditions from 1848-1870*, Princeton University Press, 1951.

Soulier, Gustave, *L'Œuvre gravé et lithographié de Alphonse Legros*, Paris, 1904.

Sorlin, Pierre, *La Société française, 1840-1910*, Arthaud, Paris, 1969.

Les Sources d'inspiration de Vincent Van Gogh, Paris, Institut néerlandais, 1972.

Stein, Donna M. and Karshan, Donald, *L'Estampe originale, a Catalogue raisonné*, The Museum of Graphic Arts, New York, 1970.

Stella, Joseph, *The Graphic Works of Renoir*, Bradford & London, Lund Humphries, 1975.

Stuffmann, Margaret, Charles Meryon, *Paris vers 1850: dessins, eaux-fortes et photographies*, Städelsches Kunstinstitut, Frankfurt, 1975.

Sudik, Thomas Joseph, *The French Administration of the Fine Arts, 1875-1914*, typewritten thesis, University of North Carolina, Chapell Hill, 1979.

Sueur, Valérie, François Chifflart, Réunion des musées nationaux, 'Les dossiers du musée d'Orsay', Paris, 1993.

'L'Album Chifflart, statut et rôle de l'image au milieu du XIXᵉ siècle', in *Nouvelles de l'estampe*, n° 131, November-December 1993.

Sutton, Denys, *James McNeill Whistler*, Phaidon Press, London, 1966.

Tabarant, Adolphe, 'Une histoire inconnue du Polichinelle', in *Bulletin de la vie artistique*, vol. IV, p. 365-369.

Pissarro, Paris, 1924.

Manet et ses œuvres, Paris, 1947.

Thomson, Richard, 'Camille Pissarro's Turpitudes sociales and the Universal Exhibition of 1889', in *Art Magazine*, vol. LVI, n° 8, August 1982, p. 82-88.

1987 *The Private Degas*, Thames & Hudson, London, 1987.

1990 *Camille Pissarro, Impressionism, Landscape and Rural Labour*, City Museum and Art Gallery, Birmingham, New York, 1990.

Thorson, Victoria, *Rodin Graphics, a Catalogue Raisonné of Drypoints and Book Illustrations*, San Francisco Fine Arts Museum, 1975.

'Reassessing Rodin's Drypoints, Lithograph and Book Illustrations', in *Nouvelles de l'estampe*, n° 25, January-February 1976, p. 17-18.

Toulouse-Lautrec, Henri de, *Unpublished Correspondance of Henri de Toulouse-Lautrec* edited by Lucien Goldschmidt and Herbert Schimmel with an introduction and notes by Jean Adhémar and Theodore Reff, Phaidon Press, London, 1969.

Valéry, Paul, *Degas, ine, dessin*, Paris, 1936.

Van Gelder, Dirk, *Rodolphe Bresdin, catalogue raisonné de l'œuvre gravé*, 2 vol., éd. du Chêne, Paris, 1976.

Van Gogh, Vincent, *Correspondance complète de Vincent Van Gogh*, 3 vol., Gallimard-Grasset, Paris, 1960.

Varnadoe, Kirk, *Gustave Caillebotte*, Adam Biro, Paris, 1988 (English Edition, Yale University Press, New Haven and London, 1987.)

Vollard, Ambroise, *Tableaux, pastels et dessins de P.-A. Renoir*, 2 vol., Paris, 1918.

La Vie et l'Œuvre de P.-A. Renoir, Paris, 1919.

Souvenirs d'un marchand de tableaux, Paris, 1937.

Way, Thomas R., and Dennis, G.R., *The Art of James McNeill Whistler*, London, 1903.

Wedmore, Frederic, *Four Masters of Etching*, Fine Arts Society, London, 1883.

Wentworth, Michael Justin, *James Tissot. Catalogue Raisonné of His Prints*, The Minneapolis Institute of Art, 1978.

Weisberg, Gabriel, 'Philippe Burty, a notable critic of the nineteenth century', in *Apollo Magazine n° 91* (1970), p. 296-300 (précis of his thesis *The Early Years of Philippe Burty: Art Critic, Amateur and Japonist*, John Hopkins University, 1967.)

1972 *The Etching Renaissance in France, 1850-1880*, Utah Museum of Fine Arts, 1972.

1975 'Japonism: early sources and the French printmaker 1854-1882', in *Japonism. Japanese Influence on French Art 1854-1910*, Cleveland Museum of Art, 1975.

1980 *The Realist Tradition, French Painting and Drawing, 1830-1900*, Cleveland Museum of Art, 1980.

Weitzenhoffer, Frances, 'Estampes impressionnistes de peintres américains', in *Nouvelles de l'estampe*, n° 28, July-August 1976, p. 7-14.

The Havemayers, Abrams, New York, 1986.

Werness, Hope B., *Vincent Van Gogh: the Influences of Nineteenth Century Illustrations*, Tallahassee, University Fine Arts Gallery, 1980.

White, Harrison and Cynthia, *La Carrière des peintres au XIXᵉ siècle*, introduction by Jean-Paul Bouillon, Flammarion, Paris, 1991 (Translation of *Canvases and Careers*, Institutional Change in the French Painting World, 1965.)

Wichmann, Siegfried, *Japonismus Ostasien und Europa begegnungen in der Kunst des 19 und 20 Jahrunderts*, Schuler Verlaggesellshaft, Herrshing, 1980 (English translation: *Japonism*, Thames & Hudson, London, 1980.)

Wilson Bareau, see Bareau, Juliet.

Wittrock, Wolfgang, *Toulouse-Lautrec. Catalogue complet des estampes*, 2 vol., Paris, ACR Éditions-Les Éditions de l'amateur, 1985 (original edition, Sotheby's Publications, London,1985).

Zigrosser, Carl, 'Manet's Etching and Lithograph», in *Print's Connoisseur*, vol. I, 1921, p. 380-398.

Zola, Émile, *Le bon combat, de Courbet aux impressionnistes*, anthologie d'écrits sur l'art, introducton and preface by de Gaëtan Picon, critical edition, chronology, bibliography and index by Jean-Paul Bouillon, Hermann, Paris, 1974.

Écrits sur l'art, definitive edition, introduced and annotated by Jean-Pierre Leduc-Adine, Gallimard, Paris, 1991.

INDEX

PHOTOGRAPHIC CREDITS

Numbers refer to the pages on which illustrations appear.

Aix-les-Bains, Musée Faure: 242; Amsterdam, Van Gogh Museum: 251; Boston, Museum of Fine Art: 69, 109, 150, 162, 174, 241, 247; Bremen, Kunsthalle: 162, 166; Chicago, Art Institute: 86, 185, 185; Cincinnati, Art Museum: 177; Frankfurt, Städelschen Kunstinstituts: 167; Glasgow, University of Glasgow, Hunterian Art Gallery: 186; Kansas City, Nelson-Atkins Museum of Art: 238; London, British Museum: 30, 40, 111, 243, 259; New Haven, Yale University Art Gallery: 166; New York, collection Mr & Mrs Eugene Thaw: 168; New York, Metropolitan Museum of Art: 45, 239; Ottawa, National Gallery of Canada: 182; Oxford, Ashmolean Museum, 172, 183, 193, 194, 195, 234, 235, 259; Paris, Flammarion: 10, 33, 47, 57, 60, 82, 83, 134, 145, 149, 200, 201, 202, 213, 230, 237, 242, 244, 262, 264, 265, 272, 273; Paris, Bibliothèque nationale: 12, 13, 14, 15, 16, 17, 18, 19, 21, 22, 23, 24, 25, 26, 27, 28, 29, 31, 32, 34, 35, 37, 38, 39, 42, 43, 44, 46, 50, 51, 53, 54, 56, 58, 59, 60, 62, 63, 64, 65, 66, 67, 68, 71, 72, 73, 74, 75, 76, 77, 79, 80, 81, 87, 88, 89, 90, 91, 92, 93, 95, 98, 99, 101, 102, 103, 104, 105, 106. 107, 108, 110, 111, 112, 113, 114, 115, 117, 119, 120, 121, 122, 124, 125, 126, 127, 129, 130, 131, 132, 133, 135, 136, 137, 139, 140, 141, 142, 143, 144, 146, 147, 148, 151, 152, 153, 154, 155, 156, 157, 158, 159, 163, 167, 168, 169, 170, 171, 172, 174, 176, 178, 179, 182, 184, 187, 189, 190, 191, 192, 196, 203, 204, 208, 209, 210, 211, 212, 214, 215, 216, 217, 218, 219, 221, 222, 223, 226, 228, 229, 230, 231, 240, 245, 246, 248, 249, 250, 253, 254, 255, 256, 257, 258, 260, 261, 268, 269, 271; Paris Musée Rodin: 205, 206; Paris, Réunion des musées nationaux: 41, 52, 161, 164, 169, 179, 234; Paris, Société des amis de la BAA: 43, 175, 180, 185c, 222, 223, 225, 251; Philadelphia, Museum of Art: 173; Richmond, Virginia Museum of Fine Arts: 226; Rutgers, The State University of New Jersey, Zimmerli Art Museum: 233; San Francisco, The Museum of Fine Arts: 241; Washington, Library of Congress: 96, 150; Washington, National Gallery of Art: 45, 186, 227, 238.